SAMUEL RICHARDSON

Pamela

IN TWO VOLUMES · VOLUME TWO

INTRODUCTION BY

M. KINKEAD-WEEKES
B.A. (*Capetown*), M.A. (*Oxon*)

Senior Lecturer in
English and American Literature
in the University of Kent at Canterbury

DENT: LONDON

EVERYMAN'S LIBRARY

DUTTON: NEW YORK

All rights reserved
Made in Great Britain
at the
Aldine Press · Letchworth · Herts
for
J. M. DENT & SONS LTD
Aldine House · Albemarle Street · London
This edition was first published in
Everyman's Library in 1914
Last reprinted 1976

Published in the U.S.A. by arrangement
with J. M. Dent & Sons Ltd

No. 684   Hardback ISBN 0 460 00684 3
No. 1684   Paperback ISBN 0 460 01684 9

AUTHOR'S ORIGINAL PREFACE
TO VOLUME II

THE First part of PAMELA met with a success greatly exceeding the most sanguine expectations: and the Editor hopes, that the Letters which compose this Part will be found equally written to NATURE, avoiding all romantic flights, improbable surprises, and irrational machinery; and the passions are touched, where requisite; and rules, equally *new* and *practicable*, inculcated throughout the whole, for the *general conduct of life ;* and, therefore, he flatters himself, that they may expect the good fortune, which *few continuations* have met with, to be judged not unworthy the *First* Part; nor disproportioned to the more exalted condition in which PAMELA was destined to shine as an affectionate *wife*, a faithful *friend*, a polite and kind *neighbour*, an indulgent *mother*, and a beneficent *mistress ;* after having in the former Part supported the character of a dutiful *child*, a spotless *virgin*, and a modest and amiable *bride*.

The reader will easily see, that in so great a choice of materials, as must arise from a multitude of important subjects, in a married life, to such geniuses and friendships as those of Mr. and Mrs. B. the Editor's greatest difficulty was how to bring them within the compass which he was determined not to exceed. And it having been left to his own choice, in what manner to digest and publish the letters, and where to close the work, he had intended, at first, in regard to his other avocations, to have carried the piece no farther than the First Part.

It may be expected, therefore, that he should enter into an explanation of the reasons whereby he was provoked into a necessity of altering his intention. But he is willing to decline saying any thing upon so well-known a subject.

The Editor has been much pressed with importunities and conjectures, in relation to the person and family of the gentleman, who are the principal persons in the work; all he thinks himself at liberty to say, or is necessary to be said, is only to repeat what has already been hinted, that the story has its foundation in truth : and that there was a necessity, for obvious reasons, to vary and disguise some facts and circumstances, as also the names of persons, places, &c.

LETTER I

My dear Father and Mother,

We arrived here last night, highly pleased with our journey, and the occasion of it. May God bless you both with long life and health, to enjoy your sweet farm, and pretty dwelling, which is just what I wished it to be. And don't make your grateful hearts too uneasy in the possession of it, by your modest diffidence of your own unworthiness: for, at the same time, that it is what will do honour to the best of men, it is not so *very* extraordinary, considering his condition, as to cause any one to censure it as the effect of a too partial and injudicious kindness for the parents of one whom he *delighteth to honour*.

My dear master (why should I not still call him so, bound to reverence him as I am, in every light he can shine in to the most obliging and sensible heart?) still proposes to fit up the large parlour, and three apartments in the commodious dwelling he calls yours, for his entertainment and mine, when I pay my duty to you both, for a few happy days; and he has actually given orders to that effect; and that the three apartments be *so* fitted up, as to be rather suitable to *your* condition, than his *own;* for, he says, the plain simple elegance, which he will have observed in the rooms, as well as the furniture, will be a variety in his retirement to this place, that will make him return to his own with the greater pleasure; and, at the same time, when we are not there, will be of use for the reception of any of your friends; and so he shall not, as he kindly says, rob the good couple of any of their accommodations.

The old bow-windows he will have preserved, but will not have them sashed, nor the woodbines, jessamines, and vines, that run up against them, destroyed: only he will have larger panes of glass, and more convenient casements to let in the sweet air and light, and make amends for that obstructed by the shades of those fragrant climbers. For he has mentioned, three or four times, how gratefully they dispensed their inter-mingled odours to us, when, the last evening we stood at the window, to hear the responsive songs of two warbling nightin-

I

gales, one at a distance, the other near, which delighted us for above two hours, and the more, as we thought their season had been over. And when they had done, he made *me* sing him one, for which he rewarded me with a kiss, saying, "How greatly do the innocent pleasures I now hourly taste, exceed the guilty tumults that used formerly to agitate my unequal mind!—Never talk, my Pamela, as you frequently do, of obligation to me: one such hour as I now enjoy is an ample reward for all the benefits I can confer on you and yours in my whole life!"

The parlour will indeed be more elegant; though that is to be rather plain than rich, as well in its wainscot as furniture, and to be new-floored. The dear gentleman has already given orders, and you will soon have workmen to put them in execution. The parlour-doors are to have brass-hinges and locks, and to shut as close, he tells them, as a watch-case: "For who knows," said he, "my dear, but we shall have still added blessings, in two or three charming boys and girls, to place there in their infancy, before they can be of age to be benefited by your lessons and example? And besides, I shall no doubt entertain there some of my chosen friends, in their excursions for a day or two."

How am I, every hour of my life, overwhelmed with instances of God Almighty's goodness and his! O spare, blessed Father of Mercies, the precious life of this excellent man; increase my thankfulness, and my worthiness;—and then—But what shall I say?—Only that I may *continue* to be what I am; for more blessed and happy, in my own mind, I cannot be.

The beds he will have of cloth, as he thinks the situation a little cold, especially when the wind is easterly, and purposes to be down in the early spring season, now and then, as well as in the latter autumn; and the window curtains of the same, in one room red, in the other green; but plain, lest you should be afraid to use them occasionally. The carpets for them will be sent with the other furniture; for he will not alter the old oaken floors of the bed-chamber, nor the little room he intends for my use, when I choose not to join in such company as may happen to fall in: "Which, my dear," says he, "shall be as little as is possible, only particular friends, who may be disposed, once in a year or two, to see when I am there, how I live with my Pamela and her parents, and how I pass my time in my retirement, as I shall call this: or, perhaps, they will be apt to think me ashamed of company I shall always be pleased with. Nor are you, my dear, to take this as a compliment to yourself,

2

but a piece of requisite policy in me : for who will offer to reproach me with marrying, as the world thinks, below me, when they shall see that I not only pride myself in my Pamela, but take pleasure in owning her relations as mine, and visiting them, and receiving visits from them : and yet offer not to set them up in such a glaring light, as if I would have the world forget (who in that case would always take the more pleasure in remembering) what they were ! And how will it anticipate low reflection, when they shall see, I can bend my mind to partake with them the pleasure of their humble but decent life ?—Ay," continued he, " and be rewarded for it too, with better health, better spirits, and a better mind ; so that, my dear," added he, " I shall reap more benefit by what I propose to do, than I shall confer."

In this generous manner does this best of men endeavour to disclaim (though I must be very ungrateful, if, with me, it did not enhance) the proper merit of a beneficence natural to him ; and which, indeed, as I tell him, may be in one respect deprecated, inasmuch as (so excellent is his nature) he cannot help it if he would. O that it was in my power to recompense him for it ! But I am poor, as I have often said, in every thing but will—and that is *wholly* his : and what a happiness is it to me, a happiness I could not so early have hoped for, that I can say so without *reserve ;* since the dear object of it requires nothing of me but what is consistent with my duty to the Supreme Benefactor, the first mover and cause of all his own happiness, of my happiness, and that of my dear, my ever dear parents,

Your dutiful and happy daughter,

LETTER II

My dearest Daughter,

I need not repeat to you the sense your good mother and I have of our happiness, and of our obligations to your honoured spouse ; you both were pleased witnesses of it every hour of the happy fortnight you passed with us. Yet, my dear, we hardly know how to address ourselves even to *you*, much less to the *'squire*, with the freedom he so often invited us to take : for I don't know how it is, but though you are our daughter, and so far from being lifted up by your high condition, that we see no difference in your behaviour to us, your poor parents, yet, viewing you as the lady of so fine a gentleman, we

3

cannot forbear having a kind of respect, and—I don't know what to call it—that lays a little restraint upon us. And yet, we should not, methinks, let our minds be run away with the admiration of worldly grandeur, so as to set too much by it. But your merit and prudence are so much above all we could ever have any notion of : and to have gentry come only to behold and admire you, not so much for your gentleness, and amiableness, or for your behaviour, and affability to poor as well as rich, and to hear every one calling you an angel, and saying, you *deserve* to be what you are, make us hardly know how to look upon you, but as an angel indeed ! I am sure you have been a good angel to us ; since, for your sake, God Almighty has put it into your honoured husband's heart to make us the happiest couple in the world. But little less we should have been, had we only in some far distant land heard of our dear child's happiness and never partaken of the benefits of it our-selves. But thus to be provided for ! thus kindly to be owned, and called Father and Mother by such a brave gentleman ! and so placed as to have nothing to do but to bless God, him, and you, and hourly pray for you *both*, is a providence too mighty to be borne by us, with equalness of temper : we kneel together every morning, noon, and night, and weep and rejoice, and rejoice and weep, to think how our unworthiness is distin-guished, and how God has provided for us in our latter days ; when all our fear was, that, as we grew older and more infirm, and worn out by hard labour, we should be troublesome where, not our pride, but our industrious wills, would have made us wish not to be so ;—but to be entitled to a happier lot : for this would have grieved us the more, for the sake of you, my dear child, and your unhappy brother's children : for it is well known, that, though we pretend not to boast of our family, and indeed have no reason, yet none of us were ever sunk so low as I was : to be sure, partly by my own fault ; for, had it been for your poor aged mother's sake only, I ought not to have done what I did for John and William ; for so unhappy were they, poor lads ! that what I could do, was but as a drop of water to a bucket.

You command me—Let me, as writing to Mr. B.'s lady, say *command*, though, as to my dear *daughter*, I will only say *desire* : and, indeed, I will not, as you wish me not to do, let the one condition, which was accidental, put the other, which was natural, out of my thought : you spoke it in better words, but this was the sense. But you have the gift of utterance ; and education is a fine thing, where it meets with such talents to

4

improve upon, as God has given you. Yet let me not forget what I was going to say—You *command*—or, if you please—you *desire* me to write long letters, and often—And how can I help it, if I would? For when here, in this happy dwelling, and this well-stocked farm, in these rich meadows, and well-cropt acres, we look around us, and which way soever we turn our head, see blessings upon blessings, and plenty upon plenty, see barns well stored, poultry increasing, the kine lowing and crowding about us: and are bid to call them our own. Then think, that all is the reward of our child's virtue !—O my dear daughter, who can bear these things !—Excuse me ! I must break off a little ! For my eyes are as full as my heart : and I will retire to bless God, and your honoured husband.

So, my dear child, I now again take up my pen : but reading what I had written, in order to carry on the thread, I can hardly forbear again being in one sort affected. But do you think I will call all these things my own ?—Do you think I would live rent-free ? Can the honoured 'squire believe, that having such a generous example before me, if I had no gratitude in my temper before, I could help being touched by such an one as he sets me ? If this goodness makes him know no mean in giving, shall I be so greedy as to know none in receiving ? Come, come, my dear child, your poor father is not so sordid a wretch, neither. He will shew the world that all these benefits are not thrown away upon one, who will disgrace you as much by his temper, as by his condition. What though I cannot be as worthy of all these favours as I wish, I will be as worthy as I can. And let me tell you, my dear child, if the king and his royal family (God bless 'em !) be not ashamed to receive taxes and duties from his subjects; if dukes and earls, and all the top gentry, cannot support their bravery, without having their rents paid; I hope I shall not affront the 'squire, to pay to his steward, what any other person would pay for his noble stock, and improving farm : and I will do it, if it please God to bless me with life and health. I should not be worthy to crawl upon the earth, if I did not. And what did I say to Mr. Longman, the faithful Mr. Longman ! Sure no gentleman had ever a more worthy steward than he : it was as we were walking over the grounds together, and observing in what good order every thing was, he was praising some little contrivances of my own, for the improvement of the farm, and saying, how comfortably he hoped we might live upon it. " Ay, Mr. Longman," said I, " comfortably indeed : but do you think I could be properly said to *live*, if I was not to pay as much rent for it as another ? "

—" I can tell you," said he, " the 'squire will not receive any thing from you, Goodman Andrews. Why, man, he has no occasion for it : he's worth a power of money, besides a noble and clear estate in land. Ad's-heartlikens, you must not affront him, I can tell you that : he's as generous as a prince, where he takes; but he is hasty, and will have his own way."— " Why, for that reason, Mr. Longman," said I, " I was thinking to make *you* my friend ! "—" Make *me* your friend ! You have not a better in the world, to my power, I can tell you that, nor your dame neither : for I love such honest hearts : I wish my own brother would let me love him as well; but let that pass. What I can do for you, I will, and here's my hand upon it."

" Well, then," said I, " it is this : let me account to you at the rent Farmer Dickens offered, and let me know what the stock cost, and what the crops are valued at; and pay the one as I can, and the other quarterly; and not let the 'squire know it till you can't choose; and I shall be as happy as a prince; for I doubt not, by God's blessing, to make a comfortable livelihood of it besides."—" Why, dost believe, Goodman Andrews," said he, " that I would do such a thing? Would not his honour think if I hid one thing from him, I might hide another? Go to, honest heart, I love thee dearly; but can Mr. B. do too much for his lady, think'st thou? Come, come " (and he jeered me so, I knew not what to say), " I wish at bottom there is not some pride in this. What, I warrant, you would not be too much beholden to his honour, would you ? "— " No," said I, " it is not that, I'm sure. If I have any pride, it is only in my dear child—to whom, under God, all this is owing. But some how or other it shall be so."

And so, my dear daughter, I resolve it shall; and it will be, over and above, one of the greatest pleasures to me, to do the good 'squire service, as well as to be so much benefited and obliged by him.

Our eldest grandson Thomas desires to come and live with us : the boy is honest, and, I hear, industrious. And cousin Borroughs wants me to employ his son Roger, who understands the business of a farm very well. It is no wonder, that all one's relations should wish to partake of our happy lot; and if they *can* and *will* do their business as well as others, I see not why relationship should be an objection : but, yet, I think, one should not *beleaguer*, as one may say, your honoured husband with one's relations. You, my best child, will give me always your advice, as to my carriage in this my new lot; for I would not for the world be thought an encroacher. And you have so

6

much prudence, that there is nobody's advice fitter to be followed than yours.

Our blessing (I am sure you have blessed us !) attend you, my dearest child; and may you be as happy as you have made us (I cannot wish you to be happier, because I have no notion how it can be in this life). Conclude us, *your ever-loving father and mother,*

JOHN *and* ELIZ. ANDREWS.

May we hope to be favoured now and then with a letter from you, my dear child, like some of your former, to let us know how you go on? It would be a great joy to us; indeed it would. But we know you'll have enough to do without obliging us in this way. So must acquiesce.

LETTER III

MY DEAR FATHER AND MOTHER,

I have shewed your letter to my beloved. Don't be uneasy that I have; for you need not be ashamed of it, since it is my pride to have such honest and grateful parents : and I'll tell you what he said to it, as the best argument I can use, why you should not be uneasy, but enjoy without pain or anxiety all the benefits of your happy lot.

" Dear good souls ! " said he, " now every thing they say and write manifests the worthiness of their hearts ! No wonder, Pamela, you love and revere such honest minds; for that you would do, were they not your parents : and tell them, that I am so far from having them believe what I have done for them were only from my affection for their daughter, that let 'em find out another couple as worthy as they are, and I will do as much for them. I would not place them," he continued, " in the *same* county, because I would wish *two* counties to be blessed for their sakes. Tell them, my dear, that they have a right to what they enjoy on the foot of their own *proper* merit; and *bid* them enjoy it as their patrimony; and if any thing arise that is more than they themselves can wish for, in their way of life, let them look among their own relations, where it may be acceptable, and communicate to them the like solid reasons for rejoicing in the situation they are pleased with : and do you, my dear, still farther enable them, as you shall judge proper, to gratify their enlarged hearts, for fear

7

they should deny any comfort to themselves, in order to do good to others."

I could only fly to his generous bosom (for this is a subject which most affects me), and, with my eyes swimming in tears of grateful joy, and which overflowed as soon as my bold lips touched his dear face, bless God, and bless him, with my whole heart; for speak I could not! But, almost chok'd with my joy, sobb'd to him my grateful acknowledgments. He clasped me in his arms, and said, " How, my dearest, do you overpay me for the little I have done for your parents! if it be thus to be bless'd for conferring benefits so insignificant to a man of my fortune, what joys is it not in the power of rich men to give themselves, whenever they please!—Foretastes, indeed, of those we are bid to hope for: which can surely only exceed these, as *then* we shall be all intellect, and better fitted to receive them."—" 'Tis too much!—too much," said I, in broken accents: "how am I oppressed with the pleasure you give me!—O, Sir, bless me more gradually, and more cautiously—for I cannot bear it!" And, indeed, my heart went flutter, flutter, flutter, at his dear breast, as if it wanted to break its too narrow prison, to mingle still more intimately with his own.

Surely, my beloved parents, nobody's happiness is so great as mine!—If it proceeds thus from degree to degree, and is to be augmented by the charming hope, that the dear second author of our blessings, be the uniformly good as well as the partially kind man to us, what a felicity will this be! and if our prayers shall be heard, and we shall have the pleasure to think, that his advances in piety are owing not a little to them, and to the example God shall give us grace to set; then, indeed, may we take the pride to think, we have repaid his goodness to us, and that we have satisfied the debt, which nothing less can discharge.

Forgive me, my worthy parents, if my style on this subject be raised above the natural simplicity, more suited to my humble talents. But how can I help it! For when the mind is elevated, ought not the sense we have of our happiness to make our expressions soar equally? Can the affections be so highly raised as mine are on these occasions, and the thoughts creep grovelling like one's ordinary self? No, indeed!—Call not this, therefore, the gift of utterance, if it should appear to you in a better light than it deserves. It is the gift of gratitude; a gift which makes you and me to *speak* and *write*, as I hope it will make us *act*, above ourselves. Thus will our gratitude be the inspirer of joy to our common benefactor; and his joy will heighten our gratitude; and so we shall proceed, as cause and effect to each other's happiness, to bless the dear man who blesses us. And will it be right then to say, you are uneasy under such (at least as to your wills) returned and discharged obligations? God Almighty requires only a thankful heart for all the mercies he heaps upon the children of men; my dear Mr. B., who in these particulars imitates Divinity, desires no more. You *have* this thankful heart; and that to such a high degree of gratitude, that nobody can exceed you.

But yet, when your worthy minds would be too much affected with your gratitude, so as to lay under the restraints you mention, to the dear gentleman, and for his sake, to your dependent daughter; let me humbly advise you, with more particular, more abstracted aspirations, than at other times, to raise your thoughts upwards, and consider who it is that gives *him* the opportunity; and pray for him and for me; for *him*, that all his future actions may be of a piece with this noble disposition of mind; for *me*, that I may continue humble, and consider myself blest for your sakes, and in order that I may be, in some sort, a rewarder, in the hands of Providence, of this its dear excellent agent; and then we shall look forward, all of us, with pleasure, *indeed*, to that state, where there is no distinction of degree, and where the humble cottager shall be upon a par with the proudest monarch.

O my dear parents, how can you, as in your *postscript*, say, " May we not be *favoured* now-and-then with a letter? " Call *me* your daughter, your Pamela—I am no lady to you. I have more pleasure to be called your comfort, and thought to act worthy of the sentiments with which your example and instructions have inspired me, than in any other thing in this life; my determined duty to our common benefactor, the best of gentlemen and husbands, excepted. God has blessed me for your sakes, and has thus answered for me all your prayers; nay, *more* than answered all you or I could have wished or hoped for. We only prayed, only hoped, that God would preserve *you* honest, and *me* virtuous : and, O see, my excellent parents, how we are crowned with blessings upon blessings, till we are the talk of all that know us.

Hence, my dear parents (I mean, from the delight I have in writing to you, which transports me far above my own sphere), you'll see, that I *must* write, and cannot help it, if I would. And *will* it be a great joy to you?—And is there any thing that can add to your joy, think you, in the power of your Pamela, that she would not *do*? O that the lives and healths

9

of my dearest Mr. B. and you, my parents, may be continued to me ! And who can then be so blest as your Pamela?

I *will* write, *depend* upon it, on every occasion—and you augment my joys to think it is in my power to add to your comforts. Nor can you conceive my pleasure in hoping that this your new happy lot may, by relieving you from corroding care, and the too wearying effects of hard labour, add, in these your advanced years, to both your days. For, so happy am I, I can have no grief, no pain, in looking forward, but from reflecting, that one day we must be separated.

But it is fit that we so comport ourselves as not to embitter our present happiness with prospects too gloomy—but bring our minds to be cheerfully thankful for the present, wisely to enjoy that *present* as we go along—and at last, when all is to be wound up—lie down, and say, " *Not mine*, but *Thy will be done*."

I have written much; yet have still more to say relating to other parts of your kind acceptable letter; and so will soon write again : for I must think every opportunity happy, whereby I can assure you, how much I am, and will ever be, without any addition to my name, if it will make you easier, *your dutiful*
PAMELA.

LETTER IV

MY DEAREST FATHER AND MOTHER,

I now write again, as I told you I should in my last; but I am half afraid to look at the copy of it; for your worthy hearts, so visible in your letter and my beloved's kind deportment upon shewing it to him, raised me into a frame of mind, bordering on ecstasy : yet I wrote my heart. But you must not, my dear father, write to your Pamela so affectingly. Your *steadier* mind could hardly bear your own moving strain, and you were forced to lay down your pen, and retire : how then could I, who love you so dearly, if you had not *increased* that love by fresh and stronger instances of your worthiness, forbear being affected, and raised above myself ! But I will not again touch upon this subject.

You must know then, that my dearest spouse commands me, with his kind respects, to tell you, he has thought of a method to make your *worthy hearts* easy; those were his words : " And this is," said he, " by putting that whole estate, with the new purchase, under your father's care, as I at first intended : he shall receive and pay, and order every thing as he pleases : and Longman, who grows in years, shall be eased of that burden.

Your father writes a very legible hand, and shall take what assistants he pleases; and do you, Pamela, see that this new task be made as easy and pleasant to him as possible. He shall make up his accounts only to you, my dear. And there will be several pleasures arise to me upon it: first, that it will be a relief to honest Longman, who has business enough on his hands. Next, it will make the good couple easy, to have an opportunity of enjoying that as their due, which now their too grateful hearts give them so many causeless scruples about. Thirdly, it will employ your father's time, more suitably to *your* liking and *mine*, because with more ease to himself; for you see his industrious will cannot be satisfied without doing something. In the fourth place, the management of this estate will gain him more respect and reverence among the tenants and his neighbours: and yet be all in his own way. For," added he, " you'll see, that it is always one point in view with me, to endeavour to convince every one, that I esteem and value them for their own intrinsic merit, and want not any body to distinguish them in any other light than that in which they have been accustomed to appear."

So, my dear father, the instrument will be drawn, and brought you by honest Mr. Longman, who will be with you in a few days to put the last hand to the new purchase, and to give you possession of your new commission, if you accept it, as I hope you will; and the rather, for my dear Mr. B.'s third reason; and knowing that this trust will be discharged as worthily and as sufficiently, after you are used to it, as if Mr. Longman himself was in it—and better it cannot be. Mr. Longman is very fond of this relief, and longs to be down to settle every thing with you, as to the proper powers, the method, &c. And he says, in his usual phrase, that he'll make it as easy to you as a glove.

If you do accept it, my dear Mr. B. will leave every thing to you, as to rent, where not already fixed, and, likewise, as to acts of kindness and favour to be done where you think proper; and he says, that, with his bad qualities, he was ever deemed a kind landlord; and that I can confirm in fifty instances to his honour: " So that the old gentleman," said he, " need not be afraid of being put upon severe or harsh methods of proceeding, where things will do without; and he can always befriend an honest man; by which means the province will be entirely such a one as suits with his inclination. If any thing difficult or perplexing arises," continued he, " or where a little knowledge in law-matters is necessary, Longman shall do all that: and your father will see that he will not have in those points a coadjutor too hard-hearted for his wish; for it was a rule my father set me, and I have strictly followed, that although I have a lawyer for my steward, it was rather to know how to do *right* things, than oppressive ones; and Longman has so well answered this intention, that he was always more noted for composing differences, than promoting lawsuits."

I dare say, my dear father, this will be acceptable to you, on the several accounts my dearest Mr. B. was pleased to mention: and what a charming contrivance is here! God for ever bless his considerate heart for it! To make you useful to him, and easy to yourself: as well as respected by, and even a benefactor to all around you! What can one say to all things? But what signifies exulting on one's gratitude for *one* benefit;—every hour the dear man heaps new ones upon us, and we can hardly thank him for one, but a second, and a third, and so on to countless degrees, confound one, and throw back our words upon our hearts before they are well formed, and oblige us to sit down under all with profound silence and admiration.

As to the desire of cousin Thomas, and Roger, to live with you, I endeavoured to sound what our dear benefactor's opinion was. He was pleased to say, " I have no choice in this case, my dear. Your father is his own master: he may employ whom he pleases; and, if they shew respect to him and your mother, I think, as he rightly observes, relationship should rather have the preference; and as he can remedy inconveniences, if he finds any, by all means to let every branch of your family have reason to rejoice with him."

But I have thought of this matter a good deal, since I had the favour of your letter; and I hope, since you condescend to ask my advice, you will excuse me, if I give it freely; yet entirely submitting all to your liking.

First, then, I think it better to have *any body* than relations; and for these reasons:

One is apt to expect more regard from them, and they more indulgence than strangers can hope for.

That where there is such a difference in the expectations of both, uneasiness cannot but arise.

That this will subject you to bear it, or to resent it, and to part with them. If you bear it, you will know no end of impositions: if you dismiss them, it will occasion ill-will. They will call you unkind; and you them ungrateful: and as your prosperous lot may raise you enviers, such will be apt to believe *them* rather than *you*.

Then the world will be inclined to think that we are crowding upon a generous gentleman a numerous family of indigent people; and it will be said, "The girl is filling every place with her relations, and *beleaguering*," as you significantly express it, "a worthy gentleman;" should one's kindred behave ever so worthily. So, in the next place, one would not, for *their* sakes, that this should be done; who may live with *less* reproach, and *equal* benefit, any where else; for I would not wish any one of them to be lifted out of his station, and made independent, at Mr. B.'s expense, if their industry will not do it; although I would never scruple to do any thing reasonable to promote or assist that industry, in the way of their callings.

Then, my dear father, I apprehend, that our honoured benefactor would be under some difficulty, from his natural politeness, and regard for you and me. You see how kindly, on all occasions, he treats you both, not only as the parents of his Pamela, but as if you were his own; and if you had any body as your servants there, who called you cousin, or grandfather, or uncle, he would not care, when he came down, to treat them on the foot of common servants, though they might think themselves honoured (as they would be, and as I shall always think *myself*) with his commands. And would it not, if they are modest and worthy, be as great a difficulty upon *them*, to be thus distinguished, as it would be to *him* and to *me*, for *his* sake? For otherwise (believe me, I hope you will, my dear father and mother), I could sit down and rejoice with the meanest and remotest relation I have. But in the world's eye, to every body but my best of parents, I must, if ever so reluctant to it, appear in a light that may not give discredit to his choice.

Then again, as I hinted, you will be able, without the least injury to our common benefactor, to do kinder things by any of our relations, when *not* with you, than you can do, if they *live* with you.

You may lend them a little money to put them in a way, if any thing offers that you think will be to their advantage. You can fit out my she-cousins to good reputable places. The younger you can put to school, or, when fit, to trades, according to their talents; and so they will be of course in a way to get an honest and creditable livelihood.

But, above all things, one would discourage such a proud and ambitious spirit in any of them, as should want to raise itself by favour instead of merit; and this the rather, for, undoubtedly, there are many more happy persons in low than in high life, take number for number all the world over.

I am sure, although four or five years of different life had passed with me, I had so much pride and pleasure in the thought of working for my living with you, if I could but get honest to you, that it made my confinement the more grievous, and, if possible, aggravated the apprehensions attending it.

But I beg of you, not to think these my reasons proceed from the bad motives of a heart tainted with pride on its high condition. Indeed there can be no reason for it, to one who thinks after this manner—the greatest families on earth have some among them who are unhappy and low in life; and shall such a one reproach me with having twenty low relations, because they have, peradventure, not above five?

Let us then, my dear parents, endeavour to judge of one another, as God, at the last day, will judge of us all: and then the honest peasant will stand fairer in our esteem than the guilty peer.

In short, this shall be my own rule—Every one who acts justly and honestly, I will look upon as my relation, whether so or not; and the more he wants my assistance, the more entitled to it he shall be, as well as to my esteem; while those who deserve it not, must expect only compassion from me, and my prayers were they my brothers or sisters. 'Tis true had I not been poor and lowly, I might not have thought thus: but if it be a right way of thinking, it is a blessing that I was so; and that shall never be matter of reproach to me, which one day will be matter of justification.

Upon the whole, I should think it advisable, my dear father and mother, to make such kind excuses to the offered service of my cousins, as your better reason shall suggest to you; and to do any thing else for them of *more* value, as their circumstances may require, or occasions offer to serve them.

But if the employing and having them about you, will add comfort to your lives, I give up entirely my own opinion, and doubt not every thing will be thought well of, that you shall think fit to do.

And so I conclude with assuring you, that I am, my ever-dear parents, *your dutiful and happy daughter*.

The copy of this letter I will keep to myself, till I have your answer, that you may be under no difficulty how to act in either of the cases mentioned in it.

My dearest Daughter,

How shall I do to answer, as they deserve, your two last letters? Sure no happy couple ever had such a child as we have! But it is in vain to aim at words like yours: and equally in vain for us to offer to set forth the thankfulness of our hearts, on the kind office your honoured husband has given us; for no reason but to favour us still more, and to quiet our minds in the notion of being useful to him. God grant I may be able to be so!—Happy shall I be, if I can! But I see the generous drift of his proposal; it is only to make me more easy from the nature of my employment, and, in my mind too, over-loaded as I may say, with benefits; and at the same time to make me more respected in my new neighbourhood.

I can only say, I most gratefully accept of the kind offer; and since it will ease the worthy Mr. Longman, shall with still greater pleasure do all I can in it. But I doubt I shall want ability; but I will be just and honest, however. That, by God's grace, will be within my own capacity; and that, I hope, I may answer for.

It is kind, indeed, to put it in my power to do good to those who shall deserve it; and I will take *double* pains to find out the true merit of such as I shall recommend to favour, and that their circumstances be really such as I shall represent them.

But one thing let me desire, that I make up my accounts to Mr. Longman, or to his honour himself, when he shall be here with us. I don't know how—but it will make me uneasy, if I am to make up my accounts to you: for so well known is your love to us, that though you would no more do an unjust thing, than, by God's grace, we should desire you; yet this same ill-willing world might think it was like making up accounts to one's self.

Do, my dearest child, get me off this difficulty, and I can have no other; for already I am in hopes I have hit upon a contrivance to improve the estate, and to better the condition of the tenants, at least not to worst them, and which, I hope, will please every body; but I will acquaint Mr. Longman with this, and take his advice; for I will not be too troublesome either to you, my dear child, or to your spouse.—If I could act so for his interest, as not to be a burden, what happy creatures should we both be in our own minds!—We find ourselves more and more respected by every one; and so far as shall be consistent with our new trust, we will endeavour to deserve it, that we may interest as many as know us in our own good wishes and prayers for the happiness of you both.

But let me say, how much convinced I am by your reasons for not taking to us any of our relations. Every one of those reasons has its force with us. How happy are we to have so prudent a daughter to advise with ! And I think myself obliged to promise this, that whatever I do for any of them above the amount of forty shillings at one time, I will take your direction in it, that your wise hints, of making every one continue their industry, and not to rely upon favour instead of merit, may be followed. I am sure this is the way to make them *happier* as well as *better* men and women; for, as I have often thought, if one were to have a hundred pounds a year, it would not do without industry; and with it, one may do with a quarter of it, and less.

In short, my dear child, your reasons are so good, that I wonder they came not into my head before, and then I needed not to have troubled you about the matter : but yet it ran in my own thought, that I could not like to be an encroacher :— for I hate a dirty thing; and, in the midst of my distresses, never could be guilty of one. Thank God for it.

You rejoice our hearts beyond expression at the hope you give us of receiving letters from you now-and-then : it will be the chief comfort of our lives, next to seeing you, as we expect we sometimes shall. But yet, my dear child, don't let us inconvenience you neither. Pray don't : you'll have enough upon your hands without—to be sure you will.

The workmen have made a good progress, and wish for Mr. Longman to come down ; as we also do.

You need not be afraid we should think you proud, or lifted up with your condition. You have weathered the first dangers, and but for your fine clothes and jewels, we should not see any difference between our dear Pamela and the much respected Mrs. B. But God has given you too much sense to be proud or lifted up. I remember, in your former writings, a saying of your 'squire's, speaking of you, that it was for persons not used to praise, and who did not deserve it, to be proud of it.

Every day brings us instances of the good name his honour and you, my dear child, have left behind you in this country. Here comes one, and then another, and a third, and a fourth; " Goodman Andrews," cries one, and, " Goody Andrews," cries another—(and some call us Mr. and Mrs., but we like the other full as well) " when heard you from his honour ? How does his lady do?—What a charming couple are they !—How lovingly do they live !—What an example do they give to all about them ! " Then one cries, " God bless them both," and another cries, " Amen; " and so says a third and a fourth; and all say, " But when do you expect them down again?—Such-a-one longs to see 'em—and will ride a day's journey, to have but a sight of 'em at church." And then they say, " How this gentleman praises them, and that lady admires them."—O what a happiness is this ! How do your poor mother and I stand fixed to the earth to hear both your praises, our tears trickling down our cheeks, and our hearts heaving as if they would burst with joy, till we are forced to take leave in half words, and hand-in-hand go in together to bless God, and bless you both. O my daughter, what a happy couple have God and you made us !

Your poor mother is very anxious about her dear child. I will not touch upon a matter so very irksome to you to hear of. But, though the time may be some months off, she every hour prays for your safety and happiness, and all the increase of felicity that his honour's generous heart can wish for.—That is all we will say at present; only, that we are, with continued prayers and blessings, my dearest child, *your loving father and mother,*

J. *and* E. ANDREWS.

LETTER VI

From Lady Davers to Mrs B.

MY DEAR PAMELA,

I intended to have been with you before this : but my lord has been a little indisposed with the gout, and Jackey has had an intermitting fever : but they are pretty well recovered, and it shall not be long before I see you, now I understand you are returned from your Kentish expedition.

We have been exceedingly diverted with your papers. You have given us, by their means, many a delightful hour, that otherwise would have hung heavy upon us; and we are all charmed with you. Lady Betty, and her noble mamma, has been of our party, whenever we have read your accounts. She is a dear generous lady, and has shed with us many a tear over them; and my lord has not been unmoved, nor Jackey neither, at some of your distresses and reflections. Indeed,

Pamela, you are a charming creature, and an ornament to your sex. We wanted to have had you among us a hundred times, as we read, that we might have loved, and kissed, and thanked you.

But after all, my brother, generous and noble as he seemed, when your trials were over, was a strange wicked young fellow; and happy it was for you both, that he was so cleverly caught in the trap he had laid for your virtue.

I can assure you, my lord longs to see you, and will accompany me; for, he says, he has but a faint idea of your person. I tell him, and them all, that you are the finest girl, and the most improved in person and mind, I ever beheld; and I am not afraid although they should imagine all they can in your favour, from my account, that they will be disappointed when they see and converse with you. But one thing more you must do, and then we will love you still more; and that is, send us the rest of your papers, down to your marriage at least; and farther, if you have written farther; for we all long to see the rest, as you relate it, though we know in general what has passed.

You leave off with an account of an angry letter I wrote to my brother, to persuade him to give you your liberty, and a sum of money; not doubting but his designs would end in your ruin, and, I own, not wishing he would marry you; for little did I know of your merit and excellence, nor could I, but for your letters so lately sent me, have had any notion of either. I don't question, but if you have recited my passionate behaviour to you, when at the hall, I shall make a ridiculous figure enough; but I will forgive all that, for the sake of the pleasure you *have* given me, and will still farther give me, if you comply with my request.

Lady Betty says, it is the best story she has heard, and the most instructive; and she longs to have the conclusion of it in your own words. She says now and then, "What a hopeful brother you have, Lady Davers! O these intriguing gentlemen!—What rogueries do they not commit! I should have had a fine husband of him, had I received your proposal! The *dear* Pamela would have run in his head, and had I been the first lady in the kingdom, I should have stood but a poor chance in his esteem; for, you see, his designs upon her began early."

She says, you had a good heart to go back again to him, when the violent wretch had driven you from him on such a slight occasion : but yet, she thinks the reasons you give in your relation, and your love for him (which then you began

18

to discover was your case), as well as the event, shewed you did right.

But we'll tell you all our judgments, when we have read the rest of your accounts. So pray send them as soon as you can, to (I won't write myself *sister* till then) *your affectionate*, &c.

B. DAVERS.

LETTER VII

MY GOOD DEAR LADY,

You have done me great honour in the letter your ladyship has been pleased to send me; and it is a high pleasure to me, now all is so happily over, that my poor papers in the least diverted you, and such honourable and worthy persons as your ladyship mentions. I could wish I might be favoured with such remarks on my conduct, so nakedly set forth (without any imagination that they would ever appear in such an assembly), as may be of use to me in my future life, and thus make me more worthy than it is otherwise possible I can be, of the honour to which I am raised. Do, dearest lady, favour me so far. I am prepared to receive blame, and to benefit by it, and cannot expect praise so much from my *actions* as from my *intentions ;* for indeed, these were always just and honourable : but why, even for these do I talk of praise, since, being prompted by impulses I could not resist, it can be no merit in me to have been governed by them ?

As to the papers following those in your hands, when I say, that they must needs appear impertinent to such judges, after what you know, I dare say, your ladyship will not insist upon them : yet I will not scruple briefly to mention what they contain.

All my dangers and trials were happily at an end : so that they only contain the conversations that passed between your ladyship's generous brother and me; his kind assurances of honourable love to me; my acknowledgments of unworthiness to him; Mrs. Jewkes's respectful change of behaviour towards me; Mr. B.'s reconciliation to Mr. Williams; his introducing me to the good families in the neighbourhood, and avowing before them his honourable intentions. A visit from my honest father, who (not knowing what to conclude from my letter to him before I returned to your honoured brother, desiring my papers from him) came in great anxiety of heart to know the worst, doubting I had at last been caught by a stratagem,

19

ending in my ruin. His joyful surprise to find how happy I was likely to be. All the hopes given me, answered by the private celebration of our nuptials—an honour so much above all that my utmost ambition could make me aspire to, and which I never can deserve ! Your ladyship's arrival, and anger, not knowing I was actually married, but supposing me a vile wicked creature; in which case I should have deserved the worst of usage. Mr. B.'s angry lessons to me, for daring to interfere; though I thought in the tenderest and most dutiful manner, between your ladyship and himself. The most acceptable goodness and favour of your ladyship afterwards to me, of which, as becomes me, I shall ever retain the most grateful sense. My return to this sweet mansion in a manner so different from my quitting it, where I had been so happy for four years, in paying my duty to the best of mistresses, your ladyship's excellent mother, to whose goodness, in taking me from my poor honest parents, and giving me what education I have, I owe, under God, my happiness. The joy of good Mrs. Jervis, Mr. Longman, and all the servants, on this occasion. Mr. B.'s acquainting me with Miss Godfrey's affair, and presenting to me the pretty Miss Goodwin, at the dairy-house. Our appearance at church; the favour of the gentry in the neighbourhood, who, knowing your ladyship had not disdained to look upon me, and to be favourable to me, came the more readily into a neighbourly intimacy with me, and still so much the more readily, as the continued kindness of my dear benefactor, and his condescending deportment to me before them (as if I had been worthy of the honour done me), did credit to his own generous act.

These, my lady, down to my good parents setting out to this place, in order to be settled, by my honoured benefactor's bounty, in the Kentish farm, are the most material contents of my remaining papers : and though they might be the most agreeable to those for whom only they were written, yet, *as* they were principally matters of course, after what your ladyship has with you; *as* the joy of my fond heart can be better judged of by your ladyship than described by me; and as you are acquainted with all the particulars that can be worthy of any other person's notice but my dear parents : I am sure your ladyship will dispense with your commands; and I make it my humble request that you will.

For, Madam, you must needs think, that *when* my doubts were dispelled; *when* confident all my trials were over; *when* I had a prospect of being so abundantly rewarded for what I suffered;

when every hour rose upon me with new delight, and fraught with fresh instances of generous kindness from such a dear gentleman, my master, my benefactor, the son of my honoured lady : your ladyship must needs think, I say, that I must be *too* much affected, my heart *too* much opened ; and especially as it then (relieved from its past anxieties and fears, which had kept down and damped the latent flame) first discovered impressions of which before I hardly thought it susceptible.—So that it is scarce possible, that my *joy* and my *prudence,* if I were to be tried by such judges of delicacy and decorum as Lord and Lady Davers, the honoured countess, and Lady Betty, could be so *intimately,* so *laudably* coupled, as were to be wished : although the continued sense of my unworthiness, and the disgrace the dear gentleman would bring upon himself by his generous goodness to me, always went hand in hand with my *joy* and my *prudence ;* and what these considerations took from the *former,* being added to the *latter,* kept me steadier and more equal to myself, than otherwise it was possible such a young creature as I could have been.

Wherefore my good lady, I hope I stand excused, and shall not bring upon myself the censure of being disobedient to your commands.

Besides, Madam, since you inform me that my good Lord Davers will attend you hither, I should never dare to look his lordship in the face, if all the emotions of my heart, on such affecting occasions, stood confessed to his lordship; and if I am ashamed they should to your ladyship, to the countess, and Lady Betty, whose goodness must induce you all three to think favourably, in such circumstances, of one who is of your own sex, how would it concern me, for the same to appear before such gentlemen as my lord and his nephew?—Indeed I could not look up to either of them in the sense of this.—And give me leave to hope, that some of the scenes, in the letters your ladyship had, were not read to gentlemen ; your ladyship must needs know which I mean, and will think of my two grand trials of all. For though I was the innocent subject of wicked attempts, and so cannot, I hope, suffer in any one's opinion for what I could not help ; yet, for your dear brother's sake, as well as for the decency of the matter, one would not, when having the honour to appear before my lord and his nephew, he looked upon, methinks, with that levity of eye and thought, which, perhaps, hard-hearted gentlemen may pass upon one, by reason of those very scenes, which would move pity and concern in a good lady's breast, for a poor creature so attempted.

21

So, my dear lady, be pleased to tell me, if the gentlemen *have* heard all—I hope not—and also to point out to me such parts of my conduct as deserve blame : indeed, I will try to make a good use of your censure, and am sure I shall be thankful for it ; for it will make me hope to be more and more worthy of the honour I have, of being exalted into such a distinguished family, and the right the best of gentlemen has given me to style myself *your ladyship's most humble, and most obliged servant,*

P. B.

LETTER VIII

From Lady Davers, in reply.

MY DEAR PAMELA,

You have given us all a great disappointment in declining to oblige me with the sequel of your papers. I was a little out of humour with you at first ;—I must own I was :—for I cannot bear denial, when my heart is set upon any thing. But Lady Betty became your advocate, and said, she thought you very excusable : since, no doubt, there might be many tender things, circumstanced as you were, well enough for your parents to see, but for nobody else ; and relations of our side, the least of all, whose future intimacy, and frequent visits, might give occasions for raillery and remarks, not otherwise agreeable. I regard her apology for you the more, because I knew it was a great baulk to her, that you did not comply with my request. But now, child, when you know me more, you'll find, that if I am obliged to give up one point, I always insist on another, as near it as I can, in order to see if it be only *one* thing I am to be refused, or *every* thing ; in which last case, I know how to take my measures, and resent.

Now this is what I insist upon ; that you correspond with me the same as you did with your parents, and acquaint me with every passage that is of concern to you ; beginning with your account how both of you spent your time when in Kent ; for you must know we are all taken with your duty to your parents, and the discretion of the good couple, and think you have given a very edifying example of filial piety to all who shall hear your story : for if so much duty is owing to parents, where nothing can be done for one, how much more is it to be expected, where there is power to add to the natural obligation, all the comforts and conveniences of life ? We people in upper life love to hear how gratitude and unexpected benefits operate upon honest minds, who have little more than plain artless nature for their guide; and we flatter ourselves with the hopes of many a delightful hour, by your means, in this our solitary situation, if obliged to pass the next winter in it, as my lord and the earl threaten me, and the countess, and Lady Betty, that we shall. Then let us hear of every thing that gives you joy or trouble : and if my brother carries you to town, for the winter, while he attends parliament, the advices you can give us of what passes in London, and of the public entertainments and diversions he will take you to, related in your own artless and natural observations, will be as diverting to us, as if at them ourselves. For a young creature of your good understanding, to whom all these things will be quite new, will give us, perhaps, a better taste of them, their beauties and defects, than we might have before; for we people of quality go to those places, dressed out and adorned in such a manner, outvying one another, as if we considered ourselves as so many parts of the public entertainment, and are too much pleased with ourselves to be able so to attend to what we see, as to form a right judgment of it; but some of us behave with so much indifference to the entertainment, as if we thought ourselves above being diverted by what we come to see, and as if our view was rather to trifle away our time, than improve ourselves by attending to the story of the action.

See, Pamela, I shall not make an unworthy correspondent altogether, for I can get into thy grave way, and moralize a little now and then : and if you'll promise to oblige me by your constant correspondence in this way, and divest yourself of all restraint, as if you were writing to your parents (and I can tell you, you'll write to one who will be as candid and as favourable to you as they can be), then I am sure we shall have truth and nature from you; and these are things which we are generally so much lifted above, by our conditions, that we hardly know what they are.

But I have written enough for one letter; and yet, having more to say, I will, after this, send another, without waiting for your answer, which you may give to both together; and am, *yours,* &c.   B. DAVERS.

LETTER IX

DEAR PAMELA,

I am very glad thy honest man has let thee into the affair of Sally Godfrey. But pr'ythee, Pamela, tell us how he

23

did it, and thy thoughts upon it, for that is a critical case; and as he has represented it, so shall I know what to say of it before you and him : for I would not make mischief between you for the world.

This, let me tell you, will be a trying part of your conduct. For he loves the child, and will judge of you by your conduct towards it. He dearly loved her mother; and notwithstanding her fault, she well deserved it : for she was a sensible, ay, and a modest lady, and of an ancient and genteel family. But he was heir to a noble estate, was of a bold and enterprising spirit, fond of intrigue—Don't let this concern you—You'll have the greater happiness, and merit too, if you can hold him; and, 'tis my opinion, if any body can, you will. Then he did not like the young lady's mother, who sought artfully to entrap him. So that the poor girl, divided between her inclination for him, and her duty to her designing mother, gave into the plot upon him : and he thought himself—vile wretch as he was for all that !—at liberty to set up plot against plot, and the poor lady's honour was the sacrifice.

I hope you spoke well of her to him—I hope you received the child kindly—I hope you had presence of mind to do this—For it is a nice part to act; and all his observations were up, I dare say, on the occasion—Do let me hear how it was. And write without restraint; for although I am not your mother, yet am I *his* eldest sister, you know, and as such—Come, I will say so, in hopes you'll oblige me—*your* sister, and so entitled to expect a compliance with my request : for is there not a duty, in degree, to elder sisters from younger?

As to our remarks upon your behaviour, they have been much to your credit : but nevertheless, I will, to encourage you to enter into this requested correspondence with me, consult Lady Betty, and will go over your papers again, and try to find fault with your conduct, and if we see any thing censurable, will freely let you know our minds.

But, before-hand, I can tell you, we shall be agreed in one opinion; and that is, that we know not who would have acted as you have done, upon the whole. So, Pamela, you see I put myself upon the same foot of correspondence with you. Not that I will promise to answer every latter : no, you must not expect that. Your part will be a kind of narrative, purposely designed to entertain us here; and I hope to receive six, seven, eight, or ten letters, as it may happen, before I return one : but such a part I will bear in it, as shall let you know our opinion of your proceedings, and relations of things. And as you wish to be found fault with, you shall freely have it (though not in a splenetic or ill-natured way), as often as you give occasion. Now, Pamela, I have two views in this. One is to see how a man of my brother's spirit, who has not denied himself any genteel liberties (for it must be owned he never was a common town rake, and had always a dignity in his roguery), will behave himself to you, and in wedlock, which used to be freely sneered at by him; the next, that I may love you more and more as by your letters, I shall be more and more acquainted with you, as well as by conversation; so that you can't be off, if you would.

I know, however, you will have one objection to this; and that is, that your family affairs will require your attention, and not give the time you used to have for this employment. But consider, child, the station you are raised to does not require you to be quite a domestic animal. You are lifted up to the rank of a lady, and you must act up to it, and not think of setting such an example, as will draw upon you the ill-will and censure of other ladies. For will any of our sex visit one who is continually employing herself in such works as either must be a reproach to herself, or to them?—You'll have nothing to do but to give orders. You will consider yourself as the task-mistress, and the common herd of female servants as so many negroes directing themselves by your nod; or yourself as the master-wheel, in some beautiful pieces of mechanism, whose dignified grave motions is to set a-going all the under-wheels, with a velocity suitable to their respective parts. Let your servants, under your direction, do all that relates to household management; they cannot write to entertain and instruct as you can : so what will you have to do?—I'll answer my own question : In the first place, endeavour to please your sovereign lord and master; and let me tell you, any other woman in England, be her quality ever so high, would have found enough to do to succeed in that. Secondly, to receive and pay visits, in order, for his credit as well as your own, to make your fashionable neighbours fond of you. Then, thirdly, you will have time upon your hands (as your monarch himself rises early, and is tolerably regular for such a brazen face as he has been) to write to me in the manner I have mentioned, and expect; and I see plainly, by your style, nothing can be easier for you than to do this.

Thus, and with reading, may your time be filled up with reputations to yourself, and delight to others, till a fourth employment puts itself upon you : and that is (shall I tell you in one word, without mincing the matter?) a succession of brave boys, to perpetuate a family, for many hundred years esteemed worthy and eminent, which, being now reduced, in the direct line, to him and me, *expects* it from you; or else let me tell you (nor will I baulk it), my brother, by descending to the wholesome cot—excuse me, Pamela—will want one apology for his conduct, be as excellent as you may.

I say this, child, not to reflect upon you, since the thing is done; for I love you dearly, and will love you more and more—but to let you know what is expected from you, and encourage you in the prospect already opening to you both, and to me, who have the welfare of the family I sprung from so much at heart, although I know this will be attended with some anxieties to a mind so thoughtful and apprehensive as yours seems to be.

O but this puts me in mind of your solicitude, lest the gentlemen should have seen every thing contained in your letters—But this I will particularly speak to in a third letter, having filled my paper on all sides: and am, till then, *yours*, &c.

B. DAVERS.

You see, and I hope will take it as a favour, that I break the ice, and begin first in the indispensably expected correspondence between us.

LETTER X

From the same.

And so, Pamela, you are solicitous to know, if the gentlemen have seen every part of your papers? I can't say but they have: nor, except in regard to the reputation of your saucy man, do I see why the part you hint at might not be read by those to whom the rest might be shewn.

I can tell you, Lady Betty, who is a very nice and delicate lady, had no objection to any part, though read before men: only now and then crying out, "O the vile man!—See, Lord Davers, what wretches you men are!" And, commiserating you, "Ah! the poor Pamela!" And expressing her impatience to hear how you escaped at this time, and at that, and rejoicing in your escape. And now-and-then, "O, Lady Davers, what a vile brother you have!—I hate him perfectly. The poor girl cannot be made amends for all this, though he has married her. Who, that knows these things of him, would wish him to be hers, with all his advantages of person, mind, and fortune?"

And such-like expressions in your praise, and condemning him and his wicked attempts.

But I can tell you this, that except one had heard every tittle of your danger, how near you were to ruin, and how little he stood upon taking any measures to effect his vile purposes, even daring to attempt you in the presence of a *good* woman, which was a wickedness that every *wicked* man could not be guilty of; I say, except one had known these things, one could not have judged of the merit of your resistance, and how shocking those attempts were to your virtue, for that life itself was endangered by them : nor, let me tell you, could I, in particular, have so well justified him for marrying you (I mean with respect to his own proud and haughty temper of mind), if there had been room to think he could have had you upon easier terms.

It was necessary, child, on twenty accounts, that we, your and his well-wishers and his relations, should know that he had tried every stratagem to subdue you to his purpose, before he married you : and how would it have answered to his intrepid character, and pride of heart, had we not been particularly led into the nature of those attempts, which you so nobly resisted, as to convince us all, that you have deserved the good fortune you have met with, as well as all the kind and respectful treatment he can possibly shew you ?

Nor ought you to be concerned who sees any the most tender parts of your story, except, as I said, for *his* sake ; for it must be a very unvirtuous mind that can form any other ideas from what you relate than those of terror and pity for you. Your expressions are too delicate to give the nicest ear offence, except at him. You paint no scenes but such as make his wickedness odious : and that gentleman, much more lady, must have a very corrupt heart, who could from such circumstances of distress, make any reflections, but what should be to your honour, and in abhorrence of such actions. I am so convinced of this, that by this rule I would judge of any man's heart in the world, better than by a thousand declarations and protestations. I do assure you, rakish as Jackey is, and freely as I doubt not that Lord Davers has formerly lived (for he has been a man of pleasure), they gave me, by their behaviour on these tender occasions, reason to think they had more virtue than not to be very apprehensive for your safety ; and my lord often exclaimed, that he could not have thought his brother such a libertine, neither.

Besides. child, were not these things written in confidence

to your mother? And, bad as his actions were to you, if you had not recited all you could recite, would there not have been room for any one, who saw what you wrote, to imagine they had been still worse? And how could the terror be supposed to have had such effects upon you, as to endanger your life, without imagining you had undergone the worst a vile man *could* offer, unless you had told us what that was which he *did* offer, and so put a bound, as it were, to one's fears of what you suffered, which otherwise must have been injurious to your purity, though you could not help it?

Moreover, Pamela, it was but doing justice to the libertine himself to tell your mother the whole truth, that she might know he was not so very abandoned, but he could stop short of the execution of his wicked purposes, which he apprehended, if pursued, would destroy the life, that, of all lives, he would choose to preserve; and you owed also thus much to your parents' peace of mind, that, after all their distracting fears for you, they might see they had reason to rejoice in an uncontaminated daughter. And one cannot but reflect, now he has made you his wife, that it must be satisfaction to the wicked man, as well as to yourself, that he was not more guilty than he *was*, nor took more liberties than he *did*.

For my own part, I must say, that I could not have accounted for your fits, by any descriptions short of those you give; and had you been less particular in the circumstances, I should have judged he had been still *worse*, and your person, though not your mind, less pure, than his pride would expect from the woman he should marry; for this is the case of all rakes, that though they indulge in all manner of libertinism themselves, there is no class of men who exact greater delicacy from the persons they marry, though they care not how bad they make the wives, the sisters, and daughters of others.

I will only add (and send all my three letters together), that we all blame you in some degree for bearing the wicked Jewkes in your sight, after her most impudent assistance in his lewd attempt: much less, we think, ought you to have left her in her place, and rewarded her; for her vileness could hardly be equalled by the worst actions of the most abandoned procuress.

I know the difficulties you labour under, in his arbitrary will, and intercession for her: but Lady Betty rightly observes, that he knew what a vile woman she was, when he put you into her power, and no doubt employed her, being sure she would answer all his purposes: and that therefore she should have had very

28

little opinion of the sincerity of his reformation, while he was so solicitous in keeping her, and having her put upon a foot, in the present on your nuptials, with honest Jervis.

She would, she says, had she been in your case, have had *one* struggle for her dismission, let it have been taken as it would; and he that was so well pleased with your virtues, must have thought this a natural consequence of it, if he was in earnest to reclaim.

I know not whether you shew him all I write : but I have written this last part in the cover, as well for want of room, as that you may keep it from him, if you please. Though if you think it will serve any good end, I am not against shewing to him all I write. For I must ever speak my mind, though I were to smart for it ; and that nobody can or has the heart to make me do, but my bold brother. So, Pamela, for this time, *Adieu.*

LETTER XI

My good Lady,

I am honoured with your ladyship's three letters, the contents of which are highly obliging to me : and I should be inexcusable if I did not comply with your injunctions, and be very proud and thankful for your ladyship's condescension in accepting of my poor scribble, and promising such a rich and valuable return ; of which you have already given such ample and delightful instances. I will not plead my defects, to excuse my obedience. I only fear that the awe which will be always upon me, when I write to your ladyship, will lay me under so great a restraint, that I shall fall short even of the merit my papers have already made for me, through your kind indulgence.—Yet, sheltering myself under your goodness, I will cheerfully comply with every thing your ladyship expects from me, that it is in my power to do.

You will give me leave, Madam, to put into some little method, the particulars of what you desire of me, that I may speak to them all : for, since you are so good as to excuse me from sending the rest of my papers (which indeed would not bear in many places), I will omit nothing that shall tend to convince you of my readiness to obey you in every thing else.

First, then, your ladyship would have the particulars of the happy fortnight we passed in Kent, on one of the most agreeable occasions that could befall me.

Secondly, an account of the manner in which your dear

brother acquainted me with the affecting story of Miss Godfrey, and my behaviour upon it.

And, thirdly, I presume your ladyship, and Lady Betty, expect me to say something upon your welcome remarks on my conduct towards Mrs. Jewkes.

The other particulars your ladyship mentions, will naturally fall under one or other of these three heads—But expect not, my lady, though I begin in method thus, that I shall keep up to it. If you will not allow for me, and keep in view the poor Pamela Andrews in all I write, but have Mrs. B. in your eye, what will become of me?—But I promise myself so much improvement from this correspondence, that I enter upon it with a greater delight than I can express, notwithstanding the mingled awe and diffidence that will accompany me, in every part of the agreeable task. To begin with the first article:

Your dear brother and my honest parents (I know your ladyship will expect from me, that on all occasions I should speak of them with the duty that becomes a good child) with myself, set out on the Monday morning for Kent, passing through St. Albans to London, at both which places we stopped a night; for our dear benefactor would make us take easy journeys: and on Wednesday evening we arrived at the sweet place allotted for the good couple. We were attended only by Abraham and John, on horseback: for Mr. Colbrand, having sprained his foot, was in the travelling-coach, with the cook, the housemaid, and Polly Barlow, a genteel new servant, whom Mrs. Brooks recommended to wait on me.

Mr. Longman had been there a fortnight, employed in settling the terms of an additional purchase of this pretty well-wooded and well-watered estate : and his account of his proceedings was very satisfactory to his honoured principal. He told us, he had much ado to dissuade the tenants from pursuing a formed resolution of meeting their landlord on horseback, at some miles distance ; for he had informed them when he expected us : but knowing how desirous Mr. B. was of being retired, he had ventured to assure them, that when every thing was settled, and the new purchase actually entered upon, they would have his presence among them often ; and that he would introduce them all at different times to their worthy landlord, before we left the country.

The house is large, and very commodious ; and we found every thing about it, and in it, exceeding neat and convenient ; owing to the worthy Mr. Longman's care and direction. The ground is well-stocked, the barns and outhouses in excellent repair ;

and my poor parents have only to wish, that they and I may be deserving of half the goodness we experience from your bountiful brother.

But, indeed, Madam, I have the pleasure of discovering every day more and more, that there is not a better disposed and more generous man in the world than himself, for I verily think he has not been so careful to conceal his *bad* actions as his *good* ones. His heart is naturally beneficent, and his beneficence is the gift of God for the most excellent purposes, as I have often freely told him. Pardon me, my dear lady; I wish I may not be impertinently grave : but I find a great many instances of his considerate charity, which few knew of, and which, since I have been his almoner, could not avoid coming to my knowledge. But this, possibly, is no news to your ladyship. Every body knows the generous goodness of your *own* heart : every one wanting relief tasted the bounty of your excellent *mother* my late honoured lady : so that 'tis a *family grace*, and I have no need to speak of it to you, Madam.

This cannot, I hope, be construed as if I would hereby suppose ourselves less obliged. I know nothing so godlike in human nature as this disposition to do good to our fellow-creatures : for is it not following immediately the example of that generous Providence which every minute is conferring blessings upon us all, and by giving power to the rich, makes them but the dispensers of its benefits to those that want them ? Yet, as there are but too many objects of compassion, and as the most beneficent cannot, like Omnipotence, do good to all, how much are they obliged who are distinguished from others !—And this being kept in mind, will always contribute to make the benefited receive, as thankfully as they *ought*, the favours of the obliger.

I know not if I write to be understood, in all I mean; but my grateful heart is so over-filled when on this subject, that methinks I want to say a great deal more at the same time that I am apprehensive I say too much. Yet, perhaps, the copies of the letters I here inclose (that marked [I.] written by me to my parents, on our return to Kent; that marked [II.] from my dear father in answer to it; and that marked [III.] mine in reply to his) will (at the same time that they may convince your ladyship that I will conceal nothing from you in the course of this correspondence, which may in the least amuse and divert you, or better explain our grateful sentiments), in a great measure, answer what your ladyship expects from me, as to the happy fortnight we passed in Kent.

31

I will now conclude, choosing to suspend the correspondence, till I know from your ladyship, whether it will not be too low, too idle for your attention; whether you will not dispense with your own commands when you see I am so little likely to answer what you may possibly expect from me: or whether, if you insist upon my scribbling, you would have me write in any other way, be less tedious, less serious—in short, less or more any thing. For all that is in my power, your ladyship may command from, *Madam, your obliged and faithful servant,*

P. B.

Your dearest brother, from whose knowledge I would not keep any thing that shall take up any considerable portion of my time, gives me leave to proceed in this correspondence, if you command it; and is pleased to say, he will content himself to see such parts of it, and *only* such parts, as I shall shew him, or read to him.—Is not this very good, Madam?—O, my lady, you don't know how happy I am!

LETTER XII

From Lady Davers to Mrs. B.

MY DEAR PAMELA,

You very much oblige me by your cheerful compliance with my request: I leave it entirely to you to write as you shall be in the humour, when you take up your pen; and then I shall have you write with less restraint: for, you must know, that what we admire in *you*, are truth and nature, not studied or elaborate epistles. We can hear at church, or read in our closets, fifty good things that we expect not from you: but we cannot receive from any body else the pleasure of sentiments flowing with that artless ease, which so much affects us when we read your letters. Then, my sweet girl, your gratitude, prudence, integrity of heart, your humility, shine so much in all your letters and thoughts, that no wonder my brother loves you as he does.

But I shall make you proud, I doubt, and so by praise ruin those graces which we admire, and, but for that, cannot praise you too much. In my conscience, if thou canst hold as thou hast begun, I believe thou wilt have him *all to thyself;* and that was more than I once thought any woman on this side the seventieth year of his age would ever be able to say. The letters to and from your parents, we are charmed with, and the communicating of them to me, I take to be as great an instance of your confidence in me, as it is of your judgment and prudence; for you cannot but think, that we, his relations, are a little watchful over your conduct, and have our eyes upon you, to observe what use you are likely to make of your power over your man, with respect to your own relations.

Hitherto all is unexampled prudence, and you take the right method to reconcile even the proudest of us to your marriage, and make us not only love you, but respect your parents : for their honesty will, I perceive, be their distinguishing character, and they will not forget themselves, nor their former condition.

I can tell you, you are exactly right; for if you were to be an *encroacher*, as the good old man calls it, my brother would be the first to see it, and would gradually think less and less of you, till possibly he might come to despise you, and to repent of his choice : for the least shadow of an imposition, or low cunning, or mere selfishness, he cannot bear.

In short, you are a charming girl; and Lady Betty says so too; and moreover adds, that if he makes you not the best and *faithfullest* of husbands, he cannot deserve you, for all his fortune and birth. And in my heart, I begin to think so too.

But won't you oblige me with the sequel of your letter to your father? For, you promise, my dear charming scribbler, in that you sent me, to write again to his letter; and I long to see how you answer the latter part of it, about your relations desiring already to come and live with him. I know what I *expect* from you. But let it be what it will, send it to me exactly as you wrote it; and I shall see whether I have reason to praise or reprove you. For surely, Pamela, you must leave one room to blame you for something. Indeed I can hardly bear the thought, that you should so much excel as you do, and have more prudence, by nature, as it were, than the best of us get in a course of the genteelest educations and with fifty advantages, at least, in conversation, that *you* could not have, by reason of my mother's retired life, while you were with her, and your close attendance on her person.

But I'll tell you what has been a great improvement to you; it is your own writings. This itch of scribbling has been a charming help. For here, having a natural fund of good sense, and prudence above your years, you have, with the observations these have enabled you to make, been flint and steel too, as I may say, to yourself : so that you have struck *fire* when you pleased, wanting nothing but a few dry leaves, like the first pair in old Du Bartas, to serve as tinder to catch your animating sparks. So that reading constantly, and thus using yourself to write, and enjoying besides a good memory, every thing you heard and read became your own; and not only so, but was improved by passing through more salubrious ducts and vehicles; like some fine fruit grafted upon a common free-stock, whose more exuberant juices serve to bring to quicker and greater perfection the downy peach, or the smooth nectarine, with its crimson blush.

Really, Pamela, I believe, I, too, shall improve by writing to you—Why, you dear saucy-face, at this rate, you'll make every one that converses with you, better, and wiser, and *wittier* too, as far as I know, than they ever before thought there was *room* for 'em to be.

As to my own part, I begin to like what I have written myself, I think; and your correspondence may revive the poetical ideas that used to fire my mind, before I entered into the drowsy married life; for my good Lord Davers's turn happens not to be to books; and so by degrees my imagination was in a manner quenched, and I, as a dutiful wife should, endeavoured to form my taste by that of the man I chose.—But, after all, Pamela, you are not to be a little proud of my correspondence; and I could not have thought it ever would have come to this; but you will observe, that I am the more free and unreserved, to encourage *you* to write without restraint : for already you have made us a family of writers and readers; so that Lord Davers himself is become enamoured of your letters, and desires of all things he may hear read every one that passes between us. Nay, Jackey, for that matter, who was the most thoughtless, whistling, sauntering fellow you ever knew, and whose delight in a book ran no higher than a song or a catch, now comes in with an enquiring face, and vows he'll set pen to paper, and turn letter-writer himself; and intends (if my brother won't take it amiss, he says) to begin to *you*, provided he could be sure of an answer.

I have twenty things still to say; for you have unlocked all our bosoms. And yet I intended not to write above ten or a dozen lines when I began; only to tell you, that I would have you take your own way, in your subjects, and in your style. And if you will but give me hope, that you are in the way I so much wish to have you in, I will then call myself your affectionate sister; but till then, it shall only barely be *your correspondent*,

B. DAVERS.

You'll proceed with the account of your Kentish affair, I doubt not.

LETTER XIII

My dear good Lady,

What kind, what generous things are you pleased to say of your happy correspondent! And what reason have I to value myself on such an advantage as is now before me, if I am capable of improving it as I ought, from a correspondence with so noble and so admired a lady! To be praised by such a genius, and my honoured benefactor's worthy sister, whose favour, next to his, it was always my chief ambition to obtain, is what would be enough to fill with vanity a steadier and a more equal mind than mine.

I have heard from my late honoured lady, what a fine pen her beloved daughter was mistress of, when she pleased to take it up. But I never could have presumed, but from your ladyship's own motion, to hope to be in any manner the subject of it, much less to be called your correspondent.

Indeed, Madam, I *am* very proud of this honour, and consider it as such a heightening to my pleasures, as only *that* could give; and I will set about obeying your ladyship without reserve.

But, first, permit me to disclaim any merit, from my own poor writings, to that improvement which your goodness imputes to me. What I have to boast, of that sort, is owing principally, if it deserves commendation, to my late excellent lady.

It is hard to be imagined what pains her ladyship took with her poor servant. Besides making me keep a book of her charities dispensed by me, I always set down, in my way, the cases of the distressed, their griefs from misfortunes, and their joys of her bountiful relief; and so I entered early into the various turns that affected worthy hearts, and was taught the better to regulate my own, especially by the help of her fine observations, when I read what I wrote. For many a time has her generous heart overflowed with pleasure at my remarks, and with praises; and I was her good girl, her dear Pamela, her hopeful maiden; and she would sometimes snatch my hand with transport, and draw me to her, and vouchsafe to kiss me; and always was saying, what she would do for me, if God spared her, and I continued to be deserving.

O my dear lady! you cannot think what an encouragement

35

this condescending behaviour and goodness was to me. Indeed, Madam, you *cannot* think it.

I used to throw myself at her feet, and embrace her knees; and, my eyes streaming with tears of joy, would often cry, " O continue to me, my dearest lady, the blessing of your favour, and kind instructions, and it is all your happy Pamela can wish for."

But I will proceed to obey your ladyship, and write with as much freedom as I possibly *can :* for you must not expect, that I can entirely divest myself of that awe which will necessarily lay me under a greater restraint, than if writing to my parents, whose partiality for their daughter made me, in a manner, secure of their good opinions.

To shorten the work before me, in the account I am to give of the sweet fortnight that we passed in Kent, I enclose not only the copy of the letter your ladyship requested, but my father's answer to it.

The letters I sent before, and those I now send, will afford several particulars; such as a brief description of the house and farm, and your honoured brother's intentions of retiring thither now-and-then; of the happiness and gratitude of my dear parents, and their wishes to be able to deserve the comfort his goodness has heaped upon them; and that in stronger lights than I am able to set them; I will only, in a summary manner, mention the rest; and, particularly, the behaviour of my dear benefactor to me, and my parents. He seemed always to delight in being particularly kind to them before strangers, and before the tenants, and before Mr. Sorby, Mr. Bennet, and Mr. Shepherd, three of the principal gentlemen in the neighbourhood, who, with their ladies, came to visit us, and whose visits we *all* returned; for your dear brother would not permit my father and mother to decline the invitation of those worthy families.

Every day we rode out, or walked a little about the grounds; and while we were there, he employed hands to cut a vista through a coppice, as they call it, or rather a little wood, to a rising ground, which, fronting an old-fashioned balcony, in the middle of the house, he ordered it to be planted like a grove, and a pretty alcove to be erected on its summit, of which he has sent them a draught, drawn by his own hand. This and a few other alterations, mentioned in my letter to my father, are to be finished against we go down next.

The dear gentleman was every hour pressing me, while there, to take one diversion or other, frequently upbraiding me, that

36

I seemed not to *choose* any thing; urging me to propose sometimes what I could *wish* he should oblige me in, and not always
to leave it to him to choose for me : saying, he was half afraid
that my constant compliance with every thing he proposed,
laid me sometimes under a restraint : and he would have me
have a will of my own, since it was impossible, that it could be
such as he should not take a delight in conforming to it.

I will not trouble your ladyship with any further particulars
relating to this happy fortnight, which was made up all of
white and unclouded days, to the very last; and your ladyship
will judge better than I can describe, of the parting between
my dear parents, and their honoured benefactor and me.

We set out, attended with the good wishes of crowds of
persons of all degrees; for your dear brother left behind him
noble instances of his bounty; it being the *first* time, as he bid
Mr. Longman say, that he had been down among them since
that estate had been in his hands.

But permit me to observe, that I could not forbear often, very
often, in this happy period, to thank God in private, for the
blessed terms upon which I was there, to what I should have
been, had I gracelessly accepted of those which formerly were
tendered to me; for your ladyship will remember, that the
Kentish estate was to be part of the purchase of my infamy.

We returned through London, by the like easy journeys, but
tarried not to see any thing of that vast metropolis, any more
than we did in going through it before; your beloved brother
only stopping at his banker's, and desiring him to look out for a
handsome house, which he proposes to take for his winter
residence. He chooses it to be about the new buildings called
Hanover Square; and he left Mr. Longman there to see one,
which his banker believed would be fit for him.

And thus, my dear lady, I have answered your first commands,
by the help of the letters which passed between my dear parents
and me; and conclude this with the assurance that I am, with
high respect, *your ladyship's most obliged and faithful servant,*

P. B.

LETTER XIV

My dearest Lady,

I now set myself to obey your ladyship's second command,
which is, to give an account in what manner your dear brother
broke to me the affair of the unfortunate Miss Godfrey, with my
behaviour upon it; and this I cannot do better, than by tran-

scribing the relation I gave at that time, in letters to my dear parents, which your ladyship has not seen, in these very words.

[See Vol. I, p. 431, beginning "My dear Mr. B.," down to p. 441.]

Thus far, my dear lady, the relation I gave to my parents, at the time of my being first acquainted with this melancholy affair.

It is a great pleasure to me, that I can already flatter myself, from the hints you kindly gave me, that I behaved as you wished I should behave. Indeed, Madam, I could not help it, for I pitied most sincerely the unhappy lady; and though I could not but rejoice, that I had had the grace to escape the dangerous attempts of the dear intriguer, yet never did the story of any unfortunate lady make such an impression upon me as hers did: she loved *him*, and believed, no doubt, he loved *her* too well to take ungenerous advantages of her soft passion for him: and so, by degrees, put herself into his power; and too seldom, alas! have the noblest-minded of the seducing sex the mercy or the goodness to spare the poor creatures that do!

Then 'tis another misfortune of people in love; they always think highly of the beloved object, and lowly of themselves, such a dismal mortifier is love!

I say not this, Madam, to excuse the poor lady's fall; nothing can do that; because virtue is, and ought to be, preferable to all considerations, and to life itself. But, methinks, I love this dear lady so well for the sake of her edifying penitence, that I would fain extenuate her crime, if I could; and the rather, as in all probability, it was a *first love* on *both* sides; and so he could not appear to her as a *practised* deceiver.

Your ladyship will see, by what I have transcribed, how I behaved myself to the dear Miss Goodwin; and I am so fond of the little charmer, as well for the sake of her unhappy mother, though personally unknown to me, as for the relation she bears to the dear gentleman whom I am bound to love and honour, that I must beg your ladyship's interest to procure her to be given up to my care, when it shall be thought proper. I am sure I shall act by her as tenderly as if I was her own mother. And glad I am, that the poor unfaulty baby is so justly beloved by Mr. B.

But I will here conclude this letter, with assuring your ladyship, and I am *your obliged and humble servant,*

P. B.

38

My good Lady,

I now come to your ladyship's remarks on my conduct to Mrs. Jewkes : which you are pleased to think too kind and forgiving considering the poor woman's baseness.

Your ladyship says, that I ought not to have borne her in my sight, after the impudent assistance she gave to his lewd attempts; much less to have left her in her place, and rewarded her. Alas ! my dear lady, what could I do ? a poor prisoner as I was made, for weeks together, in breach of all the laws of civil society; without a soul who durst be my friend; and every day expecting to be ruined and undone, by one of the haughtiest and most determined spirits in the world !—and when it pleased God to turn his heart, and incline him to abandon his wicked attempts, and to profess honourable love to me, his poor servant, can it be thought I was to insist upon conditions with such a gentleman, who had me in his power; and who, if I had provoked him, might have resumed all his wicked purposes against me ?

Indeed, I was too much overjoyed, after all my dangers past (which were so great, that I could not go to rest, nor rise, but with such apprehensions, that I wished for death rather than life), to think of refusing any terms that I could yield to, and keep my honour.

And though such noble ladies, as your ladyship and Lady Betty, who are born to independency, and are hereditarily, as I may say, on a foot with the highest-descended gentleman in the land, might have exerted a spirit, and would have a right to choose your own servants, and to distribute rewards and punishments to the deserving and undeserving, at your own good pleasure; yet what had I, a poor girl, who owed even my title to common notice, to the bounty of my late good lady, and had only a kind of imputed sightliness of person, though enough to make me the subject of vile attempts; who, from a situation of terror and apprehension, was lifted up to an hope, beyond my highest ambition, and was bid to pardon the bad woman, as an instance, that I could forgive his own hard usage of me; who had experienced so often the violence and impetuosity of his temper, which even his beloved mother never ventured to oppose till it began to subside, and then, indeed, he was all goodness and acknowledgment; of which I could give your ladyship more than one instance.

What, I say, had I to do, to take upon me lady-airs, and to resent ?

But, my dear ladies (let me, in this instance, bespeak the attention of you both), I should be inexcusable, if I did not tell you all the truth; and that is, that I not only forgave the poor wretch, in regard to *his commands*, but from *my own inclination* also. If I am wrong in saying this, I must submit it to your ladyships; and, as I pretend not to perfection, am ready to take the blame I deserve in your ladyships' judgments: but indeed, were it to be again, I verily think, I could not help forgiving her.—And were I not able to say this, I should be thought to have made a mean court to my master's passions, and to have done a wrong thing with my eyes open: which I humbly conceive, no one should do.

When full power was given me over this poor creature (seemingly at least, though it might possibly have been resumed, and I might have been re-committed to hers, had I given him reason to think I made an arrogant use of it), you cannot imagine what a triumph I had in my mind over the mortified guilt, which (from the highest degree of insolence and imperiousness, that before had hardened her masculine features) appeared in her countenance, when she found the tables likely to be soon turned upon her.

This change of behaviour, which at first discovered itself in a sullen awe, and afterwards in a kind of silent respect, shewed me, what an influence power had over her: and that when she could treat her late prisoner, when taken into favour, so obsequiously, it was the less wonder the bad woman could think it her duty to obey commands so unjust, when her obedience to them was required from her master.

To be sure, if a look could have killed her, after some of her bad treatment, she had been slain over and over, as I may say: but to me, who was always taught to distinguish between the person and the action, I could not hold my resentment against the poor passive machine of mischief one day together, though her actions were so odious to me.

I should indeed except that time of my grand trial when she appeared so much a wretch to me, that I saw her not (even after two days that she was kept from me) without great flutter and emotion of heart: and I had represented to your brother before, how hard a condition it was for me to forgive so much unwomanly wickedness.

But, my dear ladies, when I considered the latter in *one* particular light, I could the more easily forgive her; and *having* forgiven her, *bear her in my sight*, and act by her (as a consequence of that forgiveness) as if she had not so horridly offended.

Else how would it have been forgiveness? especially as she was ashamed of her crime, and there was no fear of her repeating it.

Thus then I thought on the occasion : "Poor wretched agent, for purposes little less than infernal ! I *will* forgive thee, since *thy* master and *my* master will have it so. And indeed thou art beneath the resentment even of such a poor girl as I. I will *pity* thee, base and abject as thou art. And she who is the object of my *pity* is surely beneath my *anger*."

Such were then my thoughts, my proud thoughts, so far was I from being guilty of *intentional* meanness in forgiving, at Mr. B.'s interposition, the poor, low, creeping, abject *self*-mortified, and *master*-mortified, Mrs. Jewkes.

And do you think, ladies, when you revolve in your thoughts, *who* I was, and *what* I was, and what I had been *designed* for; when you revolve the amazing turn in my favour, and the prospects before me (so much above my hopes, that I left them entirely to Providence to direct for me, as it pleased, without daring to look forward to what those prospects seemed naturally to tend); when I could see my haughty persecutor become my repentant protector; the lofty spirit that used to make me tremble, and to which I never could look up without awe, except in those animating cases, where his guilty attempts, and the concern I had to preserve my innocence, gave a courage more than natural to my otherwise dastardly heart : when this impetuous spirit could stoop to request one whom he had sunk beneath even her usual low character of his servant, who was his prisoner, under sentence of a ruin worse than death, as he had intended it, and had seized her for that very purpose, could stoop to acknowledge the vileness of that purpose; could say, at one time, that my forgiveness of Mrs. Jewkes should stand me in greater stead than I was aware of : could tell her, before me, that she must for the future shew me all the respect due to one he must love; at another, acknowledged before her, that he had been stark naught, and that I was very forgiving; again, to Mrs. Jewkes, putting himself on a level with her, as to guilt, "We are both in generous hands : and, indeed, if Pamela did not pardon *you*, I should think she but half forgave *me*, because you acted by my instructions : " another time to the same, "We have been both sinners, and must be both included in one act of grace : "—when I was thus lifted up to the state of a sovereign forgiver, and my lordly master became a petitioner for himself, and the guilty creature, whom he put under my feet; what a triumph was here for the poor Pamela? and could I have been guilty of so mean a pride, as to trample upon the poor abject creature, when I found her thus lowly, thus mortified, and wholly in my power?

Then, my dear ladies, while I was enjoying the soul-charming fruits of that innocence which the Divine Grace had enabled me to preserve, in spite of so many plots and contrivances on my master's side, and such wicked instigations and assistances on hers, and all my prospects were improving upon me beyond my wishes; when all was unclouded sunshine, and I possessed my mind in peace, and had only to be thankful to Providence, which had been so gracious to my unworthiness; when I saw my persecutor become my protector, my active enemy no longer my enemy, but creeping with slow, doubtful feet, and speaking to me with awful hesitating doubt of my acceptance; a stamp of an insolent foot now turned into curtseying half-bent knees; threatening hands into supplicating folds; and the eye unpitying to innocence, running over with the sense of her own guilt; a faltering accent on her late menacing tongue, and uplifted handkerchief, " I see she will be my lady: and then I know how it will go with me ! "—Was not this, my ladies, a triumph of triumphs to the late miserable, now exalted, Pamela !—could I do less than pardon her? And having declared that I did so, was I not to shew the sincerity of my declaration?

Would it not have shewn my master, that the low-born Pamela was incapable of a generous action, had she refused the *only* request her humble condition had given her the opportunity of granting, at that time, with innocence? Would he not have thought the humble cottager as capable of insolence, and vengeance too, in her turn, as the better born? and that she wanted but the power, to shew the like unrelenting temper, by which she had so grievously suffered? And might not this have given him room to think me (and to have resumed and prosecuted his purposes accordingly) fitter for an arrogant kept mistress, than an humble and obliged wife !

" I see " (might he not have said?), " the girl has strong passions and resentments; and she that has, will be sometimes *governed* by them. I will improve upon the hint she herself has now given me, by her inexorable temper : I will gratify her revenge, till I turn it upon herself : I will indulge her pride, till I make it administer to her fall; for a wife I cannot think of in the low-born cottager, especially when she has lurking in her all the pride and arrogance " (you know, my ladies, his haughty way of speaking of our sex) " of the better descended. And by a little perseverance, and watching her unguarded hours, and applying temptations to her passions, I shall first discover them, and then make my advantage of them."

Might not this have been the language, and this the resolution, of such a dear wicked intriguer?—For, my lady, you can hardly conceive the struggles he apparently had to bring down his high spirit to so humble a level. And though, I hope, all would have been, even in this *worst* case, ineffectual, through Divine Grace, yet how do I know what lurking vileness might have appeared by degrees in this frail heart, to encourage his designs, and to augment my trials and my dangers? And perhaps down-right violence might have been used, if he could not, on one hand, have subdued his passions, nor, on the other, have over-come his pride—a pride, that every one, reflecting upon the disparity of birth and condition between us, would have dignified with the name of *decency ;* a pride that was become such an essential part of the dear gentleman's character, in this instance of a wife, that although he knew he could not keep it up, if he made *me* happy, yet it was no small motive of his choosing me, in one respect, because he expected from me more humility, more submission, than he thought would be paid him by a lady equally born and educated; and of this I will send you an instance, in a transcription from that part of my journal you have not seen, of his lessons to me, on my incurring his dis-pleasure by interposing between yourself and him in your mis-understanding at the Hall: for, Madam, I intend to send, at times, any thing I think worthy of your ladyship's attention, out of those papers you were so kind as to excuse me from sending you in a lump, and many of which must needs have appeared very impertinent to such judges.

Thus (could your ladyship have thought it?) have I ventured upon a strange paradox, that even this strongest instance of his debasing himself, is not the weakest of his pride : and he ventured once at Sir Simon Darnford's to say, in your hearing, as you may remember, that, in his conscience, he thought he should hardly have made a tolerable husband to any body but Pamela : and why? For the reasons you will see in the in-closed papers, which give an account of the noblest and earliest curtain-lecture that ever girl had : one of which is, that he expects to be *borne* with (*complied* with, he meant) even when in the wrong : another, that a wife should never so much as expostulate with him, though he *was* in the wrong, till, by com-plying with all he insisted upon, she should have shewn him, she designed rather to convince him, for his *own* sake, than for

43

contradiction's sake; and then, another time, perhaps he might take better resolutions.

I hope, from what I have said, it will appear to your ladyship, and to Lady Betty too, that I am justified, or at least excused, in pardoning Mrs. Jewkes.

But your dear brother has just sent me word, that supper waits for me: and the post being ready to go off, I defer till the next opportunity which I have to say as to these good effects: and am, in the mean time, *your ladyship's most obliged and faithful servant,*

P. B.

LETTER XVI

My dear Lady,

I will now acquaint you with the good effects my behaviour to Mrs. Jewkes has had upon her, as a farther justification of my conduct towards the poor woman.

That she began to be affected as I wished, appeared to me before I left the Hall, not only in the conversations I had with her after my happiness was completed; but in her general demeanour also to the servants, to the neighbours, and in her devout behaviour at church: and this still further appears by a letter I have received from Miss Darnford. I dare say your ladyship will be pleased with the perusal of the whole letter, although a part of it would answer my present design; and in confidence, that you will excuse, for the sake of its other beauties, the high and undeserved praises which she so lavishly bestows upon me, I will transcribe it all.

From Miss Darnford to Mrs. B.

" My dear Neighbour that was,

" I must depend upon your known goodness to excuse me for not writing before now, in answer to your letter of compliment to us, for the civilities and favours, as you call them, which you received from us in Lincolnshire, where we were infinitely more obliged to you than you to us.

" The truth is, my papa has been much disordered with a kind of rambling rheumatism, to which the physicians, learnedly speaking, give the name of *arthritici vaga*, or the flying gout; and when he ails ever so little (it signifies nothing concealing his infirmities, where they are so well known, and when he cares not who knows them), he is so peevish, and wants so much attendance, that my mamma, and her two girls (one

44

of which is as waspish as her papa; you may be sure I don't mean myself) have much ado to make his worship keep the peace; and I being his favourite, when he is indisposed, having most patience, if I may give myself a good word, he calls upon me continually, to read to him when he is grave, which is not often, and to tell him stories, and sing to him when he is merry; and so I have been employed as a principal person about him, till I have frequently become sad to make him cheerful, and happy when I could do it at any rate. For once, in a pet, he flung a book at my head, because I had not attended him for two hours, and he could not bear to be slighted by little bastards, that was his word, that were fathered upon him for his vexation! O these men! Fathers or husbands, much alike! the one tyrannical, the other insolent: so that, between one and t'other, a poor girl has nothing for it, but a few weeks' court-ship, and perhaps a first month's bridalry, if that: and then she is as much a slave to her husband, as she was a vassal to her father—I mean if the father be a Sir Simon Darnford, and the spouse a Mr. B.

" But I will be a little more grave; for a graver occasion calls for it, yet such as will give you real pleasure. It is the very great change that your example has had upon your house-keeper.

" You desired her to keep up as much regularity as she could among the servants there; and she is next to exemplary in it, so that she has every one's good word. She speaks of her lady not only with respect, but reverence; and calls it a blessed day for all the family, and particularly for herself, that you came into Lincolnshire. She reads prayers, or makes one of the servants read them, every Sunday night; and never misses being at church, morning and afternoon; and is pre-paring herself, by Mr. Peters's advice and direction, for receiving the sacrament; which she earnestly longs to receive, and says it will be the seal of her reformation.

" Mr. Peters gives us this account of her, and says she is full of contrition for her past mis-spent life, and is often asking him, if such and such sins can be forgiven? and among them, names her vile behaviour to her angel lady, as she calls you.

" It seems she has written a letter to you, which passed Mr. Peters's revisal, before she had the courage to send it; and prides herself that you have favoured her with an answer to it, which, she says, when she is dead, will be found in a cover of black silk next her heart; for any thing from your hand, she is sure, will contribute to make her keep her good purposes:

and for that reason she places it there; and when she has had any bad thoughts, or is guilty of any faulty word, or passionate expression, she recollects her lady's letter, which recovers her to a calm, and puts her again into a better frame.

"As she has written to you 'tis possible I might have spared you the trouble of reading this account of her : but yet you will not be displeased, that so free a liver and speaker should have some testimonial besides her own assurances, to vouch for the sincerity of her reformation.

"What a happy lady are you, that persuasion dwells upon your tongue, and reformation follows your example ! "

Your ladyship will forgive me what may appear like vanity in this communication. Miss Darnford is a charming young lady. I always admired her; but her letters are the sweetest, kindest !—Yet I am too much the subject of her encomiums, and so will say no more; but add here a copy of the poor woman's letter to me; and your ladyship will see what an ample correspondence you have opened to yourself, if you go on to countenance it.

"HONOURED MADAM,

"I have been long labouring under two difficulties; the desire I had to write to you, and the fear of being thought presumptuous if I did. But I will depend on your goodness, so often tried; and put pen to paper, in that very closet, and on that desk, which once were so much used by yourself, when I was acting a part that now cuts me to the heart to think of. But you forgave me, Madam, and shewed me you had too much goodness to revoke your forgiveness; and could I have silenced the reproaches of my heart, I should have had no cause to think I had offended.

"But, Oh ! Madam, how has your goodness to me, which once filled me with so much gladness, now, on reflection, made me sorrowful, and at times, miserable.—To think I should act so barbarously as I did, by so much sweetness, and so much forgiveness. Every place that I remember to have used you hardly in, how does it now fill me with sadness, and makes me often smite my breast, and sit down with tears and groans, bemoaning my vile actions, and my hard heart !—How many places are there in this melancholy fine house, that call one thing or other to my remembrance, that give me remorse ! But the pond, and the woodhouse, whence I dragged you so mercilously, after I had driven you to despair almost, what

46

thoughts do they bring to my remembrance ! Then my wicked instigations.—What an odious wretch was I !

"Had his honour been as abandoned as myself, what virtue had been destroyed between *his* orders and *my* too rigorous execution of them; nay, stretching them to shew my wicked zeal, to serve a master, whom, though I honoured, I should not (as you more than once hinted to me, but with no effect at all, so resolutely wicked was my heart) have so well obeyed in his unlawful commands !

"His honour has made you amends, has done justice to your merits, and so atoned for *his* fault. But as for *me*, it is out of my power ever to make reparation.—All that is left me, is, to let your ladyship see, that your pious example has made such an impression upon me, that I am miserable now in the reflection upon my past guilt.

"*You* have forgiven me, and *GOD* will, I hope; for the creature cannot be more merciful than the Creator; that is all my hope !—Yet, sometimes, I dread that I am forgiven here, at least not punished, in order to be punished the more hereafter !—What then will become of the unhappy wretch, that has thus lived in a state of sin, and so qualified herself by a course of wickedness, as to be thought a proper instrument for the worst of purposes !

"Pray your ladyship, let not my honoured master see this letter. He will think I have the boldness to reflect upon him : when, God knows my heart, I only write to condemn myself, and my *unwomanly* actions, as you were pleased often most justly to call them.

"But I might go on thus for ever accusing myself, not considering whom I am writing to, and whose precious time I am taking up. But what I chiefly write for is, to beg your ladyship's prayers for me. For, oh ! Madam, I fear I shall else be ever miserable ! We every week hear of the good you do, and the charity you extend to the bodies of the miserable. Extend, I beseech you, good Madam, to the unhappy Jewkes, the mercy of your prayers, and tell me if you think I have not sinned beyond hope of pardon; for there is a woe denounced against the presumptuous sinner.

"Your ladyship assured me, at your departure, on the confession of my remorse for my misdoings, and my promise of amendment, that you would take it for proof of my being in earnest, if I would endeavour to keep up a regularity among the servants here; if I would subdue them with kindness, as I had owned myself subdued; and if I would endeavour to make every one think, that the best security they could give of doing their duty to their master in his *absence*, was by doing it to God Almighty, from whose all-seeing eye nothing can be hid. This, I remember, your ladyship told me, was the best test of fidelity and duty, that any servants could shew; since it was impossible, without religion, but that worldly convenience, or self-interest, must be the main tie; and so the worst actions might succeed, if servants thought they should find their sordid advantage in sacrificing their duty.

"So well am I convinced of this truth, that I hope I have begun the example to good effect: and as no one in the family was so wicked as I, it was therefore less difficult to reform them; and you will have the pleasure to know, that you have now servants here, whom you need not be ashamed to call yours.

"'Tis true, I found it a little difficult at first to keep them within sight of their duty, after your ladyship departed: but when they saw I was in earnest, and used them courteously, as you advised, and as your usage of me convinced me was the rightest usage; when they were told I had your commands to acquaint you how they conformed to your injunctions; the task became easy: and I hope we shall all be still more and more worthy of the favour of so good a lady and so bountiful a master.

"I dare not presume upon the honour of a line to your unworthy servant. Yet it would pride me much, if I could have it. But I shall ever pray for your ladyship's and his honour's felicity, as becomes *your undeserving servant,*

"K. JEWKES."

I have already, with these transcribed letters of Miss Darnford and Mrs. Jewkes, written a great deal: but nevertheless, as there yet remains one passage in your ladyship's letter, relating to Mrs. Jewkes, that seems to require an answer, I will take notice of it, if I shall not quite tire your patience.

That passage is this; Lady Betty rightly observes, says your ladyship, that he knew what a vile woman she [Mrs. Jewkes] was, when he put you into her power; and no doubt, employed her, because he was sure she would answer all his purposes: and therefore she should have had very little opinion of the sincerity of his reformation, while he was so solicitous in keeping her there.

She would, she says, had she been in your case, have had one struggle for her dismission, let it have been taken as it would;

48

and he that was so well pleased with your virtue, must have thought this a natural consequence of it, if in earnest to become virtuous himself.

But, alas ! Madam, he was not so well pleased with my virtue for virtue's sake, as Lady Betty thinks he was.—He would have been glad, even then, to have found me less resolved on that score. He did not so much as *pretend* to any disposition to virtue. No, not he !

He had entertained, as it proved, a strong passion for me, which had been heightened by my *resisting* it. His pride, and his advantages both of person and fortune, would not let him brook control; and when he could not have me upon his own terms, God turned his evil purposes to good ones; and he resolved to submit to mine, or rather to such as he found I would not yield to him without.

But Lady Betty thinks, I was to blame to put Mrs. Jewkes upon a foot, in the present I made on my nuptials, with Mrs. Jervis. But I rather put Mrs. Jervis on a foot with Mrs. Jewkes; for the dear gentleman had *named* the sum for me to give Mrs. Jewkes, and I would not give Mrs. Jervis *less*, because I loved her better; nor *more* could I give her, on that occasion, without making such a difference between two persons equal in station, on a solemnity too where one was present and assisting, the other not, as would have shewn such a partiality, as might have induced their master to conclude, I was not so sincere in my forgiveness, as he hoped from me, and as I really was. ·

But a stronger reason still was behind; that I could, much more agreeably, both to Mrs. Jervis and myself, shew my love and gratitude to the dear good woman : and this I have taken care to do, in the manner I will submit to your ladyship; at the tribunal of whose judgment I am willing all my actions, respecting your dear brother, shall be tried. And I hope you will not have reason to think me a too profuse or lavish creature ; yet, if you have, pray, my dear lady, don't spare me ; for if you shall judge me profuse in one article, I will endeavour to save it in another.

But I will make what I have to say on this head the subject of a letter by itself : and am, mean time, *your ladyship's most obliged and obedient servant,*

P. B.

My dear Lady,

It is needful, in order to let you more intelligibly into the subject where I left off in my last, for your ladyship to know that your generous brother has made me his almoner, as I was my late dear lady's; and ordered Mr. Longman to pay me fifty pounds quarterly, for purposes of which he requires no account, though I have one always ready to produce.

Now, Madam, as I knew Mrs. Jervis was far from being easy in her circumstances, thinking herself obliged to pay old debts for two extravagant children, who are both dead, and maintaining in schooling and clothes three of their children, which always keeps her bare, I said to her one day, as she and I sat together, at our needles (for we are always running over old stories, when alone)—" My good Mrs. Jervis, will you allow me to ask you after your own private affairs, and if you are tolerably easy in them? "

" You are very good, Madam," said she, " to concern yourself about my poor matters, so much as your thoughts are employed, and every moment of your time is taken up, from the hour you rise, to the time of your rest. But I can with great pleasure attribute it to your bounty, and that of my honoured master, that I am easier and easier every day."

" But tell me, my dear Mrs. Jervis," said I, " how your matters *particularly* stand. I love to mingle concerns with my friends, and as I hide nothing from *you*, I hope you'll treat *me* with equal freedom; for I always loved you, and always will; and nothing but death shall divide our friendship."

She had tears of gratitude in her eyes, and taking off her spectacles, " I cannot bear," she said, " so much goodness !— Oh ! my lady ! "

" Oh ! my Pamela, say," replied I. " How often must I chide you for calling me any thing but your Pamela, when we are alone together? "

" My heart," said she, " will burst with your goodness ! I cannot bear it ! "

" But you *must* bear it, and bear still greater exercises to your grateful heart, I can tell you that. A pretty thing, truly ! Here I, a poor helpless girl, raised from poverty and distress by the generosity of the best of men, only because I was young and sightly, shall put on lady-airs to a gentlewoman born, the wisdom of whose years, her faithful services, and good management, make her a much greater merit in this family, than I can pretend to have ! And shall I return, in the day of my power, insult and haughtiness for the kindness and benevolence I received from her in that of my indigence !—Indeed, I won't forgive you, my dear Mrs. Jervis, if I think you capable of looking upon me in any other light than as your daughter; for you have been a mother to me, when the absence of my own could not afford me the comfort and good counsel I received every day from you."

Then moving my chair nearer, and taking her hand, and wiping, with my handkerchief in my other, her reverend cheek, "Come, my dear second mother," said I, "call me your daughter, your Pamela: I have passed many sweet hours with you under that name; and as I have but too seldom such an opportunity as this, open to me your worthy heart, and let me know, if I cannot make my *second* mother as easy and happy as our dear master has made my *first*."

She hung her head, and I waited till the discharge of her tears gave time for utterance to her words; provoking only her speech, by saying, "You used to have three grand-children to provide for in clothes and schooling. They are all living, I hope?"

"Yes, Madam, they are living: and your last bounty (twenty guineas was a great sum, and all at once!) made me very easy and very happy!"

"How easy and how happy, Mrs. Jervis?"

"Why, my dear lady, I paid five to one old creditor of my unhappy sons: five to a second; and two and a half to two others, in proportion to their respective demands; and with the other five I paid off all arrears of the poor children's schooling and maintenance; and all are satisfied and easy, and declare they will never do harsh things by me, if they are paid no more."

"But tell me, Mrs. Jervis, the whole you owe in the world; and you and I will contrive, with justice to our best friend, to do all we can to make you quite easy; for, at your time of life, I cannot bear that you shall have any thing to disturb you, which I can remove, and so, my dear Mrs. Jervis, let me know all. I know your debts (dear, just, good woman, as you are!) like David's sins, are ever before you: so come," putting my hand in her pocket, "let me be a friendly pick-pocket; let me take out your memorandum-book, and we will see how all matters stand, and what can be done. Come, I see you are too much moved; your worthy heart is too much affected (pulling out her book, which she always had about her); "I will go to my closet, and return presently."

So I left her, to recover her spirits, and retired with the good woman's book to my closet.

Your dear brother stepping into the parlour just after I had gone out, "Where's your lady, Mrs. Jervis?" said he. And being told, came up to me:—"What ails the good woman below, my dear?" said he: "I hope you and she have had no words?"

"No, indeed, Sir," answered I. "If we had, I am sure it would have been my fault: but I have picked her pocket of her memorandum-book, in order to look into her private affairs, to see if I cannot, with justice to our common benefactor, make her as easy as you, Sir, have made my other dear parents."

"A blessing," said he, "upon my charmer's benevolent heart!—I will leave every thing to your discretion, my dear.— Do all the good you prudently can to your Mrs. Jervis."

I clasped my bold arms about him, the starting tear testifying my gratitude.—"Dearest Sir," said I, "you affect me as much as I did Mrs. Jervis; and if any one but you had a right to ask, what ails your Pamela? as you do, what ails Mrs. Jervis? I must say, I am hourly so much oppressed by your goodness, that there is hardly any bearing one's own joy."

He saluted me, and said, I was a dear obliging creature. "But," said he, "I came to tell you, that after dinner we'll take a turn, if you please, to Lady Arthur's: she has a family of London friends for her guests, and begs I will prevail upon you to give her your company, and attend you myself, only to drink tea with her; for I have told her we are to have friends to sup with us."

"I will attend you, Sir," replied I, "most willingly; although I doubt I am to be made a shew of."

"Something like it," said he, "for she has promised them this favour."

"I need not dress otherwise than I am?"

"No," he was pleased to say, I was always what he wished me to be.

So he left me to my *good works* (those were his kind words), and I ran over Mrs. Jervis's accounts, and found a balance drawn of all her matters in one leaf, and a thankful acknowledgment to God, for her master's last bounty, which had enabled her to give satisfaction to others, and to do herself great pleasure, written underneath.

The balance of all was thirty-five pounds eleven shillings and odd pence; and I went to my escritoir, and took out forty pounds, and down I hasted to my good Mrs. Jervis, and I said to her, " Here, my dear good friend, is your pocket-book; but are thirty-five or thirty-six pounds all you owe, or are bound for in the world? "

" It is, Madam," said she, " and enough too. It is a great sum; but 'tis in four hands, and they are all in pretty good circumstances, and so convinced of my honesty, that they will never trouble me for it; for I have reduced the debt every year something, since I have been in my master's service."

" Nor shall it ever be in any body's *power*," said I, " to trouble you : I'll tell you how we'll order it."

So I sat down, and made her sit by me. " Here, my dear Mrs. Jervis, is forty pounds. It is not so much to me now, as the two guineas were to you, that you would have given me at my going away from this house to my father's, as I thought. I will not *give* it you neither, at least at *present*, as you shall hear : indeed I won't make you so uneasy as that comes to. But take this, and pay the thirty-five pounds odd money to the utmost farthing; and the remaining four pounds odd will be a little fund in advance towards the children's schooling. And thus you shall repay it; I always designed, as our dear master added five guineas per annum to your salary, in acknowledgment of the pleasure he took in your services, when I was Pamela Andrews, to add five pounds per annum to it from the time I became Mrs. B. But from that time, for so many years to come, you shall receive no more than you did, till the whole forty pounds be repaid. So, my dear Mrs. Jervis, you won't have any obligation to me, you know, but for the advance; and that is a poor matter, not to be spoken of : and I will have leave for it, for fear I should die."

Had your ladyship seen the dear good woman's behaviour, on this occasion, you would never have forgotten it. She could not speak; tears ran down her cheeks in plentiful currents : her modest hand put gently from her my offering hand, her bosom heav'd, and she sobb'd with the painful tumult that seemed to struggle within her, and which, for some few moments, made her incapable of speaking.

At last, I rising, and putting my arm round her neck, wiping her eyes, and kissing her cheek, she cried, " My excellent lady ! 'tis too much ! I cannot bear all this."—She then threw herself at my feet; for I was not strong enough to hinder it; and with uplifted hands—" May God Almighty," said she—I kneeled by her, and clasping her hands in mine, both uplifted together—" May God Almighty," said I, drowning her voice with my

louder voice, " bless us both together, for many happy years !
And bless and reward the dear gentleman, who has thus enabled
me to make *the widow's heart to sing for joy !* "

And thus, my lady, did I force upon the good woman's
acceptance the forty pounds.

Permit me, Madam, to close this letter here, and to resume
the subject in my next : till when I have the honour to be *your
ladyship's most obliged and faithful servant,*

P. B.

LETTER XVIII

MY DEAR LADY,

I now resume my last subject where I left off, that your
ladyship may have the whole before you at one view.

I went after dinner, with my dear benefactor, to Lady
Arthur's; and met with fresh calls upon me for humility,
having the two natural effects of the praises and professed
admiration of that lady's guests, as well as my dear Mr. B.'s,
and those of Mr. and Mrs. Arthur, to guard myself against :
and your good brother was pleased to entertain me in the
chariot, going and coming, with an account of the orders he
had given in relation to the London house, which is actually
taken, and the furniture he should direct for it; so that I had no
opportunity to tell him what I had done in relation to Mrs.
Jervis.

But after supper, retiring from company to my closet, when
his friends were gone, he came up to me about our usual bed-
time : he enquired kindly after my employment, which was
trying to read in the French Telemachus : for, my lady, I'm
learning French, I'll assure you ! And who, do you think,
is my master?—Why, the best I *could* have in the world, your
dearest brother, who is pleased to say, I am no dunce : how
inexcusable should I be, if I was, with such a master, who
teaches me on his knee, and rewards me with a kiss whenever
I do well, and says, I have already nearly mastered the accent
and pronunciation, which he tells me is a great difficulty got
over.

I requested him to render for me into English two or three
places that were beyond my reach; and when he had done it,
he asked me, in French, what I had done for Mrs. Jervis.

I said, " Permit me, Sir (for I am not proficient enough to
answer you in my new tongue), in English, to say, I have made
the good woman quite happy; and it I have your approbation,

54

I shall be as much so myself in this instance, as I am in all others."

" I dare answer for your prudence, my dear," he was pleased to say : " but this is your favourite : let me know, when you have so bountiful a heart to strangers, what you do for your favourites ? "

I then said, " Permit my bold eye, Sir, to watch yours, as I obey you; and you know you must not look full upon me then; for if you do, how shall I look at you again; how see, as I proceed, whether you are displeased ? for you will not chide me in words, so partial have you the goodness to be to all I do."

He put his arm round me, and looked down now and then, as I desired ! for O ! Madam, he is all condescension and goodness to his unworthy, yet grateful Pamela ! I told him all I have written to you about the forty pounds.—" And now, dear Sir," said I, half hiding my face on his shoulder, " you have heard what I have done, chide or beat your Pamela, if you please : it shall be all kind from you, and matter of future direction and caution."

He raised my head, and kissed me two or three times, saying, " Thus then I chide, I beat, my angel !—And yet I have one fault to find with you; and let Mrs. Jervis, if not in bed, come up to us, and hear what it is; for I will *expose* you, as you deserve, before her."—My Polly being in hearing, attending to know if I wanted her assistance to undress, I bade her call Mrs. Jervis. And though I thought from his kind looks, and kind words, as well as tender behaviour, that I had not much to fear, yet I was impatient to know what my fault was, for which I was to be exposed.

The good woman came; and as she entered with all that modesty which is so graceful in her, he moved his chair further from me, and, with a set aspect, but not unpleasant, said, " Step in, Mrs. Jervis : your lady " (for so, Madam, he will always call me to Mrs. Jervis, and to the servants) " has incurred my censure, and I would not tell her in what, till I had you face to face."

She looked surprised—now on me, now on her dear master; and I, not knowing what he would say, looked a little attentive. " I am sorry—I am very sorry for it, Sir," said she, curtseying low :—" but should be more sorry, if *I* were the unhappy occasion."

" Why, Mrs. Jervis, I can't say but it is on your account that I must blame her."

This gave us both confusion, but especially the good woman; for still I hoped much from his kind behaviour to me just before —and she said, " Indeed, Sir, I could never deserve——"

He interrupted her—" My charge against you, Pamela," said he, " is that of niggardliness, and no other; for I will put you both out of your pain : you ought not to have found out the method of repayment.

" The dear creature," said he, to Mrs. Jervis, " seldom does any thing that can be mended; but, I think, when your good conduct deserved an annual acknowledgment from me, in addition to your salary, the lady should have shewed herself no less pleased with your service than the gentleman. Had it been for old acquaintance-sake, for sex-sake, she should not have given me cause to upbraid her on this head. But I will tell you, that you must look upon the forty pounds you have, as the effect of just distinction on many accounts : and your salary from last quarter-day shall be advanced, as the dear niggard intended it some years hence; and let me only add, that when my Pamela first begins to shew a coldness to her Mrs. Jervis, I shall then suspect she is beginning to decline in that humble virtue, which is now peculiar to herself and makes her the delight of all who converse with her."

He was thus pleased to *say* : thus, with the most graceful generosity, and a nobleness of mind *truly* peculiar to himself, was he pleased to *act* : and what could Mrs. Jervis or I say to him?—Why, indeed, nothing at all !—We could only look upon one another, with our eyes and our hearts full of a gratitude that would not permit either of us to speak, but which expressed itself at last in a manner he was pleased to call more elegant than words—with uplifted folded hands, and tears of joy.

O my dear lady ! how many opportunities have the beneficent *rich* to make *themselves*, as well as their *fellow-creatures*, happy ! All that I could think, or say, or act, was but my duty before; what a sense of obligation then must I lie under to this most generous of men !

But here let me put an end to this tedious subject; the principal part of which can have no excuse, if it may not serve as a proof of my cheerful compliance with your ladyship's commands, that I recite *every* thing of concern to me, and with the same freedom as I used to do to my dear parents.

I have done it, and at the same time offered what I had to plead in behalf of my conduct to the two housekeepers, which you expected from me; and I shall therefore close this my humble defence, if I may so call it, with the assurance that I am, *my dearest lady, your obliged and faithful servant,*

P. B.

LETTER XIX

From Lady Davers to Mrs. B. in answer to the six last Letters.

"*Where she had it, I can't tell! but I think I never met with the fellow of her in my life, at any age;*" are, as I remember, my brother's words, speaking of his Pamela in the early part of your papers. In truth, thou art a surprising creature; and every letter we have from you, we have new subjects to admire you for.—"Do you think, Lady Betty," said I, when I had read to the end of the subject about Mrs. Jervis, "I will not soon set out to hit this charming girl a box of the ear or two?" —"For what, Lady Davers?" said she.

"For what!" replied I.—"Why, don't you see how many slaps of the face the bold slut hits me! *I'll* LADY-AIRS her! I will. *I'll* teach her to reproach me, and so many of her betters, with her cottage excellencies, and improvements, that shame our education."

Why, you dear charming Pamela, did you only excel me in *words,* I could forgive you: for there may be a knack, and a volubility, as to *words,* that a natural talent may supply; but to be thus out-done in *thought* and in *deed,* who can bear it? And in so young an insulter too!

Well, Pamela, look to it, when I see you: you shall feel the weight of my hand, or—the pressure of my lip, one or t'other, depend on it, very quickly: for here, instead of my stooping, as I thought I would be, to call *you* sister, I shall be forced to think, in a little while, that you ought not to own *me* as *yours,* till I am nearer your standard.

But to come to business, I will summarily take notice of the following particulars in all your obliging letters, in order to convince you of my friendship, by the freedom of my observations on the subjects you touch upon.

First, then, I am highly pleased with what you write of the advantages you received from the favour of my dear mother; and as you know many things of her by your attendance upon her the last three or four years of her life, I must desire you will give me, as opportunity shall offer, all you can recollect in relation to the honoured lady, and of her behaviour and kindness to you, and with a retrospect to your own early beginnings, the

57

dawnings of this your bright day of excellence: and this not only I, but the countess, and Lady Betty, with whom I am going over your papers again, and her sister, Lady Jenny, request of you.

2. I am much pleased with your Kentish account; though we wished you had been more particular in some parts of it; for we are greatly taken with your descriptions: and your conversation pieces: yet I own, your honest father's letters, and yours, a good deal supply that *defect*.

3. I am highly delighted with your account of my brother's breaking to you the affair of Sally Godfrey, and your conduct upon it. 'Tis a sweet story as he brought it in, and as you relate it. The wretch has been very just in his account of it. We are in love with your charitable reflections in favour of the poor lady; and the more, as she certainly deserved them, and a better mother too than she had, and a faithfuller lover than she met with.

4. You have exactly hit his temper in your declared love of Miss Goodwin. I see, child, you know your man; and never fear but you'll hold him, if you can go on thus to act, and outdo your sex. But I should think you might as well not insist upon having her with you; you'd better see her now and then at the dairy-house, or at school, than have her with you. But this I leave to your own discretion.

5. You have satisfactorily answered our objections to your behaviour to Mrs. Jewkes. We had not considered your circumstances quite so thoroughly as we ought to have done. You are a charming girl, and all your motives are so just, that we shall be a little more cautious for the future how we censure you.

In short, I say with the countess, "This good girl is not without her pride; but it is the pride that becomes, and can only attend the innocent heart; and I'll warrant," said her ladyship, " nobody will become her station so well, as one who is capable of so worthy a pride as this."

But what a curtain-lecture hadst thou, Pamela! A noble one, dost thou call it?—Why, what a wretch hast thou got, to expect thou shouldst never expostulate against his lordly will, even when in the wrong, till thou hast obeyed it, and of consequence, joined in the evil he imposes!

Much good may such a husband do you, says Lady Betty!— Every body will *admire* you, but no one will have reason to *envy* you upon those principles.

6. I am pleased with your promise of sending what you think

58

I shall like to see, out of those papers you choose not to shew me collectively : this is very obliging. You're a good girl; and I love you dearly.

7. We have all smiled at your paradox, Pamela, that his marrying you was an instance of his pride.—The thought, though, is pretty enough, and ingenious; but whether it will hold or not, I won't just now examine.

8. Your observation on the *forget* and *forgive* we are much pleased with.

9. You are very good in sending me a copy of Miss Darnford's letter. She is a charming young lady. I always had a great opinion of her merit; her letter abundantly confirms me in it. I hope you'll communicate to me every letter that passes between you, and pray send in your next a copy of your answer to her letter : I must insist upon it, I think.

10. I am glad, with all my heart, to hear of poor Jewkes's reformation : Your example carries all before it. But pray oblige me with your answer to her letter, don't think me unreasonable : 'tis all for your sake.

Pray—have you shewn Jewkes's letter to your good friend ?—Lady Betty wants to know (if you *have*) what he could say to it ? For, she says, it cuts him to the quick. And I think so too, if he takes it as he ought : but, as you say, he's above loving virtue for *virtue's sake*.

11. Your manner of acting by Mrs. Jervis, with so handsome a regard to my brother's interest, her behaviour upon it, and your relation of the whole, and of his generous spirit in approving, reproving, and improving, your prudent generosity, make no inconsiderable figure in your papers. And Lady Betty says, " Hang him, he has some excellent qualities too.—It is impossible not to think well of him; and his good actions go a great way towards atoning for his bad." But you, Pamela, have the glory of all.

12. I am glad you are learning French : thou art a happy girl in thy teacher, and he is a happy man in his scholar. We are pleased with your pretty account of his method of instructing and rewarding. 'Twould be strange, if you did not thus learn any language quickly, with such encouragements, from the man you love, were your genius less apt than it is. But we wished you had enlarged on that subject : for such fondness of men to their wives, who have been any time married, is so rare, and so unexpected from *my* brother, that we thought you should have written a side upon that subject at least.

What a bewitching girl art thou ! What an exemplar to wives

59

now, as well as thou wast before to maidens ! Thou canst tame lions, I dare say, if thoud'st try.—Reclaim a rake in the meridian of his libertinism, and make such an one as my brother, not only marry thee, but love thee better at several months' end, than he did the first day, if possible !

Now, my dear Pamela, I think I have taken notice of the most material articles in your letters, and have no more to say to you; but write on, and oblige us; and mind to send me the copy of your letter to Miss Darnford, of that you wrote to poor penitent Jewkes, and every article I have written about, and all that comes into your head, or that passes, and you'll oblige *yours, &c.*

B. DAVERS.

LETTER XX

MY DEAR LADY,

I read with pleasure your commands, in your last kind and obliging letter : and you may be sure of a ready obedience in every one of them, that is in my power.

That which I can most easily do, I will first do; and that is, to transcribe the answer I sent to Miss Darnford, and that to Mrs. Jewkes, the former of which, (and a long one it is) is as follows :

" DEAR MISS DARNFORD,

" I begin now to be afraid I shall not have the pleasure and benefit I promised myself of passing a fortnight or three weeks at the Hall, in your sweet conversation, and that of your worthy family, as well as those others in your agreeable neighbourhood, whom I must always remember with equal honour and delight.

" The occasion will be principally, that we expect, very soon, Lord and Lady Davers, who propose to tarry here a fortnight at least; and after that, the advanced season will carry us to London, where Mr. B. has taken a house for his winter residence, and in order to attend parliament : a service he says, which he has been more deficient in hitherto, than he can either answer to his constituents, or to his own conscience; for though he is but one, yet if any good motion should be lost by *one*, every absent member, who is independent, has to reproach himself with the consequence of the loss of that good which might otherwise redound to the commonwealth. And besides, he says, such excuses as *he* could make, *every one* might plead ; and then public affairs might as well be left to the administration, and no parliament be chosen.

"See you, my dear Miss Darnford, from the humble cottager, what a public person your favourite friend is grown! How easy is it for a bold mind to look forward, and, perhaps, forgetting what she was, now she imagines she has a stake in the country, takes upon herself to be as important, as significant, as if, like my dear Miss Darnford, she had been born to it !

"Well; but may I not ask, whether, if the mountain cannot come to Mahomet, Mahomet will not come to the mountain? Since Lady Davers's visit is so uncertain as to its beginning and duration, and so great a favour as I am to look upon it, and really shall, it being her first visit to *me :*—and since we must go and take possession of our London residence, why can't Sir Simon spare to us the dear lady whom he could use hardly, and whose attendance (though he is indeed entitled to all her duty) he did not, just in that instance, quite so much deserve ?

"'Well, but after all, Sir Simon,' would I say, if I had been in presence at his peevish hour, ' you are a fine gentleman, are you not? to take such a method to shew your good daughter, that because she did not come *soon enough* to you, she came *too soon !* And did ever papa before you put a *good book* (for such I doubt not it was, *because* you were in affliction, though so little affected by its precepts) to such a *bad use ?* As parents' examples are so prevalent, suppose your daughter had taken it, and flung it at her sister; Miss Nancy at her waiting-maid; and so it had gone through the family; would it not have been an excuse for every one to say, that the father, and head of the family had set the example ?

"'You almost wish, my dear Miss tells me, that I would undertake *you !*—This is very good of you, Sir Simon,' I might (would his patience have suffered me to run on thus) have added; ' but I hope, since you are so sensible that you *want* to be undertaken, (and since this peevish rashness convinces me that you *do*) that you will undertake *yourself ;* that you will not, when your indisposition requires the attendance and duty of your dear lady and daughter, make it more uncomfortable to them, by *adding* a difficulty of being pleased, and an impatience of spirit, to the concern their duty and affection make them have for you; and, *at least,* resolve never to take a book into your hand again, if you cannot make a better use of it, than you did then.'

"But Sir Simon will say, I have *already undertaken* him, were he to see this. Yet my Lady Darnford once begged I would give him a hint or two on this subject, which, she was pleased to say, would be better received from me than from any body: and if it be a little too severe, it is but a just reprisal made by one whose ears, he knows, he has cruelly wounded more than once, twice, or thrice, besides, by what he calls his *innocent* double entendres, and who, if she had not resented it, when an opportunity offered, must have been believed, by him, to be neither more nor less than a hypocrite. There's for you, Sir Simon: and so here ends all my malice; for now I have spoken my mind.

"Yet I hope your dear papa will not be so angry as to deny me, for this my freedom, the request I make to *him*, to your *mamma*, and to your *dear self*, for your beloved company, for a month or two in Bedfordshire, and at London: and if you might be permitted to winter with us at the latter, how happy should I be! It will be half done the moment you desire it. Sir Simon loves you too well to refuse you, if you are earnest in it. Your honoured mamma is always indulgent to your requests: and Mr. B. as well in kindness to me, as for the great respect he bears you, joins with me to beg this favour of you, and of Sir Simon and my lady.

"If it can be obtained, what pleasure and improvement may I not propose to myself, with so polite a companion, when we are carried by Mr. B. to the play, the opera, and other of the town diversions! We will work, visit, read, and sing together, and improve one another; you *me*, in every word you shall speak, in every thing you shall do; I *you*, by my questions, and desire of information, which will make you open all your breast to me: and so unlocking that dear storehouse of virtuous knowledge, improve your own notions the more for communicating them. O my dear Miss Darnford! how happy is it in your power to make me!

"I am much affected with your account of Mrs. Jewkes's reformation, I could have wished, had I not *other* and *stronger* inducements (in the pleasure of so agreeable a neighbourhood, and so sweet a companion), I could have been down at the Hall, in hopes to have confirmed the poor woman in her newly assumed penitence. God give her grace to persevere in it!—To be an humble means of saving a soul from perdition! O my dear Miss Darnford, let me enjoy that heart-ravishing hope!—To pluck such a brand as this out of the fire, and to assist to quench its flaming susceptibility for mischief, and make it useful to edifying purposes, what a pleasure does this afford one! How does it encourage one to proceed in the way one has been guided to pursue! How does it make me hope, that I am raised to my present condition, in order to be an humble instrument in the hand of Providence to communicate great good to others, and so extend to many those benefits I have received, which, were they to go no further than myself, what a vile, what an ungrateful creature should I be !

" I see, my dearest Miss Darnford, how useful in every condition of life a virtuous and a serious turn of mind may be !

" In hopes of seeing you with us, I will not enlarge on several agreeable subjects, which I could touch upon with pleasure, besides what I gave you in my former (of my reception here, and of the kindness of our genteel neighbours) : such, particularly, as the arrival here of my dear parents, and the kind, generous entertainment they met with from my best friend ; his condescension in not only permitting me to attend them to Kent, but accompanying us thither, and settling them in a most happy manner, beyond their wishes and my own ; but yet so much in character, as I may say, that every one must approve his judicious benevolence ; the favours of my good Lady Davers to me, who, pleased with my letters, has vouchsafed to become my correspondent ; and a thousand things, which I want personally to communicate to my dear Miss Darnford.

" Be pleased to present my humble respects to Lady Darnford, and to Miss Nancy ; to good Madam Jones, and to your kind friends at Stamford ; also to Mr. and Mrs. Peters, and their kinswoman : and beg of that good gentleman from me to encourage his new proselyte all he can ; and I doubt not, she will do credit, poor woman ! to the pains he shall take with her. In hopes of your kind compliance with my wishes for your company, I remain, *dearest Miss Darnford, your faithful and obliged friend and servant*,

" P. B."

This, my good lady, is the long letter I sent to Miss Darnford, who, at parting, engaged me to keep up a correspondence with her, and put me in hopes of passing a month or two at the Hall, if we came down, and if she could persuade Sir Simon and her mamma to spare her to my wishes. Your ladyship will excuse me for so faintly mentioning the honours you confer upon me : but I would not either add or diminish in the communications I make to you.

The following is the copy of what I wrote to Mrs. Jewkes :

" You give me, Mrs. Jewkes, very great pleasure, to find, that, at length, God Almighty has touched your heart, and

63

let you see, while health and strength lasted, the error of your ways. Many an unhappy one has not been so graciously touched, till they have smarted under some heavy afflictions, or been confined to the bed of sickness, when, perhaps, they have made vows and resolutions, that have held them no longer than the discipline lasted; but you give me much better hopes of the sincerity of your conversion; as you are so well convinced, before some sore evil has overtaken you : and it ought to be an earnest to you of the Divine favour, and should keep you from despondency.

" As to me, it became me to forgive you, as I most cordially did; since your usage of me, as it proved, was but a necessary means in the hand of Providence, to exalt me to that state of happiness, in which I have every day more and more cause given me to rejoice, by the kindest and most generous of gentlemen.

" As I have often prayed for you, even when you used me the most unkindly, I now praise God for having heard my prayers, and with high delight look upon you as a reclaimed soul given to my supplication. May the Divine goodness enable you to persevere in the course you have begun ! And when you can taste the all-surpassing pleasure that fills the worthy breast, on being placed in a station where your example may be of advantage to the souls of others, as well as to your own—a pleasure that every good mind glories in, and none else can truly relish; then may you be assured, that nothing but your perseverance, and the consequential improvement resulting from it, is wanted to convince you, that you are in a right way, and that the woe that is pronounced against the presumptuous sinner, belongs not to you.

" Let me, therefore, dear Mrs. Jewkes (for now *indeed* you are dear to me), caution you against two things; the one, that you return not to your former ways, and wilfully err after this repentance; for the Divine goodness will then look upon itself as mocked by you, and will withdraw itself from you; and more dreadful will your state then be, than if you had never repented : the 'other, that you don't despair of the Divine mercy, which has so evidently manifested itself in your favour, and has awakened you out of your deplorable lethargy, without those sharp medicines and operations, which others, and perhaps *not more faulty* persons, have suffered. But go on cheerfully in the same happy path. Depend upon it, you are now in the right way, and turn not either to the right hand or to the left; for the reward is before you, in reputation and a good fame in this life, and everlasting felicity beyond it.

"Your letter is that of a sensible woman, as I always thought you; and of a truly contrite one, as I hope you will prove yourself to be : and I the rather hope it, as I shall be always desirous, then of taking every opportunity that offers of doing you real service, as well with regard to your present as future life : for I am, *good* Mrs. Jewkes, as I now hope I may call you, *your loving friend to serve you,*   P. B.

"Whatever good books the worthy Mr. Peters will be so kind as to recommend to you, and to those under your direction, send for them either to Lincoln, Stamford, or Grantham, and place them to my account : and may they be the effectual means of confirming you and them in the good way you are in ! I have done as much for all here : and, I hope, to no bad effect : for I shall now tell them, by Mrs. Jervis, if there be occasion, that I hope they will not let me be out-done in Bedfordshire, by Mrs. Jewkes in Lincolnshire ; but that the servants of both houses may do credit to the best of masters. Adieu, *good* woman ; as once more I take pleasure to style you."

Thus, my good lady, have I obeyed you, in transcribing these two letters. I will now proceed to your ladyship's twelve articles. As to the

1. I will oblige your ladyship, as I have opportunity, in my future letters, with such accounts of my dear lady's favour and goodness to me, as I think will be acceptable to you, and to the noble ladies you mention.

2. I am extremely delighted, that your ladyship thinks so well of my dear honest parents : they are good people, and ever had minds that set them above low and sordid actions : and God and your good brother has rewarded them most amply in this world, which is more than they ever expected, after a series of unprosperousness in all they undertook.

Your ladyship is pleased to say, that people in upper life love to see how plain nature operates in honest minds, who have hardly any thing else for their guide : and if I might not be thought to descend too low for your ladyship's attention (for, as to myself, I shall, I hope, always look back with pleasure to what I *was*, in order to increase my thankfulness for what I *am*), I would give you a scene of resignation, and contented poverty, of which otherwise you can hardly have a notion. I *will* give it, because it will be a scene of nature, however low, which your ladyship loves, and it shall not tire you by its length.

It was upon occasion of a great loss and disappointment which happened to my dear parents; for though they were never high in life, yet they were not always so low as my honoured lady found them, when she took me. My poor father came home; and as the loss was of such a nature, as that he could not keep it from my mother, he took her hand, and said, after he had acquainted her with it, " Come, my dear, let us take comfort, that we did for the best. We left the issue to Providence, as we ought, and that has turned it as it pleased; and we must be content, though not favoured as we wished.—All the business is, our lot is not cast for this life. Let us resign ourselves to the Divine will, and continue to do our duty, and this short life will soon be past. Our troubles will be quickly overblown; and we shall be happy in a better, I make no doubt."

Then my dear mother threw her arms about his neck, and said, with tears, " God's will be done, my dear love ! All cannot be rich and happy. I am contented, and had rather say, I have a poor honest husband, than a guilty rich one. What signifies repining : let the world go as it will, we shall have our length and our breadth at last. And Providence, I doubt not, will be a better friend to our good girl here, because she is good, than we could be, if this had not happened," pointing to me, who, then about eleven years old (for it was before my lady took me), sat weeping in the chimney corner, over a few dying embers of a fire, at their moving expressions.

I arose, and kissing both their hands, and blessing them, said, " And this length and breadth, my dear parents, will be, one day, all that the rich and the great can possess; and, it may be, their ungracious heirs will trample upon their ashes, and rejoice they are gone : while such a poor girl as I, am honouring the memories of mine, who, in their good names, and good lessons, will have left me the best of portions."

And then they both hugged me to their fond bosoms, by turns; and all three were filled with comfort in one another.

For a farther proof that *honest poverty* is not such a deplorable thing as some people imagine, let me ask, what pleasure can those over-happy persons know, who, from the luxury of their tastes, and their affluent circumstances, always eat before they are hungry, and drink before they are thirsty? This may be illustrated by the instance of a certain eastern monarch, who, as I have read, marching at the head of a vast army, through a wide extended desert, which afforded neither river nor spring, for the first time, found himself (in common with his soldiers) overtaken by a craving thirst, which made him pant after a cup of water. And when, after diligent search, one of his soldiers found a little dirty puddle, and carried him some of the filthy water in his nasty helmet, the monarch greedily swallowing it, cried out, that in all his life he never tasted so sweet a draught!

But when I talk or write of my worthy parents, how I run on!—Excuse me, my good lady, and don't think me, in this respect, too much like the cat in the fable, turned into a fine lady; for though I would never forget what I was, yet I would be thought to know *how* gratefully to enjoy my present happiness, as well with regard to my obligations to God, as to your dear brother. But let me proceed to your ladyship's third particular.

3. And you cannot imagine, Madam, how much you have set my heart at rest, when you say, that my dear Mr. B. gave me a just narrative of this affair with Miss Godfrey: for when your ladyship desired to know how he had recounted that story, lest you should make a misunderstanding between us unawares, I knew not what to think. I was afraid some blood had been shed on the occasion by him: for the lady was ruined, and as to her, nothing could have happened worse. The regard I have for Mr. B.'s future happiness, which, in my constant supplication for him in private, costs me many a tear, gave me great apprehensions, and not a little uneasiness. But as your ladyship tells me that he gave me a just account, I am happy again.

I now come to your ladyship's fourth particular.

And highly delighted I am for having obtained your approbation of my conduct to the child, as well as of my behaviour towards the dear gentleman, on the unhappy lady's score. Your ladyship's wise intimations about having the child with me, make due impressions upon me; and I see in them, with grateful pleasure, your unmerited regard for me. Yet, I don't know how it is, but I have conceived a strange passion for this dear baby; I cannot but look upon her poor mamma as my sister in point of trial; and shall not the prosperous sister pity and love the poor dear sister that, in so slippery a path, has *fallen*, while *she* had the happiness to keep her feet?

The rest of your ladyship's articles give me the greatest pleasure and satisfaction; and if I can but continue myself in the favour of your dear brother, and improve in that of his noble sister, how happy shall I be! I will do all I can to deserve both. And I hope you will take as an instance of it, my cheerful obedience to your commands, in writing to so fine a judge, such crude and indigested stuff, as, otherwise I ought to be ashamed to lay before you.

I am impatient for the honour of your presence here; and yet I perplex myself with the fear of appearing so unworthy in your eye when near you, as to suffer in your opinion; but I promise myself, that however this may be the case on your first visit, I shall be so much improved by the benefits I shall reap from your lessons and good example, that whenever I shall be favoured with a *second*, you shall have fewer faults to find with me; till, as I shall be more and more favoured, I shall in time be just what your ladyship will wish me to be, and, of consequence, more worthy than I am of the honour of stiling myself *your ladyship's most humble and obedient servant,*

P. B.

LETTER XXI

From Miss Darnford, in answer to Mrs. B.'s, p. 60.

MY DEAR MRS. B.,

You are highly obliging in expressing so warmly your wishes to have me with you. I know not any body in this world, out of our own family, in whose company I should be happier; but my papa won't part with me, I think; though I have secured my mamma in my interest; and I know Nancy would be glad of my absence, because the dear, perversely envious, thinks *me* more valued than *she* is; and yet, foolish girl, she don't consider, that if her envy be well grounded, I should return with more than double advantages to what I now have, improved by your charming conversation.

My papa affects to be in a fearful pet, at your lecturing of him so justly; for my mamma would shew him the letter; and he says he will positively demand satisfaction of Mr. B. for your treating him so freely. And yet he shall hardly think him, he says, on a rank with him, unless Mr. B. will, on occasion of the new commission, take out his Dedimus: and then if he will bring you down to Lincolnshire, and join with him to commit you prisoner for a month at the Hall, all shall be well.

It is very obliging in Mr. B. to join in your kind invitation: but—yet I am loth to say it to you—the character of your worthy gentleman, I doubt, stands a little in the way with my papa.

My mamma pleaded his being married. " Ads-dines, Madam," said he, " what of all that ! "

"But, Sir," said I, "I hope, if I may not go to Bedfordshire, you'll permit me to go to London, when Mrs. B. goes?"

"No," said he, "positively no!"

"Well, Sir, I have done. I could hope, however, you would enable me to give a better reason to good Mrs. B. why I am not permitted to accept of the kind invitation, than that which I understand you have been pleased to assign."

He stuck his hands in his sides, with his usual humourous positiveness. "Why, then tell her she is a very saucy lady, for her last letter to you; and her lord and master is not to be trusted; and it is my absolute will and pleasure that you ask me no more questions about it."

"I will very faithfully make this report, Sir."—"Do so." And so I have. And your poor Polly Darnford is disappointed of one of the greatest pleasures she could have had.

I can't help it—if you truly pity me you can make me easier under the disappointment, than otherwise possible, by favouring me with an epistolary conversation, since I am denied a personal one; and my mamma joins in the request; particularly let us know how Lady Davers's first visit passes; which Mrs. Peters and Mrs. Jones, who know my lady so well, likewise long to hear. And this will make us the best amends in your power for the loss of your good neighbourhood, which we had all promised to ourselves.

This denial of my papa comes out, since I wrote the above, to be principally owing to a proposal made him of an humble servant to one of his daughters: he won't say which, he tells us, in his usual humourous way, lest we should fall out about it.

"I suppose," I tell him, "the young gentleman is to pick and choose which of the two he likes best." But be he a duke, 'tis all one to Polly, if he is not something above our common Lincolnshire class of fox-hunters.

I have shewn Mr. and Mrs. Peters your letter. They admire you beyond expression; and Mr. Peters says, he does not know, that ever he did any thing in his life, that gave him so much inward reproach, as his denying you the protection of his family, which Mr. Williams sought to move him to afford you, when you were confined at the Hall, before Mr. B. came down to you, with his heart bent on mischief; and all he comforts himself with is, that very denial, as well as the other hardships you have met with, were necessary to bring about that work of Providence which was to reward your unexampled virtue.

69

Yet, he says, he doubts he shall not be thought excusable by you, who are so exact in *your* own duty, since he had the unhappiness to lose such an opportunity to have done honour to his function, had he had the fortitude to have done *his;* and he has begged of me to hint his concern to you on this head; and to express his hopes, that neither religion nor his cloth may suffer in your opinion, for the fault of one of its professors, who never was wanting in his duty so much before.

He had it often upon his mind, he says, to write to you on this very subject; but he had not the courage; and besides, did not know *how* Mr. B. might take it, if he should see that letter, as the case had such delicate circumstances in it, that in blaming himself, as he should very freely have done, he must, by implication, have cast still greater blame upon him.

Mr. Peters is certainly a very good man, and my favourite for that reason; and I hope *you,* who could so easily forgive the late wicked, but now penitent Jewkes, will overlook with kindness a fault in a good man, which proceeded more from pusillanimity and constitution, than from want of principle: for once, talking of it to my mamma, before me, he accused himself on this score, to her, with tears in his eyes. She, good lady, would have given you this protection at Mr. Williams's desire; but wanted the power to do it.

So you see, my dear Mrs. B., how your virtue has shamed every one into such a sense of what they ought to have done, that good, bad, and indifferent, are seeking to make excuses for past misbehaviour, and to promise future amendment, like penitent subjects returning to their duty to their conquering sovereign, after some unworthy defection.

Happy, happy lady! May you ever be so! May you always convert your enemies, invigorate the lukewarm, and every day multiply your friends, wishes *your most affectionate,*

POLLY DARNFORD.

P.S. How I rejoice in the joy of your honest parents! God bless 'em! I am glad Lady Davers is so wise. Every one I have named desire their best respects. Write oftener, and omit not the minutest thing: for every line of yours carries instruction with it.

LETTER XXII

From Sir Simon Darnford to Mr. B.

SIR,

Little did I think I should ever have occasion to make a formal complaint against a person very dear to you, and who I believe deserves to be so; but don't let her be so proud and so vain of obliging and pleasing you, as to make her not care how she affronts every body else.

The person is no other than the wife of your bosom, who has taken such liberties with me as ought not to be taken, and sought to turn my own child against me, and make a dutiful girl a rebel.

If people will set up for virtue, and all that, let 'em be uniformly virtuous, or I would not give a farthing for their pretences.

Here I have been plagued with gouts, rheumatisms, and nameless disorders, ever since you left us, which have made me call for a little more attendance than ordinary; and I had reason to think myself slighted, where an indulgent father can least bear to be so, that is, where he most loves; and that by young upstarts, who are growing up to the enjoyment of those pleasures which have run away from me, fleeting rascals as they are ! before I was willing to part with them. And I rung and rung, and " Where's Polly ? " (for I honour the slut with too much of my notice), " Where's Polly ? " was all my cry, to every one who came up to ask what I rung for. And, at last, in burst the pert baggage, with an air of assurance, as if she thought all must be well the moment she appeared, with " Do you want me, papa ? "

" Do I want you, Confidence ? Yes, I do. Where have you been these two hours, that you never came near me, when you knew 'twas my time to have my foot rubbed, which gives me mortal pain ? " For you must understand, Mr. B., that nobody's hand's so soft as Polly's.

She gave me a saucy answer, as I was disposed to think it, because I had just then a twinge, that I could scarce bear; for pain is a plaguy thing to a man of my lively spirits.

She gave me, I say, a careless answer, and turning upon her heel; and not coming to me at my first word, I flung a book which I had in my hand, at her head. And, this fine lady of your's, this paragon of meekness and humility, in so many words, bids me, or, which is worse, tells my own daughter to bid me, never to take a book into my hands again, if I won't make a better use of it :—and yet, what better use can an offended father make of the best books, than to correct a rebellious child with them, and oblige a saucy daughter to jump into her duty all at once?

Mrs. B. reflects upon me for making her blush formerly, and saying things before my daughters, that, truly, I ought to be ashamed of? then avows malice and revenge. Why neighbour, are these things to be borne?—Do you allow your lady to set up for a general corrector of every body's morals but your own?—Do you allow her to condemn the only instances of wit that remain to this generation; that dear polite *double entendre*, which keeps alive the attention, and quickens the apprehension, of the best companies in the world, and is the salt, the sauce, which gives a poignancy to all our genteeler entertainments!

Very fine, truly! that more than half the world shall be shut out of society, shall be precluded their share of conversation amongst the gay and polite of both sexes, were your lady to have her will! Let her first find people who can support a conversation with wit and good sense like her own, and then something may be said : but till then, I positively say, and will swear upon occasion, that *double entendre* shall not be banished from our tables; and where this won't raise a blush, or create a laugh, we will, if we please, for all Mrs. B. and her new-fangled notions, force the one and the other by still plainer hints; and let her help herself how she can.

Thus, Sir, you find my complaints are of a high nature, regarding the quiet of a family, the duty of a child to a parent, and the freedom and politeness of conversation; in all which your lady has greatly offended; and I insist upon satisfaction from you, or such a correction of the fair transgressor, as is in your power to inflict, and which may prevent worse consequences from *your offended friend and servant,*

Simon Darnford.

LETTER XXIII

From Mr. B. in Answer to the preceding one.

Dear Sir Simon,

You cannot but believe that I was much surprised at your letter, complaining of the behaviour of my wife. I could no more have expected such a complaint from such a gentleman, than I could, that she would have deserved it : and I am very sorry on *both* accounts. I have talked to her in such a manner, that, I dare say, she will never give you like cause to appeal to me.

It happened, that the criminal herself received it from her servant, and brought it to me in my closet; and, making her honours (for I can't say but she is very obliging to me, though she takes such saucy freedoms with my friends) away she tript; and I, inquiring for her, when, with surprise, as you may believe, I had read your charge, found she was gone to visit a poor sick neighbour; of which indeed I knew before because she took the chariot; but I had forgot it in my wrath.

At last, in she came, with that sweet composure in her face which results from a consciousness of doing *generally* just and generous things. I resumed, therefore, that sternness and displeasure which her entrance had almost dissipated. I took her hand; her charming eye (you know what an eye she has, Sir Simon) quivered at my overclouded aspect; and her lips, half drawn to a smile, trembling with apprehension of a countenance so changed from what she left it.

And then, all stiff and stately as I could look, did I accost her—" Come along with me, Pamela, to my closet. I want to talk with you."

" What have I done? Let me know, good Sir!" looking round, with her half-affrighted eyes, this way and that, on the books, and pictures, and on me, by turns.

" You shall know soon," said I, " the *crime* you have been guilty of."—" *Crime*, Sir! Pray let me—This closet, I hoped, would not be a *second* time witness to the flutter you put me in."

There hangs a tale, Sir Simon, which I am not very fond of relating, since it gave beginning to the triumphs of this little sorceress. I still held one hand, and she stood before me, as criminals ought to do before their judge, but said, " I see, Sir, sure I do,—or what will else become of me!—less severity in your eyes, than you affect to put on in your countenance. Dear Sir, let me but know my fault: I will repent, acknowledge, and amend."

" You must have great presence of mind, Pamela, such is the nature of your fault, if you can look me in the face, when I tell it you."

" Then let me," said the irresistible charmer, hiding her face in my bosom, and putting her other arm about my neck, " let me thus, my dear Mr. B., hide this guilty face, while I hear my

73

fault told; and I will not seek to extenuate it, by my tears, and my penitence."

I could hardly hold out. What infatuating creatures are these women, when they thus soothe and calm the tumults of an angry heart! When, instead of *scornful* looks darted in return for *angry* ones, words of *defiance* for words of *peevishness*, persisting to defend *one* error by *another*, and returning *vehement wrath* for *slight indignation*, and all the hostile provocations of the marriage warfare; they can thus hide their dear faces in our bosoms, and wish but to *know* their faults, to *amend* them!

I could hardly, I say, resist the sweet girl's behaviour; nay, I believe, I did, and in defiance to my resolved displeasure, press her forehead with my lips, as the rest of her face was hid on my breast; but, considering it was the cause of my *friend*, I was to assert, my *injured* friend, wounded and insulted, in so various a manner by the fair offender, thus haughtily spoke I to the trembling mischief, in a pomp of style theatrically tragic:

"I will not, too inadvertent, and undistinguishing Pamela, keep you long in suspense, for the sake of a circumstance, that, on this occasion, ought to give you as much joy, as it has, till now, given me—since it becomes an advocate in your favour, when otherwise you might expect very severe treatment. Know then, that the letter you gave me before you went out, is a letter from a friend, a neighbour, a worthy neighbour, complaining of your behaviour to him;—no other than Sir Simon Darnford" (for I would not amuse her too much), "a gentleman I must always respect, and whom, as my friend, I expected *you* should : since, by the value a wife expresses for one esteeemd by her husband, whether she thinks so well of him herself, or not, a man ought always to judge of the sincerity of her regards to himself."

She raised her head at once on this :—" Thank Heaven," said she, " it is no worse !—I was at my wit's end almost, in apprehension : but I know how this must be. Dear Sir, how could you frighten me so?—I know how all this is !—I can now look you in the face, and hear all that Sir Simon can charge me with! For I am sure, I have not so affronted him as to make him angry indeed. And truly " (ran she on, secure of pardon as she seemed to think), " I should respect Sir Simon not only as your friend, but on his own account, if he was not so sad a rake at a time of life——"

Then I interrupted her, you must needs think, Sir Simon; for how could I bear to hear my worthy friend so freely treated ! " How now, Pamela !" said I; " and is it thus, by *repeating*

74

your fault, that you *atone* for it? Do you think I can bear to hear my friend so freely treated?"

"Indeed," said she, "I do respect Sir Simon very much as your *friend*, permit me to repeat; but cannot for his wilful failings. Would it not be, in some measure, to approve of faulty conversation, if one can hear it, and not discourage it, when the occasion comes in so pat?—And, indeed, I was glad of an opportunity," continued she, "to give him a little rub; I must needs own it: but if it displeases you, or has made him angry in earnest, I am sorry for it, and will be less bold for the future."

"Read then," said I, "the heavy charge, and I'll return instantly to hear your answer to it." So I went from her, for a few minutes. But, would you believe it, Sir Simon? she seemed, on my return, very little concerned at your just complaints. What self-justifying minds have the meekest of these women!—Instead of finding her in repentant tears, as one would expect, she took your angry letter for a jocular one; and I had great difficulty to convince her of the heinousness of *her* fault, or the reality of your resentment. Upon which, being determined to have justice done to my friend, and a due sense of her own great error impressed upon her, I began thus:

"Pamela, take heed that you do not suffer the purity of your own mind, in breach of your charity, to make you too rigorous a censurer of other people's actions: don't be so puffed up with your own perfections, as to imagine, that, because other persons allow themselves liberties you cannot take, *therefore* they must be wicked. Sir Simon is a gentleman who indulges himself in a pleasant vein, and, I believe, as well as you, *has been* a great rake and libertine:" (You'll excuse me, Sir Simon, because I am taking your part), "but what then? You see it is all over with him now. He says, that he *must*, and therefore he *will* be virtuous: and is a man for ever to hear the faults of his youth, when so willing to forget them?"

"Ah! but, Sir, Sir," said the bold slut, "can you say he is *willing* to forget them?—Does he not repine in this very letter, that he *must* forsake them; and does he not plainly cherish the *inclination*, when he owns——" She hesitated—"Owns what?" —"You know what I mean, Sir, and I need not speak it: and can there well be a more censurable character?—Then *before* his maiden daughters! his virtuous lady! *before* any body!— What a sad thing is this, at a time of life, which should afford a better example!

"But, dear Sir," continued the bold prattler, (taking advantage of a silence more owing to displeasure than approbation) " let me, for I would not be too *censorious* " (No, not she ! in the very act of censoriousness to say this !), " let me offer but one thing : don't you think Sir Simon himself would be loth to be thought a reformed gentleman ? Don't you see his delight, when speaking of his former pranks, as if sorry he could not play them over again ? See but how he simpers, and *enjoys*, as one may say, the relations of his own rakish actions, when he tells a bad story ! "

" But," said I, " were this the case " (for I profess, Sir Simon, I was at a grievous loss to defend you), " for you to write all these free things against a father to his daughter, is that right, Pamela ? "

" O, Sir ! the *good* gentleman himself has taken care, that such a character as I presumed to draw to Miss of her papa, was no strange one to her. You have seen yourself, Mr. B., whenever his arch leers, and his humourous attitude on those occasions, have taught us to expect some shocking story, how his lady and daughters (used to him as they are), have suffered in their apprehensions of what he would say, before he spoke it : how, particularly, dear Miss Darnford has looked at me with concern, desirous, as it were, if possible, to save her papa from the censure, which his faulty expressions must naturally bring upon him. And, dear Sir, is it not a sad thing for a young lady, who loves and honours her papa, to observe, that he is discrediting himself, and *wants* the example he ought to *give ?* And pardon me, Sir, for smiling on so serious an occasion ; but is it not a fine sight to see a gentleman, as we have often seen Sir Simon, when he has thought proper to read a passage in some bad book, pulling off *his spectacles*, to talk filthily upon it ? Methinks I see him now," added the bold slut, " splitting his arch face with a broad laugh, shewing a mouth, with hardly a tooth in it, and making obscene remarks upon what he has read."

And then the dear saucy-face laughed out, to bear *me* company ; for I could not, for the soul of me, avoid laughing heartily at the figure she brought to my mind, which I have seen my old friend more than once make, with his dismounted spectacles, arch mouth, and gums of shining jet, succeeding those of polished ivory, of which he often boasts, as one ornament of his youthful days.—And I the rather in my heart, Sir Simon, gave you up, because, when I was a sad fellow, it was always my maxim to endeavour to touch a lady's heart without wounding her ears. And, indeed, I found my account sometimes in observing it.

But, resuming my gravity—" Hussy," said I, " do you think I will have my old friend thus made the object of your ridicule? —Suppose a challenge should have ensued between us on your account—what might have been the issue of it? To see an old gentleman, stumping, as he says, on crutches, to fight a duel in defence of his wounded honour ! "—" Very bad, Sir, to be sure : I see that, and am sorry for it : for had you carried off Sir Simon's crutch, as a trophy, he must have lain sighing and groaning like a wounded soldier in the field of battle, till another had been brought him, to have stumped home with."

But, dear Sir Simon, I have brought this matter to an issue, that will, I hope, make all easy :—Miss Polly, and my Pamela, shall both be punished as they deserve, if it be not your own fault. I am told, that the sins of your youth don't sit so heavily upon your limbs, as in your imagination; and I believe change of air, and the gratification of your revenge, a fine help to such lively spirits as yours, will set you up. You shall then take coach, and bring your pretty criminal to mine; and when we have them together, they shall humble themselves before us, and you can absolve or punish them, as you shall see proper. For I cannot bear to have my worthy friend insulted in so heinous a manner, by a couple of saucy girls, who, if not taken down in time, may proceed from fault to fault, till there will be no living with them.

If (to be still more serious) your lady and you will lend Miss Darnford to my Pamela's wishes, whose heart is set upon the hope of her wintering with us in town, you will lay an obligation upon us both; which will be acknowledged with great gratitude by, dear Sir, *your affectionate and humble servant.*

LETTER XXIV

From Sir Simon Darnford in reply.

Hark ye, Mr. B.—A word in your ear :—to be plain : I like neither you nor your wife well enough to trust my Polly with you.

But here's war declared against my poor gums, it seems. Well, I will never open my mouth before your lady as long as I live, if I can help it. I have for these ten years avoided to put on my cravat; and for what reason, do you think?—Why, because I could not bear to see what ruins a few years have made in a visage, that used to inspire love and terror as it pleased. And here your—what-shall-I-call-her of a wife, with all the insolence of youth and beauty on her side, follows me with a glass, and would make me look in it, whether I will or not. I'm a plaguy good-humoured old fellow—if I *am* an old fellow—or I should not bear the insults contained in your letter. Between you and your lady, you make a wretched figure of me, that's certain.—And yet 'tis *taking my part*.

But what must I do?—I'd be glad at any rate to stand in your lady's graces, that I would; nor would I be the last rake libertine unreformed by her example, which I suppose will make virtue the fashion, if she goes on as she does. But here I have been used to cut a joke and toss the squib about; and, as far as I know, it has helped to keep me alive in the midst of pains and aches, and with two women-grown girls, and the rest of the mortifications that will attend on *advanced years*; for I won't (hang me if I will) give it up as absolute *old age !*

But now, it seems, I must leave all this off, or I must be mortified with a looking glass held before me, and every wrinkle must be made as conspicuous as a furrow—And what, pray, is to succeed to this reformation?—I can neither fast nor pray, I doubt.—And besides, if my stomach and my jest depart from me, farewell, Sir Simon Darnford !

But cannot I pass as one necessary character, do you think : as a foil (as, by-the-bye, some of your own actions have been to your lady's virtue) to set off some more edifying example, where variety of characters make up a feast in conversation ?

Well, I believe I might have trusted you with my daughter, under your lady's eye, rake as you have been yourself; and fame says wrong, if you have not been, for your time a bolder sinner than ever I was, with your maxim of touching ladies' hearts, without wounding their ears, which made surer work with them, that was all; though 'tis to be hoped you are now reformed; and if you are, the whole country round you, east, west, north, and south, owe great obligations to your fair reclaimer. But here is a fine prim young fellow, coming out of Norfolk, with one estate in one county, another in another, and jointures and settlements in his hand, and more wit in his head, as well as more money in his pocket, than he can tell what to do with, to visit our Polly; though I tell her I much question the former quality, his wit, if he is for marrying.

Here then is the reason I cannot comply with your kind Mrs. B.'s request. But if this matter should go off; if he should not like *her*, or she *him ;* or if I should not like *his* terms, or he *mine ;*—or still another *or*, if he should like Nancy better—

78

why, then perhaps, if Polly be a good girl, I may trust to her virtue, and to your honour, and let her go for a month or two.

Now, when I have said this, and when I say, further, that I can forgive your severe lady, and yourself too, (who, however, are less to be excused in the airs you assume, which looks like one chimney-sweeper calling another a sooty rascal) I gave a proof of my charity, which I hope with Mrs. B. will cover a multitude of faults; and the rather, since, though I cannot be a *follower* of her virtue in the strictest sense, I can be an *admirer* of it; and that is some little merit : and indeed all that can be at present pleaded by *yourself*, I doubt, any more than *your humble servant*,

SIMON DARNFORD.

LETTER XXV

My Honoured and dear Parents,

I hope you will excuse my long silence, which has been owing to several causes, and having had nothing new to entertain you with : and yet this last is but a poor excuse to you, who think every trifling subject agreeable from your daughter.

I daily expect here my Lord and Lady Davers. This gives me no small pleasure, and yet it is mingled with some uneasiness at times; lest I should not, when viewed so intimately near, behave myself answerably to her ladyship's expectations. But I resolve not to endeavour to move out of the sphere of my own capacity, in order to emulate her ladyship. She must have advantages, by conversation, as well as education, which it would be arrogance in me to assume, or to think of imitating.

All that I will attempt to do, therefore, shall be, to shew such a respectful obligingness to my lady, as shall be consistent with the condition to which I am raised; so that she may not have reason to reproach me of pride in my exaltation, nor her dear brother to rebuke me for meanness in condescending : and, as to my family arrangement, I am the less afraid of inspection, because, by the natural bias of my own mind, I bless God, I am above dark reserves, and have not one selfish or sordid view, to make me wish to avoid the most scrutinising eye.

I have begun a correspondence with Miss Darnford, a young lady of uncommon merit. But yet you know her character from my former writings. She is very solicitous to hear of all that concerns me, and particularly how Lady Davers and I agree together. I loved her from the moment I saw her first;

for she has the least pride, and the most benevolence and solid thought, I ever knew in a young lady, and does not envy any one. I shall write to her often: and as I shall have so many avocations besides to fill up my time, I know you will excuse me, if I procure from this lady the return of my letters to her, for your perusal, and for the entertainment of your leisure hours. This will give you, from time to time, the accounts you desire of all that happens here. But as to what relates to our own particulars, I beg you will never spare writing, as I shall not answering; for it is one of my greatest delights, that I have such worthy parents (as I hope in God, I long shall) to bless me and to correspond with me.

The papers I send herewith will afford you some diversion, particularly those relating to Sir Simon Darnford; and I must desire, that when you have perused them (as well as what I shall send for the future), you will return them to me.

Mr. Longman greatly pleased me, on his last return, in his account of your health, and the satisfaction you take in your happy lot; and I must recite to you a brief conversation on this occasion, which, I dare say, will please you as much as it did me.

After having adjusted some affairs with his dear principal, which took up two hours, my best beloved sent for me. "My dear," said he, seating me by him, and making the good old gentleman sit down, (for he will always rise at my approach) "Mr. Longman and I have settled, in two hours, some accounts, which would have taken up as many months with some persons: for never was there an exacter or more methodical accomptant. He gives me (greatly to my satisfaction, because I know it will delight you) an account of the Kentish concern, and of the pleasure your father and mother take in it.—Now, my charmer," said he, "I see your eyes begin to glisten: O how this subject raises your whole soul to the windows of it!—Never was so dutiful a daughter, Mr. Longman; and never did parents better deserve a daughter's duty."

I endeavoured before Mr. Longman to rein in a gratitude, that my throbbing heart confessed through my handkerchief, as I perceived: but the good old gentleman could not hinder his from shewing itself at his worthy eyes, to see how much I was favoured—*oppressed*, I should say—with the tenderest goodness to me, and kind expressions.—"Excuse me," said he, wiping his cheeks: "my delight to see such merit so justly rewarded will not be contained, I think." And so he arose and walked to the window.

" Well, good Mr. Longman," said I, as he returned towards us, " you give me the pleasure to know that my father and mother are well; and happy then they *must* be, in a goodness and bounty, that I, and many more, rejoice in."

" Well and happy, Madam;—ay, that they are, indeed ! A worthier couple never lived. Most nobly do they go on in the farm. Your honour is one of the happiest gentlemen in the world. All the good you do, returns upon you in a trice. It may well be said *you cast your bread upon the waters ;* for it presently comes to you again, richer and heavier than when you threw it in. All the Kentish tenants, Madam, are hugely delighted with their good steward : every thing prospers under his management : the gentry love both him and my dame; and the poor people adore them."

Thus ran Mr. Longman on, to my inexpressible delight, you may believe; and when he withdrew—" 'Tis an honest soul," said my dear Mr. B. " I love him for his respectful love to my angel, and his value for the worthy pair. Very glad I am, that every thing answers *their* wishes. May they long live, and be happy ! "

The dear man makes me spring to his arms, whenever he touches this string : for he speaks always thus kindly of you; and is glad to hear, he says, that you don't live only to yourselves; and now and then adds, that he is as much satisfied with your prudence, as he is with mine; that parents and daughter do credit to one another : and that the praises he hears of you from every mouth, make him take as great pleasure in you, as if you were his own relations. How delighting, how transporting rather, my dear parents, must this goodness be to your happy daughter ! And how could I forbear repeating these kind things to you, that you may see how well every thing is taken that you do ?

When the expected visit from Lord and Lady Davers is over, the approaching winter will call us to London; and as I shall then be nearer to you, we may oftener hear from one another, which will be a great heightening to my pleasures.

But I hear such an account of the immoralities which persons may observe there, along with the public diversions, that it takes off a little from the satisfaction I should otherwise have in the thought of going thither. For, they say, quarrels, and duels, and gallantries, as they are called, so often happen in London, that those enormities are heard of without the least wonder or surprise.

This makes me very thoughtful at times. But God, I hope,

will preserve our dearest benefactor, and continue to me his affection, and then I shall be always happy; especially while your healths and felicity confirm and crown the delights of *your ever dutiful daughter,*   P. B.

LETTER XXVI

My dearest Child,

It may not be improper to mention ourselves, what the nature of the kindnesses is, which we confer on our poor neighbours, and the labouring people, lest it should be surmised, by any body, that we are lavishing away wealth that is not our own. Not that we fear either your honoured husband or you will suspect so, or that the worthy Mr. Longman would insinuate as much; for he saw what we did, and was highly pleased with it, and said he would make such a report of it as you write he did. What we do is in small things, though the good we hope from them is not small perhaps: and if a very distressful case should happen among our poor neighbours, requiring any thing considerable, and the objects be deserving, we would acquaint you with it, and leave it to you to do as God should direct you.

My dear child, you are very happy, and if it *can* be, may you be happier still! Yet I verily think you cannot be more happy than your father and mother, except in this one thing, that all *our* happiness, under God, proceeds from you; and, as other parents bless their children with plenty and benefits, you have blessed your parents (or your honoured husband rather for your sake) with all the good things this world can afford.

Your papers are the joy of our leisure hours; and you are kind beyond all expression, in taking care to oblige us with them. We know how your time is taken up, and ought to be very well contented, if but now and then you let us hear of your health and welfare. But it is not enough with such a good daughter, that you have made our lives *comfortable,* but you will make them *joyful* too, by communicating to us, all that befals you: and then you write so piously, and with such a sense of God's goodness to you, and intermix such good reflections in your writings, that whether it be our partial love or not, I cannot tell, but, truly, we think nobody comes up to you: and you make our hearts and eyes so often overflow, as we read, that we join hand in hand, and say to each other, in the same breath—" Blessed be God, and blessed be you, my love,"—" For such a daughter," says the one—" For such a daughter," says the other—" And she has your own sweet temper," cry I.—" And she has your own honest heart," cries she : and so we go on, blessing God, and you, and blessing your spouse, and ourselves !—Is any happiness like ours, my dear daughter?

We are really so enraptured with your writings, that when our spirits flag, through the infirmity of years, which hath begun to take hold of us, we have recourse to some of your papers :— " Come, my dear," cry I, " what say you to a banquet now ? "— She knows what I mean. " With all my heart," says she. So I read although it be on a Sunday, so good are your letters; and you must know, I have copies of many, and after a little while we are as much alive and brisk, as if we had no flagging at all, and return to the duties of the day with double delight.

Consider then, my dear child, what joy your writings give us : and yet we are afraid of oppressing you, who have so much to do of other kinds; and we are heartily glad you have found out a way to save trouble to yourself, and rejoice us, and oblige so worthy a young lady as Miss Darnford, all at one time. I never shall forget her dear goodness, and notice of me at the Hall, kindly pressing my rough hands with her fine hands, and looking in my face with *so* much kindness in her eyes !— What good people, as well as bad, there are in high stations !— Thank God there are; else our poor child would have had a sad time of it too often, when she was obliged to *step out of herself*, as once I heard you phrase it, into company you could not *live with*.

Well, but what shall I say more ? and yet how shall I end ?— Only, with my prayers, that God will continue to you the blessing and comforts you are in possession of !—And pray now, be not over-thoughtful about London ; for why should you let the dread of future evils lessen your present joys?—There is no absolute perfection in this life, that's true; but one would make one's self as easy as one could. 'Tis time enough to be troubled when troubles come—" *Sufficient unto the day is the evil thereof.*"

Rejoice, then, as you have often said you would, in your present blessings, and leave the event of things to the Supreme Disposer of all events. And what have *you* to do but to rejoice ? *You*, who cannot see a sun rise, but it is to bless you, and to raise up from their beds numbers to join in the blessing ! *You* who can bless your high-born friends, and your low-born parents, and obscure relations ! the rich by your example, and the poor

83

by your bounty; and bless besides so good and so brave a husband;—O my dear child, what, let me repeat it, have *you* to do but rejoice?—*For many daughters have done wisely, but you have excelled them all.*

I will only add, that every thing the 'squire ordered is just upon the point of being finished. And when the good time comes, that we shall be again favoured with his presence and yours, what a still greater joy will this afford to the already overflowing hearts of *your ever loving father and mother,*

JOHN *and* ELIZ. ANDREWS.

LETTER XXVII

MY DEAREST MISS DARNFORD,

The interest I take in everything that concerns you, makes me very importunate to know how you approve the gentleman, whom some of your best friends and well-wishers have recommended to your favour. I hope he will deserve your good opinion, and then he must excel most of the unmarried gentlemen in England.

Your papa, in his humourous manner, mentions his large possessions and riches; but were he as rich as Crœsus, he should not have my consent, if he has no greater merit; though that is what the generality of parents look out for first; and indeed an easy fortune is so far from being to be disregarded, that, when attended with equal merit, I think it ought to have a *preference* given to it, supposing affections disengaged. For 'tis certain, that a man or woman may stand as good a chance for happiness in marriage with a person of fortune, as with one who has not that advantage; and notwithstanding I had neither riches nor descent to boast of, I must be of opinion with those who say, that they never knew any body despise either, that had them. But to permit riches to be the *principal* inducement, to the neglect of superior merit, that is the fault which many a one smarts for, whether the choice be their own, or imposed upon them by those who have a title to their obedience.

Here is a saucy body, might some who have not Miss Darnford's kind consideration for her friend, be apt to say, who being thus meanly descended, nevertheless presumes to give her opinion, in these high cases, unasked.—But I have this to say; that I think myself so entirely divested of partiality to my own case, that, as far as my judgment shall permit, I will never have that in view, when I am presuming to hint my opinion of general rules. For, most surely, the honours I have received, and the debasement to which my best friend had subjected himself, have, for their principal excuse, that the gentleman was entirely independent, had no questions to ask, and had a fortune sufficient to make himself, as well as the person he chose, happy, though she brought him nothing at all; and that he had, moreover, such a character for good sense, and knowledge of the world, that nobody could impute to him any other inducement, but that of a noble resolution to reward a virtue he had so frequently, and, I will say, so wickedly, tried, and could not subdue.

My dear Miss, let me, as a subject very pleasing to me, touch upon your kind mention of the worthy Mr. Peters's sentiments to that part of his conduct to me, which (oppressed by the terrors and apprehensions to which I was subjected) once I censured; and the readier, as I had so great an honour for his cloth, that I thought, to be a clergyman, and all that was compassionate, good, and virtuous, was the same thing.

But when I came to know Mr. Peters, I had a high opinion of his worthiness, and as no one can be perfect in this life, thus I thought to myself: How hard was then my lot, to be the cause of stumbling to so worthy a heart. To be sure, a gentleman, one who knows, and practises so well, his duty, in every other instance, and preaches it so efficaciously to others, must have been *one day* sensible, that it would not have mis-become his function and character to have afforded that protection to oppressed innocence, which was requested of him: and how would it have grieved his considerate mind, had my ruin been completed, that he did not!

But as he had once a namesake, as one may say, that failed in a much greater instance, let not *my* want of charity exceed *his* fault; but let me look upon it as an infirmity, to which the most perfect are liable; I was a stranger to him; a servant girl carried off by her master, a young gentleman of violent and lawless passions, who, in this very instance, shewed how much in earnest he was set upon effecting all his vile purposes; and whose heart, although *God* might touch, it was not probable any lesser influence could. Then he was not sure, that, though he might assist my escape, I might not afterwards fall again into the hands of so determined a violator: and that difficulty would not, with such an one, enhance his resolution to overcome all obstacles.

Moreover, he might think, that the person, who was moving

him to this worthy measure, possibly sought to gratify a view of his own, and that while endeavouring to save, to outward appearance, a virtue in danger, he was, in reality, only helping another to a wife, at the hazard of exposing himself to the vindictiveness of a violent temper, and a rich neighbour, who had power as well as will to resent; for such was his apprehension, entirely groundless as it was, though not improbable, as it might seem to him.

For all these considerations, I must pity, rather than too rigorously censure, the worthy gentleman, and I will always respect him. And thank him a thousand times, my dear, in my name, for his goodness in condescending to acknowledge, by your hand, his infirmity, as such; for this gives an excellent proof of the natural worthiness of his heart; and that it is beneath him to seek to extenuate a fault, when he thinks he has committed one.

Indeed, my dear friend, I have so much honour for the clergy of all degrees, that I never forget in my prayers one article, that God will make them shining lights to the world; since so much depends on their ministry and examples, as well with respect to our public as private duties. Nor shall the faults of a few make impression upon me to the disadvantage of the order; for I am afraid a very censorious temper, in this respect, is too generally the indication of an uncharitable and perhaps a profligate heart, levelling characters, in order to cover some inward pride, or secret enormities, which they are ashamed to avow, and will not be instructed to amend.

Forgive, my dear, this tedious scribble; I cannot for my life write short letters to those I love. And let me hope that you will favour me with an account of your new affair, and how you proceed in it; and with such of your conversations, as may give me some notion of a polite courtship. For, alas! your poor friend knows nothing of this. All her courtship was sometimes a hasty snatch of the hand, a black and blue gripe of the arm, and—" Whither now? "—" Come to me when I bid you!" And Saucy-face, and Creature, and such like, on his part—with fear and trembling on mine; and——" I will, I will!—Good Sir, have mercy!" At other times a scream, and nobody to hear or mind me; and with uplift hands, bent knees, and tearful eyes—" For God's sake, pity your poor servant."

This, my dear Miss Darnford, was the hard treatment that attended my courtship—pray, then, let me know, how gentlemen court their equals in degree; how they look when they address you, with their knees bent, sighing, supplicating, and *all that*, as Sir Simon says, with the words Slave, Servant, Admirer, continually at their tongue's end.

But after all, it will be found, I believe, that be the language and behaviour ever so obsequious, it is all designed to end alike— The English, the plain English, of the politest address, is,—" I am now, dear Madam, your humble servant : pray be so good as to let me be your master,"—" Yes, and thank you too," says the lady's heart, though not her lips, if she likes him. And so they go to church together ; and, in conclusion, it will be happy, if these obsequious courtships end no worse than my frightful one.

But I am convinced, that with a man of sense, a woman of tolerable prudence *must* be happy.

That whenever you marry, it may be to such a man, who then must value you as you deserve, and make you happy as I now am, notwithstanding all that's past, wishes and prays *your obliged friend and servant,*

P. B.

[N.B.—Although Miss Darnford could not receive the above letter so soon, as to answer it before others were sent to her by her fair correspondent; yet we think it not amiss to dispense with the order of time, that the reader may have the letter and answer at one view, and shall on other occasions take the like liberty.]

LETTER XXVIII

In answer to the preceding

My dear Mrs. B.,

You charm us all with your letters. Mr. Peters says, he will never go to bed, nor rise, but he will pray for you, and desires I will return his thankful acknowledgment for your favourable opinion of him, and kind allowances. If there be an angel on earth, he says, you are one. My papa, although he has seen your stinging reflection upon his refusal to protect you, is delighted with you too ; and says, when you come down to Lincolnshire again, he will be *undertaken* by you in good earnest : for he thinks it was wrong in him to deny you his protection.

We all smiled at the description of your own uncommon courtship. And, as they say the days of courtship are the happiest part of life, if we had not known that your days of marriage are happier by far than any other body's courtship, we must needs have pitied. But as the one were days of trial and temptation, the others are days of reward and happiness: may the last always continue to be so, and you'll have no occasion to think any body happier than Mrs. B. !

I thank you heartily for your good wishes as to the man of sense. Mr. Murray has been here, and continues his visits. He is a lively gentleman, well enough in his person, has a tolerable character, yet loves company, and will take his bottle freely; my papa likes him ne'er the worse for that: he talks a good deal; dresses gay, and even richly, and seems to like his own person very well—no great pleasure this for a lady to look forward to; yet he falls far short of that genteel ease and graceful behaviour, which distinguish your Mr. B. from any body I know.

I wish Mr. Murray would apply to my sister. She is an ill-natured girl; but would make a good wife, I hope; and fancy she'd like him well enough. I can't say I do. He laughs too much; has something boisterous in his conversation: his complaisance is not pretty; he is, however, well versed in country sports; and my papa loves him for that too, and says—" He is a most accomplished gentleman."—" Yes Sir," cry I, " as gentle-men go."—" You *must* be saucy," says Sir Simon, " because the man offers himself to your acceptance. A few years hence, perhaps, if you remain single, you'll alter your note, Polly, and be willing to jump at a much less worthy tender."

I could not help answering that, although I paid due honour to all my papa was pleased to say, I could not but hope he would be mistaken in this. But I have broken my mind to my dear mamma, who tells me, she will do me all the pleasure she can; but would be loth the youngest daughter should go *first*, as she calls it. But if I could come and live with you a little now and then, I did not care who married, unless such an one offered as I never expect.

I have great hopes the gentleman will be easily persuaded to quit me for Nancy; for I see he has not delicacy enough to love with any great distinction. He says, as my mamma tells me by the bye, that I am the handsomest, and best humoured, and he has found out as he thinks, that I have some wit, and have ease and freedom (and he tacks innocence to them) in my address and conversation. 'Tis well for me, *he* is of this opinion: for if he thinks justly, which I must question, *any body* may think so still much more; for I have been far from taking pains to

88

engage his good word, having been under more reserve to him, than ever I was before to any body.

Indeed, I can't help it: for the gentleman is forward without delicacy; and (pardon me, Sir Simon) my papa has not one bit of it neither; but is for pushing matters on, with his rough raillery, that puts me out of countenance, and has already adjusted the sordid part of the preliminaries, as he tells me.

Yet I hope Nancy's three thousand pound fortune more than I am likely to have, will give her the wished-for preference with Mr. Murray; and then, as to a brother-in-law, in prospect, I can put off all restraint, and return to my usual freedom.

This is all that occurs worthy of notice from us: but from you, we expect an account of Lady Davers's visit, and of the conversations that offer among you; and you have so delightful a way of making every thing momentous, either by your subject or reflections, or both, that we long for every post-day, in hopes of the pleasure of a letter. And yours I will always carefully preserve, as so many testimonies of the honour I receive in this correspondence: which will be always esteemed as it deserves, by, my dear Mrs. B., *your obliged and faithful*

POLLY DARNFORD.

Mrs. Peters, Mrs. Jones, my papa, mamma, and sister, present their respects. Mr. Peters I mentioned before. He continues to give a very good account of poor Jewkes; and is much pleased with her.

LETTER XXIX

MY DEAR MISS DARNFORD,

At your desire, and to oblige your honoured mamma, and your good neighbours, I will now acquaint you with the arrival of Lady Davers, and will occasionally write what passes among us, I will not say worthy of notice; for were I only to do so, I should be more brief, perhaps, by much, than you seem to expect. But as my time is pretty much taken up, and I find I shall be obliged to write a bit now, and a bit then, you must excuse me, if I dispense with some forms, which I ought to observe, when I write to one I so dearly love; and so I will give it journal-wise, as it were, and have no regard, when it would fetter or break in upon my freedom of narration, to inscription or subscription; but send it as I have opportunity, and if you please to favour me so far, as to lend it me, after you have read the stuff, for the perusal of my father and mother, to whom my duty, and promise require me to give an account of my proceedings, it will save me transcription, for which I shall have no time; and then you will excuse blots and blurs, and I will trouble myself no farther for apologies on that score, but this once for all.

If you think it worth while when they have read it, you shall have it again.

WEDNESDAY MORNING, SIX O'CLOCK.

For my dear friend permits me to rise an hour sooner than usual, that I may have time to scribble; for he is always pleased to see me so employed, or in reading; often saying, when I am at my needle, (as his sister once wrote) " Your maids can do this, Pamela : but they cannot write as you can." And yet, as he says, when I choose to follow my needle, as a diversion from too intense study, (but, alas ! I know not what study is, as may be easily guessed by my hasty writing, putting down every thing as it comes) I shall then do as I please. But I promised at setting out, what a good wife I'd endeavour to make : and every honest body should try to be as good as her word, you know, and such particulars as I then mentioned, I think I ought to dispense with as little as possible; especially as I promised no more than what was my duty to perform, if I had *not* promised. But what a preamble is here? Judge by it what impertinences you may expect as I proceed.

Yesterday evening arrived here my Lord and Lady Davers, their nephew, and the Countess of C., mother of Lady Betty, whom we did not expect, but took it for the greater favour. It seems her ladyship longed, as she said, to see *me ;* and this was her principal inducement. The two ladies, and their two women, were in Lord Davers's coach and six, and my lord and his nephew rode on horseback, attended with a train of servants.

We had expected them to dinner; but they could not reach time enough; for the countess being a little incommoded with her journey, the coach travelled slowly. My lady would not suffer her lord, nor his nephew, to come hither before her, though on horseback, because she would be present, she said, when his lordship first saw me, he having quite forgot *her mother's Pamela ;* that was her word.

It rained when they came in; so the coach drove directly to the door, and Mr. B. received them there; but I was in a little sort of flutter, which Mr. B. observing, made me sit down in the parlour to compose myself. " Where's Pamela? " said my lady, as soon as she alighted.

I stept out, lest she should take it amiss : and she took my hand, and kissed me : " Here, my lady countess," said she, presenting me to her, " here's the girl : see if I said too much in praise of her person."

The countess saluted me with a visible pleasure in her eye, and said, " Indeed, Lady Davers, you have not. 'Twould have been strange (excuse me, Mrs. B., for I know your story), if such a fine flower had not been transplanted from the field to the garden."

I made no return, but by a low curtsey, to her ladyship's compliment. Then Lady Davers taking my hand again, presented me to her lord : " See here, my lord, my mother's Pamela."—" And see here, my lord," said her generous brother, taking my other hand most kindly, " see here your brother's Pamela too ! "

My lord saluted me : " I do," said he to his lady, and to his brother; " and I see the first person in her, that has exceeded my expectation, when every mouth had *prepared* me to expect a wonder."

Mr. H., whom every one calls Lord Jackey, after his aunt's example, when she is in good humour with him, and who is a very *young* gentleman, though about as old as my best friend, came to me next, and said, " Lovelier and lovelier, by my life ! —I never saw your peer, Madam."

Will you excuse me, my dear, all this seeming vanity, for the sake of repeating exactly what passed ?

" Well, but," said my lady, taking my hand, in her free quality way, which quite dashed me, and holding it at a distance, and turning me half round, her eye fixed to my waist, " let me observe you a little, my sweet-faced girl;—I hope I am right : I hope you will do credit to my brother, as he has done you credit. Why do you let her lace so tight, Mr. B. ? "

I was unable to look up, as you may believe, Miss : my face, all over scarlet, was hid in my bosom, and I looked so *silly !*—

" Ay," said my naughty lady, " you may well look down, my good girl : for works of this nature will not be long hidden. —And, oh ! my lady," (to the countess) " see how like a pretty *thief* she looks ! "

" Dear my lady ! " said I : for she still kept looking at me : and her good brother, seeing my confusion, in pity to me, pressed my blushing face a moment to his generous breast, and said, " Lady Davers, you should not be thus hard upon my dear girl, the moment you see her, and before so many witnesses :—but

91

look up, my best love, take your revenge of my sister, and tell her, you wish her in the same way."

"It is so then?" said my lady. "I'm glad of it with all my heart. I will now love you better and better: but I almost doubted it, seeing her still so slender. But if, my good child, you lace too tight, I'll never forgive you." And so she gave me a kiss of congratulation, as she said.

Do you think I did not look very silly? My lord, smiling, and gazing at me from head to foot; Lord Jackey grinning and laughing, like an oaf, as I then, in my spite, thought. Indeed the countess said, encouragingly to me, but severely in persons of birth, "Lady Davers, you are as much too teazing, as Mrs. B. is too bashful. But you are a happy man, Mr. B., that your lady's bashfulness is the principal mark by which we can judge she is not of quality." Lord Jackey, in the language of some character in a play, cried out, "*A palpable hit, by Jupiter!*" and laughed egregiously, running about from one to another, repeating the same words.

We talked only upon common topics till supper-time, and I was all ear, as I thought it became me to be; for the countess had, by her first compliment, and by an aspect as noble as intelligent, overawed me, as I may say, into a respectful silence, to which Lady Davers's free, though pleasant raillery (which she could not help carrying on now-and-then) contributed. Besides, Lady Davers's letters had given me still greater reason to revere her wit and judgment than I had before, when I reflected on her passionate temper, and such parts of the conversation I had had with her ladyship in your neighbourhood; which (however to be admired) fell short of her letters.

When we were to sit down at table, I looked, I suppose, a little diffidently: for I really then thought of my lady's anger at the Hall, when she would not have permitted me to sit at table with her; and Mr. B. saying, "Take your place, my dear; you keep our friends standing;" I sat down in my usual seat. And my lady said, "None of your reproaching eye, Pamela; I know what you hint at by it; and every letter I have received from you has made me censure myself for my *lady-airs*, as you call 'em, you sauce-box you: I told you, I'd *lady-airs* you when I saw you; and you shall have it all in good time."

"I am sure," said I, "I shall have nothing from your ladyship, but what will be very agreeable: but, indeed, I never meant any thing particular by that, or any other word that I wrote; nor could I think of any thing but what was highly respectful to your ladyship."

Lord Davers was pleased to say, that it was impossible I should either write or speak any thing that could be taken amiss.

Lady Davers, after supper, and the servants were withdrawn, began a discourse on titles, and said, " Brother, I think you should hold yourself obliged to my Lord Davers; for he has spoken to Lord S. who made him a visit a few days ago, to procure you a baronet's patent. Your estate, and the figure you make in the world, are so considerable, and your family besides is so ancient, that, methinks, you should wish for some distinction of that sort."

" Yes, brother," said my lord, " I did mention it to Lord S. and told him, withal, that it was without your knowledge or desire that I spoke about it; and I was not very sure you would accept of it; but 'tis a thing your sister has wished for a good while."

" What answer did my Lord S. make to it? " said Mr. B.

" He said, ' We,' meaning the ministers, I suppose, ' should be glad to oblige a man of Mr. B.'s figure in the world; but you mention it so slightly, that you can hardly expect courtiers will tender it to any gentleman that is so indifferent about it; for, Lord Davers, we seldom grant honours without a view : I tell you that,' added he, smiling."

" My Lord S. might mention this as a jest," returned Mr. B., " but he spoke the truth. But your lordship said well, that I was indifferent about it. 'Tis true, 'tis an hereditary title; but the rich citizens, who used to be satisfied with the title of Knight, (till they made it so common, that it is brought into as great contempt almost as that of the French knights of St. Michael,[1] and nobody cares to accept of it) now are ambitious of this; and, as I apprehend, it is hastening apace into like disrepute. Besides, 'tis a novel honour, and what the ancestors of our family, who lived at its institution, would never accept of. But were it a peerage, which has some essential privileges and splendours annexed to it, to make it desirable to some men, I would not enter into conditions for it. Titles at best," added he, " are but shadows; and he that has the substance should be above valuing them; for who that has the whole bird, would pride himself upon a single feather? "

" But," said my lady, " although I acknowledge that the institution is of late date, yet, as abroad, as well as at home,

---

[1] This order was become so scandalously common in France, that, in order to suppress it, the hangman was vested with the ensigns of it, which effectually abolished it.

it is regarded as a title of dignity, and the best families among the gentry are supposed to be distinguished by it, I should wish you to accept of it. And as to citizens who have it, they are not many; and some of this class of people, or their immediate descendants, have bought themselves into the peerage itself of the one kingdom or the other."

"As to what it is looked upon abroad," said Mr. B., "this is of no weight at all; for when an Englishman travels, be he of what degree he will, if he has an equipage, and squanders his money away, he is a lord of course with foreigners: and therefore Sir Such-a-one is rather a diminution to him, as it gives him a lower title than his vanity would perhaps make him aspire to be thought in the possession of. Then, as to citizens, in a trading nation like this, I am not displeased in the main, with seeing the overgrown ones creeping into nominal honours; and we have so many of our first titled families, who have allied themselves to trade, (whose inducements were money only) that it ceases to be either a wonder as to the fact, or a disgrace as to the honour."

"Well, brother," said my lady, "I will tell you farther, the thing may be had for asking for; if you will but go to court, and desire to kiss the king's hand, that will be all the trouble you'll have: and pray now oblige me in it."

"If a title would make me either a better or a wiser man," replied Mr. B., "I would embrace it with pleasure. Besides, I am not so satisfied with some of the measures now pursuing, as to owe any obligation to the ministers. Accepting of a small title from them, is but like putting on their badge, or listing under their banners; like a certain lord we all know, who accepted of one degree more of title to shew he was theirs, and would not have an higher, lest it should be thought a satisfaction tantamount to half the pension he demanded: and could I be easy to have it supposed, that I was an ungrateful man for voting as I pleased, because they gave me the title of a baronet?"

The countess said, the world always thought Mr. B. to be a man of steady principles, and not attached to any party; but, in her opinion, it was far from being inconsistent with any gentleman's honour and independency, to accept of a title from a prince he acknowledged as his sovereign.

"'Tis very true, Madam, that I am attached to no party, nor ever will. I will be a *country gentleman*, in the true sense of the word, and will accept of no favour that shall make any one think I would *not* be of the opposition when I think it a necessary one; as, on the other hand, I should scorn to make myself a round to any man's ladder of preferment, or a caballer for the sake of my own."

"You say well, brother," returned Lady Davers; "but you may undoubtedly keep your own principles and independency, and yet pay your duty to the king, and accept of this title; for your family and fortune will be a greater ornament to the title, than the title to you."

"Then what occasion have I for it, if that be the case, Madam?"

"Why, I can't say, but I should be glad you had it, for your family's sake, as it is an heriditary honour. Then it would mend the style of your spouse here; for the good girl is at such a loss for an epithet when she writes, that I see the constraint she lies under. It is, '*My dear gentleman, my best friend, my benefactor, my dear Mr. B.*' whereas Sir William would turn off her periods more roundly, and no other softer epithets would be wanting."

"To me," replied he, "who always desire to be distinguished as my Pamela's best friend, and think it an honour to be called *her dear Mr. B. and her dear man*, this reason weighs very little, unless there were no other Sir William in the kingdom than *her* Sir William: for I am very emulous of her favour, I can tell you, and think it no small distinction."

I blushed at this too great honour, before such company, and was afraid my lady would be a little picqued at it. But after a pause, she said, "Well, then, brother, will you let Pamela decide upon this point?"

"Rightly put," said the countess. "Pray let Mrs. B. choose for you, Sir. My lady has hit the thing."

"Very good, by my soul," says Lord Jackey; let my *young aunt*," that was his word, "choose for you, Sir."

"Well, then, Pamela," said Mr. B., "give us your opinion, as to this point."

"But, first," said Lady Davers, "say you will be determined by it; or else she will be laid under a difficulty."

"Well, then," replied he, "be it so—I will be determined by your opinion, my dear; give it me freely."

Lord Jackey rubbed his hands together, "Charming, charming, as I hope to live! By Jove, this is just as I wished!"

"Well, now, Pamela," said my lady, "speak your true heart without disguise: I charge you do."

"Why then, gentlemen and ladies," said I, "if I must be so bold as to speak on a subject, upon which on several accounts, it would become me to be silent, I should be *against* the title;

95

but perhaps my reason is of too private a nature to weigh any thing: and if so, it would not become me to have any choice at all."

They all called upon me for my reason; and I said, looking down a little abashed, "It is this: Here my dear Mr. B. has disparaged himself by distinguishing, as he has done, such a low creature as I; and the world will be apt to say, he is seeking to repair *one way* the honour he has lost *another!* and then, perhaps, it will be attributed to my pride and ambition: 'Here,' they will perhaps say, 'the proud cottager will needs be a lady, in hopes to conceal her descent;' whereas, had I such a vain thought, it would be but making it the more remembered against both Mr. B. and myself. And indeed, as to my own part, I take too much pride in having been lifted up into this distinction, for the causes to which I owe it, your brother's *bounty* and *generosity*, than to be ashamed of what I *was:* only now-and-then I am concerned for his own sake, lest he should be too much censured. But this would not be prevented, but rather be promoted by the title. So I am humbly of opinion against the title."

Mr. B. had hardly patience to hear me out, but came to me, and folding his arms about me, said, "Just as I wished, have you answered, my beloved Pamela: I was never yet deceived in you; no, not once."

"Madam," said he to the countess, "Lord Davers, Lady Davers, do we want any titles, think you, to make us happy, but what we can confer upon ourselves?" And he pressed my hand to his lips, as he always honours me most in company; and went to his place highly pleased; while his fine manner drew tears from my eyes, and made his noble sister's and the countess's glisten too.

"Well, for my part," said Lady Davers, "thou art a strange girl: where, as my brother once said, gottest thou all this?" Then pleasantly humorous, as if she was angry, she changed her tone, "What signify thy *meek* words and *humble* speeches, when by thy *actions*, as well as *sentiments*, thou reflectest upon us all? Pamela," said she, "have less merit, or take care to conceal it better: I shall otherwise have no more patience with thee, than thy monarch has just now shewn."

The countess was pleased to say, "You're a happy couple indeed!"

Such sort of entertainment as this you are to expect from your correspondent. I cannot do better than I can; and it may appear such a mixture of self-praise, vanity, and impertinence, that I expect you will tell me freely, as soon as this comes to your hand, whether it be tolerable to you. Yet I must write on, for my dear father and mother's sake, who require it of me, and are prepared to approve of every thing that comes from me, for no other reason but that : and I think you ought to leave me to write to them only, as I cannot hope it will be entertaining to any body else, without expecting as much partiality and favour from others, as I have from my dear parents. Mean time I conclude here my first conversation-piece; and am, and will be, *always yours, &c.*   P. B.

LETTER XXX

THURSDAY MORNING, SIX O'CLOCK.

Our breakfast conversation yesterday (at which only Mrs. Worden, my lady's woman, and my Polly attended) was so whimsically particular, (though I doubt some of it, at least, will appear too trifling) that I must acquaint my dear Miss Darnford with it, who is desirous of knowing all that relates to Lady Davers's conduct towards me.

You must know, then, I have the honour to stand very high in the graces of Lord Davers, who on every occasion is pleased to call me his *good Sister*, his *dear Sister*, and sometimes his *charming Sister*, and he says, he will not be out of my company for an hour together, while he stays here, if he can help it.

My lady seems to relish this very well in the main, though she cannot quite so readily, yet, frame her mouth to the sound of the word *Sister*, as my lord does; of which this that follows is one instance.

His lordship had called me by that tender name twice before, and saying, " I will drink another dish, I think, my *good Sister*." My lady said, " Your lordship has got a word by the end, that you seem mighty fond of : I have taken notice, that you have called Pamela *Sister*, *Sister*, *Sister*, no less than three times in a quarter of an hour."

My lord looked a little serious : " I shall one day," said he, " be allowed to choose my own words and phrases, I hope— Your sister, Mr. B.," added he, " often questions whether I am at age or not, though the House of Peers made no scruple of admittting me among them some years ago."

Mr. B. said severely, but with a smiling air, " 'Tis well she has such a gentleman as your lordship for a husband, whose affectionate indulgence to her makes you overlook all her saucy sallies! I am sure, when you took her out of our family into your own, we all thought ourselves, I in particular, bound to pray for you."

I thought this a great trial of my lady's patience: but it was from Mr. B. And she said, with a half-pleasant, half-serious air, "How now, Confidence!—None but my brother could have said this, whose violent spirit was always much more intolerable than mine: but I can tell you, Mr. B., I was always thought very good-humoured and obliging to every body, till your impudence came from college, and from your travels; and then, I own, your provoking ways made me now-and-then a little out of the way."

"Well, well, sister, we'll have no more of this subject; only let us see that my Lord Davers wants not his proper authority with you, although you used to keep *me* in awe formerly."

"Keep *you* in awe!—That nobody could ever do yet, boy or man. But, my lord, I beg your pardon; for this brother will make mischief betwixt us if he can—I only took notice of the word *Sister* so often used, which looked more like affectation than affection."

"Perhaps, Lady Davers," said my lord, gravely, "I have two reasons for using the word so frequently."

"I'd be glad to hear them," said the dear taunting lady; "for I don't doubt they're mighty good ones. What are they, my lord?"

"One is, because I love, and am fond of my new relation: the other, that you are so sparing of the word, that I call her so for us both."

"Your lordship says well," replied Mr. B., smiling: "and Lady Davers can give two reasons why she does *not*."

"Well," said my lady, "now we are in for't, let us hear *your* two reasons likewise; I doubt not they're wise ones too."

"If they are *yours*, Lady Davers, they must be so. One is, That every condescension (to speak in a proud lady's dialect) comes with as much difficulty from her, as a favour from the House of Austria to the petty princes of Germany. The second, Because those of your sex—(Excuse me, Madam," to the countess) "who have once made scruples, think it inconsistent with themselves to be over hasty to alter their own conduct, choosing rather to persist in an error, than own it to be one."

This proceeded from his impatience to see me in the least slighted by my lady; and I said to Lord Davers, to soften matters, "Never, my lord, were brother and sister so loving in earnest, and yet so satirical upon each other in jest, as my good lady and Mr. B. But your lordship knows their way."

My lady frowned at her brother, but turned it off with an air: "I love the mistress of this house," said she, "very well; and am quite reconciled to her: but methinks there is such a hissing sound in the word *Sister*, that I cannot abide it. 'Tis a true English word, but a word I have not been used to, having never had a sis-s-s-ter before, as you know."—Speaking the first syllable of the word with an emphatical hiss.

Mr. B. said, "Observe you not, Lady Davers, that you used a word (to avoid that) which had twice the hissing in it that *sister* has? And that was mis-s-s-tress, with two other hissing words to accompany it, of this-s-s hous-s-e: but to what childish follies does not pride make one stoop!—Excuse, Madam" (to the countess), "such poor low conversation as we are dwindled into."

"O Sir," said her ladyship, "the conversation is very agreeable;—and I think, Lady Davers, you're fairly caught."

"Well," said my lady, "then help me, good *sister*—there's for you!—to a little sugar. Will that please you, Sir?"

"I am always pleased," replied her brother, smiling, "when Lady Davers acts up to her own character, and the good sense she is mistress of."

"Ay, ay, my good brother, like other wise men, takes it for granted that it is a mark of good sense to approve of whatever *he* does.—And so, for this one time, I am a very sensible body with him—And I'll leave off, while I have his good word. Only one thing I must say to you, my dear," turning to me, "that though I call you Pamela, as I please, be assured, I love you as well as if I called you *sister*, as Lord Davers does, at every word."

"Your ladyship gives me great pleasure," said I, "in this kind assurance; and I don't doubt but I shall have the honour of being called by that tender name, if I can be so happy as to deserve it; and I'll lose no opportunity that shall be afforded me, to show how sincerely I will endeavour to do so."

She was pleased to rise from her seat: "Give me a kiss, my dear girl; you deserve every thing: and permit me to say Pamela sometimes, as the word occurs: for I am not used to speak in print; and I will call you *sister* when I think of it, and love you as well as ever sister loved another."

"These proud and passionate folks," said Mr. B., "how

99

good they can be, when they reflect a little on what becomes their characters!"

"So, then," rejoined my lady, "I am to have no merit of my own, I see, do what I will. This is not quite so generous in my brother, as one might expect."

"Why, you saucy sister—excuse me, Lord Davers—what merit *would* you assume? Can people merit by doing their duty? And is it so great a praise, that you think fit to own for a sister so deserving a girl as this, whom I take pride in calling my wife?"

"Thou art what thou always wert," returned my lady; "and were I in this my imputed pride to want an excuse, I know not the creature living, that ought so soon to make one for me, as you."

"I *do* excuse you," said he, "for *that* very reason, if you please: but it little becomes either your pride, or mine, to do any thing that wants excuse."

"Mighty moral! mighty grave, truly!—Pamela, friend, sister,—there's for you!—thou art a happy girl to have made such a reformation in thy honest man's way of *thinking* as well as *acting*. But now we are upon this topic, and only friends about us, I am resolved to be even with thee, brother— Jackey, if you are not for another dish, I wish you'd withdraw. Polly Barlow, we don't want you. Beck, you may stay." Mr. H. obeyed; and Polly went out; for you must know, Miss, that my Lady Davers will have none of the men-fellows, as she calls them, to attend upon us at tea. And I cannot say but I think her entirely in the right, for several reasons that might be given.

When they were withdrawn, my lady repeated, "Now we are upon this topic of reclaiming and reformation, tell me, thou bold wretch; for you know I have seen all your rogueries in Pamela's papers; tell me, if ever rake but thyself made such an attempt as thou didst, on this dear good girl, in presence of a virtuous woman, as Mrs. Jervis was always noted to be? As to the other vile creature, Jewkes, 'tis less wonder, although in *that* thou hadst the impudence of *him* who set thee to work: but to make thy attempt before Mrs. Jervis, and in spite of *her* struggles and reproaches, was the very stretch of shameless wickedness."

Mr. B. seemed a little disconcerted, and said, "Surely, Lady Davers, this is going too far! Look at Pamela's blushing face, and downcast eye, and wonder at yourself for this question, as much as you do at me for the action you speak of."

The countess said to me, "My dear Mrs. B., I wonder not

at this sweet confusion on so affecting a question !—but, indeed, since it is come in so naturally, I must say, Mr. B., that we have all, and my daughters too, wondered at this, more than at any part of your attempts; because, Sir, we thought you one of the most civilized men in England, and that you could not but wish to have saved appearances at least."

"Though this is to you, my Pamela, the renewal of griefs; yet hold up your dear face. You may—The triumph was yours —the shame and the blushes ought to be mine—And I will humour my saucy sister in all she would have me say."

"Nay," said Lady Davers, "you know the question; I cannot put it stronger."

"That's very true," replied he : "But would you expect I should give you a *reason* for an attempt that appears to you so very shocking?"

"Nay, Sir," said the countess, "don't say *appears* to Lady Davers; for (excuse me) it will appear so to every one who hears of it."

"I think my brother is too hardly used," said Lord Davers; "he has made all the amends he could make :—and *you*, my sister, who were the person offended, forgive him now, I hope; don't you?"

I could not answer; for I was quite confounded; and made a motion to withdraw : but Mr. B. said, "Don't go, my dear : though I ought to be ashamed of an action set before me in so full a glare, in presence of Lord Davers and the countess; yet I will not have you stir because I forget how you represented it, and you must tell me."

"Indeed, Sir, I cannot," said I : "pray, my dear ladies— pray, my good lord—and, dear Sir, don't thus *renew my griefs*, as you were pleased justly to phrase it."

"I have the representation of that scene in my pocket," said my lady; "for I was resolved, as I told Lady Betty, to shame the wicked wretch with it the first opportunity; and I'll read it to you; or rather, you shall read it yourself, Bold-face, if you can."

So she pulled those leaves out of her pocket, wrapped up carefully in a paper. "Here,—I believe he who could act thus, must read it; and, to spare Pamela's confusion, read it to yourself; for we all know how it was."

"I think," said he, taking the papers, "I can say something to abate the heinousness of this heavy charge, or else I should not stand thus at the insolent bar of my sister, answering her interrogatories."

I send you, my dear Miss Darnford, a transcript of the charge. To be sure, you'll say, he was a very wicked man.

Mr. B. read it to himself, and said, " This is a dark affair, as here stated; and I can't say, but Pamela, and Mrs. Jervis too, had great reason to apprehend the worst: but surely readers of it, who were less parties in the supposed attempt, and not determined at all events to condemn me, might have made a more favourable construction for me, than you, Lady Davers, have done in the strong light in which you have set this heinous matter before us.

" However, since my lady," bowing to the countess, " and Lord Davers seem to expect me particularly to answer this black charge, I will, at a proper time, if agreeable, give you a brief history of my passion for this dear girl; how it commenced and increased, and my .own struggles with it, and this will introduce, with some little advantage to myself perhaps, what I have to say, as to this supposed attempt: and at the same time enable you the better to account for some facts which you have read in my pretty accuser's papers."

This pleased every one, and they begged him to begin *then;* but he said, it was time we should think of dressing, the morning being far advanced; and if no company came in, he would, in the afternoon, give them the particulars they desired to hear.

The three gentlemen rode out, and returned to dress before dinner: my lady and the countess also took an airing in the chariot. Just as they returned, compliments came from several of the neighbouring ladies to our noble guests, on their arrival in these parts; and to as many as sent, Lady Davers desired their companies for to-morrow afternoon, to tea; but Mr. B. having fallen in with some of the gentlemen likewise, he told me, we should have most of our visiting neighbours at dinner, and desired Mrs. Jervis might prepare accordingly for them.

After dinner Mr. H. took a ride out, attended by Mr. Colbrand, of whom he is very fond, ever since he frightened Lady Davers's footmen at the Hall, threatening to chine them, if they offered to stop his lady: for, he says, he loves a man of courage: very probably knowing his own defects that way, for my lady often calls him a chicken-hearted fellow. And then Lord and Lady Davers, and the countess, revived the subject of the morning; and Mr. B. was pleased to begin in the manner I shall mention by-and-bye. For here I am obliged to break off.

Now, my dear Miss Darnford, I will proceed.

" I began," said Mr. B., " very early to take notice of this lovely girl, even when she was hardly thirteen years old; for her charms increased every day, not only in my eye, but in the eyes of all who beheld her. My mother, as *you* (Lady Davers) know, took the greatest delight in her, always calling her, her Pamela, her good child : and her waiting-maid and her cabinet of rarities were her boasts, and equally shewn to every visitor : for besides the beauty of her figure, and the genteel air of her person, the dear girl had a surprising memory, a solidity of judgment above her years, and a docility so unequalled, that she took all parts of learning which her lady, as fond of instructing her as she of improving by instruction, crowded upon her; insomuch that she had masters to teach her to dance, sing, and play on the spinnet, whom she every day surprised by the readiness wherewith she took every thing.

" I remember once, my mother praising her girl before me, and my aunt B. (who is since dead), I could not but notice her fondness for her, and said, 'What do you design, Madam, to do *with* or *for*, this Pamela of yours? The accomplishments you give her will do her more hurt than good; for they will set her so much above her degree, that what you intend as a kindness, may prove her ruin.'

" My aunt joined with me, and spoke in a still stronger manner against giving her such an education : and added, as I well remember, 'Surely, sister, you do wrong. One would think, if one knew not my nephew's discreet pride, that you design her for something more than your own waiting-maid.'

" ' Ah ! sister,' said the old lady, ' there is no fear of what you hint at; his family pride, and stately temper, will secure my son : he has too much of his father in him. And as for Pamela, you know not the girl. She has always in her thoughts, and in her mouth, too, her parents' mean condition, and I shall do nothing for *them*, at least at present, though they are honest folks, and deserve well, because I will keep the girl humble.'

" ' But what can I do with the little baggage?' continued my mother; ' she conquers every thing so fast, and has such a thirst after knowledge, and the more she knows, I verily think, the humbler she is, that I cannot help letting go, as my son, when a little boy, used to do to his kite, as fast as she pulls; and to what height she'll soar, I can't tell.

" ' I intended,' proceeded the good lady, ' at first, only to make her mistress of some fine needle-work, to qualify her (as she has a delicacy in her person, that makes it a pity ever to put her to hard work) for a genteel place; but she masters that so fast, that now as my daughter is married and gone from me, I am desirous to qualify her to divert and entertain me in my thoughtful hours: and were *you*, sister, to know what she is capable of, and how diverting her innocent prattle is to me, and her natural simplicity, which I encourage her to preserve amidst all she learns, you would not, nor my son neither, wonder at the pleasure I take in her. Shall I call her in?'

"'I don't want,' said I, 'to have the girl called in: if you, Madam, are diverted with her, that's enough. To be sure, Pamela is a better companion for a lady, than a monkey or a harlequin: but I fear you'll set her above herself, and make her vain and pert; and that, at last, in order to support her pride, she may fall into temptations which may be fatal to herself, and others too.'

"'I'm glad to hear this from my *son*,' replied the good lady. 'But the moment I see my favour puffs her up, I shall take other measures.'

"'Well,' thought I to myself, 'I only want to conceal my views from your penetrating eye, my good mother; and I shall one day take as much delight in your girl, and her accomplishments, as you now do: so go on, and improve her as fast as you will. I'll only now and then talk against her, to blind you: and doubt not that all you do will qualify her the better for my purpose. Only,' thought I, 'fly swiftly on, two or three more tardy years, and I'll nip this bud by the time it begins to open, and place it in my bosom for a year or two at least: for so long, if the girl behaves worthy of her education, I doubt not, she'll be new to me.—Excuse me, ladies;—excuse me, Lord Davers;—if I am not ingenuous, I had better be silent.''

I will not interrupt this affecting narration, by mentioning my own alternate blushes, confusions, and exclamations, as the naughty man went on; nor the censures, and many *Out upon you's* of the attentive ladies, and *Fie, brother's*, of Lord Davers; nor yet with apologies for the praises on myself, so frequently intermingled—contenting myself to give you, as near as I can recollect, the very sentences of the dear relator. And as to our occasional exclaimings and observations, you may suppose what they were.

"So," continued Mr. B., "I went on dropping hints against her now and then; and whenever I met her in the passages about the house, or in the garden, avoiding to look at, or to speak to her, as she passed me, curtseying, and putting on a thousand bewitching airs of obligingness and reverence; while I (who thought the best way to demolish the influence of such an education, would be not to alarm her fears on one hand, or to familiarize myself to her on the other, till I came to strike the blow) looked haughty and reserved, and passed by her with a stiff nod at most. Or, if I spoke, ' How does your lady this morning, girl?—I hope she rested well last night : ' then, covered with blushes, and curtseying at every word, as if she thought herself unworthy of answering my questions, she'd trip away in a kind of confusion, as soon as she had spoken. And once I heard her say to Mrs. Jervis, ' Dear Sirs, my young master spoke to me, and called me by my name, saying—How slept your lady last night, Pamela?—Was not that very good, Mrs. Jervis?'—' Ay,' thought I, ' I am in the right way, I find : this will do in proper time. Go on, my dear mother, improving as fast as you will : I'll engage to pull down in three hours, what you'll be building up in as many years, in spite of all the lessons you can teach her.'

" 'Tis enough for me, that I am establishing in you, ladies, and in you, my lord, a higher esteem for my Pamela (I am but too sensible I shall lose a good deal of my own reputation) in the relation I am now giving you.

" I dressed, grew more confident, and as insolent withal, as if, though I had not Lady Davers's wit and virtue, I had all her spirit—(excuse me, Lady Davers;) and having a pretty bold heart, which rather put me upon courting than avoiding a danger or difficulty, I had but too much my way with every body; and many a menaced complaint have I *looked down*, with a haughty air, and a promptitude, like that of Colbrand's to your footmen at the Hall, to clap my hand to my side; which was of the greater service to my bold enterprise, as two or three gentlemen had found I knew how to be in earnest."

" Ha ! " said my lady, " thou wast ever an impudent fellow : and many a vile roguery have I kept from my poor mother.— Yet, to my knowledge, she thought you no saint."

" Ay, poor lady," continued he, " she used now-and-then to catechize me; and was *sure* I was not so good as I ought to be :—' For, son,' she would cry ' these late hours, these all night works, and to come home so *sober* cannot be right.—I'm not sure, if I were to know all, (and yet I'm afraid of inquiring after your ways) whether I should not have reason to wish you were brought home in wine, rather than to come in so sober, and so late, as you do.'

" Once, I remember, in the summer-time, I came home about six in the morning, and met the good lady unexpectedly by the garden back-door, of which I had a key to let myself in at all hours. I started, and would have avoided her : but she called me to her, and then I approached her with an air, ' What brings

you, Madam, into the garden at so early an hour?' turning my
face from her; for I had a few scratches on my forehead—with
a thorn, or so—which I feared she would be more inquisitive
about than I cared she should.

"'And what makes you,' said she, 'so early here, Billy?—
What a rakish figure dost thou make!—One time or other these
courses will yield you but little comfort, on reflection: would
to God thou wast but happily married!'

"'So, Madam, the old wish!—I'm not so bad as you think
me:—I hope I have not merited so great a punishment.'

"These hints I give, not as matter of glory, but shame: yet
I ought to tell you all the truth, or nothing. 'Meantime,'thought
I, (for I used to have some compunction for my vile practices,
when cool reflection, brought on by satiety, had taken hold
of me) 'I wish this sweet girl was grown to years of susceptibility, that I might reform this wicked course of life, and not
prowl about, disturbing honest folks' peace, and endangering
myself.' And as I had, by a certain very daring and wicked
attempt, in which, however, I did not succeed, set a hornet's
nest about my ears, which I began to apprehend would sting
me to death, having once escaped an ambush by dint of mere
good luck; I thought it better to remove the seat of my warfare
into another kingdom, and to be a little more discreet for the
future in my amours. So I went to France a second time, and
passed a year there in the best of company, and with some
improvement both to my morals and understanding; and had
a very few sallies, considering my love of intrigue, and the
ample means I had to prosecute successfully all the desires of
my heart.

"When I returned, several matches were proposed to me,
and my good mother often requested me to make her so happy,
as she called it, as to see me married before she died; but I
could not endure the thoughts of the state: for I never saw a
lady whose temper and education I liked, or with whom I
thought I could live tolerably. She used in vain therefore to
plead family reasons to me:—like most young fellows, I was too
much a self-lover, to pay so great a regard to posterity; and, to
say truth, had little solicitude at that time, whether my name
were continued or not, in my own descendants. However, I
looked upon my mother's Pamela with no small pleasure, and
I found her so much improved, as well in person as behaviour,
that I had the less inducement either to renew my intriguing
life, or to think of a married state.

"Yet, as my mother had all her eyes about her, as the phrase is, I affected great shyness, both before her, and to the girl; for I doubted not, my very looks would be watched by them both; and what the one discovered would not be a secret to the other; and laying myself open too early to a suspicion, I thought, would but ice the girl over, and make her lady more watchful.

"So I used to go into my mother's apartment, and come out of it, without taking the least notice of her, but put on stiff airs; and as she always withdrew when I came in, I never made any pretence to keep her there.

"Once, indeed, my mother, on my looking after her, when her back was turned, said, 'My dear son, I don't like your eye following my girl so intently.—Only I know that sparkling lustre natural to it, or I should have some fear for my Pamela, as she grows older.'

"'I look after her, Madam !—My eyes sparkle at such a girl as that ! No indeed ! She may be your favourite as a waiting-maid; but I see nothing but clumsy curtseys and awkward airs about her. A little rustic affectation of innocence, that to such as cannot see into her, may pass well enough.'

"'Nay, my dear,' replied my mother, 'don't say that, of all things. She has no affectation, I am sure.'

"'Yes, she has, in my eye, Madam, and I'll tell you how it is; you have taught her to assume the airs of a gentlewoman, to dance, and to enter a room with a grace; and yet bid her keep her low birth and family in view : and between the one character, which she wants to get into, and the other she dares not get out of, she trips up and down mincingly, and knows not how to set her feet : so 'tis the same in every gesture : her arms she knows not whether to swim with, or to hold before her, nor whether to hold her head up or down; and so does neither, but hangs it on one side : a little awkward piece of one-and-t'other I think her. And, indeed, you'd do the girl more kindness to put her into your dairy, than to keep her about your person; for she'll be utterly spoiled, I doubt, for any useful purpose.'

"'Ah, son !' said she, 'I fear, by your description, you have minded her too much in one sense, though not enough in another. 'Tis not my intention to recommend her to your notice, of all men; and I doubt not, if it please God I live, and she continues a good girl, but she will make a man of some middling, genteel business, very happy.'

"Pamela came in just then, with an air so natural, so humble, and yet so much above herself, that I was forced to turn my head from her, lest my mother should watch my eye again, and I be inclined to do her that justice, which my heart assented to, but which my lips had just before denied her.

"All my difficulty, in apprehension, was my good mother; the effect of whose lessons to her girl, I was not so much afraid of as her vigilance. 'For,' thought I, 'I see by the delicacy of her person, the brilliancy of her eye, and the sweet apprehensiveness that plays about every feature of her face, she must have tinder enough in her constitution, to catch a well-struck spark; and I'll warrant I shall know how to set her in a blaze, in a few months more.'

"Yet I wanted, as I passed, to catch her attention too : I expected her to turn after me, and look so as to shew a liking towards me; for I had a great opinion of my person and air, which had been fortunately distinguished by the ladies, whom, of course, my vanity made me allow to be very good judges of these outward advantages.

"But to my great disappointment, Pamela never, by any favourable glance, gave the least encouragement to my vanity. 'Well,' thought I, 'this girl has certainly nothing ethereal in her mould : all unanimated clay !—But the dancing and singing airs my mother is teaching her, will better qualify her in time, and another year will ripen her into my arms, no doubt of it. Let me only go on thus, and make her *fear* me : that will enhance in her mind every favour I shall afterwards vouchsafe to shew her : and never question old *humdrum* Virtue,' thought I, ' but the tempter *without*, and the tempter *within*, will be too many for the perversest nicety that ever the sex boasted.'

"Yet, though I could not once attract her eye towards me, she never failed to draw mine after her, whenever she went by me, or wherever I saw her, except, as I said, in my mother's presence; and particularly when she had passed me, and could not see me look at her, without turning her head, as I expected so often from her in vain.

"You will wonder, Lord Davers, who, I suppose, was once in love, or you'd never have married such an hostile spirit as my sister's there—"

"Go on, sauce-box," said she, "I won't interrupt you."

"You will wonder how I could behave so coolly as to escape all discovery so long from a lady so watchful as my mother, and from the apprehensiveness of the girl.

"But, to say nothing of her tender years, and that my love was not of this bashful sort, I was not absolutely determined, so great was my pride, that I ought to think her worthy of being my *mistress*, when I had not much reason, as I thought,

108

to despair of prevailing upon persons of higher birth (were I disposed to try) to live with me upon my own terms. My pride, therefore, kept my passion at bay, as I may say: so far was I from imagining I should ever be brought to what has since happened! But to proceed:

"Hitherto my mind was taken up with the beauties of her person only. My EYE had drawn my HEART after it, without giving myself any trouble about that sense and judgment which my mother was always praising in her Pamela, as exceeding her years and opportunities: but an occasion happened, which, though slight in itself, took the HEAD into the party, and I thought of her, young as she was, with a distinction, that before I had not for her. It was this:

"Being with my mother in her closet, who was talking to me on the old subject, *matrimony*, I saw Pamela's commonplace book, as I may call it; in which, by her lady's direction, from time to time, she had transcribed from the Bible, and other good books, such passages as most impressed her as she read— A method, I take it, my dear" (*turning to me*), "of great service to you, as it initiated you into writing with that freedom and ease, which shine in your saucy letters and journals; and to which my present fetters are not a little owing: just as pedlars catch monkeys in the baboon kingdoms, provoking the attentive fools, by their own example, to put on shoes and stockings, till the apes of imitation, trying to do the like, entangle their feet, and so cannot escape upon the boughs of the tree of liberty, on which before they were wont to hop and skip about, and play a thousand puggish tricks.

"I observed the girl wrote a pretty hand, and very swift and free; and affixed her points or stops with so much judgment (her years considered), that I began to have an high opinion of her understanding. Some observations likewise upon several of the passages were so just and solid, that I could not help being tacitly surprised at them.

"My mother watched my eye, and was silent: I seemed not to observe that she did; and after a while, laid down the book, shutting it with great indifference, and talking of another subject.

"Upon this, my mother said, 'Don't you think Pamela writes a pretty hand, son?'

"'I did not mind it much,' said I, with a careless air. 'This is her writing, is it?' taking the book, and opening it again, at a place of Scripture. 'The girl is mighty pious!' said I.

"'I wish *you* were so, child.'

" ' I wish so too, Madam, if it would please *you*.'

" ' I wish so, for your *own* sake, child.'

" ' So do I, Madam;' and down I laid the book again very carelessly.

" ' Look once more in it,' said she, ' and see if you can't open it upon some place that may strike you.'

" I opened it at—' *Train up a child in the way it should go*,' &c. ' I fancy,' said I, ' when I was of Pamela's age, I was pretty near as good as she.'

" ' Never, never,' said my mother; ' I am sure I took great pains with you; but, alas ! to very little purpose. You had always a violent headstrong will.'

" ' Some allowances for boys and girls, I hope, Madam; but you see I am as good for a man as my sister for a woman.'

" ' No indeed, you are not, I do assure you.'

" ' I am sorry for that, Madam : you give me a sad opinion of myself.' "

" Brazen wretch !" said my lady; " but go on."

" ' Turn to one of the girl's observations on some text,' said my mother.

" I did; and was pleased with it more than I would own. ' The girl's well enough,' said I, ' for what she is; but let's see what she'll be a few years hence. Then will be the trial.'

" ' She'll be always good, I doubt not.'

" ' So much the better for her. But can't we talk of any other subject? You complain how seldom I attend you; and when you are always talking of matrimony, or of this low-born, raw girl, it must needs lessen the pleasure of approaching you.'

" But now, as I hinted to you, ladies, and my lord, I had a still higher opinion of Pamela; and esteemed her more worthy of my attempts. ' For,' thought I, ' the girl has good sense, and it will be some pleasure to watch by what gradations she may be made to rise into love, and into a higher life, than that to which she was born.' And so I began to think she would be worthy in time of being my *mistress*, which, till now, as I said before, I had been a little scrupulous about.

" I took a little tour soon after this in company of some friends, with whom I had contracted an intimacy abroad, into Scotland and Ireland, they having a curiosity to see those countries, and we spent six or eight months on this expedition; and when I had landed them in France, I returned home, and found my good mother in a very indifferent state of health, but her Pamela arrived to a height of beauty and perfection which exceeded all my expectations. I was so taken with her charms when I first saw her, which was in the garden, with a book in her hand, just come out of a little summer-house, that I then thought of obliging her to go back again, in order to begin a parley with her: but while I was resolving, she tript away with her curtesies and reverences, and was out of my sight before I could determine.

"I was resolved, however, not to be long without her; and Mrs. Jewkes having been recommended to me a little before, by a brother-rake, as a woman of tried fidelity, I asked her if she would be faithful, if I had occasion to commit a pretty girl to her care?

"She hoped, she said, it would be with the lady's own consent, and she should make no scruple in obeying me.

"So I thought I would way-lay the girl, and carry her first to a little village in Northamptonshire, to an acquaintance of Mrs. Jewkes's. And when I had brought her to be easy and pacified a little, I designed that Jewkes should attend her to Lincolnshire: for I knew there was no coming at her here, under my mother's wing, by her own consent, and that to offer terms to her, would be to blow up my project all at once. Besides, I was sensible, that Mrs. Jervis would stand in the way of my proceedings as well as my mother.

"The method I had contrived was quite easy, as I imagined, and such as could not have failed to answer my purpose, as to carrying her off; and I doubted not of making her well satisfied in her good fortune very quickly; for, having a notion of her affectionate duty to her parents, I was not displeased that I could make the terms very easy and happy to them all.

"What most stood in my way, was my mother's fondness for her: but supposing I had got her favourite in my hands, which appeared to me, as I said, a task very easy to be conquered, I had actually formed a letter for her to transcribe, acknowledging a love-affair, and laying her withdrawing herself so privately, to an implicit obedience to her husband's commands, to whom she was married that morning, and who, being a young gentleman of genteel family, and dependent on his friends, was desirous of keeping it all a profound secret; and begging, on that account, her lady not to divulge it, so much as to Mrs. Jervis.

"And to prepare for this, and make her escape the more probable, when matters were ripe for my plot, I came in one night, and examined all the servants, and Mrs. Jervis, the latter in my mother's hearing, about a genteel young man, whom I pretended to find with a pillion on the horse he rode upon,

waiting about the back door of the garden, for somebody to
come to him; and who rode off, when I came up to the door,
as fast as he could. Nobody knew any thing of the matter,
and they were much surprised at what I told them: but I
begged Pamela might be watched, and that no one would say
any thing to her about it.

"My mother said, she had two reasons not to speak of it to
Pamela: one to oblige me: the other and chief, because it
would break the poor innocent girl's heart, to be suspected.
'Poor dear child!' said she, 'whither can she go, to be so
happy as with me? Would it not be inevitable ruin to her
to leave me? There is nobody comes after her: she receives
no letters, but now-and-then one from her father and mother,
and those she shews me.'

"'Well,' replied I, 'I hope she can have no design; 'twould
be strange if she had formed any to leave so good a mistress;
but you can't be *sure* all the letters she receives are from her
father; and her shewing to you those he writes, looks like a
cloak to others she may receive from another hand. But it
can be no harm to have an eye upon her. You don't know,
Madam, what tricks there are in the world.'

"'Not I, indeed; but only this I know, that the girl shall
be under no restraint, if she is resolved to leave me, well as I
love her.'

"Mrs. Jervis said, she would have an eye upon Pamela, in
obedience to my command, but she was sure there was no
need; nor would she so much wound the poor child's peace, as
to mention the matter to her.

"This I suffered to blow off, and seemed to my mother to
have so good an opinion of her Pamela, that I was sorry, as I
told her, I had such a surmise: saying, that though the fellow
and the pillion were odd circumstances, yet I dared to say,
there was nothing in it: for I doubted not, the girl's duty
and gratitude would hinder her from doing a foolish or rash
thing.

"This my mother heard with pleasure: although my motive
was but to lay Pamela on the thicker to her, when she was to
be told she had escaped.

"She was glad I was not an enemy to the poor child.
'Pamela has no friend but me,' continued she; 'and if I don't
provide for her, I shall have done her more harm than good (as
you and your aunt B. have often said,) in the accomplishments I
have given her: and yet the poor girl, I see that,' added she,
'would not be backward to turn her hand to any thing for the

sake of an honest livelihood, were she put to it; which, if it please God to spare me, and she continues good, she never shall be.'

"I wonder not, Pamela, at your tears on this occasion. Your lady was an excellent woman, and deserved this tribute to her memory. All my pleasure now is, that she knew not half my wicked pranks, and that I did not vex her worthy heart in the prosecution of this scheme; which would have given me a severe sting, inasmuch as I might have apprehended, with too much reason, that I had shortened her days by the knowledge of the one and the other.

"I had thus every thing ready for the execution of my project: but my mother's ill state of health gave me too much concern, to permit me to proceed. And, now-and-then, as my frequent attendance in her illness gave me an opportunity of observing more and more of the girl; her affectionate duty, and continual tears (finding her often on her knees, praying for her mistress,) I was moved to pity her; and while those scenes of my mother's illness and decline were before me, I would resolve to conquer, if possible, my guilty passion, as those scenes taught me, while their impressions held, justly to call it; and I was much concerned to find it so difficult a task; for, till now, I thought it principally owing to my usual enterprising temper, and a love of intrigue; and that I had nothing to do but to resolve against it, and to subdue it.

"But I was greatly mistaken: for I had insensibly brought myself to admire her in every thing she said or did; and there was so much gracefulness, humility, and innocence in her whole behaviour, and I saw so many melting scenes between her lady and her, that I found I could not master my esteem for her.

"My mother's illness increasing beyond hopes of recovery, and having settled all her greater affairs, she talked to me of her servants; I asked what she would have done for Pamela and Mrs. Jervis.

"'Make Mrs. Jervis, my dear son, as happy as you can: she is a gentlewoman born, you know; let her always be treated as such; but for your own sake, don't make her independent; for then you'll want a faithful manager. Yet if you marry, and your lady should not value her as she deserves, allow her a competency for the rest of her life, and let her live as she pleases.

"'As for Pamela, I hope you will be her protector!—She is a good girl: I love her next to you and your dear sister. She is just arriving at a trying time of life. I don't know what

113

to say for her. What I had designed was, that if any man of a genteel calling should offer, I would give her a little pretty portion, had God spared my life till then. But were she made independent, some idle fellow might snap her up; for she is very pretty: or if she should carry what you give her to her poor parents, as her duty would lead her to do, they are so unhappily involved, that a little matter would be nothing to them, and the poor girl might be to seek again. Perhaps Lady Davers will take her. But I wish she was not so pretty ! She may be the bird for which some wicked fowler will spread his snares; or, it may be, every lady will not choose to have such a waiting-maid. You are a young gentleman, and I am sorry to say, not better than I wish you to be—Though I hope my Pamela would not be in danger from her master, who owes all his servants protection, as much as the king does to his subjects. Yet I don't know how to wish her to stay with you, for your own reputation's sake, my dear son;—for the world will censure as it lists.—Would to God !' said she, 'the dear girl had the small-pox in a mortifying manner: she'd be lovely though in the genteelness of her person and the excellencies of her mind; and more out of danger of suffering from the tran-scient beauties of countenance. Yet I think,' added she, 'she might be safe and happy under Mrs. Jervis's care; and if you marry, and your lady parts with Mrs. Jervis, let 'em go together, and live as they like. I think that will be the best for both. And you have a generous spirit enough: I will not direct you in the *quantum*. But, my dear son, remember that I am the less concerned, that I have not done for the poor girl myself, because I depend upon you: the manner how fitly to provide for her, has made me defer it till now, that I have so much more important concerns on my hands; life and strength ebbing so fast, that I am hardly fit for any thing, or to wish for any thing, but to receive the last releasing stroke.' "

Here he stopped, being under some concern himself, and we in much more. At last he resumed the subject.

" You will too naturally think, my lord—and you, my good ladies—that the mind must be truly diabolical, that could break through the regard due to the solemn injunctions of a dying parent. They *did* hold me a good while indeed; and as fast as I found any emotions of a contrary nature rise in my breast, I endeavoured for some time to suppress them, and to think and act as I ought; but the dear bewitching girl every day rose in her charms upon me: and finding she still continued the use of her pen and ink, I could not help entertaining a jealousy, that she was writing to somebody who stood well in her opinion; and my love for her, and my own spirit of intrigue, made it a sweetheart of course. And I could not help watching her emotions; and seeing her once putting a letter she had just folded up, into her bosom, at my entrance into my mother's dressing-room, I made no doubt of detecting her, and her correspondent; and so I took the letter from her stays, she trembling and curtseying with a sweet confusion : and highly pleased I was to find it contained only innocence and duty to the deceased mistress, and the loving parents, expressing her joy that, in the midst of her grief for losing the one, she was not obliged to return to be a burden to the other; and I gave it her again, with words of encouragement, and went down much better satisfied than I had been with her correspondence.

"But when I reflected upon the innocent simplicity of her style, I was still more in love with her, and formed a stratagem, and succeeded in it, to come at her other letters, which I sent forward, after I had read them, all but three or four, which I kept back, when my plot began to ripen for execution; although the little slut was most abominably free with my character to her parents.

"You will censure me, no doubt, that my mother's injunctions made not a more lasting impression. But really I struggled hard with myself to give them their due force : and the dear girl, as I said, every day grew lovelier, and more accomplished. Her letters were but so many links to the chains in which she had bound me; and though once I had resolved to part with her to Lady Davers, and you, Madam, had an intention to take her, I could not for my life give her up; and thinking more honourably then of the state of a mistress than I have done since, I could not persuade myself (since I intended to do as handsomely by her as ever man did to a lady in that situation) but that I should do better for her than my mother had wished me to do, and so *more* than answer all her injunctions, as to the providing for her : and I could not imagine I should meet with a resistance I had seldom encountered from persons much her superiors as to descent; and was amazed at it; for it confounded me in all the notions I had of her sex, which, like a true libertine, I supposed wanted nothing but *importunity* and *opportunity*, a bold attempter, and a mind not ungenerous. Sometimes I admired her for her virtue; at other times, impetuous in my temper, and unused to control, I could have beat her. She well, I remember, describes the tumults of my soul, repeating what once passed between us, in words like these :—'Take the little witch from me, Mrs. Jervis.—I can neither bear, nor forbear her.—But stay—you shan't go—Yet be gone !—No, come back again.'—She thought I was mad, she says in her papers. Indeed I was little less. She says, I took her arm, and griped it black and blue, to bring her back again; and then sat down and looked at her as silly as such a poor girl as she !—Well did she describe the passion I struggled with; and no one can conceive how much my pride made me despise myself at times for the little actions my love for her put me upon, and yet to find that love increasing every day, as her charms and her resistance increased.—I have caught myself in a raging fit, sometimes vowing I would have her, and, at others, jealous that, to secure herself from my attempts, she would throw herself into the arms of some menial or inferior, whom otherwise she would not have thought of.

" Sometimes I soothed, sometimes threatened her; but never was such courage, when her virtue seemed in danger, mixed with so much humility, when her fears gave way to her hopes of a juster treatment.—Then I would think it impossible (so slight an opinion had I of woman's virtue) that such a girl as this, cottage-born, who owed every thing to my family, and had an absolute dependence upon my pleasure : myself not despicable in person or mind, as I supposed; she unprejudiced in any man's favour, at an age susceptible of impressions, and a frame and constitution not ice or snow : ' Surely,' thought I, ' all this frost must be owing to the want of fire in my attempts to thaw it : I used to dare more, and succeed better. Shall such a girl as this awe me by her rigid virtue ? No, she shall not.'

" Then I would resolve to be more in earnest. Yet my love was a traitor, that was more faithful to *her* than to *me ;* it had more honour in it at bottom than I had designed. Awed by her unaffected innocence, and a virtue I had never before encountered, so uniform and immovable, the moment I *saw* her I was half disarmed; and I courted her consent to that, which, though I was not likely to obtain, yet it went against me to think of extorting by violence. Yet marriage was never in my thoughts : I scorned so much as to promise it.

" To what numberless mean things did not this unmanly passion subject me !—I used to watch for her letters, though mere prittle-prattle and chit-chat, received them with delight, though myself was accused in them, and stigmatized as I deserved.

" I would listen meanly at her chamber-door, try to overhear her little conversation; in vain attempted to suborn Mrs. Jervis to my purposes, inconsistently talking of honour, when no one step I took, or action I attempted, shewed any thing like it: lost my dignity among my servants; made a party in her favour against me, of every body, but whom my money corrupted, and that hardly sufficient to keep my partisans steady to my interest; so greatly did the virtue of the servants triumph over the vice of the master, when confirmed by such an example!

"I have been very tedious, ladies and my Lord Davers, in my narration: but I am come within view of the point for which I now am upon my trial at your dread tribunal (*bowing to us all*).

"After several endeavours of a smooth and rough nature, in which my devil constantly failed me, and her good angel prevailed, I had talked to Mrs. Jervis to seduce the girl (to whom, in hopes of frightening her, I had given warning, but which she rejected to take, to my great disappointment) to desire to stay; and suspecting Mrs. Jervis played me booty, and rather confirmed her in her coyness, and her desire of leaving me, I was mean enough to conceal myself in the closet in Mrs. Jervis's room, in order to hear their private conversation; but really not designing to make any other use of my concealment, than to tease her a little, if she should say any thing I did not like; which would give me a pretence to treat her with greater freedoms than I had ever yet done, and would be an introduction to take off from her unprecedented apprehensiveness another time.

"But the dear prattler, not knowing I was there, as she undressed herself, begun such a bewitching chit-chat with Mrs. Jervis, who, I found, but ill kept my secret, that I never was at such a loss what to resolve upon. One while I wished myself, unknown to them, out of the closet, into which my inconsiderate passion had meanly led me; another time I was incensed at the freedom with which I heard myself treated: but then, rigidly considering that I had no business to hearken to their private conversation, and it was such as became *them*, while I ought to have been ashamed to give occasion for it, I excused them both, and admired still more and more the dear prattler.

"In this suspense, the undesigned rustling of my night-gown, from changing my posture, alarming the watchful Pamela, she in a fright came towards the closet to see who was there. What could I then do, but bolt out upon the apprehensive charmer;

and having so done, and she running to the bed, screaming to Mrs. Jervis, would not any man have followed her thither, detected as I was? But yet, I said, if she forbore her screaming, I would do her no harm; but if not, she should take the consequence. I found, by their exclamations, that this would pass with both for an attempt of the worst kind; but really I had no such intentions as they feared. When I found myself detected; when the dear frightened girl ran to the bed; when Mrs. Jervis threw herself about her; when they would not give over their hideous squallings; when I was charged by Mrs. Jervis with the worst designs; it was enough to make me go farther than I designed; and could I have prevailed upon Mrs. Jervis to go up, and quiet the maids, who seemed to be rising, upon the other screaming, I believe, had Pamela kept out of her fit, I should have been a little freer with her, than ever I had been; but, as it was, I had no thought but of making as honourable a retreat as I could, and to save myself from being exposed to my whole family: and I was not guilty of any freedoms, that her modesty, unaffrighted, could reproach herself with having suffered; and the dear creature's fainting fits gave *me* almost as great apprehensions as I could give *her*.

"Thus, ladies—and, my lord—have I tediously, and little enough to my own reputation, given you my character, and told you more against myself than any *one* person could accuse me of. Whatever redounds to the credit of my Pamela, redounds in part to my own; and so I have the less regret to accuse myself, since it exalts her. But as to a formed intention to hide myself in the closet, in order to attempt the girl by violence, and in the presence of a good woman, as Mrs. Jervis is, which you impute to me, bad as I was, I was not so vile, so abandoned as that.

"Love, as I said before, subjects its inconsiderate votaries to innumerable meannesses, and unlawful passion to many more. I could not live without this dear girl. I hated the thoughts of matrimony with any body: and to be brought to the state by my mother's waiting-maid.—' Forbid it, pride !' thought I; ' forbid it, example ! forbid it, all my past sneers, and constant ridicule, both on the estate, and on those who descended to inequalities in it ! and, lastly, forbid it my family spirit, so visible in Lady Davers, as well as in myself, to whose insults, and those of all the world, I shall be obnoxious, if I take such a step !'

"All this tends to demonstrate the strength of my passion:

I could not conquer my love; so I conquered a pride, which every one thought unconquerable; and since I could not make an innocent heart vicious, I had the happiness to follow so good an example; and by this means, a vicious heart is become virtuous. I have the pleasure of rejoicing in the change, and hope I shall do so still more and more; for I really view with contempt my past follies; and it is now a greater wonder to me how I could act as I did, than that I should detest those actions, which made me a curse, instead of a benefit to society. I am not yet so pious as my Pamela; but that is to come; and it is one good sign, that I can truly say, I delight in every instance of her piety and virtue: and now I will conclude my tedious narration."

Thus he ended his affecting relation: which in the course of it gave me a thousand different emotions; and made me often pray for him, that God will entirely convert a heart so generous and worthy, as his is on most occasions. And if I can but find him not deviate, when we go to London, I shall greatly hope that nothing will affect his morals again.

I have just read over again the foregoing account of himself. As near as I remember (and my memory is the best faculty I have), it is pretty exact; only he was fuller of beautiful similitudes, and spoke in a more flowery style, as I may say. Yet don't you think, Miss (if I have not done injustice to his spirit), that the beginning of it, especially, is in the saucy air of a man too much alive to such notions? For so the ladies observed in his narration.—Is it very like the style of a true penitent?—But indeed he went on better, and concluded best of all.

But don't you observe what a dear good lady I had? A thousand blessings on her beloved memory! Were I to live to see my children's children, they should be all taught to lisp her praises before they could speak. *My* gratitude should always be renewed in *their* mouths; and God, and my dear father and mother, my lady, and my master that was, my best friend that is, but principally, as most due, the FIRST, who inspired all the rest, should have their morning, their noontide, and their evening praises, as long as I lived!

I will only observe farther, as to this my third conversation-piece, that my Lord Davers offered to extenuate some parts of his dear brother-in-law's conduct, which he did not himself vindicate; and Mr. B. was pleased to say, that my lord was always very candid to him, and kind in his allowances for the sallies of ungovernable youth. Upon which my lady said, a little tartly, " Yes, and for a very good reason, I doubt not; for who cares to condemn himself ? "

" Nay," said my lord pleasantly, " don't put us upon a foot, neither : for what sallies I made before I knew your ladyship, were but like those of a fox, which now and then runs away with a straggling pullet, when nobody sees him, whereas those of my brother were like the invasions of a lion, breaking into every man's fold, and driving the shepherds, as well as the sheep, before him."—" Ay," said my lady, " but I can look round me, and have reason, perhaps, to think the invading lion has come off, little as he deserved it, better than the creeping fox, who, with all his cunning, sometimes suffers for his pilfering theft."

O, my dear, these gentlemen are strange creatures !—What can they think of themselves ? for they say, there is not one virtuous man in five; but I hope, for our sex's sake, as well as for the world's sake, all is not true that evil fame reports; for you know every man-trespasser must *find* or *make* a woman-trespasser !—And if so, what a world is this !—And how must the innocent suffer from the guilty ! Yet, how much better is it to suffer one's self, than to be the cause of another's sufferings ? I long to hear of you, and must shorten my future accounts, or I shall do nothing but write, and tire *you* into the bargain, though I cannot my dear father and mother. I am, my dear Miss, *always yours,*   P. B.

LETTER XXXI

From Miss Darnford to Mrs. B.

DEAR MRS. B.,

Every post you more and more oblige us to admire and love you : and let me say, I will gladly receive your letters upon your own terms : only when your worthy parents have perused them, see that I have every line of them again.

Your account of the arrival of your noble guests, and their behaviour to you, and yours to them; your conversation, and wise determination, on the offered title of Baronet; the just applauses conferred upon you by all, particularly the good countess; your breakfast conversation, and the narrative of your saucy abominable *master*, though amiable *husband ;* all delight us beyond expression.

Do go on, dear excellent lady, with your charming journals, and let us know all that passes.

As to the state of matters with us, I have desired my papa to allow me to decline Mr. Murray's addresses. The good man loved me most violently, nay, he could not live without me : life was no life, unless I favoured him : but yet, after a few more of these flights, he is trying to sit down satisfied without my papa's foolish perverse girl, as Sir Simon calls me, and to transpose his affections to a worthier object, my sister Nancy ; and it would make you smile to see how, a little while before he *directly* applied to her, she screwed up her mouth to my mamma, and, truly, she'd have none of Polly's leavings ; no, not she !—But no sooner did he declare himself in form, than the *gaudy wretch*, as he was before with her, became a *well-dressed* gentleman ;—the *chattering magpie* (for he talks and laughs much), *quite conversable*, and has something *agreeable* to say upon *every subject*. Once he would make a good master of the buck-hounds ; but now, really, the *more* one is in his company, the *more polite* one finds him.

Then, on his part,—he happened to see Miss Polly first ; and truly, he could have thought himself very happy in so agreeable a young lady ; yet there was always something of majesty (what a stately name for ill nature !) in Miss Nancy, something so awful ; that while Miss Polly engaged the affections at first sight, Miss Nancy struck a man with reverence ; insomuch, that the one might be loved as a woman, but the other revered as something more : a goddess, no doubt !

I do but think, that when he comes to be lifted up to her celestial sphere, as her fellow constellation, what a figure Nancy and her *ursus major* will make together ; and how will they glitter and shine to the wonder of all beholders !

Then she must make a brighter appearance by far, and a more pleasing one too : for why ? She has three thousand *satellites*, or little stars, in her train more than poor Polly can pretend to. Won't there be a fine twinkling and sparkling, think you, when the greater and lesser bear-stars are joined together ?

But excuse me, dear Mrs. B.; this saucy girl has vexed me just now, by her ill-natured tricks ; and I am even with her, having thus vented my spite, though she knows nothing of the matter.

So, fancy you see Polly Darnford abandoned by her own fault ; her papa angry at her ; her mamma pitying her, and calling her silly girl ; Mr. Murray, who is a rough lover, growling over his mistress, as a dog over a bone he fears to lose ; Miss Nancy, putting on her prudish pleasantry, snarling out a kind word, and breaking through her sullen gloom, for a smile now and then in return; and I laughing at both in my sleeve, and thinking I shall soon get leave to attend you in town, which will be better than twenty humble servants of Mr. Murray's cast: or, if I can't, that I shall have the pleasure of your correspondence here, and enjoy, unrivalled, the favour of my dear parents, which this ill-tempered girl is always envying me.

Forgive all this nonsense. I was willing to write something, though worse than nothing, to shew how desirous I am to oblige you, had I a capacity or subject, as you have. But nobody can love you better, or admire you more, of this you may be assured (however unequal in all other respects), than
your   POLLY DARNFORD.

I send you up some of your papers for the good couple in Kent. Pray, pay my respects to them: and beg they'll let me have 'em again as soon as they can, by your conveyance.

Our Stamford friends desire their kindest respects; they mention you with delight in every letter.

LETTER XXXII

The Journal continued.

THURSDAY, FRIDAY EVENING.

MY DEAR MISS DARNFORD,

I am returned from a very busy day, having had no less than fourteen of our neighbours, gentlemen and ladies, to dinner: the occasion, principally, to welcome our noble guests into these parts; Mr. B. having, as I mentioned before, turned the intended visit into an entertainment, after his usual generous manner.—He and Lord Davers are gone part of the way with them home; and Lord Jackey, mounted with his favourite Colbrand, as an escort to the countess and Lady Davers, who are taking an airing in the chariot. They offered to take the coach, if I would have gone; but being fatigued, I desired to be excused. So I retired to my closet; and Miss Darnford, who is seldom out of my thoughts, coming into my mind, I had a new recruit of spirits, which enabled me to resume my pen, and thus I proceed with my journal.

Our company was, the Earl and Countess of D., who are so fashionable a married couple, that the earl made it his boast, and his countess bore it like one accustomed to such treatment, that he had not been in his lady's company an hour abroad before for seven years. You know his lordship's character: every body does; and there is not a worse, as report says, in the peerage.

Sir Thomas Atkyns, a single gentleman, not a little finical and ceremonious, and a mighty beau, though of the tawdry sort, and affecting foreign airs; as if he was afraid it would not be judged by any other mark that he had travelled.

Mr. Arthur and his lady, a moderately happy couple, who seem always, when together, to behave as if upon a compromise; that is, that each should take it in turn to say free things of the other; though some of their freedoms are of so cutting a nature, that it looks as if they intended to divert the company at their own expense. The lady, being of a noble family, strives to let every one know that she values herself not a little upon that advantage: but otherwise has many good qualities.

Mr. Brooks and his lady. He is a free joker on serious subjects, but a good-natured man, and says sprightly things with no ill grace: the lady a little reserved, and haughty, though to-day was freer than usual; as was observed at table by

Lady Towers, who is a maiden lady of family, noted for her wit and repartee, and who says many good things, with so little doubt and really so good a grace, that one cannot help being pleased with her. This lady is generally gallanted by

Mr. Martin of the Grove, so called, to distinguish him from a rich citizen of that name, settled in these parts, but being covetous and proud, is seldom admitted among the gentry in their visits or parties of pleasure.

Mr. Dormer, one of a very courteous demeanour, a widower, was another, who always speaks well of his deceased lady, and of all the sex for her sake. Mr. Chapman and his lady, a well-behaved couple, not ashamed to be very tender and observing to each other, but without that censurable fondness which sits so ill upon some married folks in company.

Then there was the dean, our good minister, whom I name last, because I would close with one of the worthiest; and his daughter, who came to supply her mamma's place, who was indisposed; a well-behaved prudent young lady. And here were our fourteen guests.

The Countess of C., Lord and Lady Davers, Mr. H., my dear Mr. B. and your humble servant, made up the rest of the company. Thus we had a capacious and brilliant circle; and all the avenues to the house were crowded with their equipages.

123

The subjects of discourse at dinner were various, as you may well suppose; and the circle was too large to fall upon any regular or very remarkable topics. A good deal of sprightly wit, however, flew about, between the Earl of D., Lady Towers, and Mr. Martin, in which that lord suffered as he deserved; for he was no match for the lady, especially as the presence of the dean was a very visible restraint upon him, and Mr. Brooks too: so much awe will the character of a good clergyman always have upon even forward spirits, where he is known to have had an inviolable regard to it himself.—Besides, the good gentleman has, naturally, a genteel and inoffensive vein of raillery, and so was too hard for them at their own weapons. But after dinner, and the servants being withdrawn, Mr. Martin singled me out, as he loves to do, for a subject of encomium, and made some high compliments to my dear Mr. B. upon his choice; and wished (as he often does), he could find just such another for himself.

Lady Towers told him it was a thing as unaccountable as it was unreasonable, that every rake who loved to destroy virtue, should expect to be rewarded with it: and if his *brother* B. had come off so well, she thought no one else ought to expect it.

Lady Davers said, it was a very just observation: and she thought it a pity there was not a law, that every man who made a harlot of an honest woman, should be obliged to marry one of another's making.

Mr. B. said, that would be too severe; it would be punishment enough, if he was to marry his own; and especially if he had not seduced her under promise of marriage.

" Then you'd have a man be obliged to stand to his promise, I suppose, Mr. B.? " replied Lady Davers. " Yes, madam."— " But," said she, " the proof would be difficult perhaps: and the most unguilty heart of our sex might be least able to make it out.—But what say you, my Lord D.; will you, and my Lord Davers, join to bring a bill into the House of Peers, for the purposes I mentioned? I fancy my brother would give it all the assistance he could in the Lower House."

" Indeed," said Mr. B., " if I may be allowed to speak in the plural number, *we* must not pretend to hold an argument on this subject.—What say you, Mr. H.? Which side are you of? "—" Every gentleman," replied he, " who is not of the ladies' side, is deemed a criminal; and I was always of the side that had the power of the gallows."

" That shews," returned Lady Towers, " that Mr. H. is more afraid of the *punishment*, than of deserving it."—" 'Tis well," said Mr. B., " that any consideration deters a man of Mr. H.'s time of life. What may be *fear* now, may improve to *virtue* in time."

" Ay," said Lady Davers, " Jackey is one of his uncle's *foxes :* he'd be glad to snap up a straggling pullet, if he was not well looked after, perhaps."—" Pray, my dear," said Lord Davers, " forbear : you ought not to introduce two different conversations into different companies."

" Well, but," said Lady Arthur, " since you seem to have been so hard put to it, as *single* men, what's to be done with the married man who ruins an innocent body?—What punishment, Lady Towers, shall we find out for such an one ; and what reparation to the injured? " This was said with a particular view to the earl, on a late scandalous occasion ; as I afterwards found.

" As to the punishment of the gentleman," replied Lady Towers, " where the law is not provided for it, it must be left, I believe, to his conscience. It will then one day be heavy enough. But as to the reparation to the woman, so far as it can be made, it will be determinable as the unhappy person *may* or may *not* know, that her seducer is a married man : if she knows he is, I think she neither deserves redress nor pity, though it elevate not *his* guilt. But if the case be otherwise, and *she* had no means of informing herself that he was married, and he promised to make her his wife, to be sure, though *she* cannot be acquitted, *he* deserves the severest punishment that can be inflicted.—What say you, Mrs. B.? "

" If I must speak, I think that since custom now exacts so little regard to virtue from men, and so much from women, and since the designs of the former upon the latter are so flagrantly avowed and known, the poor creature, who suffers herself to be seduced, either by a *single* or *married* man, *with* promises, or *without*, has only to sequester herself from the world, and devote the rest of her days to penitence and obscurity. As to the gentleman," added I, " he must, I doubt, be left to his conscience, as you say, Lady Towers, which he will one day have enough to do to pacify."

" Every young lady has not your angelic perfection, Madam," said Mr. Dormer. " And there are cases in which the fair sex deserve compassion, ours execration. Love may insensibly steal upon a soft heart ; when once admitted, the oaths, vows, and protestations of the favoured object, who declaims against the deceivers of his sex, confirm her good opinion of him, till having lull'd asleep her vigilance, in an unguarded hour he takes advantage of her unsuspecting innocence. Is not such a poor creature to be pitied? And what punishment does not such a seducer deserve?"

"You have put, Sir," said I, "a moving case, and in a generous manner. What, indeed, does not such a deceiver deserve?" —"And the more," said Mrs. Chapman, "as the most innocent heart is generally the most credulous."—"Very true," said my countess; "for such an one as would do no harm *to* others, seldom suspects any *from* others; and her lot is very unequally cast; admired for that very innocence which tempts some brutal ravager to ruin it."—"Yet, what is that virtue," said the dean, "which cannot stand the test?"

"But," said Lady Towers, very satirically, "whither, ladies, are we got? We are upon the subject of virtue and honour. Let us talk of something in which the *gentlemen* can join with us. This is such an one, you see, that none but the dean and Mr. Dormer can discourse upon."—"Let us then," retorted Mr. Martin, "to be even with *one* lady at least find a subject that will be *new* to her: and that is CHARITY."

"Does what I said concern Mr. Martin more than any other gentleman," returned Lady Towers, "that he is disposed to take offence at it?"

"You must pardon me, Lady Towers," said Mr. B., "but I think a lady should never make a motion to wave such subjects as those of virtue and honour; and less still, in company, where there is so much occasion, as she seems to think, for enforcing them."

"I desire not to wave the subject, I'll assure you," replied she. "And if, Sir, you think it may do good, we will continue it for the sakes of all *you* gentlemen" (looking round her archly), "who are of opinion you may be benefited by it."

A health to the king and royal family, brought on public affairs and politics; and the ladies withdrawing to coffee and tea, I have no more to say as to this conversation, having repeated all that I remember was said to any purpose.

SATURDAY MORNING.

The countess being a little indisposed, Lady Davers and I took an airing this morning in the chariot, and had a long discourse together. Her ladyship was pleased to express great favour and tenderness towards me; gave me much good advice, as to the care she would have me take of myself; and told me, that her hopes, as well as her brother's, all centred in my welfare; and that the way I was in made her love me better and better.

She was pleased to tell me, how much she approved of the domestic management; and to say, that she never saw such regularity and method in any family in her life, where was the like number of servants: every one, she said, knew their duty, and did it without speaking to, in such silence, and with so much apparent cheerfulness and delight, without the least hurry or confusion, that it was her surprise and admiration: but kindly would have it that I took too much care upon me. "Yet," said she, "I don't see but you are always fresh and lively, and never seem tired or fatigued; and are always dressed and easy, so that no company find you unprepared, or unfit to receive them, come when they will, whether it be to breakfast or dinner."

I told her ladyship, I owed all this and most of the conduct for which she was pleased to praise me, to her dear brother, who, at the beginning of my happiness, gave me several cautions and instructions for my behaviour; which had been the rule of my conduct ever since, and I hoped ever would be:—"To say nothing," added I, "which yet would be very unjust, of the assistance I received from worthy Mrs. Jervis, who is an excellent manager."

Good Creature, Sweet Pamela, and *Charming Girl,* were her common words; and she was pleased to attribute to me a graceful and unaffected ease, and that I have a natural dignity in my person and behaviour, which at once command love and reverence; so that, my dear Miss Darnford, I am in danger of being proud. For you must believe, that her ladyship's approbation gives me great pleasure; and the more, as I was afraid, before she came, I should not have come off near so well in her opinion. As the chariot passed along, she took great notice of the respects paid me by people of different ranks, and of the blessings bestowed upon me, by several, as we proceeded; and said, she should fare well, and be rich in good wishes, for being in my company.

"The good people who know us, *will* do so, Madam," said I; "but I had rather have their silent prayers than their audible ones; and I have caused some of them to be told so. What I apprehend is, that you will be more uneasy to-morrow, when at church you'll see a good many people in the same way. Indeed my story, and your dear brother's tenderness to me, are so much talked of, that many strangers are brought hither to see us: 'tis the only thing," continued I (and so it is, Miss), "that makes me desirous to go to London; for by the time we return, the novelty, I hope, will cease."

Then I mentioned some verses of Mr. Cowley, which were laid under my cushion in our seat at church, two Sundays ago, by some unknown hand; and how uneasy they have made me. I will transcribe them, my dear, and give you the particulars of our conversation on that occasion. The verses are these:

> " Thou robb'st my days of bus'ness and delights,
>   Of sleep thou robb'st my nights.
> Ah ! lovely thief ! what wilt thou do?
> What ! rob me of heaven too?
> Thou ev'n my prayers dost steal from me,
> And I, with wild idolatry,
> Begin to GOD, and end them all to thee.
>
> No, to what purpose should I speak?
> No, wretched heart, swell till you break.
> She cannot love me, if she would,
> And, to say truth, 'twere pity that she should.
> No, to the grave thy sorrow bear,
> As silent as they will be there;
> Since that lov'd hand this mortal wound does give,
> So handsomely the thing contrive
> That she may guiltless of it live;
> So perish, that her killing thee
> May a chance-medley, and no murder, be."

I had them in my pocket, and read them to my lady; who asked me, if her brother had seen them? I told her, it was he that found them under the cushion I used to sit upon; but did not shew them to me till I came home; and that I was so vexed at them, that I could not go to church in the afternoon.

" What should you be vexed at, my dear?" said she: " how could you help it? My brother was not disturbed at them, was he?"—" No, indeed," replied I: " he chid *me* for being so; and was pleased to make me a fine compliment upon it; that he did not wonder that every body who saw me loved me. But I said, this was all that wicked wit is good for, to inspire such boldness in bad hearts, which might otherwise not dare to set pen to paper to affront any one. But pray, Madam," added I, " don't own I have told you of them, lest the least shadow of a thought should arise, that I was prompted by some vile secret vanity, to tell your ladyship of them, when I am sure, they have vexed me more than enough. For is it not a sad thing, that the church should be profaned by such actions, and such thoughts, as ought not to be brought into it? Then, Madam, to have any wicked man *dare* to think of one with impure notions ! It gives me the less opinion of myself, that I should be so much as *thought of* as the object of any wicked body's wishes. I have called myself to account upon it, whether any levity in my looks, my dress, my appearance, could embolden such an offensive insolence. And I have thought upon this occasion better of Julius Cæsar's delicacy than I did, when I read of it; who, upon an attempt made on his wife, to which, however, it does not appear she gave the least encouragement, said to those who pleaded for her against the divorce he was resolved upon, *that the wife of Cæsar ought not to be suspected.*— Indeed, Madam," continued I, " it would extremely shock me, but to know that any wicked heart had conceived a design upon me; upon *me*, give me leave to repeat, whose only glory and merit is, that I have had the grace to withstand the greatest of trials and temptations, from a gentleman more worthy to be beloved, both for person and mind, than any man in England."

" Your observation, my dear, is truly delicate, and such as becomes your mind and character. And I really think, if any lady in the world is secure from vile attempts, it must be you; not only from your story, so well known, and the love you bear to your man, and his merit to you, but from the prudence, and natural *dignity*, I will say, of your behaviour, which, though easy and cheerful, is what would strike dead the hope of any presumptuous libertine the moment he sees you."

" How can I enough," returned I, and kissed her hand, " acknowledge your ladyship's polite goodness in this compliment? But, my lady, you see by the very instance I have mentioned, that a liberty is taken, which I cannot think of without pain."

" I am pleased with your delicacy, my dear, as I said before. You can never err, whilst thus watchful over your conduct: and I own you have the more reason for it, as you have married a mere Julius Cæsar, an open-eyed rake " (that was her word), " who would, on the least surmise, though ever so causeless on your part, have all his passions up in arms, in fear of liberties being offered like those he has not scrupled to take."—" O but, Madam," said I, " he has given me great satisfaction in one point; for you must think I should not love him as I ought, if I had not a concern for his future happiness, as well as for his present; and that is, he has assured me, that in all the liberties he has taken, he never attempted a married lady, but always abhorred the thought of so great an evil."—" 'Tis pity," said her ladyship, " that a man who could conquer his passions *so far*, could not subdue them entirely. This shews it was in his own power to do so; and increases his crime: and what a wretch is he, who scrupling, under pretence of conscience or honour, to attempt ladies *within* the pale, boggles not to ruin a poor creature *without;* although he knows, he thereby, most probably, for ever deprived her of that protection, by preventing her marriage, which even among such rakes as himself, is deemed, he owns, inviolable; and so casts the poor creature headlong into the jaws of perdition."

"Ah! Madam," replied I, "this was the very inference I made upon the occasion."—"And what could he say?"—"He said, my inference was just; but called me *pretty preacher;*—and once having cautioned me not to be over-serious to him, so as to cast a gloom, as he said, over our innocent enjoyments, I never dare to urge matters farther, when he calls me by that name."

"Well," said my lady, "thou'rt an admirable girl! God's goodness was great to our family, when it gave thee to it. No wonder," continued she, "as my brother says, every body that sees you, and has heard your character, loves you. And this is some excuse for the inconsiderate folly even of this unknown transcriber."—"Ah! Madam," replied I, "but is it not a sad thing, that people, if they must take upon them to like one's behaviour in general, should have the *worst,* instead of the *best* thoughts upon it? If I were as good as I *ought* to be, and as some *think* me, must they wish to make me bad for that reason?"

Her ladyship was pleased to kiss me as we sat. "My charming Pamela, my *more than sister.*"—(Did she say?)—Yes, she did say so! and made my eyes overflow with joy to hear the sweet epithet. "How your conversation charms me!—I charge you, when you get to town, let me have your remarks on the diversions you will be carried to by my brother. Now I know what to expect from *you,* and you know how acceptable every thing from you will be *to me,* I promise great pleasure, as well to myself as to my worthy friends, particularly to Lady Betty, in your unrestrained free correspondence.—Indeed, Pamela, I must bring you acquainted with Lady Betty: she is one of the worthies of our sex, and has a fine understanding. —I'm sure you'll like her.—But (for the world say it not to my brother, nor let Lady Betty know I tell you so, if ever you should be acquainted) I had carried the matter so far by my officious zeal to have my brother married to so fine a lady, not doubting his joyful approbation, that it was no small disappointment to *her,* when he married you: and this is the best excuse I can make for my furious behaviour to you at the

Hall. For though I am naturally very hasty and passionate, yet then I was almost mad.—Indeed my disappointment had given me so much indignation both against you and him, that it is well I did not do some violent thing by you. I believe you did feel the weight of my hand : but what was that ? 'Twas well I did not *kill you dead*."—These were her ladyship's words —" For how could I think the wild libertine capable of being engaged by such noble motives, or thee what thou art !—So this will account to thee a little for my violence then."

" Your ladyship," said I, " all these things considered, had but too much reason to be angry at your dear brother's proceedings, so well as you always loved him, so high a concern as you always had to promote his honour and interest, and so far as you had gone with Lady Betty."

" I tell thee, Pamela, that the old story of Eleanor and Rosamond run in my head all the way of my journey, and I almost wished for a potion to force down thy throat : when I found thy lewd paramour absent, (for little did I think thou wast married to him, though I expected thou wouldst try to persuade me to believe it) fearing that his intrigue with thee would effectually frustrate my hopes as to Lady Betty and him : ' Now,' thought I, ' all happens as I wish !—Now will I confront this brazen girl !—Now will I try her innocence, as I please, by offering to take her away with me ; if she refuses, take that refusal for a demonstration of her guilt ; and then,' thought I, ' I will make the creature provoke me, in the presence of my nephew and my woman,' (and I hoped to have got that woman Jewkes to testify for me too), and I cannot tell what I might have done, if thou hadst not escaped out of the window, especially after telling me thou wast as much married as I was, and hadst shewn me his tender letter to thee, which had a quite different effect upon me than you expected. But if I had committed any act of violence, what remorse should I have had on reflection, and knowing what an excellence I had injured ! Thank God thou didst escape me ! " And then her ladyship folded her arms about me, and kissed me.

This was a sad story, you'll say, my dear : and I wonder what her ladyship's passion would have made her do ! Surely she would not have *killed me dead !* Surely she would not !— Let it not, however, Miss Darnford—nor you, my dear parents —when you see it—go out of your own hands, nor be read, for my Lady Davers's sake, to any body else—No, not to your own mamma. It made me tremble a little, even at this distance, to think what a sad thing passion is, when way is given to its ungovernable tumults, and how it deforms and debases the noblest minds.

We returned from this agreeable airing just in time to dress before dinner, and then my lady and I went together into the countess's apartment, where I received abundance of compliments from both. As this brief conversation will give you some notion of that management and economy for which they heaped upon me their kind praises, I will recite to you what passed in it, and hope you will not think me too vain; and the less, because what I underwent formerly from my lady's indignation, half entitles me to be proud of her present kindness and favour.

Lady Davers said, "Your ladyship must excuse us, that we have lost so much of your company; but here, this sweet girl has so entertained me, that I could have staid out with her all day; and several times did I bid the coachman prolong his circuit."—"My good Lady Davers, Madam," said I, "has given me inexpressible pleasure, and has been all condescension and favour, and made me as proud as proud can be."—"You, my dear Mrs. B.," said she, "may have given great pleasure to Lady Davers, for it cannot be otherwise—But I have no great notion of her ladyship's condescension, as you call it—(pardon me, Madam," said she to her, smiling) "when she cannot raise her style above the word *girl*, coming off from a tour you have made so delightful to her."—"I protest to you, my Lady C.," replied her ladyship, with great goodness, "that word, which once I used through pride, as you'll call it, I now use for a very different reason. I begin to doubt, whether to call her *sister*, is not more honour to myself than to her; and to this hour am not quite convinc'd. When I am, I will call her so with pleasure." I was quite overcome with this fine compliment, but could not answer a word: and the countess said, "I could have spared you longer, had not the time of day compelled your return; for I have been very agreeably entertained, as well as you, although but with the talk of your woman and mine. For here they have been giving me such an account of Mrs. B.'s economy, and family management, as has highly delighted me. I never knew the like; and in so young a lady too.—We shall have strange reformations to make in our families, Lady Davers, when we go home, were we to follow so good an example.— Why, my dear Mrs. B.," continued her ladyship, "you out-do all your neighbours. And indeed I am glad I live so far from you :—for were I to try to imitate you, it would still be *but* imitation, and you'd have the honour of it."—"Yet you hear,

132

and you see by yesterday's conversation," said Lady Davers, " how much her best neighbours, of both sexes, admire her : they all yield to her the palm, unenvying."—" Then, my good ladies," said I, " it is a sign I have most excellent neighbours, full of generosity, and willing to encourage a young person in doing right things : so it makes, considering what I was, more for their honour than my own. For what censures should not such a one as I deserve, who have not been educated to fill up my time like ladies of condition, were I not to employ myself as I do? I, who have so little other merit, and who brought no fortune at all."—" Come, come, Pamela, none of your self-denying ordinances," that was Lady Davers's word; " you must know something of your own excellence : if you do not, I'll tell it you, because there is no fear you will be proud or vain upon it. I don't see, then, that there is the lady in yours, or any neighbourhood, that behaves with more decorum, or better keeps up the part of a lady, than you do. How you manage it, I can't tell; but you do as much by a look, and a pleasant one too, that's the rarity ! as I do by high words, and passionate exclamations : I have often nothing but blunder upon blunder, as if the wretches were in a confederacy to try my patience."—" Perhaps," said I, " the awe they have of your ladyship, because of your high qualities, makes them commit blunders; for I myself was always more afraid of appearing before your ladyship, when you have visited your honoured mother, than of any body else, and have been the more sensibly awkward through that very awful respect."—" Psha, psha, Pamela, that is not it : 'tis all in yourself. I used to think my mamma, and my brother too, had as awkward servants as ever I saw any where—except Mrs. Jervis—Well enough for a bachelor, indeed !—But, here !—thou hast not parted with one servant— Hast thou ? "—" No, Madam."—" How ! " said the countess; " what excellence is here !—All of them, pardon me, Mrs. B., your fellow-servants, as one may say, and all of them so respectful, so watchful of your eye; and you, at the same time, so gentle to them, so easy, so cheerful."

Don't you think me, my dear, insufferably vain? But 'tis what they were pleased to say. 'Twas their goodness to me, and shewed how much they can excel in generous politeness. So I will proceed. " Why this," continued the countess, " must be *born* dignity—*born* discretion—Education cannot give it :— if it could, why should not *we* have it ? "

The ladies said many more kind things of me then ; and after dinner they mentioned all over again, with additions, before my best friend, who was kindly delighted with the encomiums given me by two ladies of such distinguishing judgment in all other cases. They told him, how much they admired my family management: then they would have it that my genius was universal, for the employments and accomplishments of my sex, whether they considered it as employed in penmanship, in needlework, in paying or receiving visits, in music, and I can't tell how many other qualifications, which they were pleased to attribute to me, over and above the family management: saying, that I had an understanding which comprehended every thing, and an eye that penetrated into the very bottom of matters in a moment, and never was at a loss for the *should be*, the *why* or *wherefore*, and the *how*—these were their comprehensive words; that I did every thing with celerity, clearing all as I went, and left nothing, they observed, to come over again, that could be dispatched at once: by which means, they said, every hand was clear to undertake a new work, as well as my own head to direct it; and there was no hurry nor confusion: but every coming hour was fresh and ready, and unincumbered (so they said), for its new employment; and to this they attributed that ease and pleasure with which every thing was performed, and that I could *do* and *cause* to be done, so much business without hurry either to myself or servants.

Judge how pleasing this was to my best beloved, who found, in their kind approbation, such a justification of his own conduct as could not fail of being pleasing to him, especially as Lady Davers was one of the kind praisers. Lord Davers was so highly delighted, that he rose once, begging his brother's excuse, to salute me, and stood over my chair, with a pleasure in his looks that cannot be expressed, now-and-then lifting up his hands, and his good-natured eye glistening with joy, which a pier-glass gave me the opportunity of seeing, as sometimes I stole a bashful glance towards it, not knowing how or which way to look. Even Mr. H. seemed to be touched very sensibly; and recollecting his behaviour to me at the Hall, he once cried out, " What a sad whelp was *I*, to behave as I formerly did, to so much excellence !—Not, Mr. B., that I was any thing uncivil neither;—but in unworthy sneers, and nonsense.—You know me well enough.—You called me, *tinsell'd boy*, though, Madam, don't you remember that? and said, *twenty or thirty years hence, when I was at age, you'd give me an answer*. Egad ! I shall never forget your looks, nor your words neither !—they were severe speeches, were they not, Sir ? "—" O you see, Mr. H.," replied my dear Mr. B., " Pamela is not quite perfect. We must not provoke her; for she'll call us both so, perhaps; for I wear a laced coat, sometimes, as well as you."

"Nay, I can't be angry," said he. "I deserved it richly, that I did, had it been worse."—"Thy silly tongue," said my lady, "runs on without fear or wit. What's past is past."—"Why, Madam, I was plaguily wrong; and I said nothing of any body but *myself*:—and have been ready to hang myself since, as often as I have thought of my nonsense."—"My nephew," said my lord, "must bring in hanging, or the gallows in every speech he makes, or it will not be he." Mr. B., smiling, said, with severity enough in his meaning, as I saw by the turn of his countenance, "Mr. H. knows that his birth and family entitle him more to the *block*, than the rope, or he would not make so free with the latter."—"Good! very good, by Jupiter!" said Mr. H. laughing. The countess smiled. Lady Davers shook her head at her brother, and said to her nephew, "Thou'rt a good-natured foolish fellow, that thou art."—"For what, Madam? Why the word *foolish*, aunt? What have I said now?"

"Nothing to any purpose, indeed," said she; "when thou dost, I'll write it down."—"Then, Madam," said he, "have your pen and ink always about you, when I am present; and put that down to begin with!" This made every one laugh. "What a happy thing is it," thought I, "that good nature generally accompanies this character; else, how would some people be supportable?"

But here I'll break off. 'Tis time, you'll say. But you know to whom I write, as well as to yourself, and they'll be pleased with all my silly scribble. So excuse one part for that, and another for friendship's sake, and then I shall be wholly excusable to you.

Now the trifler again resumes her pen. I am in some pain, Miss, for to-morrow, because of the rules we observe of late in our family on Sundays, and of going through a crowd to church; which will afford new scenes to our noble visitors, either for censure or otherwise: but I will sooner be censured for doing what I think my duty, than for the want of it; and so will omit nothing that we have been accustomed to do.

I hope I shall not be thought ridiculous, or as one who aims at works of supererogation, for what I think is very short of my duty. Some order, surely, becomes the heads of families; and besides, it would be discrediting one's own practice, if one did not appear at one time what one does at another. For that which is a reason for discontinuing a practice for some company, would seem to be a reason for laying it aside for ever, especially in a family visiting and visited as ours. And I remember well a hint given me by my dearest friend once on another subject, that it is in every one's power to prescribe rules to himself, after a while, and persons to see what is one's way, and that one is not to be put out of it. But my only doubt is, that to ladies, who have not been accustomed perhaps to the *necessary* strictness, I should make myself censurable, as if I aimed at too much perfection : for, however one's duty is one's duty, and ought not to be dispensed with; yet, when a person, who uses to be remiss, sees so hard a task before them, and so many great points to get over, all to be no more than tolerably regular, it is rather apt to frighten and discourage, than to allure; and one must proceed, as I have read soldiers do, in a difficult siege, inch by inch, and be more studious to entrench and fortify themselves, as they go on gaining upon the enemy, than by rushing all at once upon an attack of the place, be repulsed, and perhaps obliged with great loss to abandon a hopeful enterprise. And permit me to add, that young as I am, I have often observed, that over-great strictnesses all at once enjoined and insisted upon, are not fit for a beginning reformation, but for stronger Christians only; and therefore generally do more harm than good.

But shall I not be too grave, my dear friend?—Excuse me; for this is Saturday night : and as it was a very good method which the ingenious authors of the Spectator took, generally to treat their more serious subjects on this day; so I think one should, when one can, consider it as the preparative eve to a still better.

SUNDAY.

Now, my dear, by what I have already written, it is become in a manner necessary to acquaint you briefly with the method my dear Mr. B. not only permits, but encourages me to take, in the family he leaves to my care, as to the Sunday *duty*.

The worthy dean, at my request, and my beloved's permission, recommended to me, as a sort of family chaplain, for Sundays, a young gentleman of great sobriety and piety, and sound principles, who having but lately taken orders, has at present no other provision. And this gentleman comes, and reads prayers to us about seven in the morning, in the lesser hall, as we call it, a retired apartment, next the little garden; for we have no chapel with us here, as in your neighbourhood; and this generally, with some suitable exhortation, or meditation out of some good book, which he is so kind as to let me choose now-and-then, when I please, takes up little more than half an hour. We have a great number of servants of both sexes: and myself, Mrs. Jervis, and Polly Barlow, are generally in a little closet, which, when we open the door, is but just a separation from the hall.—Mr. Adams (for that is our young clergyman's name) has a desk at which sometimes Mr. Jonathan makes up his running accounts to Mr. Longman, who is very scrupulous of admitting any body to the use of his office, because of the writing in his custody, and the order he values himself upon having every thing in. About seven in the evening he comes again, and I generally, let me have what company I will, find time to retire for about another half hour; and my dear Mr. B. connives at, and excuses my absence, if enquired after; though for so short a time, I am seldom missed.

To the young gentleman I shall present, every quarter, five guineas, and Mr. B. presses him to accept of a place at his table at his pleasure: but, as we have generally much company, his modesty makes him decline it, especially at those times.—Mr. Longman joins with us very often in our Sunday office, and Mr. Colbrand seldom misses: and they tell Mrs. Jervis that they cannot express the pleasure they have to meet me there; and the edification they receive.

My best beloved dispenses as much as he can with the servants, for the evening part, if he has company; or will be attended only by John or Abraham, perhaps by turns; and sometimes looks upon his watch, and says, "'Tis near seven;" and if he says so, they take it for a hint that they may be dispensed with for half an hour; and this countenance which he gives me, has contributed not a little to make the matter easy and delightful to me, and to every one.—When I part from them, on the breaking up of our assembly, they generally make a little row on each side of the hall-door; and when I have made my compliments, and paid my thanks to Mr. Adams, they whisper, as I go out, "God bless you, Madam!" and bow and curtsey with such pleasure in their honest countenances as greatly delights me: and I say, "So my good friends—I am glad to see you—Not one absent!" or but one—(as it falls out)—"This is very obliging," I cry: and thus I shew them, that I take notice, if any body be not there. And back again I go to pay my duty to my earthly benefactor: and he is pleased to say sometimes, that I come to him with such a radiance in my countenance, as gives him double pleasure to behold me; and often tells me, that but for appearing too fond before company, he could meet me as I enter, with embraces as pure as my own heart.

I hope in time, I shall prevail upon the dear man to give me his company.—But, thank God, I am enabled to go thus far already!—I will leave the rest to his providence. For I have a point very delicate to touch upon in this particular; and I must take care not to lose the ground I have gained, by too precipitately pushing at too much at once. This is my comfort, that next to being uniform *himself*, is that permission and encouragement he gives *me* to be so, and his pleasure in seeing me so delighted—and besides, he always gives me his company to church. O how happy should I think myself, if he would be pleased to accompany me to the divine office, which yet he has not done, though I have urged him as much as I durst.— Mrs. Jervis asked me on Saturday evening, if I would be concerned to see a larger congregation in the lesser hall next morning than usual? I answered, "No, by no means." She said, Mrs. Worden, and Mrs. Lesley (the two ladies' women), and Mr. Sidney, my Lord Davers's gentleman, and Mr. H.'s servant, and the coachmen and footmen belonging to our noble visitors, who are, she says, all great admirers of our family management and good order, having been told our method, begged to join in it. I knew I should be a little dashed at so large a company; but the men being orderly for lords' servants, and Mrs. Jervis assuring me that they were very earnest in their request, I consented to it.

When, at the usual time, (with my Polly) I went down, I found Mr. Adams here (to whom I made my first compliments), and every one of our own people waiting for me, Mr. Colbrand excepted (whom Mr. H. had kept up late the night before), together with Mrs. Worden and Mrs. Lesley, and Mr. Sidney, with the servants of our guests, who, as also worthy Mr. Longman, and Mrs. Jervis, and Mr. Jonathan, paid me their respects: and I said, "This is early rising, Mrs. Lesley and Mrs. Worden; you are very kind to countenance us with your companies in this our family order. Mr. Sidney, I am glad to see you.—How do you do, Mr. Longman?" and looked round with complacency on the servants of our noble visitors. And then I led Mrs. Worden and Mrs. Lesley to my little retiring place, and Mrs. Jervis and my Polly followed; and throwing the door open, Mr. Adams began some select prayers; and as he reads with great emphasis and propriety, as if his heart was in what he read, all the good folks were exceedingly attentive.—After prayers, Mr. Adams reads a meditation, from a collection made

138

for private use, which I shall more particularly mention by-and-by; and ending with the usual benediction, I thanked the worthy gentleman, and gently chid him in Mr. B.'s name, for his modesty in declining our table; and thanking Mr. Longman, Mrs. Worden, and Mrs. Lesley, received their kind wishes, and hastened, blushing through their praises, to my chamber, where, being alone, I pursued the subject for an hour, till breakfast was ready, when I attended the ladies, and my best beloved, who had told them of the verses placed under my cushion at church. —We set out, my Lord and Lady Davers, and myself, and Mr. H. in our coach, and Mr. B. and the countess in the chariot; both ladies and the gentlemen splendidly dressed; but I avoided a glitter as much as I could, that I might not seem to vie with the two peeresses.—Mr. B. said, " Why are you not full-dressed, my dear? " I said, I hoped he would not be displeased : if he was, I would do as he commanded. He kindly answered, " As you like best, my love. You are charming in every dress."

The chariot first drawing up to the church door, Mr. B. led the countess into church. My Lord Davers did me that honour; and Mr. H. handed his aunt through a crowd of gazers, many of whom, as usual, were strangers. The neighbouring gentlemen and their ladies paid us their silent respects; but the thoughts of the wicked verses, or rather, as Lady Davers will have me say, wicked action of the transcriber of them, made me keep behind the pew; but my lady sat down by me, and whisperingly talked between whiles, to me, with great tenderness and freedom in her aspect; which I could not but take kindly, because I knew she intended by it, to shew every one she was pleased with me.

Afterwards she was pleased to add, taking my hand, and Mr. B. and the countess heard her (for she raised her voice to a more audible whisper), " I'm proud to be in thy company, and in this solemn place, I take thy hand, and acknowledge with pride, my *sister*." I looked down; and indeed, at church, I can hardly at any time look up; for who can bear to be gazed at so?—and softly said, " Oh ! my good lady ! how much you honour me; the place, and these surrounding eyes, can only hinder me from acknowledging as I ought."

My best friend, with pleasure in his eyes, said, pressing his hand upon both ours, as my lady had mine in hers—" You are two beloved creatures : both excellent in your way. God bless you both."—" And you too, my dear brother," said my lady.

The countess whispered, " You should spare a body a little ! You give one, ladies, and Mr. B., too much pleasure all at once.

Such company, and such behaviour adds still more charms to devotion; and were I to be here a twelvemonth, I would never miss once accompanying you to this good place."

Mr. H. thought he must say something, and addressing himself to his noble uncle, who could not keep his good-natured eye off me—" I'll be *hang'd*, my lord, if I know how to behave myself! Why this outdoes the chapel!—I'm glad I put on my new suit!" And then he looked upon himself, as if he would support, as well as he could, his part of the general admiration.

But think you not, my dear Miss Darnford, and my dearest father and mother, that I am now in the height of my happiness in this life, thus favoured by Lady Davers? The dean preached an excellent sermon; but I need not have said that; only to have mentioned, that *he* preached, was saying enough.

My lord led me out when divine service was over; and being a little tender in his feet, from a gouty notice, walked very slowly. Lady Towers and Mrs. Brooks joined us in the porch, and made us their compliments, as did Mr. Martin. " Will you favour us with your company home, my old acquaintance?" said Mr. B. to him.—" I can't, having a gentleman, my relation, to dine with me; but if it will be agreeable in the evening, I will bring him with me to taste of your Burgundy: for we have not any such in the county."—" I shall be glad to see you, or any friend of yours," replied Mr. B.

Mr. Martin whispered—" It is more, however, to admire your lady, I can tell you that, than your wine.—Get into your coaches, ladies," said he, with his usual freedom; " our maiden and widow ladies have a fine time of it, wherever you come: by my faith they must every one of them quit this neighbourhood, if you were to stay in it: but all their hopes are, that while you are in London, they'll have the game in their own hands."—" *Sister*," said Lady Davers, most kindly to me, in presence of many, who (in a respectful manner) gathered near us, " Mr. Martin is the same gentleman he used to be, I see."

" Mr. Martin, Madam," said I, smiling, " has but one fault: he is too apt to praise whom he favours, at the expense of his absent friends."

" I am always proud of your reproofs, Mrs. B.," replied he. —" Ay," said Lady Towers, " that I believe.—And, therefore, I wish, for all our sakes, you'd take him oftener to task, Mrs. B."

Lady Towers, Lady Arthur, Mrs. Brooks, and Mr. Martin, all claimed visits from us; and Mr. B. making excuses, that he must husband his time, being obliged to go to town soon, proposed to breakfast with Lady Towers the next morning, dine with Mrs. Arthur, and sup with Mrs. Brooks; and as there cannot be a more social and agreeable neighbourhood any where, his proposal, after some difficulty, was accepted; and our usual visiting neighbours were all to have notice accordingly, at each of the places.

I saw Sir Thomas Atkyns coming towards us, and fearing to be stifled with compliments, I said—" Your servant, ladies and gentlemen; and giving my hand to Lord Davers, stept into the chariot, instead of the coach; for people that would avoid bustle, sometimes make it. Finding my mistake, I would have come out, but my lord said, " Indeed you shan't : for I'll step in, and have you all to myself."

Lady Davers smiled—" Now," said she (while the coach drew up), " is my Lord Davers pleased ;—but I see, sister, you were tired with part of your company in the coach."—" 'Tis well contrived, my dear," said Mr. B., " as long as you have not deprived me of this honour; " taking the countess's hand, and leading her into the coach.

Will you excuse all this impertinence, my dear?—I know my father and mother will be pleased with it; and you will therefore bear with me; for their kind hearts will be delighted to hear every minute thing in relation to Lady Davers and myself.—When Mr. Martin came in the evening, with his friend (who is Sir William G., a polite young gentleman of Lincolnshire), he told us of the praises lavished away upon me by several genteel strangers; one saying to his friend, he had travelled twenty miles to see me.—My Lady Davers was praised too for her goodness to me, and the gracefulness of her person; the countess for the noble serenity of her aspect, and that charming ease and freedom, which distinguished her birth and quality. My dear Mr. B., he said, was greatly admired too : but he would not make *him* proud; for he had superiorities enough already, that was his word, over his neighbours : " But I can tell you," said he, " that for most of your praises you are obliged to your lady, and for having rewarded her excellence as you have done : for one gentleman," added he, " said, he knew no one but *you* could deserve her; and he believed *you* did, from that tenderness in your behaviour to her, and from that grandeur of air, and majesty of person, that seemed to shew you formed for her protector, as well as rewarder.—Get you gone to London, both of you," said he. " I did not intend to tell you, Mr. B., what was said of you."

The women of the two ladies had acquainted their ladyships with the order I observed for the day, and the devout behaviour of the servants. And about seven, I withdrawing as silently and as unobserved as I could, was surprised, as I was going through the great hall, to be joined by both.

"I shall come at all your secrets, Pamela," said my lady, "and be able, in time, to cut you out in your own way. I know whither you are going."

"My good ladies," said I, "pardon me for leaving you. I will attend you in half an hour."

"No, my dear," said Lady Davers, "the countess and I have resolved to attend you for that half hour, and we will return to company together."

"Is it not descending too much, my ladies, as to the company?"—"If it is for us, it is for you," said the countess; "so we will either act up to you, or make you come down to us; and we will judge of all your proceedings."

Every one, but Abraham (who attended the gentlemen), and all their ladyships' servants, and their two women, were there; which pleased me, however, because it shewed, that even the strangers, by this their second voluntary attendance, had no ill opinion of the service. But they were all startled, ours and theirs, to see the ladies accompanying me.

I stept up to Mr. Adams.—"I was in hopes, Sir," said I, "we should have been favoured with your company at our table." He bowed.—"Well, Sir," said I, "these ladies come to be obliged to you for your good offices; and you'll have no better way of letting them return their obligations, than to sup, though you would not dine with them."—"Mr. Longman," said my lady, "how do you do?—We are come to be witnesses of the family decorum."—"We have a blessed lady, Madam," said he : " and your ladyship's presence augments our joys."

I should have said, we were not at church in the afternoon; and when I do not go, we have the evening service read to us, as it is at church; which Mr. Adams performed now, with his usual distinctness and fervour.

When all was concluded, I said, "Now, my dearest ladies, excuse me for the sake of the delight I take in seeing all my good folks about me in this decent and obliging manner.—Indeed, I have no ostentation in it, if I know my own heart."

The countess and Lady Davers, delighted to see such good behaviour in every one, sat a moment or two looking upon one another in silence : and then my Lady Davers took my hand : "Beloved, deservedly beloved of the kindest of husbands, what a blessing art thou to this family!"—"And to every family," said the countess, "who have the happiness to know, and the grace to follow, her example!"—"But where," said Lady Davers, "collectedst thou all this good sense, and fine spirit in thy devotion?"—"The Bible," said I, "is the foundation of all."—Lady Davers then turning herself to Mrs. Jervis—"How do you, good woman?" said she. "Why you are now made ample amends for the love you bore to this dear creature formerly."

"You have an angel, and not a woman, for your lady, my good Mrs. Jervis," said the countess.

Mrs. Jervis, folding her uplifted hands together—"O my good lady, you know not our happiness; no, not one half of it. We were before blessed with plenty, and a bountiful indulgence, by our good master; but our plenty brought on wantonness and wranglings: but now we have peace as well as plenty; and peace of mind, my dear lady, in doing all in our respective powers, to shew ourselves thankful creatures to God, and to the best of masters and mistresses."

"Good soul!" said I, and was forced to put my handkerchief to my eyes: "your heart is always overflowing thus with gratitude and praises, for what you so well merit from us."

"Mr. Longman," said my lady, assuming a sprightly air, although her eye twinkled, to keep within its lids the precious water, that sprang from a noble and well-affected heart, "I am glad to see you here, attending your pious young lady.—Well might you love her, honest man!—I did not know there was so excellent a creature in any rank."

"Madam," said the other worthy heart, unable to speak but in broken sentences, "you don't know—indeed you don't, what a—what a—hap—happy—family we are!—Truly, we are like unto Alexander's soldiers, every one fit to be a general; so well do we all know our duties, and *practise* them too, let me say.—Nay, and please your ladyship, we all of us long till morning comes, thus to attend my lady; and after that is past, we long for evening, for the same purpose: for she is so good to us—You cannot think how good she is! But permit your honoured father's old servant to say one word more, that though we are always pleased and joyful on these occasions; yet we are in transports to see our master's noble sister thus favouring us—with your ladyship too," (to the countess)—"and approving our young lady's conduct and piety."

" Blessing on you all ! " said my lady. " Let us go, my lady ; —let us go, sister, for I cannot stop any longer ! "

As I slid by, following their ladyships—" How do you, Mr. Colbrand ? " said I softly : " I feared you were not well in the morning." He bowed—" Pardon me, Madam—I was leetel indispose, dat ish true ! "

Now, my dear friend, will you forgive me all this self-praise, as it may seem ?—Yet when you know I give it you, and my dear parents, as so many instances of my Lady Davers's reconciliation and goodness to me, and as it will shew what a noble heart she has at bottom, when her pride of quality and her passion have subsided, and her native good sense and excellence taken place, I flatter myself, I may be the rather excused ; and especially, as I hope to have your company and countenance one day, in this my delightful Sunday employment.

I should have added, for I think a good clergyman cannot be too much respected, that I repeated my request to Mr. Adams, to oblige us with his company at supper ; but he so very earnestly begged to be excused, and with so much concern of countenance, that I thought it would be wrong to insist upon it ; though I was sorry for it, sure as I am that modesty is always a sign of merit.

We returned to the gentlemen when supper was ready, as cheerful and easy, Lady Davers observed, as if we had not been present at so solemn a service. " And this," said she, after they were gone, " makes religion so pleasant and delightful a thing, that I profess I shall have a much higher opinion of those who make it a regular and constant part of their employment, than ever I had."

" Then," said she, " I was once, I remember, when a girl, at the house of a very devout man, for a week, with his granddaughter, my school-fellow ; and there were such preachments *against* vanities, and *for* self-denials, that were we to have followed the good man's precepts, (though indeed not his practice, for well did he love his belly), half God Almighty's creatures and works would have been useless, and industry would have been banished the earth.

" Then," added her ladyship, " have I heard the good man confess himself guilty of such sins, as, if true (and by his hiding his face with his broad-brimmed hat, it looked a little bad against him), he ought to have been hanged on a gallows fifty feet high."

These reflections, as I said, fell from my lady, after the gentlemen were gone, when she recounted to her brother, the entertainment, as she was pleased to call it, I had given her. On which she made high encomiums, as did the countess; and they praised also the natural dignity which they imputed to me, saying, I had taught them a way they never could have found out, to descend to the company of servants, and yet to secure, and even augment, the respect and veneration of inferiors at the same time. "And, Pamela," said my lady, "you are certainly very right to pay so much regard to the young clergyman; for that makes all he reads, and all he says, of greater efficacy with the auditors, facilitates the work you have in view to bring about, and in your own absence (for your monarch may not always dispense with you, perhaps) strengthens his influence, and encourages him, beside."

MONDAY.

I am to thank you, my dear Miss Darnford, for your kind letter, approving of my scribble. When you come to my Saturday's and Sunday's accounts, I shall try your patience. But no more of that; for as you can read them, or let them alone, I am the less concerned, especially as they will be more indulgently received somewhere else, than they may merit; so that my labour will not be wholly lost.

I congratulate you with all my heart on your dismissing Mr. Murray; I could not help shewing your letter to Mr. B. And what do you think the free gentleman said upon it? I am half afraid to tell you: but do, now you are so happily disengaged, get leave to come, and let us two contrive to be even with him for it. You are the only lady in the world that I would join with against him.

He said, that your characters of Mr. Murray and Miss Nancy, which he called severe (but I won't call them so, without your leave), looked a little like petty spite, and as if you were sorry the gentleman took you at your word. That was what he said —Pray let us punish him for it. Yet, he called you charming lady, and said much in your praise, and joined with me, that Mr. Murray, who was so easy to part with you, could not possibly deserve you.

"But, Pamela," said he, "I know the sex well enough. Miss Polly may not love Mr. Murray; yet, to see her sister addressed and complimented, and preferred to herself, by one whom she so lately thought she could choose or refuse, is a mortifying thing.—And young ladies cannot bear to sit by neglected, while two lovers are playing pug's tricks with each other.

145

"Then," said he, "all the preparations to matrimony, the clothes to be bought, the visits to be paid and received, the compliments of friends, the busy novelty of the thing, the day to be fixed, and all the little foolish humours and nonsense attending a concluded courtship, when *one sister* is to engross all the attention and regard, the new equipages, and so forth; these are all subjects of mortification to the *other*, though she has no great value for the man perhaps."

"Well, but, Sir," said I, "a lady of Miss Darnford's good sense, and good taste, is not to be affected by these parades, and has well considered the matter, no doubt; and I dare say, rejoices, rather than repines, at missing the gentleman."

I hope you will leave the happy pair (for they are so, if they think themselves so) together, and Sir Simon to rejoice in his accomplished son-in-law elect, and give us your company to London. For who would stay to be vexed by that ill-natured Miss Nancy, as you own you were, at your last writing?—But I will proceed, and the rather, as I have something to tell you of a conversation, the result of which has done me great honour, and given inexpressible delight; of which in its place.

We pursued Mr. B.'s proposal, returning several visits in one day; for we have so polite and agreeable a neighbourhood, that all seem desirous to accommodate each other.

We came not home till ten in the evening, and then found a letter from Sir Jacob Swynford, uncle by the half blood to Mr. B., acquainting him, that hearing his niece, Lady Davers, was with him, he would be here in a day or two (being then upon his journey) to pay a visit to both at the same time. This gentleman is very particularly odd and humoursome: and his eldest son being next heir to the maternal estate, if Mr. B. should have no children, was exceedingly dissatisfied with his debasing himself in marrying me; and would have been better pleased had he not married at all, perhaps.

There never was any cordial love between Mr. B.'s father and him, nor between the uncle, and nephew and niece: for his positiveness, roughness, and self-interestedness too, has made him, though very rich, but little agreeable to the generous tempers of his nephew and niece; yet when they meet, which is not above once in four or five years, they are very civil and obliging to him. Lady Davers wondered what could bring him hither now: for he lives in Herefordshire, and seldom stirs ten miles from home. Mr. B. said, he was sure it was not to compliment him and me on our nuptials. "No, rather," said my lady, "to satisfy himself if you are in a way to cut out his

146

own cubs."—"Thank God, we are," said he. "Whenever I was strongest set against matrimony, the only reason I had to weigh against my dislike to it was, that I was unwilling to leave so large a part of my estate to that family. My dear," said he to me, "don't be uneasy; but you'll see a relation of mine much more disagreeable than you can imagine; but no doubt you have heard his character."

"Ah, Pamela," said Lady Davers, "we are a family that value ourselves upon our ancestry; but, upon my word, Sir Jacob, and all his line, have nothing else to boast of. And I have been often ashamed of my relation to them."—"No family, I believe, my lady, has every body excellent in it," replied I: "but I doubt I shall stand but poorly with Sir Jacob."

"He won't dare to affront you, my dear," said Mr. B., "although he'll say to you, and to me, and to my sister too, blunt and rough things. But he'll not stay above a day or two, and we shall not see him again for some years to come; so we'll bear with him."

I am now, Miss, coming to the conversation I hinted at.

TUESDAY.

On Tuesday, Mr. Williams came to pay his respects to his kind patron. I had been to visit a widow gentlewoman, and, on my return, went directly to my closet, so knew not of his being here till I came to dinner; for Mr. B. and he were near two hours in discourse in the library. When I came down, Mr. B. presented him to me. "My friend Mr. Williams, my dear," said he. "Mr. Williams, how do you do?" said I; "I am glad to see you."

He rejoiced, he said, to see me look so well; and had longed for an opportunity to pay his respects to his worthy patron and me before: but had been prevented twice when upon the point of setting out. Mr. B. said, "I have prevailed upon my old acquaintance to reside with us, while he stays in these parts. Do you, my dear, see that every thing is made agreeable to him."—"To be sure, Sir, I will."

Mr. Adams being in the house, Mr. B. sent to desire he would dine with us: if it were but in respect to a gentleman of the same cloth, who gave us his company.

Mr. B., when dinner was over, and the servants were withdrawn, said, "My dear, Mr. Williams's business, in part, was to ask my advice as to a living that is offered him by the Earl of ——, who is greatly taken with his preaching and conversation."

"And to quit yours, I presume, Sir," said Lord Davers. "No, the earl's is not quite so good as mine, and his lordship would procure him a dispensation to hold both. What would *you* advise, my dear?"

"It becomes not me, Sir, to meddle with such matters as these."—"Yes, my dear, it does, when I ask your opinion."—"I beg pardon, Sir.—My opinion then is, that Mr. Williams will not care to do any thing that *requires* a dispensation, and which would be unlawful without it."—"Madam," said Mr. Williams, "you speak exceedingly well."

"I am glad, Mr. Williams, that you approve of my sentiments, required of me by one who has a right to command me in every thing: otherwise this matter is above my sphere; and I have so much good will to Mr. Williams, that I wish him every thing that will contribute to make him happy."

"Well, my dear," said Mr. B., "but what would you advise in this case? The earl proposes, that Mr. Williams's present living be supplied by a curate; to whom, no doubt, Mr. Williams will be very genteel; and, as we are seldom or never there, his lordship thinks we shall not be displeased with it, and insists upon proposing it to me; as he has done."

Lord Davers said, "I think this may do very well, brother. But what, pray, Mr. Williams, do you propose to allow to your curate? Excuse me, Sir, but I think the clergy do so hardly by one another generally, that they are not to be surprised that some of the laity treat them as they do."

Said Mr. B., "Tell us freely, Pamela, what you would advise your friend Mr. Williams to do."

"And must I, Sir, speak my mind on such a point, before so many better judges?"

"Yes, *sister*," said her ladyship (a name she is now pleased to give me freely before strangers, after her dear brother's example, who is kindest, though always kind, at such times) "you *must*; if I may be allowed to say *must*."—"Why then," proceeded I, "I beg leave to ask Mr. Williams one question; that is, whether his present parishioners do not respect and esteem him in that particular manner, which I think every body must, who knows his worth?"

"I am very happy, Madam, in the good-will of all my parishioners, and have great acknowledgments to make for their civilities to me."—"I don't doubt," said I, "but it will be the same wherever you go; for bad as the world is, a prudent and good clergyman will never fail of respect. But, Sir, if you think your ministry among them is attended with good effects;

if they esteem your person with a preference, and listen to your doctrines with attention; methinks, for *their* sakes, 'tis pity to leave them, were the living of less value, as it is of *more*, than the other. For, how many people are there who can benefit by one gentleman's preaching, rather than by another's; although, possibly, the one's abilities may be no way inferior to the other's? There is much in a *delivery*, as it is called, in a manner, a deportment, to engage people's attention and liking; and as you are already in possession of their esteem, you are sure to do much of the good you aim and wish to do. For where the flock loves the shepherd, all the work is easy, and more than half done; and without that, let him have the tongue of an angel, and let him live the life of a saint, he will be heard with indifference, and, oftentimes, as his subject may be, with disgust."

I paused here; but every one being silent—" As to the earl's friendship, Sir," continued I, " you can best judge what force that ought to have upon you; and what I have mentioned would be the only difficulty with me, were I in Mr. Williams's case. To be sure, it will be a high compliment to his lordship, and so he ought to think it, that you quit a better living to oblige him. And he will be bound in honour to make it up to you. For I am far from thinking that a prudent regard to worldly interest misbecomes the character of a good clergyman; and I wish all such were set above the world, for their own sakes, as well as for the sakes of their hearers; since independency gives a man respect, besides the power of doing good, which will enhance that respect, and of consequence, give greater efficacy to his doctrines.

" As to strengthening of a good man's influence, a point always to be wished, I would not say so much as I have done, if I had not heard Mr. Longman say, and I heard it with great pleasure, that the benefice Mr. Williams so worthily enjoys is a clear two hundred pounds a year.

" But, after all, does happiness to a gentleman, a scholar, a philosopher, rest in a greater or lesser income? On the contrary, is it not oftener to be found in a happy competency or mediocrity? Suppose my dear Mr. B. had five thousand pounds a year added to his present large income, would that increase his happiness? That it would add to his cares, is no question; but could it give him one single comfort which he has not already? And if the dear gentleman had two of three thousand less, might he be less happy on that account? No, surely; for it would render a greater prudence on my humble part necessary.

and a nearer inspection, and greater frugality, on his own; and he must be contented (if he did not, as now, perhaps, lay up every year) so long as he lived within his income.—And who will say, that the obligation to greater prudence and economy is a misfortune?

"The competency, therefore, the golden mean, is the thing; and I have often considered the matter, and endeavoured to square my actions by the result of that consideration. For a person who, being not born to an estate, is not satisfied with a competency, will probably know no limits to his desires. One whom an acquisition of one or two hundred pounds a year will not satisfy, will hardly sit down contented with any sum. For although he may propose to himself at a distance, that such and such an acquisition will be the height of his ambition; yet he will, as he approaches to that, advance upon himself farther and farther, and know no bound, till the natural one is forced upon him, and his life and his views end together.

"Now let me humbly beg pardon of you all, ladies and gentlemen," turning my eyes to each; "but most of you, my good lady."

"Indeed, Madam," said Mr. Williams, "after what I have heard from you, I would not, for the world, have been of another mind."

"You are a good man," said I; "and I have such an opinion of your worthiness, and the credit you do your function, that I can never suspect either your judgment or your conduct. But pray, Sir, may I ask, what have you determined to do?"—"Why, Madam," replied he, "I am staggered in that too, by the observation you just now made, that where a man has the love of his parishioners, he ought not to think of leaving them."—"Else, Sir, I find you was rather inclined to oblige the earl, though the living be of *less* value! This is very noble, Sir; it is more than generous."

"My dear," said Mr. B., "I'll tell you (for Mr. Williams's modesty will not let him speak it before all the company) what *is* his motive; and a worthy one you'll say it is. Excuse me, Mr. Williams;"—for the reverend gentleman blushed.

"The earl has of late years—we all know his character—given himself up to carousing, and he will suffer no man to go from his table sober. Mr. Williams has taken the liberty to expostulate, as became his function, with his lordship on this subject, and upon some other irregularities, so agreeably, that the earl has taken a great liking to him, and promises, that he will suffer his reasonings to have an effect upon him, and that he shall reform his whole household, if he will come and live near him, and regulate his table by his own example. The countess is a very good lady, and privately presses Mr. Williams to oblige the earl : and this is our worthy friend's main inducement ; with the hope, which I should mention, that he has, of preserving untainted the morals of the two young gentlemen, the earl's son, who, he fears, will be carried away by the force of such an example : and he thinks, as the earl's living has fallen, mine may be better supplied than the earl's, if he, as he kindly offers, gives it me back again ; otherwise the earl, as he apprehends, will find out for his, some gentleman, if such an one can be found, as will rather further, than obstruct his own irregularities, as was the unhappy case of the last incumbent."

"Well," said Lady Davers, "I shall always have the highest respect for Mr. Williams, for a conduct so genteel and so prudent. But, brother, will you—and will you, Mr. Williams—put this whole affair into Mrs. B.'s hands, since you have such testimonies, *both* of you, of the rectitude of her thinking and acting ? " —" With all my heart, Madam," replied Mr. Williams ; "and I shall be proud of such a direction."—" What say *you*, brother ? You are to suppose the living in your own hands again ; will you leave the whole matter to my *sister* here ? "—" Come, my dear," said Mr. B., " let us hear how you'd wish it to be ordered. I know you have not need of one moment's consideration, when once you are mistress of a point."

"Nay," said Lady Davers, "that is not the thing. I repeat my demand : shall it be as Mrs. B. lays it out, or not ? "— "Conditionally," said Mr. B., "provided I cannot give satisfactory reasons, why I *ought* not to conform to her opinion ; for this, as I said, is a point of conscience with me ; and I made it so, when I presented Mr. Williams to the living : and have not been deceived in that presentation."—" To be sure," said I, " that is very reasonable, Sir ; and on that condition, I shall the less hesitate to speak my mind, because I shall be in no danger to commit an irreparable error."

"I know well, Lady Davers," added Mr. B., "the power your sex have over ours, and their subtle tricks : and so will never, in my weakest moments, be drawn in to make a blindfold promise. There have been several instances, both in sacred and profane story, of mischiefs done by such surprises : so you must allow me to suspect myself, when I know the dear slut's power over me, and have been taught, by the inviolable regard she pays to her own word, to value mine—And now, Pamela, speak all that is in your heart to say."

"With your *requisite* condition in my eye, I will, Sir. But let me see that I state the matter right. And, preparative to it, pray, Mr. Williams, though you have not been long in possession of this living, yet, may-be, you can compute what it is likely, by what you know of it, to bring in clear?"

"Madam," said he, "by the best calculation I can make—I thank *you* for it, good Sir—it may, one year with another, be reckoned at three hundred pounds per annum; and is the best within twenty miles of it, having been improved within these two last years."

"If it was five hundred pounds, and would make you happier—(for *that*, Sir, is the thing) I should wish it you," said I, "and think it short of your merits. But pray, Sir, what is the earl's living valued at?"

"At about two hundred and twenty pounds, Madam."—"Well, then," replied I, very pertly, "I believe now I have it.

"Mr. Williams, for motives most excellently worthy of his function, inclines to surrender up to Mr. B. his living of three hundred pounds per annum, and to accept of the earl's living of two hundred and twenty. Dear Sir, I am going to be very bold; but under *your* condition nevertheless :—let the gentleman, to whom you shall present the living of E. allow eighty pounds per annum out of it to Mr. Williams, till the earl's favour shall make up the difference to him, and no longer. And—but I dare not name the gentleman :—for how, dear Sir, were I to be so bold, shall I part with my chaplain?"—"Admirable! most admirable!" said Lord and Lady Davers, in the same words. The countess praised the decision too; and Mr. H. with his "Let me be hang'd," and his "Fore Gad's," and such exclamations natural to him, made his plaudits. Mr. Williams said, he could wish with all his heart it might be so; and Mr. Adams was so abashed and surprised, that he could not hold up his head;—but joy danced in his silent countenance, for all that.

Mr. B. having hesitated a few minutes, Lady Davers called out for his objection, or consent, according to condition, and he said, "I cannot so soon determine as that prompt slut did. I'll withdraw one minute."

He did so, as I found afterwards to advise, like the considerate and genteel spirit he possesses, with Mr. Williams, whom he beckoned out, and to examine whether he was in *earnest* willing to give it up, or very desirous for any one to succeed him; saying, that if he had, he thought himself obliged, in return for his worthy behaviour to him, to pay a particular regard to his recommendation. And so being answered as he desired, in they came together again.

But I should say, that his withdrawing with a very serious aspect, made me afraid I had gone too far : and I said, " What shall I do, if I have incurred Mr. B.'s anger by my over-forwardness ! Did he not look displeased ? Dear ladies, if he be so, plead for me, and I'll withdraw when he comes in; for I cannot stand his anger : I have not been used to it."

" Never fear, Pamela," said my lady; " he can't be angry at any thing you say or do. But I wish, for the sake of what I have witnessed of Mr. Adams's behaviour and modesty, that such a thing could be done for him." Mr. Adams bowed, and said, " O my good ladies ! 'tis too considerable a thing : I cannot expect it—I do not—it would be presumption if I did."

Just then re-entered Mr. B. and Mr. Williams : the first with a stately air, the other with a more peace-portending smile on his countenance.

But Mr. B. sitting down, " Well, Pamela," said he, very gravely, " I see that power is a dangerous thing in any hand."— " Sir, Sir ! " said I—" My dear lady," whispering to Lady Davers, " I will withdraw, as I said I would." And I was getting away as fast as I could : but he arose and took my hand, " Why is my charmer so soon frightened ? " said he, most kindly; and still more kindly, with a noble air, pressed it to his lips. " I must not carry my jest too far upon a mind so apprehensive, as I otherwise might be inclined to do." And leading me to Mr. Adams and Mr. Williams, he said, taking Mr. Williams's hand with his left, as he held mine in his right, " Your worthy brother clergyman, Mr. Adams, gives me leave to confirm the decision of my dear wife, whom you are to thank for the living of E. upon the condition she proposed; and may you give but as much satisfaction *there*, as you have done in *this* family, and as Mr. Williams has given to his flock; and they will then be pleased as much with your ministry as they have hitherto been with his."

Mr. Adams trembled with joy, and said, he could not tell how to bear this excess of goodness in us both : and his countenance and eyes gave testimony of a gratitude too high for further expression.

As for myself, you, my honoured and dear friends, who know how much I am always raised, when I am made the dispenser of acts of bounty and generosity to the deserving; and who now instead of incurring blame, as I had apprehended, found myself applauded by every one, and most by the gentleman whose approbation I chiefly coveted to have : you, I say, will judge how greatly I must be delighted.

But I was still more affected, when Mr. B. directing himself to me, and to Mr. Williams at the same time, was pleased to say, " Here, my dear, you must thank this good gentleman for enabling you to give such a shining proof of your excellence : and whenever I put power into your hands for the future, act but as you have now done, and it will be impossible that I should have any choice or will but yours."

" O Sir," said I, pressing his hand with my lips, forgetting how many witnesses I had of my grateful fondness, " how shall I, oppressed with your goodness, in such a signal instance as this, find words equal to the gratitude of my heart !—But here," patting my bosom, " just here, they stick ;—and I cannot—"

And, indeed, I could say no more ; and Mr. B. in the delicacy of his apprehensiveness for me, led me into the next parlour ; and placing himself by me on the settee, said, " Take care, my best beloved, that the joy, which overflows your dear heart, for having done a beneficent action to a deserving gentleman, does not affect you too much."

My Lady Davers followed us : " Where is my angelic sister ? " said she. " I have a share in her next to yourself, my noble brother." And clasping me to her generous bosom, she ran over with expressions of favour to me, in a style and words, which would suffer, were I to endeavour to repeat them.

Coffee being ready, we returned to the company. My Lord Davers was pleased to make me a great many compliments, and so did Mr. H. after his manner. But the countess exceeded *herself* in goodness.

Mr. B. was pleased to say, " It is a rule with me, not to leave till to-morrow what can be done to-day :—and *when*, my dear, do you propose to dispense with Mr. Adams's good offices in your family ? Or did you intend to induce him to go to town with us ? "

" I had not proposed anything, Sir, as to that, for I had not asked your kind direction : but the good dean will supply us, I doubt not, and when we set out for London, Mr. Adams will be at full liberty, with his worthy friend, Mr. Williams, to pursue the happy scheme your goodness has permitted to take effect."

" Mr. Adams, my dear, who came so lately from the university, can, perhaps, recommend such another young gentleman as himself, to perform the functions he used to perform in your family."

I looked, it seems, a little grave; and Mr. B. said, "What have you to offer, Pamela?—What have I said amiss?"

"Amiss! dear Sir!—"

"Ay, and dear Madam too! I see by your bashful seriousness, in place of that smiling approbation which you always shew when I utter any thing you *entirely* approve, that I have said something which would rather meet with your acquiescence, than choice. So, as I have often told you, none of your reserves; and never *hesitate* to me your consent in any thing, while you are sure I will conform to your wishes, or pursue my own liking, as *either* shall appear reasonable to me, when I have heard *your* reasons."

"Why, then, dear Sir, what I had presumed to think, but I submit it to your better judgment, was, whether, since the gentleman who is so kind as to assist us in our family devotions, in some measure acts in the province of the worthy dean, it were not right, that our own parish-minister, whether here or in London, should name, or at least approve *our* naming, the gentleman?"

"Why could not I have thought of that, as well as you, sauce-box?—Lady Davers, I am entirely on your side: I think she deserves a slap now from us both."

"I'll forgive her," said my lady, "since I find her sentiments and actions as much a reproof to others as to me."

"Mr. Williams, did you ever think," said Mr. B., "it would have come to this?—Did you ever know such a saucy girl in your life?—Already to give herself these reproaching airs?"— "No, never, if your honour is pleased to call the most excellent lady in the world by such a name, nor any body else."

"Pamela, I charge you," said the dear gentleman, "if you *study* for it, be sometimes in the wrong, that one may not always be taking lessons from such an assurance; but in our turns, have something to teach *you*."

"Then, dear Sir," said I, "must I not be a strange creature? For how, when you, and my good ladies, are continually giving me such charming examples, can I do a wrong thing?"

I hope you will forgive me, my dear, for being so tedious on the foregoing subject, and its most agreeable conclusion. It is an important one, because several persons, as conferers or receivers, have found their pleasure and account in it; and it would be well, if conversation were often attended with like happy consequences. I have one merit to plead in behalf even of my prolixity; that in reciting the delightful conferences I have the pleasure of holding with our noble guests and Mr. B., I am careful not to write twice upon one topic, although several which I omit, may be more worthy of your notice than those I give; so that you have as much variety from me, as the nature of the facts and cases will admit of.

But here I will conclude, having a very different subject, as a proof of what I have advanced, to touch in my next. Till when, I am *your most affectionate and faithful,*

P. B.

LETTER XXXIII

My dear Miss Darnford,

I now proceed with my journal, which I brought down to Tuesday evening; and of course I begin with

WEDNESDAY.

Towards evening came Sir Jacob Swynford, on horseback, attended by two servants in liveries. I was abroad; for I had got leave for a whole afternoon, attended by my Polly; which time I passed in visiting no less than four poor sick families, whose hearts I made glad. But I should be too tedious, were I to give you the particulars; besides, I have a brief list of cases, which, when you'll favour me with your company, I may shew you: for I oblige myself, though not desired, to keep an account of what I do with no less than two hundred pounds a year, that Mr. B. allows me to expend in acts of charity and benevolence.

Lady Davers told me afterwards, that Sir Jacob carried it mighty stiff and formal when he alighted. He strutted about the court-yard in his boots, with his whip in his hand; and though her ladyship went to the great door, in order to welcome him, he turned short, and, whistling, followed the groom into the stable, as if he had been at an inn, only, instead of taking off his hat, pulling its broad brim over his eyes, for a compliment. In she went in a pet, as she says, saying to the countess, " A surly brute he always was ! *My* uncle ! He's more of an ostler than a gentleman; I'm resolved I'll not stir to meet him again. And yet the wretch loves respect from others, though he never practises common civility himself."

The countess said, she was glad he was come, for she loved to divert herself with such odd characters now-and-then.

And now let me give you a short description of him as I found him, when I came in, that you may the better conceive what sort of a gentleman he is.

He is about sixty-five years of age, a coarse, strong, big-boned man, with large irregular features; he has a haughty supercilious look, a swaggering gait, and a person not at all bespeaking one's favour in behalf of his mind; and his mind, as you shall hear by and bye, not clearing up those prepossessions in his disfavour, with which his person and features at first strike one. His voice is big and surly; his eyes little and fiery; his mouth large, with yellow and blackish teeth, what are left of them being broken off to a tolerable regular height, looked as if they were ground down to his gums, by constant use. But with all these imperfections, he has an air that sets him somewhat above the mere vulgar, and makes one think half his disadvantages rather owing to his own haughty humour, than to nature; for he seems to be a perfect tyrant at first sight, a man used to prescribe, and not to be prescribed to; and has the advantage of a shrewd penetrating look, but which seems rather acquired than natural.

After he had seen his horses well served, and put on an old-fashioned gold-buttoned coat, which by its freshness shewed he had been very chary of it, a better wig, but in stiff buckle, and a long sword, stuck stiffly, as if through his coat lappets, in he came, and with an imperious air entering the parlour, " What, nobody come to meet me ! " said he; and saluting her ladyship. " How do you do, niece? " and looked about haughtily, she says, as if he expected to see me. My lady presenting the countess, said, " The Countess of C., Sir Jacob ! "—" Your most obedient humble servant, Madam. I hope his lordship is well."—" At your service, Sir Jacob."

" I wish he was," said he, bluntly; " he should not have voted as he did last sessions, I can tell you that."

" Why, Sir Jacob," said she, " *servants*, in this free kingdom, don't always do as their *masters* would have 'em."—" *Mine* do, I can tell you that, Madam."

" Right or wrong, Sir Jacob? "—" It can't be wrong if I command them."—" Why, truly, Sir Jacob, there's many a private gentleman carries it higher to a servant, than he cares his *prince* should to him; but I thought, till now, it was the king only that could do no wrong."

" But I always take care to be right."—" A good reason—because, I dare say, you never think you *can* be in the wrong."— " Your ladyship should spare me : I'm but just come off a journey. Let me turn myself about, and I'll be up with you, never fear, Madam.—But where's my nephew, Lady Davers? And where's your lord? I was told you were all here, and young

H. too upon a very extraordinary occasion; so I was willing to see how causes went among you. It will be long enough before you come to see me."—" My brother, and Lord Davers, and Mr. H. have all rode out."—" Well, niece," strutting with his hands behind him, and his head held up—" Ha !—He has made a fine kettle on't—han't he ?—that ever such a rake should be so caught ! They tell me, she's plaguy cunning, and quite smart and handsome. But I wish his father were living. Yet what could he have done ? Your brother was always unmanageable. I wish he'd been my son; by my faith, I do ! What ! I hope, niece, he locks up his baby, while you're here ? You don't keep her company, do you ? "

" Yes, Sir Jacob, I do : and you'll do so too, when you see her."—" Why, thou countenancest him in his folly, child : I'd a better opinion of thy spirit ! Thou married to a lord, and thy brother to a —— Can'st tell me what, Barbara ? If thou can'st, pr'ythee do."—" To an angel; and so you'll say presently."

" What, dost think I shall look through *his* foolish eyes? What a disgrace to a family ancienter than the Conquest ! *O Tempora ! O Mores !* What will this world come to ? " The countess was diverted with this odd gentleman, but ran on in my praise, for fear he should say some rude things to me when I came in; and Lady Davers seconded her. But all signified nothing. He would tell us both his mind, let the young whelp (that was his word) take it as he would—" And pray," said he, " can't I see this fine body before he comes in? Let me but turn her round two or three times, and ask her a question or two; and by her answer I shall know what to think of her in a twinkling."—" She is gone to take a little airing, Sir Jacob, and won't be back till supper-time."

" Supper-time ! Why, she is not to sit at table, is she ? If she does, I won't; that's positive. But now you talk of a supper, what have you ?—I must have a boiled chicken, and shall eat it all myself. Who's housekeeper now ? I suppose all's turned upside down."

" No, there is not one new servant, except a girl that waits upon her own person : all the old ones remain."—" That's much ! These creatures generally take as great state upon them as a born lady; and they're in the right. If they can make the man stoop to the great point, they'll hold his nose to the grindstone : and all the little ones come about in course."—" Well, Sir Jacob, when you see her, you'll alter your mind."—" Never, never; that's positive."

"Ay, Sir Jacob, I was as positive as you once; but I love her now as well as if she were my own sister."

"O hideous, hideous! All the fools he has made wherever he has travelled, will clap their hands at him, and at you too, if you talk at this rate. But let me speak to Mrs. Jervis, if she be here: I'll order my own supper."

So he went out, saying, he knew the house, though in a better mistress's days. The countess said, if Mr. B. as she hoped, kept his temper, there would be good diversion with the old gentleman. "O yes," said my lady, "my brother will, I dare say. He despises the surly brute too much to be angry with him, say what he will." He talked a great deal against me to Mrs. Jervis. You may guess, my dear, that she launched out in my praises; and he was offended at her, and said, "Woman! woman! forbear these ill-timed praises; her birth's a disgrace to our family. What! my sister's waiting-maid, taken upon charity! I cannot bear it." I mention all these things, as I afterwards heard them, because it shall prepare you to judge what a fine time I was likely to have of it. When Mr. B. and my Lord Davers, and Mr. H. came home, which they did about half an hour after six, they were told who was there, just as they entered the parlour; and Mr. B. smiled at Lord Davers, and entering, "Sir Jacob," said he, "welcome to Bedfordshire; and thrice welcome to this house; I rejoice to see you."

My lady says, never was so odd a figure as the old baronet made, when thus accosted. He stood up indeed; but as Mr. B. offered to take his hand, he put 'em both behind him. "Not that you know of, Sir!" And then looking up at his face, and down at his feet, three or four times successively, "Are you my brother's son? That very individual son, that your good father used to boast of, and say, that for handsome person, true courage, noble mind, was not to be matched in any three counties in England?"

"The very same, dear Sir, that my honoured father's partiality used to think he never praised enough."

"And what is all of it come to at last?—He paid well, did he not, to teach you to know the world, nephew! hadst thou been born a fool, or a raw greenhead, or a doating greyhead—"—"What then, Sir Jacob?"—"Why then thou wouldst have done just as thou hast done!"—"Come, come, Sir Jacob, you know not my inducement. You know not what an angel I have in person and mind. Your eyes shall by and bye be blest with the sight of her: your ears with hearing her speak: and then you'll call all you have said, profanation."—"What is it I hear? You talk in the language of romance; and from the housekeeper to the head of the house, you're all stark staring mad. Nephew, I wish, for thy own credit, thou wert—But what signifies wishing?—I hope you'll not bring your syren into my company."

"Yes, I will, Sir, because I love to give you pleasure. And say not a word more, for your own sake, till you see her. You'll have the less to unsay, Sir Jacob, and the less to repent of."

"I'm in an enchanted castle, that's certain. What a plague has this little witch done to you all? And how did she bring it about?"

The ladies and Lord Davers laughed, it seems; and Mr. B. begging him to sit down, and answer him some family questions, he said, (for it seems he is very captious at times), "What, am I to be laughed at!—Lord Davers, I hope *you're* not bewitched, too, are you?"—"Indeed, Sir Jacob, I am. My sister B. is my doating-piece."

"Whew!" whistled he, with a wild stare: "and how is it with you, youngster?"—"With me, Sir Jacob?" said Mr. H., "I'd give all I'm worth in the world, and ever shall be worth, for such another wife." He ran to the window, and throwing up the sash looking into the court-yard, said, "Hollo—So-ho! Groom—Jack—Jonas—Get me my horse!—I'll keep no such company!—I'll be gone! Why, Jonas!" calling again.

"You're not in earnest, Sir Jacob," said Mr. B.

"I am!—I'll away to the village this night! Why you're all upon the high game! I'll—But who comes here?"—For just then, the chariot brought me into the court-yard—"Who's this? who is she?"—"One of *my* daughters," started up the countess; "my youngest daughter Jenny!—She's the pride of my family, Sir Jacob!"—"I was running; for I thought it was the grand enchantress." Out steps Lady Davers to me; "Dear Pamela," said she, "humour all that's said to you. Here's Sir Jacob come. You're the Countess of C.'s youngest daughter Jenny—That's your cue."—"Ah? but, Madam," said I, "Lady Jenny is not married," looking (before I thought) on a circumstance that I think too much of sometimes, though I carry it off as well as I can. She laughed at my exception: "Come, Lady Jenny," said she, (for I just entered the great door), "I hope you've had a fine airing."—"A very pretty one, Madam," said I, as I entered the parlour. "This is a pleasant country, Lady Davers." (" *Wink when I'm wrong,*" *whispered I*), "Where's Mrs. B.?" Then, as seeing a strange gentleman, I started half back, into a more reserved air; and made him a low curt'sy. Sir Jacob looked as if he did not know what to think of it, now at me, now at Mr. B. who put him quite out of doubt, by taking my hand: "Well, Lady Jenny, did you meet my fugitive in your tour?"

"No, Mr. B. Did she go my way? I told you I would keep the great road."—"Lady Jenny C.," said Mr. B., presenting me to his uncle. "A charming creature!" added he: "Have you not a son worthy of such an alliance?"—"Ay, nephew, this is a lady indeed! Why the plague," whispered he, "could you not have pitched your tent here? Miss, by your leave," and saluting me, turned to the countess. "Madam, you've a charming daughter! Had my rash nephew seen this lovely creature, and you condescended, he'd never have stooped to the cottage as he has done."—"You're right, Sir Jacob," said Mr. B.; "but I always ran too fast for my fortune: yet these ladies of family never bring out their jewels into bachelors' company; and when, too late, we see what we've missed, we are vexed at our precipitation."

"Well said, however, boy. I wish thee repentance, though 'tis out of thy power to mend. Be that one of thy curses, when thou seest this lady; as no doubt it is." Again surveying me from head to foot, and turning me round, which, it seems, is a mighty practice with him to a stranger lady, (and a modest one too, you'll say, Miss)—"Why, truly, you're a charming creature, Miss—Lady Jenny I would say—By your leave, once more !—My Lady Countess, she is a charmer! But—but—" staring at me, "Are you married, Madam?" I looked a little silly; and my new mamma came up to me, and took my hand: "Why, Jenny, you are dressed oddly to-day !—What a hoop you wear; it makes you look I can't tell how!"

"Madam, I thought so; what signifies lying?—But 'tis only the hoop, I see—Really, Lady Jenny, your hoop is enough to make half a hundred of our sex despair, lest you should be married. I thought it was something! Few ladies escape my notice. I always kept a good look-out; for I have two daughters of my own. But 'tis the hoop, I see plainly enough. You are so slender every where but *here*," putting his hand upon my hip which quite dashed me; and I retired behind my Lady Countess's chair.

"Fie, Sir Jacob!" said Mr. B.; "before us young gentlemen, to take such liberties with a maiden lady! You give a bad example."—"Hang him that sets you a bad example, nephew. But I see you're right; I see Lady Jenny's a maiden lady, or she would not have been so shamefaced. I'll swear for her on occasion. Ha, ha, ha!—I'm sure," repeated he, "she's a maiden—For our sex give the married ladies a freer air in a trice."—"How, Sir Jacob!" said Lady Davers.

"O fie!" said the countess. "Can't you praise the maiden ladies, but at the expense of the married ones! What do you see of freedom in me?"—"Or in me?" said Lady Davers. "Nay, for that matter you are very well, I must needs say. But will you pretend to blush with that virgin rose?—Od's my life, Miss—Lady Jenny I would say, come from behind your mamma's chair, and you two ladies stand up now together. There, so you do—Why now, blush for blush, and Lady Jenny shall be three to one, and a deeper crimson by half. Look you there else! An hundred guineas to one against the field." Then stamping with one foot, and lifting up his hands and eyes "Lady Jenny has it all to nothing—Ha, ha, ha! You may well sit down both of you; but you're a blush too late, I can tell you that. Well hast thou done, Lady Jenny," tapping my shoulder with his rough paw.

I was hastening away, and he said, "But let's see you again, Miss; for now will I stay, if they bring nobody else." And away I went; for I was quite out of countenance, "What a strange creature," thought I, "is this!" Supper being near ready, he called out for Lady Jenny, for the sight of her, he said, did him good; but he was resolved not to sit down to table with *somebody else.* The countess said, she would fetch her daughter; and stepping out, returned saying, "Mrs. B. understands that Sir Jacob is here, and does not choose to see her; so she begs to be excused; and my Jenny and she desire to sup together."

"The very worst tidings I have heard this twelvemonth. Why, nephew, let your girl sup with any body, so we may have Lady Jenny back with us."—"I know," said the countess, (who was desirous to see how far he could carry it), "Jenny won't leave Mrs. B.; so if you see *one,* you must see *t'other.*"—"Nay, then I must sit down contented. Yet I should be glad to see Lady Jenny. But I will not sit at table with Mr. B.'s girl—that's positive."

"Well, well, let 'em sup together, and there's an end of it," said Mr. B. "I see my uncle has as good a judgment as any body of fine ladies."—("*That I have, nephew.*")—"But he can't forgo his humour, in compliment to the finest lady in England."

"Consider, nephew, 'tis not thy doing a foolish thing, and calling a girl wife, shall cram a niece down my throat, that's positive. The moment she comes down to take place of these ladies, I am gone, that's most certain."—"Well then, shall I go up, and oblige Pamela to sup by herself, and persuade Lady Jenny to come down to us?"—"With all my soul, nephew,—a good notion.—But, Pamela—did you say?—A *queer* sort of name! I have heard of it somewhere!—Is it a Christian or a Pagan name?—Linsey-woolsey—half one, half t'other—like thy girl—Ha, ha, ha."—"Let me be *hang'd*," whispered Mr. H. to his aunt, "if Sir Jacob has not a power of wit; though he is so whimsical with it. I like him much."—"But hark ye, nephew," said Sir Jacob, "one word with you. Don't fob upon us your girl with the Pagan name for Lady Jenny. I have set a mark upon her, and should know her from a thousand, although she had changed her hoop." Then he laughed again, and said, he hoped Lady Jenny would come—and without any body with her—"But I smell a plot," said he—"By my soul I won't stay, if they both come together. I won't be put upon—But here is one or both—Where's my whip?—I'll go."—"Indeed, Mr. B., I had rather have staid with Mrs. B.," said I, as I entered, as he had bid me.

"'Tis she! 'tis she! You've nobody behind you!—No, she han't—Why now, nephew, you are right; I was afraid you'd have put a trick upon me.—You'd *rather*," repeated he to me, "have staid with Mrs. B.!—Yes, I warrant—But you shall be placed in better company, my dear child."—"Sister," said Mr. B., "will you take that chair; for Pamela does not choose to give my uncle disgust, who so seldom comes to see us." My lady took the upper end of the table, and I sat next below my new mamma. "So, Jenny," said she, "how have you left Mrs. B.?"—"A little concerned; but she was the easier, as Mr. B. himself desired I'd come down."

My Lord Davers sat next me, and Sir Jacob said, "Shall I beg a favour of you, my lord, to let me sit next to Lady Jenny?" Mr. B. said, "Won't it be better to sit over-against her, uncle?"—"Ay, that's right. I' faith, nephew, thou know'st what's right. Well, so I will." He accordingly removed his seat, and I was very glad of it; for though I was sure to be stared at by him, yet I feared if he sat next me, he would not keep his hands off my hoop.

He ran on a deal in my praises, after his manner, but so rough at times, that he gave me pain; and I was afraid too, lest he should observe my ring; but he stared so much in my face, that it escaped his notice. After supper, the gentlemen sat down to their bottle, and the ladies and I withdrew, and about twelve they broke up; Sir Jacob talking of nothing but Lady Jenny, and wished Mr. B. had happily married such a charming creature, who carried tokens of her high birth in her face, and whose every feature and look shewed her to be nobly descended.

They let him go to bed with his mistake : but the countess said next morning, she thought she never saw a greater instance of stupid pride and churlishness; and should be sick of the advantage of birth or ancestry, if this was the natural fruit of it. "For a man," said her ladyship, "to come to his nephew's house, and to suffer the mistress of it to be closetted up (as he thinks), in order to humour his absurd and brutal insolence, and to behave as he has done, is such a ridicule upon the pride of descent, that I shall ever think of it.—O Mrs. B.," said she, "what advantages have you over every one that sees you; but most over those who pretend to treat you unworthily!" I expect to be called to breakfast every minute, and shall then, perhaps, see how this matter will end. I wish, when it is revealed, he may not be in a fury, and think himself imposed on. I fear it won't go off so well as I wish; for every body seems to be grave, and angry at Sir Jacob.

THURSDAY.

I now proceed with my tale. At breakfast-time, when every one was sat, Sir Jacob began to call out for Lady Jenny. "But," said he, "I'll have none of your girl, nephew : although the chair at the tea-table is left for somebody."—"No," said Mr. B., "we'll get Lady Jenny to supply Mrs. B.'s place, since you don't care to see her."—"With all my heart," replied he.—"But, uncle," said Mr. B., "have you really no desire, no curiosity to see the girl I have married ?"—"No, none at all, by my soul."

Just then I came in, and paying my compliments to the company, and to Sir Jacob—"Shall I," said I, "supply Mrs. B.'s place in her absence?" And down I sat. After breakfast, and the servants were withdrawn—"Lady Jenny," said Lady Davers, "you are a young lady, with all the advantages of birth and descent; and some of the best blood in the kingdom runs in your veins; and here Sir Jacob Swynford is your great admirer : cannot *you*, from whom it will come with a double grace, convince him that he acts unkindly at my brother's house, to keep the person he has thought worthy of making the mistress of it, out of company? And let us know your opinion, whether my brother himself does right, to comply with such an unreasonable distaste ?"—"Why, how now, Lady Davers ! This from you ! I did not expect it !"

"My uncle," said Mr. B., "is the only person in the kingdom

164

that I would have humoured thus : and I made no doubt, when he saw how willing I was to oblige him in such a point, he would have acted a more generous part than he has yet done.—But, Lady Jenny, what say you to my sister's questions?"

"If I must speak my mind," replied I, "I should take the liberty to be very serious with Sir Jacob, and to say, that when a thing is done, and cannot be helped, he should take care how he sows the seeds of indifference and animosity between man and wife, and makes a gentleman dissatisfied with his choice, and perhaps unhappy as long as he lives."—"Nay, Miss," said he, "if all are against me, and you, whose good opinion I value most, you may e'en let the girl come, and sit down.—If she is but half as pretty, and half as wise, and modest, as you, I shall, as it cannot be helped, as you say, be ready to think better of the matter. For 'tis a little hard, I must needs say, if she has hitherto appeared before all the good company, to keep her out of the way on my account."—"Really, Sir Jacob," said the countess, "I have blushed for you more than once on this occasion. But the mistress of this house is more than half as wise, and modest, and lovely : and in hopes you will return me back some of the blushes I have lent you, see *there*, in my daughter Jenny, whom you have been so justly admiring, the mistress of the house, and the lady with the Pagan name." Sir Jacob sat aghast, looking at us all in turn, and then cast his eyes on the floor. At last, up he got, and swore a sad oath : "And am I thus tricked and bamboozled," that was his word; "am I? There's no bearing this house, nor her presence, now, that's certain; and I'll begone."

Mr. B. looking at me, and nodding his head towards Sir Jacob, as he was in a flutter to begone, I rose from my chair, and went to him, and took his hand. "I hope, Sir Jacob, you will be able to bear *both*, when you shall see no other difference but that of descent, between the supposed Lady Jenny you so kindly praised, and the girl your dear nephew has so much exalted."—"Let me go," said he; "I am most confoundedly bit. I cannot look you in the face ! By my soul, I cannot ! For 'tis impossible you should forgive me."—"Indeed it is not, Sir; you have done nothing but what I can forgive you for, if your dear nephew can; for to him was the wrong, if any, and I am sure he can overlook it. And for his sake, to the uncle of so honoured a gentleman, to the brother of my late good lady, I can, with a bent knee, *thus*, ask your blessing, and your excuse for joining to keep you in this suspense."—"Bless you !" said he, and stamped —"Who can choose but bless you?"—and he kneeled down, and wrapped his arms about me.—" But, curse me," that was his strange word, " if ever I was so touched before ! " My dear Mr. B., for fear my spirits should be too much affected (for the rough baronet, in his transport, had bent me down lower than I kneeled), came and held my arm; but permitted Sir Jacob to raise me; only saying, " How does my angel ? Now she has made this conquest, she has completed all her triumphs."— " Angel, did you call her ?—I'm confounded with her goodness, and her sweet carriage !—Rise, and let me see if I can stand myself ! And, believe me, I am sorry I have acted thus so much like a bear; and the more I think of it, the more I shall be ashamed of myself." And the tears, as he spoke, ran down his rough cheeks; which moved me much; for to see a man with so hard a countenance weep, was a touching sight.

Mr. H. putting his handkerchief to his eyes, his aunt said, " What's the matter, Jackey ? "—" I don't know how 'tis," answered he; " but here's strange doings, as ever I knew—For, day after day, one's ready to cry, without knowing whether it be for joy or sorrow !—What a plague's the matter with me, I wonder ! " And out he went, the two ladies, whose charming eyes, too, glistened with pleasure, smiling at the effect the scene had upon Mr. H. and at what he said.—" Well, Madam," said Sir Jacob, approaching me; for I had sat down, but then stood up—" You will forgive me; and from my heart I wish you joy. By my soul I do,"—and saluted me.—" I could not have believed there had been such a person breathing. I don't wonder at my nephew's loving you !—And you call her sister, Lady Davers, don't you ?—If you do, I'll own her for my niece."

" Don't I !—Yes, I do," said she, coming to me, " and am proud so to call her. And this I tell you, for *your* comfort, though to *my own shame*, that I used her worse than you have done, before I knew her excellence; and have repented of it ever since."

I bowed to her ladyship, and kissed her hand—" My dearest lady," said I, " you have made me such rich amends since, that I am sure I may say, ' *It was good for me that I was afflicted !* ' "— " Why, nephew, she has the fear of God, I perceive, before her eyes too ! I'm sure I've heard those words. They are somewhere in the Scripture, I believe !—Why, who knows but she may be a means to save your soul !—Hey, you know ! "—" Ay, Sir Jacob, she'll be a means to save a hundred souls, and might go a great way to save yours if you were to live with her but one month."

" Well, but, nephew, I hope you forgive me too; for now I think

of it, I never knew you take any matter so patiently in my life."
—" I knew," said Mr. B., " that every extravagance you insisted upon, was heightening my charmer's triumph, and increasing your own contrition; and, as I was not *indeed* deprived of her company, I could bear with every thing you said or did—Yet, don't you remember my caution, that the less you said against her, the less you'd have to unsay, and the less to repent of ! "

" I do; and let me ride out, and call myself to account for all I have said against her, in her own hearing; and when I can think of but one half, and how she has taken it, by my soul, I believe 'twill make me *more* than half mad."

At dinner (when we had Mr. Williams's company), the baronet told me, he admired me now, as much as when he thought me Lady Jenny; but complained of the trick put upon him by us all, and seemed now and then a little serious upon it.

He took great notice of the dexterity which he imputed to me, in performing the honours of the table. And every now and then, he lifted up his eyes—" Very clever.—Why, Madam, you seem to me to be born to these things !—I will be helped by nobody but you—And you'll have a task of it, I can tell you; for I have a whipping stomach, and were there fifty dishes, I always taste of every one." And, indeed, John was in a manner wholly employed in going to and fro between the baronet and me, for half an hour together.—He went from us afterwards to Mrs. Jervis, and made her answer many questions about me, and how all these matters had *come about*, as he phrased it; and returning, when we drank coffee, said, " I have been *confabbing* with Mrs. Jervis, about you, niece. I never heard the like ! She says you can play on the harpsichord, and sing too; will you let a body have a tune or so? My Mab can play pretty well, and so can Dolly; I'm a judge of music, and would fain hear you." I said, if he was a judge, I should be afraid to play before him; but I would not be asked twice, after our coffee. Accordingly he repeated his request. I gave him a tune, and, at his desire, sung to it : " Od's my life," said he, " you do it purely !—But I see where it is. My girls have got *my* fingers ! " Then he held both hands out, and a fine pair of paws shewed he. " Plague on't, they touch two keys at once; but those slender and nimble fingers, how they sweep along ! My eye can't follow 'em—Whew," whistled he, " they are here and there, and every where at once !—Why, nephew, I believe you have put another trick upon me. My niece is certainly of quality ! And report has not done her justice.—One more tune, one more song—By my faith, your voice goes sweetly to your fingers. 'Slife—I'll thrash

167

my jades," that was his polite phrase, " when I get home.—
Lady Davers, you know not the money they have cost me to
qualify them; and here's a mere baby to them outdoes 'em by a
bar's length, without any expense at all bestowed upon her.
Go over that again—Confound me for a puppy! I lost it by
my prating.—Ay, there you have it! Oh! that I could but
dance as well as thou sing'st! I'd give you a saraband, old as
I am."

After supper, we fell into a conversation, of which I must
give you some account, being on a topic that Mr. B. has been
blamed for in his marrying me, and which has stuck by some of
his friends, even after they have, in kindness to me, acquitted
him in every other respect; and that is, *the example he has set to
young gentlemen of family and fortune to marry beneath them.*—It
was begun by Sir Jacob, who said, " I am in love with my new
niece, that I am : but still one thing sticks with me in this affair,
which is, what will become of degree or distinction, if this practice
of gentlemen marrying their mothers' waiting-maids—excuse
me, Madam—should come into vogue? Already, young ladies
and young gentlemen are too apt to be drawn away thus, and
disgrace their families. We have too many instances of this.
You'll forgive me, both of you."

" That," said Lady Davers, " is the *only* thing!—Sir Jacob
has hit upon the point that would make one wish this example
had not been set by a gentleman of such an ancient family, till
one becomes acquainted with this dear creature; and then
every body thinks it should not be otherwise than it is."

" Ay, Pamela," said Mr. B., " what can you say to this?
Cannot you defend me from this charge? This is a point that
has been often objected to me; try for one of your pretty
arguments in my behalf."

" Indeed, Sir," replied I, looking down, " it becomes not me to
say any thing to this."—" But indeed it does, if you can : and
I beg you'll help me to some excuse, if you have any at hand."—
" Won't you, Sir, dispense with me on this occasion? I know,
not what to say. Indeed I should not, if I may judge for myself,
speak one *word* to this subject.—For it is my absolute opinion,
that degrees in general should be kept up; although I must
always deem the present case an happy exception to the rule."
Mr. B. looked as if he still expected I should say something.—
" Won't you, Sir, dispense with me? " repeated I. " Indeed
I should not speak to this point, if I may be my own judge."

" I always intend, my dear, you shall judge for yourself; and,
you know, I seldom urge you farther, when you use those words.

168

But if you have any thing upon your mind to say, let's have it; for your arguments are always new and unborrowed."

"I would then, if I *must*, Sir, ask, if there be not a nation, or if there has not been a law in some nation, which, whenever a young gentleman, be *his* degree what it would, has seduced a poor creature, be *her* degree what it would, obliges him to marry that unhappy person?"—"I think there is such a law in some country, I can't tell where," said Sir Jacob.

"And do you think, Sir, whether it be so or not, that it is equitable it should be so?"

"Yes, by my troth. Though I must needs own, if it were so in England, many men, that I know, would not have the wives they now have."—"You speak to your knowledge, I doubt not, Sir Jacob?" said Mr. B.

"Why, truly—I don't know but I do."

"All then," said I, "that I would infer, is, whether another law would not be a still more just and equitable one, that the gentleman who is repulsed, from a principle of virtue and honour, should not be censured for marrying a person he could *not* seduce? And whether it is not more for both their honours, if he does: since it is nobler to reward a virtue, than to repair a shame, were that shame to be repaired by matrimony, which I take the liberty to doubt. But I beg pardon: you commanded me, Sir, else this subject should not have found a speaker to it, in me."

"This is admirably said," cried Sir Jacob.—"But yet this comes not up to the objection," said Mr. B. "The setting an example to waiting-maids to aspire, and to young gentlemen to descend. And I will enter into the subject myself; and the rather, because as I go along, I will give Sir Jacob a faint sketch of the merit and character of my Pamela, of which he cannot be so well informed as he has been of the disgrace which he imagined I had brought upon myself by marrying her.—I think it necessary, that as well those persons who are afraid the example should be taken, as those who are inclined to follow it, should consider *all* the material parts of it; otherwise, I think the precedent may be justly cleared; and the fears of the one be judged groundless, and the plea of the other but a pretence, in order to cover a folly into which they would have fallen, whether they had this example or not. For instance, in order to lay claim to the excuses, which my conduct, if I may suppose it of force enough to do either good or hurt, will furnish, it is necessary, that the object of their wish should be a girl of exquisite beauty (and that not only in their own blinded and partial judgments, but in the opinion of *every one* who sees her, friend or foe), in order to justify the force which the *first* attractions have upon him : that she be descended of honest and conscientious, though poor and obscure parents; who having preserved their integrity, through great trials and afflictions, have, by their examples, as well as precepts, laid deep in the girl's mind the foundations of piety and virtue.

" It is necessary that, to the charms of person, this waiting-maid, should have an humble, teachable mind, fine natural parts, a sprightly, yet inoffensive wit, a temper so excellent, and a judgment so solid, as should promise (by the love and esteem these qualities should attract to herself from her fellow-servants, superior and inferior) that she would become a higher station, and be respected in it.—And that, after so good a foundation laid by her parents, she should have all the advantages of female education conferred upon her; the example of an excellent lady, improving and building upon so worthy a foundation : a capacity surprisingly ready to take in all that is taught her : an attention, assiduity, and diligence almost peculiar to herself, at her time of life; so as, at fifteen or sixteen years of age, to be able to vie with any young ladies of rank, as well in the natural genteelness of her person, as in her acquirements : and that in nothing but her humility she should manifest any difference between herself and the high-born.

" It will be necessary, moreover, that she should have a mind above temptation; that she should resist the *offers* and *menaces* of one upon whom all her worldly happiness seemed to depend; the son of a lady to whom she owed the greatest obligations; a person whom she did not *hate*, but greatly *feared*, and whom her grateful heart would have been *glad* to oblige; and who sought to prevail over her virtue, by all the inducements that could be thought of, to *attract* a young unexperienced virgin at one time, or to *frighten* her at another, into his purposes; who offered her very high terms, her circumstances considered, as well for herself, as for parents she loved better than herself, whose circumstances were low and distressful; yet, to all these *offers* and *menaces*, that she should be able to answer in such words as these, which will always dwell upon my memory —' I reject your proposals with all my soul. May God desert me, whenever I make worldly grandeur my chiefest good ! I know I am in your power; I dread your will to ruin me is as great as your power. Yet, will I dare to tell you, I will make no free-will offering of my virtue. All that I *can* do, poor as it is, I *will* do, to shew you, that my will bore no part in the violation of me.' And when future marriage was intimated to her, to induce her to yield, to be able to answer, ' The moment I yield to your proposals, there is an end of all merit, if now I have any. And I should be so far from *expecting* such an honour that I will pronounce I should be most *unworthy* of it.'

" If, I say, such a girl can be found, thus beautifully attractive in *every one's* eye, and not partially so only in a young gentleman's *own ;* and after that (what good persons would infinitely prefer to beauty), thus piously principled ; thus genteely educated and accomplished ; thus brilliantly witty ; thus prudent, modest, generous, undesigning ; and having been thus tempted, thus tried, by the man she hated not, pursued (not intriguingly pursuing), be thus inflexibly virtuous, and proof against temptation : let her reform her libertine, and let him marry her ; and were he of princely extraction, I dare answer for it, that no *two* princes in *one age,* take the world through, would be in danger. For, although I am sensible it is not to my credit, I will say, that I never met with a repulse, nor a conduct like this ; and yet I never sunk very low for the subjects of my attempts, either at home or abroad. These are obvious inferences," added he, " not refinements upon my Pamela's story ; and if the gentlemen were capable of thought and comparison, would rather make such an example, as is apprehended, *more* than *less* difficult than *before.*

" But if, indeed, the young fellow be such a booby, that he cannot *reflect* and *compare,* and take the case *with all its circumstances* together, I think his good papa or mamma should get him a wife to their own liking, as soon as possible ; and the poorest girl in England, who is honest, should rather bless herself for escaping such a husband, than glory in the catch she would have of him. For he would hardly do honour to his family in any one instance."—" Indeed," said the countess, " it would be pity, after all, that such an one should marry any lady of prudence and birth ; for 'tis enough in conscience, that he is a disgrace to *one* worthy family ; it would be pity he should make *two* unhappy."

" Why, really, nephew," said Sir Jacob, " I think you have said much to the purpose. There is not so much danger, from the example, as I apprehended, from *sensible* and *reflecting* minds. I did not consider this matter thoroughly, I must needs say."

" And the business is," said Lady Davers—" You'll excuse me, sister—There will be more people hear that Mr. B. has married his mother's waiting-maid, than will know his inducements."—"Not many, I believe, sister. For when 'tis known, I have some character in the world, and am not quite an idiot (and my faults, in having not been one af the most virtuous of men, will stand me in some stead in *this* case, though hardly in *any other*) they will naturally enquire into my inducements.—But see you not, when we go abroad, what numbers of people her character draws to admire the dear creature? Does not this shew, that her virtue has made her more conspicuous than my fortune has made me? For I passed up and down quietly enough before (handsome as my equipage always was) and attracted not any body's notice: and indeed I had as lieve these honours were not so publicly paid *her;* for even, were I fond to shew and parade, what are they, but a reproach to me? And can I have any excellence, but a secondary one, in having, after all my persecutions of her, done but common justice to her merit?—This answers your objection, Lady Davers, and shews that *my* inducements and *her* story must be equally known. And I really think (every thing I have said considered, and that might still farther be urged, and the conduct of the dear creature in the station she adorns, so much exceeding all I hoped or could expect from the most promising appearances), that she does *me* more honour than I have done *her;* and if I could put myself in a third person's place, I think I should be of the same opinion, were I to determine upon such another pair, exactly circumstanced as we are."

You may believe, my friend, how much this generous defence of the step he had taken, attributing every thing to me, and deprecating his worthy self, affected me. I played with a cork one while, with my rings another; looking down, and every way but on the company; for they gazed too much upon me all the time; so that I could only glance a tearful eye now and then upon the dear man; and when it would overflow, catch in my handkerchief the escaped fugitives that would start unbidden beyond their proper limits, though I often tried, by a twinkling motion, to disperse the gathering water, before it had formed itself into drops too big to be restrained. All the company praised the dear generous speaker; and he was pleased to say farther, "Although, my good friends, I can truly say, that with all the pride of family, and the insolence of fortune, which once made me doubt whether I should not sink too low, if I made my Pamela my mistress (for I should then have treated her not ungenerously, and should have suffered her, perhaps, to call herself by my name), I have never once repented of what I have done; on the contrary, always rejoiced in it, and it has been, from the first day of our marriage, my pride and my boast (and shall be, let others say what they will), that I can call such an excellence, and such a purity, which I so little deserve, mine; and I look down with contempt upon the rashness of all who reflect upon me; for they can have no notion of my happiness or her merit."

"O dear Sir, how do you overrate my poor merit!—Some persons are happy in a life of *comforts*, but mine's a life of *joy!*—One rapturous instance follows another so fast, that I know not how to bear them."

"Whew!" whistled Sir Jacob. "Whereabouts am I?—I hope by-and-by you'll come down to our pitch, that one may put in a word or two with you."

"May you be long thus blest and happy together!" said Lady Davers. "I know not which to admire most, the dear girl that never was bad, or the dear man, who, having been bad, is now so good!"

Said Lord Davers, "There is hardly any bearing these moving scenes, following one another so quick, as my sister says."

The countess was pleased to say, that till now she had been at a loss to form any notion of the happiness of the first pair before the Fall; but now, by so fine an instance as this, she comprehended it in all its force. "God continue you to one another," added she, "for a credit to the state, and to human nature."

Mr. H., having his elbows on the table, folded his hands, shaking them, and looking down—"Egad, this is uncommon life, that it is! Your two souls, I can see that, are like well-tuned instruments; but they are too high set for me, a vast deal."

"The best thing," said Lady Davers (always severe upon her poor nephew), "thou ever saidst. The music must be equal to that of Orpheus, which can make such a savage as thee dance to it. I charge thee, say not another word to-night."—"Why, indeed, aunt," returned he, laughing, "I believe it *was* pretty well said for your foolish fellow: though it was by chance, I must confess; I did not think of it."—"That I believe," replied my lady; "if thou hadst, thou'dst not have spoken so well."

Sir Jacob and Mr. B. afterwards fell into a family discourse; and Sir Jacob told us of two or three courtships *by* his three sons, and *to* his two daughters, and his reasons for disallowing them: and I could observe, he is an absolute tyrant in his family, though they are all men and women grown, and he seemed to please himself how much they stood in awe of him.

173

I would not have been so tediously trifling, but for the sake of my dear parents; and there is so much self-praise, as it may seem, from a person on repeating the fine things said of herself, that I am half of opinion I should send them to Kent only, and to think you should be obliged to me for saving you so much trouble and impertinence.

Do, dear Miss, be so free as to forbid me to send you any more long journals, but common letters only, of how you do? and who and who's together, and of respects to one another, and so forth—letters that one might dispatch, as Sir Jacob says, in a *twinkling*, and perhaps be more to the purpose than the tedious scrawl which kisses your hands, from *yours most sincerely,*   P. B.

Do, dear good Sir Simon, let Miss Polly add to our delights, by her charming company. Mr. Murray, and the new affair will divert *you*, in her absence.—So pray, since my good Lady Darnford has consented, and she is willing, and her sister can spare her; don't be so cross as to deny me.

LETTER XXXIV

From Miss Darnford to Mrs. B.

My dear Mrs. B.,

You have given us great pleasure in your accounts of your conversations, and of the verses put so wickedly under your seat; and in your just observations on the lines, and occasions.

I am quite shocked, when I think of Lady Davers's passionate intentions at the hall, but have let nobody into the worst of the matter, in compliance with your desire. We are delighted with the account of your family management, and your Sunday's service. What an excellent lady you are! And how happy and good you make all who know you, is seen by the ladies joining in your evening service, as well as their domestics.

We go on here swimmingly with our courtship. Never was there a fonder couple than Mr. Murray and Miss Nancy. The modest girl is quite alive, easy, and pleased, except now-and-then with me. We had a sad falling out t'other day. Thus it was :—She had the assurance, on my saying, they were so fond and free before-hand, that they would leave nothing for improvement afterwards, to tell me, she had long perceived, that my envy was very disquieting to me. This she said before

Mr. Murray, who had the good manners to retire, seeing a storm rising between us. " Poor foolish girl ! " cried I, when he was gone, provoked to great contempt by her expression before him, " thou wilt make me despise thee in spite of my heart. But, pr'ythee, manage thy matters with common decency, at least."—" Good lack ! *Common decency*, did you say? When my sister Polly is able to shew me what it is, I shall hope to be better for her example."—" No, thou'lt never be better for any body's example ! Thy ill-nature and perverseness will continue to keep thee from that."—" My ill-temper, you have often told me, is *natural* to me; so it must become *me :* but upon such a sweet-tempered young lady as Miss Polly, her late assumed petulance sits but ill ! "

" I must have had no bad temper, and that every one says, to bear with thy sullen and perverse one, as I have done all my life."

" But why can't you bear with it a little longer, sister? Does any thing provoke you *now* " (with a sly leer and affected drawl) " that did not *formerly ?* "

" Provoke me !—What should provoke me? I gave thee but a hint of thy fond folly, which makes thee behave so before company, that every one smiles at thee; and I'd be glad to save thee from contempt for thy *new* good humour, as I used to try to do, for thy *old* bad nature."

" Is that it? What a kind sister have I ! But I see it vexes you; and *ill-natured* folks love to teaze, you know. But, dear Polly, don't let the affection Mr. Murray expresses for me, put such a good-tempered body out of humour, pray don't— Who knows " (continued the provoker, who never says a tolerable thing that is not ill-natured) " but the gentleman may be happy that he has found a way, with so much ease, to dispense with the difficulty that eldership laid him under? But, as he did you the favour to let the repulse come from you, don't be angry, sister, that he took you at the first word."

" Indeed," said I, with a contemptuous smile, " thou'rt in the right, Nancy, to take the gentleman at *his* first word. Hold him fast, and play over all thy monkey tricks with him, with all my heart; who knows but it may engage him more? For, should *he* leave thee, I might be too much provoked at thy ingratitude, *to turn over* another gentleman to thee. And let me tell thee, without such an introduction, thy temper would keep any body from thee, that knows it ! "

" Poor Miss Polly—Come, be as easy as you can ! Who knows but we may find out some cousin or friend of Mr. Murray's between us, that we may persuade to address you? Don't make us your enemies: we'll try to make you easy, if we can. 'Tis a little hard, that you should be so cruelly taken at your word, that it is."—"Dost think," said I, "poor, stupid, ill-judging Nancy, that I can have the same regret for parting with a man I could not like, that thou hadst, when thy vain hopes met with the repulse they deserved from Mr. B.?"—"Mr. B. come up again? I have not heard of him a great while."—"No, but it was necessary that one nail should drive out another; for thou'dst been repining still, had not Mr. Murray been *turned over* to thee."—"*Turned over!* You used that word once before: such great wits as you, methinks, should not use the same word twice."

"How dost thou know what wits *should* or should *not* do? Thou hast no talent but ill-nature; and 'tis enough for thee, that *one* view takes up thy whole thought. Pursue that— But I would only caution thee, not to *satiate* where thou wouldst *oblige*, that's all; or, if thy man can be so gross as to like thy fondness, to leave something for *hereafter*."

"I'll call him in again, sister, and you shall acquaint us how you'd have it. Bell" (for the maid came in just then), "tell Mr. Murray I desire him to walk in."—"I'm glad to see thee so teachable all at once!—I find now what was the cause of thy constant perverseness: for had the unavailing lessons my mamma was always inculcating into thee, come from a *man* thou couldst have had hopes of, they had succeeded better."

In came Sir Simon with his crutch-stick—But can you bear this nonsense, Mrs. B.?—"What sparring, jangling again, you sluts!—O what fiery eyes on one side! and contemptuous looks on t'other!"

"Why, papa, my sister Polly has *turned over* Mr. Murray to me, and she wants him back again, and he won't come—That's all the matter!"

"You know Nancy, papa, never could *bear* reproof, and yet would always *deserve* it!—I was only gently remarking for her instruction, on her fondness before company, and she is as she *used to be!*—Courtship, indeed, is a new thing to the poor girl, and so she knows not how to behave herself in it."

"So, Polly, because you have been able to run over a long list of humble servants, you must insult your sister, must you? —But are you really concerned, Polly?—Hey!"—"Sir, this or anything is very well from you. But these imputations of envy, before Mr. Murray, must make the man very considerable with himself. Poor Nancy don't consider that. But, indeed, how should she? How should *she* be able to reflect, who knows not what reflection is, except of the spiteful sort? But, papa, should the poor thing add to *his* vanity, which wants no addition, at the expense of that pride, which can only preserve her from contempt?"

I saw her affected, and was resolved to pursue my advantage.

"Pr'ythee, Nancy," continued I, "canst thou not have a *little* patience, child—My papa will set the day as soon as he shall think it proper. And don't let thy man toil to keep pace with thy fondness; for I have pitied him many a time, when I have seen him stretched on the tenters to keep thee in countenance."

This set the ill-natured girl in tears and fretfulness; all her old temper came upon her, as I designed it should, for she had kept me at bay longer than usual; and I left her under the dominion of it, and because I would not come into fresh dispute, got my mamma's leave, and went in the chariot, to beg a dinner at Lady Jones's; and then came home as cool and as easy as I used to be; and found Nancy as sullen and silent, as was her custom, before Mr. Murray tendered himself to her ready acceptance. But I went to my spinnet, and suffered her to swell on.

We have said nothing but No and Yes ever since; and I wish I was with you for a month, and all their nonsense over without me. I am, my dear, obliging, and excellent Mrs. B., *your faithful and affectionate*

POLLY DARNFORD.

The two following anticipating the order of time, for the reasons formerly mentioned, we insert here.

LETTER XXXV

From Miss Darnford to Mrs. B.

MY DEAR MRS B.,

Pray give my service to your Mr. B. and tell him he is very impolite in his reflections upon me, as to Mr. Murray, when he supposes I regret the loss of him. You are much more favourable and *just* too, I will say, to your Polly Darnford. These gentlemen, the very best of them, are such indelicates! They think so highly of their saucy selves, and confident sex, as if a lady cannot from *her* heart despise them; but if she turns them off, as they deserve, and continues her dislike, what should be interpreted in her favour, as a just and *regular* conduct, is turned against her, and it must proceed from spite. Mr. B. may think he knows much of the sex. But were I as malicious as he is reflecting (and yet, if I have any malice, he has raised it), I could say, that his acquaintance, was not with the most unexceptionable, till he knew you: and he has not long enough been happy in you, I find, to do justice to those who are proud to emulate your virtues.

I say, Mrs. B., there can be no living with these men upon such beginnings. They ought to know their distance, or be taught it, and not to think it in their power to confer that as a favour, which they should esteem it an honour to receive.

But neither can I bear, it seems, the preparatives to matrimony, the fine clothes, the compliments, the *busy novelty*, as he calls it, the new equipages, and so forth.

That's his mistake again, tell him: for one who can look forwarder than the nine days of wonder, can easily despise so flashy and so transient a glare. And were I fond of compliments, it would not, perhaps, be the way to be pleased, in that respect, if I were to marry.

Compliments in the single state are a lady's due, whether courted or not; and she receives, or ought always to receive them, as such; but in courtship they are poured out upon one, like a hasty shower, soon to be over. A mighty comfortable consideration this, to a lady who *loves to be complimented!* Instead of the refreshing April-like showers, which beautify the sun-shine, she shall stand a deluge of complaisance, be wet to the skin with it; and what then? Why be in a Lybian desert ever after!—experience a constant parching drought and all her attributed excellencies will be swallowed up in the quicksands of matrimony. It may be otherwise with you; and it *must* be so; because there is such an infinite variety in your excellence. But does Mr. B. think it must be so in *every* matrimony?

'Tis true, he improves every hour, as I see in his fine speeches to you. But it could not be Mr. B. if he did not: your merit *extorts* it from him: and what an ungrateful, as well as absurd churl, would he be, who should seek to obscure a meridian lustre, that dazzles the eyes of every one else?

I thank you for your delightful narratives, and beg you to continue them. I told you how your Saturday's conversation

178

with Lady Davers, and your Sunday employments, charm us all: so regular, and so easy to be performed—That's the delightful thing—What every body may do;—and yet so beautiful, so laudable, so uncommon in the practice, especially among people in genteel life!—Your conversation and decision in relation to the two parsons (more than charm) transport us. Mr. B. judges right, and acts a charming part, to throw such a fine game into your hands. And so excellently do you play it, that you do as much credit to your partner's judgment as to your own. Never was so happy a couple.

Mr. Williams is more my favourite than ever; and the amply rewarded Mr. Adams, how did that scene affect us! Again and again, I say (for what can I say else or more—since I can't find words to speak all I think?), you're a charming lady! Yet, methinks, poor Mr. H. makes but a sorry figure among you. We are delighted with Lady Davers; but still more, if possible, with the countess: she is a fine lady, as you have drawn her: but your characters, though truth and nature, are the most shocking, or the most amiable, that I ever read.

We are full of impatience to hear of the arrival of Sir Jacob Swynford. We know his character pretty well: but when he has sat for it to your pencil, it must be an original indeed. I will have another trial with my papa, to move him to let me attend you. I am rallying my forces, and have got my mamma on my side again; who is concerned to see her girl vexed and insulted by her younger sister; and who yet minds no more what *she* says to her, than what I say; and Sir Simon loves to make mischief between us, instead of interposing to silence either: and truly, I am afraid his delight of this kind will make him deny his Polly what she so ardently wishes for. I had a good mind to be sick, to be with you. I could fast two or three days, to give it the better appearance; but then my mamma, who loves not deceit, would blame me, if she knew my stratagem; and be grieved, if she thought I was really ill. I know, fasting, when one has a stomach to eat, gives one a very gloomy and mortified air. What would I not do, in short, to procure to myself the inexpressible pleasure that I should have in your company and conversation? But continue to write to me till then, however, and that will be *next best*. I am *your most obliged and obedient*   POLLY DARNFORD.

From the same.

MY DEAREST MRS. B.,

I am all over joy and rapture. My good papa permits me to say, that he will put his Polly under your protection, when you go to London. If you have but a *tenth part* of the pleasure I have on this occasion, I am sure, I shall be as welcome as I wish. But he will insist upon it, he says, that Mr. B. signs some acknowledgment, which I am to carry along with *me*, that I am intrusted to his honour and yours, and to be returned to him *heart-whole* and *dutiful*, and with a reputation as unsullied as he receives me. But do continue your journals till then; for I have promised to take them up where you leave off, to divert our friends here. There will be presumption! But yet I will write nothing but what I will shew you, and have your consent to send! For I was taught early not to tell tales out of school; and a school, the best I ever went to, will be your charming conversation.

We were greatly diverted with the trick put upon that *barbarian* Sir Jacob. His obstinacy, repentance, and amendment, followed so irresistibly in one half hour, from the happy thought of the excellent lady countess, that I think no plot was ever more fortunate. It was like springing a lucky mine in a siege, that blew up twenty times more than was expected from it, and answered all the besiegers' ends at once.

Mr. B.'s defence of his own conduct towards you is quite noble; and he judges with his usual generosity and good sense, when, by adding to your honour, he knows he enhances his own.

You bid me skim over your writings lightly; but 'tis impossible. I will not flatter you, my dear Mrs. B., nor will I be suspected to do so; and yet I cannot find words to praise, so much as I think you deserve : so I will only say that your good parents, for whose pleasure you write, as well as for mine, cannot receive or read them with more delight than I do. Even my sister Nancy (judge of their effect by this!) will at any time leave Murray, and forget to frown or be ill-natured, while she can hear read what you write. And, angry as she makes me some times, I cannot deny her this pleasure, because possibly, among the innumerable improving reflections they abound with, some one may possibly dart in upon her, and illuminate her, as your conversation and behaviour did Sir Jacob.

But your application in P. S. to my papa pleased him; and confirmed his resolution to let me go. He snatched the sheet that contained this, "That's to me," said he : "I must read this myself." He did, and said, "She's a sweet one : '*Do dear good Sir Simon,*'" repeated he aloud, "'*let Miss Polly add to our delights!*' So she shall, then;—if that will do it!—And yet this same Mrs. B. has so many delights already, that I should think she might be contented. But, Dame Darnford, I think I'll let her go. These sisters then, you'll see, how they'll love at a distance, though always quarrelling when together." He read on, "'*The new affair will divert you—Lady Darnford has consented—Miss is willing; and her sister can spare her;*' —Very prettily put, faith—'*And don't you be cross*'—Very sweet '*to deny me.*'—Why, dear Mrs. B., I won't be so cross then; indeed I won't!—And so, Polly, let 'em send word when they set out for London, and you shall join 'em there with all my heart; but I'll have a letter every post, remember that, girl."

"Any thing, any thing, dear papa," said I : "so I can but go!" He called for a kiss, for his compliance. I gave it most willingly, you may believe.

Nancy looked envious, although Mr. Murray came in just then. She looked almost like a great glutton, whom I remember; one Sir Jonathan Smith, who killed himself with eating : he used, while he was heaping up his plate from one dish, to watch the others, and follow the knife of every body else with such a greedy eye, as if he could swear a robbery against any one who presumed to eat as well as he.

Well, let's know when you set out, and you shan't have been a week in London, if I can help it, but you shall be told by my tongue, as now by my pen, how much I am *your obliged admirer and friend,*

POLLY DARNFORD.

LETTER XXXVII

MY DEAR FRIEND,

I now proceed with my journal, which I had brought down to Thursday night.

FRIDAY.

The two ladies resolving, as they said, to inspect all my proceedings, insisted upon it, that I would take them with me in my *benevolent round* (as they, after we returned, would call

181

it), which I generally take once a week, among my poor and sick neighbours; and finding I could not get off, I set out with them, my lady countess proposing Mrs. Worden to fill up the fourth place in the coach. We talked all the way of charity, and the excellence of that duty; and my Lady Davers took notice of the text, that it would hide a *multitude of faults*.

The countess said she had once a much better opinion of herself, than she found she had reason for, within these *few* days past: " And indeed, Mrs. B.," said she, " when I get home, I shall make a good many people the better for your example." And so said Lady Davers; which gave me no small inward pleasure; and I acknowledged, in suitable terms, the honour they both did me. The coach set us down by the side of a large common, about five miles distant from our house; and we alighted, and walked a little way, choosing not to have the coach come nearer, that we might be taken as little notice of as possible; and they entered with me into two mean cots with great condescension and goodness; one belonging to a poor widow and five children, who had been all down in agues and fevers; the other to a man and his wife bed-rid with age and infirmities, and two honest daughters, one a widow with two children, the other married to an husbandman, who had also been ill, but now, by comfortable cordials, and good physic, were pretty well to what they had been.

The two ladies were well pleased with my demeanour to the good folks: to whom I said, that as I should go so soon to London, I was willing to see them before I went, to wish them better and better, and to tell them, that I should leave orders with Mrs. Jervis concerning them, to whom they must make known their wants: and that Mr. Barrow would take care of them, I was sure; and do all that was in the power of physic for the restoration of their healths.

Now you must know, Miss, that I am not so good as the old ladies of former days, who used to distil cordial waters, and prepare medicines, and dispense them themselves. I knew, if I were so inclined, my dear Mr. B. would not have been pleased with it, because in the approbation he has kindly given to my present method, he has twice or thrice praised me, that I don't carry my charity to extremes, and make his house a dispensatory. I would not, therefore, by aiming at doing too much, lose the opportunity of doing any good at all in these respects; and besides, as the vulgar saying is, One must creep before one goes. But this is my method :

I am upon an agreement with this Mr. Barrow, who is deemed a very skilful and honest apothecary, and one Mr. Simmonds, a surgeon of like character, to attend to all such cases and persons as I shall recommend; Mr. Barrow, to administer physic and cordials, as he shall judge proper, and even, in necessary cases, to call in a physician. And now and then, by looking in upon them one's self, or sending a servant to ask questions, all is kept right.

My Lady Davers observed a Bible, a Common Prayer-book, and a Whole Duty of Man, in each cot, in leathern outside cases, to keep them clean, and a Church Catechism or two for the children; and was pleased to say, it was right; and her ladyship asked one of the children, a pretty girl, who learnt her her catechism? And she curtsey'd and looked at me; for I do ask the children questions, when I come, to know how they improve: " 'Tis as I thought," said my lady; " my sister provides for both parts. God bless you, my dear!" said she, and tapped my neck.

My ladies left tokens of their bounty behind them to both families, and all the good folks blessed and prayed for us at parting: and as we went out, my Lady Davers, with a serious air, was pleased to say to me, " Take care of your health, my dear sister; and God give you, when it comes, a happy hour: for how many real mourners would you have, if you were to be called early to reap the fruits of your piety!"

" God's will must be done, my lady," said I. " The same Providence that has so wonderfully put it in my power to do a little good, will raise up new friends to the honest hearts that rely upon him."

This I said, because some of the good people heard my lady, and seemed troubled, and began to redouble their prayers, for my safety and preservation.

We walked thence to our coach, and stretched a little farther, to visit two farmers' families, about a mile distant from each other. One had the mother of the family, with two sons, just recovering, the former from a fever, the latter from tertian agues; and I asked, when they saw Mr. Barrow? They told me, with great commendations of him, that he had but just left them. So, having congratulated their hopeful way, and wished them to take care of themselves, and not go too early to business, I said I should desire Mr. Barrow to watch over them, for fear of a relapse, and should hardly see 'em again for some time; and so I slid, in a manner not to be observed, a couple of guineas into the good woman's hand; for I had a hint given me by Mrs. Jervis, that their illness had made it low with them.

We proceeded then to the other farm, where the case was a married daughter, who had a very dangerous lying-in, and a wicked husband who had abused her, and run away from her; but she was mending apace, by good comfortable things, which from time to time I had caused to be sent her. Her old father had been a little unkind to her, before I took notice of her; for she married against his consent; and indeed the world went hard with the poor man, and he could not do much; and besides, he had a younger daughter, who had lost all her limbs, and was forced to be tied in a wicker chair, to keep her up in it; which (having expended much to relieve her) was a great *pull-back*, as the good old woman called it. And having been a year in arrear to a harsh landlord, who, finding a good stock upon the ground, threatened to distress the poor family, and turn them out of all, I advanced the money upon the stock; and the poor man has already paid me half of it (for, Miss, I must keep within compass too), which was fifty pounds at first, and is in a fair way to pay me the other half, and make as much more for himself.

Here I found Mr. Barrow, and he gave me an account of the success of two other cases I had recommended to him; and told me, that John Smith, a poor man, who, in thatching a barn, had tumbled down, and broken his leg, and bruised himself all over, was in a fair way of recovery. This poor creature had like to have perished by the cruelty of the parish officers, who would have passed him away to Essex, where his settlement was, though in a burning fever, occasioned by his misfortune; but hearing of the case, I directed Mr. Simmonds to attend him, and to provide for him at my expense, and gave my word, if he died, to bury him.

I was glad to hear he was in so good a way, and told Mr. Barrow, I hoped to see him and Mr. Simmonds together at Mr. B.'s, before I set out for London, that we might advise about the cases under their direction, and that I might acquit myself of some of my obligations to them.

"You are a good man, Mr. Barrow," added I: "God will bless you for your care and kindness to these poor destitute creatures. They all praise you, and do nothing but talk of your humanity to them."

"O my good lady," said he, "who can forbear following such an example as you set? Mr. Simmonds can testify as well as I (for now and then a case requires us to visit together) that we can hardly hear any complaints from our poor patients, let 'em be ever so ill, for the praises and blessings they bestow upon you."

"It is good Mr. B. that enables and encourages me to do what I do. Tell them, they must bless God, and bless him, and pray for me, and thank you and Mr. Simmonds : we all join together, you know, for their good."

The countess and Lady Davers asked the poor lying-in woman many questions, and left with her, and for her poor sister, a miserable object indeed !—(God be praised that I am not such an one !) marks of their bounty in gold, and looking upon one another, and then upon me, and lifting up their hands, could not say a word till we were in the coach : and so we were carried home, after we had just looked in upon a country school, where I pay for the learning of eight children. And here (I hope I recite not this with pride, though I do with pleasure) is a cursory account of my *benevolent weekly round*, as my ladies will call it. I know you will not be displeased with it; but it will highly delight my worthy parents, who, in their way, do a great deal of discreet good in their neighbourhood : for indeed, Miss, a little matter, *prudently* bestowed, and on true objects of compassion (whose cases are soon at a crisis, as are those of most labouring people), will go a great way, and especially if laid out properly for 'em, according to the exigencies of their respective cases.—For such poor people, who live generally low, want very seldom any thing but reviving cordials at first, and good wholesome kitchen physic afterwards : and then the wheels of nature, being unclogged, new oiled, as it were, and set right, they will go round again with pleasantness and ease for a good while together, by virtue of that exercise which their labour gives them; while the rich and voluptuous are forced to undergo great fatigues to keep theirs clean and in order.

SATURDAY MORNING.

It is hardly right to trouble either of you, my honoured correspondents, with an affair that has vexed me a good deal; and, indeed, *should* affect me more than any other mistress of a family, for reasons which will be obvious to you, when I tell you the case. And this I cannot forbear doing.

A pretty genteel young body, my Polly Barlow, as I call her, having been well recommended, and behaved with great prudence till this time, is the cause.

My dear Mr. B. and the two ladies, agreed with me to take a little airing in the coach, and to call in upon Mr. Martin, who

185

had a present made him for his menagerie, in which he takes a great delight, of a rare and uncommon creature, a native of the East Indies. But just as Sir Jacob was on horseback to accompany them, and the ladies were ready to go, I was taken with a sudden disorder and faintishness; so that Lady Davers, who is very tender of me, and watches every change of my countenance, would not let me go with them, though my disorder was going off: and my dear Mr. B. was pleased to excuse me; and just meeting with Mr. Williams, as they went to the coach, they took him with them, to fill up the vacant place. So I retired to my closet, and shut myself in.

They had asked Mr. H. to go with them, for company to Sir Jacob; but he (on purpose, as I believe by what followed) could not be found, when they set out: so they supposed he was upon some ramble with Mr. Colbrand, his great favourite.

I was writing to you, being pretty well recovered, when I heard Polly, as I supposed, and as it proved, come into my apartment: and down she sat, and sung a little catch, and cried, "Hem!" twice; and presently I heard two voices. But suspecting nothing, I wrote on, till I heard a kind of rustling and struggling, and Polly's voice crying, "Fie—How can you do so !—Pray, Sir."

This alarmed me much, because we have such orderly folks about us; and I looked through the key-hole; and, to my surprise and concern, saw Mr. H.—foolish gentleman !—taking liberties with Polly, that neither became him to offer, nor, more foolish girl ! her to suffer. And having reason to think, that this was not their first interview, and freedom—and the girl sometimes encouragingly laughing, as at other times, inconsistently, struggling and complaining, in an accent that was too tender for the occasion, I forced a faint cough. This frighted them both: Mr. H. swore, and said, "Who can that be ?—Your lady's gone with them, isn't she ? "

" I believe so !—I hope so ! " said the silly girl—" yet that was like her voice !—Me'm, are you in your closet, Me'm ? " said she, coming up to the door; Mr. H. standing like a poor thief, half behind the window-curtains, till he knew whether it was I.

I opened the door : away sneaked Mr. H., and she leaped with surprise, not hoping to find me there, though she asked the question.

" I thought—Indeed—Me'm—I thought you were gone out."—" It is plain you did, Polly.—Go and shut the chamber door, and come to me again."

She did, but trembled, and was so full of confusion, that I pitied the poor creature, and hardly knew how to speak to her. For my compassion got the upper hand of my resentment; and as she stood quaking and trembling, and looking on the ground with a countenance I cannot describe, I now and then cast my eye upon her, and was as often forced to put my handkerchief to it.

At last I said, " How long have these freedoms past between you and Mr. H.?—I am loth to be censorious, Polly; but it is too plain, that Mr. H. would not have followed you into my chamber, if he had not met you at other places."—The poor girl said never a word.—" Little did I expect, Polly, that you would have shewn so much imprudence. You have had instances of the vile arts of men against poor maidens : have you any notion that Mr. H. intends to do honourably by you ? " —" Me'm—Me'm—I believe—I hope—I dare say, Mr. H. would not do otherwise."—" So much the worse that you believe so, if you have not very good reason for your belief. Does he pretend that he will marry you ? "—She was silent.— " Tell me, Polly, if he does ? "—" He says he will do honourably by me."—" But you know there is but one word necessary to explain that other precious word *honour*, in this case. It is *matrimony*. That word is as soon spoken as any other, and if he *means* it, he will not be shy to *speak* it."—She was silent.— " Tell me, Polly (for I am really greatly concerned for you), what you think *yourself ;* do you *hope* he will marry you ? " —She was silent.—" Do, good Polly (I hope I may call you *good* yet !), answer me."—" Pray, Madam ! " and she wept, and turned from me, to the wainscot—" Pray, excuse me."— " But, indeed, Polly, I cannot *excuse* you. You are under my protection. I was once in as dangerous a situation as you can be in. And I did not escape it, child, by the language and conduct I heard from you."—" Language and conduct, Me'm ! "— " Yes, Polly, language and conduct. Do you think, if I had set me down in my lady's bed-chamber, sung a song, and hemm'd twice, and Mr. B. coming to me, upon that signal (for such I doubt it was), I had kept my place, and suffered myself to be rumpled, and only, in a soft voice, and with an encouraging laugh, cried—' How can you do so ? ' that I should have been what I am ? "—" Me'm, I dare say, my lord " (so all the servants call him, and his aunt often, when she puts Jackey to it), " means no hurt."—" No hurt, Polly ! What, and make you cry ' *Fie !* '—or do you intend to trust your honour to his mercy, rather than to your own discretion ? "—" I hope not, Me'm ! "

—" I hope not too, Polly !—But you know he was free enough with you, to make you say ' Fie ! ' And what might have been the case, who knows ? had I not coughed on purpose : unwilling, for your sake, Polly, to find matters so bad as I feared, and that you would have been led beyond what was reputable."

" Reputable, Me'm ! "—" Yes, Polly : I am sorry you oblige me to speak so plain. But your good requires it. Instead of flying from him, you not only laughed when you cried out, ' Fie ! ' and ' How can you do so ? ' but had no other care than to see if any body heard you ; and you observe how he slid away, like a guilty creature, on my opening the door—Do these things look well, Polly ? Do you think they do ?—And if you hope to emulate my good fortune, do you think this is the way ? "

" I wish, Me'm, I had never seen Mr. H. For nobody will look upon me, if I lose your favour ! "

" It will still, Polly " (and I took her hand, with a kind look), " be in your power to keep it : I will not mention this matter, if you make me your friend, and tell me all that has passed."— Again she wept, and was silent.—This made me more uneasy. —" Don't think, Polly," said I, " that I would envy any other person's preferment, when I have been so much exalted myself. If Mr. H. has talked to you of marriage, tell me."—" No, Me'm, I can't say he has yet."—" Yet, Polly ! Then he never will. For when men do talk of it, they don't always mean it : but whenever they mean it, how can they confirm a doubting maiden, without mentioning it : but alas for you, poor Polly !— The freedoms you have permitted, no doubt, previous to those I heard, and which might have been greater, had I not surprised you with my cough, shew too well, that he need not make any promises to you."—" Indeed, Me'm," said she, sobbing, " I might be too little upon my guard ; but I would not have done any ill for the world."

" I hope you would not, Polly ; but if you suffer these free-doms, you can't tell what you'd have permitted—Tell me, do you love Mr. H. ? "

" He is very good-humoured, Madam, and is not proud."— " No, 'tis not his business to be proud, when he hopes to humble you—humble you, indeed !—beneath the lowest person of the sex, that is honest."—" I hope——"—" You hope ! " interrupted I. " You hope too much ; and I fear a great deal for you, because you fear so little for yourself.—But say, how often have you been in private together ? "

" In private, Me'm ! I don't know what your ladyship calls

private !"—"Why that is *private*, Polly, when, as just now, you neither imagined nor intended any body should see you."

She was silent; and I saw by this, poor girl, how true lovers are to their secret, though, perhaps, their ruin depends upon keeping it. But it behoved me, on many accounts, to examine this matter narrowly; because if Mr. H. should marry her, it would have been laid upon Mr. B.'s example.—And if Polly were ruined, it would be a sad thing, and people would have said, "Aye, she could take care enough of herself, but none at all of her servant : *her* waiting-maid had a much more remiss mistress than Pamela found, or the matter would not have been thus."

"Well, Polly, I see," continued I, "that you will not speak out to me. You may have *several* reasons for it, possibly, though not *one* good one. But as soon as Lady Davers comes in, who has a great concern in this matter, as well as Lord Davers, and are answerable to Lord H. in a matter of so much importance as this, I will leave it to her ladyship's consideration, and shall no more concern myself to ask you questions about it—For then I must take her ladyship's directions, and part with you, to be sure."

The poor girl, frighted at this (for every body fears Lady Davers), wrung her hands, and begged, for God's sake, I would not acquaint Lady Davers with it.

"But how can I help it?—Must I not connive at your proceedings, if I do not? You are no fool, Polly, in other cases. Tell me, how it is possible for me, in my situation, to avoid it?"

"I will tell your ladyship the whole truth; indeed I will—if you will not tell Lady Davers. I am ready to sink at the thoughts of Lady Davers knowing any thing of this."

This looked sadly. I pitied her, but yet was angry in my mind; for I saw, too plainly, that her conduct could not bear a scrutiny, not even in *her own* opinion, poor creature.

I said, "Make me acquainted with the whole."—"Will your ladyship promise——"—"I'll promise nothing, Polly. When I have heard all you think proper to say, I will do what befits me to do; but with as much tenderness as I can for you—and that's all you ought to expect me to promise."—"Why then, Madam—But how can I speak it?—I can speak sooner to any body, than to Lady Davers and you, Madam : for her ladyship's passion, and your ladyship's virtue—How shall I?"—And then she threw herself at my feet, and hid her face with her apron.

I was in agonies for her, almost; I wept over her, and raised

189

her up, and said, " Tell me all. You cannot tell me worse than I apprehend, nor I hope so bad ! O Polly, tell me soon.—For you give me great pain."

And my back, with grief and compassion for the poor girl, was ready to open, as it seemed to me.—In my former distresses, I have been overcome by fainting next to death, and was deprived of sense for some moments—But else, I imagine, I must have felt some such affecting sensation, as the unhappy girl's case gave me.

" Then, Madam, I own," said she, " I have been too faulty." —" As how?—As what?—In what way?—How faulty ? "— asked I, as quick as thought : " you are not ruined, are you? —Tell me, Polly ! "—" No, Madam, but——"—" But what?— Say, but what ? "—" I had consented——"—" To what ? "— " To his proposals, Madam."—" What proposals ? "—" Why, Madam, I was to live with Mr. H."

" I understand you too well—But is it too late to break so wretched a bargain ;—have you already made a sacrifice of your honour ? "

" No, Madam : but I have given it under my hand."

" Under your *hand !*—Ah ! Polly, it is well if you have not given it under your *heart* too. But what foolishness is this !— What consideration has he made you ? "—" He has given it under his hand, that he will always love me; and when his lordship's father dies, he will own me."

" What foolishness is this on both sides !—But are you willing to be released from this bargain ? "

" Indeed I am, Madam, and I told him so yesterday. But he says he will sue me, and ruin me, if I don't stand to it."

" You are ruined if you do !—And I wish—But tell me, Polly, are you not ruined as it is ? "

" Indeed I am not, Madam."

" I doubt, then, you were upon the brink of it, had not this providential indisposition kept me at home.—You met, I suppose, to conclude your shocking bargain.—O poor unhappy girl !—But let me see what he has given under his hand ! "

" He has 'em both, Madam, to be drawn up fair, and in a strong hand, that shall be like a record."

Could I have thought, Miss, that a girl of nineteen could be so ignorant in a point so important, when in every thing else she has shewn no instances like this stupid folly ?

" Has he given you money ? "

" Yes, Madam, he gave me—he gave me—a note. Here it is. He says any body will give me money for it."

And this was a bank note of fifty pounds, which she pulled out of her stays.

The result was, he was to settle one hundred pounds a year upon her and *hers*, poor, poor girl—and was to *own* her, as he calls it (but as wife or mistress, she stipulated not), when his father died, and he came into the title and estate.

I told her, it was impossible for me to conceal the matter from Lady Davers, if she would not, by her promises to be governed entirely by me, and to abandon all thoughts of Mr. H., give me room to conclude, that the wicked bargain was at an end.

And to keep the poor creature in some spirits, and to enable her to look up, and to be more easy under my direction, I blamed *him* more than I did *her*: though, considering what virtue requires of a woman, and custom has made shameless in a man, I think the poor girl inexcusable, and shall not be easy while she is about me. For she is more to blame, because, of the two, she has more wit than the man.

"But what can I do?" thought I. "If I put her away, 'twill be to throw her directly into his hands. He won't stay here long: and she *may* see her folly. But yet her eyes were open; she knew what she had to trust to—and by their wicked beginning, and her encouraging repulses, I doubt she would have been utterly ruined that very day."

I knew the rage Lady Davers would be in with both. So this was another embarrassment. Yet should my good intentions fail, and they conclude their vile bargain, and it appeared that I knew of it, but would not acquaint her, then should I have been more blamed than any mistress of a family, circumstanced as I am. Upon the whole, I resolved to comfort the girl as well as I could, till I had gained her confidence, that my advice might have the more weight, and, by degrees, be more likely to reclaim her: for, poor soul! there would be an end of her reputation, the most precious of all jewels, the moment the matter was known; and that would be a sad thing.

As for the man, I thought it best to take courage (and you, that know me, will say, I must have a good deal more than usual) to talk to Mr. H. on this subject. And she consenting I should, and, with great protestations, declaring her sorrow and repentance, begging to get her note of hand again, and to give him back his note of fifty pounds, I went down to find him.

He shunned me, as a thief would a constable at the head of a hue-and-cry. As I entered one room, he went into another, looking with conscious guilt, yet confidently humming a tune. At last I fixed him, bidding Rachel tell Polly he wanted to send a message by her to her lady. By which I doubted not he was desirous to know what she had owned, in order to govern himself accordingly.

His back was towards me; and I said—

" Mr. H., here I am myself, to take your commands."

He gave a caper half a yard high—" Madam, I wanted—I wanted to speak to—I would have spoken with——"

" You wanted to send Polly to me, perhaps, Mr. H., to ask if I would take a little walk with you in the garden."

" Very true, Madam !—Very true indeed !—You have guessed the matter. I thought it was pity, this fine day, as every body was taking airing——"

" Well then, Sir, please to lead the way, and I'll attend you."

" Yet I fancy, Madam, the wind is a little too high for you.—Won't you catch cold ? "—" No, never fear, Mr. H., I am not afraid of a little air."

" I will attend you presently, Madam : you'll be in the great gravel walk, or on the terrace.—I'll wait upon you in an instant."

I had the courage to take hold of his arm, as if I had like to have slipt.—For, thought I, thou shalt not see the girl till I have talked to thee a little, if thou dost then.—" Excuse me, Mr. H. —I hope I have not hurt my foot—I must lean upon you."

" Will you be pleased, Madam, to have a chair ? I fear you have sprained your foot.—Shall I help you to a chair ? "

" No, no, Sir, I shall walk it off, if I hold by you."

So he had no excuse to leave me, and we proceeded into the garden. But never did any thing look so like a *foolish fellow*, as his aunt calls him. He looked, if possible, half a dozen ways at once, hemm'd, coughed, turned his head behind him every now and then, started half a dozen silly subjects, in hopes to hinder me from speaking.

I appeared, I believe, under some concern how to begin with him ; for he would have it I was not very well, and begged he might step in one minute to desire Mrs. Jervis to attend me.

So I resolved to begin with him ; lest I should lose the opportunity, seeing my eel so very slippery. And placing myself on a seat, asked him to sit down. He declined, and would wait upon me presently, he said, and seemed to be going. So I began—" It is easy for me, Mr. H., to penetrate into the reason why you are so willing to leave me : but 'tis for your own sake, that I desire you to hear me, that no mischief may ensue among friends and relations, on an occasion to which you are no stranger."

" O, Madam, what can you mean? Surely, Madam, you don't think amiss of a little innocent liberty, or so!"

" Mr. H.," replied I, " I want not any evidence of your inhospitable designs upon a poor unwary young creature, whom your birth and quality have found it too easy a task to influence."

" *Inhospitable designs!* Madam!—A harsh word! You very nice ladies cannot admit of the least freedom in the world! —Why, Madam, I have kiss'd a lady's woman before now, in a civil way or so, and never was called to an account for it, as a breach of hospitality."

" 'Tis not for me, Mr. H., to proceed to *very nice* particulars with a gentleman who can act as you have done, by a poor girl, that dare not have looked up to a man of your quality, had you not levelled all distinction between you in order to level the weak creature to the common dirt of the highway. I must say, that the poor girl heartily repents of her folly; and, to shew you, that it signifies nothing to deny it, she begs you will return the note of her hand you extorted from her foolishness; and I hope you'll be so much of a gentleman, as not to keep in your power such a testimony of the weakness of any of the sex."

" Has she told you that, Madam?—Why, may be—indeed— I can't but say—Truly, it mayn't look so well to you, Madam: but young folks will have frolics. It was nothing but a frolic. Let me *be hanged*, if it was!"

" Be pleased then, Sir, to give up her note to me, to return to her. Reputation should not be frolicked with, Sir; especially that of a poor girl, who has nothing else to depend upon."

" I'll give it her myself, if you please, Madam, and laugh at her into the bargain. Why, 'tis comical enough, if the little pug thought I was earnest, I must have a laugh or two at her, Madam, when I give it her up."

" Since, 'tis but a frolic, Mr. H., you won't take it amiss, that when we are set down to supper, we call Polly in, and demand a sight of her note, and that will make every one merry as well as you."

" Not so, Madam, that mayn't be so well neither! For, perhaps, they will be apt to think it is in earnest; when, as I hope to live, 'tis but a jest: nothing in the world else, upon honour!"

I put on then a still more serious air—" As you *hope to live*, say you, Mr. H.!—and *upon your honour!* How! fear you not an instant punishment for this appeal? And what is the *honour* you swear by? Take that, and answer me, Sir: do gentlemen give away bank-notes for *frolics*, and for *mere jests*, and *nothing in the world* else !—I am sorry to be obliged to deal thus with you. But I thought I was talking to a gentleman who would not forfeit his veracity; and that in so solemn an instance as this ! "

He looked like a man thunderstruck. His face was distorted, and his head seemed to turn about upon his neck, like a weather-cock in a hurricane, to all points of the compass; his hands clenched as in a passion, and yet shame and confusion struggling in every limb and feature. At last he said, " I am confoundedly betrayed. But if I am exposed to my uncle and aunt " (for the wretch thought of nobody but himself), " I am undone, and shall never be able to look them in the face. 'Tis true, I had a design upon her; and since she has betrayed me, I think I may say, that she was as willing, almost, as I."

" Ungenerous, contemptible wretch !" thought I—" But such of our sex as can thus give up their virtue, ought to expect no better: for he that sticks not at *one* bad action, will not scruple at *another* to vindicate himself: and so, devil-like, become the attempter and the accuser too ! "

" But if you will be so good," said he, with hands uplifted, " as to take no notice of this to my uncle, and especially to my aunt and Mr. B., I swear to you, I never will think of her as long as I live."

" And you'll bind this promise, will you, Sir, by *your honour*, and as you *hope to live* ? "

" Dear, good Madam, forgive me, I beseech you; don't be so severe upon me. By all that's—"

" Don't swear, Mr. H. But as an earnest that I may believe you, give me back the girl's foolish note, that, though 'tis of no significance, she may not have *that* to witness her folly."— He took out his pocket-book : " There it is, Madam ! And I beg you'll forgive this attempt : I see I ought not to have made it. I doubt it was a breach of the laws of hospitality, as you say. But to make it known, will only expose me, and it can do no good; and Mr. B. will perhaps resent it; and my aunt will never let me hear the last of it, nor my uncle neither— And I shall be sent to travel again—And " (added the poor creature) " I was once in a storm, and the crossing the sea again would be death to me."

" What a wretch art thou ! " thought I. " What could such an one as thou find to say, to a poor creature that, if put in the scale against considerations of virtue, should make the latter

194

kick the beam? Poor, poor Polly Barlow! thou art sunk indeed! Too low for excuse, and almost beneath pity!"

I told him, if I could observe that nothing passed between them, that should lay me under a necessity of revealing the matter, I should not be forward to expose him, nor the maiden either: but that he must, in his own judgment, excuse me, if I made every body acquainted with it, if I were to see the correspondence between them likely to be renewed or carried on: "For," added I, " in that case I should owe it to myself, to Mr. B., to Lord and Lady Davers, and to you, and the unhappy body too, to do so."

He would needs drop down on one knee, to promise this; and with a thousand acknowledgments, left me to find Mr. Colbrand, in order to ride to meet the coach on its return. I went in, and gave the foolish note to the silly girl, which she received eagerly, and immediately burnt; and I told her, I would not suffer her to come near me but as little as possible, when I was in company while Mr. H. staid; but consigned her entirely to the care of Mrs. Jervis, to whom only, I said, I would hint the matter as tenderly as I could: and for this, I added, I had more reasons than one; first, to give her the benefit of a good gentlewoman's advice, to which I had myself formerly been beholden, and from whom I concealed nothing; next, to keep out of Mr. H.'s way; and lastly that I might have an opportunity, from Mrs. Jervis's opinion, to judge of the sincerity of her repentance: " For, Polly," said I, " you must imagine, so regular and uniform as all our family is, and so good as I thought all the people about me were, that I could not suspect, that she, the duties of whose place made her nearest to my person, was the farthest from what I wished."

I have set this matter so strongly before her, and Mrs. Jervis has so well seconded me, that I hope the best; for the grief the poor creature carries in her looks, and expresses in her words, cannot be described; frequently accusing herself, with tears, saying often to Mrs. Jervis, she is not worthy to stand in the presence of her mistress, whose example she has made so bad an use of, and whose lessons she had so ill followed.

I am sadly troubled at this matter, however; but I take great comfort in reflecting that my sudden indisposition looked like a providential thing, which may save one poor soul, and be a seasonable warning to her, as long as she lives.

Meantime I must observe, that at supper last night, Mr. H. looked abject and mean, and like a poor thief, as I thought; and conscious of his disappointed folly (though I seldom glanced my eye upon him), had less to say for himself than ever.

And once my Lady Davers, laughing, said, "I think in my heart, my nephew looks more foolish every time I see him, than the last." He stole a look at me, and blushed; and my lord said, "Jackey has some grace! He blushes! Hold up thy head, nephew! Hast thou nothing at all to say for thyself?"

Sir Jacob said, "A blush becomes a young gentleman! I never saw one before though, in Mr. H.—What's the matter, Sir?"—"Only," said Lady Davers, "his skin or his conscience is mended, that's all."

"Thank you, Madam," was all he said, bowing to his aunt, and affecting a careless yet confused air, as if he whispered a whistle. "O, wretch!" thought I, "see what it is to have a condemning conscience; while every *innocent* person looks round easy, smiling, and erect!"—But yet it was not the shame of a bad action, I doubt, but being discovered and disappointed, that gave him his confusion of face.

What a sad thing for a person to be guilty of such actions, as shall put it in the power of another, even by a look, to mortify him! And if poor souls can be thus abjectly struck at such a discovery by a fellow-creature, how must they appear before an unerring and omniscient Judge, with a conscience standing in the place of a thousand witnesses? and calling in vain upon the *mountains to fall upon them*, and the *hills to cover them!*— How serious this subject makes one!

SATURDAY EVENING.

I am just retired from a fatiguing service; for who should come to dine with Mr. B. but that sad rake Sir Charles Hargrave; and Mr. Walgrave, Mr. Sedley, and Mr. Floyd, three as bad as himself; inseparable companions, whose whole delight is drinking, hunting, and lewdness; but otherwise gentlemen of wit and large estates. Three of them broke in upon us at the Hall, on the happiest day of my life, to our great regret; and they had been long threatening to make this visit, in order to see me, as they told Mr. B.

They whipt out two bottles of champagne instantly, for a *whet*, as they called it; and went to view the stud and the kennel, and then walked in the garden till dinner was ready; my Lord Davers, Mr. H. and Sir Jacob, as well as Mr. B. (for they are all acquainted) accompanying them.

Sir Charles, it seems, as Lord Davers told me afterwards,

said, he longed to see Mrs. B. She was the talk wherever he went, and he had conceived a high opinion of her beforehand.

Lord Davers said, " I defy you, gentlemen, to think so highly of her as she deserves, take mind and person together."

Mr. Floyd said, he never saw any woman yet, who came up to what he expected, where fame had been lavish in her praise.

" But how, brother baronet," said Sir Charles to Sir Jacob, " came *you* to be reconciled to her? I heard that you would never own her."

" Oons man ! " said Sir Jacob, " I was taken in.—They contrived to clap her upon me as Lady Jenny C. and pretended they'd keep t'other out of my sight; and I was plaguily bit, and forced to get off as well as I could."

" That was a bite indeed," said Mr. Walgrave; " and so you fell a praising Lady Jenny, I warrant, to the skies."

" Ye—s " (drawling out the affirmative monosyllable), " I was used most scurvily : faith I was. I bear 'em a grudge for it still, I can tell 'em that; for I have hardly been able to hold up my head like a man since—but am forced to go and come, and to do as they bid me. By my troth, I never was so manageable in my life."

" Your Herefordshire neighbours, Sir Jacob," said Mr. Sedley, with an oath, " will rejoice to hear this; for the whole county there cannot manage you."

" I am quite cow'd now, as you will see by-and-by; nay, for that matter, if you can set Mrs. B. a talking, not one of you all will care to open your lips, except to say as she says."

" Never fear, old boy," said Sir Charles, " we'll bear our parts in conversation. I never saw the woman yet, who could give me either awe or love for six minutes together. What think you, Mr. B.? Have you any notion, that your lady will have so much power over us? "

" I think, Sir Charles, I have one of the finest women in England; but I neither expect nor desire you rakes should see her with my eyes."

" You know, if I have a mind to love her, and make court to her too, Mr. B., I will : and I am half in love with her already, although I have not seen her."

They came in when dinner was near ready, and the four gentlemen took each a large bumper of old hock for another whet.

The countess, Lady Davers, and I came down together. The gentlemen knew our two noble ladies, and were known to them in person, as well as by character. Mr. B., in his usual

197

kind and encouraging manner, took my hand, and presented the four gentlemen to me, each by his name. Sir Charles said, pretty bluntly, that he hoped he was more welcome to me now, than the last time he was under the same roof with me; for he had been told since, that *that* was our happy day.

I said, Mr. B.'s friends were always welcome to me.

" 'Tis well, Madam," said Mr. Sedley, "we did not know how it was. We should have quartered ourselves upon Mr. B. for a week together, and kept him up day and night."

I thought this speech deserved no answer, especially as they were gentlemen who wanted no countenance, and addressed myself to Lord Davers, who is always kindly making court to me : "I hope, my good lord, you find yourself quite recovered of your head-ache?" (of which he complained at breakfast).

"I thank you, my dear sister, pretty well."

"I was telling Sir Charles and the other gentlemen, niece," said Sir Jacob, "how I was cheated here, when I came first, with a Lady Jenny."

"It was a very lucky cheat for me, Sir Jacob; for it gave you a prepossession in my favour under so advantageous a character, that I could never have expected otherwise."

"I wish," said the countess, "my daughter, for whom Sir Jacob took you, had Mrs. B.'s qualities to boast of."—"How am I obliged to your ladyship's goodness," returned I, "when you treat me with even greater indulgence than you use to so beloved a daughter!"

"Nay, now you talk of treating," said Sir Charles, "when, ladies, will you treat our sex with the politeness which you shew to one another?"

"When your sex deserve it, Sir Charles," answered Lady Davers.

"Who is to be judge of that?" said Mr. Walgrave.

"Not the gentlemen, I hope," replied my lady.

"Well then, Mrs. B.," said Sir Charles, "we bespeak your good opinion of *us ;* for you have *ours.*"

"I am obliged to you, gentlemen ; but I must be more cautious in declaring *mine,* lest it should be thought I am influenced by your kind, and perhaps too hasty, opinions of me."

Sir Charles swore they had *seen* enough of me the moment I entered the parlour, and heard enough the moment I opened my lips to answer for *their* opinions of me.

I said, I made no doubt, when *they* had as good a subject to expatiate upon, as I had, in the pleasure before me, of seeing so many agreeable friends of Mr. B.'s, they would maintain the title they claimed of every one's good opinion.

"This," said Sir Jacob, "is binding you over, gentlemen, to your good behaviour. You must know, my niece never shoots flying, as *you* do."

The gentlemen laughed: "Is it shooting flying, Sir Jacob," returned Sir Charles, "to praise that lady?"

"Ads-bud, I did not think of that."

"Sir Jacob," said the countess, "you need not be at a fault; —for a good sportsman always hits his mark, flying or not; and the gentlemen had so fair an one, that they could not well miss it."

"You are fairly helped over the stile, Sir Jacob," said Mr. Floyd.

"And, indeed, I wanted it; though I limped like a puppy before I was lame. One can't think of every thing as one used to do at your time of life, gentlemen." This flippant stuff was all that passed, which I *can* recite; for the rest, at table, and after dinner, was too polite by half for me; such as, the quantity of wine each man could *carry off* (that was the phrase), dogs, horses, hunting, racing, cock-fighting, and all accompanied with swearing and cursing, and that in good humour, and out of wantonness (the least excusable and more profligate sort of swearing and cursing of all).

The gentlemen liked the wine so well, that we had the felicity to drink tea and coffee by ourselves; only Mr. B. (upon our inviting the gentlemen to partake with us) sliding in for a few minutes to tell us, they would stick by what they had, and taking a dish of coffee with us.

I should not omit one observation; that Sir Jacob, when they were gone, said they were *pure company ;* and Mr. H. that he never was so delighted in his *born days.*—While the two ladies put up their prayers, that they might never have such another entertainment. And being encouraged by their declaration, I presumed to join in the same petition.

Yet it seems, these are men of wit! I believe they must be so—for I could neither like nor understand them. Yet, if their conversation had much wit, I should think my ladies would have found it out.

The gentlemen, permit me to add, went away very merry, to ride ten miles by owl-light; for they would not accept of beds here. They had two French horns with them, and gave us a flourish or two at going off. Each had a servant besides: but the way they were in would have given me more concern than it did, had they been related to Mr. B. and less used to it. And, indeed, it is a happiness, that such gentlemen take no more care than they generally do, to interest any body intimately in their healths and preservation; for these are all single men. Nor need the public, any more than the private, be much concerned about them; for let such persons go when they will, if they continue single, their next heir cannot well be a worse commonwealth's man; and there is a great chance he may be better.

You know I end my Saturdays seriously. And this, to what I have already said, makes me add, that I cannot express how much I am, my dear Miss Darnford, *your faithful and affectionate*

P. B.

LETTER XXXVIII

From Mrs. B. to Miss Darnford. In Answer to Letters XXXV and XXXVI.

MY DEAR MISS DARNFORD,

I skip over the little transactions of several days, to let you know how much you rejoice me, in telling me Sir Simon has been so kind as to comply with my wishes. Both your most agreeable letters came to my hand together, and I thank you a hundred times for them; and I thank your dear mamma, and Sir Simon too, for the pleasure they have given me in this obliging permission. How happy shall we be !—But how long will you be permitted to stay, though? All the winter, I hope :—and then, when that is over, let us set out together, if God shall spare us, directly for Lincolnshire; and to pass most of the summer likewise in each other's company. What a sweet thought is this !—Let me indulge it a little while.

Mr. B. read your letters, and says, you are a charming young lady, and surpass yourself in every letter. I told him, that he was more interested in the pleasure I took in this favour of Sir Simon's than he imagined. " As how, my dear? " said he. " A plain case, Sir," replied I: " for endeavouring to improve myself by Miss Darnford's conversation and behaviour, I shall every day be more worthy of your favour." He kindly would have it, that nobody, no, not Miss Darnford herself, excelled me.

'Tis right, you know, Miss, that Mr. B. should think so, though I must know nothing at all, if I was not sensible how inferior I am to my dear Miss Darnford: and yet, when I look

200

abroad now-and-then, I could be a proud slut, if I would, and not yield the palm to many others.

Well, my dear Miss,

SUNDAY

Is past and gone, as happy as the last; the two ladies, and, at *their* earnest request, Sir Jacob bearing us company, in the evening part. My Polly was there morning and evening, with her heart broken almost, poor girl!—I put her in a corner of my closet, that her concern should not be minded. Mrs. Jervis gives me great hopes of her.

Sir Jacob was much pleased with our family order, and said, 'twas no wonder I *kept* so good myself, and made others so: and he thought the four rakes (for he run on how much they admired me) would be converted, if they saw how well I passed my time, and how cheerful and easy every one, as well as myself was under it! He said, when he came home, he must take such a method himself in *his* family; for, he believed, it would make not only better masters and mistresses, but better children, and better servants too. But, poor gentleman! he has, I doubt, a great deal to mend in *himself*, before he can begin such a practice with efficacy in his *family*.

MONDAY.

In the afternoon, Sir Jacob took his leave of us, highly satisfied with us both, and *particularly* (so he said) with me; and promised that my two cousins, as he called his daughters, and his sister, an old maiden lady, if they went to town this winter, should visit me, and be improved by me; that was his word. Mr. B. accompanied him some miles on his journey, and the two ladies, and Lord Davers, and I, took an airing in the coach.

Mr. B. was so kind as to tell me, when he came home, with a whisper, that Miss Goodwin presented her duty to me.

I have got a multitude of fine things for the dear little creature, and Mr. B. promises to give me a dairy-house breakfast, when our guests are gone.

I enclose the history of this little charmer, by Mr. B.'s consent, since you are to do us the honour, as he (as well as I) pleases himself, to be one of our family—but keep it to yourself, whatever you do. I am guarantee that you will; and have put it in a separate paper, that you may burn it when read. For I may want your advice on this subject, having a great desire to get this child in my possession; and yet Lady Davers has given a hint, that dwells a little with me. When I have the pleasure I hope for, I will lay all before you, and be determined, and proceed, as far as I have power, by you. You, my good father and mother, have seen the story in my former papers.

TUESDAY.

You must know, I pass over the days thus swiftly, not that I could not fill them up with writing, as amply as I have done the former; but intending only to give you a general idea of our way of life and conversation; and having gone through a whole week and more, you will be able, from what I have recited, to form a judgment how it is with us, one day with another. As for example, now and then neighbourly visits received and paid—Needlework between whiles—Music—Cards sometimes, though I don't love them—One more benevolent round—Improving conversations with my dear Mr. B. and my two good ladies—A lesson from him, when alone, either in French or Latin—A new pauper case or two—A visit from the good dean—Mr. Williams's departure, in order to put the new projected alteration in force, which is to deprive me of my chaplain—(By the way, the dean is highly pleased with this affair, and the motives to it, Mr. Adams being a favourite of his, and a distant relation of his lady)—Mr. H.'s and Polly's mutual endeavour to avoid one another—My lessons to the poor girl, and cautions, as if she were my sister——

These, my dear Miss Darnford, and my honoured parents, are the pleasant employments of our time; so far as we females are concerned: for the gentlemen hunt, ride out, and divert themselves in their way, and bring us home the news and occurrences they meet with abroad, and now-and-then a straggling gentleman they pick up in their diversions. And so I shall not enlarge upon these articles, after the tedious specimens I have already given.

WEDNESDAY, THURSDAY.

Could you ever have thought, my dear, that husbands have a dispensing power over their wives, which kings are not allowed over the laws? I have had a smart debate with Mr. B., and I fear it will not be the only one upon this subject. Can you believe, that if a wife thinks a thing her duty to do, which her husband does not approve, he can dispense with her performing it, and no sin shall lie at her door? Mr. B. maintains this point. I have great doubts about it; particularly one; that if a matter be my duty, and he dispenses with my performance of it, whether, even although that were to clear *me*

202

of the sin, it will not fall upon *himself* ? And a good wife would be as much concerned at this, as if it was to remain upon *her*. Yet he seems set upon it. What can one do?—Did you ever hear of such a notion, before? Of such a prerogative in a husband? Would you care to subscribe to it?

He says, the ladies are of his opinion. I'm afraid they are, and so will not ask them. But, perhaps, I mayn't live, and other things may happen; and so I'll say no more of it at present.

Mr. H. and my Lord and Lady Davers and the excellent Countess of C. having left us this day, to our mutual regret, the former put the following letter into my hands, with an air of respect and even reverence. He says, he spells most lamentably; and this obliges me to give it you *literally* :

" DEARE GOOD MADAM,

"I cannott contente myself with common thankes, on leaving youres, and Mr. B.'s hospitabel house, because of *thatt there* affaire, which I neede not mention ! and truly am *ashamed* to mention, as I *have been* to looke you in the face ever since it happen'd. I don't knowe *how itt came aboute*, butt I thought butt att first of *joking* a littel, *or soe ;* and seeing Polley heard me with more attentiveness than I expected, I was encouraged to proceede; and *soe*, now I recollecte, itt *camn aboute*.

" But she is innosente for me : and I don't knowe how *thatt* came about neither; for wee were oute one moonelighte nighte in the garden, walking aboute, and afterwards tooke a *napp* of two houres, as I beliefe, in the summer-house in the littel gardin, being over-powered with sleepe; for I woulde make her lay her head uppon my breste, till before we were awar, wee felle asleepe. Butt before thatt, wee had agreed on whatt you discovered.

" This is the whole truthe, and all the intimasies we ever hadde, to *speake off*. But I beleefe we should have been better acquainted, hadd you nott, luckily *for mee !* prevented itt, by being at home, when we thought you abroad. For I was to come to her when shee hemm'd *two or three times ;* for having made a contract, you knowe, Madam, it was naturall enough to take the first occasion to putt itt in force.

" Poor Polley ! I pity her too. Don't thinke the worse of her, deare Madam, so as to turn her away, because it may bee her ruin. I don't desire too see her. I might have been *drawne in* to do strange foolish things, and been ruin'd at the long run; for who knows where this thing mought have ended? My *unkell* woulde have never seene me. My *father* too (his lordshipp, you have hearde, Madam, is a very *crosse man*, and never loved *me much*) mought have cutt off the intaile. My *aunte* would have dispis'd mee and scorn'd mee. I should have been her foolishe fellowe in *earneste*, nott in *jeste*, as now. You woulde have resented itt, and Mr. B. (who knows?) mought have called me to account.

"Butt cann you forgive me? You see how happy I am in my disappointment. I did nott think too write so much;—for I don't love it: but on this occasion, know not how too leave off. I hope you can read my letter. I know I write a *clumsy* hand, and *spelle most lamentabelly ;* for I never had a tallent for these things. I was readier by half to admire the *orcherd robbing picture in* Lillie's grammar, then any other part of the book.

"But, hey, whether am I running! I never writt to you before, and never may again, unless you, or Mr. B. command it, for your service. So pray excuse me, Madam.

"I knowe I neede give no advice to Polley, to take care of *first* encouragements. Poor girl! she mought have suffer'd sadly, as welle as I. For iff my father, and my unkell and aunte, had requir'd mee to turne her off, you know itt woulde have been undutifull to have refused them, notwithstanding our bargaine. And want of duty to them woulde have been to have added faulte too faulte : as you once observed, I remember, that one faulte never comes alone, but drawes after itt generally five or six, to hide or vindicate itt, and *they* every one perhapps as many more *eache*.

"I shall never forgett severall of youre wise sayinges. I have been vex'd, may I be *hang'd* if I have not, many a time, thatt I coulde not make such observations as you make; who am so much *older* too, and a *man* besides, and a *peere's son*, and a *peere's nephew !* but my tallents lie *another way ;* and by that time my father dies, I hope to improve myselfe, in order to *cutt* such a figure, as may make me be no disgrase to my *name* or *countrey*.

"Well, but whatt is all this to the purpose?—I will keep close to my text; and that is, to thank you, good Madam, for all the favours I have received in your house; to thank you for disappointing mee, and for convincing mee, in so *kinde*, yet so *shameing* a manner, how wrong I was in the matter of *that there* Polley; and for not exposing my folly to any boddy but *myselfe* (for I should have been ready to *hang* myselfe, if you hadd);

and to beg youre pardon for itt, assuring you, that I will never offerr the like as long as I breathe. I am, Madam, with the greatest respecte, *youre most, obliged, moste faithful, and most obedient humbell servante,*   J. H.

" Pray excuse blotts and blurs."

Well, Miss Darnford, what shall we say to this fine letter?— You'll allow it to be an original, I hope. Yet, may-be not. For it may be as well written, and as sensible a letter as this class of people generally write !

Mr. H. dresses well, is not a contemptible figure of a man, laughs, talks, where he can be heard, and his aunt is not present; and *cuts*, to use his own word, a considerable figure in a country town.—But see—Yet I will not say what I might—He is Lord Davers's nephew; and if he makes his *observations*, and *forbears* his *speeches* (I mean, can be silent, and only laugh when he sees somebody of more sense laugh, and never *approve* or *condemn* but in *leading-strings*), he may possibly pass in a crowd of gentlemen. But poor, poor Polly Barlow !   What *can* I say for Polly Barlow ?

I have a time in view, when my papers may fall under the inspection of a dear gentleman, to whom, next to God, I am accountable for all my actions and correspondences; so I will either write an account of the matter, and seal it up separately, for Mr. B., or, at a fit opportunity, break it to him, and let him know (under secrecy, if he will promise it) the steps I took in it; lest something arise hereafter, when I cannot answer for myself, to render any thing dark or questionable in it. A method, I believe, very proper to be taken by every married lady; and I presume the rather to say so, having had a good example for it : for I have often thought of a little sealed up parcel of papers, my lady made me burn in her presence, about a month before she died.   " They are, Pamela," said she, " such as would not concern me, let who will see them, could they know the springs and causes of them : but, for want of a clue, my son might be at a loss what to think of several of those letters were he to find them, in looking over my other papers, when I am no more."

Let me add, that nothing could be more endearing than our parting with our noble guests.   My lady repeated her commands for what she often engaged me to promise, that is to say, to renew the correspondence begun between us, so much (as she was pleased to say) to her satisfaction.

I could not help shewing her ladyship, who was always enquiring after my writing employment, most of what passed between you and me : she admires you much, and wished Mr. H. had more wit, that was her word : she should in that case, she said, be very glad to set on foot a treaty between you and him.

But that, I fancy, can never be tolerable to you; and I only mention it *en passant.*—There's a French woman for you !

The countess was full of her kind wishes for my happiness; and my Lady Davers told me, that if I could give her timely notice, she would be present on a *certain* occasion.

But, my dear Miss, what could I say ?—I know nothing of the matter !—Only, I am a sad coward, and have a thousand anxieties which I cannot mention to any body.

But, if I have such in the honourable estate of matrimony, what must those poor souls have, who are seduced, and have all manner of reason to apprehend, that the crime shall be followed by a punishment so *natural* to it ? A punishment *in kind*, as I may say; which if it only ends in forfeiture of life, following the forfeiture of fame, must be thought merciful and happy beyond expectation : for how shall they lay claim to the hope given to persons in their circumstances that *they shall be saved in child-bearing,* since the condition is, *if they* CONTINUE *in faith and charity, and* HOLINESS *with* SOBRIETY.

Now, my honoured mother, and my dear Miss Darnford, since I am upon this affecting subject, does not this text seem to give a comfortable hope to a good woman, who shall thus die, of being happy in the Divine mercies? For the Apostle, in the context, says, that *he suffers not a woman to teach, nor usurp authority over the man, but to be in silence.*—And what is the reason he gives? Why, a reason that is a natural consequence of the curse on the first disobedience, that she shall be in subjection to her husband. " For," says he, " *Adam was* NOT *deceived; but the woman, being deceived, was in the transgression.*" As much as to say—Had it not been for the woman, Adam had kept his integrity, and therefore her punishment shall be, as it is said, " *I will greatly multiply thy sorrow in thy conception : in sorrow shalt thou bring forth children—and thy husband shall rule over thee.*" But nevertheless, if thou shalt not survive the sharpness of thy sorrow, thy death shall be deemed to be such an alleviation of thy part of the entailed transgression, that thou shalt *be saved*, if thou hast CONTINUED in faith and charity, and HOLINESS with SOBRIETY.

This, my honoured parents, and my dear friend, is *my* paraphrase; and I reap no small comfort from it, when I meditate upon it.

But I shall make you as serious as myself; and, my dear

206

friend, perhaps, frighten you from entering into a state, in which our poor sex suffer so much, from the bridal morning, let it rise as gaily as it will upon a thoughtful mind, to that affecting circumstance, (throughout its whole progression), for which nothing but a tender, a generous, and a worthy husband can make them any part of amends.

But a word or two more, as to the parting with our honoured company. I was a little indisposed, and they all would excuse me, against my will, from attending them in the coach some miles, which their dear brother did. Both ladies most tenderly saluted me, twice or thrice a-piece, folding their kind arms about me, and wishing my safety and health, and charging me to *think* little, and *hope* much; for they saw me thoughtful at times, though I endeavoured to hide it from them.

My Lord Davers said, with a goodness of temper that is peculiar to him, " My dearest sister,—May God preserve you, and multiply your comforts ! I shall pray for you more than ever I did for myself, though I have so much more need of it : —I *must* leave you—But I leave one whom I love and honour next to Lady Davers, and ever shall."

Mr. H. looked consciously silly. " I can say nothing, Madam, but " (saluting me) " that I shall never forget your goodness to me."

I had before, in Mrs. Jervis's parlour, taken leave of Mrs. Worden and Mrs. Lesley, my ladies' women : they each stole a hand of mine, and kissed it, begging pardon for the freedom. But I answered, taking each by her hand, and kissing her, " I shall always think of you with pleasure, my good friends; for you have encouraged me constantly by your presence in my private duties; and may God bless you, and the worthy families you so laudably serve, as well for your sakes, as their own ! "

They turned away with tears; and Mrs. Worden would have said something to me, but could not.—Only both taking Mrs. Jervis by the hand, " Happy Mrs. Jervis ! " said they, almost in a breath. " And happy I too," repeated I, " in my Mrs. Jervis, and in such kind well-wishers as Mrs. Worden and Mrs. Lesley. Wear this, Mrs. Worden;—wear this, Mrs. Lesley, for my sake : " and to each I gave a ring, with a crystal and brilliants set about it, which Mr. B. had bought a week before for this purpose : he has a great opinion of both the good folks, and often praised their prudence, and quiet and respectful behaviour to every body, so different from the impertinence (that was his word) of most ladies' women who are favourites.

Mrs. Jervis said, " I have enjoyed many happy hours in your

conversation, Mrs. Worden and Mrs. Lesley: I shall miss you very much."

"I must endeavour," said I, taking her hand, "to make it up to you, my good friend, as well as I can. And of late we have not had so many opportunities together as I should have wished, had I not been so agreeably engaged as you know. So we must each try to comfort the other, when we have lost, I such noble, and you such worthy companions."

Mrs. Jervis's honest heart, before touched by the parting, shewed itself at her eyes. "Wonder not," said I, to the two gentlewomen, wiping with my handkerchief her venerable cheeks, "that I always thus endeavour to dry up all my good Mrs. Jervis's tears;" and then I kissed her, thinking of *you*, my dear mother; and I was forced to withdraw a little abruptly, lest I should be too much moved myself; for had our departing company enquired into the occasion, they would perhaps have thought it derogatory (though I should not) to my present station, and too much retrospecting to my former.

I could not, in conversation between Mr. B. and myself, when I was gratefully expatiating upon the amiable characters of our noble guests, and of their behaviour and kindness to me, help observing, that I had little expected, from some hints which formerly dropt from Mr. B., to find my good Lord Davers so polite and so sensible a man.

"He is a very good-natured man," replied Mr. B. "I believe I might once or twice drop some disrespectful words of him. But it was the effect of passion at the time, and with a view to two or three points of his conduct in public life; for which I took the liberty to find fault with him, and received very unsatisfactory excuses. One of these, I remember, was in a conference between a committee of each house of parliament, in which he behaved in a way I could not wish from a man so nearly allied to me by marriage; for all he could talk of, was the dignity of their house, when the reason of the thing was strong with the other; and it fell to my lot to answer what he said; which I did with some asperity; and this occasioned a coolness between us for some time.

"But no man makes a better figure in private life than Lord Davers; especially now that my sister's good sense has got the better of her passions, and she can behave with tolerable decency towards him. For once, Pamela, it was not so: the violence of her spirit making him appear in a light too little advantageous either to his quality or merit. But now he improves upon me every time I see him.

"You know not, my dear, what a disgrace a haughty and passionate woman brings upon her husband, and upon herself too, in the eyes of her own sex, as well as ours. Nay, even those ladies, who would be as glad of dominion as she, if they might be permitted to exercise it, despise others who do, and the man *most* who suffers it.

"And let me tell you," said the dear man, with an air that shewed he was satisfied with his own conduct in this particular, "that you cannot imagine how much a woman owes to her husband, as well with regard to *her own* peace of mind, as to *both* their reputations (however it may go against the grain with her sometimes), if he be a man who has discretion to keep her encroaching passions under a genteel and reasonable control!"

How do you like this doctrine, Miss?—I'll warrant, you believe, that I could do no less than drop Mr. B. one of my best curt'sies, in acknowledgment of my obligation to him, for so considerately preserving to me *my* peace of mind, and *my* reputation, as well as *his own*, in this case.

But after all, when one duly weighs the matter, what he says may be right in the main; for I have not been able to contradict him, partial as I am to my sex, when he has pointed out to me instances in the behaviour of certain ladies, who, like children, the more they have been humoured, the more humoursome they have grown; which must have occasioned as great uneasiness to themselves, as to their husbands. Will you excuse me, my dear? This is between ourselves; for I did not own so much to Mr. B. For one should not give up one's sex, you know, if one can help it: for the men will be as apt to impose, as the women to encroach, I doubt.

Well, but here, my honest parents, and my dear Miss Darnford, at last, I end my journal-wise letters, as I may call them; our noble guests being gone, and our time and employments rolling on in much the same manner, as in past days, of which I have given an account. I am, *my dearest father and mother, and best beloved Miss Darnford, your dutiful and affectionate*

P. B.

LETTER XXXIX

My dear Miss Darnford,

I hear that Mrs. Jewkes is in no good state of health. I am very sorry for it. I pray for her life, that she may be a credit (if it please God) to the penitence she has so lately assumed.

209

Do, my dear *good* Miss, vouchsafe to the poor soul the honour of a visit : she may be low-spirited.—She may be too much sunk with the recollection of past things. Comfort, with that sweetness which is so natural to Miss Darnford, her drooping heart; and let her know, that I have a true concern for her, and give it her in charge to take care of herself, and spare nothing that will administer either to her health or peace of mind.

You'll pardon me that I put you upon an office so unsuitable from a lady in your station, to a person in hers; but not to your piety and charity, where a duty so eminent as that of visiting the sick, and cheering the doubting mind, is in the question.

I know your condescension will give her great comfort; and if she should be hastening to her account, what a pleasure will it give such a lady as you, to have illuminated a benighted mind, when it was tottering on the verge of death !

I know she will want no spiritual help from good Mr. Peters; but then the kind notice of so generally esteemed a young lady, will raise her more than can be imagined : for there is a tenderness, a sympathy, in the good persons of our sex to one another, that (while the best of the other seem but to act as in office, saying those things, which, though edifying and convincing, one is not certain proceeds not rather from the fortitude of their minds, than the tenderness of their natures) mingles with one's very spirits, thins the animal mass, and runs through one's heart in the same lify current (I can't clothe my thought suitably to express what I would), giving assurance, as well as pleasure, in the most arduous cases, and brightening our misty prospects, till we see the Sun of Righteousness rising on the hills of comfort, and dispelling the heavy fogs of doubt and diffidence.

This it is makes me wish and long as I do, for the company of my dear Miss Darnford. O when shall I see you? When shall I?—To speak to my present case, it is *all I long for ;* and, pardon my freedom of expression, as well as thought, when I let you know in this instance, how *early* I experience the *ardent longings* of one in the way I am in.

But I ought not to set my heart upon any thing not in my own power, and which may be subject to accidents, and the control of others. But let whatever interventions happen, so I have your *will* to come, I must be rejoiced in your kind intention, although your *power* should not prove answerable.

But I will say no more, than that I am, my honoured father and mother, your ever dutiful daughter; and, my dear Miss Darnford, *your affectionate and obliged*   P. B.

LETTER XL

From Miss Darnford to Mrs. B.

MY DEAR MRS. B.,

We are greatly obliged to you for every particular article in your entertaining journal, which you have brought, sooner than we wished, to a conclusion. We cannot express how much we admire you for your judicious charities, so easy to be practised, yet so uncommon in the manner; and for your inimitable conduct in the affair of your frail Polly and the silly Mr. H.

Your account of the visit of the four rakes; of your parting with your noble guests; Mr. H.'s letter (an original indeed!) have all greatly entertained us, as your prerogative hints have amused us: but we defer our opinion of those hints, till we have the case more fully explained.

But, my dear friend, are you not in danger of falling into a too thoughtful and gloomy way? By the latter part of your last letter, we are afraid you are; and my mamma, and Mrs. Jones, and Mrs. Peters, enjoin me to write, to caution you on that head. But there is the less need of it, because your prudence will always suggest to you reasons, as it does in that very letter, that must out-balance your fears. *Think* little, and *hope* much, is a good lesson in your case, and to a lady of your temper; and I hope Lady Davers will not in vain have given you that caution. After all, I dare say your thoughtfulness is but symptomatical, and will go off in proper time.

But to wave this: let me ask you, is Mr. B.'s conduct to you as *respectful*, I don't mean fond, when you are alone together, as in company?—Forgive me—But you have hinted two or three times, in your letters, that he always is most complaisant to you in company; and you observe, that *wisely* does he act in this, as he thereby does credit with every body to his own choice. I make no doubt, that the many charming scenes which your genius and fine behaviour furnish out to him, must, as often as they happen, inspire him with joy, and even rapture: and must make him love you more for your mind than for your person:—but these rapturous scenes last very little longer than the present moment. What I want to know is, whether in the *steadier* parts of life, when you are both nearer the level of us common folks, he give up any thing of his own will in compliment to yours? Whether he acts the part of a respectful, polite gentleman, in his behaviour to you; and breaks not into your retirements, in the dress, and with the brutal roughness of a fox-hunter?—Making no difference, perhaps, between the field or his stud (I will not say kennel) and your chamber or closet?—Policy, for his own credit-sake, as I mentioned, accounts to me well, for his complaisance to you in public. But his regular and uniform behaviour to you, in your retirement, when the conversation between you turns upon usual and common subjects, and you have not obliged him to rise to admiration of you, by such scenes as those of your two parsons, Sir Jacob Swynford, and the like : is what would satisfy my curiosity, if you please to give me an instance or two of it.

Now, my dearest Mrs. B., if you can give me a case, partly or nearly thus circumstanced, you will highly oblige me :

First, where he has borne with any infirmity of your own; and I know of none where you can give him such an opportunity, except you get into a vapourish habit, by giving way to a temper too thoughtful and apprehensive :

Next, that, in complaisance to *your* will, he recedes from his *own* in any one instance :

Next, whether he breaks not into your retirements unceremoniously, and without apology or concern, as I hinted above.

You know, my dear Mrs. B., all I mean, by what I have said; and if you have any pretty conversation in memory, by the recital of which, this my bold curiosity may be answered, pray oblige me with it; and we shall be able to judge by it, not only of the in-born generosity which all that know Mr. B. have been willing to attribute to him, but of the likelihood of the continuance of both your felicities, upon terms suitable to the characters of a fine lady and fine gentleman : and, of consequence, worthy of the imitation of the most delicate of our own sex.

Your obliging *longings*, my beloved dear lady, for my company, I hope, will very soon be answered. My papa was so pleased with your sweet earnestness on this occasion, that he joined with my mamma; and both, with equal cheerfulness, said, you should not be many days in London before me. Murray and his mistress go on swimmingly, and have not yet had one quarrel. The only person, he, of either sex, that ever knew Nancy so intimately, and so long, without one !

This is all I have to say, at present, when I have assured you, my dear Mrs. B., how much I am *your obliged and affectionate*

POLLY DARNFORD.

My dearest Miss Darnford,

I was afraid I ended my last letter in a gloomy way; and I am obliged to you for the kind and friendly notice you take of it. It was owing to a train of thinking which sometimes I get into, of late; I hope only symptomatically, as you say, and that the cause and effect will soon vanish together.

But what a task, my dear friend, I'll warrant, you think you have set me! I thought, in the progress of my journal, and in my letters, I had given so many instances of Mr. B.'s polite tenderness to me, that no new ones would be required at my hands; and when I said he was always *most* complaisant before company, I little expected, that such an inference would be drawn from my words, as would tend to question the uniformity of his behaviour to me, when there were no witnesses to it. But I am glad of an opportunity to clear up all your doubts on this subject.

To begin then:

You first desire an instance, where Mr. B. has borne with some infirmity of mine:

Next, that in complaisance to my will, he has receded from his own:

And lastly, whether he breaks not into my retirements unceremoniously; and without apology or concern, making no difference between the field or the stud, and my chamber or closet?

As to the first, his bearing with my infirmities; he is daily giving instances of his goodness to me on this head; and I am ashamed to say, that of late I give him so much occasion for them as I do; but he sees my apprehensiveness, at times, though I endeavour to conceal it; and no husband was ever so soothing and so indulgent as Mr. B. He gives me the best advice, as to my malady, if I may call it one: treats me with redoubled tenderness: talks to me upon the subjects I most delight to dwell upon: as of my worthy parents; what they are doing at this time, and at that; of our intended journey to London; of the diversions of the town; of Miss Darnford's company; and when he goes abroad, sends up my good Mrs. Jervis to me, because I should not be alone: at other times, takes me abroad with him; brings this neighbour and that neighbour to visit; and carries me to visit them; talks of our journey to Kent, and into Lincolnshire, and to my Lady Davers's, to Bath, to Tunbridge, and I can't tell whither, when the apprehended time shall be over.—In fine, my dear Miss Darnford, you cannot imagine one half of his tender goodness and politeness to me !—Then he hardly ever goes to any distance, but brings some pretty present he thinks will be grateful to me. When at home, he is seldom out of my company; delights to teach me French and Italian, and reads me pieces of manuscript poetry, in several of the modern tongues (for he speaks them all); explains to me every thing I understand not; delights to answer all my questions, and to encourage my inquisitiveness and curiosity, tries to give me a notion of pictures and medals, and reads me lectures upon them, for he has a fine collection of both; and every now and then will have it, that he has been improved by my questions and observations.

What say you to these things, my dear? Do they come up to your first question? or do they not? Or is not what I have said, a full answer, were I to say no more, to *all* your enquiries?

O my dear, I am thoroughly convinced, that half the mis-understandings, among married people, are owing to trifles, to petty distinctions, to mere words, and little captious follies, to over-weenings, or unguarded petulances : and who would forego the solid satisfaction of life, for the sake of triumphing in such poor contentions, if one could triumph?

But you next require of me an instance, where, in complaisance to *my* will, he has receded from *his own ?* I don't know what to say to this. When Mr. B. is all tenderness and indulgence, and requires of me nothing, that I can have a material objection to, ought I *not* to oblige him? Can I have a will that is not his? Or would it be excusable if I *had ?* All little matters I cheerfully give up : great ones have not yet occurred between us, and I hope never will. One point, indeed, I have some apprehension *may* happen; and that, to be plain with you, is, we have had a debate or two on the subject (which I maintain) of a mother's duty to nurse her own child; and I am sorry to say it, he seems more determined than I wish he were, against it.

I hope it will not proceed so far as to awaken the sleeping dragon I mentioned, *Prerogative* by name; but I doubt I cannot give up this point very contentedly. But as to lesser points, had I been a duchess born, I think I would not have contested them with my husband.

I could give you many respectful instances too, of his receding, when he has desired to see what I have been writing, and I have told him to whom, and begged to be excused. One such instance I can give since I began this letter. This is it :

I put it in my bosom, when he came up : he saw me do so :

"Are you writing, my dear, what I must not see?"

"I am writing to Miss Darnford, Sir: and she begged you might not at present."

"This augments my curiosity, Pamela. What can two such ladies write, that I may not see?"

"If you won't be displeased, Sir, I had rather you would not, because she desires you may not see her letter, nor this my answer, till the letter is in her hands."

"Then I will not," returned Mr. B.

Will this instance, my dear, come up to your demand for one, where he recedes from his own will, in complaisance to mine?

But now, as to what both our notions and our practice are on the article of my retirements, and whether he breaks in upon them unceremoniously, and without apology, let the conversation I promised inform you, which began on the following occasion.

Mr. B. rode out early one morning, within a few days past, and did not return till the afternoon; an absence I had not been used to of late; and breakfasting and dining without him being also a new thing with me, I had such an impatience to see him, having expected him at dinner, that I was forced to retire to my closet, to try to divert it, by writing; and the gloomy conclusion of my last was then the subject. He returned about four o'clock, and indeed did *not* tarry to change his riding-dress, as your politeness, my dear friend, would perhaps have expected; but came directly up to me, with an impatience to see me, equal to my own, when he was told, upon enquiry, that I was in my closet.

I heard his welcome step, as he came up stairs; which generally, after a longer absence than I expect, has such an effect upon my fond heart, that it gives a responsive throb for every step he takes towards me, and beats quicker and faster, as he comes nearer.

I met him at my closet door. "So, my dear love," says he, "how do you?" folding his kind arms about me, and saluting me with ardour. "Whenever I have been but a few hours from you, my impatience to see my beloved, will not permit me to stand upon the formality of a message to know how you are engaged; but I break in upon you, even in my riding-dress, as you see."

"Dear Sir, you are very obliging. But I have no notion of *mere* formalities of this kind"—(How unpolite this, my dear, in your friend?)—"in a married state, since 'tis impossible a

215

virtuous wife can be employed about any thing that her husband may not know, and so need not fear surprises."

"I am glad to hear you say this, my Pamela; for I have always thought the extraordinary civilities and distances of this kind which I have observed among several persons of rank, altogether unaccountable. For if they are exacted by the lady, I should suspect she had reserves, which she herself believed I could not approve. If not exacted, but practised of choice by the gentleman, it carries with it, in my opinion, a false air of politeness, little less than affrontive to the lady, and dishonourable to himself; for does it not look as if he supposed, and *allowed*, that she might be so employed that it was necessary to apprise her of his visit, lest he should make discoveries not to her credit or his own?"

"One would not, Sir" (for I thought his conclusion too severe), "make such a harsh supposition as this neither : for there are little delicacies and moments of retirement, no doubt, in which a modest lady would wish to be indulged by the tenderest husband."

"It may be so in an *early* matrimony, before the lady's confidence in the honour and discretion of the man she has chosen has disengaged her from her bridal reserves."

"Bridal reserves, dear Sir ! permit me to give it as my humble opinion, that a wife's behaviour ought to be as pure and circumspect, in degree, as that of a bride, or even of a maiden lady, be her confidence in her husband's honour and discretion ever so great. For, indeed, I think a gross or a careless demeanour little becomes that modesty which is the peculiar excellency and distinction of our sex."

"You account very well, my dear, by what you now say for your own over-nice behaviour, as I have sometimes thought it. But are we not all apt to argue for a practice we make our own, because we *do* make it our own, rather than from the reason of the thing?"

"I hope, Sir, that is not the present case with me; for, permit me to say, that an over-free or negligent behaviour of a lady in the married state, must be a mark of disrespect to her consort, and would shew as if she was very little solicitous about what appearance she made in his eye. And must not this beget in him a slight opinion of her sex too, as if, supposing the gentleman had been a free liver, she would convince him there was no other difference in the sex, but as they were within or without the pale, licensed by the law, or acting in defiance of it?"

216

"I understand the force of your argument, Pamela. But you were going to say something more."

"Only, Sir, permit me to add, that when, in my particular case, you enjoin me to appear before you always dressed, even in the early part of the day, it would be wrong, if I was less regardful of my behaviour and actions, than of my appearance."

"I believe you are right, my dear, if a precise or unnecessary scrupulousness be avoided, and where all is unaffected, easy, and natural, as in my Pamela. For I have seen married ladies, both in England and France, who have kept a husband at a greater distance than they have exacted from some of his sex, who have been more entitled to his resentment, than to his wife's intimacies.

"But to wave a subject, in which, as I can with pleasure say, neither of us have much concern, tell me, my dearest, how you were employed before I came up? Here are pen and ink: here, too, is paper; but it is as spotless as your mind. To whom were you directing your favours now? May I not know your subject?"

Mr. H.'s letter was a part of it; and so I had put it by, at his approach, and not choosing he should see that—"I am writing," replied I, "to Miss Darnford: but I think you must not ask me to see what I have written *this* time. I put it aside that you should not, when I heard your welcome step. The subject is our parting with our noble guests; and a little of my apprehensiveness, on an occasion upon which our sex may write to one another; but, for some of the reasons we have been mentioning, gentlemen should not desire to see."

"Then I will not, my dearest love." (So here, my dear, is another instance—I could give you an hundred such—of his receding from his own will, in complaisance to mine.) "Only," continued he, "let me warn you against too much apprehensiveness, for your own sake, as well as mine; for such a mind as my Pamela's I cannot permit to be habitually over-clouded. And yet there now hangs upon your brow an over-thoughtfulness, which you must not indulge."

"Indeed, Sir, I was a little too thoughtful, from my subject, before you came; but your presence, like the sun, has dissipated the mists that hung upon my mind. See you not," and I pressed his hand with my lips, "they are all gone already?" smiling upon him with a delight unfeigned.

"Not quite, my dearest Pamela; and therefore, if you have no objection, I will change my dress, and attend you in the chariot for an hour or two, whither you please, that not one

217

shadow may remain visible in this dear face;" tenderly saluting me.

"Whithersoever you please, Sir. A little airing with you will be highly agreeable to me."

The dear obliger went and changed his dress in an instant; and he led me to the chariot, with his usual tender politeness, and we had a charming airing of several miles; returning quite happy, cheerful, and delighted with each other's conversation, without calling in upon any of our good neighbours : for what need of that, my dear, when we could be the best company in the world to each other?

Do these instances come up to your questions, my dear? or, do they not?—If you think not, I could give you our conversation in the chariot : for I wrote it down at my first leisure, so highly was I delighted with it : for the subject was my dearest parents; a subject started by himself, because he knew it would oblige me. But being tired with writing, I may reserve it, till I have the pleasure of seeing you, if you think it worth asking for. And so I will hasten to a conclusion of this long letter.

I have only farther to add, for my comfort, that next Thursday se'n-night, if nothing hinders, we are to set out for London. And why do you think I say *for my comfort*? Only that I shall then soon have the opportunity, to assure you personally, as you give me hope, how much I am, my dear Miss Darnford, *your truly affectionate.*   P. B.

LETTER XLII

My dear Miss Darnford,

One more letter, and I have done for a great while, because I hope your presence will put an end to the occasion. I shall now tell you of my second visit to the dairy-house, where we went to breakfast, in the chariot and four, because of the distance, which is ten pretty long miles.

I transcribed for you, from letters written formerly to my dear parents, an account of my former dairy-house visit, and what the people were, and whom I saw there; and although I besought you to keep that affair to yourself, as too much affecting the reputation of my Mr. B. to be known any farther, and even to destroy that account, when you had perused it; yet, I make no doubt, you remember the story, and so I need not repeat any part of it.

When we arrived there, we found at the door, expecting us

(for they heard the chariot-wheels at a distance), my pretty Miss Goodwin, and two other Misses, who had earned their ride, attended by the governess's daughter, a discreet young gentle-woman. As soon as I stepped out, the child ran into my arms with great eagerness, and I as tenderly embraced her, and leading her into the parlour, asked her abundance of questions about her work, and her lessons; and among the rest if she had merited this distinction of the chaise and dairy-house breakfast, or if it was owing to her uncle's favour, and to that of her governess? The young gentlewoman assured me it was to both, and shewed me her needleworks, and penmanship; and the child was highly pleased with my commendations.

I took a good deal of notice of the other two Misses, for their school-fellow's sake, and made each of them a present of some little toys; and my Miss, of a number of pretty trinkets, with which she was highly delighted; and I told her, that I would wait upon her governess, when I came from London into the country again, and see in what order she kept her little matters; for, above all things, I love pretty house-wifely Misses; and then, I would bring her more.

Mr. B. observed, with no small satisfaction, the child's be-haviour, which is very pretty; and appeared as fond of her, as if he had been *more* than her *uncle*, and yet seemed under some restraint, lest it should be taken, that he *was* more. Such power has secret guilt, poor gentleman! to lessen and restrain a pleasure, that would, in a happier light, have been so laudable to have manifested!

I am going to let you into a charming scene, resulting from this perplexity of the dear gentleman. A scene that has afforded me high delight ever since; and always will, when I think of it.

The child was very fond of her uncle, and told him she loved him dearly, and always would love and honour him, for giving her such a good aunt. " You talked, Madam," said she, " when I saw you before, that I should come and live with you—Will you let me, Madam? Indeed I will be very good, and do every thing you bid me, and mind my book, and my needle; indeed I will."

" Ask your uncle, my dear," said I; " I should like your pretty company of all things."

She went to Mr. B. and said, " Shall I, Sir, go and live with my aunt?—Pray let me, when you come from London again."

" You have a very good governess, child," said he; " and she can't part with you."

" Yes, but she can, Sir; she has a great many Misses, and can

219

spare me well enough; and if you please to let me ride in your coach sometimes, I can go and visit my governess, and beg a holiday for the Misses, now-and-then, when I am almost a woman, and then all the Misses will love me."

" Don't the Misses love you now, Miss Goodwin ? " said he.

" Yes, they love me well enough, for matter of that; but they'll love me better, when I can beg them a holiday. Do, dear Sir, let me go home to my new aunt, next time you come into the country."

I was much pleased with the dear child's earnestness; and permitted her to have her full argument with her beloved uncle; but was much moved, and he himself was under some concern, when she said, " But you should, in pity, let me live with you, Sir, for I have no papa, nor mamma neither : they are so far off !—But I will love you both as if you were my own papa and mamma; so, dear now, my good uncle, promise the poor girl that has never a papa nor mamma ! "

I withdrew to the door : " It will rain, I believe," said I, and looked up. And, indeed, I had almost a shower in my eye : and had I kept my place, could not have refrained shewing how much I was affected.

Mr. B., as I said, was a little moved; but for fear the young gentlewoman should take notice of it—" How ! my dear," said he, " no papa and mamma !—Did they not send you a pretty black boy to wait upon you, a while ago ? Have you forgot that ? "—" That's true," replied she : " but what's a black boy to living with my new aunt ?—That's better a great deal than a black boy ! "

" Well, your aunt and I will consider of it, when we come from London. Be a good girl, meantime, and do as your governess would have you, and then you don't know what we may do for you."

" Well then, Miss," said she to her young governess, " let me be set two tasks instead of one, and I will learn all I can to deserve to go to my aunt."

In this manner the little prattler diverted herself. And as we returned from them, the scene I hinted at, opened as follows :

Mr. B. was pleased to say, " What a poor figure does the proudest man make, my dear Pamela, under the sense of a concealed guilt, in company of the innocent who know it, and even of those who do not !—Since the casual expression of a baby shall overwhelm him with shame, and make him unable to look up without confusion. I blushed for myself," continued he, " to see how you were affected for me, and yet withdrew, to avoid reproaching me so much as with a look. Surely, Pamela, I must then make a most contemptible appearance in your eye ! Did you not disdain me at that moment ? "

" Dearest Sir ! how can you speak such a word ? A word I cannot repeat after you ! For at that very time, I beheld you with the more reverence, for seeing your noble heart touched with a sense of your error; and it was such an earnest to me of the happiest change I could ever wish for, and in so young a gentleman, that it was one half joy for that, and the other half concern at the little charmer's accidental plea, to her best and nearest friend, for coming home to her new aunt, that affected me so sensibly as you saw."

" You must not talk to me of the child's coming home, after this visit, Pamela; for how, at this rate, shall I stand the reproaches of my own mind, when I see the little prater every day before me, and think of what her poor mamma has suffered on my account ! 'Tis enough, that in *you*, my dear, I have an hourly reproach before me, for my attempts on your virtue; and I have nothing to boast of, but that I gave way to the triumphs of your innocence : and what then is my boast ? "

" What is your boast, dearest Sir ? You have everything to boast, that is worthy of being boasted of.

" You are the best of husbands, the best of landlords, the best of masters, the best of friends; and, with all these excellencies, and a mind, as I hope, continually improving, and more and more affected with the sense of its past mistakes, will you ask, dear Sir, what is your boast ?

" O my dearest, dear Mr. B.," and then I pressed his hands with my lips, " whatever you are to yourself, when you give way to reflections so hopeful, you are the glory and the boast of your grateful Pamela ! And permit me to add," tears standing in my eyes, and holding his hand between mine, " that I never beheld you in my life, in a more amiable light, than when I saw that noble consciousness which you speak of, manifest itself in your eyes, and your countenance—O Sir ! this was a sight of joy, of true joy ! to one who loves you for your dear soul's sake, as well as for that of your person; and who looks forward to a companionship with you beyond the term of this transitory life."

Putting my arms round his arms, as I sat, my fearful eye watching his, " I fear, Sir, I have been too serious ! I have, perhaps, broken one of your injunctions ! Have cast a gloominess over your mind ! And if I have, dear Sir, forgive me ! "

He clasped his arms around me: "O my beloved Pamela," said he; "thou dear confirmer of all my better purposes! How shall I acknowledge your inexpressible goodness to me? I see every day more and more, my dear love, what confidence I may repose in your generosity and discretion! You want no forgiveness; and my silence was owing to much better motives than to those you were apprehensive of."

He saw my grateful transport, and kindly said, "Struggle not, my beloved Pamela, for words to express sentiments which your eyes and your countenance much more significantly express than any words *can* do. Every day produces new instances of your affectionate concern for my *future* as well as *present* happiness: and I will endeavour to confirm to you all the hopes which the present occasion has given you of me, and which I see by these transporting effects are so desirable to you."

The chariot brought us home sooner than I wished, and Mr. B. handed me into the parlour.

"Here, Mrs. Jervis," said he, meeting her in the passage, "receive your angelic lady. I must take a little tour without you, Pamela; for I have had *too much* of your dear company, and must leave you, to descend again into myself; for you have raised me to such a height, that it is with pain I look down from it."

He kissed my hand, and went into his chariot again; for it was but half an hour after twelve; and said he would be back by two at dinner. He left Mrs. Jervis wondering at his words, and at the solemn air with which he uttered them. But when I told that good friend the occasion, I had a new joy in the pleasure and gratulations of the dear good woman, on what had passed.

My next letter will be from London, and to you, my honoured parents; for to you, my dear, I shall not write again, expecting to see you soon. But I must now write seldomer, because I am to renew my correspondence with Lady Davers; with whom I cannot be so free, as I have been with Miss Darnford; and so I doubt, my dear father and mother, you cannot have the particulars of that correspondence; for I shall never find time to transcribe.

But every opportunity that offers, you may assure yourselves, shall be laid hold of by your ever-dutiful daughter.

And now, my dear Miss Darnford, as I inscribed this letter to you, let me conclude it, with the assurance, that I am, and ever will be *your most affectionate friend and servant,*   P. B.

My dear Father and Mother,

I know you will be pleased to hear that we arrived safely in town last night. We found a stately, well-furnished, and convenient house; and I had my closet, or library, and my withdrawing room, all in complete order, which Mr. B. gave me possession of in the most obliging manner.

I am in a new world, as I may say, and see such vast piles of building, and such a concourse of people, and hear such a rattling of coaches in the day, that I hardly know what to make of it, as yet. Then the nightly watch, going their hourly rounds, disturbed me. But I shall soon be used to that, and sleep the sounder, perhaps, for the security it assures to us.

Mr. B. is impatient to shew me what is curious in and about this vast city, and to hear, as he is pleased to say, my observations upon what I shall see. He has carried me through several of the fine streets this day in his chariot; but, at present, I have too confused a notion of things, to give any account of them: nor shall I trouble you with descriptions of that kind; for you being within a day's journey of London, I hope for the pleasure of seeing you oftener than I could expect before; and shall therefore leave these matters to your own observations, and what you'll hear from others.

I am impatient for the arrival of my dear Miss Darnford, whose company and conversation will reconcile me, in a great measure, to this new world.

Our family at present are Colbrand, Jonathan, and six men servants, including the coachman. The four maids are also with us.

But my good Mrs. Jervis was indisposed; so came not up with us; but we expect her and Mr. Longman in a day or two: for Mr. B. has given her to my wishes; and as Mr. Longman's business will require him to be up and down frequently, Mrs. Jervis's care will be the better dispensed with. I long to see the dear good woman, and shall be more in my element when I do.

Then I have, besides, my penitent Polly Barlow, who has never held up her head since that deplorable instance of her weakness, which I mentioned to you and to Miss Darnford, yet am I as kind to her as if nothing had happened. I wish, however, some good husband would offer for her.

Mr. Adams, our worthy chaplain, is now with Mr. Williams. He purposes to give us his company here till Christmas, when probably matters will be adjusted for him to take possession of his living. Meantime, not to let fall a good custom, when perhaps we have most occasion for it, I make Jonathan, who is reverend by his years and silver hairs, supply his place, appointing him the prayers he is to read.

God preserve you both in health, and continue to me, I beseech you, your prayers and blessings, concludes *your ever dutiful daughter*,

P. B.

LETTER XLIV

From Mrs. B. to Lady Davers.

MY DEAREST LADY,

I must beg pardon, for having been in this great town more than a week, and not having found an opportunity to tender my devoirs to your ladyship. You know, dear Madam, what hurries and fatigues must attend such a journey, to one in my way, and to an entire new settlement in which an hundred things must be done, and attended to, with a preference to other occasions, however delightful. Yet, I must own, we found a stately, well-ordered, and convenient house : but, although it is not far from the fields, and has an airy opening to its back part, and its front to a square, as it is called, yet I am not reconciled to it, so entirely as to the beloved mansion we left.

My dear Mr. B. has been, and is, busily employed in ordering some few alterations, to make things still more commodious. He has furnished me out a pretty library ; and has allotted me very convenient apartments besides : the furniture of every place is rich, as befits the mind and fortune of the generous owner. But I shall not offer at particulars, as we hope to have the honour of a visit from my good lord, and your ladyship, before the winter weather sets in, to make the roads too dirty and deep : but it is proper to mention, that the house is so large, that we can make a great number of beds, the more conveniently to receive the honours of your ladyship, and my lord, and Mr. B.'s other friends will do us.

I have not yet been at any of the public diversions. Mr. B. has carried me, by gentle turns, out of his workmen's way, ten miles round this overgrown capital, and through the principal of its numerous streets. The villages that lie spangled about this vast circumference, as well on the other side the noble Thames (which I had before a notion of, from Sir John Denham's celebrated Cooper's Hill), as on the Middlesex side, are beautiful, both by buildings and situation, beyond what I had imagined, and several of them seem larger than many of our country towns of note. But it would be impertinent to trouble your ladyship with these matters, who are no stranger to what is worthy of notice in London. But I was surprised, when Mr. B. observed to me, that this whole county, and the two cities of London and Westminster, are represented in parliament by no more than eight members, when so many borough towns in England are inferior to the meanest villages about London.

I am in daily expectation of the arrival of Miss Darnford, and then I shall wish (accompanied by a young lady of so polite a taste) to see a good play. Mr. B. has already shewn me the opera-house, and the play-houses, though silent, as I may say; that, as he was pleased to observe, they should not be new to me, and that the sight might not take off my attention from the performance, when I went to the play; so that I can conceive a tolerable notion of every thing, from the disposition of the seats, the boxes, galleries, pit, the music, scenes, and the stage; and so shall have no occasion to gaze about me, like a country novice, whereby I might attract a notice that I would not wish, either for my own credit, or your dear brother's honour.

I have had a pleasure which I had not in Bedfordshire; and that is, that on Sunday I was at church, without gaping crowds to attend us, and blessings too loud for my wishes. Yet I was more gazed at (and so was Mr. B.) than I expected, considering there were so many well-dressed gentry, and some nobility there, and *they* stared as much as any body, but will not, I hope, when we cease to be a novelty.

We have already had several visitors to welcome Mr. B. to town, and to congratulate him on his marriage; but some, no doubt, to see, and to find fault with his rustic; for it is impossible, you know, Madam, that a gentleman so distinguished by his merit and fortune should have taken a step of such consequence to himself and family, and not to have been known by every body so to have done.

Sir Thomas Atkyns is in town, and has taken apartments in Hanover Square; and he brought with him a younger brother of Mr. Arthur's, who, it seems, is a merchant.

Lord F. has also been to pay his respects to Mr. B. whose school fellow he was at Eton, the little time Mr. B. was there. His lordship promises, that his lady shall make me a visit, and accompany me to the opera, as soon as we are fully settled.

A gentleman of the Temple, Mr. Turner by name, and Mr. Fanshow of Gray's Inn, both lawyers, and of Mr. B.'s former acquaintance, very sprightly and modish gentlemen, have also welcomed us to town, and made Mr. B. abundance of gay compliments on my account to my face, all in the common frothy run.

They may be polite gentlemen, but I can't say I over-much like them. There is something so opiniated, so seemingly insensible of rebuke, either from *within* or *without*, and yet not promising to avoid deserving one occasionally, that I could as *lieve* wish Mr. B. and they would not renew their former acquaintance.

I am very bold your ladyship will say—But you command me to write freely: yet I would not be thought to be uneasy, with regard to your dear brother's morals, from these gentlemen; for, oh, Madam, I am a blessed creature, and am hourly happier and happier in the confidence I have as to that particular: but I imagine they will force themselves upon him, more than he may wish, or would permit, were the acquaintance now to begin; for they are not of his turn of mind, as it seems to me; being, by a sentence or two that dropt from them, very free, and very frothy in their conversation; and by their laughing at what they say themselves, taking that for wit which will not stand the test, if I may be allowed to say so.

But they have heard, no doubt, what a person Mr. B.'s goodness to me has lifted into notice; and they think themselves warranted to say any thing before his country girl.

He was pleased to ask me, when they were gone, how I liked his two lawyers? And said, they were persons of family and fortune.

" I am glad of it, Sir," said I; " for their own sakes."

" Then you don't approve of them, Pamela?"

" They are *your* friends, Sir; and I cannot have any dislike to them."

" They say good things *sometimes*," returned he.

" I don't doubt it, Sir; but you say good things *always*."

" 'Tis happy for me, my dear, you think so. But tell me, what you think of 'em?"

" I shall be better able, Sir, to answer your questions, if I see them a second time."

" But we form notions of persons at first sight, sometimes, my dear; and you are seldom mistaken in yours."

" I only think, Sir, that they have neither of them any diffidence: but their profession, perhaps, may set them above that."

" They don't *practise*, my dear; their fortunes enable them
226

to live without it; and they are too studious of their pleasures, to give themselves any trouble they are not obliged to take."

"They seem to me, Sir, *qualified* for practice : they would make great figures at the bar, I fancy."

"Why so?"

"Only, because they seem prepared to think *well* of what they say *themselves ;* and *lightly* of what *other people* say, or may think, *of them.*"

"That, indeed, my dear, is the necessary qualifications of a public speaker, be he lawyer, or what he will : the man who cannot doubt *himself,* and can think meanly of his *auditors,* never fails to speak with *self-applause* at least."

"But you'll pardon me, good Sir, for speaking my mind so freely, and so early of these *your friends.*"

"I never, my love, ask you a question, I wish you not to answer; and always expect your answer should be without reserve; for many times I may ask your opinion, as a corrective or a confirmation of my own judgment."

How kind, how indulgent was this, my good lady! But you know, how generously your dear brother treats me, on all occasions; and this makes me so bold as I often am.

It may be necessary, my dear lady, to give you an account of our visitors, in order to make the future parts of my writing the more intelligible; because what I have to write may turn sometimes upon the company we see : for which reason, I shall also just mention Sir George Stuart, a Scottish gentleman, with whom Mr. B. became acquainted in his travels, who seems to be a polite (and Mr. B. says, is a learned) man, and a virtuoso : he, and a nephew of his, of the same name, a bashful gentleman, and who, for that reason, I imagine, has a merit that lies deeper than a first observation can reach, are just gone from us, and were received with so much civility by Mr. B. as entitles them to my respectful regard.

Thus, Madam, do I run on, in a manner, without materials; and only to shew you the pleasure I take in obeying you. I hope my good Lord Davers enjoys his health, and continues me in his favour; which I value extremely, as well as your ladyship's. Mr. H., I hope, likewise enjoys his health. But let me not forget my particular and thankful respects to the Countess, for her favour and goodness to me, which I shall ever place next, in my grateful esteem, to the honours I have received from your ladyship, and which bind me to be, with the greatest respect, *your faithful and obliged servant,*   P. B.

My dear Father and Mother,

I write to you both, at this time, for your advice in a particular dispute, which is the only one I have had, or I hope ever shall have, with my dear benefactor; and as he is pleased to insist upon his way, and it is a point of conscience with me, I must resolve to be determined by your joint advice; for, if my father and mother, and husband, are of one opinion, I must, I think, yield up my own.

This is the subject :—I think a mother ought, if she can, to be the nurse to her own children.

Mr. B. says, he will not permit it.

It is the first *will not* I have heard from him, or given occasion for : and I tell him, that it is a point of conscience with me, and I hope he will indulge me : but the dear gentleman has an odd way of arguing, that sometimes puzzles me. He pretends to answer me from Scripture; but I have some doubts of *his* exposition; and he gives me leave to write to you, though yet he won't promise to be determined by your opinions if they are not the same with his own; and I say to him, " Is this fair, my dearest Mr. B. ? Is it ? "

He has got the dean's opinion with him; for our debate began before we came to town : and then he would not let me state the case; but did it himself; and yet 'tis but an half opinion, as I may, neither. For it is, that if the husband is set upon it, it is a wife's duty to obey.

But I can't see how that is; for if it be the *natural* duty of a mother, it is a *divine* duty; and how can a husband have power to discharge a divine duty? As great as a wife's obligation is to obey her husband, which is, I own, one indispensable of the marriage contract, it ought not to interfere with what one takes to be a superior duty : and must not one be one's own judge of actions, by which we must stand or fall?

I'll tell you my plea :

I say, that where a mother is unhealthy; subject to communicative distempers, as scrophulous or scorbutic, or consumptive disorders, which have infected the blood or lungs; or where they have not plenty of nourishment for the child, that in these cases, a dispensation lies of course.

But where there is good health, free spirits, and plentiful nourishment, I think it an indispensable duty.

For this was the custom of old, of all the good wives we read of in Scripture.

Then the nourishment of the mother must be most natural to the child.

These were my pleas, among others : and this is his answer which he gave to me in writing :

" As to what you allege, my dear, of old customs; times and fashions are much changed. If you tell me of Sarah's, or Rachel's, or Rebecca's, or Leah's nursing their children, I can answer, that the one drew water at a well, for her father's flocks; another kneaded cakes, and baked them on the hearth; another dressed savoury meat for her husband ; and all of them performed the common offices of the household : and when our modern ladies shall follow such examples in *every thing*, their plea ought to be allowed in this.

" Besides, my fondness for your personal graces, and the laudable, and, I will say, honest pleasure, I take in that easy, genteel form, which every body admires in you, at first sight, oblige me to declare, that I can by no means consent to sacrifice these to the carelessness into which I have seen very nice ladies sink, when they became nurses. Moreover, my chief delight in you is for the beauties of your mind ; and unequalled as they are, in my opinion, you have still a genius capable of great improvement ; and I shan't care, when I want to hear my Pamela read her French and Latin lessons, which I take so much delight to teach her (and to endeavour to improve myself from her virtue and piety, at the same time), to seek my beloved in the nursery; or to permit her to be engrossed by those baby offices, which will better befit weaker minds.

" No, my dear, you must allow me to look upon you as my scholar, in one sense; as my companion in another; and as my instructress, in a third. You know I am not governed by the worst motives : I am half overcome by your virtue : and you must take care, that you leave not your work half done. But I cannot help looking upon the nurse's office, as an office beneath Pamela. Let it have your inspection, your direction, and your sole attention, if you please, when I am abroad : but when I am at home, even a son and heir, so jealous am I of your affections, shall not be my rival in them : nor will I have my rest broken in upon, by your servants bringing to you your dear little one, at times, perhaps, as unsuitable to my repose and your own, as to the child's necessities.

" The chief thing with you, my dear, is that you think it unnatural in a mother not to be a nurse to her own child, if she can ; and what is unnatural, you say, is sin.

" Some men may be fond of having their wives undertake this

229

province, and good reasons may be assigned for such their fondness; but it suits not me at all. And yet no man would be thought to have a greater affection for children than myself, or be more desirous to do them justice; for I think every one should look forward to posterity with a preference: but if my Pamela can be *better* employed; if the office can be equally well performed; if your direction and superintendence will be sufficient; and if I cannot look upon you in that way with equal delight, as if it was otherwise; I insist upon it, my Pamela, that you acquiesce with my *dispensation*, and don't think to let me lose my beloved wife, and have a nurse put upon me instead of her.

"As to that (the nearest to me of all) of dangers to your constitution: there is as much reason to hope it may not be so, as to fear that it *may*. For children sometimes bring health with them as well as infirmity; and it is not a little likely, that the *nurse's* office may affect the health of one I hold most dear, who has no very robust constitution, and thinks it so much her duty to attend to it, that she will abridge herself of half the pleasures of life, and on that account confine herself within doors, or, in the other case, must take with her her infant and her nursery-maid wherever she goes; and I shall either have very fine company (shall I not?) or be obliged to deny myself yours.

"Then, as I propose to give you a smattering of the French and Italian, I know not but I may take you on a little tour into France and Italy; at least, to Bath, Tunbridge, Oxford, York, and the principal places of England. Wherefore, as I love to look upon you as the companion of my pleasures, I advise you, my dearest love, not to weaken, or, to speak in a phrase proper to the present subject, *wean* me from that love *to* you, and admiration *of* you, which hitherto has been rather increasing than otherwise, as your merit, and regard for me have increased."

These, my dear parents, are charming allurements, almost irresistible temptations! And what makes me mistrust myself the more, and be the more diffident; for we are but too apt to be persuaded into any thing, when the motives are so tempting as the last.

I take it for granted, that many wives will not choose to dispute this point so earnestly as I have done; for we have had several little debates about it; and it is the only point I have ever yet debated with him; but one would not be altogether implicit neither. It is no compliment to him to be quite passive, and to have no will at all of one's own : yet would I not dispute one point, but in supposition of a superior obligation : and this, he says, he can *dispense* with. But alas ! my dear Mr. B. was never yet thought so entirely fit to fill up the character of a casuistical divine, as that one may absolutely rely upon his decisions in these serious points : and you know we must stand or fall by our own judgments.

Upon condition, therefore, that he requires not to see this my letter, nor your answer to it, I write for your advice. But this I see plainly, that he will have his own way; and if I cannot get over my scruples, what shall I do? For if I think it a *sin* to submit to the dispensation he insists upon as in his power to grant, and to submit to it, what will become of my peace of mind? For it is not in our power to believe as one will.

As to the liberty he gives me for a month, I should be loath to take it; for one knows not the inconveniences that may attend a change of nourishment; or if I did, I should rather—But I know not what I would say; for I am but a young creature to be in this way, and so very unequal to it in every respect ! So I commit myself to God's direction, and your advice, as becomes *your ever dutiful daughter,*   P. B.

LETTER XLVI

My dearest Child,
        Your mother and I have as well considered the case you put as we are able; and we think your own reasons very good; and it is a thousand pities your honoured husband will not allow them, as you, my dear, make it such a point with you. Very few ladies would give their spouses, we believe, the trouble of this debate; and few gentlemen are so very nice as yours in this respect; for I (but what signifies what such a mean soul as I think, compared to so learned and brave a gentleman; yet I) always thought your dear mother, and she has been a pretty woman too, in her time, never looked so lovely, as when I saw her, like the pelican in the wilderness, feeding her young ones from her kind breast :—and had I never so noble an estate, I should have had the same thoughts.

But since the good 'squire cannot take this pleasure; since he so much values your person; since he gives you warning, that it may estrange his affections; since he is impatient of denial, and thinks so highly of his prerogative; since he may, if dis-obliged, resume some bad habits, and so you may have all your

231

prayers and hopes in his perfect reformation frustrated, and find your own power to do good more narrowed : we think, besides the obedience you have vowed to him, and is the duty of every good wife, you ought to give up the point, and acquiesce; for this seemeth to us to be the lesser evil : and God Almighty, if it should be your duty, will not be less merciful than men; who, as his honour says, by the laws of the realm, excuses a wife, when she is faulty by the command of the husband; and we hope, the fault he is pleased to make you commit (if a fault, for he really gives very praise-worthy motives for his dispensation) will not be laid at his own door. So e'en resolve, my dearest child, to submit to it, and with cheerfulness too.

God send you an happy hour ! But who knows, when the time comes, whether it may not be proper to dispense with this duty, as you deem it, on other accounts? For every young person is not enabled to perform it. So, to shew his honour, that you will cheerfully acquiesce, your dear mother advises you to look out for a wholesome, good-humoured, honest body, as near your complexion and temper, and constitution, as may be; and it may not be the worse, she thinks, if she is twenty, or one- or two-and-twenty; for she will have more strength and perfection, as one may say, than even you can have at your tender age : and, above all, for the wise reason you give from your reading, that she may be brought to-bed much about your time, if possible. We can look out, about us, for such an one. And, as Mr. B. is not adverse to have the dear child in the house, you will have as much delight, and the dear baby may fare as well, under your prudent and careful eye, as if you were obliged in the way you would choose.

So God direct you, my child, in all your ways, and make you acquiesce in this point with cheerfulness (although, as you say, one cannot believe, as one pleases; for we verily are of opinion you safely may, as matters stand) and continue to you, and your honoured husband, health, and all manner of happiness, are the prayers of *your most affectionate father and mother,*

J. *and* E. ANDREWS.

LETTER XLVII

I thank you, my dearest parents, for your kind letter; it was given to Mr. B. and he brought it to me himself, and was angry with me : indeed he was, as you shall hear :

" 'Tis from the good couple, my dear, I see. I hope they are of my opinion—But whether they be or not—But I will leave you; and do you, Pamela, step down to my closet, when you have perused it."

He was pleased to withdraw; and I read it, and sat down, and considered it well; but, as you know I made it always my maxim to do what I could not avoid to do, with as good a grace as possible, I waited on the dear gentleman.

"Well, Pamela," said he, a little seriously, "what say the worthy pair?"

"O Sir! they declare for you. They say, it is best for me to yield up this point."

"They are certainly in the right—But were you not a dear perverse creature, to give me all this trouble about your saucy scruples?"

"Nay, Sir, don't call them so," said I, little thinking he was displeased with me. "I still am somewhat wavering; though they advise me to acquiesce; and, as it is your will, and you have determined, it is my duty to yield up the point."

"But do you yield it up cheerfully, my dear?"

"I do, Sir; and will never more dispute it, let what will happen. And I beg pardon for having so often entered into this subject with you. But you know, Sir, if one's weakness of mind gives one scruples, one should not yield implicitly, till they are satisfied; for that would look as if one gave not you the obedience of a free mind."

"You are very obliging, *just now*, my dear: but I can tell you, you had made me half serious; yet I would not shew it, in compliment to your present condition; for I did not expect that you would have thought *any* appeal necessary, though to your parents, in a point that I was determined upon, as you must see, every time we talked of it."

This struck me all in a heap. I looked down to the ground: having no courage to look up to his face, for fear I should behold his aspect as mortifying to me as his words. But he took both my hands, and drew me kindly to him, and saluted me, "Excuse me, my dearest love: I am not angry with you. Why starts this precious pearl?" and kissed my cheek: "speak to me, Pamela!"

"I will, Sir—I will—as soon as I can:" for this being my first check, so seriously given, my heart was full. But as I knew he would be angry, and think me obstinate, if I did not speak, I said, full of concern, "I wish, Sir—I wish—you had been pleased to spare me a little longer, for the same kind, very kind, consideration."

233

"But is it not better, my dear, to tell you I *was* a little out of humour with you, than that I *am ?*—But you were very earnest with me on this point more than once; and you put me upon a hated, because ungenerous, necessity of pleading my prerogative, as I call it; yet this would not do, but you appealed against me in the point I was determined upon, for reasons altogether in your favour : and if this was not like my Pamela, excuse me, that I could not help being a little unlike myself."

"Ah !" thought I, " this is not so very unlike your dear self, were I to give the least shadow of an occasion; for it is of a piece with your lessons formerly."

"I am sure," said I, " I was not in the least aware, that I had offended. But I was too little circumspect. I had been used to your goodness for so long a time, that I expected it, it seems; and thought I was sure of your favourable construction."

"Why, so you may be, my dear, in every thing *almost*. But I don't love to speak twice my mind on the same subject; you know I don't ! and you have really disputed this point with me five or six times; insomuch, that I wondered what was come to my dearest."

"I thought, Sir, you would have distinguished between a command where my *conscience* was concerned, and a *common* point : you know, Sir, I never had any will but yours in *common* points. But, indeed, you make me fearful because my task is rendered too difficult for my own weak judgment."

I was silent, but by my tears.

"Now, I doubt, Pamela, your spirit is high. You won't speak, because you are out of humour at what I say. I will have no sullen reserves, my dearest. What means that heaving sob ? I know that this is the time with your sex, when, saddened with your apprehensions, and indulged because of them, by the fond husband, it is needful, for both their sakes, to watch over the changes of their temper. For ladies in your way are often like encroaching subjects; apt to extend what they call their privileges, on the indulgence shewed them ; and the husband never again recovers the ascendant he had before."

"You know these things better than I, Mr. B. But I had no intention to invade your province, or to go out of my own. Yet I thought I had a right to a little free will, on some greater occasions."

"Why, so you have, my dear. But you must not plead in behalf of your own will, and refuse to give due weight to mine."

" Well, Sir, I must needs say, I have one advantage above others of my sex; for if wives, in my circumstances, are apt to grow upon indulgence, I am very happy that your kind and watchful care will hinder me from falling into that error."

He gave me a gentle tap on the neck : " Let me beat my beloved sauce-box," said he : " is it thus you rally my watchful care over you for your own good ? But tell me, truly, Pamela, are you not a little sullen ? Look up to me, my dear. Are you not ? "

" I believe I am ; but 'tis but very little, Sir. It will soon go off. Please to let me withdraw, that I may take myself to task about it;—for at present, I know not what to do, because I did not expect the displeasure I have incurred."

" Is it not the same thing," replied he, " if this our first quarrel end here, without your withdrawing?—I forgive you heartily, my Pamela ; and give me one kiss, and I will think of your saucy appeal against me no more."

" I will comply with your condition, Sir; but I have a great mind to be saucy. I wish you would let me for this once."

" What would you say, my dearest?—Be saucy then, as you call it, as saucy as you can."

" Why; then I *am* a little sullen at present, that I am; and I am not fully convinced, whether it must be I that forgive you, or you me. For, indeed, if I can recollect, I cannot think my fault so great in this point, that was a point of conscience to me, as (pardon me Sir), to stand in need of your forgiveness."

" Well, then, my dearest," said he, " we will forgive one another? but take this with you, that it is my love to you that makes me more delicate than otherwise I should be; and you have inured me so much to a faultless conduct, that I can hardly bear with natural infirmities from you.—But," giving me another tap, " get you gone; I leave you to your recollection; and let me know what fruits it produces : for I must not be put off with a half-compliance; I must have your whole will with me, if possible."

So I went up, and recollecting every thing, *sacrificed to my sex*, as Mr. B. calls it, when he talks of a wife's reluctance to yield a favourite point : for I shed many tears, because my heart was set upon it.

And so, my dear parents, twenty charming ideas and pleasures I had formed to myself, are vanished from me, and my measures are quite broken. But after my heart was relieved by my eye, I was lighter and easier. And the result is, we have heard of a good sort of woman, that is to be my poor *baby's mother*, when it comes; so your kindly-offered enquiries are needless, I believe.

'Tis well for our sex in general, that there are not many husbands who distinguish thus nicely. For, I doubt, there are but very few so well entitled to their ladies' observances as Mr. B. is to mine, and who would act so generously and so tenderly by a wife as he does, in every material instance on which the happiness of life depends.

But we are quite reconciled; although as I said, upon his own terms: and so I can still style myself, *my dear honoured parents, your* happy, *as well as your dutiful daughter,*   P. B

LETTER XLVIII

From Lady Davers to Mrs. B.

MY DEAR PAMELA,

I have sent you a present, the completest I could procure, of every thing that may suit your approaching happy circumstance; as I hope it will be to you, and to us all: but it is with a hope annexed, that although both sexes are thought of in it, you will not put us off with a girl: no, child, we will not permit you, may we have our wills, to *think* of giving us a girl, till you have presented us with half a dozen fine boys. For our line is gone so low, we expect that human security from you in your first seven years, or we shall be disappointed.

I will now give you their names, if my brother and you approve of them: your first shall be BILLY; my Lord Davers, and the Earl of C——, godfathers; and it must be doubly godmothered too, or I am afraid the countess and I shall fall out about it. Your second DAVERS; be sure remember that.—— Your third, CHARLEY; your fourth, JEMMY; your fifth, HARRY; your sixth—DUDLEY, if you will—and your girl, if you had not rather call it PAMELA, shall be called BARBARA.—The rest name as you please.——And so, my dear, I wish all seven happily over with you.

I am glad you got safe to town: and long to hear of Miss Darnford's arrival, because I know you'll be out of your bias in your new settlement till then. She is a fine lady, and writes the most to my taste of any one of her sex that I know, next to you. I wish she'd be so kind as to correspond with me. But be sure don't omit to give me the sequel of her sister's and Murray's affair, and what you think will please me in relation

236

to her.—You do well to save yourself the trouble of describing the town and the public places. We are no strangers to them; and they are too much our table talk, when any country lady has for the first time been carried to town, and returned : besides, what London affords, is nothing that deserves mention, compared to what we have seen at Paris and at Versailles, and other of the French palaces. You exactly, therefore, hit our tastes, and answer our expectations, when you give us, in your peculiar manner, sentiments on what we may call the *soul of things*, and such characters as you draw with a pencil borrowed from the hand of nature, intermingled with those fine lights and shades of reflections and observations, that make your pictures glow, and instruct as well as delight.

There, Pamela, is encouragement for you to proceed in obliging us. We are all of one mind in this respect; and more than ever, since we have seen your actions so well answered to your writings; and that theory and practice, as to every excellence that can adorn a lady, is the same thing with you.

We are pleased with your lawyers' characters. There are life and nature in them; but never avoid giving all that occur to you, for that seems to be one of your talents; and in the ugliest, there will be matter of instruction; especially as you seem naturally to fall upon such as are so general, that no one who converses, but must see in them the picture of one or other he is acquainted with.

By this time, perhaps, Miss Darnford will be with you.—Our respects to her, if so.—And you will have been at some of the theatrical entertainments : so will not want subjects to oblige us.—'Twas a good thought of your dear man's, to carry you to see the several houses, and to make you a judge, by that means, of the disposition and fashion of every thing in them.— Tell him, I love him better and better. I am proud of my brother, and do nothing but talk of what a charming husband he makes. But then, he gives an example to all who know him, and his uncontrollable temper (which makes against many of us), that it is possible for a good wife to make even a bad man a worthy husband : and this affords an instruction, which may stand all our sex in good stead.—But then they must have been cautious first, to choose a man of natural good sense, and good manners, and not a brutal or abandoned debauchee.

But hark-ye-me, my sweet girl, what have I done, that you won't write yourself *sister* to me? I could find in my heart to be angry with you. Before my last visit, I was scrupulous to subscribe myself so to *you*. But since I have seen myself so much surpassed in every excellence, that I would take pleasure in the name, you assume a pride in your turn, and may think it under-valuing yourself, to call *me* so—Ay, that's the thing, I doubt—Although I have endeavoured by several regulations since my return (and the countess, too, keeps your example in distant view, as well as I), to be more worthy of the appellation. If, therefore, you would avoid the reproaches of secret pride, under the shadow of so remarkable an humility, for the future never omit subscribing as I do, with great pleasure, *your truly affectionate sister and friend,*   B. DAVERS.

I always take it for granted, that my worthy brother sends his respects to us; as you must, that Lord Davers, the Countess of C. and Jackey (who, as well as his uncle, talks of nothing else but you), send theirs; and so unnecessary compliments will be always excluded our correspondence.

LETTER XLIX

In answer to the preceding.

How you overwhelm me with your goodness, my dearest lady, in every word of your last welcome letter, is beyond my power to express ! How nobly has your ladyship contrived, in your ever-valued present, to encourage a doubting and apprehensive mind ! And how does it contribute to my joy and my glory, that I am deemed the noble sister of my best beloved, not wholly unworthy of being the humble means to continue, and, perhaps, to perpetuate, a family so ancient and so honourable !

When I contemplate this, and look upon what I was—How shall I express a sense of the honour done me !—And when, reading over the other engaging particulars in your ladyship's letter, I come to the last charming paragraph, I am doubly affected to see myself seemingly upbraided, but so politely emboldened to assume an appellation, that otherwise I hardly dared.

I—*humble* I—who never had a sister before—to find one now in Lady Davers ! O Madam, you, and *only* you, can teach me words fit to express the joy and the gratitude that filled my delighted heart !—But thus much I am taught, that there is some thing more than the low-born can imagine in birth and education. This is so evident in your ladyship's actions, words, and manner, that it strikes one with a becoming reverence; and we look up with awe to a condition we emulate in vain, when raised by partial favour, like what I have found; and are confounded when we see grandeur of soul joined with grandeur of birth and condition; and a noble lady acting thus nobly, as Lady Davers acts.

My best wishes, and a thousand blessings, attend your ladyship in all you undertake! And I am persuaded the latter will, and a peace and satisfaction of mind incomparably to be preferred to whatever else this world can afford, in the new regulations, which you, and my dear lady countess, have set on foot in your families: and when I can have the happiness to know what they are, I shall, I am confident, greatly improve my own methods by them.

Were we to live for ever in this life, we might be careless and indifferent about these matters: but when such an uncertainty as to the time, and such a certainty as to the event is before us, a prudent mind will be always preparing, till prepared; and what can be a better preparative, than charitable actions to our fellow-creatures in the eye of that Majesty, which wants nothing of us himself, but to do just the merciful things to one another.

Pardon me, my dearest lady, for this my free style. Methinks I am out of myself! I know not how to descend all at once from the height to which you have raised me: and you must forgive the reflections to which you yourself and your own noble actions have given birth.

Here, having taken respite a little, I naturally sink into *body* again.—And will not your ladyship confine your expectations from me within narrower limits?—For, O, I cannot even with my wishes, so swiftly follow your expectations, if such they are! But, however, leaving futurity to HIM, who only governs futurity, and who conducts us all, and our affairs, as shall best answer his own divine purposes, I will proceed as well as I can, to obey you in those articles, which are, at present, more within my own power.

My dear Miss Darnford, then, let me acquaint your ladyship, arrived on Thursday last: she had given us notice, by a line, of the day she set out; and Sir Simon and Lady Darnford saw her ten miles on the way to the stage coach in Sir Simon's coach, Mr. Murray attending her on horseback. They parted with her, as was easy to guess from her merit, with great tenderness; and we are to look upon the visit (as we do) as a high favour from her papa and mamma; who, however, charge her not to exceed a month in and out, which I regret much. Mr. B. kindly proposed to me, as she came in the stage coach, attended with one maid-servant, to meet her part of the way in his coach and six, if, as he was pleased to say, it would not be too fatiguing to me; and we would go so early, as to dine at St. Alban's. I gladly consented, and we got thither about one o'clock; and while dinner was preparing, he was pleased to shew me the great church there, and the curious vault of the good Duke of Gloucester, and also the monument of the great Lord Chancellor Bacon in St. Michael's church; all which, no doubt, your lady-ship has seen.

There happened to be six passengers in the stage coach, including Miss Darnford and her maid; she was exceeding glad to be relieved from them, though the weather was cold enough, two of the passengers being not very agreeable company, one a rough military man, and the other a positive humoursome old gentlewoman: and the others two sisters—"who jangled now and then," said she, "as much as *my* sister, and my sister's *sister*."

Judge how joyful this meeting was to us both. Mr. B. was no less delighted, and said, he was infinitely obliged to Sir Simon for this precious trust.

"I come with double pleasure," said she, "to see the greatest curiosity in England, a husband and wife, who have not, in so many months as you have been married, if I may believe report, and your letters, Mrs. B., once repented."

"You are severe, Miss Darnford," replied Mr. B., "upon people in the married state: I hope there are many such instances."

"There might, if there were more such husbands as Mr. B. makes.—I hated you once, and thought you very wicked; but I revere you now."

"If you will *revere* any body, my dear Miss Darnford," said he, "let it be this good girl; for it is all owing to her conduct and direction, that I make a tolerable husband: were there more such wives, I am persuaded, there would be more such husbands than there are."

"You see, my dear," said I, "what it is to be wedded to a generous man. Mr. B., by his noble treatment of me, creates a merit in me, and disclaims the natural effects of his own goodness."

"Well, you're a charming couple—person and mind. I know not any equal either of you have.—But, Mr. B., I will not compliment you too highly. I may make *you* proud, for men are saucy creatures; but I cannot make your *lady* so: and in this doubt of the one, and confidence in the other, I must join with you, that *her* merit is the greatest.—Since, excuse me, Sir, her example has reformed her rake; and you have only confirmed in her the virtues you found ready formed to your hand."

"That distinction," said Mr. B., "is worthy of Miss Darnford's judgment."

"My dearest Miss Darnford—my dearest Mr. B.," said I, laying my hand upon the hand of each, "how can you go on thus !—As I look upon every kind thing, two such dear friends say of me, as incentives for me to endeavour to deserve it, you must not ask me too high; for then, instead of encouraging, you'll make me despair."

He led us into the coach; and in a free, easy, joyful manner, not in the least tired or fatigued, did we reach the town and Mr. B.'s house; with which and its furniture, and the apartments allotted for her, my dear friend is highly pleased.

But the dear lady put me into some little confusion, when she saw me first, taking notice of my *improvements*, as she called them, before Mr. B. I looked at him and her with a downcast eye. He smiled, and said, "Would *you*, my good Miss Darnford, look so silly, after such a length of time, with a husband you need not be ashamed of ? "

"No, indeed, Sir, not I, I'll assure you; nor will I forgive those maiden airs in a wife so happy as you are."

I said nothing. But I wished myself, in mind and behaviour, to be just what Miss Darnford is.

But, my dear lady, Miss Darnford has had those early advantages from conversation, which I had not; and so must never expect to know how to deport myself with that modest freedom and ease, which I know I want, and shall always want, although some of my partial favourers think I do not. For I am every day more and more sensible of the great difference there is between being used to the politest conversation as an inferior, and being born to bear a part in it : in the one, all is set, stiff, awkward, and the person just such an ape of imitation as poor I; in the other, all is natural ease and sweetness—like Miss Darnford.

Knowing this, I don't indeed aim at what I am sensible I cannot attain; and so, I hope, am less exposed to censure than I should be if I did. For, I have heard Mr. B. observe with regard to gentlemen who build fine houses, make fine gardens, and open fine prospects, that art should never take place of, but be subservient to, nature; and a gentleman, if confined to a situation, had better conform his designs to that, than to do as at Chatsworth, level a mountain at a monstrous expense;

which, had it been suffered to remain, in so wild and romantic a scene as Chatsworth affords, might have been made one of the greatest beauties of the place.

So I think I had better endeavour to make the best of those natural defects I cannot master, than, by assuming airs and dignities in appearance, to which I was not born, act neither part tolerably. By this means, instead of being thought neither gentlewoman nor rustic, as Sir Jacob hinted (*linsey-wolsey*, I think was his term too), I may be looked upon as an original in my way; and all originals pass well enough, you know, Madam, even with judges.

Now I am upon this subject, I can form to myself, if your ladyship will excuse me, two such polite gentlemen as my lawyers mentioned in my former, who, with a true London magnanimity and penetration (for, Madam, I fancy your London critics will be the severest upon the country girl), will put on mighty significant looks, forgetting, it may be, that they have any faults themselves, and apprehending that they have nothing to do, but to sit in judgment upon others, one of them expressing himself after this manner—" Why, truly, Jack, the girl is well enough—*considering*—I can't say——" (then a pinch of snuff, perhaps, adds importance to his air)—" but a man might love her for a month or two." (These sparks talked thus of other ladies before me.) " She behaves better than I expected from her—*considering*——" again will follow.

" So I think," cries the other, and tosses his tie behind him, with an air partly of contempt, and partly of rakery.

" As you say, Jemmy, I expected to find an awkward country girl, but she tops her part, I'll assure you!—Nay, for that matter, behaves very tolerably for *what she was*—And is right, not to seem desirous to drown the remembrance of her original in her elevation—And, I can't but say " (for something like it he did say), " is mighty pretty, and passably genteel." And thus with their poor praise of Mr. B.'s girl, they think they have made a fine compliment to his judgment.

But for *his* sake (for as to my own, I am not solicitous about *such* gentlemen's good opinions), I owe them a spite; and believe, I shall find an opportunity to come out of their debt. For I have the vanity to think, now you have made me proud by your kind encouragements and approbation, that the country girl will make 'em look about them, with all their *genteel contempts*, which they miscall *praise*.

But how I run on ! Your ladyship expects that I shall write as freely to you as I used to do to my parents. I have the merit of obeying you, that I have; but, I doubt, too much to the exercise of your patience.

This (like all mine) is a long letter; and I will only add to it Miss Darnford's humble respects, and thanks for your lady-ship's kind mention of her, which she receives as no small honour.

And now, Madam, with a greater pleasure than I can express, will I make use of the liberty you so kindly allow me to take, of subscribing myself with that profound respect which becomes me, *your ladyship's most obliged sister, and obedient servant,*

P. B.

Mr. Adams, Mr. Longman, and Mrs. Jervis, are just arrived; and our household is now complete.

LETTER L

From Lady Davers to Mrs. B.

MY DEAR PAMELA,

After I have thanked you for your last agreeable letter, which has added the Earl and Lady Jenny to the number of your admirers (you know Lady Betty, her sister, was so before), I shall tell you, that I now write, at their requests, as well as at those of my Lord Davers, the countess you so dearly love, and Lady Betty, for your decision of an odd dispute, that, on reading your letter, and talking of your domestic excellencies, happened among us.

Lady Betty says, that, notwithstanding any awkwardness you attribute to yourself, she cannot but decide, by all she has seen of your writings, and heard from us, that yours is the perfectest character she ever found in the sex.

The countess said, that you wrong yourself in supposing you are not every thing that is polite and genteel, as well in your behaviour, as in your person; and that she knows not any lady in England who better becomes her station than you do.

" Why, then," said Lady Jenny, " Mrs. B. must be quite perfect: that's certain." So said the earl; so said they all. And Lord Davers confirmed that you were.

Yet, as we are sure, there cannot be such a character in this life as has not one fault, although we could not tell where to fix it, the countess made a whimsical motion : " Lady Davers," said she, " pray do you write to Mrs. B. and acquaint her with our subject; and as it is impossible, for one who can act as she does, not to know herself better than any body else can do, desire her to acquaint us with some of those secret foibles, that leave room for her to be still more perfect."

"A good thought," said they all. And this is the present occasion of my writing; and pray see that you accuse yourself, of no more than you know yourself guilty : for over-modesty borders nearly on pride, and too liberal self-accusations are generally but so many traps for acquittal with applause : so that (whatever other ladies might) you will not be forgiven, if you deal with us in a way so poorly artful; let your faults, therefore, be such as you think we can subscribe to, from what we have *seen* of *you* and what we have *read* of *yours ;* and you must try to extenuate them too, as you give them, lest we should think you above that nature, which, in the *best* cases, is your undoubted talent.

I congratulate you and Miss Darnford on her arrival : she is a charming young lady; but tell her, that we shall not allow her to take you at your word, and to think that she excels you in any one thing : only, indeed, we think you nicer in some points than you need be to, as to your present agreeable circumstance. And yet, let me tell you, that the easy, unaffected, conjugal purity, in word and behaviour, between your good man and you, is worthy of imitation, and what the countess and I have with pleasure contemplated since we left you, an hundred times, and admire in you both : and it is good policy too, child, as well as high decorum; for it is what will make you ever new and respectful to one another.

But *you* have the honour of it all, whose sweet, natural, and easy modesty, in person, behaviour, and conversation, forbid indecency, even in thought, much more in word, to approach you : insomuch that no rakes can be rakes in your presence, and yet they hardly know to what they owe their restraint.

However, as people who see you at this time, will take it for granted that you and Mr. B. have been very intimate together, I should think you need not be ashamed of your appearance, because, as he rightly observes, you have no reason to be ashamed of your husband.

Excuse my pleasantry, my dear : and answer our demand upon you, as soon as you can; which will oblige us all; particularly *your affectionate sister,*

B. DAVERS.

My dearest Lady,

What a task have you imposed upon me! And according to the terms you annex to it, how shall I acquit myself of it, without incurring the censure of affectation, if I freely accuse myself as I may deserve, or of vanity, if I do not? Indeed, Madam, I have a great many failings: and you don't know the pain it costs me to keep them under; not so much for fear the world should see them, for I bless God, I can hope they are not capital, as for fear they should become capital, if I were to let them grow upon me.

And this, surely, I need not have told your ladyship, and the Countess of C., who have read my papers, and seen my behaviour in the kind visit you made to your dear brother, and had from *both* but too much reason to censure me, did not your generous and partial favour make you overlook my greater failings, and pass under a kinder name many of my lesser; for surely, my good ladies, you must both of you have observed, in what you have read and seen, that I am naturally of a saucy temper: and with all my appearance of meekness and humility, can resent, and sting too, when I think myself provoked.

I have also discovered in myself, on many occasions (of some of which I will by-and-by remind your ladyship), a malignancy of heart, that, it is true, lasts but a little while—nor had it need—but for which I have often called myself to account —to very little purpose hitherto.

And, indeed, Madam (now for a little extenuation, as you expect from me), I have some difficulty, whether I ought to take such pains to subdue myself in some instances, in the station to which I am raised, that otherwise it would have become me to attempt to do: for it is no easy task, for one in my circumstances, to distinguish between the *ought* and the *ought not;* to be humble without meanness, and decent without arrogance. And if all persons thought as justly as I flatter myself I do, of the inconveniences, as well as conveniences, which attend their being raised to a condition above them, they would not imagine all the world was their own, when they came to be distinguished as I have been: for, what with the contempts of superior relations on one side, the envy of the world, and low reflections arising from it, on the other, from which no one must hope to be totally exempted, and the awkwardness, besides, with which they support their elevated condition, if they have sense to judge of their own imperfections; and if the gentleman be not such an one as mine—(and where

245

will such another be found?)—On all these accounts, I say, they will be made sensible, that, whatever they might once think, happiness and an high estate are two very different things.

But I shall be too grave, when your ladyship, and all my kind and noble friends, expect, perhaps, I should give the uncommon subject a pleasanter air : yet what must that mind be, that is not serious, when obliged to recollect, and give account of its defects?

But I must not only accuse myself, it seems, I must give *proofs*, such as your ladyship can subscribe to, of my imperfections. There is so much *real kindness* in this *seeming hardship*, that I will obey you, Madam, and produce proofs in a moment, which cannot be controverted.

As to my *sauciness*, those papers will give an hundred instances against me, as well to your dear brother, as to others. Indeed, to extenuate, as you command me, as I go along, these were mostly when I was apprehensive for my honour, they were.

And then, I have a little tincture of *jealousy*, which sometimes has made me more uneasy than I ought to be, as the papers you have not seen would have demonstrated, particularly in Miss Godfrey's case, and in my conversation with your ladyships, in which I have frequently betrayed my fears of what might happen when in London : yet, to extenuate again, I have examined myself very strictly on this head; and really think, that I can ascribe a great part of this jealousy to laudable motives; no less than to my concern for your dear brother's future happiness, in the hope, that I may be a humble means, through Providence, to induce him to abhor those crimes of which young gentlemen too often are guilty, and bring him over to the practice of those virtues, in which he will ever have cause to rejoice.—Yet, my lady, some other parts of the charge must stand against me; for as I love his person, as well as his mind, I have pride in my jealousy, that would not permit me, I verily think, to support myself as I ought, under trial of a competition, in this very tender point.

And this obliges me to own, that I have a little spark—not a little one, perhaps—of *secret pride* and *vanity*, that will arise, now and then, on the honours done me; but which I keep under as much as I can; and to this pride, let me tell your ladyship, I know no one contributes, or can contribute, more largely than yourself.

So you see, my dear lady, what a naughty heart I have, and how far I am from being a faultless creature—I hope I shall be better and better, however, as I live longer, and have more grace, and more wit: for here to recapitulate my faults, is in the first place, *vindictiveness*, I will not call it downright revenge —And how much room do all these leave for amendment, and greater perfection?

Had your ladyship, and the countess, favoured us longer in your kind visit, I must have so improved, by your charming conversations, and by that natural ease and dignity which accompany everything your ladyships do and say, as to have got over such of these foibles as are not rooted in nature: till in time I had been able to do more than emulate those perfections, which at present, I can only at an awful distance revere; as becomes, *my dear ladies, your most humble admirer, and obliged servant,*

P. B.

LETTER LII

From Miss Darnford to her Father and Mother.

MY EVER-HONOURED PAPA AND MAMMA,

I arrived safely in London on Thursday, after a tolerable journey, considering Deb and I made six in the coach (two having been taken up on the way, after you left me), and none of the six highly agreeable. Mr. B. and his lady, who looks very stately upon us (from the circumstance of *person*, rather than of *mind*, however), were so good as to meet me at St. Alban's, in their coach and six. They have a fine house here, richly furnished in every part, and have allotted me the best apartment in it.

We are happy beyond expression. Mr. B. is a charming husband; so easy, so pleased with, and so tender of his lady: and she so much all that we saw her in the country, as to humility and affability, and improved in every thing else which we hardly thought possible she could be—that I never knew so happy a matrimony.—All that *prerogative sauciness*, which we apprehended would so eminently display itself in his behaviour to his wife, had she been ever so distinguished by birth and fortune, is vanished. I did not think it was in the power of an angel, if our sex could have produced one, to have made so tender and so fond a husband of Mr. B. as he makes. And should I have the sense to follow Mrs. B.'s example, if ever I marry, I should not despair of making myself happy, let it be to whom it would, provided he was not a brute, nor sordid in his temper; which

247

two characters are too obvious to be concealed, if persons take due care, and make proper inquiries, and if they are not led by blind passion. May Mr. Murray and Miss Nancy make just such a happy pair!

You commanded me, my honoured mamma, to write to you an account of every thing that pleased me—I said I would: but what a task should I then have!—I did not think I had undertaken to write volumes.—You must therefore allow me to be more brief than I had intended.

In the first place, it would take up five or six long letters to do justice to the economy observed in this happy family. You know that Mrs. B. has not changed one of her servants, and only added her Polly to them. This is an unexampled thing, especially as they were her *fellow-servants* as we may say: but since they have the sense to admire so good an example, and are proud to follow it, each to his and her power, I think it one of her peculiar facilities to have continued them, and to choose to reform such as were exceptionable rather than dismiss them.

Their mouths, Deb tells me, are continually full of their lady's praises, and prayers, and blessings, uttered with such delight and fervour for the happy pair, that it makes her eyes, she says, ready to run over to hear them.

Moreover, I think it an extraordinary degree of policy (whether designed or not) to keep them, as they were all worthy folks; for had she turned them off, what had she done but made as many enemies as she had discarded servants; and as many more as those had friends and acquaintance? And we all know, how much the reputation of families lies at the mercy of servants; and it is easy to guess to what cause each would have imputed his or her dismission. And so she has escaped, as she ought, the censure of pride; and made every one, instead of reproaching her with her descent, find those graces in her, which turn that very disadvantage to her glory.

She is exceedingly affable; always speaks to them with a smile; but yet has such a dignity in her manner, that it secures her their respect and reverence; and they are ready to fly at a look, and seem proud to have her commands to execute: insomuch, that the words—" *My lady commands so, or so,*" from one servant to another, are sure to meet with an indisputable obedience, be the duty required what it will.

If any of them are the least indisposed, her care and tenderness for them engage the veneration and gratitude of all the rest, who see how kindly they will be treated, should they ail any thing themselves. And in all this she is very happy in

Mrs. Jervis, who is an excellent second to her admirable lady; and is treated by her with as much respect and affection, as if she was her mother.

You may remember, Madam, that in the account she gave us of her *benevolent round*, as Lady Davers calls it, she says, that as she was going to London, she should instruct Mrs. Jervis about some of her *clients*, as I find she calls her poor, to avoid a word which her delicacy accounts harsh with regard to them, and ostentatious with respect to herself. I asked her, how (since, contrary to her then expectation, Mrs. Jervis was permitted to be in town with her) she had provided to answer her intention as to those her clients, whom she had referred to the care of that good woman?

She said, that Mr. Barlow, her apothecary, was a very worthy man, and she had given him a plenary power in that particular, and likewise desired him to recommend any new and worthy case to her that no deserving person among the destitute sick poor, might be unrelieved by reason of her absence.

And here in London she has applied herself to Dr. —— (her parish minister, a fine preacher, and sound divine, who promises on all opportunities to pay his respects to Mr. B.) to recommend to her any poor housekeepers, who would be glad to accept of some private benefactions, and yet, having lived creditably, till reduced by misfortunes, are ashamed to apply for public relief : and she has several of these already on her *benevolent list*, to some of whom she sends coals now at the entrance on the wintry season, to some a piece of Irish or Scottish linen, or so many yards of Norwich stuff, for gowns and coats for the girls, or Yorkshire cloth for the boys; and money to some, who she is most assured will lay it out with care. And she has moreover *mortified*, as the Scots call it, one hundred and fifty pounds as a fund for loans, without interest, of five, ten, or fifteen, but not exceeding twenty pounds, to answer some present exigence in some honest families, who find the best security they can, to repay it in a given time; and this fund, she purposes, as she grows richer, she says, to increase; and estimates pleasantly her worth by this sum, saying sometimes, " Who would ever have thought I should have been worth one hundred and fifty pounds so soon? I shall be a rich body in time." But in all these things, she enjoins secresy, which the doctor has promised.

She told the doctor what Mr. Adams's office is in her family; and hoped, she said, he would give her his sanction to it; assuring him, that she thought it her duty to ask it, as she was one of his flock, and he, on that account, her principal shepherd, which made a spiritual relation between them, the requisites of which, on her part, were not to be dispensed with. The good gentleman very cheerfully and applaudingly gave his consent; and when she told him how well Mr. Adams was provided for, and that she would apply to him to supply her with a town chaplain, when she was deprived of him, he wished that the other duties of his function (for he has a large parish) would permit him to be the happy person himself, saying, that till she was supplied to her mind, either he or his curate would take care that so laudable a method should be kept up.

You will do me the justice, Madam, to believe, that I very cheerfully join in my dear friend's Sunday duties; and I am not a little edified, with the good example, and the harmony and good-will that this excellent method preserves in the family.

I must own I never saw such a family of love in my life : for here, under the eye of the best of mistresses, they twice every Sunday see one another all together (as they used to do in the country), superior as well as inferior servants; and Deb tells me, after Mrs. B. and I are withdrawn, there are such friendly salutations among them, that she never heard the like—" Your servant, good Master Longman : "—" Your servant, Master Colbrand," cries one and another :—" How do you, John ? "—" I'm glad to see you, Abraham ! "—" All blessedly met once more ! " cries Jonathan, the venerable butler, with his silver hairs, as Mrs. B. always distinguishes him :—" Good Madam Jervis," cries another, " you look purely this blessed day, thank God ! " And they return to their several vocations, so light, so easy, so pleased, so even-tempered in their minds, as their cheerful countenances, as well as expressions, testify, that it is a heaven of a house : and being wound up thus constantly once a week, at least, like a good eight-day clock, no piece of machinery that ever was made is so regular and uniform as this family is.

What an example does this dear lady set to all who see her, know her, and who hear of her; how happy they who have the grace to follow it ! What a public blessing would such a mind as hers be, could it be vested with the robes of royalty, and adorn the sovereign dignity ! But what are the princes of the earth, look at them in every nation, and what they have been for ages past, compared to this lady? who acts from the impulses of her own heart, unaided in most cases, by any human example. In short, when I contemplate her innumerable excellencies, and that sweetness of temper, and universal benevolence, which shine in every thing she says and does, I cannot sometimes help looking upon her in the light of an angel, dropped down from heaven, and received into bodily organs, to live among men and women, in order to shew what the first of the species was designed to be.

And, here, is the admiration, that one sees all these duties performed in such an easy and pleasant manner, as any body may perform them; for they interfere not with any parts of the family management; but rather aid and inspirit every one in the discharge of all their domestic services; and, moreover, keep their minds in a state of preparation for the more solemn duties of the day; and all without the least intermixture of affectation, enthusiasm, or ostentation. O my dear papa and mamma, permit me but to tarry here till I am perfect in all these good lessons, and how happy shall I be !

As to the town, and the diversions of it, I shall not trouble you with any accounts, as, from your former thorough knowledge of both, you will want no information about them; for, generally speaking, all who reside constantly in London, allow, that there is little other difference in the diversions of one winter and another, than such as are in clothes; a few variations of the fashions only, which are mostly owing to the ingenious contrivances of persons who are to get their bread by diversifying them.

Mrs. B. has undertaken to give Lady Davers an account of the matters as they pass, and her sentiments on what she sees. There must be something new in her observations, because she is a stranger to these diversions, and unbiassed entirely by favour or prejudice; and so will not play the partial critic, but give to a beauty its due praise, and to a fault its due censure, according to that truth and nature which are the unerring guides of her actions as well as sentiments. These I will transcribe for you; and you'll be so good as to return them when perused, because I will lend them, as I used to do her letters, to her good parents; and so I shall give her a pleasure at the same time in the accommodating them with the knowledge of all that passes, which she makes it a point of duty to do, because they take delight in her writings.

My papa's observation, that a woman never takes a journey but she forgets something, is justified by me; for, with all my care, I have left my diamond buckle, which Miss Nancy will find in the inner till of my bureau, wrapt up in cotton; and I beg it may be sent me by the first opportunity. With my humble duty to you both, my dear indulgent papa and mamma, thanks for the favour I now rejoice in, and affectionate respects to Miss Nancy (I wish she would love me as well as I love her), and service to Mr. Murray, and all our good neighbours, conclude *me your dutiful, and highly-favoured daughter,*

M. DARNFORD.

Mr. B. and Mrs. B. desire their compliments of congratulation to Mr. and Mrs. Peters, on the marriage of their worthy niece; also to your honoured selves they desire their kind respects and thanks for the loan of your worthless daughter. I experience every hour some new token of their politeness and affection; and I make no scruple to think I am with such a brother, and such a sister as any happy creature may rejoice in, and be proud of. Mr. B. I cannot but repeat, is a charming husband, and a most polite gentleman. His lady is always accusing herself to me of awkwardness and insufficiency; but not a soul who sees her can find it out; she is all genteel ease; and the admiration of every one who beholds her. Only I tell her, with such happiness in possession, she is a little of the gravest sometimes.

LETTER LIII

From Mrs. B. to Lady Davers.

MY GOOD LADY,

You command me to acquaint you with the proceedings between Mr. Murray and Miss Nanny Darnford: and Miss Polly makes it easy for me to obey you in this particular, and in very few words; for she says, every thing was adjusted before she came away, and the ceremony, she believes, may be performed by this time. She rejoices that she was out of the way of it: for, she says, love is so awkward a thing to Mr. Murray, and good-humour so uncommon an one to Miss Nancy, that she hopes she shall never see such another courtship.

We have been at the play-house several time; and, give me leave to say, Madam, (for I have now read as well as seen several), that I think the stage, by proper regulations, might be made a profitable amusement.—But nothing more convinces one of the truth of the common observation, that the best things, corrupted, prove the worst, than these representations. The terror and compunction for evil deeds, the compassion for a just distress, and the general beneficence which those lively exhibitions are so capable of raising in the human mind, might be of great service, when directed to right ends, and induced by proper motives: particularly where the actions which the catastrophe is designed to punish, are not set in such advantageous lights, as shall destroy the end of the moral, and make the vice that ought to be censured, imitable; where instruction is kept in view all the way, and where vice is punished, and virtue rewarded.

But give me leave to say, that I think there is hardly one play I have seen, or read hitherto, but has too much of love in it, as that passion is generally treated. How unnatural in some, how inflaming in others, are the descriptions of it!—In most, rather rant and fury, like the loves of the fiercer brute animals, as Virgil, translated by Dryden, describes them, than the soft, sighing, fearfully hopeful murmurs, that swell the bosoms of our gentler sex: and the respectful, timorous, submissive complainings of the other, when the truth of the passion humanizes, as one may say, their more rugged hearts.

In particular, what strange indelicates do these writers of tragedy often make of our sex! They don't enter into the passion at all, if I have any notion of it; but when the authors want to paint it strongly (at least in those plays I have seen and read) their aim seems to raise a whirlwind, as I may say, which sweeps down reason, religion, and decency; and carries every laudable duty away before it; so that all the examples can serve to shew is, how a disappointed lover may rage and storm, resent and revenge.

The play I first saw was the tragedy of *The Distressed Mother*; and a great many beautiful things I think there are in it: but half of it is a tempestuous, cruel, ungoverned rant of passion, and ends in cruelty, bloodshed, and desolation, which the truth of the story not warranting, as Mr. B. tells me, makes it the more pity, that the original author (for it is a French play, translated, you know, Madam), had not conducted it, since it was his choice, with less terror, and with greater propriety, to the passions intended to be raised, and actually raised in many places.

But the epilogue spoken after the play, by Mrs. Oldfield, in the character of Andromache, was more shocking to me, than the most terrible parts of the play; as by lewd and even senseless *double entendre*, it could be calculated only to efface all the tender, all the virtuous sentiments, which the tragedy was designed to raise.

The pleasure this gave the men was equally barbarous and insulting; all turning to the boxes, pit, and galleries, where ladies were, to see how they looked, and stood an emphatical and too-well pronounced ridicule, not only upon the play in general, but upon the part of Andromache in particular, which had been so well sustained by an excellent actress; and I was extremely mortified to see my favourite (and the only perfect) character debased and despoiled, and the widow of Hector, prince of Troy, talking nastiness to an audience, and setting it out with all the wicked graces of action, and affected archness of look, attitude, and emphasis.

I stood up—" Dear Sir !—Dear Miss ! " said I.

" What's the matter, my love ? " said Mr. B. smiling.

" Why have I wept the distresses of the injured Hermione ? " whispered I : " why have I been moved by the murder of the brave Pyrrhus, and shocked by the madness of Orestes ! Is it for this ? See you not Hector's widow, the noble Andromache, inverting the design of the whole play, satirizing her own sex, but indeed most of all ridiculing and shaming, in *my* mind, that part of the audience, who can be delighted with this vile epilogue, after such scenes of horror and distress ? "

He was pleased to say, smiling, " I expected, my dear, that your delicacy, and Miss Darnford's too, would be shocked on this preposterous occasion. I never saw this play, rake as I was, but the impropriety of the epilogue sent me away dissatisfied with it, and with human nature too : and you only see, by this one instance, what a character that of an actor or actress is, and how capable they are to personate any thing for a sorry subsistence."

" Well, but, Sir," said I, " are there not, think you, extravagant scenes and characters enough in most plays to justify the censures of the virtuous upon them, that the wicked friend of the author must crown the work in an epilogue, for fear the audience should go away improved by the representation ? It is not, I see, always narrowness of spirit, as I have heard some say, that opens the mouths of good people against these diversions."

In this wild way talked I ; for I was quite out of patience at this unnatural and unexpected piece of ridicule, tacked to so serious a play, and coming after such a moral.

Here is a specimen, my dear lady, of my observations on the first play I saw. How just or how impertinent, I must leave to your better judgment. I very probably expose my ignorance and folly in them, but I will not say presumption, because you have put me upon the task, which otherwise I should hardly have attempted. I have very little reason therefore to blame myself on this score ; but, on the contrary, if I can escape your ladyship's censure, have cause to pride myself in the opportunity you have thereby given me to shew my readiness to obey you ; and the rather, since I am sure of your kindest indulgence, now you have given me leave to style myself *your ladyship's obliged sister, and humble servant,*

P. B.

LETTER LIV

MY DEAR LADY,

I gave you in my last my bold remarks upon a TRAGEDY —*The Distressed Mother*. I will now give you my shallow notions of a COMEDY—*The Tender Husband*.

I liked this part of the title; though I was not pleased with the other, explanatory of it; *Or—The Accomplished Fools*. But when I heard it was written by Sir Richard Steele, and that Mr. Addison had given some hints towards it, if not some characters—" O, dear Sir," said I, " give us your company to this play; for the authors of the Spectator cannot possibly produce a faulty scene."

Mr. B. indeed smiled; for I had not then read the play: and the Earl of F., his countess, Miss Darnford, Mr. B. and myself, agreed to meet with a niece of my lord's in the stage-box, which was taken on purpose.

There seemed to me to be much wit and satire in the play: but, upon my word, I was grievously disappointed as to the morality of it; nor, in some places, is *probability* preserved; and there are divers speeches so very free, that I could not have expected to meet with such, from the names I mentioned.

In short the author seems to have forgotten the moral all the way; and being put in mind of it by some kind friend (Mr. Addison, perhaps), was at a loss to draw one from such characters and plots as he had produced; and so put down what came uppermost, for the sake of custom, without much regard to propriety. And truly, I should think, that the play was begun with a design to draw more amiable characters, answerable to the title of *The Tender Husband ;* but that the author, being carried away by the luxuriancy of a genius, which he had not the heart to prune, on a general survey of the whole, distrusting the propriety of that title, added the under one : with an OR, *The Accomplished Fools*, in justice to his piece, and compliment to his audience. Had he called it *The Accomplished Knaves*, I would not have been angry at him, because there would have been more propriety in the title.

I wish I could, for the sake of the authors, have praised every scene of this play : I hoped to have reason for it. Judge then, my dear lady, my mortification, not to be able to say I liked above one, the *Painter's scene*, which too was out of time, being on the wedding-day; and am forced to disapprove of every character in it, and the views of every one. I am, dear Madam, *your most obliged sister and servant,*

P. B.

LETTER LV

MY DEAR LADY,

Although I cannot tell how you received my observations on the tragedy of *The Distressed Mother*, and the comedy of *The Tender Husband*, yet will I proceed to give your ladyship my opinion of the opera I was at last night.

But what can I say, after mentioning what you so well know, the fine scenes, the genteel and splendid company, the charming voices, and delightful music?

If, Madam, one were all ear, and lost to every sense but that of harmony, surely the Italian opera would be a transporting thing!—But when one finds good sense, and instruction, and propriety, sacrificed to the charms of sound, what an unedifying, what a mere temporary delight does it afford! For what does one carry home, but the remembrance of having been pleased so many hours by the mere vibration of air, which, being but sound, you cannot bring away with you; and must therefore enter the time passed in such a diversion, into the account of those blank hours, from which one has not reaped so much as one improving lesson?

Mr. B. observes, that when once sound is preferred to sense, we shall depart from all our own worthiness, and, at best, be but the apes, yea, the dupes, of those whom we may strive to imitate, but never can reach, much less excel.

Mr. B. says, sometimes, that this taste is almost the only good fruit our young nobility gather, and bring home from their foreign tours; and that he found the English nation much ridiculed on this score, by those very people who are benefited by their depravity. And if this be the best, what must the other qualifications be, which they bring home?—Yet every one does not return with so little improvement, it is to be hoped.

But what can I say of an Italian opera?—For who can describe sound! Or what words shall be found to embody air? And when we return, and are asked our opinion of what we have seen or heard, we are only able to answer, as I hinted above, the scenery is fine, the company splendid and genteel, the music charming for the time, the action not extraordinary, the language unintelligible, and, for all these reasons—the instruction none at all.

This is all the thing itself gives me room to say of the Italian opera; very probably, for want of a polite taste, and a knowledge of the language.

In my next, I believe, I shall give you, Madam, my opinion of a diversion, which, I doubt, I shall like still less, and that is a masquerade; for I fear I shall not be excused going to one, although I have no manner of liking to it, especially in my present way. I am, Madam, *your ladyship's most obliged and faithful* P. B.

I must add another half sheet to this letter on the subject matter of it, the opera; and am sure you will not be displeased with the addition.

Mr. B. coming up just as I had concluded my letter, asked me what was my subject? I told him I was giving your ladyship my notions of the Italian opera. "Let me see what they are, my dear; for this is a subject that very few of those who admire these performances, and fewer still of those who decry them, know any thing of."

He read the above, and was pleased to commend it. "Operas," said he, "are very sad things in England, to what they are in Italy; and the translations given of them abominable : and indeed, our language will not do them justice.

"Every nation, as you say, has its excellencies; and ours should not quit the manly nervous sense, which is the distinction of the English drama. One play of our celebrated Shakespeare will give infinitely more pleasure to a sensible mind than a dozen English-Italian operas. But, my dear, in Italy, they are quite another thing : and the sense is not, as here, sacrificed so much to the sound, but that they are both very compatible."

"Be pleased, Sir, to give me your observations on this head in writing, and then I shall have something to send worthy of Lady Davers's acceptance."

"I will, my dear;" and he took a pen, and wrote the inclosed; which I beg your ladyship to return me; because I will keep it for my instruction, if I should be led to talk of this subject in company. "Let my sister know," said he, "that I have given myself no time to re-peruse what I have written. She will do well, therefore, to correct it, and return it to you."

"In Italy, judges of operas are so far from thinking the drama or poetical part of their operas nonsense, as the unskilled in Italian rashly conclude in England, that if the Libretto, as they call it, is not approved, the opera, notwithstanding the excellence

257

of the music, will be condemned. For the Italians justly determine, that the very music of an opera cannot be complete and pleasing, if the drama be incongruous, as I may call it, in its composition, because, in order to please, it must have the necessary contrast of the grave and the light, that is, the diverting equally blended through the whole. If there be too much of the first, let the music be composed ever so masterly in that style, it will become heavy and tiresome; if the latter prevail, it will surfeit with its levity: wherefore it is the poet's business to adapt the words for this agreeable mixture: for the music is but secondary, and subservient to the words; and if there be an artful contrast in the drama, there will be the same in the music, supposing the composer to be a skilful master.

"Now, since in England, the practice has been to mutilate, curtail, and patch up a drama in Italian, in order to introduce favourite airs, selected from different authors, the contrast has always been broken thereby, without every one's knowing the reason: and since ignorant mercenary prompters, though Italians, have been employed in hotch-potch, and in translating our dramas from Italian into English, how could such operas appear any other than incongruous nonsense?"

Permit me, dear Madam, to repeat my assurances, that I am, and must ever be, *your obliged sister and servant,*

P. B.

LETTER LVI

Well, now, my dear lady, I will give you my poor opinion of a masquerade, to which Mr. B. persuaded me to accompany Miss Darnford; for, as I hinted in my former, I had a great indifference, or rather dislike, to go, and Miss therefore wanted so powerful a second, to get me with her; because I was afraid the freedoms which I had heard were used there, would not be very agreeable to my apprehensive temper, at *this* time especially.

But finding Mr. B. chose to have me go, if, as he was pleased to say, I had no objection, "I said, I *will* have none, I *can* have none, when you tell me it is your choice; and so send for the habits you like, and that you would have me appear in, and I will cheerfully attend you."

The habit Mr. B. pitched upon was that of a Spanish Don, and it well befitted the majesty of his person and air; and Miss Darnford chose that of a young Widow; and Mr. B. recommended that of a Quaker for me. We all admired one another in our dresses; and Mr. B. promising to have me always in his eye, we went thither.

But I never desire to be present at another. Mr. B. was singled out by a bold Nun, who talked Italian to him with such free airs, that I did not much like it, though I knew not what she said; for I thought the dear gentleman no more kept to his Spanish gravity, than she to the requisites of the habit she wore : when I had imagined that all that was tolerable in a masquerade, was the acting up to the character each person assumed : and this gave me no objection to the Quaker's dress; for I thought I was prim enough for that naturally.

I said softly, " Dear Miss Darnford " (for Mr. B. and the Nun were out of sight in a moment), " what is become of that Nun ? "—" Rather," whispered she, " what is become of the Spaniard ? "

A Cardinal attacked me instantly in French : but I answered in English, not knowing what he said, " Quakers are not fit company for Red-hats."

" They are," said he, in the same language; " for a Quaker and a Jesuit is the same thing."

Miss Darnford was addressed by the name of the Sprightly Widow : another asked, how long she intended to wear those weeds ? And a footman, in a rich livery, answered for her eyes, through her mask, that it would not be a month.

But I was startled when a Presbyterian Parson came up, and bid me look after my Musidorus—So that I doubted not by this, it must be one who knew my name to be Pamela; and I soon thought of one of my lawyers, whose characters I gave before.

Indeed, he needed not to bid me; for I was sorry, on more accounts than that of my timorousness, to have lost sight of him. " Out upon these nasty masquerades ! " thought I; " I can't abide them already ! "

An egregious beauish appearance came up to Miss, and said, " You hang out a very pretty *sign*, Widow."

" Not," replied she, " to invite such fops as you to my shop."

" Any customer would be welcome," returned he, " in my opinion. I whisper this as a secret."

" And I whisper another," said she, but not whisperingly, " that no place warrants ill manners."

" Are you angry, Widow ? "

She affected a laugh : " No, indeed, it i'n't worth while."

He turned to me—and I was afraid of some such hit as he

gave me. "I hope, friend, thou art prepared with a father for the light within thee?"

"Is this wit?" said I, turning to Miss Darnford: "I have enough of this diversion, where nothing but coarse jests appear *barefac'd.*"

At last Mr. B. accosted us, as if he had not known us. "So lovely a widow, and so sweet a friend! no wonder you do not separate: for I see not in this various assembly a third person of your sex fit to join with you."

"Not *one*, Sir!" said I. "Will not a penitent Nun make a good third with a mournful Widow, and a prim Quaker?"

"Not for more than ten minutes at most."

Instantly the Nun, a fine person of a lady, with a noble air, though I did not like her, joined us, and spoke in Italian something very free, as it seemed by her manner, and Mr. B.'s smiling answer; but neither Miss Darnford nor I understood that language, and Mr. B. would not explain it to us.

But she gave him a signal to follow her, seeming to be much taken with his person and air; for though there were three other Spanish habits there, he was called *The stately Spaniard* by one, *The handsome Spaniard* by another, in our hearing, as he passed with us to the dessert, where we drank each of us a glass of Champaign, and eat a few sweetmeats, with a crowd about us; but we appeared not to know one another: while several odd appearances, as one Indian Prince, one Chinese Mandarin, several Domino's, of both sexes, a Dutch Skipper, a Jewish Rabbi, a Greek Monk, a Harlequin, a Turkish Bashaw, and Capuchin Friar, glided by us, as we returned into company, signifying that we were strangers to them by squeaking out— "*I know you!*"—Which is half the wit of the place.

Two ladies, one in a very fantastic party-coloured habit, with a plume of feathers, the other in a rustic one, with a garland of flowers round her head, were much taken notice of for their freedom, and having something to say to every body. They were as seldom separated as Miss Darnford and I, and were followed by a crowd wherever they went.

The party-coloured one came up to me: "Friend," said she, "there is something in thy person that attracts every one's notice: but if a sack had not been a profane thing, it would have become thee almost as well."—"I thank thee, friend," said I, "for thy counsel; but if thou hadst been pleased to look at home, thou wouldst not have taken so much pains to join such advice, and such an appearance, together, as thou makest!"

This made every one that heard it laugh.—One said, the butterfly hath met with her match.

She returned, with an affected laugh, " Smartly said !—But art thou come hither, friend, to make thy light shine before men or women ? "

" Verily, friend, neither," replied I : " but out of mere curiosity, to look into the *minds* of both sexes; which I read in their *dresses*."

" A general satire on the assemblée, by the mass ! " said a fat Monk.

The Nun whisked to us : " We're all concerned in my friend's remark."—

" And no disgrace to a fair Nun," returned I, " if her behaviour answer her dress—Nor to a reverend Friar," turning to the Monk, " if his mind be not a discredit to his appearance—Nor yet to a Country-girl," turning to the party-coloured lady's companion, " if she has not weeds in her heart to disgrace the flowers on her head."

An odd figure, representing a *Merry Andrew*, took my hand, and said, I had the most piquant wit he had met with that night : " And, friend," said he, " let us be better acquainted ! "

" Forbear," said I, withdrawing my hand; " not a companion for a Jack-pudding, neither ! "

A Roman Senator just then accosted Miss Darnford; and Mr. B. seeing me so much engaged, " 'Twere hard," said he, " if our nation, in spite of Cervantes, produced not one cavalier to protect a fair lady thus surrounded."

" Though surrounded, not distressed, my good knight-errant," said the Nun : " the fair Quaker will be too hard for half-a-dozen antagonists, and wants not your protection :—but your poor Nun bespeaks it," whispered she, " who has not a word to say for herself." Mr. B. answered her in Italian (I wish I understood Italian !)—and she had recourse to her beads.

You can't imagine, Madam, how this Nun haunted him !—I don't like these masquerades at all. Many ladies, on these occasions, are so very free, that the censorious will be apt to blame the whole sex for *their* conduct, and to say, their hearts are as faulty as those of the most culpable men, since they scruple not to shew as much, when they think they cannot be known by their faces. But it is my humble opinion, that could a standard be fixed, by which one could determine readily what *is*, and what is *not* wit, decency would not be so often wounded by attempts to be witty, as it is. For here every one, who can say things that shock a modester person, not meeting

261

with due rebuke, but perhaps a smile, (without considering whether it be of contempt or approbation) mistakes courage for wit; and every thing sacred or civil becomes the subject of his frothy jest.

But what a moralizer am I ! will your ladyship say : indeed I can't help it :—and especially on such a subject as a *masquerade*, which I dislike more than any thing I ever saw. I could say a great deal more on this occasion; but, upon my word, I am quite out of humour with it : for I liked my English Mr. B. better than my Spaniard : and the Nun I approved not by any means; though there were some who observed, that she was one of the gracefullest figures in the place. And, indeed, in spite of my own heart, I could not help thinking so too.

Your ladyship knows so well what *masquerades* are, that I may well be excused saying any thing further on a subject I am so little pleased with : for you only desire my notions of those diversions, because I am a novice in them; and this, I doubt not, will doubly serve to answer that purpose.

I shall only therefore add, that after an hundred other impertinences spoken to Miss Darnford and me, and retorted with spirit by her, and as well as I could by myself, quite sick of the place, I feigned to be more indisposed than I was, and so got my beloved Spaniard to go off with us, and reached home by three in the morning. And so much for *masquerades*. I hope I shall never have occasion to mention them again to your ladyship. I am, my dearest Madam, *your ever obliged sister and servant*,

P. B.

LETTER LVII

My dearest Lady,

My mind is so wholly engrossed by thoughts of a very different nature from those which the diversions of the town and theatres inspire, that I beg to be excused, if, for the present, I say nothing further of those lighter matters. But as you do not disapprove of my remarks, I intend, if God spares my life, to make a little book, which I will present to your ladyship, of my poor observations on all the dramatic entertainments I have seen, and shall see, this winter : and for this purpose I have made brief notes in the margin of the printed plays I have bought, as I saw them, with a pencil; by referring to which, as helps to my memory, I shall be able to state what my thoughts were at the time of seeing them pretty nearly with the same advantage, as if I had written them at my return from each.

I have obtained Sir Simon, and Lady Darnford's permission for Miss to stay with me till it shall be seen how it will please God to deal with me, and I owe this favour partly to a kind letter written in my behalf to Sir Simon, by Mr. B., and partly to the young lady's earnest request to her papa, to oblige me; Sir Simon having made some difficulty to comply, as Mr. Murray and his bride have left them, saying, he could not live long, if he had not the company of his beloved daughter.

But what shall I say, when I find my frailty so much increased, that I cannot, with the same intenseness of devotion I used to be blest with, apply myself to the throne of Grace, nor, of consequence, find my invocations answered by that delight and inward satisfaction, with which I used when the present near prospect was more remote?

I hope I shall not be deserted in the hour of trial, and that this my weakness of mind will not be punished with a spiritual dereliction, for suffering myself to be too much attached to those worldly delights and pleasures, which no mortal ever enjoyed in a more exalted degree than myself. And I beseech you, my dearest lady, let me be always remembered in your prayers—*only* for a resignation to the Divine will; a *cheerful* resignation! I presume not to prescribe to his gracious Providence; for if one has but *that*, one has every thing that one need to have.

Forgive me, my dearest lady, for being so deeply serious. I have just been contending with a severe pang, that is now gone off; what effect its return may have, God only knows. And if this is the last line I shall ever write, it will be the more satisfactory to me, as (with my humble respects to my good Lord Davers, and my dear countess, and praying for the continuance of all your healths and happiness, both here and hereafter), I am permitted to subscribe myself *your ladyship's obliged sister and humble servant,*

P. B.

LETTER LVIII

From Lady Davers to Mr. B.

MY DEAREST BROTHER,

Although I believe it needless to put a man of your generous spirit in mind of doing a worthy action; yet, as I do not know whether you have thought of what I am going to hint to you, I cannot forbear a line or two with regard to the good old couple in Kent.

I am sure, if, for our sins, God Almighty should take from us my incomparable sister (forgive me, my dear brother, but to intimate what *may* be, although I hourly pray, as her trying minute approaches, that it will not), you will, for her sake, take care that her honest parents have not the loss of your favour, to deepen the inconsolable one, they will have, in such a case, of the best of daughters.

I say, I am sure you will do as generously by them as ever : and I dare say your sweet Pamela doubts it not : yet, as you know how sensible she is of every favour done them, it is the countess's opinion and mine, and Lady Betty's too, that you give *her* this assurance, in some *legal* way : for, as she is naturally apprehensive, and thinks more of her present circumstances, than, for your sake, she chooses to express to you, it will be like a cordial to her dutiful and grateful heart; and I do not know, if it will not contribute, more than any *one* thing, to make her go through her task with ease and safety.

I know how much your heart is wrapped up in the dear creature : and you are a worthy brother to let it be so ! You will excuse me therefore, I am sure, for this my officiousness.

I have no doubt but God will spare her to us, because, although we may not be worthy of such excellence, yet we all now unite so gratefully to thank him, for such a worthy relation, that I hope we shall not be deprived of an example so necessary to us all.

I can have but one fear, and that is, that, young as she is, she seems ripened for glory : she seems to have lived long enough for *herself*. But for *you*, and for *us*, that God will *still* spare her, shall be the hourly prayer of, *my dear worthy brother, your ever affectionate sister,*   B. DAVERS.

Have you got her mother with you ? I hope you have. God give you a son and heir, if it be his blessed will ! But, however that be, preserve your Pamela to you ! for you never can have such *another* wife.

LETTER LIX

From Mrs. B. to Mr. B.

MY DEAR AND EVER-HONOURED MR. B.,
        Since I know not how it may please God Almighty to dispose of me on the approaching occasion, I should think myself

inexcusable, not to find one or two select hours to dedicate to you, out of the very many, in the writing way, which your goodness has indulged me, because you saw I took delight in it.

But yet, think not, O best beloved of my heart! that I have any boon to beg, any favour to ask, either for myself or for my friends, or so much as the *continuance* of your favour, to the one or the other. As to them, you have prevented and exceeded all my wishes: as to myself, if it please God to spare me, I know I shall always be rewarded beyond my desert, let my deservings be what they will. I have only therefore to acknowledge with the deepest sense of your goodness to me, and with the most heart-affecting gratitude, that from the happy, the thrice happy hour, that you so generously made me yours, till *this* moment, you have not left one thing, on my own part, to wish for, but the continuance and increase of your felicity, and that I might be still worthier of the unexampled goodness, tenderness, and condescension, wherewith you have always treated me.

No, my dearest, my best beloved master, friend, husband, my *first*, my *last*, and *only* love! believe me, I have nothing to wish for but your honour and felicity, temporal and eternal; and I make no doubt, that God, in his infinite goodness and mercy, will perfect his own good work, begun in your dear heart; and, whatever may now happen, give us a happy meeting, never more to part from one another.

Let me then beg of you, my dearest protector, to pardon all my imperfections and defects; and if, ever since I have had the honour to be yours, I have in *looks*, or in *word*, or in *deed*, given you cause to wish me other than I was, that you will kindly put it to the score of natural infirmity (for in *thought* or *intention*, I can truly boast, I have never wilfully erred). Your tenderness, and generous politeness to me, always gave me apprehension, that I was not what you wished me to be, because you would not find fault with me so often as I fear I deserved: and this makes me beg of you to do, as I hope God Almighty will, pardon all my involuntary errors and omissions.

But let me say one word for my dear worthy Mrs. Jervis. Her care and fidelity will be very necessary for your affairs, dear Sir, while you remain single, which I hope will not be long. But, whenever you make a second choice, be pleased to allow her such an annuity as may make her independent, and pass away the remainder of her life with ease and comfort. And this I the rather presume to request, as my late honoured lady once intimated the same thing to you. If I were to name what that may be, it would not be with the thought of *heightening*, but of *limiting* rather, the natural bounty of your heart; and fifty pounds a-year would be a rich provision, in her opinion, and will entail upon you, dear Sir, the blessings of one of the faithfullest and worthiest hearts in the kingdom.

Nor will Christian charity permit me to forget the once wicked, but now penitent Jewkes. I understand by Miss Darnford, that she begs for nothing but to have the pleasure of dying in your service, and by that means to atone for some small slips and mistakes in her accounts, which she had made formerly, and she accuses herself; for she will have it, that Mr. Longman has been better to her than she deserved, in passing one account particularly, to which he had, with too much reason, objected; do, dear Sir, if your *future* happy lady has no great dislike to the poor woman, be pleased to grant her request, except her own mind should alter, and she desire her dismission.

And now I have to beg of God to shower down his most precious blessings upon you, my dearest, my *first*, my *last*, and my *only* love ! and to return to you an hundred fold, the benefits which you have conferred upon me and mine, and upon so many poor souls, as you have blessed through my hands ! And that you may in your next choice be happy with a lady, who may have every thing I want; and who may love and honour you, with the same affectionate duty, which has been my delight and my glory to pay you : for in this I am sure, no one *can* exceed me !—And after having given you long life, prosperity, and increase of honour, translate you into a blessed eternity, where, through the merits of our common Redeemer, I hope I shall be allowed a place, and be permitted (O let me indulge that pleasing, that *consolatory* thought !) to receive and rejoice in my restored spouse, for ever and ever : are the prayers, the *last* prayers, if it so please God ! of, my dearest dear Mr. B., *your dutiful and affectionate wife, and faithful servant,*

P. B.

LETTER LX

From Miss Darnford to Lady Darnford.

MY HONOURED MAMMA,

You cannot conceive how you and my dear papa have delighted my good Mrs. B. and obliged her Mr. B. by the permission you have given me to attend her till the important hour shall be over with her; for she is exceedingly apprehensive, and one can hardly blame her; since there is hardly such another happy couple in the world.

I am glad to hear that the ceremony is over, so much to both your satisfactions : may this matrimony be but a *tenth part* as happy as that I am witness to here; and Mr. and Mrs. Murray will have that to boast of, which few married people have, even among those we call happy !

For my part, I believe I shall never care to marry at all; for though I cannot be so deserving as Mrs. B. yet I shall not bear to think of a husband much less excellent than hers. Nay, by what I see in *her* apprehensions, and conceive of the condition she hourly expects to be in, I don't think a lady can be requited with a *less* worthy one, for all she is likely to suffer on a husband's account, and for the sake of *his* family and name.

Mrs. Andrews, a discreet worthy soul as ever I knew, and who in her aspect and behaviour is far from being a disgrace even to Mr. B.'s lady, is with her dear daughter, to her no small satisfaction, as you may suppose.

Mr. B. asked my advice yesterday, about having in the house a midwife, to be at hand, at a moment's warning. I said I feared the sight of such a person would terrify her : and so he instantly started an expedient, of which her mother, Mrs. Jervis, and myself, approved, and have put into practice; for this day, Mrs. Harris, a distant relation of *mine*, though not of yours, Sir and Madam, is arrived from Essex to make me a visit; and Mr. B. has prevailed upon her, in *compliment to me*, as he pretended, to accept of her board in his house, while she stays in town, which she says, will be about a week.

Mrs. Harris being a discreet, modest, matron-like person, Mrs. B. took a liking to her at first sight, and is already very familiar with her; and understanding that she was a doctor of physic's lady, and takes as much delight in administering to the health of her own sex, as her husband used to do to that of both, Mrs. B. says it is very fortunate, that she has so experienced a lady to consult, as she is such a novice in her own case.

Mr. B. however, to carry on the honest imposture the better, just now, in presence of Mrs. Harris, and Mrs. Andrews, and me, asked the former, if it was not necessary to have in the house the good woman? This frighted Mrs. B. who turned pale, and said she could not bear the thoughts of it. Mrs. Harris said it was highly necessary that Mrs. B. if she would not permit the gentlewoman to be in the house, should see her; and that then, she apprehended, there would be no necessity, as she did not live far off, to have her in the house, since Mrs. B. was so uneasy upon that account. This pleased Mrs. B. much, and Mrs. Thomas was admitted to attend her.

Now, you must know, that this is the assistant of my new relation; and she being apprised of the matter, came; but never did I see so much shyness and apprehension as Mrs. B. shewed all the time Mrs. Thomas was with her, holding sometimes her mother, sometimes Mrs. Harris, by the hand, and being ready to sweat with terror.

Mrs. Harris scraped acquaintance with Mrs. Thomas, who, pretending to recollect her, gave Mrs. Harris great praises; which increased Mrs. B.'s confidence in her : and she undertakes to govern the whole so, that the dreaded Mrs. Thomas need not come till the very moment : which is no small pleasure to the over-nice lady. And she seems every hour to be better pleased with Mrs. Harris, who, by her prudent talk, will more and more familiarize her to the circumstance, unawares to herself in a manner. But notwithstanding this precaution, of a midwife in the house, Mr. B. intends to have a gentleman of the profession in readiness, for fear of the worst.

Mrs. B. has written a letter, with this superscription : " To the ever-honoured and ever-dear Mr. B., with prayers for his health, honour, and prosperity in this world, and everlasting felicity in that to come. P.B." It is sealed with black wax, and she gave it me this moment, on her being taken ill, to give to Mr. B. if she dies. But God, of his mercy, avert that ! and preserve the dear lady, for the honour of her sex, and the happiness of all who know her, and particularly for that of your Polly Darnford; for I cannot have a greater loss, I am sure, while my honoured papa and mamma are living : and may that be for many, very many, happy years !

I will not close this letter till all is over : happily, as I hope !— Mrs. B. is better again, and has, occasionally, made some fine reflections, directing herself to me, but designed for the benefit of her Polly, on the subject of the inconsideration of some of our sex, with regard to the circumstances she is in.

I knew what her design was, and said, " Aye, Polly, let you and I, and every single young body, bear these reflections in mind, pronounced by so excellent a lady, in a moment so arduous as these ! "

The girl wept, and very movingly fell down by the door, on

her knees, praying to God to preserve her dear lady, and she should be happy for ever !

Mrs. B. is exceedingly pleased with my new relation Mrs. Harris, as we call her, who behaves with so much prudence, that she suspects nothing, and told Mrs. Jervis, she wished nobody else was to come near her. And as she goes out (being a person of eminence in her way) two or three times a day, and last night staid out late, Mrs. B. said, she hoped she would not be abroad, when she should wish her to be at home——

I have the very great pleasure, my dear papa and mamma, to acquaint you, and I know you will rejoice with me upon it, that just half an hour ago, my dear Mrs. B. was brought to-bed of a fine boy.

We are all out of our wits for joy almost. I ran down to Mr. B. myself, who received me with trembling impatience. " A boy ! a fine boy ! dear Mr. B.," said I : " a son and heir, indeed ! "

" But how does my Pamela? Is *she* safe? Is *she* like to do well? "—" We hope so," said I : " or I had not come down to you, I'll assure you." He folded me in his arms, in a joyful rapture : " How happy you make me, dearest Miss Darnford ! If my Pamela is safe, the boy is welcome, welcome, indeed !— But when may I go up to thank my jewel? "

Mrs. Andrews is so overjoyed, and so thankful, that there is no getting her from her knees.

A man and horse is dispatched already to Lady Davers, and another ordered to Kent, to the good old man.

Mrs. Jervis, when I went up, said she must go down and release the good folks from their knees; for, half an hour before, they declared they would not stir from that posture till they heard how it went with their lady; and when the happy news was brought them of her safety, and of a young master, they were quite ecstatic, she says, in their joy, and not a dry eye among them, shaking hands, and congratulating one another, men and maids; which made it one of the most affecting sights that can be imagined. And Mr. Longman, who had no power to leave the house for three days past, hasted to congratulate his worthy principal; and never was so much moving joy seen, as this honest-hearted steward ran over with.

I did a foolish thing in my joy—I gave Mr. B. the letter designed for him, had an unhappy event followed; and he won't return it : but says, he will obtain Mrs. B.'s leave, when she is better, to open it; and the happier turn will augment his thankfulness to God, and love to her, when he shall, by this means, be blest with sentiments so different from what the other case would have afforded.

Mrs. B. had a very sharp time. Never more, my dear papa, talk of a husband to me. Place all your expectations on Nancy! Not one of these men that I have yet seen, is worth running these risques for! But Mr. B.'s endearments and tenderness to his lady, his thankful and manly gratitude and politeness, when he was admitted to pay his respects to her, and his behaviour to Mrs. Andrews, and to us all, though but for a visit of ten minutes, was alone worthy of all her risque.

I would give you a description of it, had I Mrs. B.'s pen, and of twenty agreeable scenes and conversations besides: but, for want of that, must conclude. with my humble duty, as becomes, honoured Sir, and Madam, *your ever grateful*

POLLY DARNFORD,

LETTER LXI

From the Same,

MY HONOURED PAPA AND MAMMA,

We have nothing but joy and festivity in this house : and it would be endless to tell you the congratulations the happy family receives every day, from tenants and friends. Mr. B., you know, was always deemed one of the kindest landlords in England; and his tenants are overjoyed at the happy event which has given them a young landlord of his name : for all those who live in that large part of the estate, which came by Mrs. B. his mother, were much afraid of having any of Sir Jacob Swynford's family for their landlord, who, they say, are all made up of pride and cruelty, and would have racked them to death : insomuch that they had a voluntary meeting of about twenty of the principal of them, to rejoice on the occasion; and it was unanimously agreed to make a present of a piece of gilt plate, to serve as basin for the christening, to the value of one hundred guineas; on which is to be engraven the following inscription :

" *In acknowledgment of the humanity and generosity of the best of landlords, and as a token of his tenants' joy on the birth of a son and heir, who will, it is hoped, inherit his father's generosity, and his mother's virtues, this piece of plate is, with all due gratitude, presented, as a christening basin to all the children that shall proceed from such worthy parents, and their descendants, to the end of time.*

"By the obliged and joyful tenants of the maternal estate in Bedfordshire and Gloucestershire, the initials of whose names are under engraven, viz.

Then are to follow the first letters of each person's Christian and surname.

What an honour is this to a landlord! In my opinion very far surpassing the *mis-nomer'd* free gifts which we read of in some kingdoms on extraordinary occasions, some of them like this! For here it is all truly spontaneous—A free gift *indeed!* and Mr. B. took it very kindly, and has put off the christening for a week, to give time for its being completed and inscribed as above.

The Earl and Countess of C. and Lord and Lady Davers, are here, to stand in person at the christening; and you cannot conceive how greatly my Lady Davers is transported with joy, to have a son and heir to the estate: she is every hour, almost, thanking her dear sister for him; and reads in the child all the great qualities she forms to herself in him. 'Tis indeed a charming boy, and has a great deal (if one may judge of a child so very young) of his father's manly aspect. The dear lady herself is still but weak; but the joy of all around her, and her spouse's tenderness and politeness, give her cheerful and free spirits; and she is all serenity, ease, and thankfulness.

Mrs. B., as soon as the danger was over, asked me for her letter with the black seal. I had been very earnest to get it from Mr. B. but to no purpose; so I was forced to tell who had it. She said, but very composedly, she was sorry for it, and hoped he had not opened it.

He came into her chamber soon after, and I demanded it before her. He said he had designed to ask her leave to break the seal, which he had not yet done; nor would without her consent.

"Will you give me leave, my dear," said he, "to break the seal?"—"If you do, Sir, let it not be in my presence; but it is too serious."—"Not, my dear, now the apprehension is so happily over: it may now add to my joy and my thankfulness on that account."—"Then, do as you please, Sir; but I had rather you would not."

"Then here it is, Miss Darnford: it was put into your hands, and there I place it again."—"That's something like," said I, "considering the gentleman. Mrs. B., I hope we shall bring him into good order between us in time." So I returned it to the dear writer; who put it into her bosom.

I related to Lady Davers, when she came, this circumstance;

and she, I believe, has leave to take it with her. She is very proud of all opportunities now of justifying her brother's choice, and doing honour to his wife, with Lady Betty C., who is her great favourite, and who delights to read Mrs. B.'s letters.

You desire to know, my honoured papa, how Mr. B. passes his time, and whether it be in his lady's chamber? No, indeed! Catch gentlemen, the best of them, in too great a complaisance that way, if you can. "What then, does he pass his time *with you*, Polly?" you are pleased to ask. What a disadvantage a man lies under, who has been once a rake! But I am so generally with Mrs. B. that when I tell you, Sir, his visits to her are much of the polite form, I believe I answer all you mean by your questions; and especially when I remind you, Sir, that Lord and Lady Davers, and the Earl and Countess of C. and your unworthy daughter, are at dinner and supper-time generally together; for Mrs. Andrews, who is not yet gone back to Kent, breakfasts, dines, and sups with her beloved daughter, and is hardly ever out of her room.

Then, Sir, Mr. B., the Earl, and Lord Davers, give pretty constant attendance to the business of parliament; and, now and-then, sup abroad—So, Sir, we are all upon honour; and I could wish (only that your facetiousness always gives me pleasure, as it is a token that you have your much-desired health and freedom of spirits), that even in jest, my mamma's daughter might pass unquestioned.

But I know *why* you do it: it is only to put me out of heart to ask to stay longer. Yet I wish—But I know you won't permit me to go through the whole winter here. Will my dear papa grant it, do you think, if you were to lay the highest obligation upon your dutiful daughter, and petition for me? And should you care to try? I dare not hope it myself: but when one sees a gentleman here, who denies his lady nothing, it makes one wish, methinks, that Lady Darnford, was as happy in that particular as Mrs. B.

Your indulgence for this *one* winter, or, rather this small *remainder* of it, I make not so much doubt of, you see, Madam. I know you'll call me a bold girl; but then you always, when you do, condescend to grant my request: and I will be as good as ever I can be afterwards. I will fetch up all the lost time; rise an hour sooner in the morning, go to bed an hour later at night; flower my papa any thing he pleases; read him to sleep when he pleases; put his gout into good-humour, when it will be soothed—And Mrs. B., to crown all, will come down with me, by permission of her sovereign lord, who will attend her, you may be sure : and will not *all* this do, to procure me a month or two more?—If it won't, why then, I will thank you for your past goodness to me, and with all duty and cheerfulness, bid adieu to this dear London, this dearer family, and tend a *still* dearer papa and mamma; whose dutiful daughter I will ever be, whilst

POLLY DARNFORD.

LETTER LXII

To the Same.

MY HONOURED PAPA AND MAMMA,

I have received your joint commands, and intend to set out on Wednesday, next week. I hope to find my papa in better health than at present, and in better humour too; for I am sorry he is displeased with my petitioning for a little longer time in London. It is very severe to impute to me want of duty and affection, which would, if deserved, make me most unworthy of your favour.

Mr. B. and his lady are resolved to accompany me in their coach, till your chariot meets me, if you will be pleased to permit it so to do; and even set me down at your gate, if it did not; but he vows, that he will neither alight at your house, nor let his lady. But I say, that this is a misplaced resentment, because I ought to think it a favour, that you have indulged me so much as you have done. And yet even this is likewise a favour on *their* side, to me, because it is an instance of their fondness for your unworthy daughter's company.

Mrs. B. is, if possible, more lovely since her lying-in than before. She has so much delight in her nursery, that I fear it will take her off from her pen, which will be a great loss to all whom she used to oblige with her correspondence. Indeed this new object of her care is a charming child; and she is exceedingly pleased with her nurse;—for she is not permitted, as she very much desired, to suckle it herself.

She makes a great proficiency in the French and Italian languages; and well she may; for she has the best schoolmaster in the world, and one whom she loves better than any lady ever loved a tutor. He is lofty, and will not be disputed with; but I never saw a more polite and tender husband, for all that.

We had a splendid christening, exceedingly well ordered, and every body was delighted at it. The quality gossips went away

273

but on Tuesday; and my Lady Davers took leave of her charming sister with all the blessings, and all the kindness, and affectionate fondness, that could be expressed.

Mr. Andrews, that worthy old man, came up to see his grandson, yesterday. You would never have forgotten the good man's behaviour (had you seen it), to his daughter, and to the charming child: I wish I could describe it to you; but I am apt to think Mrs. B. will notice it to Lady Davers; and if she enters into the description of it while I stay, I will beg a copy of it, to bring down with me; because I know you were pleased with the sensible, plain, good man, and his ways, when at the Hall in your neighbourhood.

The child is named William, and I should have told you; but I write without any manner of connection, just as things come uppermost: but don't, my dear papa, construe this, too, as an instance of disrespect.

I see but one thing that can possibly happen to disturb the felicity of this charming couple; and that I will mention, in confidence. Mr. B. and Mrs. B. and myself were at the masquerade, before she lay-in: there was a lady greatly taken with Mr. B. She was in a nun's habit, and followed him wherever he went; and Mr. Turner, a gentleman of one of the inns of court, who visits Mr. B. and is an old acquaintance of his, tells me, by-the-bye, that the lady took an opportunity to unmask to Mr. B. Mr. Turner has since found she is the young Countess Dowager of ——, a fine lady; but not the most reserved in her conduct of late, since her widowhood. And he has since discovered, as he says, that a letter or two, if not more, have passed between Mr. B. and that lady.

Now Mrs. B., with all her perfections, has, as she *owns*, a little spice of jealousy; and should she be once alarmed, I tremble for the consequence to both their happiness.

I conceive, that if ever anything makes a misunderstanding between them, it will be from some such quarter as this. But 'tis a thousand pities it should. And I hope, as to the actual correspondence begun, Mr. Turner is mistaken.

But be it as it will, I would not for the world, that the first hints of this matter should come from me.—Mr. B. is a very enterprising and gallant man, a fine figure, and I don't wonder a lady may like him. But he seems so pleased, so satisfied with his wife, and carries it to her with so much tenderness and affection, that I hope her merit, and his affection for her, will secure his conjugal fidelity.

If it prove otherwise, and she discovers it, I know not one

that would be more miserable than Mrs. B., as well from motives of piety and virtue, as from the excessive love she bears him. But I hope for better things, for both their sakes.

My humble thanks for all your indulgence to me, with hopes, that you will not, my dear papa and mamma, hold your displeasure against me, when I throw myself at your feet, as I now soon hope to do. Conclude me *your dutiful daughter,*

P. DARNFORD.

LETTER LXIII

From Mrs. B. to Lady Davers.

MY DEAR LADY,

We are just returned from accompanying the worthy Miss Darnford as far as Bedford, in her way home, where her papa and mamma met her in their coach. Sir Simon put on his pleasant airs, and schooled Mr. B. for persuading his daughter to stay so long from him; *me* for putting her upon asking to stay longer; and *she* for being persuaded by us.

We tarried two days together at Bedford; for we knew not how to part; and then we took a most affectionate leave of each other.

We struck out of the road a little, to make a visit to the dear house, where we tarried one night; and next morning before any body could come to congratulate us (designing to be *incog.*), we proceeded on our journey to London, and found my dearest, dear boy, in charming health.

What a new pleasure has God bestowed upon me; which, after every little absence, rises upon me in a true maternal tenderness, every step I move toward the dear little blessing! Yet sometimes, I think your dear brother is not so fond of him as I wish him to be. He says, " 'tis time enough for him to mind him, when he can return his notice, and be grateful !"—A negligent word isn't it, Madam—considering—

My dear father came to town, to accompany my good mother down to Kent, and they set out soon after your ladyship left us. It is impossible to describe the joy with which his worthy heart overflowed, when he congratulated us on the happy event. And as he had been apprehensive for his daughter's safety, judge, my lady, what his transports must be, to see us all safe and well, and happy, and a son given to Mr. B. by his greatly honoured daughter.

I was in the nursery when he came. So was my mother. Miss Darnford also was there. And Mr. B., who was in his closet, at his arrival, after having received his most respectful congratulations himself, brought him up (though he has not been there since : indeed he ha'n't !) " Pamela," said the dear gentleman, " see who's here ! "

I sprang to him, and kneeled for his blessing : " O my father ! " said I, " see " (pointing to the dear baby at the nurse's breast), " how God Almighty has answered all our prayers ! "

He dropped down on his knees by me, clasping me in his indulgent arms : " O my daughter !—My blessed daughter !—And do I once more see you ! And see you safe and well ! —I do ! I do !—Blessed be thy name, O gracious God, for these thy mercies ! "

While we were thus joined, happy father, and happy daughter, in one thanksgiving, the sweet baby having fallen asleep, the nurse had put it into the cradle ; and when my father rose from me, he went to my mother, " God bless my dear Betty," said he, " I longed to see you, after this separation. Here's joy ! here's pleasure ! O how happy are we ! " And taking her hand, he kneeled down on one side the cradle, and my mother on the other, both looking at the dear baby, with eyes running over ; and, hand in hand, he prayed, in the most fervent manner, for a blessing upon the dear infant, and that God Almighty would make him an honour to his father's family, and to his mother's virtue ; and that, in the words of Scripture, " *he might grow on, and be in favour both with the Lord, and with man.*"

Mr. B. has just put into my hands Mr. Locke's Treatise on Education, and he commands me to give him my thoughts upon it in writing. He has a very high regard for this author, and tells me, that my tenderness for Billy will make me think some of the first advice given in it a little harsh ; but although he has not read it through, only having dipped into it here and there, he believes from the name of the author, I cannot have a better directory ; and my opinion of it, after I have well considered it, will inform him, he says, of my own capacity and prudence, and how far he may rely upon both in the point of a *first education*.

I asked, if I might not be excused writing, only making my observations, here and there, to himself, as I found occasion ? But he said, " You will yourself, my dear, better consider the subject, and be more a mistress of it, and I shall the better attend to your reasonings, when put into writing : and surely, Pamela, you may, in such an important point as this, as well oblige *me* with a little of your penmanship, as your other dear friends."

After this, your ladyship will judge I had not another word to say. He cuts one to the heart, when he speaks so seriously.

I have looked a little into it. It is a book quite accommodated to my case, being written to a gentleman, the author's friend, for the regulation of his conduct towards his children. But how shall I do, if in such a famed and renowned author, I see already some few things, which I think want clearing up. Won't it look like intolerable vanity in me, to find fault with such a genius as Mr. Locke?

I must, on this occasion, give your ladyship the particulars of a short conversation between your brother and me; which, however, perhaps, will not be to my advantage, because it will shew you what a teazing body I can be, if I am indulged. But Mr. B. will not spoil me neither in that way, I dare say!—Your ladyship will see this in the very dialogue I shall give you.

Thus it was. I had been reading in Mr. Locke's book, and Mr. B. asked me how I liked it?—" Exceedingly well, Sir. But I have a proposal to make, which, if you will be pleased to comply with, will give me a charming opportunity of understanding Mr. Locke."

" What is your proposal, my dear? I see it is some very particular one, by that sweet earnestness in your look."

" Why, so it is, Sir: and I must know, whether you are in high good humour, before I make it. I think you look grave upon me; and my proposal will not then do, I'm sure."

" You have all the amusing ways of your sex, my dear Pamela. But tell me what you would say? You know I don't love suspense."

" May-be you're busy, Sir. Perhaps I break in upon you. I believe you were going into your closet."

" True woman!—How you love to put one upon the tenters! Yet, my life for yours, by your parade, what I just now thought important, is some pretty trifle!—Speak it at once, or I'll be angry with you;" and tapped my cheek.

" Well, I wish I had not come just now!—I see you are not in a good humour enough for my proposal.—So, pray, Sir, excuse me till to-morrow."

He took my hand, and led me to his closet. calling me his pretty impertinent; and then urging me, I said, " You know, Sir, I have not been used to the company of children. Your dear Billy will not make me fit, for a long time, to judge of any part of education. I can learn of the charming boy nothing but the baby conduct: but now, if I might take into the house some little Master of three or four years old, or Miss of five or six, I should watch over all their little ways; and now reading a chapter in the *child*, and now one in the *book*, I can look forward, and with advantage, into the subject; and go through all the parts of education tolerably, for one of my capacity; for, Sir, I can, by my own defects, and what I have wished to mend, know how to judge of, and supply that part of life which carries a child up to eleven or twelve years of age, which was mine, when my lady took me."

"A pretty thought, Pamela! but tell me, who will part with their child, think you? Would *you*, if it were your case, although ever so well assured of the advantages your little one would reap by it?—For don't you consider, that the child ought to be wholly subjected to your authority? That its father or mother ought seldom to see it; because it should think itself absolutely dependent upon you?—And where, my dear, will you meet with parents so resigned?—Besides, one would have the child descended of genteel parents, and not such as could do nothing for it; otherwise the turn of mind and education you would give it, might do it more harm than good."

"All this, Sir, is very true. But have you no other objection, if one could find a genteely-descended young Master? And would you join to persuade his papa to give me up his power, only from three months to three months, as I liked, and the child liked, and as the papa approved of my proceedings?"

"This is so reasonable, with these last conditions, Pamela, that I should be pleased with your notion, if it could be put in practice, because the child would be benefited by your instruction, and you would be improved in an art, which I could wish to see you an adept in."

"But, perhaps, Sir, you had rather it were a girl than a boy?"
—"I had, my dear, if a girl could be found, whose parents would give her up to you; but I suppose you have some boy in your head, by your putting it upon that sex at first."

"Let me see, Sir, you say you are in a good humour! Let me see if you be;"—looking boldly in his face.

"What now," with some little impatience, "would the pretty fool be at?"

"Only, Sir, that you have nothing to do, but to speak the word, and there is a child, whose papa and mamma too, I am sure, would consent to give up to me for my own instruction, as well as for her sake; and if, to speak in the Scripture phrase,

I have found *grace in your sight,* kind Sir, speak this word to the dear child's papa."

" And have you thus come over me, Pamela !—Go, I am half angry with you, for leading me on in this manner against myself. This looks so artful, that I won't love you !"—" Dear Sir !"— " And dear Madam too ! Be gone, I say !—You have surprised me by art, when your talent is nature, and you should keep to that !"

I was sadly baulked, and had neither power to go nor stay ! At last, seeing I had put him into a kind of flutter, as now he had put me, I moved my unwilling feet towards the door.—He took a turn about the closet meantime.—" Yet stay," said he, " there is something so generous in your art, that, on recollection, I cannot part with you."

He took notice of the starting tear—" I am to blame !—You had surprised me so, that my hasty temper got the better of my consideration. Let me kiss away this pearly fugitive. Forgive me, my dearest love ! What an inconsiderate brute am I, when compared to such an angel as my Pamela ! I see at once now, all the force, and all the merit, of your amiable generosity : and to make you amends for this my hastiness, I will coolly consider of the matter, and will either satisfy you by my compliance, or by the reasons, which I will give you for the contrary.

" But, say, my Pamela, can you forgive my harshness ? "— " Can I !—Yes, indeed, Sir," pressing his hand to my lips; " and bid me Go, and Be gone, twenty times a-day, if I am to be thus kindly called back to you, thus nobly and condescendingly treated, in the same breath !—I see, dear Sir," continued I, " that I must be in fault, if ever you are lastingly displeased with me. For as soon as you turn yourself about, your anger vanishes, and you make me rich amends for a few harsh words. Only one thing, dear Sir, let me add; if I have dealt artfully with you, impute it to my fear of offending you, through the nature of my petition, and not to design; and that I took the example of the prophet, to King David, in the parable of the *Ewe-Lamb.*"

" I remember it, my dear—and you have well pointed your parable, and had nothing to do, but to say—' *Thou art the man !* ' "

I am called upon by my dear benefactor for a little airing, and he suffers me only to conclude this long letter. So I am obliged, with greater abruptness than I had designed, to mention thankfully your ladyship's goodness to me; particularly in that kind, kind letter, in behalf of my dear parents, had a certain event taken place. Mr. B. shewed it to me *this morning*, and not before—I believe, for fear I should have been so much oppressed by the sense of your unmerited goodness to me, had he let me known of it before your departure from us, that I should not have been able to look up at you; heaping favours and blessings upon me, as you were hourly doing besides. What a happy creature am I!—But my gratitude runs me into length; and sorry I am, that I cannot have time just now to indulge it.

Is there nothing, my dear Lord and Lady Davers, my dear Lady Countess, and my good Lord C., that I can do, to shew at least, that I have a *will*, and am not an ungrateful, sordid creature?

And yet, if you give me power to do any thing that will have the *appearance* of a return, even that *power* will be laying a fresh obligation upon me—Which, however, I should be very proud of, because I should thereby convince you, by more than words, how much I am (most particularly, my dearest Lady Davers, my sister, my friend, my patroness), *your most obliged and faithful servant,*   P. B.

Your dear brother joins in respectful thankfulness to his four noble gossips. And my Billy, by his lips, subscribed his. I hope so to direct his earliest notions, as to make him sensible of his dutiful obligation.

LETTER LXIV

From Lady Davers to Mrs. B.

My dearest Pamela,

Talk not to us of unreturnable obligations and all that. You do more for us, in the entertainment you give us all, by your letters, than we *have* done, or even *can* do, for you. And as to me, I know no greater pleasure in the world than that which my brother's felicity and yours gives me. God continue this felicity to you both. I am sure it will be *his* fault, and not yours, if it be at all diminished.

We have heard some idle rumours here, as if you were a little uneasy of late; and having not had a letter from you for this fortnight past, it makes me write, to ask you how you all do? and whether you expected an answer from me to your last?

I hope you won't be punctilious with me. For we have

nothing to write about, except it be how much we all love and honour you; and that you believe already, or else you don't do us justice.

I suppose you will be going out of town soon, now the parliament is rising. My Lord is resolved to put his proxy into another hand, and intends I believe, to take my brother's advice in it. Both the Earl and his Lordship are highly pleased with my brother's moderate and independent principles. He has got great credit among all unprejudiced men, by the part he acted throughout the last session, in which he has shown, that he would no more join to distress and clog the wheels of government, by an unreasonable opposition, than he would do the dirty work of any administration. As he has so noble a fortune and wants nothing of any body, he would be doubly to blame, to take any other part than that of his country, in which he has so great a stake.

May he act *out* of the house, and *in* the house with equal honour; and he will be his country's pride, and your pride, and mine too ! which is the wish of *your affectionate sister,*

B. DAVERS.

LETTER LXV

MY DEAREST LADY,

I have been a little in disorder, that I have. Some few rubs have happened. I hope they will be happily removed. I am unwilling to believe all that is said. But this is a wicked town. I wish we were out of it. Yet I see not when that will be. I wish Mr. B. would permit me and my Billy to go into Kent. But I don't care to leave him behind me, neither; and he is not inclined to go. Excuse my brevity, my dearest lady— But I must break off, with only assuring your ladyship, that I am, and ever will be, *your obliged and grateful,*   P. B.

LETTER LXVI

MY DEAREST PAMELA,

I understand things go not so well as I wish. If you think my coming up to town, and residing with you, while you stay, will be of service, or help you to get out of it, I will set out directly. I will pretend some indisposition, and a desire of consulting the London physicians; or any thing you shall think fit to be done, by *your affectionate sister, and faithful friend,*   B. DAVERS.

LETTER LXVII

My dearest Lady,

A thousand thanks for your goodness to me; but I hope all will be well. I hope God will enable me to act so prudent a part, as will touch his generous breast. Be pleased to tell me what your ladyship has heard; but it becomes not me, I think, till I cannot help it, to make any appeals; for I know those will not be excused; and I do all I can to suppress my uneasiness before him. But I pay for it, when I am alone. My nursery and my reliance on God (I should have said the latter first), are all my consolation. God preserve and bless you, my good lady, and my noble lord! (but I am apt to think your ladyship's presence will not avail), prays *your affectionate and obliged*, P. B.

LETTER LXVIII

Why does not my sweet girl subscribe *Sister*, as usual? I have done nothing amiss to you! I love you dearly, and ever will. I can't help my brother's faults. But I hope he treats you with politeness and decency. He shall be none of my brother if he don't. I rest a great deal upon your prudence: and it will be very meritorious, if you can overcome yourself, so as to act unexceptionably, though it may not be deserved on this occasion. For in doing so, you'll have a triumph over nature itself; for, my dear girl, as you have formerly owned, you have a little touch of jealousy in your composition.

What I have heard, is no secret to any body. The injured party is generally the last who hears in these cases, and you shall not first be told anything by me that must *afflict* you, but cannot *you*, more than it does *me*. God give you patience and comfort! The wicked lady has a deal to answer for, to disturb such an uncommon happiness. But no more, than that I am *your ever-affectionate sister*, B. Davers.

I am all impatience to hear how you conduct yourself upon this trying occasion. Let me know what you have heard, and *how* you came to hear it.

LETTER LXIX

Why don't I subscribe Sister? asks my dearest Lady Davers.— I have not had the courage to do it of late. For my title to that honour arises from the dear, thrice dear Mr. B. And how long I may be permitted to call him mine, I cannot say. But since you command it, I will call your ladyship by that beloved name, let the rest happen as God shall see fit.

Mr. B. cannot be unpolite, in the main; but he is cold, and a little cross, and short in his speeches to me. I try to hide my grief from everybody, and most from him: for neither my parents, nor Miss Darnford know anything from me. Mrs. Jervis, from whom I seldom hide any thing, as she is on the spot with me, hears not my complainings, nor my uneasiness; for I would not lessen the dear man. He may *yet* see the error of the way he is in. God grant it, for his own sake as well as mine.—I am even sorry your ladyship is afflicted with the knowledge of the matter.

The unhappy lady (God forgive her!) is to be pitied: she loves him, and having strong passions, and being unused to be controlled, is lost to a sense of honour and justice.—From these wicked masquerades springs all the unhappiness; my Spaniard was too amiable, and met with a lady who was no Nun, but in habit. Every one was taken with him in that habit, so suited to the natural dignity of his person!—O these wicked masquerades!

I am all patience in appearance, all uneasiness in reality. I did not think I could, especially in *this* most *affecting* point, be such an hypocrite. Your ladyship knows not what it has cost me, to be able to assume that character! Yet my eyes are swelled with crying, and look red, although I am always breathing on my hand, and patting them with it, and my warm breath, to hide the distress that will, from my overcharged heart, appear in them.

Then he says, " What's the matter with the little fool! You are always in this way of late! What ails you, Pamela?"

" Only a little vapourish, Sir!—Don't be angry at me!—Billy, I thought, was not very well!"

" This boy will spoil your temper: at this rate, what should be your joy, will become your misfortune. Don't receive me in this manner, I charge you."

" In what manner, Sir? I always receive you with a grateful heart! If any thing troubles me, it is in your absence: but see, Sir " (then I try to smile, and seem pleased), " I am all sunshine, now you are come!—don't you see I am?"

" Yes, your sunshine of late is all through a cloud! I know not what's the matter with you. Your temper will alter, and then——"

"It shan't alter, Sir—it shan't—if I can help it." And then I kissed his hand; that dear hand, that, perhaps, was last about his more beloved Countess's neck—Distracting reflection!

But come, may-be I think the worst! To be sure I do! For my apprehensions were ever aforehand with events; and bad must be the case, if it be worse than I think it.

You command me to let you know *what* I have heard, and how I *came* to hear it. I told your ladyship in one of my former that two gentlemen brought up to the law, but above the practice of it, though I doubt, not above practices less honourable, had visited us on coming to town.

They have been often here since, Mr. Turner particularly: and sometimes by himself, when Mr. B. has happened to be out: and he it was, as I guessed, that gave me, at the wicked masquerade, the advice to look after my *Musidorus*.

I did not like their visits, and *his* much less: for he seemed to be a man of intriguing spirit. But about three weeks ago, Mr. B. setting out upon a party of pleasure to Oxford, he came and pretended great business with me. I was at breakfast in the parlour, only Polly attending me, and admitted him, to drink a dish of chocolate with me. When Polly had stept out, he told me, after many apologies, that he had discovered who the nun was at the masquerade, that had engaged Mr. B.

I said it was very indifferent to me who the lady was.

He replied (making still more apologies, and pretending great reluctance to speak out), that it was no less a lady than the young Countess Dowager of ——, a lady noted for her wit and beauty, but of a gay disposition, though he believed not yet culpable.

I was alarmed; but would not let him see it; and told Mr. Turner, that I was so well satisfied in Mr. B.'s affection for me, and his well-known honour, that I could not think myself obliged to any gentleman who should endeavour to give me a less opinion of either than I ought to have.

He then bluntly told me, that the very party Mr. B. was upon, was with the Countess for one, and Lord ——, who had married her sister.

I said, I was glad he was in such good company, and wished him every pleasure in it.

He hoped, he said, he might trust to my discretion, that I would not let Mr. B. know from whom I had the information: that, indeed, his motive in mentioning it was self-interest; having presumed to make some overture of an honourable nature to the Countess, in his own behalf; which had been rejected since that masquerade night : and he hoped the prudent use I would make of the intimation, might somehow be a means to break off that correspondence, before it was attended with bad consequences.

I told him coldly, though it stung me to the heart, that I was fully assured of Mr. B.'s honour; and was sorry he, Mr. Turner, had so bad an opinion of a lady to whom he professed so high a consideration. And rising up—"Will you excuse me, Sir, that I cannot attend at all to such a subject as this? I think I ought not : and so must withdraw."

"Only, Madam, one word." He offered to take my hand, but I would not permit it. He then swore a great oath, that he had told me his true and only motive; that letters had passed between the Countess and Mr. B., adding, "But I beg you'll keep it within your own breast; else, from two such hasty spirits as his and mine, it might be attended with still worse consequences."

"I will never, Sir, enter into a subject that is not proper to be communicated every tittle of it to Mr. B.; and this must be my excuse for withdrawing." And away I went from him.

Your ladyship will judge with how uneasy a heart; which became more so, when I sat down to reflect upon what he had told me. But I was resolved to give it as little credit as I could, or that any thing would come of it, till Mr. B.'s own behaviour should convince me, to my affliction, that I had some reason to be alarmed : so I opened not my lips about it, not even to Mrs. Jervis.

At Mr. B.'s return, I received him in my usual affectionate and unreserved manner : and he behaved himself to me with his accustomed goodness and kindness : or, at least, with so little difference, that had not Mr. Turner's officiousness made me more watchful, I should not have perceived it.

But next day a letter was brought by a footman for Mr. B. He was out : so John gave it to me. The superscription was a lady's writing : the seal, the Dowager Lady's, with a coronet. This gave me great uneasiness; and when Mr. B. came in, I said, " Here is a letter for you, Sir; and from a lady too ! "

" What then," said he, with quickness.

I was baulked, and withdrew. For I saw him turn the seal about and about, as if he would see whether I had endeavoured to look into it.

He needed not to have been so afraid; for I would not have done such a thing had I known my life was to depend upon it.

I went up, and could not help weeping at his quick answer: yet I did my endeavour to hide it, when he came up.

"Was not my girl a little inquisitive upon me just now?"

"I spoke pleasantly, Sir—But you were very quick on your girl."

"'Tis my temper, my dear—You know I mean nothing. You should not mind it."

"I should not, Sir, if I had been *used* to it."

He looked at me with sternness, "Do you doubt my honour, Madam?"

"*Madam!* did you say, Sir?—I won't take that word!—Dear Sir, call it back—I won't be called *Madam!*—Call me your girl, your rustic, your Pamela—call me any thing but *Madam!*"

"My charmer, then, my life, my soul: will any of those do?" and saluted me: "but whatever you do, let me not see that you have any doubts of my honour to you."

"The very mention of the word, dear Sir, is a security to me; I want no other; I cannot doubt: but if you speak short to me, how shall I bear that?"

He withdrew, speaking nothing of the contents of his letter; as I dare say he would, had the subject been such as he chose to mention to me.

We being alone, after supper, I took the liberty to ask him, who was of his party to Oxford? He named the Viscountess ——, and her lord, Mr. Howard, and his daughter, Mr. Herbert and his lady: "And I had a partner too, my dear, to represent you."

"I am much obliged to the lady, Sir, be she who she would."

"Why, my dear, you are *so* engaged in your nursery! Then this was a sudden thing; as you know I told you."

"Nay, Sir, as long as it was agreeable to you, I had nothing to do, but to be pleased with it."

He watched my eyes, and the turn of my countenance—"You look, Pamela, as if you'd be glad to return the lady thanks in person. Shall I engage her to visit you? She longs to see you."

"Sir—Sir," hesitated I, "as you please—I can't—I can't be displeased——"

"*Displeased?*" interrupted he: "why that word? and why that hesitation in your answer? You speak very volubly, my dear, when you're not moved."

"Dear Sir," said I, almost as quick as he was, "why should I be moved? What occasion is there for it? I hope you have a better opinion of me than——"

" Than what, Pamela?—What would you say? I know you are a little jealous rogue, I know you are."

" But, dear Sir, why do you impute jealousy to me on *this* score?—What a creature must I be, if you could not be abroad with a lady, but I must be jealous of you?—No, Sir, I have reason to rely upon your honour; and I *do* rely upon it; and——"

" And what? Why, my dear, you are giving me assurances, as if you thought the case required it ! "

" Ah ! " thought I, " so it does, I see too plainly, or apprehend I do; but I durst not say so, nor give him any hint about my informant; though now confirmed of the truth of what Mr. Turner had said.

Yet I resolved, if possible, not to alter my conduct. But my frequent weepings, when by myself, could not be hid as I wished; my eyes not keeping my heart's counsel.

And this gives occasion to some of the stern words which I have mentioned above.

All that he further said at this time was, with a negligent, yet a determined air—" Well, Pamela, don't be doubtful of my honour. You know how much I love you. But, one day or other I shall gratify this lady's curiosity, and bring her to pay you a visit, and you shall see you need not be ashamed of her acquaintance."—" Whenever you please, Sir," was all I cared to say farther; for I saw he was upon the catch, and looked steadfastly upon me whenever I moved my lips; and I am not a finished hypocrite, and he can read the lines of one's face, and the motions of one's heart, I think.

I am sure mine is a very uneasy one. But till I reflected, and weighed well the matter, it was worse; and my natural imperfection of this sort made me see a necessity to be more watchful over myself, and to doubt my own prudence. And thus I reasoned when he withdrew :

" Here," thought I, " I have had a greater proportion of happiness without alloy, fallen to my share, than any of my sex; and I ought to be prepared for some trials.

" 'Tis true, this is of the sorest kind : 'tis worse than death itself to me, who had an opinion of the dear man's reformation, and prided myself not a little on that account. So that the blow is full upon my sore place. 'Tis on the side I could be the most easily penetrated. But Achilles could be touched only in his heel; and if he was to die by an enemy's hands, must not the arrow find out that only vulnerable place? My jealousy is that place with me, as your ladyship observes; but it is seated deeper than the heel: it is in my heart. The barbed dart has found that out, and there it sticks up to the very feathers.

"Yet," thought I, "I will take care, that I do not exasperate him by upbraidings, when I should try to move him by patience and forbearance. For the breach of his duty cannot warrant the neglect of *mine*. My business is to reclaim, and not to provoke. And when, if it please God, this storm shall be over-blown, let me not, by my present behaviour, leave any room for heart-burnings; but, like a skilful surgeon, so heal the wound to the bottom, though the operation be painful, that it may not fester, and break out again with fresh violence, on future misunderstandings, if any shall happen.

"Well, but," thought I, "let the worst come to the worst, he perhaps may be so good as to permit me to pass the remainder of my days with my dear Billy, in Kent, with my father and mother; and so, when I cannot rejoice in possession of a virtuous husband, I shall be employed in praying for him, and enjoy a two-fold happiness, that of doing my own duty to my dear baby—a pleasing entertainment this! and that of comforting my worthy parents, and being comforted by them—a no small consolation! And who knows, but I may be permitted to steal a visit now-and-then to dear Lady Davers, and be called Sister, and be deemed a *faultless* sister too?" But remember, my dear lady, that if ever it comes to this, I will not bear, that, for my sake, you shall, with too much asperity, blame your brother; for I will be ingenious to find excuses or extenuations for him; and I will now-and-then, in some disguised habit, steal the pleasure of seeing him and his happier Countess; and give him, with a silent tear, my blessing for the good I and mine have reaped at his hands.

But oh! if he takes from me my Billy, who must, after all, be his heir, and gives him to the cruel Countess, he will at once burst asunder the strings of my heart! For, oh, my happy rivaless! if you tear from me my husband, he is in his own disposal, and I cannot help it: nor can I indeed, if he will give you my Billy. But this I am sure of, that my child and my life must go together!

Your ladyship will think I rave. Indeed I am almost crazed at times. For the dear man is so negligent, so cold, so haughty, that I cannot bear it. He says, just now, "You are quite altered, Pamela." I believe I am, Madam. But what can I do? He knows not that I know so much. I dare not tell him. For he will have me then reveal my intelligencer: and what may be the case between them?

288

I weep in the night, when he is asleep; and in the day when he is absent: and I am happy when I can, unobserved, steal this poor relief. I believe already I have shed as many tears as would drown my baby. How many more I may have to shed, God only knows! For, O Madam, after all my fortitude, and my recollection, to fall from so much happiness, and so soon, is a trying thing!

But I will still hope the best, and should this matter blow over, I shall be ashamed of my weakness, and the trouble I must give to your generous heart, for one so undeservedly favoured by you, as *your obliged sister, and most humble servant,*

P. B.

Dear Madam, let no soul see any part of this our present correspondence, for your brother's sake, and your sake, and my sake.

LETTER LXX

My dearest Pamela,

You need not be afraid of any body's knowing what passes between us on this cutting subject. Though I hear of it from every mouth, yet I pretend 'tis all falsehood and malice. Yet Lady Betty will have it that there is more in it than I will own; and that I know my brother's wickedness by my pensive looks. She will make a vow, she says, never to marry any man living.

I am greatly moved by your affecting periods. Charming Pamela! what a tempest do you raise in one's mind, when you please, and lay it too, at your own will! Your colourings are strong; but, I hope, your imagination carries you much farther than it is possible he should go.

I am pleased with your prudent reasonings, and your wise resolutions. I see nobody can advise or help you. God only can! And his direction you beg *so* hourly, that I make no doubt you will have it.

What vexes me is, that when the noble uncle of this vile lady—(why don't you call her so as well as I?)—expostulated with her on the scandals she brought upon her character and family, she pretended to argue (foolish creature!) for polygamy: and said, she had rather be a certain gentleman's second wife, than the first to the greatest man in England.

I leave you to your own workings; but if I find your prudence unrewarded by the wretch, the storm you saw raised at the

Hall, shall be nothing to the hurricane I will excite, to tear up by the roots all the happiness the two wretches propose to themselves.

Don't let my intelligence, which is undoubted, grieve you over-much. Try some way to move the wretch. It must be done by touching his generosity : he has that in some perfection. But how in *this* case to move it, is beyond my power or skill to prescribe. God bless you, my dearest Pamela ! You shall be my *only* sister. And I will never own my brother, if he be so base to your superlative merit. Adieu once more, *from your sister and friend,* B. DAVERS.

LETTER LXXI

MY DEAREST LADY,

A thousand thanks for your kind, your truly sisterly letter and advice. Mr. B. is just returned from a tour to Portsmouth, with the Countess, I believe, but am not sure.

Here I am forced to leave off.

Let me scratch through this last surmise. It seems she was not with him. This is some comfort.

He is very kind : and Billy not being well when he came in, my grief passed off without blame. He had said many tender things to me ; but added, that if I gave myself so much uneasiness every time the child ailed any thing, he would hire the nurse to overlay him. Bless me, Madam ! what hard-hearted shocking things are these men capable of saying !—The farthest from their hearts, indeed ; so they had need—For he was as glad of the child's being better as I could be.

In the morning he went out in the chariot for about an hour, and returned in a good humour, saying twenty agreeable things to me, which makes me *so* proud, and *so* pleased !

He is gone out again.

Could I but find this matter happily conquered, for his own soul's sake !—But he seems, by what your ladyship mentions, to have carried this polygamy point with the lady.

Can I live with him, Madam—*ought* I—if this be the case ? I have it under his hand, that the laws of his country were sufficient to deter him from that practice. But alas ! he knew not this countess then !

But here I must break off.

He is returned, and coming up. " Go into my bosom for the present, O letter dedicated to dear Lady Davers—Come to

290

my hand the play employment, so unsuited to my present afflicted mind!"—Here he comes!

O, Madam! my heart is almost broken!—Just now Mr. B. tells me, that the Countess Dowager and the Viscountess, her sister, are to be here to see my Billy, and to drink tea with me, this very afternoon!

I was all confusion when he told me this. I looked around and around, and upon every thing but him.

"Will not my friends be welcome, Pamela?" said he sternly.

"O yes, very welcome! But I have these wretched vapours so, that I wish I might be excused—I wish I might be allowed to take an airing in the chariot for two or three hours; for I shall not be fit to be seen by such—ladies," said I, half out of breath.

"You'll be fit to be seen by nobody, my dear, if you go on thus. But, do as you please."

He was going, and I took his hand: "Stay, dear Sir, let me know what you would have me do. If you would have me stay, I will."

"To be sure I would."

"Well, Sir, then I will. For it is hard," thought I, "if an innocent person cannot look up in her own house too, as it now is, as I may say, to a guilty one! Guilty in her heart, at least!—Though, poor lady, I hope she is not so in fact; and, if God hears my prayers, never will, for all three of our sakes."

But, Madam, think of me, what a task I have!—How my heart throbs in my bosom! How I tremble! how I struggle with myself! What rules I form for my behaviour to this naughty lady! How they are dashed in pieces as soon as formed, and new ones taken up! And yet I doubt myself when I come to the test.

But one thing will help me. I *pity* the poor lady; and as she comes with the heart of a robber, to invade me in my lawful right, I pride myself in a superiority over this countess; and will endeavour to shew her the country girl in a light which would better become *her* to appear in.

I must be forced to leave off here; for Mr. B. is just come in to receive his guests; and I am in a sad flutter upon it. All my resolution fails me: what shall I do? O that this countess was come and gone!

I have one comfort, however, in the midst of all my griefs; and that is in your ladyship's goodness, which gives me leave to assume the honoured title, that let what may happen, will always give me equal pride and pleasure, in subscribing myself, *your ladyship's most obliged sister, and humble servant,*

P. B.

LETTER LXXII

My dear Lady,

I will now pursue my last affecting subject; for the visit is over; but a sad situation I am in with Mr. B. for all that: but, bad as it is, I'll try to forget it, till I come to it in course.

At four in the afternoon Mr. B. came in to receive his guests, whom he expected at five. He came up to me. I had just closed my last letter; but put it up, and set before me your ladyship's play subjects.

" So, Pamela !—How do you do now ? "

Your ladyship may guess, by what I wrote before, that I could not give any extraordinary account of myself—" As well—as well, Sir, as possible; " half out of breath.

" You give yourself strange melancholy airs of late, my dear. All that cheerfulness, which used to delight me whenever I saw you, I am sorry for it, is quite vanished. You and I must shortly have a little serious talk together."

" When you please, Sir. I believe it is only being used to this smoky thick air of London !—I shall be better when you carry me into the country. I dare say I shall. But I never was in London so long before, you know, Sir."

" All in good time, Pamela !—But is this the best appearance you choose to make, to receive such guests ? "

" If it displeases you, Sir, I will dress otherwise in a minute."

" You look well in any thing. But I thought you'd have been better dressed. Yet it would never have less become you; for of late your eyes have lost that brilliancy that used to strike me with a lustre, much surpassing that of the finest diamonds."

" I am sorry for it, Sir. But as I never could pride myself in deserving such a kind of compliment, I should be too happy, forgive me, my dearest Mr. B., if the failure be not rather in your eyes, than in *mine*."

He looked at me steadfastly. " I fear, Pamela—But don't be a fool."

" You are angry with me, Sir ? "

" No, not I."

" Would you have me dress better ? "

" No, not I. If your eyes looked a little more brilliant, you want no addition." Down he went.

292

Strange short speeches, these, my lady, to what you have heard from his dear mouth!—" Yet they shall not rob me of the merit of a patient sufferer, I am resolved," thought I.

Now, my lady, as I doubted not my rival would come adorned with every outward ornament, I put on only a white damask gown, having no desire to vie with her in appearance; for a virtuous and honest heart is my glory, I bless God! I wish the countess had the same to boast of!

About five, their ladyships came in the countess's new chariot: for she has not been long out of her transitory mourning, and dressed as rich as jewels, and a profusion of expense, could make her.

I saw them from the window alight. O how my heart throbbed!—" Lie still," said I, " busy thing! why all this emotion?—Those shining ornaments cover not such a guileless flatterer as thou. Why then all this emotion?"

Polly Barlow came up instantly from Mr. B.

I hastened down; tremble, tremble, tremble, went my feet, in spite of all the resolution I had been endeavouring so long to collect together.

Mr. B. presented the countess to me, both of us covered with blushes; but from very different motives, as I imagine.

" The Countess of ——, my dear."

She saluted me, and looked, as I thought, half with envy, half with shame: but one is apt to form people's countenances by what one judges of their hearts.

" O too lovely, too charming rival!" thought I—" Would to heaven I saw less attraction in you!"—For indeed she is a charming lady; yet she could not help calling me Mrs. B., that was some pride to me: every little distinction is a pride to me now—and said, she hoped I would excuse the liberty she had taken: but the character given of me by Mr. B. made her desirous of paying her respects to me.

" O these villainous masquerades," thought I!—" You would never have wanted to see me, but for them, poor naughty Nun, that was!"

Mr. B. presented also the Viscountess to me; I saluted her ladyship; her *sister* saluted *me*.

She is a graceful lady; better, as I hope, in heart, but not equal in person to her sister.

" You have a charming boy, I am told, Madam; but no wonder from such a pair!"

" O dear heart," thought I, " i'n't it so!" Your ladyship may guess what I thought farther.

293

" Will your ladyship see him now ? " said Mr. B.

He did not look down ; no, not one bit !—though the Countess played with her fan, and looked at him, and at me, and then down by turns, a little consciously : while I wrapped up myself in my innocence, my first flutters being over, and thought I was superior, by reason of that, even to a Countess.

With all her heart, she said.

I rang. " Polly, bid nurse bring *my* Billy down."—*My*, said I, with an emphasis.

I met the nurse at the stairs' foot, and brought in my dear baby in my arms : " Such a child, and such a mamma ! " said the Viscountess.

" Will you give Master to my arms, one moment, Madam ? " said the Countess.

" Yes," thought I, " much rather than my dear naughty gentleman should any other."

I *yielded* it to her : I thought she would have stifled it with her warm kisses. " Sweet boy ! charming creature," and pressed it to her too lovely bosom, with such emotion, looking on the child, and on Mr. B., that I liked it not by any means.

" Go, you naughty lady," thought I : But I durst not say so. " And go, naughty man, too ! " thought I : " for you seem to look too much gratified in your pride, by her fondness for your boy. I wish I did not love you so well as I do ! " But neither, your ladyship may believe, did I say this.

Mr. B. looked at me, but with a bravery, I thought, too like what I had been witness to, in some former scenes, in as bad a cause. " But," thought I, " God delivered me *then;* I will confide in him. He will now, I doubt not, restore thy heart to my prayers; untainted, I hope, for thy own dear sake as well as mine."

The Viscountess took the child from her sister, and kissed him with great pleasure. She is a married lady. Would to God, the Countess was so too ! for Mr. B. never corresponded, as I told your ladyship once, with married ladies : so I was not afraid of *her* love to my Billy. " But let me," said she, " have the pleasure of restoring Master to his charming mamma. I thought," added she, " I never saw a lovelier sight in my life, than when in his mamma's arms."

" Why, I *can't* say," said the Countess, " but Master and his mamma do credit to one another. Dear Madam, let us have the pleasure of seeing him still on your lap, while he is so good."

I wondered the dear baby was so quiet; though, indeed, he is generally so : but *he* might surely, if but by sympathy, have complained for his poor mamma, though she durst not for herself.

How apt one is to engage every thing in one's distress, when it is deep! and one wonders too, that things animate and inanimate look with the same face, when we are greatly moved by any extraordinary and interesting event.

I sat down with my baby on my lap, looking, I believe, with a righteous boldness (I will call it so; for well says the text, "*The righteous is as bold as a lion,*") now on my Billy, now on his papa, and now on the Countess, with such a *triumph* in my heart; for I saw her blush, and look down, and the dear gentleman seemed to eye me with a kind of conscious tenderness, as I thought.

A silence of five minutes, I believe, succeeded, we all four looking upon one another; and the little dear was awake, and stared full upon me, with such innocent smiles, as if he promised to love me, and make me amends for all.

I kissed him, and took his pretty little hand in mine—"You are very good, my charmer, in this company!" said I.

I remembered a scene, which made greatly for me in the papers you have seen, when, instead of recriminating, as I might have done, before Mr. Longman for harsh usage (for, O my lady, your dear brother has a hard heart indeed when he pleases), I only prayed for him on my knees.

And I hope I was not now too mean; for I had dignity and a proud superiority in my vain heart, over them all. Then it was not my part to be upon defiances, where I loved, and where I hoped to reclaim. Besides, what had I done by that, but justified, seemingly, by after acts in a passionate resentment, to their minds, at least, their too wicked treatment of me?—Moreover, your ladyship will remember, that Mr. B. knew not that I was acquainted with his intrigue: for I must call it so. If he had, he is too noble to insult me by such a visit; and he had told me, I should see the lady he was at Oxford with.

And this, breaking silence, he mentioned; saying, "I gave you hope, my dear, that I should procure you the honour of a visit from a lady who put herself under my care at Oxford."

I bowed my head to the Countess; but my tears being ready to start, I kissed my Billy: "Dearest baby," said I, "you are not going to cry, are you?"—I would have had him just then to cry, instead of me.

The tea equipage was brought in. "Polly, carry the child to nurse." I gave it another kiss, and the Countess desired another. I grudged it, to think her naughty lips should so closely follow mine. Her sister kissed it also, and carried him to Mr. B. "Take him away," said he, "I owe him my blessing."

"O these young gentlemen papas!" said the Countess—"They are like young unbroken horses, just put into the traces!"—"Are they so?" thought I. "Matrimony must not expect your good word, I doubt."

Mr. B. after tea, at which I was far from being talkative (for I could not tell what to say, though I tried, as much as I could not to appear sullen), desired the Countess to play one tune upon the harpsichord.—She did, and sung, at his request, an Italian song to it very prettily; too prettily, I thought. I wanted to find some faults, some great faults in her: but, O Madam, she has too many outward excellencies!—pity she wants a good heart.

He could ask nothing, that she was not ready to oblige him; indeed he could not.

She desired me to touch the keys. I would have been excused; but could not. And the ladies commended my performance; but neither my heart to play, nor my fingers in playing, deserved their praises. Mr. B. *said*, indeed—"You play better sometimes, my dear."—"Do I, Sir?" was all the answer I made.

The Countess hoped, she said, I would return her visit; and so said the Viscountess.

I replied, Mr. B. would command me whenever he pleased.

She said, she hoped to be better acquainted—("I hope not," thought I)—and that I would give her my company, for a week or so, upon the Forest: it seems she has a seat upon Windsor Forest.

"Mr. B. says," added she, "you can't ride a single horse; but we'll teach you there. 'Tis a sweet place for that purpose."

"How came Mr. B.," thought I, "to tell *you* that, Madam? I suppose you know more of me than I do myself." Indeed, my lady, this may be too true; for she may know what is to become of me!

I told her, I was very much obliged to her ladyship; and that Mr. B. directed all my motions.

"What say *you*, Sir?" said the Countess.

"I can't promise that, Madam: for Mrs. B. wants to go down to Kent, before we go to Bedfordshire, and I am afraid I can't give her my company thither."

"Then, Sir, I shan't choose to go without you."

"I suppose not, my dear. But if you are disposed to oblige the Countess for a week, as you never were at Windsor——"

"I believe, Sir," interrupted I, "what with my little nursery, and *one* thing or *another*, I must deny myself that honour, for this season."

"Well, Madam, then I'll expect you in Pall Mall."

I bowed my head, and said, Mr. B. would command me.

They took leave with a politeness natural to them.

Mr. B., as he handed them to the chariot, said something in Italian to the Countess: the word Pamela was in what he said: she answered him with a downcast look, in the same language, half-pleased, half-serious, and the chariot drove away.

"I would give," said I, "a good deal, Sir, to know what her ladyship said to you; she looked with so particular a meaning, if I may say so."

"I'll tell you, truly, Pamela: I said to her, 'Well, now your ladyship has seen my Pamela—Is she not the charmingest girl in the world?'

"She answered—'Mrs. B. is very grave, for so young a lady: but I must needs say she is a lovely creature.'"

"And did you say so, Sir? And did her ladyship so answer?" And my heart was ready to leap out of my bosom for joy.

But my folly spoiled all again; for, to my own surprise, and great regret, I burst out into tears; though I even sobbed to have suppressed them, but could not; and so I lost a fine opportunity to have talked to him while he was so kind; for he was more angry with me than ever.

What made me such a fool, I wonder? But I had so long struggled with myself; and not expecting so kind a question from the dear gentleman, or such a favourable answer from the Countess, I had no longer any command of myself.

"What ails the little fool?" said he, with a wrathful countenance. This made me worse, and he added, "Take care, take care, Pamela!—You'll drive me from you, in spite of my own heart."

So he went into the best parlour, and put on his sword, and took his hat. I followed him—"Sir, Sir!" with my arms expanded, was all I could say; but he avoided me, putting on his hat with an air; and out he went, bidding Abraham follow him.

This is the dilemma into which, as I hinted at the beginning of this letter, I have brought myself with Mr. B. How strong, how prevalent is the passion of jealousy; and thus it will shew itself uppermost, when it *is* uppermost, in spite of one's most watchful regards!

My mind is so perplexed, that I must lay down my pen : and, indeed, your ladyship will wonder, all things considered, that I could write the above account as I have done, in this cruel suspense, and with such apprehensions. But writing is all the diversion I have, when my mind is oppressed.

PAST TEN O'CLOCK AT NIGHT.

I have only time to tell your ladyship (for the postman waits) that Mr. B. is just come in. He is gone into his closet, and has shut the door, and taken the key on the inside; so I dare not go to him there. In this uncertainty and suspense, pity and pray for *your ladyship's afflicted sister and servant,*

P. B.

LETTER LXXIII

My dear Lady,

I will now proceed with my melancholy account. Not knowing what to do, and Mr. B. not coming near me, and the clock striking twelve, I ventured to send this billet to him, by Polly.

" Dear Sir,

" I know you choose not to be invaded, when retired to your closet; yet, being very uneasy, on account of your abrupt departure, and heavy displeasure, I take the liberty to write these few lines.

" I own, Sir, that the sudden flow of tears which involuntarily burst from me, at your kind expressions to the Countess in my favour, when I had thought for more than a month past, you were angry with me, and which had distressed my weak mind beyond expression, might appear unaccountable to you. But had you kindly waited but one moment till this fit, which was rather owing to my gratitude than to perverseness, had been over (and I knew the time when you would have generously soothed it), I should have had the happiness of a more serene and favourable parting.

" Will you suffer me, Sir, to attend you? (Polly shall wait your answer). I dare not come *without* your permission; for should you be as angry as you were, I know not how I shall bear it. But if you say I may come down, I hope to satisfy you, that I intended not any offence. Do, dear Sir, permit me to attend you, I can say no more, than that I am *your ever dutiful,*

" P. B."

Polly returned with the following. "So," thought I, "a letter!—I could have spared that, I am sure."

I expected no favour from it. So tremblingly, opened it.

"MY DEAR,

"I would not have you sit up for me. We are getting apace into the matrimonial recriminations. *You knew the time!*—So did I, my dear!—But it seems that the time is over with both; and I have had the mortification, for some past weeks, to come home to a very different Pamela, than I used to leave all company and all pleasure for.—I hope we shall better understand one another. But you cannot see me at present with any advantage to yourself; and I would not, that any thing farther should pass, to add to the regrets of both. I wish you good rest. I will give your cause a fair hearing, when I am more fit to hear all your pleas, and your excuses. I cannot be insensible, that the reason for the concern you have lately shewn, must lie deeper than, perhaps, you'll now own. As soon as you are prepared to speak all that is upon your mind, and I to hear it with temper, then we may come to an eclaircissement. Till when I am *your affectionate*, &c."

My busy apprehension immediately suggested to me, that I was to be terrified, with a high hand, into a compliance with some new scheme or other that was projecting; and it being near one, and hearing nothing from Mr. B., I bid Polly go to bed, thinking she would wonder at our intercourse by letter, if I should send again.

So down I ventured, my feet, however, trembling all the way, and tapped at the door of his closet.

"Who's that?"

"I, Sir: one word, if you please. Don't be more angry, however, Sir."

He opened the door: "Thus poor Hester, to her royal husband, ventured her life, to break in upon him unbidden. But that eastern monarch, great as he was, extended to the fainting suppliant the golden sceptre!"

He took my hand: "I hope, my dear, by this tragedy speech, we are not to expect any sad catastrophe to our present misunderstanding."

"I hope not, Sir. But 'tis all as God and you shall please. I am resolved to do my duty, Sir, if possible. But, indeed, I cannot bear this cruel suspense! Let me know what is to become of me. Let me know but what is designed for me, and you

299

shall be sure of all the acquiescence that my duty and conscience can give to your pleasure."

" What *means* the dear creature? What *means my* Pamela? Surely, your head, child, is a little affected ! "

" I can't tell, Sir, but it may !—But let me have my trial, that you write about. Appoint my day of hearing, and speedily too; for I would not bear such another month, as the last has been, for the world."

" Come, my dear," said he, " let me attend you to your chamber. But your mind has taken much too solemn a turn, to enter further now upon this subject. Think as well of me as I do of you, and I shall be as happy as ever."

I wept, " Be not angry, dear Sir : your kind words have just the same effect upon me now, as in the afternoon."

" Your apprehensions, my dear, must be very strong, that a kind word, as you call it, has such an effect upon you ! But let us wave the subject for a few days, because I am to set out on a little journey at four, and had not intended to go to bed, for so few hours."

When we came up, I said, " I was very bold, Sir, to break in upon you; but I could not help it, if my life had been the forfeit : and you received me with more goodness than I could have expected. But will you pardon me, if I ask, whither you go so soon? And if you had intended to have gone without taking leave of me? "

" I go to Tunbridge, my dear. I should have stept up and taken leave of you before I went."

" Well, Sir, I will not ask you, who is of your party : I will not—No," (putting my hand to his lips) " don't tell me, Sir : it mayn't be proper."

" Don't fear, my dear; I won't tell you : nor am I certain whether it be *proper* or not, till we are come to a better understanding. Only, once more, think as well of me as I do of you."

" Would to Heaven," thought I, " there was the same reason for the one as for the other ! "

I intended (for my heart was full) to enter further into this subject, so fatal to my repose : but the dear gentleman had no sooner laid his head on the pillow, but he fell asleep, or feigned to do so, and that was as prohibitory to my talking as if he had. So I had all my own entertaining reflections to myself; which gave me not one wink of sleep; but made me of so much service, as to tell him, when the clock struck four, that he should not (though I did not say so, you may think, Madam) make my ready rivaless (for I doubted not her being one of the party) wait for him.

He arose, and was dressed instantly; and saluting me, bid me be easy and happy, while it was *yet* in my own power.

He said, he should be back on Saturday night, as he believed. And I wished him, most fervently, I am sure, health, pleasure, and safety.

Here, Madam, must I end this letter. My next, will, perhaps contain my trial, and my sentence : God give me but patience and resignation, and then whatever occurs, I shall not be unhappy : especially while I can have, in the last resource, the pleasure of calling myself *your ladyship's most obliged sister and servant,*

P. B.

LETTER LXXIV

My dear Lady,

I will be preparing to write to you, as I have opportunity, not doubting but this must be a long letter; and having some apprehensions, that, as things may fall out, I may want either head or heart to write to your ladyship, were I to defer it till the catastrophe of this cruel suspense.

O what a happiness am I sunk from !—And in so few days too ! O the wicked masquerades !

The following letter, in a woman's hand, and signed, as you'll see, by a woman's name, and spelt as I spell it, will account to your ladyship for my beginning so heavily. It came by the penny-post.

" Madame,

" I ame unknowne to yowe; but yowe are not so alto-gathar to mee, becaus I haue bene edefy'd by yowre pius be-hafiorr att church, whir I see yowe with playsir everie Sabbaoth day. I ame welle acquaintid with the famely of the Coumptesse of ——; and yowe maie passiblie haue hard what you wished not to haue hard concerninge hir. Butt this verie morninge, I can assur yowe, hir ladishippe is gon with yowre spowse to Tonbrigge; and theire they are to take lodgings, or a hous; and Mr. B. is after to come to town, and settel matters to go downe to hir, where they are to liue as man and wiffe. Make what use yowe pleas of thiss informasion : and belieue me to haue no other motife, than to serue yowe, becavs of yowre vartues,

301

whiche make yowe deserue a better retorne, I am, thof I shall not set my trewe name, *yowre grete admirer and seruant,*

"THOMASINE FULLER.

"Wednesday morninge,
"9 o'clock."

Just above I called my state, a state of *cruel suspense.* But I recall the words : for now it is no longer suspense ; since, if this letter says truth, I know the worst : and there is too much appearance that it does, let the writer be who he will, or his or her motive what it will : for, after all, I am apt to fancy this a contrivance of Mr. Turner's, though, for fear of ill consequences, I will not say so.

And now, Madam, I am endeavouring, by the help of religion, and cool reflection, to bring my mind to bear this heavy evil, and to recollect what I *was*, and how much more honourable an estate I *am in*, than I could ever have expected to be in; that my virtue and good name are secured ; and I can return innocent to my dear parents : and these were once the only pride of my heart.

In addition to what I was then (and yet I pleased myself with my prospects, poor as they were), I have honest parents, bountifully provided for, thank God and your ever-dear brother for this blessing !—and not only provided for—but made useful to him, to the amount of their provision, well-nigh ! There is a pride, my lady !

Then I shall have better conditions from his generosity to support myself, than I can wish for, or make use of.

Then I have my dear Billy—O be contented, too charming, and too happy rival, with my husband ; and tear not from me my dearest baby, the pledge, the beloved pledge, of our happier affections, and the dear remembrance of what I once was !— A thousand pleasing prospects, that had begun to dawn on my mind, I can bear to have dissipated ! But I cannot, indeed I cannot ! permit my dear Mr. B.'s son and heir to be torn from me.

But I am running on in a strain that shews my impatience, rather than my resignation ; yet some struggles must be allowed me : I could not have loved, as I love, if I could easily part with my interest in so beloved a husband.—For my interest I *will* part with, and sooner die, than live with a gentleman who has another wife, though I was the first. Let countesses, if they can, and ladies of birth, choose to humble themselves to this baseness. The low-born Pamela cannot stoop to it. Pardon me; you know I only write this with a view to this poor lady's answer to her noble uncle, of which you wrote me word.

FRIDAY

Is now concluding. I hope I am much calmer. For, being disappointed, in all likelihood, in twenty agreeable schemes and projects, I am now forming new ones, with as much pleasure to myself as I may.

I am thinking to try to get good Mrs. Jervis with me. You must not, Madam, be too much concerned for me. After a while, I shall be no unhappy person; for though I was thankful for my splendid fortunes, and should have been glad, to be sure I should, of continuing in them, with so dear a gentleman; yet a high estate had never such dazzling charms with me as it has with some: if it had, I could not have resisted so many temptations, possibly, as God enabled me to resist.

SATURDAY NIGHT

Is now come. 'Tis nine, and no Mr. B.—" O why," as Deborah makes the mother of Sisera say, " is his chariot so long in coming? Why tarry the wheels of his chariot?"

I have this note now at eleven o'clock:

" MY DEAREST PAMELA,

" I dispatch the messenger, lest, expecting me this night, you should be uneasy. I shall not be with you till Monday, when I hope to dine with my dearest life. *Ever affectionately yours.*"

So I'll go up and pray for him, and then to bed.—Yet 'tis a sad thing !—I have had but poor rest for a great while; nor shall have any till my fate is decided.—Hard-hearted man, he knows under what uneasiness he left me !

MONDAY, ELEVEN.

If God Almighty hears my yesterday's, and indeed my hourly, prayers, the dear man will be good still; but my aching heart, every time I think what company he is in (for I find the Countess is *certainly* one of the party), bodes me little satisfaction.

He's come ! He's come ! now, just now, come ! I will have my trial over before this night be past, if possible. I'll go down and meet him with love unfeigned, and a duty equal to my love, although he may forget his to me. If I conquer myself on this occasion, I conquer nature, as your ladyship says: and then, by God's grace, I can conquer every thing. They have taken their house, I suppose : but what need they, when they'll have one in Bedfordshire, and one in Lincolnshire? But they know best. God bless him, and reform her ! That's all the harm I wish them, or will wish them !

My dear Mr. B. has received me with great affection and tenderness. Sure he cannot be so bad !—Sure he cannot !

" I know, my dear," said he, " I left you in great anxiety; but 'tis an anxiety you have brought upon yourself; and I have not been easy ever since I parted from you."

" I am sorry for it, Sir."

" Why, my dear love, there is still a melancholy air in your countenance : indeed, it seems mingled with a kind of joy; I hope at my return to you. But 'tis easy to see which of the two is the most natural."

" You should see nothing, Sir, that you would not wish to see, if I could help it."

" I am sorry you cannot. But I am come home to hear all your grievances, and to redress them, if in my power."

" When, Sir, am I to come upon my trial? I have much to say. I will tell you every thing I think. And, as it may be the last *grievances*, as you are pleased to call them, I may ever trouble you with, you must promise to answer me not one word till I have done. For, if it does but hold, I have great courage, indeed ! you don't know half the sauciness that is in your girl yet; but when I come upon my trial, you'll wonder at my boldness."

" What means my dearest? " taking me into his arms. " You alarm me exceedingly, by this moving sedateness."

" Don't let it alarm you, Sir ! I mean nothing but good !— But I have been preparing myself to tell you all my mind. And as an instance of what you may expect from me, sometimes, Sir, I will be your judge, and put home questions to you; and sometimes you shall be mine, and at last pronounce sentence upon me; or, if you won't, I will upon myself; a severe one to me, it shall be, but an agreeable one, perhaps, to you !—When comes on the trial, Sir? "

He looked steadily upon me, but was silent. And I said, " But don't be afraid, Sir, that I will invade your province; for though I shall count myself your judge, in some cases, you shall be judge paramount still."

" Dear charmer of my heart," said he, and clasped me to his bosom, " what a *new* PAMELA have I in my arms ! A mysterious charmer ! Let us instantly go to my closet, or yours, and come

304

upon our mutual trial; for you have fired my soul with impatience!"

"No, Sir, if you please, we will dine first. I have hardly eaten any thing these four days; and your company may give me an appetite. I shall be pleased to sit down at table with you, Sir," taking his hand, and trying to smile upon him; "for the moments I have of your company, may be, some time hence, very precious to my remembrance."

I was then forced to turn my head, to hide from him my eyes, brimful as they were of tears.

He took me again into his arms:—"My dearest Pamela, if you love me, distract not my soul thus, by your dark and mysterious speeches. You are displeased with *me*, and I thought I had reason, of late, to take something amiss in *your* conduct; but, instead of your suffering by my anger, you have words and an air that penetrate my very soul."

"O Sir, Sir, treat me not thus kindly! Put on an angrier brow, or how shall I retain my purpose? How shall I!"

"Dear, dear creature! make not use of *all* your power to melt me! *Half* of it is enough. For there is eloquence in your eyes I cannot resist; but in your present solemn air, and affecting sentences, you mould me to every purpose of your heart; so that I am a mere machine, a passive instrument, to be played upon at your pleasure."

"Dear, kind Sir, how you revive my heart, by your goodness! Perhaps I have only been in a frightful dream, and am but just now awakened.—But we will not anticipate our trial. Only, Sir, give orders, that you are not to be spoken with by any body, when we have dined; for I must have you *all* to myself, without interruption."

Just as I had said this, a gentleman calling, I retired to my chamber, and wrote to this place.

Mr. B. dismissed his friend, without asking him to dine; so I had him all to myself at dinner—But we said little, and sat not above a quarter of an hour; looking at each other: he, with impatience, and some seeming uneasiness; I with more steadiness, I believe, but now and then a tear starting.

I eat but little, though I tried all I could, and especially as he helped me, and courted me with tenderness and sweetness— O why were ever such things as *masquerades* permitted in a Christian nation!

I chose to go into *my* closet rather than into *his*; and here I sit, waiting the dear gentleman's coming up to me. If I keep but my courage, I shall be pleased. I know the worst, and that will help me; for he is too noble to use me roughly, when he sees I mean not to provoke him by upbraidings, any more than I will act, in this case, beneath the character I ought to assume as his wife.

Mr. B. came up, with great impatience in his looks. I met him at the chamber door, with a very sedate countenance, and my heart was high with my purpose, and supported me better than I could have expected.—Yet, on recollection, now I impute to myself something of that kind of magnanimity, that was wont to inspire the innocent sufferers of old, for a still worthier cause than mine; though their motives could hardly be more pure, in that one hope I had, to be an humble means of saving the man I love and honour, from errors that might be fatal to his soul.

I took his hand with boldness :—" Dear Sir," leading him to my closet, " here is the bar at which I am to take my trial," pointing to the backs of three chairs, which I had placed in a joined row, leaving just room to go by on each side. " You must give me, Sir, all my own way; this is the first, and perhaps the last time, that I shall desire it.—Nay, dear Sir," turning my face from him, " look not upon me with an eye of tenderness : if you do I may lose my purposes, important to me as they are; and however fantastic my behaviour may seem to you, I want not to move your passions (for the good impressions made upon them may be too easily dissipated by the winds of *sense,*) but *your reason ;* and if that can be done, I am safe, and shall fear no relapse."

" What means all this parade, my dear? Let me perish," that was his word, " if I know how to account for *you,* or your *humour.*"

" You *will,* presently, Sir. But give me all my ways—I pray you do—This one time only ! "

" Well, so, this is your bar, is it? There's an elbow-chair, I see; take your place in it, Pamela, and here I'll stand to answer all your questions."

" No, Sir, that must not be." So I boldly led *him* to the elbow-chair. " You are the judge, Sir; it is I that am to be tried. Yet I will not say I am a criminal. I know I am not. But that must be proved, Sir, you know."

" Well, take your way; but I fear for your head, my dear, in all this."

" I fear only my heart, Sir, that's all ! but there you must sit—So here," (retiring to the three chairs, and leaning on the backs,) " here I stand."

306

"And now, my dearest Mr. B., you must begin first; you must be my accuser, as well as my judge."

"I have nothing to accuse you of, my dear, if I *must* give in to your moving whimsy. You are everything I wish you to be. But for the last month you have seemed to be uneasy, and have not done me the justice to acquaint me with your reasons for it."

"I was in hopes my reasons might have proved to be no reasons; and I would not trouble you with my ungrounded apprehensions. But now, Sir, we are come directly to the point; and methinks I stand here as Paul did before Felix; and like that poor prisoner, if I, Sir, reason of *righteousness, temperance,* and *judgment to come,* even to make you, as the great Felix did, tremble, don't put me off to *another day,* to a *more convenient season,* as that governor did Paul; for you must bear patiently with all that I have to say."

"Strange, uncommon girl! how unaccountable is all this!— Pr'ythee, my dear," and he pulled a chair by him, "come and sit down by me, and without these romantic airs let me hear all you have to say; and teaze me not with this parade."

"No, Sir, let me stand, if you please, while I *cau* stand; when weary I will sit down at my bar.

"Now, Sir, since you are so good as to say, you have nothing but change of temper to accuse me of, I am to answer to that, and assign a cause; and I will do it without evasion or reserve; but I beseech you say not one word but Yes or No, to my questions, till I have said all I have to say, and then you shall find me all silence and resignation."

"Well, my strange dear!—But sure your head is a little turned!—What is your question?"

"Whether, Sir, the Nun—I speak boldly; the cause requires it—who followed you at the Masquerade every where, is not the Countess of —— ?"

"What then, my dear:" (speaking with quickness,)—"I *thought* the occasion of your sullenness and reserve was this!— But, Pamela——"

"Nay, Sir," interrupted I, "only Yes, or No, if you please: I will be all silence by-and-by."

"Yes, then."—"Well, Sir, then let me tell you, for I *ask* you not (it may be too bold in me to multiply questions,) that she *loves* you; that you correspond by letters with her—Yes, Sir, *before* that letter from her ladyship came, which you received from my hand in so short and angry a manner, for fear of my curiosity to see its contents, which would have been inexcusable in me, I own, if I had. You have talked over to her all your polygamy notions, and she seems so well convinced of them, as to declare to her noble uncle (who expostulated with her on the occasions she gave for talk,) that she had rather be a certain gentleman's second wife, than the first to the greatest man in England: and you are but just returned from a journey to Tunbridge, in which that lady was a party; and the motive for it, I am acquainted with, by this letter."

He was displeased, and frowned: I looked down, being resolved not to be terrified, if I could help it.

"I have cautioned you, Pamela——"

"I know you have, Sir," interrupted I; "but be pleased to answer me. Has not the Countess taken a house or lodgings at Tunbridge?"

"She has: and what then?"

"And is her ladyship there, or in town?"

"*There*—and what then?"

"Are you to go to Tunbridge, Sir, soon, or not?—Be pleased to answer but that one question."

"I *will* know," rising up in anger, "your informants, Pamela."

"Dear Sir, so you shall, in proper time: you shall know all, when I am convinced, that your wrath will not be attended with bad consequences to yourself and others. That is wholly the cause of my reserve in this point; for I have not had a thought, since I have been yours, that I wished to be concealed from you.—But your knowledge of the informants makes nothing at all as to the truth of the information—Nor will I press you too home. I doubt not, you are soon to return to Tunbridge?"

"I *am*, and what then?—Must the consequence be crime enough to warrant your jealousy?"

"Dear Sir, don't be so angry," still looking down; for I durst not trust myself to look up. "I don't do this, as your letter charged me, in a spirit of matrimonial recrimination: if you don't *tell* me, that you see the Countess with pleasure, I *ask* it not of you; nor have I anything to say by way of upbraiding. 'Tis my misfortune, that she is too lovely, and too attractive: and it is the less wonder, that a fine young gentleman as you are, and a fine young lady as she is, should engage one another's affections.

"I knew every thing, except what this letter which you shall read presently, communicates, when you brought the two noble sisters to visit me: hence proceeded my grief; and should I, Sir, have deserved to be what I am, if I was *not* grieved?

308

Religion has helped me, and God has answered my supplications, and enabled me to act this new uncommon part before you at this imaginary bar. You shall see, Sir, that as, on one hand, I want not, as I said before, to move your passions in my favour; so, on the other, I shall not be terrified by your displeasure, dreaded by me as it used to be, and as it will be again, the moment that my raised spirits sink down to their usual level, or are diverted from this my long meditated purpose, to tell you all my mind.

"I repeat, then, Sir, that I knew all this, when the two noble sisters came to visit your poor girl, and to see your Billy. Yet, *grave* as the Countess called me, (dear Sir! might I not well be grave, knowing what I knew?) did I betray any impatience of speech or action, or any discomposure?

"No, Sir," putting my hand on my breast, "*here* all my discomposure lay, vehemently struggling, now and then, and wanting that vent of my eyes, which it seems (overcome by my joy, to hear myself favourably spoken of by you and the lady,) it *too soon* made itself. But I could not help it—You might have seen, Sir, I could not!

"But I want neither to recriminate nor expostulate; nor yet, Sir, to form excuses for my general conduct; for that you accuse not in the main—but be pleased, Sir, to read this letter. It was brought by the penny-post, as you'll see by the mark. Who the writer is, I know not. And did *you*, Sir, that knowledge, and your resentment upon it, will not alter the fact, or give it a more favourable appearance."

I stepped to him, and giving him the letter, came back to my bar, and sat down on one of the chairs while he read it, drying my eyes; for they would overflow as I talked, do what I could.

He was much moved at the contents of this letter; called it malice, and hoped he might find out the author of it, saying, he would advertise 500 guineas reward for the discoverer.

He put the letter in his pocket, "Well, Pamela, you believe all you have said, no doubt : and this matter has a black appearance, indeed, if you do. But who was your *first* informant? —Was that by letter or personally? That Turner, I doubt not, is at the bottom of all this. The vain coxcomb has had the insolence to imagine the Countess would favour an address of his ; and is enraged to meet with a repulse ; and has taken liberties upon it, that have given birth to all the scandals scattered about on this occasion. Nor do I doubt but he has been the Serpent at the ear of my Eve."

I stood up at the bar, and said, "Don't be too hasty, Sir, in your judgment—You *may* be mistaken."

"But *am* I mistaken, Pamela?—You never told me an untruth in cases the most important to you to conceal. *Am* I mistaken?"

"Dear Sir, if I should tell you it is *not* Mr. Turner, you'll guess at somebody else: and what avails all this to the matter in hand? You are your own master, and must stand or fall by your own conscience. God grant that *that* may aquit you!—But my intention is not either to accuse or upbraid you."

"But, my dear, to the fact then:—This is a malicious and a villainous piece of intelligence, given you, perhaps, for the sake of designs and views, that may not yet be proper to be avowed."

"By God's grace, Sir, I defy all designs and views of any one, upon my honour!"

"But, my dear, the charge is basely false: we have not agreed upon any such way of life."

"Well, Sir, all this only proves, that the intelligence may be a little premature. But now let me, Sir, sit down one minute, to recover my failing spirits, and then I'll tell you all I purpose to do, and all I have to say, and that with as much brevity as I can, for fear neither my head nor my heart should perform the part I have been so long in endeavouring to prevail upon them to perform."

I sat down then, he taking out the letter, and reading it again with much vexation and anger in his countenance; and after a few tears and sobs, that would needs be so officious as to offer their service, unbidden, and undesired, to introduce what I had to say; I rose up, my feet trembling, as well as my knees; which, however, leaning against the seats of the chairs, that made my bar, as my hand held by the back, tolerably supported me, I cleared my voice, wiped my eyes, and said:

"You have all the excuse, dear Mr. B., that a gentleman can have in the object of your present passion."

"Present passion, Pamela!"

"Dear Sir, hear me without interruption.

"The Countess is a charming lady. She excels your poor girl in all those outward graces of form, which your kind fancy (more valued by me than the opinion of all the world besides) had made you attribute to me. And she has all those additional advantages, as nobleness of birth, of alliance, and deportment, which I want. (Happy for you, Sir, that you had known her ladyship some months ago, before you disgraced yourself by the honours you have done me!) This therefore frees you from the aggravated crime of those, who prefer, to their own ladies, less amiable and less deserving persons; and I have not the sting which those must have, who are contemned and ill-treated for the sake of their inferiors. Yet cannot the Countess love you better than your girl loves you, not even for your person, which must, I doubt, be *her* principal attachment! when I can truly say, all noble and attracting to the outward eye as it is, that is the least consideration by far with me: no, Sir, your generous and beneficent mind, is the principal object of my affection; and my pride in hoping to be an humble means, in the hands of Providence, to bless you *hereafter* as well as *here*, gave me more pleasure than all the blessings I reaped from your name or your fortune. Judge then, my dearest Mr. B., my grief and disappointment.

"But I will not expostulate: I *will not,* because it *must* be to no purpose; for could my fondness, and my watchful duty to you, have kept you steady, I should not now appear before you in this solemn manner: and I know the charms of my rival are too powerful for me to contend with. Nothing but divine grace can touch your heart: and that I expect not, from the nature of the case, should be instantaneous.

"I will therefore, Sir, dear as you are to me—(Don't look with such tender surprise upon me!) give up your person to the happier, to my *worthier* rival. For since such is your will, and seem to be your engagements, what avails it to me to oppose them?

"I have only to beg, that you will be so good as to permit me to go down to Kent, to my dear parents, who, with many more, are daily rejoicing in your favour and bounty. I will there" (holding up my folded hands) "pray for you every hour of my life; and for every one who shall be dear to you, not excepting the charming Countess.

"I will never take your name into my lips, nor suffer any other in my hearing, but with reverence and gratitude, for the good I and mine *have* reaped at your hands: nor wish to be freed from my obligations to you, except you shall choose to be divorced from me; and if so I will give your wishes all the forwardness I honourably can, with regard to my own character and yours, and that of your beloved baby.

"But you must give me something worth living for along with you; your Billy and mine!—Unless it is your desire to kill me quite! and then 'tis done, and nothing will stand in your happy Countess's way, if you tear from my arms my *second* earthly good, after I am deprived of you, my *first.*

"I will there, Sir, dedicate all my time to my first duties; happier far, than once I could have hoped to be! And if, by any accident, and misunderstanding between you, you should part by consent, and you will have it so, my heart shall be ever yours, and my hopes shall be resumed of being an instrument still for your future good, and I will receive your returning ever-valued heart, as if nothing had happened, the moment I can be sure it will be wholly mine.

"For, think not, dear Sir, whatever be your notions of polygamy, that I will, were my life to depend upon it, consent to live with a gentleman, dear as, GOD is my witness," (lifting up my tearful eyes) "you are to me, who lives in what I cannot but think open sin with another! You *know*, Sir, and I appeal to you for the purity, and I will aver piety of my motives, when I say this, that I *would not;* and as you do know this, I cannot doubt but my proposal will be agreeable to you both. And I beg of you, dear Sir, to take me at my word; and don't let me be tortured, as I have been so many weeks, with such anguish of mind, that nothing but religious considerations can make supportable to me."

"And are you in earnest, Pamela?" coming to me, and folding me in his arms over the chair's back, the seat of which supported my trembling knees, "Can you so easily part with me?"

"I can, Sir, and I will!—rather than divide my interest in you, knowingly, with any lady upon earth. But say not, can I part with you, Sir; it is you that part with me: and tell me, Sir, tell me but what you had intended should become of me?"

"You talk to me, my dearest life, as if all you had heard against me was true; and you would have me answer you, (would you?) as if it was."

"I want nothing to convince me, Sir, that the Countess loves you: you know the rest of my information: judge for me, what I can, what I ought to believe!—You know the rumours of the world concerning you: Even I, who stay so much at home, and have not taken the least pains to find out my wretchedness, nor to confirm it, since I knew it, have come to the hearing of it; and if you know the licence taken with both your characters, and yet correspond so openly, must it not look to me that you value not your honour in the world's eye, nor my lady hers? I told you, Sir, the answer she made to her uncle."

"You told me, my dear, as you were told. Be tender of a

lady's reputation—for your own sake. No one is exempted from calumny; and even words said, and the occasion of saying them not known, may bear a very different construction from what they would have done, had the occasion been told."

"This may be all true, Sir: I wish the lady would be as tender of her reputation as I would be, let her injure me in your affections as she will. But can you say, Sir, that there is nothing between you, that should *not* be, according to *my* notions of virtue and honour, and according to your *own*, which I took pride in, before that fatal masquerade?

"You answer me not," continued I; "and may I not fairly presume you cannot as I wish to be answered? But come, dearest Sir," (and I put my arms around his neck) "let me not urge you too boldly. I will never forget your benefits, and your past kindnesses to me. I have been a happy creature: no one, till within these few weeks, was ever so happy as I. I will love you still with a passion as ardent as ever I loved you. Absence cannot lessen such a love as mine: I am sure it cannot.

"I see your difficulties. You have gone too far to recede. If you can make it easy to your conscience, I will wait with patience my happier destiny; and I will wish to live (if I can be convinced you wish me not to die) in order to pray for you, and to be a directress to the first education of my dearest baby.

"You sigh, dear Sir; repose your beloved face next to my fond heart. 'Tis all your own: and ever shall be, let it, or let it not, be worthy of the honour in your estimation.

"But yet, my dear Mr. B., if one could as easily, in the prime of sensual youth, look twenty years backward, what an empty vanity, what a mere nothing, will be all those grosser satisfactions, that now give wings of desire to our debased appetites!

"Motives of religion will have their due force upon *your* mind one day, I hope; as, blessed be God, they have enabled *me* to talk to you on such a touching point (after infinite struggles, I own,) with so much temper and resignation; and then, my dearest Mr. B., when we come to that last bed, from which the piety of our friends shall lift us, but from which we shall never be able to raise ourselves; for, dear Sir, your Countess, and you, and your poor Pamela, must all come to this!—we shall find what it is will give us true joy, and enable us to support the pangs of the dying hour. Think you, my dearest Sir," (and I pressed my lips to his forehead, as his head was reclined on my throbbing bosom,) "that *then*, in that important moment, what now gives us the greatest pleasure, will have any part in our consideration, but as it may give us woe or comfort in the reflection?

"But I will not, O best beloved of my soul, afflict you farther. Why should I thus sadden all your gaudy prospects? I have said enough to such a heart as yours, if Divine grace touches it. And if not, all I can say will be of no avail!—I will leave you therefore to that, and to your own reflections. And after giving you ten thousand thanks for your indulgent patience with me, I will only beg, that I may set out in a week for Kent, with my dear Billy; that you will receive one letter at least, from me, of gratitude and blessings; it shall not be of up-braidings and exclamations.

"But my child you must not deny me; for I shall haunt, like his shadow, every place wherein you shall put my Billy, if you should be so unkind to deny him to me!—And if you will permit me to have the dear Miss Goodwin with me, as you had almost led me to hope, I will read over all the books of education, and digest them, as well as I am able, in order to send you my scheme, and to show you how fit, I hope your *indulgence*, at least, will make you think me, of having two such precious trusts reposed in me!"

I was silent, waiting in tears his answer. But his generous heart was touched, and seemed to labour within him for expression.

He came round to me at last, and took me in his arms: "Exalted creature!" said he: "noble-minded Pamela! Let no bar be put between us henceforth! No wonder, when one looks back to your first promising dawn of excellence, that your fuller day should thus irresistibly dazzle such weak eyes as mine. Whatever it costs me, and I have been inconsiderately led on by blind passion for an object too charming, but which I never thought equal to my Pamela, I will (for it is yet, I bless God, in my power), restore to your virtue a husband all your own."

"O Sir, Sir," (and I should have sunk with joy, had not his kind arms supported me,) "what have you said?—Can I be so happy as to behold you innocent as to deed! God, of his infinite goodness, continue you both so!—And, Oh! that the dear lady would make me as truly love her, for the graces of her mind, as I admire her for the advantages of her person!"

"You are virtue itself, my dearest life; and from this moment I will reverence you as my tutelary angel. I shall behold you with awe, and implicitly give up myself to all your dictates:

for what you *say*, and what you *do*, must be ever right. But I will not, my dearest life, too lavishly promise, lest you should think it the sudden effects of passions thus movingly touched, and which may subside again, when the soul, as you observed in your own case, sinks to its former level : but this I promise (and I hope you believe me, and will pardon the pain I have given you, which made me fear more than once, that your head was affected, so *uncommon*, yet so like *yourself*, has been the manner of your acting,) that I will break off a correspondence that has given you so much uneasiness : and my Pamela may believe, that if I can be as good as my word in this point, she will never more be in danger of any rival whatever.

"But say, my dear love," added he, "say you forgive me; and resume but your former cheerfulness, and affectionate regards to me, else I shall suspect the sincerity of your forgiveness : and you shall indeed go to Kent, but not without me, nor your boy neither; and if you insist upon it, the poor child you have wished so often and so generously to have, shall be given up absolutely to your disposal."

Do you think, Madam, I could speak any one distinct sentence? No indeed I could not. I was just choked with my joy; I never was so before. And my eyes were in a manner fixed, as he told me afterwards; and that he was a little startled, seeing nothing but the whites; for the sight was out of its orbits, in a manner lifted up to heaven—in ecstasy for a turn so sudden, and so unexpected !

We were forced to separate soon after; for there was no bearing each other, so excessive was my joy, and his goodness. He left me, and went down to his own closet.

Judge my employment you will, I am sure, my dear lady. I had new ecstasy to be blest with, in a thankfulness so exalted, that it left me all light and pleasant, as if I had shook off body, and trod in air; so much heaviness had I lost, and so much joy had I received. From two such extremes, how was it possible I could presently hit the medium? For when I had given up my beloved husband, as lost to me, and had dreaded the consequences to his future state : to find him not only untainted as to deed, but, in all probability, mine upon b etter and surer terms than ever—O, Madam ! must not this give a joy beyond all joy, and surpassing all expression !

About eight o'clock Mr. B. sent me up these lines from his closet, which will explain what I meant, as to the papers I must beg your ladyship to return me.

"MY DEAR PAMELA,

"I have so much real concern at the anguish I have given you, and am so much affected with the recollection of the uncommon scenes which passed between us, just now, that I write, because I know not how to look so excellent a creature in the face—You must therefore sup without me, and take your Mrs. Jervis to bed with you; who, I doubt not, knows all this affair; and you may tell her the happy event.

"You must not interfere with me just now, while writing upon a subject which takes up all my attention; and which, requiring great delicacy, I may, possibly, be all night before I can please myself in it.

"I am determined to make good my promise to you. But if you have written to your mother, Miss Darnford, or to Lady Davers, anything of this affair, you must shew me the copies, and let me into every tittle how you came by your information. I solemnly promise you, on my honour (that has not yet been violated to you, and I hope never will), that not a soul shall know or suffer by the communication, not even Turner; for I am confident he has had some hand in it. This request you must comply with, if you can confide in me; for I shall make some use of it (as prudent a one as I am able), for the sake of every one concerned, in the conclusion of the correspondence between the lady and myself. Whatever you may have said in the bitterness of your heart, in the letters I require to see, or whatever any of those, to whom they are directed, shall say, on the bad prospect, shall be forgiven, and looked upon as deserved, by *your ever-obliged and faithful*, &c."

I returned the following:

"DEAREST, DEAR SIR,

"I will not break in upon you, while you are so importantly employed. Mrs. Jervis has indeed seen my concern for some time past, and has heard rumours, as I know by hints she has given me; but her prudence, and my reserves, have kept us from saying anything to one another of it. Neither my mother nor Miss Darnford know a tittle of it from me. I have received a letter of civility from Miss, and have answered it, taking and giving thanks for the pleasure of each other's company, and best respects from her, and the Lincolnshire families, to your dear self. These, my copy, and her original, you shall see when you please. But, in truth, all that has passed, is between Lady Davers and me, and I have not kept copies of mine; but I will dispatch a messenger to her ladyship for them, if you please, in the morning, before it is light, not doubting your kind promise of excusing everything and everybody.

"I beg, dear Sir, you will take care your health suffers not by your sitting up; for the nights are cold and damp.

"I will, now you have given me the liberty, let Mrs. Jervis know how happy you have made me, by dissipating my fears, and the idle rumours, as I shall call them to her, of calumniators.

"God bless you, dear Sir, for your goodness and favour to *your ever-dutiful* P. B."

He was pleased to return me this:

"My dear Life,

"You need not be in such haste to send. If you write to Lady Davers how the matter has ended, let me see the copy of it: and be very particular in *your*, or rather, *my* trial. It shall be a standing lesson to me for my future instruction; as it will be a fresh demonstration of your excellence, which every hour I more and more admire. I am glad Lady Davers only knows the matter. I think I ought to avoid seeing you, till I can assure you, that every thing is accommodated to your desire. Longman has sent me some advices, which will make it proper for me to meet him at Bedford or Gloucester. I will not go to Tunbridge, till I have all your papers; and so you'll have three days to procure them. Your boy, and your penmanship, will find you no disagreeable employment till I return. Nevertheless, on second thoughts, I will do myself the pleasure of breakfasting with you in the morning, to re-assure you of my unalterable purpose to approve myself, *my dearest life, ever faithfully yours.*"

Thus, I hope, is happily ended this dreadful affair. My next shall give the particulars of our breakfast conversation. But I would not slip this post, without acquainting you with this blessed turn; and to beg the favour of you to send me back my letters; which will lay a new obligation upon, *dear Madam, your obliged sister, and humble servant,* P. B.

LETTER LXXV

My dearest Lady,

Your joyful correspondent has obtained leave to get every thing ready to quit London by Friday next, when your kind brother promises to carry me down to Kent, and allows me to take my charmer with me. There's happiness for you, Madam! To see, as I hope I shall see, upon one blessed spot, a dear faithful husband, a beloved child, and a father and mother, whom I so much love and honour!

Mr. B. told me this voluntarily, this morning at breakfast; and then, in the kindest manner, took leave of me, and set out for Bedfordshire.

But I should, according to my promise, give you a few particulars of our breakfast conference.

I bid Polly withdraw, when her master came up to breakfast; and I ran to the door to meet him, and threw myself on my knees: "O forgive me, dearest, dear Sir, all my boldness of yesterday!—My heart was strangely affected—or I could not have acted as I did. But never fear, my dearest Mr. B., that my future conduct shall be different from what it used to be, or that I shall keep up to a spirit, which you hardly thought had place in the heart of your dutiful Pamela, till she was thus severely tried."—"I have weighed well your conduct, my dear life," raising me to his bosom; "and I find an uniformity in it, that is surprisingly just."

He led me to the tea-table, and sat down close by me. Polly came in. "If every thing," said he, "be here, that your lady wants, you may withdraw; and let Colbrand and Abraham know I shall be with them presently. Nobody shall wait upon me but you, my dear." Polly withdrew.

"I always *loved* you, my dearest," added he, "and that with a passionate fondness, which has not, I dare say, many examples in the married life: but I *revere* you now. And so great is my reverence for your virtue, that I chose to sit up all night, to leave you for a few days, until, by disengaging myself from all intercourses that have given you uneasiness, I can convince you, that I have rendered myself as worthy as I can be, of you upon your own terms. I will account to you for every step I *shall* take, and will reveal to you every step I have taken: for this I *can* do, because the lady's honour is untainted, and wicked rumour has treated her worse than she could deserve."

I told him, that since *he* had named the lady, I would take the liberty to say, I was glad, for her own sake, to hear that. Changing the subject a little precipitately, as if it gave him pain, he told me, as above, that I might prepare on Friday for Kent; and I parted with him with greater pleasure than ever I did in my life. So necessary sometimes are afflictions, not only to teach one how to subdue one's passions, and to make us, in our happiest states, know we are still on earth, but even when they are overblown to augment and redouble our joys!

I am now giving orders for my journey, and quitting this undelightful town, as it has been, and is, to me. My next will be from Kent, I hope; and I may then have an opportunity to acquaint your ladyship with the particulars, and (if God answers my prayers), the conclusion of the affair, which has given me so much uneasiness.

Meantime, I am, with the greatest gratitude, for the kind share you have taken in my past afflictions, my good lady, *your ladyship's most obliged sister and servant,*   P. B.

LETTER LXXVI

My dearest Pamela,

Inclosed are all the letters you send for. I rejoice with you upon the turn this afflicting affair has taken, through your inimitable prudence, and a courage I thought not in you. A wretch!—to give you so much discomposure!—But I will not, if he be good now, rave against him, as I was going to do. I am impatient to hear what account he gives of the matter. I hope he will be able to abandon this—I won't call her names; for she loves the wretch; and that, if he be just to *you,* will be her punishment.

What care ought these young widows to take of their reputation?—And how watchful ought they to be over themselves!—She was hardly out of her weeds, and yet must go to a masquerade, and tempt her fate, with all her passions about her, with an independence, and an affluence of fortune, that made her able to think of nothing but gratifying them.

She has good qualities—is generous—is noble—but has strong passions, and is thoughtless and precipitant.

My lord came home last Tuesday, with a long story of my brother and her: for I had kept the matter as secret as I could, for his sake and yours. It seems he had it from Sir John——, uncle to the young Lord C., who is very earnest to bring on a treaty of marriage between her and his nephew, who is in love with her, and is a fine young gentleman; but has held back, on the liberties she has lately given herself with my brother.

I hope she is innocent, as to fact; but I know not what to say to it. He ought to be hanged, if he did not say she was. Yet I have great opinion of his veracity: and yet he is so bold a wretch!—And her inconsideration is so great!

319

But lest I should alarm your fears, I will wait till I have the account he gives you of this dark affair; till when, I congratulate you upon the leave you have obtained to quit the town, and on your setting out for a place so much nearer to Tunbridge. Forgive me, Pamela; but he is an intriguing wretch, and I would not have you to be too secure, lest the disappointment should be worse for you, than what you knew before : but assure yourself, that I am in all cases and events, *your affectionate sister and admirer*,

B. DAVERS.

LETTER LXXVII

From Mrs. B. to Lady Davers.

MY DEAREST LADY,

Mr. B. came back from Bedfordshire to his time. Every thing being in readiness, we set out with my baby, and his nurse. Mrs. Jervis, when every thing in London is settled by her direction, goes to Bedfordshire.

We were met by my father and mother in a chaise and pair, which your kind brother had presented to them unknown to me, that they might often take the air together, and go to church in it (which is at some distance) on Sundays. The driver is clothed in a good brown cloth suit, but no livery; for that my parents could not have borne, as Mr. B.'s goodness made him consider.

Your ladyship must needs think, how we were all overjoyed at this meeting : for my own part I cannot express how much I was transported when we arrived at the farm-house, to see all I delighted in, upon one happy spot together.

Mr. B. is much pleased with the alterations here : and it is a sweet, rural, and convenient place.

We were welcomed into these parts by the bells, and by the minister, and people of most note; and were at church together on Sunday.

Mr. B. is to set out on Tuesday for Tunbridge, with my papers. A happy issue, attend that affair, I pray God ! He has given me the following particulars of it, to the time of my trial, beginning at the masquerade.

He says, that at the masquerade, when, pleased with the fair Nun's shape, air and voice, he had followed her to a corner most unobserved, she said in Italian, " Why are my retirements invaded, audacious Spaniard ? "—" Because, my dear Nun, I hope you would have it so."

"I can no otherwise," returned she, "strike dead thy bold presumption, than to shew thee my scorn and anger thus!"— "And she unmasking surprised me," said Mr. B., "with a face as beautiful, but not so soft as my Pamela's."—"And I," said Mr. B., "to shew I can defy your resentment, will shew you a countenance as intrepid as yours is lovely." And so he drew aside his mask too.

He says, he observed his fair Nun to be followed wherever she went, by a mask habited like Testimony in Sir Courtly Nice, whose attention was fixed upon her and him; and he doubted not, that it was Mr. Turner. So he and the fair Nun took different ways, and he joined me and Miss Darnford, and found me engaged as I before related to your ladyship, and his Nun at his elbow unexpected.

That afterwards as he was engaged in French with a lady who had the dress of an Indian Princess, and the mask of an Ethiopian, his fair Nun said, in broken Spanish, "Art thou at all complexions?—By St. Ignatius, I believe thou'rt a rover!"

"I am trying," replied he in Italian, "whether I can meet with any lady comparable to my lovely Nun."

"And what is the result?"—"Not one: no 'not one."—"I wish you could not help being in earnest," said she; and slid from him.

He engaged her next at the sideboard, drinking under her veil a glass of Champaign. "You know, Pamela," said he, "there never was a sweeter mouth in the world than the Countess's except your own." She drew away the glass, as if unobserved by any body, to shew me the lower part of her face.

"I cannot say, but I was struck with her charming manner, and an unreservedness of air and behaviour, that I had not before seen so becoming. The place, and the freedom of conversation and deportment allowed there, gave her great advantages in my eye, although her habit required, as I thought, a little more gravity and circumspection: and I could not tell how to resist a secret pride and vanity, which is but too natural to both sexes, when they are taken notice of by persons so worthy of regard.

"Naturally fond of every thing that carried the face of an intrigue, I longed to know who this charming Nun was. And next time I engaged her, 'My good sister,' said I, 'how happy should I be, if I might be admitted to a conversation with you at your grate!'

" 'Answer me,' said she, 'thou bold Spaniard,' (for that was a name she seemed fond of, which gave me to imagine, that boldness was a qualification she was not displeased with. 'Tis

321

not unusual with our vain sex," observed he, " to construe even reproaches to our advantage,") ' is the lady here, whose shackles thou wearest ? '—' Do I look like a man shackled, my fairest Nun ? '—' No—no ! not much like such an one. But I fancy thy wife is either a *Widow* or a *Quaker*.'—' Neither,' replied I, taking, by equivocation, her question literally.

" ' And art thou not a married wretch ? Answer me quickly !— We are observed.'—' No,' said I.—' Swear to me, thou art not.'—' By St. Ignatius, then ; ' for, my dear, I was no *wretch*, you know.—' Enough ! ' said she, and slid away ; and the Fanatic would fain have engaged her, but she avoided him as industriously.

" Before I was aware, she was at my elbow, and, in Italian, said, ' That fair Quaker, yonder, is the wit of the assemblée : her eyes seem always directed to thy motions ; and her person shews some intimacies have passed with somebody : is it with thee ? '—' It would be my glory if it was,' said I, ' were her face answerable to her person.'—' Is it not ? '—' I long to know,' " replied Mr. B.—" I am glad thou dost not."—" I am glad to hear my fair Nun say that."—" Dost thou," said she, " hate shackles ? Or is it, that thy hour is not yet come ? "

" I wish," replied he, " this be not the hour, the very hour ! " pretending (naughty gentleman !—What ways these men have !) to sigh.

She went again to the side-board, and put her handkerchief upon it. Mr. B. followed, and observed all her motions. She drank a glass of lemonade, as he of Burgundy ; and a person in a domino, supposed to be the King, passing by, took up every one's attention but Mr. B.'s who eyed her handkerchief, not doubting but she laid it there on purpose to forget to take it up. Accordingly she left it there ; and slipping by him, he, unobserved, as he believes, put it in his pocket, and at the corner found the cover of a letter—" To the Right Honourable the Countess Dowager of —— "

That after this, the fair Nun was so shy, so reserved, and seemed so studiously to avoid him, that he had no opportunity to return her handkerchief ; and the Fanatic observing how she shunned him, said, in French, " What, Monsieur, have you done to your Nun ? "

" I found her to be a very coquette ; and told her so ; and she is offended."

" How could you affront a lady," replied he, " with such a *charming face ?* "

" By that I had reason to think," said Mr. B., " that he had
322

seen her unmask; and I said, 'It becomes not any character, but that you wear, to pry into the secrets of others, in order to make ill-natured remarks, and perhaps to take ungentlemanlike advantages.'"

"No man should make that observation," returned he, "whose views would bear prying into."

" I was nettled," said Mr. B., " at this warm retort, and drew aside my mask : ' Nor would any man, who wore not a mask, tell me so ! '

" He took not the challenge, and slid from me, and I saw him no more that night."

" So ! " thought I, " another instance this might have been of the glorious consequences of masquerading." O my lady, these masquerades are abominable things !

The King, they said, met with a free speaker that night : in truth, I was not very sorry for it; for if monarchs will lay aside their sovereign distinctions, and mingle thus in masquerade with the worst as well as the highest (I cannot say *best*) of their subjects, let 'em take the consequence. Perhaps they might have a chance to hear more truth here than in their palaces—the only good that possibly can accrue from them—that is to say, if they made a good use of it when they heard it. For you see, my monarch, though he told the truth, as it happened, received the hint with more resentment than thankfulness!—So, 'tis too likely did the monarch of us both.

And now, my lady, you need not doubt, that so polite a gentleman would find an opportunity to return the Nun her handkerchief !—To be sure he would : for what man of honour would rob a lady of any part of her apparel? And should he, that wanted to steal a heart content himself with a handker-chief?—No no, that was not to be expected. So, what does he do, but resolve, the very next day, after dinner, to pursue this affair : accordingly, the poor Quaker little thinking of the matter, away goes her naughty Spaniard, to find out his Nun at her grate, or in her parlour rather.

He asks for the Countess. Is admitted into the outward parlour—her woman comes down; requires his name and busi-ness. His name he mentioned not. His business was, to restore into her lady's own hands, something she had dropt the night before.—Was desired to wait.

I should have said, that he was dressed very richly—having no design at all to make conquests; no, not he !—O this wicked love of intrigue !—A kind of olive-coloured velvet, and fine brocaded waistcoat. I said, when he took leave of me, " You're

323

a charming Mr. B.," and saluted him, more pressingly than he returned it; but little did I think, when I plaited so smooth his rich laced ruffles, and bosom, where he was going, or what he had in his plotting heart. He went in his own chariot, that he did: so that he had no design to conceal who he was—But intrigue, a new conquest, vanity, pride !—O these men !—They had need talk of ladies !—But it is half our own fault, indeed it is, to encourage their vanity.

Well, Madam, he waited till his stateliness was moved to send up again, that he would wait on her ladyship some other time. So down she came, dressed most richly, jewels in her breast, and in her hair, and ears—But with a very reserved and stately air. He approached her—Methinks I see him, dear saucy gentleman. You know, Madam, what a noble manner of address he has.

He took the handkerchief from his bosom with an air; and kissing it, presented it to her, saying, " This happy estray, thus restored, begs leave, by me, to acknowledge its lovely owner ! "

" What mean you, Sir?—Who are you, Sir?—What mean you? "

" Your ladyship will excuse me : but I am incapable of meaning any thing but what is honourable."—(*No, to be sure*)— " This, Madam, you left last night, when the domino took up every one's attention but mine, which was much better engaged; and I take the liberty to restore it to you."

She turned to the mark; a coronet at one corner, " 'Tis true, Sir, I see now it is one of mine : but such a trifle was not worthy of being brought by such a gentleman as you seem to be; nor of my trouble to receive it in person. Your servant, Sir, might have delivered the bagatelle to mine."—"Nothing should be called so that belongs to the Countess of ——"—" She was no Countess, Sir, that *dropt* that handkerchief, and a gentleman would not attempt to penetrate, *unbecomingly,* through the disguises a lady thinks proper to assume; especially at such a place where every enquiry should begin and end."

This, Madam, from a lady, who had unmasked—because *she would not be known !*—Very pretty, indeed !—Oh ! these slight cobweb airs of modesty ! so easily seen through. Hence such advantages against us are taken by the men. She had looked out of her window, and seen no arms quartered with his own ; for you know, my lady, I would never permit any to be procured for me : so, she doubted not, it seems, but he was an unmarried gentleman, as he had intimated to her the night before. He told her it was impossible, after having seen the finest lady in the world, not to wish to see her again; and that he hoped he did not, *unbecomingly*, break through her ladyship's reserves: nor had he made any enquiries, either on the spot, or off it; having had a much better direction by accident.

"As how, Sir?" said she, as he told me, with so bewitching an air, between attentive and pleasant, that, bold gentleman, forgetting all manner of distance, so early too! he clasped his arms around her waist, and saluted her, struggling with anger and indignation, he says; but I think little of that!

"Whence this insolence? How, now, Sir! Begone!" were her words, and she rung the bell: but he set his back against the door—(I never heard such boldness in my life, Madam!)—till she would forgive him. And, it is plain, she was not so angry as she pretended: for her woman coming, she was calmer;—"Nelthorpe," said she, "fetch my snuff box, with the lavender in it."

Her woman went; and then she said, "You told me, Sir, last night, of your intrepidness: I think you are the boldest man I ever met with: but, Sir, surely you ought to know, that you are not now in the Haymarket."

I think, truly, Madam, the lady might have saved herself that speech: for, upon my word, they neither of them wore masks—Though they ought to have put on one of blushes—I am sure I do for them, while I am writing. Her irresistible loveliness served for an excuse, that she could not disapprove from a man she disliked not: and his irresistible—may I say, assurance, Madam?—found too ready an excuse.

"Well, but, Sir," said I, "pray, when her ladyship was made acquainted that you were a married gentleman, how then?—Pray, did *she* find it out, or did *you* tell her?"—"Patience, my dear!"—"Well pray, Sir, go on.—What was next?"

"Why, next, I put on a more respectful and tender air: I would have taken her hand indeed, but she would not permit it; and when she saw I would not go till her lavender snuff came down (for so I told her, and her woman was not in haste), she seated herself, and I sat by her, and began to talk about a charming lady I saw the night before, after parting with her ladyship, but not equal by any means to her: and I was confident this would engage her attention; for I never knew the lady who thought herself handsome, that was not taken by this topic. Flattery and admiration, Pamela, are the two principal engines by which our sex make their first approaches to yours; and if you listen to us, we are sure, either by the sap or the mine, to succeed, and blow you up when ever we please, if we do but take

325

care to suit ourselves to your particular foibles; or, to carry on the metaphor, point our batteries to your weak side—for the strongest fortresses, my dear, are weaker in one place than another."—" A fine thing, Sir," said I, "to be so learned a gentleman!"—"I wish, however," thought I, " you had always come honestly by your knowledge."

" When the lavender snuff came down, we were engaged in an agreeable disputation, which I had raised on purpose to excite her opposition, she having all the advantage in it; and in order to my giving it up, when she was intent upon it, as a mark of my consideration for her."

" I the less wonder, Sir," said I, " at your boldness (pardon the word !) with such a lady, in your first visit, because of her freedoms, when masked, her unmasking, and her handkerchief, and letter cover. To be sure, the lady, when she saw, next day, such a fine gentleman and handsome equipage, had little reason, after her other freedoms, to be so very nice with you as to decline an ensnaring conversation, calculated on purpose to engage her attention, and to lengthen out your visit. But did she not ask you who you were? "

" Her servants did of mine. And her woman (for I knew all afterwards, when we were better acquainted), whispered her lady, that I was Mr. B. of Bedfordshire; and had an immense estate, to which they were so kind as to add two or three thousand pounds a year, out of pure good will to me : I thank them."

" But pray, dear Sir, what had you in view in all this? Did you intend to carry this matter, at first, as far as ever you could?"
—" I had, at first, my dear, no view, but such as pride and vanity suggested to me. I was carried away by inconsideration, and the love of intrigue, without even thinking about the consequences. The lady, I observed, had abundance of fine qualities. I thought I could converse with her, on a very agreeable foot, and her honour I knew, at any time, would preserve me mine, if ever I should find it in danger; and, in my soul, I preferred my Pamela to all the ladies on earth, and questioned not, but that, and your virtue, would be another barrier to my fidelity.

" In a word, therefore, pride, vanity, thoughtlessness, were my misguiders, as I said. The Countess's honour and character, and your virtue and merit, my dear, and my obligations to you, were my defences : but I find one should avoid the first appearances of evil. One knows not one's own strength. 'Tis presumptuous to depend upon it, where wit and beauty are in the way on one side, and youth and strong passions on the other."

" You certainly, Sir, say right. But be pleased to tell me

what her ladyship said when she knew you were married."—
" The Countess's woman was in my interest, and let me into
some of her lady's secrets, having a great share in her confidence;
and particularly acquainted me, how loth her lady was to believe I was married. I had paid her three visits in town, and
one to her seat upon the Forest, before she heard that I was.
But when she was assured of it, and directed her Nelthorpe to
ask me about it, and I readily owned it, she was greatly incensed,
though nothing but general civilities, and intimacies not inconsistent with honourable friendship, had passed between us.
The consequence was, she forbad my ever seeing her again, and
set out with her sister and the Viscount for Tunbridge, where
she staid about three weeks.

" I thought I had already gone too far, and blamed myself
for permitting her so long to believe me single; and here the
matter had dropped, in all probability, had not a ball, given by
my Lord ——, to which, unknown to each other, we were both, as
also the Viscountess, invited, brought us again together. The
lady soon withdrew, with her sister, to another apartment;
and being resolved upon personal recrimination (which is what
a lady, who is resolved to break with a favoured object, should
never trust herself with,) sent for me, and reproached me on my
conduct, in which her sister joined.

" I owned frankly, that gaiety, rather than design, made me
give cause, at the masquerade, for her ladyship to think I was
not married; for that I had a wife, with a thousand excelliencies,
who was my pride, and my boast: that I held it very possible
for a gentleman and lady to carry on an innocent and honourable
friendship, in a *family* way; and I was sure, when she and her
sister saw my spouse, they would not be displeased with her
acquaintance; all that I had to reproach myself with, was,
that after having, at the masquerade, given reason to think I
was not married, I had been loth, *officiously*, to say I was, although I never intended to conceal it. In short, I acquitted
myself so well with both ladies, that a family intimacy was
consented to. I renewed my visits; and we accounted to one
another's honour, by entering upon a kind of Platonic system,
in which sex was to have no manner of concern.

" But, my dear Pamela, I must own myself extremely blameable, because I knew the world and human nature, I will say,
better than the lady, who never before had been trusted into
it upon her own feet: and who, notwithstanding that wit and
vivacity which every one admires in her, gave herself little
time for consideration. I ought, therefore, to have more care-

327

fully guarded against inconveniencies, which I knew were so likely to arise from such intimacies; and the rather, as I hinted, because the lady had no apprehension at all of any: so that, my dear, if I have no excuse from human frailty, from youth, and the charms of the object, I am entirely destitute of any."

"I see, Mr. B.," said I, "there is a great deal to be said for the lady. I wish I could say there was for the gentleman. But such a fine lady had been safe, with all her inconsideration; and so (forgive me, Sir,) would the gentleman, with all his intriguing spirit, had it not been for these vile masquerades. Never, dear Sir, think of going to another."—"Why, my dear, those are least of all to be trusted at these diversions, who are most desirous to go to them.—Of this I am now fully convinced."—"Well, Sir, I long to hear more particulars of this story: for this generous openness, now the affair is over, cannot but be grateful to me, as it shews me you have no reserve, and tends to convince me, that the lady was less blameable than I apprehended: for I love, for the honour of my sex, to find ladies of birth and quality innocent, who have so many opportunities of knowing and practising their duties, above what meaner persons can have."

"Well observed, my dear: this is like your generous and deep way of thinking."

"But, dear Sir, proceed—Your reconciliation is now effected: a friendship quadripartite is commenced. And the Viscountess and I are to find cement for the erecting of an edifice, that is to be devoted to Platonic love. What, may I ask, came next? And what did you design should come of it?"

"The Oxford journey, my dear, followed next; and it was my fault you were not a party in it, both ladies being very desirous of your company: but it was the time you were not going abroad, after your lying-in, so I excused you to them. Yet they both longed to see you: especially as by this time, you may believe, they knew all your story: and besides, whenever you were mentioned, I did justice, as well to your mind, as to your person."

"Well, Sir, to be sure this was very kind; and little was I disposed (knowing what I did,) to pass so favourable a construction in your generosity to me."

"My question to her ladyship at going away, whether you were not the charmingest girl in the world, which seeing you both together, rich as she was drest, and plain as you, gave me the double pleasure (a pleasure she said afterwards I exulted in,) of deciding in your favour; my readiness to explain to you what we both said, and her not ungenerous answer, I thought entitled me to a better return than a flood of tears; which confirmed me that your past uneasiness was a jealousy I was not willing to allow in you: though I should have been more indulgent to it had I known the grounds you thought you had for it: and for this reason I left you so abruptly as I did."

Here, Madam, Mr. B. broke off, referring to another time the conclusion of his narrative. I will here close this letter (though possibly I may not send it, till I send the conclusion of this story in my next,) with the assurance that I am *your ladyship's obliged sister and servant*,

P. B.

LETTER LXXVIII

My dear Lady,

Now I will proceed with my former subject: and with the greater pleasure, as what follows makes still more in favour of the Countess's character, than what went before, although that set it in a better light than it had once appeared to me in. I began as follows:

"Will you be pleased, Sir, to favour me with the continuation of our last subject?"—"I will, my dear."—"You left off, Sir, with acquitting me for breaking out into that flood of tears, which occasioned your abrupt departure. But, dear Sir, will you be pleased, to satisfy me about that affecting information, of your intention and my lady's to live at Tunbridge together?"

"'Tis absolute malice and falsehood. Our intimacy had not proceeded so far; and, thoughtless as my sister's letters suppose the lady, she would have spurned at such a proposal, I dare say."

"Well, but then, Sir, as to the expression to her uncle, that she had rather have been a certain gentleman's second wife?"

"I believe she might, in a passion, say something like it to him: he had been teazing her (from the time that I held an argument in favour of that foolish topic *polygamy*, in his company and his niece's, and in that of her sister and the Viscount,) with cautions against conversing with a man, who, having, as he was pleased to say behind my back, married beneath him, wanted to engage the affections of a lady of birth, in order to recover, by doubling that fault upon her, his lost reputation.

"She despised his insinuation enough to answer him, that she thought my arguments in behalf of *polygamy* were convincing. This set him a raving, and he threw some coarse reflections upon her, which could not be repeated, if one may

329

guess at them, by her being unable to tell me them; and then to vex him more, and to revenge herself, she said·something like what was reported : which was handle enough for her uncle; who took care to propagate it with an indiscretion peculiar to himself; for I heard it in three different companies, before I knew any thing of it from herself; and when I did, it was so repeated, as you, my dear, would hardly have censured her for it, the provocation considered."

" Well, but then, dear Sir, there is nothing at all amiss, at this rate, in the correspondence between my lady and you ? "

" Not on her side, I dare say, if her ladyship can be excused to punctilio, and for having a greater esteem for a married man, than he can deserve, or than may be strictly defended to a person of your purity and niceness."

" Well, Sir, this is very noble in you. I love to hear the gentlemen generous in points where the honour of our sex is concerned. But pray, Sir, what then was there on *your* side, in that matter, that made you give me so patient and so kind a hearing ? "

" Now, my dear, you come to the point : at first it was nothing in me but vanity, pride, and love of intrigue, to try my strength, where I had met with some encouragement, as I thought, at the masquerade; where the lady went farther, too, than she would have done, had she not thought I was a single man. For, by what I have told you, Pamela, you will observe, that she tried to satisfy herself on that head, as soon as she well could. Mrs. Nelthorpe acquainted me afterwards, when better known to each other, that her lady was so partial in my favour, (who can always govern their fancies, my dear?) as to think, so early as at the masquerade, that if every thing answered appearances, and that I were a single man, she, who has a noble and independent fortune, might possibly be induced to make me happy in her choice.

" Supposing, then, that I was unmarried, she left a signal for me in her handkerchief. I visited her; had the honour, after the customary first shyness, of being well received; and continued my visits, till, perhaps, she would have been glad I had not been married, but on finding I was, she avoided me, as I have told you, till the accident I mentioned threw us again upon each other : which renewed our intimacy upon terms you would think too inconsiderable on one side, and too designing on the other.

" For myself, what can I say? only that you gave me great disgusts (without cause, as I thought,) by your unwonted reception of me, ever in tears and grief; the Countess ever cheerful

330

and lively; and fearing that your temper was entirely changing, I believe I had no bad excuse to try to make myself easy and cheerful abroad, since my home became more irksome to me than ever I believed it could be. Then, as we naturally love those who love us, I had vanity, and some reason for my vanity (indeed all vain men believe they have,) to think the Countess had more than an indifference for me. She was so exasperated by the wrong methods taken with an independent lady of her generous spirit, to break off our acquaintance, that, in revenge, she denied me less than ever opportunities of her company. The pleasure we took in each other's conversation was reciprocal. The world's reports had united us in one common cause: and you, as I said, had made home less delightful to me than it used to be: what might not then have been apprehended from so many circumstances concurring with the lady's beauty and my frailty?

"I waited on her to Tunbridge. She took a house there. Where people's tongues will take so much liberty, without any foundation, and where the utmost circumspection is used, what will they not say, where so little of the latter is observed? No wonder, then, that terms were said to be agreed upon between us: from her uncle's story, of polygamy proposed by me, and seemingly agreed to by her, no wonder that all your Thomasine Fuller's information was surmised. Thus stood the matter, when I was determined to give your cause for uneasiness a hearing, and to take my measures according to what should result from that hearing."

"From this account, dear Sir," said I, "it will not be so difficult, as I feared, to end this affair even to her *ladyship's* satisfaction."—"I hope not, my dear."—"But if, now, Sir, the Countess should still be desirous not to break with you; from so charming a lady, who knows what may happen!"

"Very true, Pamela; but to make you still easier, I will tell you that her ladyship has a first cousin married to a person going with a public character to several of the Italian courts, and, had it not been for my persuasions, she would have accepted of their earnest invitations, and passed a year or two in Italy, where she once resided for three years together, which makes her so perfect a mistress of Italian.

"Now I will let her know, additionally to what I have written to her, the uneasiness I have given you, and, so far as it is proper, what is come to your ears, and your generous account of her, and the charms of her person, of which she will not be a little proud; for she has really noble and generous sentiments, and thinks well (though her sister, in pleasantry, will have it a little enviously,) of you; and when I shall endeavour to persuade her to go, for the sake of her own character, to a place and country of which she was always fond, I am apt to think she will come into it; for she has a greater opinion of my judgment than it deserves : and I know a young lord, who may be easily persuaded to follow her thither, and bring her back his lady, if he can obtain her consent : and what say you, Pamela, to this ? "

" O, Sir ! I believe I shall begin to love the lady dearly, and that is what I never thought I should. I hope this will be brought about.

" But I see, give me leave to say, Sir, how dangerously you might both have gone on, under the notion of this Platonic love, till two precious souls had been lost : and this shews one, as well in spirituals as temporals, from what slight beginnings the greatest mischiefs sometimes spring; and how easily at first a breach may be stopped, that, when neglected, the waves of passion will widen till they bear down all before them."

" Your observation, my dear, is just," replied Mr. B., " and though, I am confident the lady was more in earnest than myself in the notion of Platonic love, yet I am convinced, and always was, that Platonic love is Platonic nonsense : 'tis the fly buzzing about the blaze, till its wings are scorched; or, to speak still stronger, it is a bait of the devil to catch the unexperienced, and thoughtless : nor ought such notions to be pretended to, till the parties are five or ten years on the other side of their grand climateric : for age, old age, and nothing else, must establish the barriers to Platonic love. But this was my comparative consolation, though a very bad one, that had I swerved, I should not have given the only instance, where persons more scrupulous than I pretended to be, have begun friendships even with spiritual views, and ended them as grossly as I could have done, were the lady to have been as frail as her tempter."

Here Mr. B. finished his narrative. He is now set out for Tunbridge with all my papers. I have no doubt in his honour and kind assurances, and hope my next will be a joyful letter; and that I shall inform you in it, that the affair which went so near my heart, is absolutely concluded to my satisfaction, to Mr. B.'s and the Countess's; for if it be so to all three, my happiness, I doubt not, will be founded on a permanent basis. Meantime I am, my dear good lady, *your most affectionate, and obliged sister and servant,*

P. B.

332

A new misfortune, my dear lady!—But this is of God Almighty's sending; so I must bear it patiently. My dear baby is taken with the small-pox!—To how many troubles are the happiest of us subjected in this life! One need not multiply them by one's own wilful mismanagements!—I am able to mind nothing else!

I had so much joy (as I told your ladyship in the beginning of my last letter but one) to see, on our arrival at the farm-house, my dearest Mr. B., my beloved baby, and my good parents, all upon one happy spot, that I fear I was too proud—Yet I was truly thankful, I am sure!—But I had, notwithstanding too much pride, and too much pleasure, on this happy occasion.

I said, in my last, that your dear brother set out on Tuesday morning for Tunbridge with my papers; and I longed to know the result, hoping that every thing would be concluded to the satisfaction of all three: "For," thought I, "if this be so, my happiness must be permanent:" but alas! there is nothing permanent in this life. I feel it by experience now!—I knew it before by theory: but that was not so near and interesting by half.

For, with all my pleasures and hopes; in the midst of my dear parents' joy and congratulations on our arrival, and on what had passed so happily since we were last here together, (in the birth of the dear child, and my safety, for which they had been so apprehensive,) the poor baby was taken ill. It was on that very Tuesday his papa set out for Tunbridge; but we knew not it would be the small-pox till Thursday. O Madam! how are all the pleasures I had formed to myself sickened now upon me! for my Billy is very bad.

They talk of a kind sort: but alas: they talk at random: for they come not out at all!—I fear the nurse's constitution is too hale and too rich for the dear baby!—Had *I* been permitted—But hush, all my repining *ifs!*—except one *if;* and that is, *if* it be got happily over, it will be best he had it so young, and while at the breast!——

Oh! Madam, Madam! the small appearance that there was is gone in again: and my child, my dear baby, will die! The doctors seem to think so.

They wanted to send for Mr. B. to keep me from him!—But I forbid it!—For what signifies life, or any thing, if I cannot see my baby, while he is so dangerously ill!

My father and mother are, for the first time, quite cruel to me; they have forbid me, and I never was so desirous of disobeying them before, to attend the darling of my heart : and why?—For fear of this poor face !—For fear I should get it myself !—But I am living very low, and have taken proper precautions by bleeding, and the like, to lessen the distemper's fury, if I should have it; and the rest I leave to Providence. And if Mr. B.'s value is confined so much to this poor transitory sightliness, he must not break with his Countess, I think; and if I am ever so deformed in person, my poor intellects, I hope will not be impaired, and I shall, if God spare my Billy, be useful in his first education, and be helpful to dear Miss Goodwin—or to any babies—with all my heart—he may make me an humble nurse too !—How peevish, sinfully so, I doubt, does this accident, and their affectionate contradiction, make one !

I have this moment received the following from Mr. B.

Maidstone.

" MY DEAREST LOVE,

" I am greatly touched with the dear boy's malady, of which I have this moment heard. I desire you instantly to come to me hither, in the chariot with the bearer, Colbrand. I know what your grief must be : but as you can do the child no good, I beg you'll oblige me. Everything is in a happy train; but I can think only of you, and (for your sake principally, but not a little for *my own*) my boy. I will set out to meet you; for I choose not to come myself, lest you should try to persuade me to permit your tarrying about him; and I should be sorry to deny you any thing. I have taken handsome apartments for you, till the event, which I pray God may be happy, shall better determinate me what to do. I will be ever *your affectionate and faithful.*"

Maidstone indeed is not so very far off, but one may hear every day, once or twice, by a man and horse; so I will go, to shew my obedience, since Mr. B. is so intent upon it—But I cannot live, if I am not permitted to come back—Oh ! let me be enabled, gracious Father ! to close this letter more happily than I have begun it !

I have been so dreadfully uneasy at Maidstone, that Mr. B. has been so good as to return with me hither; and I find my baby's case not yet quite desperate—I am easier now I see him, in presence of his beloved papa who lets me have all my way, and approves of my preparative method for myself; and he tells me that since I will have it so, he will indulge me in my attendance on the child, and endeavour to imitate my reliance on

God—that is his kind expression—and leave the issue to him. And on my telling him, that I feared nothing in the distemper, but the loss of his love, he said, in presence of the doctors, and my father and mother, pressing my hand to his lips—" My dearest life, make yourself easy under this affliction, and apprehend nothing for yourself: I love you more, for your mind than for your face. That and your person will be the same; and were that sweet face to be covered with seams and scars, I will value you the more for the misfortune : and glad I am, that I had your picture so well drawn in town, to satisfy those who have heard of your loveliness, what you were, and hitherto are. For myself, my admiration lies deeper;" and, drawing me to the other end of the room, whisperingly he said, " The last uneasiness between us, I now begin to think, was necessary, because it has turned all my delight in you, more than ever, to the perfections of your mind : and so God preserves to me the life of my Pamela, I care not for my own part, what ravages the distemper makes here," and tapped my cheek.—How generous, how noble, how comforting was this !

When I went from my apartment, to go to my child, my dear Mr. B. met me at the nursery door, and led me back again. " You must not go in again, my dearest. They have just been giving the child other things to try to drive out the malady; and some pustules seem to promise on his breast." I made no doubt, my baby was then in extremity; and I would have given the world to have shed a few tears, but I could not.

With the most soothing goodness he led me to my desk, and withdrew to attend the dear baby himself—to see his last gaspings, poor little lamb, I make no doubt !

In this suspense, my own strange hardness of heart would not give up one tear, for the passage from *that* to my *eyes* seemed quite choaked up, which used to be so open and ready on other occasions, affecting ones too.

Two days have passed, dreadful days of suspense : and now, blessed be God ! who has given me hope that our prayers are heard, the pustules come kindly out, very thick in his breast, and on his face : but of a good sort, they tell me.—They won't let me see him; indeed they won't !—What cruel kindness is this ! One must believe all they tell one !

But, my dear lady, my spirits are so weak; I have such a violent headache, and have such a strange shivering disorder all running down my back, and I was so hot just now, and am so cold at this present—aguishly inclined—I don't know how ! that I must leave off, the post going away, with the assurance, that I am, and will be, to the last hour of my life, *your ladyship's grateful and obliged sister and servant,*

P. B.

LETTER LXXX

From Mr. B. to Lady Davers.

My dear Sister,

I take very kindly your solicitude for the health of my beloved Pamela. The last line she wrote was to you; for she took to her bed the moment she laid down her pen.

I told her your kind message, and wishes for her safety, by my lord's gentleman; and she begged I would write a line to thank you in her name for your affectionate regards to her.

She is in a fine way to do well: for with her accustomed prudence, she had begun to prepare herself by a proper regimen, the moment she knew the child's illness was the small-pox.

The worst is over with the boy, which keeps up her spirits; and her mother is so excellent a nurse to both, and we are so happy likewise in the care of a skilful physician, Dr. M. (who directs and approves of every thing the good dame does,) that it is a singular providence this malady seized them here; and affords no small comfort to the dear creature herself.

When I tell you, that, to all appearance, her charming face will not receive any disfigurement by this cruel enemy to beauty, I am sure you will congratulate me upon a felicity so desirable: but were it to be otherwise, if I were capable of slighting a person, whose principal beauties are much deeper than the skin, I should deserve to be thought the most unworthy and superficial of husbands.

Whatever your notions have been, my ever-ready censuring Lady Davers, of your brother, on a certain affair, I do assure you, that I never did, and never can, love any woman as I love my Pamela.

It is indeed impossible I can ever love her better than I do; and her outward beauties are far from being indifferent to me; yet, if I know myself, I am sure I have justice enough to love her *equally*, and generosity enough to be *more tender* of her, were she to suffer by this distemper. But, as her humility, and her affection to me, would induce her to think herself under greater obligation to me, for such my tenderness to her, were she to lose any the *least* valuable of her perfections, I rejoice that she will have no reason for mortification on that score.

336

My respects to Lord Davers, and your noble neighbours. I am, *your affectionate brother, and humble servant.*

LETTER LXXXI

From Lady Davers, in answer to the preceding.

MY DEAR BROTHER,

I do most heartily congratulate you on the recovery of Master Billy, and the good way my sister is in. I am the more rejoiced, as her sweet face is not like to suffer by the malady; for, be the beauties of the mind what they will, those of the person are no small recommendation, with some folks, I am sure; and I began to be afraid, that when it was hardly possible for *both conjoined* to keep a roving mind constant, that *one only* would not be sufficient.

This news gives me more pleasure, because I am well informed, that a certain gay lady was pleased to give herself airs upon learning of my sister's illness, as, That she would not be sorry for it; for now she should look upon herself as the prettiest woman in England.—She meant only, I suppose, as to *outward* prettiness, brother !

You give me the name of a *ready censurer.* I own, I think myself to be not a little interested in all that regards my brother, and his honour. But when some people are not readier to *censure,* than others to *trespass,* I know not whether they can with justice be styled censorious.

But however that be, the rod seems to have been held up, as a warning—and that the blow, in the irreparable deprivation, is not given, is a mercy, which I hope will be deserved; though you never can those very signal ones you receive at the Divine hands, beyond any man I know. For even (if I shall not be deemed censorious again) your very vices have been turned to your felicity, as if God would try the nobleness of the heart he has given you, by overcoming you (in answer to my sister's constant prayers, as well as mine) by mercies rather than by judgments.

I might give instances of the truth of this observation, in almost all the actions and attempts of your past life; and take care (if you *are* displeased, I *will* speak it), take care, thou bold wretch, that if this method be ungratefully slighted, the uplifted arm fall not down with double weight on thy devoted head !

I must always love and honour my brother, but cannot help

337

speaking my mind : which, after all, is the natural result of that very love and honour, and which obliges me to style myself *your truly affectionate sister,*

B. DAVERS.

LETTER LXXXII

From Mrs. B. to Lady Davers.

MY DEAREST LADY,

My first letter, and my first devoirs, after those of thankfulness to that gracious God, who has so happily conducted me through two such heavy trials, as my child's and my own illness, must be directed to you, with all due acknowledgment of your generous and affectionate concern for me.

We are now preparing for our journey to Bedfordshire; and there, to my great satisfaction, I am to be favoured with the care of Miss Goodwin.

After tarrying about a month there, Mr. B. will make a tour with me through several counties (taking the Hall in the way) for about a fortnight, and shew me what is remarkable, every where as we pass; for this, he thinks, will better contribute to my health, than any other method. The distemper has left upon me a kind of weariness and listlessness; and he proposes to be out with me till the Bath season begins; and by the aid of those healing and balsamic waters, he hopes, I shall be quite established. Afterwards to return to Bedfordshire for a little while; then to London; and then to Kent; and, if nothing hinders, has a great mind to carry me over to Paris.

Thus most kindly does he amuse and divert me with his agreeable proposals. But I have made one amendment to them; and that is, that I must not be denied to pay my respects to your ladyship, at your seat, and to my good Lady Countess in the same neighbourhood, and this will be far from being the least of my pleasures.

I have had congratulations without number upon my recovery; but one, among the rest, I did not expect; from the Countess Dowager (could you think it, Madam?) who sent me by her gentleman the following letter from Tunbridge.

" MADAM,

" I hope, among the congratulations of your numerous admirers, on your happy recovery, my very sincere ones will not be unacceptable. I have no other motive for making you

338

my compliments on this occasion, on so slender an acquaintance, than the pleasure it gives me, that the public, as well as your private friends, have not been deprived of a lady whose example, in every duty of life, is of so much concern to both.—May you, Madam, long rejoice in an uninterrupted state of happiness, answerable to your merits, and to your own wishes, are those of *your most obedient humble servant.*"

To this kind letter I returned the following:

" MADAM,
" I am under the highest obligation to your generous favour, in your kind compliments of congratulation on my recovery. There is something so noble and so condescending in the honour you have done me, on so slender an acquaintance, that it bespeaks the exalted mind and character of a lady, who, in the principles of generosity, and in true nobleness of nature, has no example. May God Almighty bless you, my dear lady, with all the good you wish me, and with increase of honour and glory, both here and hereafter, prays, and will always pray, *your ladyship's most obliged and obedient servant,*
" P. B.''

This leads me to mention, what my illness would not permit me to do before, that Mr. B. met with such a reception and audience from the Countess, when he attended her, in all he had to offer and propose to her, and in her patient hearing of what he thought fit to read her, from your ladyship's letters and mine, that he said, " Don't be jealous, my dear Pamela; but I must admire her as long as I live."

He gave me the particulars, so much to her ladyship's honour, that I told him, he should not only be welcome to admire her ladyship, but that I would admire her too.

They parted very good friends, and with great professions of esteem for each other.—And as Mr. B. had undertaken to inspect into some exceptionable accounts and managements of her ladyship's bailiff, one of her servants brought a letter for him on Monday last, wholly written on that subject. But she was so considerate, as to send it unsealed, in a cover directed to me. When I opened it, I was frightened to see it begin to Mr. B. and I hastened to find him—" Dear Sir—Here's some mistake—You see the direction is to Mrs. B.—'Tis very plain—But, upon my word, I have not read it."—" Don't be uneasy, my love.—I know what the subject must be; but I dare swear there is nothing, nor will there ever be, but what you or any body may see."

He read it, and giving it to me, said, "Answer yourself the postscript, my dear." That was—"If, Sir, the trouble I give you, is likely to subject you or your lady to uneasiness or apprehensions, I beg you will not be concerned in it. I will then set about the matter myself; for my uncle I will not trouble; yet women enter into these particulars with as little advantage to themselves as inclination."

I told him, I was entirely easy and unapprehensive; and, after all his goodness to me, should be so, if he saw the Countess every day. "That's kindly said, my dear; but I will not trust myself to see her every day, or at all, for the present. But I shall be obliged to correspond with her for a month or so, on this occasion; unless you prohibit it; and it shall be in your power to do so."

I said, with my whole heart, he might; and I should be quite easy in both their honours.

"Yet I will not," said he, "unless you see our letters: for I know she will always, now she has begun, send in a cover to you, what she will write to me, unsealed; and whether I am at home or abroad, I shall take it unkindly, if you do not read them."

He went in, and wrote an answer, which he sent by the messenger; but would make me, whether I would or not, read it, and seal it up with his seal. But all this needed not to me now, who think so much better of the lady than I did before; and am so well satisfied in his own honour and generous affection for me; for you saw, Madam, in what I wrote before, that he always loved me, though he was angry at times, at my change of temper, as he feared, not knowing that I was apprised of what had passed between him and the Countess.

I really am better pleased with his correspondence, than I should have been, had it not been carried on; because the servants, on both sides, will see, by my deportment on the occasion (and I will officiously, with a smiling countenance, throw myself in their observation), that it is quite innocent; and this may help to silence the mouths of those who have so freely censured their conduct.

Indeed, Madam, I think I have received no small good myself by that affair, which once lay so heavy upon me: for I don't believe I shall be ever jealous again; indeed I don't think I shall. And won't that be an ugly foible overcome? I see what may be done, in cases not favourable to our wishes, by the aid of proper reflection; and that the bee is not the only creature that may make honey out of the bitter flowers as well as the sweet.

My most grateful respects and thanks to my good Lord Davers; to the Earl, and his excellent Countess; and most particularly to Lady Betty (with whose kind compliments your ladyship acquaints me), and to Mr. H. for all your united congratulations on my recovery. What obligations do I lie under to such noble and generous well-wishers!—I can make no return but by my prayers, that God, by *his* goodness, will supply all my defects. And these will always attend you, from, my dearest lady, *your ever obliged sister, and humble servant,*

P. B.

Mr. H. is just arrived. He says, he comes a special messenger, to make a report how my face has come off. He makes me many compliments upon it. How kind your ladyship is, to enter so favourably into the minutest concerns, which you think, may any way affect my future happiness in your dear brother's opinion!—I want to pour out all my joy and my thankfulness to God, before you, and the good Countess of C——! For I am a happy, yea, a blessed creature! Mr. B.'s boy, your ladyship's boy, and my boy, is charmingly well; quite strong, and very forward, for his months; and his papa is delighted with him more and more.

LETTER LXXXIII

MY DEAR MISS DARNFORD,

I hope you are happy and well. You kindly say you can't be so, till you hear of my perfect recovery. And this, blessed be God! you have heard already from Mr. B.

As to your intimation of the fair Nun, 'tis all happily over. Blessed be God for that too! And I have a better and more endearing husband than ever. Did you think that could be?

My Billy too improves daily, and my dear parents seem to have their youth renewed like the eagle's. How many blessings have I to be thankful for!

We are about to turn travellers, to the northern counties. I think quite to the borders: and afterwards to the western, to Bath, Bristol, and I know not whither myself: but among the rest, to Lincolnshire, that you may be sure of. Then how happy shall I be in my dear Miss Darnford!

I long to hear whether poor Mrs. Jewkes is better or worse

for the advice of the doctor, whom I ordered to attend her from Stamford, and in what frame her mind is. Do vouchsafe her a visit in my name; tell her, if she be low spirited, what God hath done for me, as to *my* recovery, and comfort her all you can; and bid her spare neither expence nor attendance, nor any thing her heart can wish for; nor the company of any relations or friends she may desire to be with her.

If she is in her *last stage*, poor soul! how noble will it be in you to give her comfort and consolation in her dying hours! Although we can merit nothing at the hand of God, yet I have a notion, that we cannot deserve more of one another, and in some sense, for that reason, of him, than in our charities on so trying an exigence! When the poor soul stands shivering, as it were, on the verge of death, and has nothing strong, but its fears and doubts; then a little balm poured into the wounds of the mind, a little comforting advice to rely on God's mercies, from a good person, how consolatory must it be! And how, like morning mists before the sun, must all diffidences and gloomy doubts, be chased away by it!

But, my dear, the great occasion of my writing to you just now, is by Lady Davers's desire, on a quite different subject. She knows how we love one another. And she has sent me the following lines by her kinsman, who came to Kent, purposely to enquire how my face fared in the small-pox; and accompanied us hither, [*i.e.* to Bedfordshire,] and sets out to-morrow for Lord Davers's.

" MY DEAR PAMELA,

" Jackey will tell you the reason of his journey, my curiosity on your own account; and I send this letter by him, but he knows not the contents. My good Lord Davers wants to have his nephew married, and settled in the world : and his noble father leaves the whole matter to my lord, as to the person, settlements, &c. Now I, as well as he, think so highly of the prudence, the person, and family of your Miss Darnford, that we shall be obliged to you, to sound the young lady on this score.

" I know Mr. H. would wish for no greater happiness. But if she is engaged, or cannot love my nephew, I don't care, nor would my lord, that such a proposal should be received with undue slight. His birth, and the title and estate he is heir to, are advantages that require a lady's consideration. He has not so much wit as Miss, but enough for a lord, whose friends are born before him, as the phrase is; is very good-humoured, no fool, no sot, no debauchee : and, let me tell you, this is not to be met with every day in a young man of quality.

"As to settlements, fortunes, &c. I fancy there would be no great difficulties. The business is, if Miss Darnford could love him well enough for a husband? *That* we leave you to sound the young lady; and if she thinks she can, we will directly begin a treaty with Sir Simon. I am, my dearest Pamela, *your ever affectionate sister,*   B. DAVERS."

Now, my dear friend, as my lady has so well stated the case, I beg you to enable me to return an answer. I will not say one word *pro* or *con.* till I know your mind—Only, that I think he is good-humoured and might be easily persuaded to any thing a lady should think reasonable.

I must tell you another piece of news in the matrimonial way. Mr. Williams has been here to congratulate us on our multiplied blessings; and he acquainted Mr. B. that an overture has been made him by his new patron, of a kinswoman of his lordship's, a person of virtue and merit, and a fortune of three thousand pounds, to make him amends, as the earl tell him, for quitting a better living to oblige him; and that he is in great hope of obtaining the lady's consent, which is all that is wanting. Mr. B. is much pleased with so good a prospect in Mr. Williams's favour, and was in the lady's company formerly at a ball, at Gloucester; he says, she is prudent and deserving; and offers to make a journey on purpose to forward it, if he can be of service to him.

I suppose you know that all is adjusted, according to the scheme I formerly acquainted you with, between Mr. Adams and that gentleman; and both are settled in their respective livings. But I ought to have told you, that Mr. Williams, upon mature deliberation, declined the stipulated eighty pounds *per annum* from Mr. Adams, as he thought it would have a simoniacal appearance.

But now my hand's in, let me tell you of a third matrimonial proposition, which gives me more puzzle and dislike a great deal. And that is, Mr. Adams has, with great reluctance, and after abundance of bashful apologies, asked me, if I have any objection to his making his addresses to Polly Barlow? which, however, he told me, he had not mentioned to her, nor to any body living, because he would first know whether I should take it amiss, as her service was so immediately about my person.

This unexpected motion much perplexed me. Mr. Adams is a worthy man. He has now a very good living; yet just

343

entered upon it; and, I think, according to his accustomed prudence in other respects, had better have turned himself about first.

But that is not the point with me neither. I have a great regard to the function. I think it is as necessary, in order to preserve the respect due to the clergy, that their wives should be nearly, if not quite as unblemished, and as circumspect, as themselves; and this for the gentleman's own sake, as well as in the eye of the world : for how shall he pursue his studies with comfort to himself, if made uneasy at home ! or how shall he expect his female parishioners will regard his *public* preaching, if he cannot have a due influence over the *private* conduct of his wife?

I can't say, excepting in the instance of Mr. H. but Polly is a good sort of body enough so far as I know; but that is such a blot in the poor girl's escutcheon, a thing not *accidental*, nor *surprised* into, not owing to *inattention*, but to cool *premeditation*, that, I think, I could wish Mr. Adams a wife more unexceptionable.

'Tis true, Mr. Adams knows not this; but *that* is one of my difficulties. If I acquaint him with it, I shall hurt the poor girl irreparably, and deprive her of a husband, to whom she may possibly make a good wife—For she is not very meanly descended—much better than myself, as the world would say were a judgment to be made from my father's low estate, when I was exalted—I never, my dear, shall be ashamed of these retrospections ! She is genteel, has a very innocent look, a good face, is neat in her person, and not addicted to any excess that I know of. But *still*, that one *premeditated* fault, is so sad a one, though she might make a good wife for any middling man of business, yet she wants, methinks, that discretion, that purity, which I would always have in the wife of a good clergyman.

Then, she has not applied her thoughts to that sort of economy, which the wife of a country clergyman ought to know something of; and has such a turn to dress and appearance, that I can see, if indulged, she would not be one that would help to remove the scandal which some severe remarkers are apt to throw upon the wives of *parsons*, as they call them.

The maiden, I believe, likes Mr. Adams not a little. She is very courteous to every body, but most to him of any body, and never has missed being present at our Sunday's duties; and five or six times, Mrs. Jervis tells me, she has found her desirous to have Mr. Adams expound this text, and that difficulty; and the good man is taken with her piety, which, and her reformation, I hope, is sincere; but she is very sly, very subtle, as I have found in several instances, as foolish as she was in the affair I hint at.

"So," sometimes I say to myself, "the girl may love Mr. Adams."—"Ay," but then I answer, "so she did Mr. H. and on his own very bad terms too."—In short—but I won't be too censorious neither.

So I'll say no more, than that I was perplexed; and yet should be very glad to have Polly well married; for, since *that* time, I have always had some diffidences about her—Because, you know, Miss—her fault was so enormous, and, as I have said, so premeditated. I wanted you to advise with.—But this was the method I took.—I appointed Mr. Adams to drink a dish of tea with me. Polly attended, as usual; for I can't say I love men attendants in these womanly offices. A tea-kettle in a man's hand, that would, if there was no better employment for him, be fitter to hold a plough, or handle a flail, or a scythe, has such a look with it!—This is like my low breeding, some would say, perhaps,—but I cannot call things polite, that I think unseemly; and, moreover, Lady Davers keeps me in countenance in this my notion; and who doubts her politeness?

Well, but Polly attended, as I said; and there were strange simperings, and bowing, and curt'sying, between them; the honest gentleman seeming not to know how to let his mistress wait upon him; while she behaved with as much respect and officiousness, as if she could not do too much for him.

"Very well," thought I, "I have such an opinion of your veracity, Mr. Adams, that I dare say you have not mentioned the matter to Polly; but between her officiousness, and your mutual simperings and complaisance, I see you have found a language between you, that is full as significant as plain English words. Polly," thought I, "sees no difficulty in *this* text; nor need you, Mr. Adams, have much trouble to make her understand you, when you come to expound upon *this* subject."

I was forced, in short, to put on a statelier and more reserved appearance than usual, to make them avoid acts of complaisance for one another, that might not be proper to be shewn before me, for one who sat as my companion, to my servant.

When she withdrew, the modest gentleman hemmed, and looked on one side, and turned to the right and left, as if his seat was uneasy to him, and, I saw, knew not how to speak; so I began in mere compassion to him, and said—"Mr. Adams,

345

I have been thinking of what you mentioned to me, as to Polly Barlow."

"Hem! hem!" said he; and pulled out his handkerchief, and wiped his mouth—"Very well, Madam; I hope no offence, Madam!"

"No, Sir, none at all. But I am at a loss how to distinguish in this case; whether it may not be from a motive of too humble gratitude, that you don't think yourself above matching with Polly, as you may suppose her a favourite of mine; or whether it be your value for her person and qualities, that makes her more agreeable in your eyes, than any other person would be."

"Madam—Madam," said the bashful gentleman, hesitatingly —"I do—I must needs say—I can't but own—that—Mrs. Mary—is a person—whom I think very agreeable; and no less modest and virtuous."

"You know, Sir, your own circumstances. To be sure you have a very pretty house, and a good living, to carry a wife to. And a gentleman of your prudence and discretion wants not any advice; but you have reaped no benefits by your living. It has been an expence to you rather, which you will not presently get up: do you propose an early marriage, Sir? Or were it not better to suspend your intentions of that sort for a year or two more?"—"Madam, if your ladyship choose not to part with——"—"Nay, Mr. Adams," interrupted I, "I say not any thing for my own sake in this point: that is out of the question with me. I can very willingly part with Polly, were it to-morrow, for her good and yours."—"Madam, I humbly beg pardon;—but—but—delays may breed dangers." —"Oh! very well," thought I; "if the artful girl has not let him know, by some means or other, that she has another humble servant."

And so, Miss, it has proved—For, dismissing my gentleman, with assuring him, that I had no objection at all to the matter, or to parting with Polly, as soon as it suited with their conveniency—I sounded her, and asked, if she thought Mr. Adams had any affection for her?—She said he was a very good gentleman.

"I know it, Polly; and are you not of opinion he loves you a little?"—"Dear Ma'am—love me—I don't know what such a gentleman as Mr. Adams should see in me, to love me!" —"Oh!" thought I, "does the doubt lie on *that* side then?— I see 'tis not of *thine*."

"Well, but, Polly, if you have *another* sweetheart, you should do the fair thing; it would be wrong, if you encourage any

346

body else, if you thought of Mr. Adams."—"Indeed, Ma'am, I had a letter sent me—a letter that I received—from—from a young man in Bedford; but I never answered it."

"Oh !" thought I, "then thou wouldst not encourage *two at once ;* " and this was as plain a declaration as I wanted, that she had thoughts of Mr. Adams.

"But how came Mr. Adams, Polly, to know of this letter?"—"How came he to know of it, Ma'am !"—repeated she—half surprised—"Why, I don't know, I can't tell how it was—but I dropped it near his desk—pulling out my handkerchief, I believe, Ma'am, and he brought it, and gave it me again."—"Well," thought I, "thou'rt an intriguing slut, I doubt, Polly."—"*Delays may breed dangers,*" quoth the poor gentleman !—"Ah ! girl, girl !" thought I, but did not say so, "thou deservest to have thy plot spoiled, that thou dost—But if thy forwardness should expose thee afterwards to evils which thou mayest avoid if thy schemes take place, I should very much blame myself. And I see he loves thee—So let the matter take its course; I will trouble myself no more about it. I only wish, that thou wilt make Mr. Adams as good a wife as he deserves."

And so I dismissed her, telling her, that whoever thought of being a clergyman's wife, should resolve to be as good as himself; to set an example to all her sex in the parish, and shew how much his doctrines had weight with her; should be humble, circumspect, gentle in her temper and manners, frugal, not proud, nor vying in dress with the ladies of the laity; should resolve to sweeten his labour, and to be obliging in her deportment to poor as well as rich, that her husband get no discredit through her means, which would weaken his influence upon his auditors; and that she must be most of all obliging to him, and study his temper, that his mind might be more disengaged, in order to pursue his studies with the better effect.

And so much for *your* humble servant; and for Mr. Williams's and Mr. Adams's matrimonial prospect;—and don't think me so disrespectful, that I have mentioned my Polly's affair in the same letter with yours. For in high and low (I forget the Latin phrase—I have not had a lesson a long, long while, from my dear tutor) love is in all the same !—But whether you'll like Mr. H. as well as Polly does Mr. Adams, that's the question. But, leaving that to your own decision, I conclude with one observation; that, although I thought our's was a house of as little intriguing as any body's, since the dear master of it has left off that practice, yet I cannot see, that any family can be clear of some of it long together, where there are men and women worth plotting for, as husbands and wives.

My best wishes and respects attend all your worthy neighbours. I hope ere long, to assure them, severally. (to wit, Sir Simon, my lady, Mrs. Jones, Mr. Peters, and his lady and niece, whose kind congratulations make me very proud, and very thankful) how much I am obliged to them; and particularly, my dear, how much I am *your ever affectionate and faithful friend and servant,*

P. B.

LETTER LXXXIV

From Miss Darnford, in answer to the preceding.

MY DEAR MRS. B.,

I have been several times (in company with Mr. Peters) to see Mrs. Jewkes. The poor woman is very bad, and cannot live many days. We comfort her all we can; but she often accuses herself of her past behaviour to so excellent a lady; and with blessings upon blessings, heaped upon you, and her master, and your charming little boy, is continually declaring how much your goodness to her aggravates her former faults to her own conscience.

She has a sister-in-law and her niece with her, and has settled all her affairs, and thinks she is not long for this world.—Her distemper is an inward decay, all at once as it were, from a constitution that seemed like one of iron; and she is a mere skeleton : you would not know her, I dare say.

I will see her every day; and she has given me up all her keys, and accounts, to give to Mr. Longman, who is daily expected, and I hope will be here soon; for her sister-in-law, she says herself, is a woman of *this world,* as *she* has been.

Mr. Peters calling upon me to go with him to visit her, I will break off here.

Mrs. Jewkes is much as she was; but your faithful steward is come. I am glad of it—and so is she—Nevertheless I will go every day, and do all the good I can for the poor woman, according to your charitable desires.

I thank you for your communication of Lady Davers's letter. I am much obliged to my lord, and her ladyship; and should have been proud of an alliance with that noble family; but with all Mr. H.'s good qualities, as my lady paints them out, and his other advantages, I could not, for the world, make him my husband. I'll tell you one of my objections, in confidence,

348

however, (for you are only to *sound* me, you know :) and I would not have it mentioned that I have taken any thought about the matter, because a stronger reason may be given, such a one as my lord and lady will both allow; which I will communicate to you by and bye.—My objection arises even from what you intimate, of Mr. H.'s good humour, and his persuadableness, if I may so call it. Now, were I of a boisterous temper, and high spirit, such an one as required great patience in a husband to bear with me, then Mr. H.'s good humour might have been a consideration with me. But when I have (I pride myself in the thought) a temper not wholly unlike your own, and such an one as would not want to contend for superiority with a husband, it is no recommendation to me, that Mr. H. is a good-humoured gentleman, and will bear with faults I design not to be guilty of.

But, my dear Mrs. B., my husband must be a man of sense, and give me reason to think he has a superior judgment to my own, or I shall be unhappy. He will otherwise do wrong-headed things : I shall be forced to oppose him in them : he will be tenacious and obstinate, be taught to talk of prerogative, and to call himself a *man*, without knowing how to behave as one, and I to despise him, of course; so be deemed a bad wife, when, I hope, I have qualities that would make me a tolerable good one, with a man of sense for my husband.

Now you must not think I would dispense with real good-humour in a man. No, I make it one of my *indispensables* in a husband. A good-natured man will put the best constructions on what happens; but he must have sense to *distinguish* the best. He will be kind to little, unwilful, undesigned failings : but he must have judgment to distinguish what *are* or are *not so*. But Mr. H.'s good-humour is softness, as I may call it; and my husband must be such an one, in short, as I need not be ashamed to be seen with in company; one who, being my head, must not be beneath all the gentlemen he may happen to fall in with, and who, every time he is adjusting his mouth for speech, will give me pain at my heart, and blushes in my face, even before he speaks.

I could not bear, therefore, that every one we encountered should be prepared, whenever he offered to open his lips, by their contemptuous smiles, to expect some weak and silly things from him; and when he *had* spoken, that he should, with a booby grin, seem pleased that he had not disappointed them.

The only recommendatory point in Mr. H. is, that he dresses

349

exceedingly smart, and is no contemptible figure of a man. But, dear Madam, you know, that's so much the worse, *when* the man's talent is not taciturnity, except before his aunt, or before Mr. B. or you; *when* he is not conscious of internal defect, and values himself upon outward appearance.

As to his attempts upon your Polly, though I don't like him the better for it, yet it is a fault so wickedly common among men, that when a woman resolves never to marry, till a quite virtuous man addresses her, it is, in other words, resolving to die single: so that I make not this the *chief* objection; and yet, I would abate in my expectations of half a dozen other good qualities, rather than that one of virtue in a husband—But when I reflect upon the figure Mr. H. made in that affair, I cannot bear him; and, if I may judge of other coxcombs by him, what wretches are these smart, well-dressing querpo fellows, many of whom you and I have seen admiring themselves at the plays and operas!

This is one of my infallible rules, and I know it is yours too; that he who is taken up with the admiration of his own person, will never admire a wife's. His delights are centred in himself, and he will not wish to get out of that exceeding narrow circle; and, in my opinion, should keep no company but that of taylors, wig-puffers, and milliners.

But I will run on no further upon this subject; but will tell you a reason, which you *may* give to Lady Davers, why her kind intentions to me cannot be answered; and which she'll take better than what I *have said*, were she to know it, as I hope you won't let her: and this is, my papa has had a proposal made to him from a gentleman you have seen, and have thought polite. It is from Sir W. G. of this county, who is one of your great admirers, and Mr. B.'s too; and that, you must suppose, makes me have never the worse opinion of him, or of his understanding; although it requires no great sagacity or penetration to see how much you adorn our sex, and human nature too.

Every thing was adjusted between my papa and mamma, and Sir William, on condition we approved of each other, before I came down; which I knew not, till I had seen him here four times; and then my papa surprised me into half an approbation of him: and this, it seems, was one of the reasons why I was so hurried down from you. I can't say, but I like the man as well as most I have seen; he is a man of sense and sobriety, to give him his due, in very easy circumstances, and much respected by all who know him; which is no bad earnest in a marriage prospect. But, hitherto, he seems to like me better than I do him. I don't know how it is; but I often observe, that when any thing is in our power, we are not half so much taken with it, as we should be, perhaps, if we were kept in suspense! Why should this be?—But this I am convinced of, there is no comparison between Sir William and Mr. Murray.

Now I have named this brother-in-law of mine; what do you think?—Why, that good couple have had their house on fire three times already. Once it was put out by Mr. Murray's mother, who lives near them; and twice Sir Simon has been forced to carry water to extinguish it; for, truly, Mrs. Murray would go home again to her papa; she would not live with such a surly wretch: and it was with all his heart; a fair riddance! for there was no bearing the house with such an ill-natured wife:—her sister Polly was worth a thousand of her!—I am heartily sorry for their unhappiness. But could she think every body must bear with her, and her fretful ways?—They'll jangle on, I reckon, till they are better used to one another; and when he sees she can't help it, why he'll bear with her, as husbands generally do with ill-tempered wives; he'll try to make himself happy abroad, and leave her to quarrel with her maids, instead of him; for she must have somebody to vent her spleen upon—poor Nancy!—I am glad to hear of Mr. Williams's good fortune.

As Mr. Adams knows not Polly's fault, and it was prevented in time, they may be happy enough. She is a *sly* girl. I always thought her so: something so innocent, and yet so artful in her very looks: she is an odd compound. But these worthy and piously turned young gentlemen, who have but just quitted the college, are mere novices, as to the world: indeed they are *above* it, while *in* it; they therefore give themselves little trouble to study it, and so, depending on the goodness of their own hearts, are more liable to be imposed upon than people of half their understanding.

I think, since he seems to love her, you do right not to hinder the girl's fortune. But I wish she may take your advice, in her behaviour to *him*, at least: for as to her carriage to her neighbours, I doubt she'll be one of the heads of the parish, presently, in her own estimation.

'Tis pity, methinks, any worthy man of the cloth should have a wife, who, by her bad example, should pull down, as fast as he, by a good one, can build up. This is not the case of Mrs. Peters, however; whose example I wish was more generally followed by gentlewomen, who are made so by marrying good clergymen, if they were not so before.

Don't be surprised, if you should hear that poor Jewkes is

given over !—She made a very exemplary—Full of blessings—
And more easy and resigned, than I apprehended she would
be. I know you'll shed a tear for the poor woman :—I can't
help it myself. But you will be pleased that she had so much
time given her, and made so good use of it.

Mr. Peters has been every thing that one would wish one of
his function to be, in his attendance and advice to the poor
woman. Mr. Longman will take proper care of every thing.
So, I will only add, that I am, with the sincerest respect, in
hopes to see you soon (for I have a multitude of things to talk
to you about), dear Mrs. B., *your ever faithful and affectionate*
                                                POLLY DARNFORD.

LETTER LXXXV

From Mrs. B. to Lady Davers.

MY DEAR LADY DAVERS,

I understand from Miss Darnford, that before she went
down from us, her papa had encouraged a proposal made by
Sir W. G. whom you saw, when your ladyship was a kind
visitor in Bedfordshire. We all agreed, if you remember, that
he was a polite and sensible gentleman, and I find it is countenanced on all hands. Poor Mrs. Jewkes, Madam, as Miss informs me, has paid her last debt. I hope, through mercy, she
is happy !—Poor, poor woman ! But why say I so !—Since,
in *that* case, she will be richer than an earthly monarch !

Your ladyship was once mentioning a sister of Mrs. Worden's
whom you wished to recommend to some worthy family.
Shall I beg of you, Madam, to oblige Mr. B.'s in this particular?
I am sure she must have merit if your ladyship thinks well
of her; and your commands in this, as well as in every other
particular in my power, shall have their due weight with *your
ladyship's obliged sister and humble servant*,   P. B.

Just now, dear Madam, Mr. B. tells me I shall have Miss
Goodwin brought me hither to-morrow.

LETTER LXXXVI

From Lady Davers to Mrs. B. in answer to the preceding.

MY DEAR PAMELA,

I am glad Miss Darnford is likely to be so happy in a
husband, as Sir W. G. will certainly make her. I was afraid

that my proposal would not do with her, had she not had so good a tender. I want *too*, to have the foolish fellow married—for several reasons; one of which is, he is continually teasing us to permit him to go up to town, and reside there for some months, in order that he may *see the world*, as he calls it. But we are convinced he would *feel* it, as well as *see* it, if we give way to his request : for in understanding, dress, and inconsiderate vanity, he is so exactly cut out and sized for a town fop, coxcomb, or pretty fellow, that he will undoubtedly fall into all the vices of those people; and, perhaps, having such expectations as he has, will be made the property of rakes and sharpers. He complains that we use him like a child in a go-cart, or a baby with leading-strings, and that he must not be trusted out of our sight. 'Tis a sad thing, that these *bodies* will grow up to the stature of men, when the *minds* improve not at all with them, but are still those of boys and children. Yet, he would certainly make a fond husband : for he has no very bad qualities. But is such a Narcissus !—But this between ourselves, for his uncle is wrapt up in the fellow—And why? Because he is good-humoured, that's all. He has vexed me lately, which makes me write so angrily about him—But 'tis not worth troubling you with the particulars. I hope Mrs. Jewkes is happy, as you say !—Poor woman ! she seemed to promise for a longer life ! But what shall we say?

Your compliment to me, about my Beck's sister, is a very kind one. Mrs. Oldham is a sober, grave widow, a little aforehand, in the world, but not much; has lived well; understands household management thoroughly; is diligent; and has a turn to serious things, which will make you like her the better. I'll order Beck and her to wait on you, and she will satisfy you in every thing as to what you may, or may not expect of her.

You can't think how kindly I take this motion from you. You forget nothing that can oblige your friends. Little did I think you would remember me of (what I had forgotten in a manner) my favourable opinion and wishes for her expressed so long ago.—But you are what you are—a dear obliging creature.

Beck is all joy and gratitude upon it, and her sister had rather serve you than the princess. You need be under no difficulties about terms : she would serve you for nothing, if you would accept of her service.

I am glad, because it pleases you so much, that Miss Goodwin will be soon put into your care. It will be happy for the child, and I hope she will be so dutiful as to give you no pain for your generous goodness to her. Her mamma has sent me a present

353

of some choice products of that climate, with acknowledgments of my kindness to Miss. I will send part of it to you by your new servant; for so I presume to call her already.

What a naughty sister are you, however, to be so far advanced again as to be obliged to shorten your intended excursions, and yet not to send me word of it yourself? Don't you know how much I interest myself in every thing that makes for my brother's happiness and your's? more especially in so material a point as is the increase of a family that it is my boast to be sprung from. Yet I must find this out by accident, and by other hands! —Is not this very slighting!—But never do so again, and I'll forgive you now because of the joy it gives me; who am *your truly affectionate and obliged sister,* B. DAVERS.

I thank you for your book upon the plays you saw. Inclosed is a list of some others, which I desire you to read, and to oblige me with your remarks upon them at your leisure; though you may not, perhaps, have seen them by the time you will favour me with your observations.

LETTER LXXXVII

From Mrs. B. to Lady Davers.

MY DEAR LADY DAVERS,

I have a valuable present made me by the same lady; and therefore hope you will not take it amiss, that, with abundance of thanks, I return your's by Mrs. Worden, whose sister I much approve of, and thank your ladyship for your kind recommendation of so worthy a person. We begin with so much good liking to one another, that I doubt not we shall be very happy together.

A moving letter, much more valuable to me than the handsome present, was put into my hands, at the same time with that; of which the following is a copy:

From Mrs. Wrightson (formerly Miss Sally Godfrey) to Mrs. B.

" HAPPY, DESERVEDLY HAPPY, DEAR LADY,

" Permit these lines to kiss your hands from one, who, though she is a stranger to your person, is not so to your character: *that* has reached us here, in this remote part of the world, where you have as many admirers as have heard of you. But I

354

more particularly am bound to be so, by an obligation which I can never discharge, but by my daily prayers for you, and the blessings I continually implore upon you and yours.

" I can write my whole mind *to* you, though I cannot, from the most deplorable infelicity, receive *from* you the wished-for favour of a few lines in return, written with the same unreservedness : so unhappy am I, from the effects of an inconsideration and weakness on one hand, and temptation on the other, which you, at a tender age, most nobly, for your own honour, and that of your sex, have escaped : whilst I—but let my tears in these blots speak the rest—as my heart bleeds, and has constantly bled ever since, at the grievous remembrance—but believe, however, dear Madam, that 'tis shame and sorrow, and not pride and impenitence, that make me loth to speak out, to so much purity of life and manners, my own odious weakness.

" Nevertheless, I ought, and I *will* accuse myself by name. Imagine then, illustrious lady, truly illustrious for virtues, infinitely superior to all the advantages of birth and fortune !— Imagine, I say, that in this letter, you see before you the *once* guilty, and therefore, I doubt, *always* guilty, but *ever penitent*, Sarah Godfrey; the unhappy, though fond and tender mother of the poor infant, to whom your generous goodness has, I hear, extended itself, so as to make you desirous of taking her under your worthy protection : God for ever bless you for it ! prays an indulgent mother, who admires at an awful distance, that virtue in you, which she could not practise herself.

" And will you, dearest lady, take under your own immediate protection, the poor unguilty infant ? will you love her, for the sake of her suffering mamma, whom you know not; for the sake of the gentleman, now so dear to you, and so worthy of you, as I hear, with pleasure, he is ? And will you, by the best example in the world, give me a moral assurance, that she will never sink into the fault, the weakness, the crime (I ought not to scruple to call it so) of her poor inconsiderate—But you are her mamma *now :* I will not think of a *guilty* one therefore. What a joy is it to me, in the midst of my heavy reflections on my past misconduct, that my beloved Sally can boast a *virtuous* and *innocent mamma*, who has withstood the snares and temptations, that have been so fatal—elsewhere !—and whose example, and instructions, next to God's grace, will be the strongest fences to her honour !—Once more I say, and on my knees I write it, God for ever bless you here, and augment your joys hereafter, for your generous goodness to my poor, and, till now, *motherless* infant.

"I hope she, by her duty and obligingness, will do all in her little power to make you amends, and never give you cause to repent of this your *unexampled* kindness to her and to *me*. She cannot, I hope (except her mother's crime has had an influence upon her, too much like that of an original stain), be of a sordid, or an ungrateful nature. And, O my poor Sally! if you *are*, and if ever you fail in your duty to your new mamma, to whose care and authority I transfer my *whole* right in you, remember that you have no more a mamma in me, nor can you be entitled to my blessing, or my prayers, which I make now, on that *only* condition, your implicit obedience to all your new mamma's commands and directions.

"You may have the curiosity, Madam, to wish to know how I live: for no doubt you have heard all my sad, sad story!—Know, then, that I am as happy, as a poor creature can be, who has once so deplorably, so inexcusably fallen. I have a worthy gentleman for my husband, who married me as a widow, whose only child by my former was the care of her papa's friends, particularly of good Lacy Davers and her brother. Poor unhappy I! to be under such a *sad* necessity to disguise the truth!—Mr. Wrightson (whose name I am unworthily honoured by) has often entreated me to send for the poor child, and to let her be joined as his—killing thought, that it cannot be!—with two children I have by him!—Judge, my good lady, how that very generosity, which, had I been guiltless, would have added to my joys, must wound me deeper than even ungenerous or unkind usage from him could do! and how heavy that crime must lie upon me, which turns my very pleasures to misery, and fixes all the joy I *can* know, in repentance for my past misdeeds! —How happy are you, Madam, on the contrary; you, who have nothing of this sort to pall, nothing to mingle with your felicities! who, blessed in an honour untainted, and a conscience that cannot reproach you, are enabled to enjoy every well deserved comfort, as it offers itself; and can *improve* it too, by reflection on *your* past conduct! While *mine*, alas! like a winter frost, nips in the bud every rising satisfaction.

"My husband is rich as well as generous, and very tender of me—Happy, if I could think *myself* as deserving as *he* thinks me!—My principal comfort, as I hinted, is in my penitence for my past faults; and that I have a merciful God for my judge, who knows that penitence to be sincere!

"You may guess, Madam, from what I have said, in what light I *must* appear here; and if you would favour me with a line or two, in answer to the letter you have now in your hand, it

356

will be one of the greatest pleasures I *can* receive: a pleasure next to that which I *have* received in knowing, that the gentleman you love best, has had the grace to repent of all his evils; has early seen his errors; and has thereby, I hope, freed *two* persons from being, one day, mutual accusers of each other; for now I please myself to think, that the crimes of both may be washed away in the blood of that Saviour God, whom both have so grievously offended!

"May that God, who has not suffered me to be abandoned entirely to my own shame, as I deserved, continue to shower down upon you those blessings, which a virtue like yours may expect from his mercy! May you long be happy in the possession of all you wish! and late, very late (for the good of thousands, I wish this!) may you receive the reward of your piety, your generosity, and your filial, your social, and conjugal virtues! are the prayers of *your most unworthy admirer, and obliged humble servant,*

"SARAH WRIGHTSON.

"Mr. Wrightson begs your acceptance of a small present, part of which can have no value, but what its excelling qualities, for what it is, will give it at so great a distance as that dear England, which I once left with so much shame and regret; but with a laudable purpose, *however*, because I would not incur still *greater* shame, and of consequence give cause for still *greater* regret!"

To this letter, my dear Lady Davers, I have written the following answer, which Mr. B. will take care to have conveyed to her.

"DEAREST MADAM,

"I embrace with great pleasure the opportunity you have so kindly given me, of writing to a lady whose person though I have not the honour to know, yet whose character, and noble qualities, I truly revere.

"I am infinitely obliged to you, Madam, for the precious trust you have reposed in me, and the right you make over to me, of your maternal interest in a child, on whom I set my heart, the moment I saw her.

"Lady Davers, whose love and tenderness for Miss, as well for her mamma's sake, as your late worthy spouse's, had, from her kind opinion of me, consented to grant me this favour: and I was, by Mr. B.'s leave, in actual possession of my

357

pretty ward about a week before your kind letter came to my hands.

" As I had been long very solicitous for this favour, judge how welcome your kind concurrence was : and the rather, as, had I known, that a letter from you was on the way to me, I should have feared you would insist upon depriving the surviving friends of her dear papa, of the pleasure they take in the dear child. Indeed, Madam, I believe we should one and all have joined to disobey you, had *that* been the case ; and it is a great satisfaction to us, that we are not under so hard a necessity, as to dispute with a tender mamma the possession of her own child.

" Assure yourself, worthiest Madam, of a care and tenderness in me to the dear child truly maternal, and answerable, as much as in my power, to the trust you repose in me. The little boy, that God has given me, shall not be more dear to me than my sweet Miss Goodwin shall be ; and my care, by God's grace, shall extend to her *future* as well as to her *present* prospects, that she may be worthy of that piety, and *truly* religious excellence, which I admire in your character.

" We all rejoice, dear Madam, in the account you give of your present happiness. It was impossible that God Almighty should desert a lady so exemplarily deserving ; and he certainly conducted you in your resolutions to abandon every thing that you loved in England, after the loss of your dear spouse, because it seems to have been his intention that you should reward the merit of Mr. Wrightson, and meet with your own reward in so doing.

" Miss is very fond of my little Billy : she is a charming child, is easy and genteel in her shape, and very pretty ; she dances finely, has a sweet air, and is improving every day in music ; works with her needle, and reads admirably for her years ; and takes a delight in both, which gives me no small pleasure. But she is not very forward in her penmanship, as you will see by what follows : the inditing too is her own ; but in that, and the writing, she took a good deal of time, on a separate paper.

" Dearest dear Mamma,

"Your Sally is full of joy, to have any commands from her honoured mamma. I promise to follow all your directions. Indeed, and upon my word, I will. You please me mightily in giving me so dear a new mamma here. Now I know indeed I have a mamma, and I will love and obey her, as if she was you your own self. Indeed I will. You must always bless me, because I will be always good. I hope you will believe me,

358

because I am above telling fibs. I am, my honoured mamma on the other side of the water, and ever will be, as if you was here, *your dutiful daughter,*

"SALLY GOODWIN."

"Miss (permit me, dear Madam, to subjoin) is a very good tempered child, easy to be persuaded, and I hope loves me dearly; and I will endeavour to make her love me better and better; for on that love will depend the regard which, I hope, she will pay to all I shall say and do for her good.

"Repeating my acknowledgments for the kind trust you repose in me, and with thanks for the valuable present you have sent me, we all here join in respects to worthy Mr. Wrightson, and in wishing you, Madam, a continuance and increase of worldly felicity; and I particularly beg leave to assure you, that I am, and ever will be, with the highest respect and gratitude, though personally unknown, dearest Madam, *the affectionate admirer of your piety, and your obliged humble servant,*

"P. B."

Your ladyship will see how I was circumscribed and limited; otherwise I would have said (what I have mentioned more than once), how I admire and honour her for her penitence, and for that noble resolution, which enabled her to do what thousands could not have had the heart to do, abandon her country, her relations, friends, baby, and all that was dear to her, as well as the seducer, whom she too well loved, and hazard the sea, the dangers of pirates, and possibly of other wicked attempters of the mischievous sex, in a world she knew nothing of, among strangers; and all to avoid repeating a sin she had been unhappily drawn into; and for which she still abhors herself.

Must not such a lady as this, dear Madam, have as much merit as many even of those, who, having not had her temptations, have not fallen? This, at least, one may aver, that next to not committing an error, is the resolution to retrieve it all that one may, to repent of it, and studiously to avoid the repetition. But who, besides this excellent Mrs. Wrightson, having so fallen, and being still so ardently solicited and pursued, (and flattered, perhaps, by fond hopes, that her spoiler would one day do her all the justice he *could*—for who can do complete justice to a woman he has robbed of her honour?)—could resolve as she resolved, and act as she acted? Miss Goodwin is a sweet child; but, permit me to say, has a little of her papa's spirit; hasty, yet generous and acknowledging when she is convinced of her fault; a little haughtier and prouder than I wish her to be; but in every thing else deserves the character I give of her to her mamma.

She is very fond of fine clothes, is a little too lively to the servants.—Told me once, when I took notice that softness and mildness of speech became a young lady, that they were *but* servants! and she could say no more than, "Pray," and "I desire," and "I wish you'd be so kind," to her uncle or to me.

I told her, that good servants deserved any civil distinctions; and that so long as they were ready to oblige in every thing, by a kind word, it would be very wrong to give them imperative ones, which could serve for no other end but to convince observers of the haughtiness of one's own temper; and looked, as if one would question their compliance with our wills, unless we would exact it with an high hand; which might cast a slur upon the command we gave, as if we thought it was hardly so reasonable as otherwise to obtain their observation of it.

"Besides, my dear," said I, "you don't consider, that if you speak as haughtily and commandingly to them on common, as on extraordinary occasions, you weaken your own authority, if even you should be permitted to have any, and they'll regard you no more in the one case than in the other."

She takes great notice of what I say, and when her little proud heart is subdued by reasonings she cannot answer, she will sit as if she were studying what to say, to come off as flying as she can, and as the case requires, I let her go off easily, or push the little dear to her last refuge, and make her quit her post, and yield up her spirit a captive to Reason and Discretion : two excellent commanders, with whom, I tell her, I must bring her to be intimately acquainted.

Yet, after all, till I can be sure that I can inspire her with the love of virtue, for its *own* sake, I will rather try to conduct her spirit to proper ends, than endeavour totally to subdue it; being sensible that our passions are given us for excellent ends, and that they may, by a proper direction, be made subservient to the noblest purposes.

I tell her sometimes, there may be a decent pride in humility, and that it is very possible for a young lady to behave with so much *true* dignity, as shall command respect by the turn of her eye, sooner than by asperity of speech; that she may depend upon it, the person, who is always finding faults, frequently causes them; and that it is no glory to be better born than servants, if she is not better behaved too.

360

Besides, I tell her humility is a grace that shines in a *high* condition, but cannot equally in a *low* one; because that is already too much humbled, perhaps: and that, though there is a censure lies against being *poor and proud*, yet I would rather forgive pride in a poor body, than in a rich: for in the rich it is insult and arrogance, proceeding from their high condition; but in the poor it may be a defensative against dishonesty, and may shew a natural bravery of mind, perhaps, if properly directed, and manifested on right occasions, that the frowns of fortune cannot depress.

She says she hears every day things from me, which her governess never taught her.

That may very well be, I tell her, because her governess has *many* young ladies to take care of: I but *one;* and that I want to make her wise and prudent betimes, that she may be an example to other Misses; and that governesses and mammas shall say to their Misses, "When will you be like Miss Goodwin? Do you ever hear Miss Goodwin say a naughty word? Would Miss Goodwin, think you, have done so or so?"

She threw her arms about my neck, on one such occasion as this: "Oh," said she, "what a charming mamma have I got! I will be in every thing as like you, as ever I can!—and then you will love me, and so will my uncle, and so will every body else."

Mr. B. whom now-and-then, she says, she loves as well as if he was her own papa, sees with pleasure how we go on. But she tells me, I must not have any daughter but her, and is very jealous on the occasion about which your ladyship so kindly reproaches me.

There is a pride, you know, Madam, in some of our sex, that serves to useful purposes, is a good defence against improper matches, and mean actions; and is not wholly to be subdued, for that reason: for, though it is not *virtue*, yet, if it can be virtue's *substitute*, in high, rash, and inconsiderate minds, it may turn to good account. So I will not quite discourage my dear pupil neither, till I see what discretion, and riper years, may add to her distinguishing faculty. For, as some have no notion of pride, separate from imperiousness and arrogance, so others know no difference between humility and meanness.

There is a golden mean in every thing; and if it please God to spare us both, I will endeavour to point her passions, and such even of those foibles, which seem too deeply rooted to be soon eradicated, to useful purposes; choosing to imitate physicians, who, in certain chronical illnesses, as I have read in Lord Bacon, rather proceed by palliatives, than by harsh extirpatives, which, through the resistance given to them by the constitution, may create such ferments in it, as may destroy that health it was their intention to establish.

But whither am I running?—Your ladyship, I hope, will excuse this parading freedom of my pen : for though these notions are well enough with regard to Miss Goodwin, they must be very impertinent to a lady, who can so much better instruct Miss's tutoress than that vain tutoress can her pupil. And, therefore, with my humblest respects to my good Lord Davers, and your noble neighbours, and to Mr. H. I hasten to conclude myself *your ladyship's obliged sister, and obedient servant,*

P. B.

Your Billy, Madam, is a charming dear !—I long to have you see him. He sends you a kiss upon this paper. You'll see it stained, just here. The charmer has cut two teeth, and is about more : so you'll excuse the dear, pretty, slabbering boy. Miss Goodwin is ready to eat him with love : and Mr. B. is fonder and fonder of us all : and then your ladyship, and my good Lord Davers love us too. O, Madam, what a blessed creature am I !

Miss Goodwin begs I'll send her duty to her *noble* uncle and aunt; that's her just distinction always, when she speaks of you both. She asked me, pretty dear, just now, If I think there is such a happy girl in the world as she is? I tell her, God always blesses good Misses, and makes them happier and happier.

LETTER LXXXVIII

My dear Lady Davers,

I have three marriages to acquaint you with, in one letter. In the first place, Sir W. G. has sent, by the particular desire of my dear friend, that he was made one of the happiest men in England, on the 18th past; and so I have no longer my Miss Darnford to boast of. I have a very good opinion of the gentleman; but if he be but half so good a husband as she will make a wife, they will be exceedingly happy in one another.

Mr. Williams's marriage to a kinswoman of his noble patron (as you have heard was in treaty) is the next; and there is great reason to believe, from the character of both, that they will likewise do credit to the state.

The third is Mr. Adams and Polly Barlow; and I wish them, for both their sakes, as happy as either of the former. They are set out to his living, highly pleased with one another; and I hope will have reason to continue so to be.

As to the first, I did not indeed think the affair would have been so soon concluded; and Miss kept it off so long, as I understood, that her papa was angry with her: and, indeed, as the gentleman's family, circumstances, and character, were such, that there could lie no objection against him, I think it would have been wrong to have delayed it.

I should have written to your ladyship before; but have been favoured with Mr. B.'s company into Kent, on a visit to my good mother, who was indisposed. We tarried there a week, and left both my dear parents, to my thankful satisfaction, in as good health as ever they were in their lives.

Mrs. Judy Swynford, or Miss Swynford (as she refuses not being called, now and then), has been with us for this week past; and she expects her brother, Sir Jacob, to fetch her away in about a week hence.

It does not become me to write the least word that may appear disrespectful of any person related to your ladyship and Mr. B. Otherwise I should say, that the B—s and the S—s are directly the opposites of one another. But yet, as she never saw your ladyship but once, you will forgive me to mention a word or two about her, because she is a character that is in a manner new to me.

She is a maiden lady, as you know, and though she will not part with the green leaf from her hand, one sees by the grey-goose down on her brows and her head, that she cannot be less than fifty-five. But so much pains does she take, by powder, to have never a dark hair in her head, because she has one half of them white, that I am sorry to see, what is a subject for reverence, should be deemed, by the good lady, matter of concealment.

She is often seemingly reproaching herself, that she is an *old maid*, and an *old woman;* but it is very discernible, that she expects a compliment, that she is *not so*, every time she is so free with herself: and if nobody makes her one, she will say something of that sort in her own behalf.

She takes particular care, that of all the public transactions which happen to be talked of, her memory will never carry her back above thirty years! and then it is—" About thirty years ago; when I was a girl," or " when I was in hanging sleeves; " and so she makes herself, for twenty years of her life, a very useless and insignificant person.

If her teeth, which, for her age, are very good, though not

over white (and which, by her care of them, she seems to look upon as the last remains of her better days), would but fail, it might help her to a conviction, that would set her ten years forwarder at least. But, poor lady, she is so *young*, in spite of her wrinkles, that I am really concerned for her affectation; because it exposes her to the remarks and ridicule of the gentlemen, and gives one pain for her.

Surely, these ladies don't act prudently at all; since, for every year Mrs. Judy would take from her age, her censurers add two to it; and, behind her back, make her going on towards seventy; whereas, if she would lay claim to her *reverentials*, as I may say, and not try to conceal her age, she would have many compliments for looking so well at her years.—And many a young body would hope to be the better for her advice and experience, who now are afraid of affronting her, if they suppose she has lived much longer in the world than themselves.

Then she looks back to the years she owns, when more flippant ladies, at the laughing time of her life, delight to be frolic : she tries to sing too, although, if ever she had a voice, she has outlived it; and her songs are of so antique a date, that they would betray her; only, as she says, they were learnt her by her grandmother, who was a fine lady at the Restoration. She will join in a dance; and though her limbs move not so pliantly as might be expected of a lady no older than she would be thought, and whose dancing-days are not entirely over, yet that was owing to a fall from her horse some years ago, which, she doubts, she shall never recover, though she finds she grows better and better, *every year*.

Thus she loses the respect, the reverence, she might receive, were it not for this miserable affectation; takes pains, by aping youth, to make herself unworthy of her years, and is content to be thought less discreet than she might otherwise be deemed, for fear she should be imagined older if she appeared wiser.

What a sad thing is this, Madam !—What a mistaken conduct ! We pray to live to old age; and it is promised as a blessing, and as a reward for the performance of certain duties; and yet, when we come to it, we had rather be thought as foolish as youth, than to be deemed wise, and in possession of it. And so we shew how little we deserve what we have been so long coveting; and yet covet on : for what? Why, to be more and more ashamed, and more and more unworthy of that we covet !

How fantastic a character is this !—Well may irreverent, unthinking youth despise, instead of revere, the hoary head which the wearer is so much ashamed of. The lady boasts a relationship to you, and Mr. B. and, I think, I am very bold. But my reverence for years, and the disgust I have to see anybody behave unworthy of them, makes me take the greater liberty : which, however, I shall wish I had not taken, if it meets not with that allowance, which I have always had from your ladyship in what I write.

God knows whether ever I may enjoy the blessing I so much revere in others. For now my heavy time approaches. But I was so apprehensive before, and so troublesome to my best friends, with my vapourish fears, that now (with a perfect resignation to the Divine Will) I will only add, that I am *your ladyship's most obliged sister and servant,*   P. B.

My dear Billy, and Miss Goodwin, improve every day, and are all I can desire or expect them to be. Could Miss's poor mamma be here with a wish, and back again, how much would she be delighted with one of our afternoon conferences; our Sunday employments especially !—And let me add, that I am very happy in another young gentleman of the dean's recommending, instead of Mr. Adams.

LETTER LXXXIX

My dearest Lady,

I am once more, blessed be God for all his mercies to me ! enabled, on my upsitting, to thank you, and my noble lord, for all your kind solicitudes for my welfare. Billy every day improves. Miss is all I wish her to be, and my second dear boy continues to be as lovely and as fine a baby as your ladyship was pleased to think him; and their papa, the best of husbands !

I am glad to hear Lady Betty is likely to be so happy. Mr. B. says, her noble admirer is as worthy a gentleman as any in the peerage; and I beg of you to congratulate the dear lady, and her noble parents, in my name, if I should be at a distance, when the nuptials are celebrated.

I have had the honour of a visit from my lady, the Countess Dowager, on occasion of her leaving the kingdom for a year or two, for which space she designs to reside in Italy, principally at Naples or Florence; a design she took up some time ago, but which it seems she could not conveniently put into execution till now.

Mr. B. was abroad when her ladyship came, and I expected him not till the next day. She sent her gentleman, the preceding evening, to let me know that business had brought her as far as Wooburn; and if it would not be unacceptable, she would pay her respects to me at breakfast, the next morning, being speedily to leave England. I returned, that I should be very proud of that honour. And about ten her ladyship came.

She was exceedingly fond of my two boys, the little man, and the pretty baby, as she called them; and I had very different emotions from the expression of her love to Billy, and her visit to me, from what I had once before. She was sorry, she said, Mr. B. was abroad; though her business was principally with me. "For, Mrs. B.," said she, "I come to tell you all that passed between Mr. B. and myself, that you may not think worse of either of us, than we deserve; and I could not leave England till I had waited on you for this purpose; and yet, perhaps, from the distance of time, you'll think it needless now. And, indeed, I should have waited on you before, to have cleared up my character with you, had I thought I should have been so long kept on this side of the water."—I said, I was very sorry I had ever been uneasy, when I had two persons of so much honour—"Nay," said she, interrupting me, "you have no need to apologize; things looked bad enough, as they were presented to you, to justify greater uneasiness than you expressed."

She asked me, who that pretty genteel Miss was?—I said, a relation of Lord Davers, who was entrusted lately to my care. "Then, Miss," said her ladyship, and kissed her, "you are very happy."

Believing the Countess was desirous of being alone with me, I said, "My dear Miss Goodwin, won't you go to your little nursery, my love?" for so she calls my last blessing—"You'd be sorry the baby should cry for you." For she was so taken with the charming lady, that she was loth to leave us—But, on my saying this, withdrew.

When we were alone, the Countess began her story, with a sweet confusion, which added to her loveliness. She said she would be brief, because she should exact all my attention, and not suffer me to interrupt her till she had done. She began with acknowledging, that she thought, when she first saw Mr. B. at the masquerade, that he was the finest gentleman she had ever seen; that the allowed freedoms of the place had made her take liberties in following him, and engaging him wherever he went. She blamed him very freely for passing for a single man; for that, she said, since she had so splendid a fortune of her own, was all she was solicitous about; having never, as

366

she confessed, seen a man she could like so well; her former marriage having been in some sort forced upon her, at an age when she knew not how to distinguish; and that she was very loth to believe him married, even when she had no reason to doubt it. "Yet this I must say," said she, "I never heard a man, when he owned he was married, express himself with more affectionate regard and fondness than he did of you; which made me long to see you; for I had a great opinion of those personal advantages which every one flattered me with; and was very unwilling to yield the palm of beauty to you.

"I believe you will censure me, Mrs. B., for permitting his visits after I knew he was married. To be sure, that was a thoughtless, and a faulty part of my conduct. But the world's saucy censures, and my friends' indiscreet interposals, incensed me; and, knowing the uprightness of my own heart, I was resolved to disgrace both, when I found they could not think worse of me than they did.

"I am naturally of a high spirit, impatient of contradiction, always gave myself freedoms, for which, satisfied with my own innocence, I thought myself above being accountable to any body—And then Mr. B. has such noble sentiments, a courage and fearlessness, which I saw on more occasions than one, that all ladies who know the weakness of their own sex, and how much they want the protection of the brave, are taken with. Then his personal address was so peculiarly distinguishing, that having an opinion of his honour, I was embarrassed greatly how to deny myself his conversation; although, you'll pardon me, Mrs. B., I began to be afraid that my reputation might suffer in the world's opinion for the indulgence.

"Then, when I had resolved, as I did several times, to see him no more, some unforeseen accident threw him in my way again, at one entertainment or other; for I love balls and concerts, and public diversions, perhaps, better than I ought; and then I had all my resolves to begin again. Yet this I can truly say, whatever his views were, I never heard from him the least indecent expression, nor saw in his behaviour to me much to apprehend; saving, I began to fear, that by his insinuating address, and noble manner, I should be too much in his power, and too little in my own, if I went on so little doubting, and so little alarmed, if ever he should avow dishonourable designs.

"I had often lamented, that our sex were prohibited, by the designs of the other upon their honour, and by the world's censures, from conversing with the same ease and freedom with gentlemen, as with one another. And when once I asked myself, to what this conversation might tend at last? and where the pleasure each seemed to take in the other's, might possibly end? I resolved to break it off; and told him my resolution next time I saw him. But he stopped my mouth with a romantic notion, as I since think it, (though a sorry plea will have weight in favour of a proposal, to which one has no aversion) of Platonic love; and we had an intercourse by letters, to the number of six or eight, I believe, on that and other subjects.

"Yet all this time, I was the less apprehensive, because he always spoke so tenderly, and even with delight, whenever he mentioned his lady; and I could not find, that you were at all alarmed at our acquaintance: for I never scrupled to send my letters, by my own livery, to your house, sealed with my own seal. At last, indeed, he began to tell me, that from the sweetest and evenest temper in the world, you seemed to be leaning towards melancholy, were always in tears, or shewed you had been weeping, when he came home; and that you did not make his return to you so agreeable as he used to find it.

"I asked if it were not owing to some alteration in his own temper? If you might not be uneasy at our acquaintance, and at his frequent absence from you, and the like? He answered, No; that you were above disguises, were of a noble and frank nature, and would have hinted it to him, if you had. This, however, when I began to think seriously of the matter, gave me but little satisfaction; and I was more and more convinced, that my honour required it of me, to break off this intimacy.

"And although I permitted Mr. B. to go with me to Tunbridge, when I went to take a house there, yet I was uneasy, as he saw. And, indeed, so was he, though he tarried a day or two longer than he designed, on account of a little excusion my sister and her lord, and he and I, made into Sussex, to see an estate I thought of purchasing; for he was so good as to look into my affairs, and has put them upon an admirable establishment.

"His uneasiness, I found, was upon your account, and he sent you a letter to excuse himself for not waiting on you on Saturday, and to say, he would dine with you on Monday. And I remember when I said, 'Mr. B., you seem to be chagrined at something; you are more thoughtful than usual:' his answer was, 'Madam, you are right, Mrs. B. and I have had a little misunderstanding. She is so solemn, and so melancholy of late, I fear it will be no difficult matter to put her out of her right mind: and I love her so well, that then I should hardly keep my own.'

368

" ' Is there no reason, think you,' said I, ' to imagine that your acquaintance with me gives her uneasiness? You know, Mr. B., how that villain T.' (a man," said she, " whose insolent address I rejected with the contempt it deserved) ' has slandered us. How know you, but he has found a way to your wife's ear, as he has done to my uncle's, and to all my friends'? And if so, it is best for us both to discontinue a friendship, that may be attended with disagreeable consequences.'

" He said, he should find it out on his return. ' And will you,' said I, ' ingenuously acquaint me with the issue of your inquiries? for,' added I, ' I never beheld a countenance, in so young a lady, that seemed to mean more than Mrs. B.'s, when I saw her in town; and notwithstanding her prudence I could see a reserve and thoughtfulness in it, that, if it was not natural to it, must indicate too much.'

" He wrote to me, in a very moving letter, the issue of your conference, and referred to some papers of your's, that he would shew me, as soon as he could procure them, they being of your own hands; and let me know that T. was the accuser, as I had suspected.

" In brief, Madam, when you went down into Kent, he read to me some part of your account to Lady Davers, of your informant and information; your apprehensions; your prudence; your affection for him; the reason of your melancholy; and, to all appearance, reason enough you had, especially from the letter of Thomasine Fuller, which was one of T.'s vile forgeries: for though we had often, for argument's sake, talked of polygamy (he arguing for it, I against it), yet had not Mr. B. *dared*, nor was he inclined, I verily believe, to propose any such thing to me: no, Madam, I was not so much abandoned to a sense of honour, as to give reason for any one, but my impertinent and foolish uncle, to impute such a folly to me; and he had so behaved to me, that I cared not what *he* thought.

" Then, what he read to me, here and there, as he pleased, gave me reason to admire you for your generous opinion of one you had so much seeming cause to be afraid of: he told me his apprehensions, from your uncommon manner, that your mind was in some degree affected, and your strange proposal of parting with a husband every one knows you so dearly love: and we agreed to forbear seeing each other, and all manner of correspondence, except by letter, for one month, till some of my affairs were settled, which had been in great disorder, and were in his kind management then; and I had not one relation, whom I cared to trouble with them, because of their treatment of me on Mr. B.'s account. And this, I told him, should not be neither, but through your hands, and with your consent.

" And thus, Madam," said her ladyship, " have I told you the naked truth of the whole affair. I have seen Mr. B. very seldom since : and when I have, it has been either at a horse-race, in the open field, or at some public diversion, by accident, where only distant civilities have passed between us.

" I respect him greatly; you must allow me to say that. Except in the article of permitting me to believe, for some time, that he was a single gentleman, a fault he cannot be excused for, and which made me heartily quarrel with him, when I first knew it, he has behaved to me with so much generosity and honour, that I could have wished I had been of his sex, since he had a lady so much more deserving than myself; and then, had he had the same esteem for me, there never would have been a more perfect friendship. I am now going," continued she, " to embark for France, and shall pass a year or two in Italy; and then I shall, I hope, return as solid, as grave, as circumspect, though not so wise, as Mrs. B."

Thus the Countess concluded her narrative : I said, I was greatly obliged to her for the honour of this visit, and the kind and considerate occasion of it : but that Mr. B. had made me entirely happy in every particular, and had done her ladyship the justice she so well deserved, having taken upon himself the blame of passing as a single man at his first acquaintance with her.

I added, that I could hope her ladyship might be prevented, by some happy man, from leaving a kingdom, to which she was so great an ornament, as well by her birth, her quality and fortune, as by her perfections of person and mind.

She said, she had not been the happiest of her sex in her former marriage : although nobody, her youth considered, thought her a bad wife; and her lord's goodness to her, at his death, had demonstrated his own favourable opinion of her by deeds, as he had done by words upon all occasions : but that she was yet young; a little too gay and unsettled : and had her head turned towards France and Italy, having passed some time in those countries, which she thought of with pleasure, though then only twelve or thirteen : that for this reason, and having been on a late occasion still more unsettled (looking down with blushes, which often overspread her face, as she talked), she had refused some offers, not despicable : that indeed Lord C. threatened to follow her to Italy, in hopes of meeting better success there, than he had met with here : but if he did, though she would make no resolutions, she might be too much offended with him, to give him reason to boast of his journey; and this the rather, as she believed he had once entertained no very honourable notions of her friendship for Mr. B.

She wished to see Mr. B. and to take leave of him, but not out of my company, she was pleased to say.—" Your ladyship's consideration for me," replied I, " lays me under high obligation; but indeed, Madam, there is no occasion for it, from any diffidences I have in your's or Mr. B.'s honour. And if you will give me the pleasure of knowing when it will be most acceptable, I will beg of Mr. B. to oblige me with his company to return this favour, the first visit I make abroad."

" You are very kind, Mrs. B.," said she : " but I think to go to Tunbridge for a fortnight, when I have disposed of every thing for my embarkation, and so set out from thence. And if you should then be both in Kent, I should be glad to take you at your word."

To be sure, I said, Mr. B. at least, would attend her ladyship there, if any thing should happen to deprive me of that honour.

" You are very obliging," said she, " I take great concern to myself, for having caused you a moment's uneasiness formerly : but I must now try to be circumspect, in order to retrieve my character, which has been so basely traduced by that presumptuous fellow Turner, who hoped, I suppose, by that means, to bring me down to his level."

Her ladyship would not be prevailed upon to stay dinner; and, saying she would be at Wooburn all the next day, took a very tender leave of me, wishing me all manner of happiness, as I did her.

Mr. B. came home in the evening, and next morning rode to Wooburn, to pay his respects to the Countess, and came back in the evening.

Thus happily, and to the satisfaction of all three, as I hope, ended this perplexing affair.

Mr. B. asks me how I relish Mr. Locke's *Treatise on Education*? which he put into my hands some time since, as I told your ladyship. I answered, Very well; and I thought it an excellent piece in the main.

" I'll tell you," said he, " what you shall do. You have not shewed me any thing you have written for a good while. I could wish you to fill up your leisure-time with your observations on that treatise, that I may know what you can object to it ; for you say *in the main*, which shews, that you do not entirely approve of every part of it."

371

"But will not that be presumptuous, Sir?"

"I admire Mr. Locke," replied he; "and I admire my Pamela. I have no doubt of his excellencies, but I want to know the sentiments of a young mother, as well as of a learned gentleman, upon the subject of education; because I have heard several ladies censure some part of his regimen, when I am convinced, that the fault lies in their own over-great fondness for their children."

"As to myself, Sir, who, in the early part of my life, have not been brought up too tenderly, you will hardly meet with any objection to the part which I imagine you have heard most objected to by ladies who have been more indulgently treated in their first stage. But there are a few other things that want clearing up to my understanding; but, which, however, may be the fault of that."

"Then, my dear," said he, "suppose me at a distance from you, cannot you give me your remarks in the same manner, as if you were writing to Lady Davers, or to Miss Darnford, that was?"

"Yes, Sir, depending on your kind favour to me, I believe I could."

"Do then; and the less restraint you write with, the more I shall be pleased with it. But I confine you not to time or place. We will make our excursions as I once proposed; and do you write to me now-and-then upon the subject; for the places and remarkables you will see, will be new only to yourself; nor will either of those ladies expect from you an itinerary, or a particular description of countries, which are better described by authors who have made it their business to treat upon those subjects. By this means, you will be usefully employed in your own way, which may turn to good account to us both, and to the dear children, which it may please God to bestow upon us."

"You don't expect, Sir, any thing regular, or digested from me."

"I don't, my dear. Let your fancy and your judgment be both employed, and I require no method; for I know, in your easy, natural way, that would be a confinement, which would cramp your genius, and give what you write a stiff, formal air, that I might expect in a pedagogue, but not in my Pamela."

"Well, but, Sir, although I may write nothing to the purpose, yet if Lady Davers desires it, you will allow me to transmit what I shall write to her, when you have perused it yourself? For your good sister is so indulgent to my scribble, she will expect to be always hearing from me; and this way I shall oblige her ladyship while I obey her brother."

"With all my heart," he was pleased to say.

So, my lady, I shall now-and-then pay my respects to you in the writing way, though I must address myself, it seems, to my dearest Mr. B.; and I hope to be received on these my own terms, since they are your brother's also, and, at the same time, such as will convince you, how much I wish to approve myself, to the best of my poor ability, *your ladyship's most obliged sister, and humble servant,*

P. B.

LETTER XC

My dearest Mr. B.,

I have been considering of your commands, in relation to Mr. Locke's book, and since you are pleased to give me time to acquit myself of the task, I shall beg to include in a little book my humble sentiments, as I did to Lady Davers, in that I shewed you in relation to the plays I had seen. And since you confine me not to time or place, I may be three or four years in completing it, because I shall reserve some subjects to my further experience in children's ways and tempers, and in order to benefit myself by the good instructions I shall receive from your delightful conversation, in that compass of time, if God spare us to one another : and then it will, moreover, be still worthier of the perusal of the most honoured and best beloved of all my correspondents, much honoured and beloved as they all are.

I must needs say, my dear Mr. B., that this is a subject to which I was always particularly attentive; and among the charities your bountiful heart permits me to dispense to the poor and indigent, I have had always a watchful eye upon the children of such, and endeavoured, by questions put to them, as well as to their parents, to inform myself of their little ways and tempers, and how nature delights to work in different minds, and how it might be pointed to their good, according to their respective capacities; and I have for this purpose erected, with your approbation, a little school of seven or eight children, among which is four in the earliest stages, when they can but just speak, and call for what they want and love : and I am not a little pleased to observe, when I visit them in their school time that principles of goodness and virtue may be instilled into their little hearts much earlier than is usually imagined. And why should it not be so ? for may not the child, that can tell its wants, and make known its inclination, be easily made sensible of *yours,* and what you expect from it, provided you take a proper method ? For, sometimes, signs and tokens (and even looks), uniformly practised, will do as well as words; as we see in such of the young of the brute creation as we are disposed to domesticate, and to teach to practise those little tricks, of which the aptness or docility of their natures makes them capable.

But yet, dearest Sir, I know not enough of the next stage, the *maturer* part of life, to touch upon that as I wish to do: and yet there is a natural connection and progression from the one to the other: and I would not be thought a vain creature, who believes herself equal to *every* subject, because she is indulged with the good opinion of her friends, in a *few*, which are supposed to be within her own capacity.

For, I humbly conceive, that it is no small point of wisdom to know, and not to mistake, one's own talents: and for this reason, permit me, Sir, to suspend, till I am better qualified for it, even my own proposal of beginning my little book; and, in the mean time, to touch upon a few places of the admirable author, that seem to me to warrant another way of thinking, than that which he prescribes.

But, dear Sir, let me premise, that all that your dear babies can demand of my attention for some time to come, is their health; and God has blessed them with such sound limbs, and, to all appearances, good constitutions, that I have very little to do, but to pray for them every time I pray for their dear papa; and that is hourly; and yet not so often as you confer upon me benefits and favours, and new obligations, even to the prevention of all my wishes, were I to sit down and study for what must be the next.

As to this point of *health*, Mr. Locke gives these plain and easy to be observed rules.

He prescribes first, *plenty of open air*. That this is right, the infant will inform one, who, though it cannot speak, will make signs to be carried abroad, and is never so well pleased, as when enjoying the open and free air; for which reason I conclude, that this is one of those natural pointings, as I may say, that are implanted in every creature, teaching it to choose its good, and to avoid its evil.

Sleep is the next, which he enjoins to be indulged to its utmost extent: an admirable rule, as I humbly conceive; since sound sleep is one of the greatest nourishers of nature, both to the *once* young and to the *twice* young, if I may use the phrase. And I the rather approve of this rule, because it keeps the nurse unemployed, who otherwise may be doing it the greatest mischief, by cramming and stuffing its little bowels, till ready to burst. And, if I am right, what an inconsiderate and foolish,

374

as well as pernicious practice it is, for a nurse to *waken* the child from its nourishing sleep, for fear it should suffer by hunger, and instantly pop the breast into its pretty mouth, or provoke it to feed, when it has no inclination to either, and for want of digestion, must have its nutriment turned to repletion, and bad humours !

Excuse me, dear Sir, these lesser particulars. Mr. Locke begins with them; and surely they may be allowed in a young *mamma*, writing (however it be to a gentleman of genius and learning) to a *papa*, on a subject, that in its lowest beginnings ought not to be unattended to by either. I will therefore pursue my excellent author without farther apology, since you have put his work into my hands.

The next thing, then, which he prescribes, is *plain diet*. This speaks for itself, for the baby can have no corrupt taste to gratify : all is pure, as out of the hand of Nature; and what is not plain and natural, must vitiate and offend.

Then, *no wine*, or *strong drink*. Equally just; and for the same reasons.

Little or *no physic*. Undoubtedly right. For the *use* of physic, without necessity, or by way of *precaution*, as some call it, begets the *necessity* of physic; and the very *word* supposes *distemper* or *disorder ;* and where there is none, would a parent beget one; or, by frequent use, render the salutary force of medicine ineffectual, when it was wanted?

Next, he forbids *too warm* and *too strait clothing*. This is just as I wish it. How often has my heart ached, when I have seen poor babies rolled and swathed, ten or a dozen times round ; then blanket upon blanket, mantle upon that; its little neck pinned down to one posture; its head, more than it frequently needs, triple-crowned like a young pope, with covering upon covering ; its legs and arms, as if to prevent that kindly stretching, which we rather ought to promote, when it is in health, and which is only aiming at growth and enlargement, the former bundled up, the latter pinned down ; and how the poor thing lies on the nurse's lap, a miserable little pinioned captive, goggling and staring with its eyes, the only organ it has at liberty, as if supplicating for freedom to its fettered limbs ! Nor has it any comfort at all, till with a sigh or two, like a dying deer, it drops asleep ; and happy then will it be till the officious nurse's care shall awaken it for its undesired food, as if resolved to try its constitution, and willing to see how many difficulties it could overcome.

Then he advises, that the head and feet should be kept cold ; and the latter often used to cold water, and exposed to wet, in order to lay the foundation, as he says, of an healthy and hardy constitution.

Now, Sir, what a pleasure it is to your Pamela, that her notions, and her practice too, fall in so exactly with this learned gentleman's advice that, excepting one article, which is, that your Billy has not yet been accustomed to be *wet-shod*, every other particular has been observed! And don't you see what a charming, charming baby he is?—Nay, and so is your little Davers, for his age—pretty soul!

Perhaps some, were they to see this, would not be so ready, as I know *you* will be, to excuse me; and would be apt to say, " What nursery impertinences are these to trouble a man with ! " —But with all their wisdom, they would be mistaken; for if a child has not good health, (and are not these rules the moral foundation, as I may say, of that blessing?) its animal organs will play but poorly in a weak or crazy case. These, therefore, are necessary rules to be observed for the first two or three years : for then the little buds of their minds will begin to open, and their watchful mamma will be employed like a skilful gardener, in assisting and encouraging the charming flower through its several hopeful stages to perfection, when it shall become one of the principal ornaments of that delicate garden, your honoured family. Pardon me, Sir, if in the above paragraph I am too figurative. I begin to be afraid I am out of my sphere, writing to your dear self, on these important subjects.

But be that as it may, I will here put an end to this my first letter (on the earliest part of my subject), rejoicing in the opportunity you have given me of producing a fresh instance of that duty and affection, wherewith I am, and shall ever be, my dearest Mr. B., *your grateful, happy*,

P. B.

LETTER XCI

I will now, my dearest, my best beloved correspondent of all, begin, since the tender age of my dear babies will not permit me to have an eye yet to their *better* part, to tell you what are the little matters to which I am not quite so well reconciled in Mr. Locke : and this I shall be better enabled to do, by my observations upon the temper and natural bent of my dear Miss Goodwin, as well as by those which my visits to the bigger children of my little school, and those at the cottages adjacent, have enabled me to make; for human nature, Sir, you are not to be told, is human nature, whether in the high-born, or in the low.

This excellent author (§ 52), having justly disallowed of slavish and corporal punishments in the education of those we would have to be wise, good, and ingenuous men, adds, " On the other side, to flatter children by rewards of things that are pleasant to them, is as carefully to be avoided. He that will give his son apples, or sugar-plums, or what else of this kind he is most delighted with, to make him learn his book, does but authorize his love of pleasure, and cockers up that dangerous propensity, which he ought, by all means, to subdue and stifle in him. You can never hope to teach him to master it, whilst you compound for the check you give his inclination in one place, by the satisfaction you propose to it in another. To make a good, a wise, and a virtuous man, 'tis fit he should learn to cross his appetite, and deny his inclination to riches, finery, or pleasing his palate, &c."

This, Sir, is well said; but is it not a little too philosophical and abstracted, not only for the generality of children, but for the age he supposes them to be of, if one may guess by the apples and the sugar-plums proposed for the rewards of their well-doing?—Would not this require that memory or reflection in children, which, in another place, is called the concomitant of prudence and age, and not of childhood?

It is undoubtedly very right, to check an unreasonable appetite, and that at its first appearance. But if so small and so reasonable an inducement will prevail, surely, Sir, it might be complied with. A generous mind takes delight to win over others by good usage and mildness, rather than by severity; and it must be a great pain to such an one, to be always inculcating, on his children or pupils, the doctrine of self-denial, by methods quite grievous to his own nature.

What I would then humbly propose, is, that the encouragements offered to youth, should, indeed, be innocent ones, as the gentleman enjoins, and not such as would lead to luxury, either of food or apparel; but I humbly think it necessary, that rewards, *proper* rewards, should be proposed as incentives to laudable actions: for is it not by this method that the whole world is influenced and governed? Does not God himself, by rewards and punishments, make it our *interest*, as well as our *duty*, to obey him? And can we propose ourselves, for the government of our children, a better example than that of the Creator?

This fine author seems to think he had been a little of the

strictest, and liable to some exception. "I say not this," proceeds he, (§ 53) " that I would have children kept from the conveniences or pleasures of life, that are not injurious to their health or virtue. On the contrary, I would have their lives made as pleasant and as agreeable to them as may be, in a plentiful enjoyment of whatsoever might innocently delight them."—And yet he immediately subjoins a very hard and difficult proviso to this indulgence.—" Provided," says he, " it be with this caution, that they have those enjoyments only as the consequences of the state of esteem and acceptation they are in with their parents and governors."

I doubt, my dear Mr. B., this is expecting such a distinction and discretion in children, as they seldom have in their tender years, and requiring capacities not commonly to be met with: so that it is not prescribing to the *generality*, as this excellent author intended. 'Tis, I humbly conceive, next to impossible that their tender minds should distinguish beyond facts: they covet this or that play-thing, and the parent, or governor, takes advantage of its desires, and annexes to the indulgence such or such a task or duty, as a condition; and shews himself pleased with its compliance with it: so the child wins its play-thing, and receives the commendation so necessary to lead on young minds to laudable pursuits. But shall it not be suffered to enjoy the innocent reward of its compliance, unless it can give satisfaction, that its greatest delight is not in having the thing coveted, but in performing the task, or obeying the injunctions imposed upon it as a condition of its being obliged? I doubt, Sir, this is a little too strict, and not to be expected from children. A servant, full-grown, would not be able to shew, that, on condition he complied with such and such terms (which, it is to be supposed by the *offer*, he would not have complied with, but for that inducement), he should have such and such a reward; I say, he would hardly be able to shew, that he preferred the pleasure of performing the requisite conditions to the stipulated reward. Nor is it necessary he should: for he is not the less a good servant, or a virtuous man, if he own the conditions painful, and the reward necessary to his low state in the world, and that otherwise he would not undergo any service at all.— Why then should this be exacted from a child?

Let, therefore, innocent rewards be proposed, and let us be contented to lead on the ductile minds of children to a love of their duty, by obliging them with such: we may tell them what we *expect* in this case; but we ought not, I humbly conceive, to be too rigorous in *exacting* it; for, after all, the inducement will naturally be the uppermost consideration with the child: nor, as I hinted, had it been offered to it, if the parent himself had not thought so. And, therefore, we can only let the child know his duty in this respect, and that he *ought* to give a preference to that; and then rest ourselves contented, although we should discern, that the reward is the chief incentive, of it. For this, from whatever motive inculcated, may beget a habit in the child of doing it: and then, as it improves in years, one may hope, that reason will take place, and enable him, from the most solid and durable motives, to give a preference to the duty.

Upon the whole, then, can we insist upon it, that the child should so nicely distinguish away its little *innate* passions, as if we expected it to be born a philosopher? Self-denial is, indeed, a most excellent doctrine to be inculcated into children, and it must be done *early:* but we must not be too severe in our exacting it; for a duty too rigidly insisted upon, will make it odious. This Mr. Locke, too, observes in another place, on the head of too great severity; which he illustrates by a familiar comparison: " Offensive circumstances," says he, " ordinarily infect innocent things which they are joined with. And the very sight of a cup, wherein any one uses to take nauseous physic, turns his stomach; so that nothing will relish well out of it, though the cup be never so clean and well-shaped, and of the richest materials."

Permit me to add, that Mr. Locke writes still more rigorously on the subject of rewards; which I quote, to shew I have not misunderstood him: " But these enjoyments," says he, " should *never* be offered or bestowed on children, as the rewards of this or that particular performance that they shew an aversion to, or to which they would not have applied themselves without that temptation." If, dear Sir, the minds of children *can* be led on by innocent inducements to the performance of a duty, of which they are capable, what I have humbly offered, is enough, I presume, to convince one, that it *may* be done. But if ever a particular study be proposed to be mastered, or a bias to be overcome (that is not an *indispensable* requisite to his future life of morals) to which the child shews an aversion, I would not, methinks, have him be too much tempted or compelled to conquer or subdue it, especially if it appear to be a *natural* or rivetted aversion. For, permit me to observe, that the education and studies of children ought, as much as possible, to be suited to their capacities and inclination, and, by these means, we may expect to have always *useful* and often *great* men, in different professions: for that genius which does not prompt to the prosecution of one study, may shine in another no less necessary part of science. But, if the promise of innocent rewards *would* conquer this aversion, yet they should not be applied with this view; for the best consequences that can be hoped for, will be tolerable skill in one thing, instead of most excellent in another.

Nevertheless, I must repeat, that if, as the child grows up, and is capable of so much reason, that, from the love of the *inducement*, one can raise his mind to the love of the *duty*, it should be done by all means. But, my dear Mr. B., I am afraid that *that* parent or tutor will meet with but little success, who, in a child's tender years, shall refuse to comply with its foibles, till he sees it value its duty, and the pleasure of obeying his commands, beyond the little enjoyment on which his heart is fixed. For, as I humbly conceive, that mind which can be brought to prefer its duty to its appetites, will want little of the perfection of the wisest philosophers.

Besides, Sir, permit to me say, that I am afraid this perpetual opposition between the passions of the child and the duty to be enforced, especially when it sees how other children are indulged (for if this regimen could be observed by *any*, it would be impossible it should become *general*, while the fond and the inconsiderate parents are so large a part of mankind), will cow and dispirit a child, and will, perhaps produce, a necessity of making use of severity, to subdue him to this temper of self-denial; for if the child refuses, the parent must insist; and what will be the consequence? must it not introduce a harsher discipline than this gentleman allows of?—and which, I presume to say, did never yet do good to any but to slavish and base spirits, if to them; a discipline which Mr. Locke every where justly condemns.

See here, dear Sir, a specimen of the presumption of your girl: "What will she come to in time!" you will perhaps say, "Her next step will be to arraign myself." No, no, dear Sir, don't think so: for my duty, my love, and my reverence, shall be your guards, and defend you from every thing saucy in me, but the bold approaches of my gratitude, which shall always testify for me, how much I am *your obliged and dutiful servant,*

P. B.

LETTER XCII

My dearest Mr. B.,

I will continue my subject, although I have not had an opportunity to know whether you approve of my notions or not by reason of the excursions you have been pleased to allow me to make in your beloved company to the sea-ports of this kingdom, and to the more noted inland towns of Essex, Kent, Sussex, Hampshire, and Dorsetshire, which have given me infinite delight and pleasure, and enlarged my notions of the wealth and power of the kingdom, in which God's goodness has given you so considerable a stake.

My next topic will be upon a *home* education, which Mr. Locke prefers, for several weighty reasons, to a *school* one, provided such a tutor can be procured, as he makes next to an impossibility to procure. The gentleman has set forth the inconveniencies of both, and was himself so discouraged, on a review of them, that he was ready, as he says, to throw up his pen. My chief cares, dear Sir, on this head, are three : 1st, The difficulty which, as I said, Mr. Locke makes almost insuperable, to find a qualified tutor. 2ndly, The necessity there is, according to Mr. Locke, of keeping the youth out of the company of the meaner servants, who may set him bad examples. And, 3rdly, Those still greater difficulties which will arise from the example of his parents, if they are not very discreet and circumspect.

As to the qualifications of the tutor, Mr. Locke supposes, that he is to be so learned, so discreet, so wise, in short, so *perfect* a man, that I doubt, and so does Mr. Locke, such an one can hardly be met with for this *humble* and *slavish* employment. I presume, Sir, to call it so, because of the too little regard that is generally paid to these useful men in the families of the great, where they are frequently put upon a foot with the uppermost servants, and the rather, if they happen to be men of modesty.

" I would," says he, " from children's first beginning to talk, have some discreet, sober, nay, *wise* person about them, whose care it should be to fashion them right, and to keep them from all ill; especially the infection of bad company. I think this province requires great sobriety, temperance, tenderness, diligence, and discretion ; qualities hardly to be found united in persons that are to be had for ordinary salaries, nor easily to be found any where."

If this, Sir, be the case, does not this excellent author recommend a scheme that is rendered in a manner impracticable from this difficulty ?

As to these qualities being more rarely to be met with in persons that are to be had for *ordinary salaries*, I cannot help being of opinion (although, with Mr. Locke, I think no expence should be spared, if that *would* do) that there is as good a chance for finding a proper person among the needy scholars (if not of a low and sordid turn of mind) as among the more affluent: because the narrow circumstances of the former (which probably became a spur to his own improvement) will, it is likely, at first setting out in the world, make him be glad to embrace such an offer in a family which has interest enough to prefer him, and will quicken his diligence to make him *deserve* preferment; and if such an one wanted any of that requisite politeness, which some would naturally expect from scholars of better fortune, might not that be supplied to the youth by the conversation of parents, relations, and visitors, in conjunction with those other helps which young men of family and large expectations constantly have, and which few learned tutors can give him?

I say not this to countenance the wretched niggardliness (which this gentleman justly censures) of those who grudge a handsome consideration to so necessary and painful a labour as that of a tutor, which, where a deserving man can be met with, cannot be too genteelly rewarded, nor himself too respectfully treated. I only beg to deliver my opinion, that a low condition is as likely as any other, with a mind not ungenerous, to produce a man who has these good qualities, as well for the reasons I have hinted at, as for others which might be mentioned.

But Mr. Locke thus proceeds: " To form a young gentleman as he should be, 'tis fit his governor should be well bred, understand the ways of carriage, and measures of civility, in all the variety of *persons*, *times*, and *places* and keep his pupil, as far as his age requires, constantly to the observation of them. This is an art not to be learnt or taught by books.—Nothing can give it but good company and observation joined together."

And in another place says, " Besides being well-bred, the tutor should know the world well; the ways, the humours, the follies, the cheats, the faults of the age he has fallen into, and particularly of the country he lives in: these he should be able to shew to his pupil, as he finds him capable: teach him skill in men and their manners; pull off the mask which their several callings and pretences cover them with; and make his pupil discern what lies at the bottom, under such appearances, that he may not, as unexperienced young men are apt to do, if they are unwarned, take one thing for another, judge by the outside, and give himself up to show, and the insinuations of a fair carriage, or an obliging application: teach him to guess at, and beware of, the designs of men he hath to do with, neither with too much suspicion, nor too much confidence."

This, dear Sir, is excellently said: 'tis noble *theory*; and if the tutor be a man void of resentment and caprice, and will not be governed by partial considerations, in his own judgment of persons and things, all will be well: but if otherwise, may he not take advantage of the confidence placed in him, to the injury of some worthy person, and by degrees monopolize the young gentleman to himself, and govern his passions as absolutely, as I have heard some first ministers have done those of their prince, equally to his own personal disreputation, and to the disadvantage of his people? But all this, and much more, according to Mr. Locke, is the duty of a tutor: and on the finding out such an one, depends his scheme of a home education. No wonder, then, that he himself says, "When I consider the scruples and cautions I here lay in your way, methinks it looks as if I advised you to something which I would have offered at, but in effect not done," &c.—Permit me, dear Sir, in this place to express my fear that it is hardly possible for any one, with talents inferior to those of Mr. Locke himself, to come up to the rules he has laid down upon this subject; and 'tis to be questioned, whether even *he*, with all that vast stock of natural reason and solid sense, for which, as you tell me, Sir, he was so famous, had attained to these perfections, at his first setting out into life.

Now, therefore, dear Sir, you can't imagine how these difficulties perplex me, as to my knowing how to judge which is best, a *home* or a *school* education. For hear what this excellent author justly observes on the latter, among other things, no less to the purpose: "I am sure, he who is able to be at the charge of a tutor at home, may there give his son a more genteel carriage, more manly thoughts, and a sense of what is worthy and becoming, with a greater proficiency in learning, into the bargain, and ripen him up sooner into a man, than any school can do. Not that I blame the schoolmaster in this," says he, " or think it to be laid to his charge. The difference is great between two or three pupils in the same house, and three or four score boys lodged up and down: for, let the master's industry and skill be never so great, it is impossible he should have fifty or an hundred scholars under his eye any longer than they are in the school together." But then, Sir, if there be such a difficulty as Mr. Locke says, to meet with a proper tutor for the home education, which he thus prefers, what a perplexing thing is this. But still, according to this gentleman, another difficulty attends a home education; and that is, what I hinted at before, in my second article, the necessity of keeping the youth out of the company of the meaner servants, who may set him bad

examples. For thus he says, " Here is another great inconvenience, which children receive from the ill examples which
they meet with from the meaner servants. They are *wholly*, if
possible, to be kept from such conversation : for the contagion
of these ill precedents, both in civility and virtue, horribly
infects.children, as often as they come within the reach of it.
They frequently learn from unbred or debauched servants,
such language, untowardly tricks and vices, as otherwise they
would be ignorant of all their lives. 'Tis a hard matter wholly
to prevent this mischief," continues he ; " you will have very
good luck, if you never have a clownish or vicious servant,
and if from them your children never get any infection."

Then, Sir, my third point (which I mentioned in the beginning
of this letter) makes a still stronger objection, as it may happen,
against a home education ; to wit, the example of the parents
themselves, if they be not very circumspect and discreet.

All these difficulties being put together, let me, dear Sir,
humbly propose it, as a matter for your consideration and
determination, whether there be not a middle way to be found
out in a school education, that may remedy some of these inconveniencies ? For suppose you cannot get a tutor so qualified
as Mr. Locke thinks he ought to be, for your Billy as he grows
up. Suppose there is danger from your meaner servants ; or
we his parents should not be able to lay ourselves under the requisite restraints, in order to form his mind by our own examples,
which I hope, by God's grace, however, will not be the case—
Cannot some master be found, who shall be so well rewarded for
his care of a *few* young gentlemen, as to make it worth his while
to be contented with those *few ?*—suppose from five to eight
at most ; whose morals and breeding he may attend to, as well
as to their learning ? The farther this master lives from the
young gentleman's friends, the better it may be. We will hope,
that he is a man of a mild disposition, but strict in his discipline,
and who shall make it a rule not to give correction for small
faults, or till every other method has been tried ; who carries
such a just dignity in his manner, without the appearance of
tyranny, that his looks may be of greater force than the blows
of others ; and who will rather endeavour to shame than terrify,
a youth out of his faults. Then, suppose this gentleman was
to allot a particular portion of time for the *more learned* studies ;
and before the youth was tired with *them*, suppose another portion was allotted for the *writing* and *arithmetic* ; and then to
relieve his mind from both, suppose the *dancing-master* should
take his part ; and innocent exercises of mere diversion, to fill

up the rest, at his own choice, in which, diverted by such a rotation of employments (all thus rendered delightful by their successive variety), he would hardly wish to pass much time. For the dancing of itself, with the dancing-master's instruction, if a well-bred man, will answer both parts, that of breeding and that of exercise: and thus different studies at once be mastered.

Moreover, the emulation which will be inspired, where there are several young gentlemen, will be of inconceivable use both to tutor and pupil, in lessening the trouble of the one, and advancing the learning of the other, which cannot be expected where there is but a single youth to be taken care of.

Such a master will know it to be his interest, as well as duty, to have a watchful eye over the conduct and behaviour of his servants. His assistants, in the different branches of science and education, will be persons of approved prudence, for whom he will think himself answerable, since his own *reputation*, as well as *livelihood*, will depend upon their behaviour. The youths will have young gentlemen for their companions, all under the influence of the same precepts and directions; and if some chosen period were fixed, as a reward for some excellence, where, at a little desk, raised a step or two above the other seats, the excelling youth should be set to read, under the master's direction, a little portion from the best translations of the Greek and Roman historians, and even from the best English authors; this might, in a very engaging manner, initiate them into the knowledge of the history of past times, and of their own country, and give them a curiosity to pass some of their vacant hours in the same laudable pursuit: for, dear Sir, I must still insist that rewards, and innocent gratifications, as also little honours and distinctions, must needs be very attractive to the minds of youth.

For, is not the pretty ride, and dairy house breakfasting, by which Miss Goodwin's governess distinguishes the little ladies who excel in their allotted tasks, a fine encouragement to their ductile minds?—Yes, it is, to be sure!—And I have often thought of it with pleasure, and partaken of the delight with which I have supposed their pretty hearts must be filled with on that occasion. And why may not such little triumphs be, in proportion, as incentives, to children, to make them try to master laudable tasks; as the Roman triumphs, of different kinds, and their mural and civic crowns, all which I have heard you speak of, were to their heroes and warriors of old? For Mr. Dryden well observes, that—

385

> " Men are but children of a larger growth;
> Our appetites are apt to change as theirs,
> And full as craving too, and full as vain."

Permit me, Sir, to transcribe four or five lines more, for the beauty of the thought :

> " And yet the soul, shut up in her dark room,
> Viewing so clear abroad, at home sees nothing :
> But like a mole in earth, busy and blind,
> Works all her folly up, and casts it outward
> To the world's open view—"

Improving the thought : methinks I can see the dear little Miss, who has, in some eminent task, borne away the palm, make her public entry, as I may call it, after her dairy breakfast and pretty airing, into the governess's court-yard, through a row of her school-fellows, drawn out on each side to admire her; her governess and assistants receiving her at the porch, their little capitol, and lifting her out with applauses and encomiums, with a *Thus shall it be done to the Miss, whom her governess delighteth to honour!* I see not why the dear Miss in this case, as she moves through her admiring school-fellows, may not have her little heart beat with as much delight, be as gloriously elated, proportionably, as that of the greatest hero in his triumphal car, who has returned from exploits, perhaps, much less laudable.

But how I ramble !—Yet surely, Sir, you don't expect method or connection from your girl. The education of our sex will not permit that, where it is best. We are forced to struggle for knowledge, like the poor feeble infant in the month, who is pinned and fettered down upon the nurse's lap; and who, if its little arms happen, by chance, to escape its nurse's observation, and offer but to expand themselves, are immediately taken into custody, and pinioned down to their passive behaviour. So, when a poor girl, in spite of her narrow education, breaks out into notice, her genius is immediately tamed by trifling employments, lest, perhaps, she should become the envy of one sex, and the equal of the other. But you, Sir, act more nobly with your Pamela; for you throw in her way all opportunities of improvement; and she has only to regret, that she cannot make a better use of them, and, of consequence, render herself more worthy of your generous indulgence.

I know not how, Sir, to recover my thread; and so must break off with that delight which I always take when I come near the bottom of my letters to your dear self; because then I can boast of the honour which I have in being *your ever dutiful,*

P. B.

LETTER XCIII

Well, but, my dear Mr. B., you will perhaps think, from my last rambling letter, that I am most inclined to a *school* education for your Billy, and some years hence, if it should please God to spare him to us. Yet I cannot say that I am; I only lay several things together in my usual indigested way, to take your opinion upon, which, as it ought, will be always decisive with me. And indeed I am so thoroughly convinced by Mr. Locke's reasons, where the behaviour of servants can be so well answered for, as that of yours can be, and where the example of the parents will be, as I hope, rather edifying than otherwise, that without being swayed, as I think, by maternal fondness, in this case, I must needs give a preference to the home education; and the little scheme I presumed to form in my last, was only on a supposition, that those necessary points could not be so well secured.

In my observations on this head, I shall take the liberty, in one or two particulars, a little to differ from an author, that I admire exceedingly; and that is the present design of my writing these letters; for I shall hereafter, if God spare my life, in my little book (when you have kindly decided upon the points in which I presume to differ) shew you, Sir, my great reverence and esteem for him; and can then let you know all my sentiments on this important subject, and that more undoubtedly, as I shall be more improved by years and your conversation; especially, Sir, if I have the honour and happiness of a foreign tour with you, of which you give me hope; so much are you pleased with the delight I take in these improving excursions, which you have now favoured me with, at different times, through more than half the kingdom.

Well then, Sir, I will proceed to consider a little more particularly the subject of a home education, with an eye to those difficulties, of which Mr. Locke takes notice, as I mentioned in my last. As to the first, that of finding a qualified tutor; we must not expect so much perfection, I doubt, as he lays down as necessary. What, therefore, I humbly conceive is best to be done, will be to avoid choosing a man of bigoted and narrow principles; who yet shall not be tainted with sceptical or heterodox notions, nor a mere scholar or pedant; who has travelled, and yet preserved his moral character un-

387

tainted; and whose behaviour and carriage is easy, unaffected, unformal, and genteel, as well acquiredly as naturally so, if possible; who shall not be dogmatical, positive, overbearing, on one hand; nor too yielding, suppliant, fawning, on the other; who shall study the child's natural bent, in order to direct his studies to the point he is most likely to excel in; and to preserve the respect due to his own character from every one, he must not be a busy body in the family, a whisperer, a tale-bearer, but of a benevolent turn of mind, ready to compose differences; who shall avoid, of all things, that foppishness of dress and appearance, which distinguishes the *petit-maîtres*, and French ushers (that I have seen at some boarding schools), for coxcombs rather than guides of education : for, as I have heard you, my best tutor, often observe, the peculiarities of habit, where a person aims at something fantastic, or out of character, are an undoubted sign of a wrong head; for such a one is so kind as always to hang out on his sign what sort of furniture he has in his shop, to save you the trouble of asking questions about him; so that one may as easily know by his outward appearance what he *is*, as one can know a widow by her weeds.

Such a person as I have thus negatively described, may be found without very much difficulty, perhaps, because some of these requisites are personal, and others are such as are obvious at first sight, to a common penetration ; or, where not so, may be found out, by inquiry into his general character and behaviour : and to the care of such a one, dear Sir, let me suppose your Billy is committed : and so we acquit ourselves of the first difficulty, as well as we can, that of the tutor; who, to become more perfect, may form himself, as to what he wants, by Mr. Locke's excellent rules on that head.

But before I quit this subject, I beg to remind you of your opinion upon it, in a conversation with Sir George Stuart, and his nephew, in London ; in which you seemed to prefer a Scottish gentleman for a tutor, to those of your own nation, and still more than to those of France? Don't you remember it, dear Sir? And how much those gentlemen were pleased with your facetious freedom with their country, and said, you made them amends for that, in your preference to their learned and travelled youth? If you have forgot it, I will here transcribe it from my *records*, as I call my book of memorandums ; for every time I am pleased with a conversation, and have leisure, before it quits my memory, I enter it down in as near the very words as I can ; and now you have made me your correspondent, I shall some-times, perhaps, give you back some valuables from your own treasure.—Miss Darnford, and Mr. Turner, and Mr. Fanshaw, were present, I well remember. These were your words:

" Since the union of the two kingdoms, we have many persons of condition, who have taken their tutors for their sons from Scotland; which practice, to speak impartially, has been attended with some advantageous circumstances, that should not be overlooked. For, Sir George, it must be confessed that, notwithstanding your narrow and stiff manner of education in Scotland, a spirit of manly learning, a kind of poetic liberty, as I may call it, has begun to exert itself in that part of the island. The blustering north—forgive me, gentlemen—seems to have hardened the foreheads of her hungry sons; and the keenness with which they set out for preferment in the kindlier south, has taught them to know a good deal of the world betimes. Through the easy terms on which learning is generally attained there, as it is earlier inculcated, so it may, probably, take deeper root: and since 'tis hardly possible—forgive me, dear Sirs—they can go to a worse country on this side Greenland, than some of the northern parts of Scotland; so their education, with a view to travel, and to better themselves by settlements in other countries, may, perhaps, be so many reasons to take greater pains to qualify themselves for this employment, and may make them succeed better in it; especially when they have been able to shake off the fetters which are rivetted upon them under the narrow influence of a too tyrannical kirk discipline, which you, Sir George, have just now so freely censured.

" To these considerations, when we add the necessity, which these remote tutors lie under, of behaving well; first, because they seldom wish to return to their own country; and next, because *that* cannot prefer them, if it would; and thirdly, because it would not, if it could, if the gentleman be of an enlarged genius, and generous way of thinking; I say, when we add to the premises these considerations, they all make a kind of security for their good behaviour: while those of our own country have often friends or acquaintances on whose favour they are apt to depend, and for that reason give less attention to the duties requisite for this important office.

" Besides, as their kind friend Æolus, who is accustomed to spread and strengthen the bold muscles of the strong-featured Scot, has generally blown away that inauspicious bashfulness, which hangs a much longer time, commonly, on the faces of the southern students; such a one (if he fall not too egregiously into the contrary extreme, so as to become insufferable) may still be the more eligible person for a tutor, as he may teach a young

389

gentleman, betimes, that necessary presence of mind, which those who are confined to a private education sometimes want.

"But, after all, if a gentleman of this nation be chosen for this employment, it may be necessary that he should be one who has had as genteel and free an education himself, as his country will afford; and the native roughness of his climate filed off by travel and conversation; who has made, at least, the tour of France and Italy, and has a taste for the politeness of the former nation : but from the boisterousness of a North Britain, and the fantastic politeness of a Frenchman, if happily blended, such a mixture may result, as will furnish out a more complete tutor, than either of the two nations, singly, may be able to produce. But it ought to be remembered that this person must have conquered his native brogue, as I may call it, and be a master of the English pronunciation; otherwise his conversation will be disagreeable to an English ear.

"And permit me to add, that, as an acquaintance with the Muses contributes not a little to soften the manners, and give a graceful and delicate turn to the imagination, and a kind of polish to severer studies, it would not be amiss that he should have a taste of poetry, although perhaps it were not to be wished he had such strong inclinations that way, as to make that lively and delectable amusement his predominant passion : for we see very few poets, whose warm imaginations do not run away with their judgments. And yet, in order to learn the dead languages in their purity, it will be necessary to inculcate both the love and the study of the ancient poets, which cannot fail of giving the youth a taste for poetry, in general."

Permit me, dear Sir, to ask you, whether you advanced this for argument sake, as sometimes you love to amuse and entertain your friends in an uncommon way ? For I should imagine, that our two universities, which you have shewn me, and for which I have ever since had a greater reverence than I had before, are capable of furnishing as good tutors as any nation in the world : for here the young gentlemen seem to me to live both in the *world* and in the *university ;* and we saw several gentlemen who had not only fine parts, but polite behaviour, and deep learning, as you assured me; some of whom you entertained, and were entertained by, in so elegant a manner, that no travelled gentleman, if I may be allowed to judge, could excel them ! And besides, my dear Mr. B., I know who is reckoned one of the politest and best-bred gentlemen in England by every body, and learned as well as polite, and yet had his education in one of those celebrated seats of learning. I wish your Billy may never fall short of the gentleman I mean, in all these acquirements; and he will be a very happy creature, I am sure.

But how I wander again from my subject. I have no other way to recover myself, when I thus ramble, but by returning to that one delightful point of reflection, that I have the honour to be, dearest Sir, *your ever dutiful and obliged,*

P. B.

LETTER XCIV

Dearest Sir,

I now resume my subject. I had gone through the article of the tutor, as well as I could; and will now observe upon what Mr. Locke says, That children are wholly, if possible, to be kept from the conversation of the meaner servants; whom he supposes to be, as too frequently they are, *unbred* and *debauched*, to use his own words.

Now, Sir, I think it is very difficult to keep children from the conversation of servants at all times. The care of personal attendance, especially in the child's early age, must fall upon servants of one denomination or other, who, little or much, must be conversant with the inferior servants, and so be liable to be tainted by their conversation; and it will be difficult in this case to prevent the taint being communicated to the child. Wherefore it will be a *surer*, as well as a more *laudable* method, to insist upon the regular behaviour of the whole family, than to expect the child, and its immediate attendant or tutor, should be the only good ones in it.

Nor is this so difficult to effect, as may be imagined. Your family affords an eminent instance of it: the good have been confirmed, the remiss have been reformed, the passionate have been tamed; and there is not a family in the kingdom, I will venture to say, to the honour of every individual in it, more uniform, more regular, and freer from evil, and more regardful of what they say and do, than yours. And you will allow, that though always honest, yet they were not always so laudable, so exemplarily virtuous, as of late: which I mention only to shew the practicableness of a reformation, even where bad habits have taken place—For your Pamela, Sir, arrogates not to herself the honour of this change: 'tis owing to the Divine grace shining upon hearts naturally good; for else an example so easy, so plain, so simple, from so young a mistress, who moreover had been exalted from their own station, could not have been attended with such happy effects.

You see, dear Sir, what a master and mistress's example could do, with a poor soul so far gone as Mrs. Jewkes. And I dare be confident, that if, on the hiring of a new servant, sobriety of manners and a virtuous conversation were insisted upon, and a general inoffensiveness in words as well as actions was required from them, as indispensable conditions of their service : and that a breach of that kind would be no more passed over, than a wilful fraud, or an act of dishonesty; and if, added to these requisites, their principals take care to support these injunctions by their own example; I say, then, I dare be confident, that if such a service did not *find* them good, it would *make* them so.

And why should we not think this a very practicable scheme, considering the servants we take are at years of discretion, and have the strong ties of *interest* superadded to the obligations we require of them? and which, they must needs know (let 'em have what bad habits they will) are right for *themselves* to discharge, as well as for *us* to exact.

We all know of how much force the example of superiors is to inferiors. It is too justly said, that the courts of princes abound with the most profligate of men, insomuch that a man cannot well have a more significantly bad title, than that of COURTIER : yet even among these, one shall see the force of *example*, as I have heard you, Sir, frequently observe : for, let but the land be blest with a pious and religious prince, who makes it a rule with him to countenance and promote men of virtue and probity; and to put the case still stronger, let such a one even succeed to the most libertine reign, wherein the manners of the people are wholly depraved : yet a wonderful change will be immediately effected. The flagitious livers will be chased away, or reformed; or at least will think it their duty, or their *interest*, which is a stronger tie with such, to *appear* reformed; and not a man will seek for the favour or countenance of his prince, but by laudable pretences, or by worthy actions.

In the reign of King Richard III, as I have read, deformity of body was the fashion, and the nobility and gentry of the court thought it an indispensable requisite of a graceful form to pad for themselves a round shoulder, because the king was crooked. And can we think human nature so absurdly wicked, that it would not much rather have tried to imitate a personal perfection, than a deformity so shocking in its appearance, in people who were naturally straight?

'Tis melancholy to reflect, that of all professions of men, the mariners, who most behold the wonders of Almighty power displayed in the great deep (a sight that has struck me with awe and reverence only from a coast prospect), and who every moment, while at sea, have but one frail plank betwixt themselves and inevitable destruction, are yet, generally speaking, said to be the most abandoned invokers and blasphemers of the name of that God, whose mercies they every moment unthankfully, although so visibly, experience. Yet, as I once heard at your table, Sir, on a particular occasion, we have now a commander in the British navy, who, to his honour, has shewn the force of an excellent example supporting the best precepts : for, on board of his ship, not an oath or curse was to be heard ; while volleys of both (issued from impious mouths in the same squadron, out of his knowledge) seemed to fill the sails of other ships with guilty breath, calling aloud for that perdition to overtake them, which perhaps his worthy injunctions and example, in his own, might be of weight to suspend.

If such then, dear Sir, be the force of a good example, what have parents to do, who would bring up a child at home under their own eye, according to Mr. Locke's advice, but, first, to have a strict regard to *their* conduct ! This will not want its due influence on the servants ; especially if a proper enquiry be first made into their characters, and a watchful eye had over them, to keep them up to those characters afterwards. And when they know they must forfeit the favour of a worthy master, and their places too (which may be thought to be the best of places, because an *uniform* character must make all around it easy and happy), they will readily observe such rules and directions, as shall be prescribed to them—Rules and directions, which their own consciences will tell them are *right* to be prescribed ; and even *right* for them to follow, were they not insisted upon by their superiors : and this conviction must go a great way towards their *thorough* reformation : for a person wholly convinced is half reformed. And thus the hazard a child will run of being corrupted by conversing with the servants, will be removed, and all Mr. Locke's other rules be better enforced.

I have the boldness, Sir, to make another objection ; and that is, to the distance which Mr. Locke prescribes to be kept between children and servants : for may not this be a means to fill the minds of the former with a contempt of those below them, and an arrogance that is not warranted by any rank or condition, to their inferiors of the same species?

I have before transcribed what Mr. Locke has enjoined in relation to this distance, where he says, that the children are by all means to be kept *wholly* from the conversation of the meaner servants. But how much better advice does the same author give for the behaviour of children to servants in the following words which, I humbly think, are not so entirely consistent with the former, as might be expected from so admirable an author.

"Another way," says he (§ 111), "to instil sentiments of humanity, and to keep them lively in young folks, will be, to accustom them to civility in their language and deportment towards their inferiors, and meaner sort of people, particularly servants. It is not unusual to observe the children in gentlemen's families treat the servants of the house with domineering words, names of contempt, and an imperious carriage, as if they were of another race, or species beneath them. Whether ill example, the advantage of fortune or their natural vanity, inspire this haughtiness, it should be prevented or weeded out; and a gentle, courteous, affable carriage towards the lower ranks of men placed in the room of it. No part of their superiority will be hereby lost, but the distinction increased, and their authority strengthened, when love in inferiors is joined to outward respect, and the esteem of the person has a share in their submission : and domestics will pay a more ready and cheerful service, when they find themselves not spurned, because fortune has laid them below the level of others at their master's feet."

These, dear Sir, are certainly the sentiments of a generous and enlarged spirit : but I hope, I may observe, that the great distance Mr. Locke before enjoins to be kept between children and servants, is not very consistent with the above-cited paragraph : for if we would prevent this undue contempt of inferiors in the temper of children, the best way, as I humbly presume to think, is not to make it so unpardonable a fault for them, especially in their early years, to be in their company. For can one make the children shun the servants without rendering them odious or contemptible to them, and representing them to the child in such disadvantageous light, as must needs make the servants vile in their eyes, and themselves lofty and exalted in their own? and thereby cause them to treat them with "domineering words, and an imperious carriage, as if they were of another race or species beneath them; and so," as Mr. Locke says, "nurse up their natural pride into an habitual contempt of those beneath them; and then," as he adds, "where will that probably end, but in oppression and cruelty?" But this matter, dear Sir, I presume to think, will all be happily accommodated and reconciled, when the servants' good behaviour is secured by the example and injunctions of the principals.

Upon the whole, then, of what Mr. Locke has enjoined, and what I have taken the liberty to suggest on this head, it shall be my endeavour, in that early part of your dear Billy's education, which you will intrust to me, to inculcate betimes in his mind the principles of universal benevolence and kindness to others, especially to inferiors.

Nor shall I fear, that the little dear will be wanting to himself in assuming, as he grows up, an air of superiority and distance of behaviour equal to his condition, or that he will descend too low for his station. For, Sir, there is a pride and self-love natural to human minds, that will seldom be kept so low, as to make them humbler than they ought to be.

I have observed, before now, instances of this, in some of the families we visit, between the young Masters or Misses, and those children of lower degree, who have been brought to play with them, or divert them. On the Masters' and Misses' side I have always seen, they lead the play and prescribe the laws of it, be the diversion what it will; while, on the other hand, their lower-rank play-fellows have generally given into their little humours, though ever so contrary to their own; and the difference of dress and appearance, and the notion they have of the more eminent condition of their play-fellows' parents, have begot in them a kind of awe and respect, that perhaps more than sufficiently secures the superiority of the one, and the subordination of the other.

The advantage of this universal benevolence to a young gentleman, as he grows up, will be, as I humbly conceive, so to diffuse itself over his mind, as to influence all his actions, and give a grace to every thing he does or says, and make him admired and respected from the best and most durable motives; and will be of greater advantage to him for his attaining a handsome address and behaviour (for it will make him conscious that he *merits* the distinction he will meet with, and encourage him still *more* to merit it), than the best rules that can be given him for that purpose.

I will therefore teach the little dear courteousness and affability, from the properest motives I am able to think of; and will instruct him in only one piece of pride, that of being above doing a mean or low action. I will caution him not to behave in a lordly or insolent manner, even to the lowest servants. I will tell him that that superiority is the most commendable, and will be the best maintained, which is owing to humanity and kindness, and grounded on the perfections of the *mind*, rather than on the *accidental* advantage of *fortune* and *condition* : that if his conduct be such as it ought to be, there will be no occasion to tell a servant, that he will be observed and respected : that *humility*, as I once told my Miss Goodwin, is a charming grace, and most conspicuously charming in persons of distinction; for that the poor, who are humbled by their condition, cannot glory in it, as the rich may; and that it makes the lower ranks of people love and admire the high-born, who can so condescend : whereas *pride*, in such, is meanness and insult, as it owes its boast and its being to accidental advantages; which, at the same time, are seldom of *his* procuring, who can be so mean as to be proud : that even I would sooner forget pride in a low degree than in a high; for it may be a security in the first against doing a base thing : but in the rich, it is a base thing itself, and an impolitic one too; for the more distinction a proud mind grasps at, the less it will have; and every poor despised person can whisper such a one in the ear, when surrounded with, and adorned by, all his glittering splendours, that he *was* born, and *must* die, in the *same manner* with those whom he despises.

Thus will the doctrine of benevolence and affability, implanted early in the mind of a young gentleman, and duly cultivated as he grows up, inspire him with the requisite conduct to command respect from *proper* motives; and while it will make the servants observe a decorum towards him, it will oblige them to have a guard upon their words and actions in presence of one, whose manner of education and training-up would be so great a reproach to them, if they were grossly faulty : so thus, I conceive, a mutual benefit will flow to the manners of each; and *his* good behaviour will render him, in some measure, an instructive monitor to the whole family.

But permit me, Sir, to enlarge on the hint I have already given, in relation to the example of parents, in case a preference be given to the home education. For if this point cannot be secured, I should always imagine it were best to put the child to such a school, as I formerly mentioned. But yet the subject might be spared by me in this case, as I write with a view only to your family; though you will remember, that while I follow Mr. Locke, whose work is public, I must be considered as directing myself to the generality of the world : for, Sir, I have the pleasure to say, that your conduct in your family is unexceptionable; and the pride to think that mine is no disgrace to it. No one hears a word from your mouth unbecoming the character of a polite gentleman; and I shall always be very regardful of what falls from mine. Your temper, Sir, is equal and kind to all your servants, and they love you, as well as awfully respect you : and well does your beautiful and considerate mind, deserve it of them all : and they, seeing I am watchful over my own conduct, so as not to behave unworthy of your kind example, regard me as much as I could wish they should; for well do they know, that their beloved master will have it so, and greatly honours and esteems me himself. Your table-talk is such as persons of the strictest principles may hear, and join in : your guests, and your friends are, generally speaking, persons of the genteelest life, and of the best manners. So that Mr. Locke would have advised *you*, of all gentlemen, had he been living, and known you, to give your children a home education, and assign these, and still stronger reasons for it.

But were we to speak to the generality of parents, I fear this would be an almost insuperable objection to a home education. For (I am sorry to say it) when one turns one's eyes to the bad precedents given by the heads of some families, it is hardly to be wondered at, that there is so little virtue and religion among men. For can those parents be surprised at the ungraciousness of their *children*, who hardly ever shew them, that their *own* actions are governed by reasonable or moral motives? Can the gluttonous father expect a self-denying son? With how ill a grace must a man who will often be disguised in liquor, preach sobriety? a passionate man, patience? an irreligious man, piety? How will a parent, whose hands are seldom without cards, or dice in them, be observed in lessons against the pernicious vice of gaming? Can the profuse father, who is squandering away the fortunes of his children, expect to be regarded in a lesson of frugality? 'Tis impossible he should, except it were that the youth, seeing how pernicious his father's example is, should have the grace to make a proper use of it, and look upon it as a sea-mark, as it were, to enable him to shun the dangerous rocks, on which he sees his father splitting. And even in this *best* case, let it be considered, how much shame and disgrace his thoughtless parent ought to take to himself, who can admonish his child by nothing but the *odiousness* of his own vice; and how little it is owing to him, that his guilt is not *doubled*, by his son's treading in his steps ! Let such an unhappy parent duly weigh this, and think how likely he is to be, by his bad example, the cause of his child's perdition, as well as his own, and stand unshocked and unamended, if he can !

It is then of no avail to wish for discreet servants, if the conduct of the parents is faulty. If the fountain-head be polluted, how shall the under-currents run clear? That master and mistress, who would exact from their servants a behaviour which they themselves don't practice, will be but ill observed. And that child, who discovers excesses and errors in his parents, will be found to be less profited by their good precepts, than prejudiced by bad examples. Excessive fondness this hour; violent passions and perhaps execrations, the next; unguarded jests, and admiration of fashionable vanities, rash censures, are perhaps the best, that the child sees in, or hears from those, who are most concerned to inculcate good precepts into his mind. And where it is so, a home education must not surely be chosen.

Having thus, as well as my slender abilities will permit, presumed to deliver my opinion upon three great points, *viz.* the qualifications of a tutor; the necessity of having an eye to the morals of servants; and the example of parents (all which, being taken care of, will give a preference, as I imagine, to a home education); permit me, dear Sir, to speak a little further to a point, that I have already touched upon.

It is that of *emulation;* which I humbly conceive to be of great efficacy to lead children on in their duties and studies. And how, dear Sir, shall this advantage be procured for a young master, who has no school-fellows and who has no example to follow, but that of his tutor, whom he cannot, from the disparity of years, and other circumstances, without pain (because of this disparity), think of emulating? And this, I conceive, is a very great advantage to such a school education, as I mentioned in my former letter, where there are no more scholars taken in, than the master can with ease and pleasure instruct.

But one way, in my humble opinion, is left to answer this objection, and still preserve the reason for the preference which Mr. Locke gives to a home education; and that is, what I formerly hinted, to take into your family the child of some honest neighbour of but middling circumstances, and like age of your own, but who should give apparent indications of his natural promptitude, ingenuous temper, obliging behaviour and good manners; and to let him go hand-in-hand with yours in his several studies and lessons under the same tutor.

The child would be sensible of the benefit, as well as of the distinction, he received, and consequently of what was expected from him, and would double his diligence, and exert all his good qualities, which would inspire the young gentleman with the wished-for emulation, and, as I imagine, would be so promotive of his learning, that it would greatly compensate the tutor for his pains with the additional scholar; for the young gentleman would be ashamed to be outdone by one of like years and stature with himself. And little rewards might be proposed to the greatest proficient, in order to heighten the emulation.

Then, Sir, the *generosity* of such a method, to a gentleman of your fortune, and beneficent mind, would be its own reward, were there no other benefit to be received from it.

Moreover, such an ingenious youth might, by his good morals and industry, hereafter be of service, in some place of trust in the family; or it would be easy for a gentleman of your interest in the world, if such a thing offered not, to provide for the youth in the navy, in some of the public offices, or among your private friends. If he proved faulty in his morals, his dismission would be in your own power, and would be punishment enough.

But, if on the other hand, he proved a sober and hopeful youth, he would make an excellent companion for your Billy in riper years; as he would be, in a manner, a corroborator of his morals; for, as his circumstances would not support him in any extravagance, so they would be a check upon his inclination; and this being seconded by the hopes of future preferment from your favour and interest, which he could not expect but upon the terms of his perseverance in virtue, he would find himself under a necessity of setting such an example, as might be of great benefit to his companion, who should be watched, as he grew up, that he did not (if his ample fortune became dangerous to his virtue) contribute out of his affluence to draw the other after him into extravagance. And to this end, as I humbly conceive, the noble doctrine of *independence* should be early instilled into both their minds, and upon all occasions, inculcated and inforced; which would be an inducement for the one to endeavour to *improve* his fortune by his honest industry, lest he never be enabled to rise out of a state of dependence; and to the other, to *keep*, if not to *improve*, his own, lest he ever fall into such a servile state, and thereby lose the glorious power of conferring happiness on the deserving, one of the highest pleasures that a generous mind can know; a pleasure, Sir, which you have oftener experienced than thousands of gentlemen: and which may you still continue to experience for a long and happy succession of years, is the prayer of one, the most obliged of all others in her own person, as well as in the persons of her dearest relations, and who owes to this glorious beneficence the honour she boasts, of being *your ever affectionate and grateful* **P. B.**

But now, my dear Mr. B., if you will indulge me in a letter or two more, preparative to my little book, I will take the liberty to touch upon one or two other places, wherein I differ from this learned gentleman. But first, permit me to observe, that if parents are, above all things, to avoid giving bad examples to their children, they will be no less careful to shun the practice of such fond fathers and mothers, as are wont to indulge their children in bad habits, and give them their head, at a time when, like wax, their tender minds may be moulded into what shape they please. This is a point that, if it please God, I will carefully attend to, because it is the foundation on which the superstructure of the whole future man is to be erected. For, according as he is indulged or checked in his childish follies, a ground is laid for his future happiness or misery; and if once they are suffered to become habitual to him, it cannot but be expected, that they will grow up with him, and that they will hardly ever be eradicated. "Try it," says Mr. Locke, speaking to this very point, "in a dog, or a horse, or any other creature, and see whether the ill and resty tricks they have learned when young, are easily to be mended, when they are knit; and yet none of these creatures are half so wilful and proud, or half so desirous to be masters of themselves, as men."

And this brings me, dear Sir, to the head of *punishments*, in which, as well as in the article of *rewards*, which I have touched upon, I have a little objection to what Mr. Locke advances.

But permit me, however, to premise, that I am exceedingly pleased with the method laid down by this excellent writer, rather to shame the child out of his fault, than beat him: which latter serves generally for nothing but to harden his mind.

Obstinacy, and telling a *lie*, and committing a *wilful* fault, and then persisting in it, are, I agree with this gentleman, the only causes for which the child should be punished with stripes : and I admire the reasons he gives against a too rigorous and severe treatment of children.

But I will give Mr. Locke's words, to which I have some objection.

"It may be doubted," says he, "concerning whipping, when, as the *last* remedy, it comes to be necessary, at *what time*, and by whom, it should be done; whether presently, upon the committing the fault, whilst it is yet fresh and hot. I think it should not be done presently," adds he, "lest passion mingle with it; and so, though it exceed the just proportion, yet it lose of its due weight. For even children discern whenever we do things in a passion."

I must beg leave, dear Sir, to differ from Mr. Locke in this point; for I think it ought rather to be a rule with parents, who shall chastise their children, to conquer what would be extreme in *their own* passion on this occasion (for those who cannot do it, are very unfit to be the punishers of the wayward passions of their children), than to *defer* the punishment, especially if the child knows its fault has reached its parent's ear. It is otherwise, methinks, giving the child, if of an obstinate disposition, so much more time to harden its mind, and bid defiance to its punishment.

Just now, dear Sir, your Billy is brought into my presence, all smiling, crowing to come to me, and full of heart-cheering promises; and the subject I am upon goes to my heart. Surely I can never beat your Billy !—Dear little life of my life ! how can I think thou canst ever deserve it, or that I can ever inflict it ?—No, my baby, that shall be thy papa's task, if ever thou art so heinously naughty; and whatever *he* does, must be right. Pardon my foolish fondness, dear Sir !—I will proceed.

If, then, the fault be so atrocious as to deserve whipping, and the parent be resolved on this exemplary punishment, the child ought not, as I imagine, to come into one's presence without meeting with it : or else, a fondness too natural to be resisted, will probably get the upper hand of one's resentment, and how shall one be able to whip the dear creature one had ceased to be angry with? Then after he has once seen one without meeting his punishment, will he not be inclined to hope for connivance at his fault, unless it should be repeated? And may he not be apt (for children's resentments are strong) to impute to cruelty a correction (when he thought the fault had been forgotten) that should always appear to be inflicted with reluctance, and through motives of love?

If, from anger at his fault, one should go *above the due proportion,* (I am sure I might be trusted for this !) let it take its course ! —How barbarously, methinks, I speak !—He ought to *feel* the lash, first, because he *deserves* it, poor little soul? Next, because it is *proposed* to be exemplary. And, lastly, because it is not intended to be *often* used : and the very passion or displeasure one expresses (if it be not enormous) will shew one is in earnest, and create in him a necessary awe, and fear to offend again. The *end* of the correction is to shew him the difference between right and wrong. And as it is proper to take him at his first offer of a full submission and repentance (and not before), and instantly dispassionate one's self, and shew him the difference by acts of pardon and kindness (which will let him see that one punishes him out of necessity rather than choice), so one would not be afraid to make him smart so sufficiently, that he should not soon forget the severity of the discipline, nor the disgrace of it. There's a cruel mamma for you, Mr. B.! What my *practice* may be, I cannot tell; but this *theory*, I presume to think, is right.

As to the *act* itself, I much approve Mr. Locke's advice, to do it by pauses, mingling stripes and expostulations together, to shame and terrify the more; and the rather, as the parent, by this slow manner of inflicting the punishment, will less need to be afraid of giving too violent a correction; for those pauses will afford *him*, as well as the *child*, opportunities for consideration and reflection.

But as to the *person*, by whom the discipline should be performed, I humbly conceive, that this excellent author is here also to be objected to.

"If you have a discreet servant," says he, "capable of it, and has the place of governing your child (for if you have a tutor, there is no doubt), I think it is best the smart should come immediately from another's hand, though by the parent's order, who should see it done, whereby the parent's authority will be preserved, and the child's aversion for the pain it suffers, rather be turned on the person that immediately inflicts it. For I would have a father seldom strike a child, but upon very urgent necessity, and as the last remedy."

'Tis in such an urgent case that we are supposing that it should be done at all. If there be not a reason strong enough for the father's whipping the child himself, there cannot be one for his ordering another to do it, and standing by to see it done. But I humbly think, that if there be a necessity, no one can be so fit as the father himself to do it. The child cannot dispute his authority to punish, from whom he receives and expects all the good things of his life : he cannot question *his* love to him, and after the smart is over, and his obedience secured, must believe that so tender, so indulgent a father could have no other end in whipping him, but his good. Against *him*, he knows he has no remedy, but must passively submit; and when he is convinced he *must*, he will in time conclude that he *ought*.

But to have this severe office performed by a servant, though at the father's command, and that professedly, that the aversion of the child for the pain it suffers should be turned on the person who immediately inflicts it, is, I humbly think, the *reverse* of what ought to be done. And *more* so, if this servant has any direction of the child's education; and still much *more* so, if it be his tutor, though Mr. Locke says, there is no doubt, if there be a tutor, that it should be done by him.

For, dear Sir, is there no doubt, that the tutor should lay himself open to the aversion of the child, whose manners he is to form? Is not the best method a tutor can take, in order to enforce the lessons he would inculcate, to try to attract the love and attention of his pupil by the most winning ways he can possibly think of? And yet is *he*, this very tutor *out of all doubt*, to be the instrument of doing an harsh and disgraceful thing, and that in the last resort, when all other methods are found ineffectual; and that too, because he ought to incur the child's resentment and aversion, rather than the father? No, surely, Sir, it is not reasonable it should be so : quite contrary, in my humble notion, there can be no doubt, but that it should be *otherwise*.

It should, methinks, be enough for a tutor, in case of a fault in the child, to threaten to complain to his father; but yet not to make such a complaint, without the child obstinately persists in his error, which, too, should be of a nature to merit such an appeal : and this might highly contribute to preserve the parent's authority; who, on this occasion, should never fail of extorting a promise of amendment, or of instantly punishing him with his own hands. And, to soften the distaste he might conceive in resentment of too rigid complainings, it might not be amiss, that his interposition in the child's favour, were the fault not too flagrant, should be permitted to save him once or twice from the impending discipline.

'Tis certain that the passions, if I may so call them, of affection and aversion, are very early discoverable in children; insomuch that they will, even before they can speak, afford us marks for the detection of an hypocritical appearance of love to it before the parents' faces. For the fondness or averseness of the child to some servants, will at any time let one know, whether their love to the baby is uniform and the same, when one is absent, as present. In one case the child will reject with sullenness all the little sycophancies made to it in one's sight; while on the other, its fondness of the person, who generally obliges it, is an infallible rule to judge of such an one's sincerity behind one's back. This little observation shews the strength of a child's resentments, and its sagacity, at the earliest age, in discovering who obliges, and who disobliges it : and hence one may infer, how improper a person *he* is, whom we would have a child to love and respect, or by whose precepts we would have it directed, to be the punisher of its faults, or to do any harsh or disagreeable office to it.

For my own part, I beg to declare, that if the parent were not to inflict the punishment himself, I think it much better it should be given him, in the parent's presence, by the servant of the lowest consideration in the family, and whose manners and example one would be the least willing of any other he should follow. Just as the common executioner, who is the lowest and most flagitious officer of the commonwealth, and who frequently deserves, as much as the criminal, the punishment he is chosen to inflict, is pitched upon to perform, as a mark of greater ignominy, sentences intended as examples to deter others from the commission of heinous crimes. The Almighty took this method when he was disposed to correct severely his chosen people; for, in that case, he generally did it by the hands of the most profligate nations around them, as we read in many places of the Old Testament.

But the following rule I admire in Mr. Locke: "When," says he (for any misdemeanour), "the father or mother looks sour on the child, every one else should put on the same coldness to him, and nobody give him countenance till forgiveness is asked, and a reformation of his fault has set him right again, and restored him to his former credit. If this were constantly observed," adds he, "I guess there would be little need of blows or chiding: their own ease or satisfaction would quickly teach children to court commendation, and avoid doing that which they found every body condemned, and they were sure to suffer for, without being chid or beaten. This would teach them modesty and shame, and they would quickly come to have a natural abhorrence for that which they found made them slighted and neglected by every body."

This affords me a pretty hint; for if ever your charming Billy shall be naughty, I will proclaim throughout your worthy family, that the little dear is in disgrace! And one shall shun him, another decline answering him, a third say, "No, master, I cannot obey you, till your mamma is pleased with you"; a fourth, "Who shall mind what little masters bid them do, when they won't mind what their mammas say to them?" And when the dear little soul finds this, he will come in my way, (and I see, pardon me, my dear Mr. B., he has some of his papa's spirit, already, indeed he has!) and I will direct myself with double kindness to your beloved Davers, and to my Miss Goodwin, and not notice the dear creature, if I can help it, till I can see his *papa* (forgive my boldness) banished from his little sullen brow, and all his *mamma* rise to his eyes. And when his musical tongue shall be unlocked to own his fault, and promise amendment—O then ! how shall I clasp him to my bosom ! and tears of joy, I know, will meet his tears of penitence !

How these flights, dear Sir, please a body !—What delights have those mammas (which some fashionable dear ladies are quite unacquainted with) who can make their babies, and their first educations, their entertainment and diversion ! To watch the dawnings of reason in them, to direct their little passions, as they shew themselves, to this or that particular point of benefit or use ; and to prepare the sweet virgin soil of their minds to receive the seeds of virtue and goodness so early, that, as they grow up, one need only now a little pruning, and now a little water, to make them the ornaments and delights of the garden of this life ! And then their pretty ways, their fond and grateful endearments, some new beauty every day rising to observation—O my dearest Mr. B., whose enjoyments and pleasures are so great, as those of such mothers as can bend their minds two or three hours every day to the duties of the nursery ?

I have a few other things to observe upon Mr. Locke's treatise, which, when I have done, I shall read, admire, and improve by the rest, as my years and experience advance ; of which, in my proposed little book, I shall give you better proofs than I am able to do at present ; raw, crude, and indigested as the notions of so young a mamma must needs be.

But these shall be the subjects of another letter ; for now I am come to the pride and the pleasure I always have, when I subscribe myself, dearest Sir, *your ever dutiful and grateful*

P. B.

LETTER XCVI

Dear Sir,

Mr. Locke gives a great many very pretty instructions relating to the play-games of children : but I humbly presume to object to what he says in one or two places.

He would not indulge them in any playthings, but what they make themselves, or endeavour to make. "A smooth pebble, a piece of paper, the mother's bunch of keys, or any thing they cannot hurt themselves with," he rightly says, "serve as much to divert little children, as those more chargeable and curious toys from the shops, which are presently put out of order, and broken."

These playthings may certainly do for little ones : but me-thinks, to a person of easy circumstances, since the making these toys employs the industrious poor, the buying them for the child might be complied with, though they *were* easily broken ; and especially as they are of all prices, and some less costly, and more durable than others.

" Tops, gigs, battledores," Mr. Locke observes, " which are to be used with labour, should indeed be procured them—not for variety, but exercise ; but if they had a top, the scourge-stick and leather strap should be left to their own making and fitting."

But I may presume to say, that whatever be the good Mr. Locke proposes by this, it cannot be equal to the mischief children may do themselves in making these playthings ! For must they not have implements to work with ? and is not a knife, or other edged tool, without which it is impossible they can make or shape a scourge-stick, or *any* of their playthings, a fine instrument in a child's hands ! This advice is the reverse of the caution warranted from all antiquity, *That it is dangerous to meddle with edged tools !* and I am afraid, the tutor must often act the surgeon, and follow the indulgence with a styptic and plaister ; and the young gentleman's hands might be so often bound up as to be one way to cure him of his earnest desire to play ; but I can hardly imagine any other good that it can do him ; for I doubt the excellent consequences proposed by our author from this doctrine, such as to teach the child moderation in his desires, application, industry, thought, contrivance, and good husbandry, qualities that, as he says, will be useful to him when he is a man, are too remote to be ingrafted upon such beginnings : although it must be confessed, that, as Mr. Locke wisely observes, good habits and industry cannot be too early inculcated.

But then, Sir, may I ask, Are not the very plays and sports, to which children accustom themselves, whether they make their own playthings or not, equivalent to the work or labour of grown persons ! Yes, Sir, I will venture to say, they are, and more than equivalent to the exercises and labour of many.

Mr. Locke advises, that the child's playthings should be as few as possible, which I entirely approve : that they should be in his tutor's power, who is to give him but one at once. But since it is the nature of the human mind to court most what is prohibited, and to set light by what is in its own power ; *I* am half doubtful (only that Mr. Locke says it, and it may not be so very important as other points, in which I have ventured to differ from that gentleman), whether the child's absolute possession of his own playthings in some little repository, of which he may be permitted to keep the key, especially if he makes no bad use of the privilege, would not make him more indifferent to them : while the contrary conduct might possibly enhance his value of them. And if, when he had done with any plaything, he were obliged to put it into its allotted place, and were accustomed to keep account of the number and places of them severally; this would teach him order, and at the same time instruct him to keep a proper account of them, and to avoid being a squanderer or waster : and if he should omit to put his playthings in their places, or be careless of them, the taking them away for a time, or threatening to give them to others, would make him the more heedful.

Mr. Locke says, that he has known a child so distracted with the number and variety of his playthings, that he tired his maid every day to look them over : and was so accustomed to abundance, that he never thought he had enough, but was always asking, " What more? What new thing shall I have? "—" A good introduction," adds he, ironically, " to moderate desires, and the ready way to make a contented happy man."

All that I shall offer to this, is, that few *men* are so philosophical as one would wish them to be, much less *children*. But, no doubt, this variety engaged the child's activity; which, of the two might be turned to better purposes than sloth or indolence; and if the maid was tired, it might be, because she was not so much *alive* as the child; and perhaps this part of the grievance might not be so great, because if she was his attendant, 'tis probable she had nothing else to do.

However, in the main, as Mr. Locke says, it is no matter how few playthings the child is indulged with : but yet I can hardly persuade myself, that plenty of them can have such bad consequences as he apprehends; and the rather, because they will excite his attention, and promote his industry and activity. His enquiry after new things, let him have few or many, is to be expected as a consequence to those natural desires which are implanted in him, and will every day increase : but this may be observed, that as he grows in years, he will be above some playthings, and so the number of the old ones will be always reducible, perhaps in a greater proportion, than the new ones will increase

On the head of good-breeding, he observes, that, " there are two sorts of ill-breeding; the one a sheepish bashfulness, and the other a misbecoming negligence and disrespect in our carriage; both which," says he, " are avoided by duly observing this one rule, not to think meanly of ourselves, and not to think meanly of others." I think, as Mr. Locke explains this rule, it is an excellent one. But I would beg to observe upon it, that however discommendable a bashful temper is, in some instances, where it must be deemed a weakness of the mind, yet, in my humble opinion, it is generally the mark of an ingenuous one, and is always to be preferred to an undistinguishing and hardy confidence, which, as it seems to me, is the genuine production of invincible ignorance.

What is faulty in it, which he calls *sheepishness*, should indeed be shaken off as soon as possible, because it is an enemy to merit in its advancement in the world : but, Sir, were I to choose a companion for your Billy, as he grows up, I should not think the worse of the youth, who, not having had the opportunities of knowing men, or seeing the world, had this defect. On the contrary, I should be apt to look upon it as an outward fence or inclosure to his virtue, which might keep off the lighter attacks of immorality, the *Hussars* of vice, as I may say, who are not able to carry on a formal siege against his morals; and I should expect such a one to be docile, humane, good-humoured, diffident of himself, and therefore most likely to improve as well in mind as behaviour : while a hardened mind, that never doubts itself, must be a stranger to its own infirmities, and suspecting none, is impetuous, over-bearing, incorrigible; and, if rich, a tyrant; if not, possibly an invader of other men's properties; or at least, such a one as allows itself to walk so near the borders of injustice, that where *self* is concerned, it hardly ever does right things.

Mr. Locke proposes (§ 148) a very pretty method to cheat children, as it were, into learning : but then he adds, " There may be dice and playthings, with the letters on them, to teach children the alphabet by playing." And (§ 151) " I know a person of great quality, who, by pasting on the six sides of a dice, and the remaining eighteen consonants on the sides of three other dice, has made this a play for his children, that *he* shall win, who at one cast throws most words on these four dice; whereby his eldest son, yet in coats, has *played* himself *into spelling* with great eagerness, and without once having been chid for it, or forced to it."

But I had rather your Billy should be a twelvemonth backwarder for want of this method, than forwarded by it. For what may not be feared from so early inculcating the use of dice and gaming, upon the minds of children? Let Mr. Locke himself speak to this in his § 208, and I wish I could reconcile the two passages in this excellent author. "As to cards and dice," says he, "I think the safest and best way is, never to learn any play upon them, and so to be incapacitated for these dangerous temptations, and encroaching wasters of useful time." And, he might have added, of the noblest estates and fortunes; while sharpers and scoundrels have been lifted into distinction upon their ruins. Yet, in § 153, Mr. Locke proceeds to give directions in relation to the dice he recommends.

But after all, if some innocent plays were fixed upon to cheat children into reading, that, as he says, should look as little like a task as possible, it must needs be of use for that purpose. But let every gentleman, who has a fortune to lose, and who, if he games, is on a foot with the vilest company, who generally have nothing at all to risque, tremble at the thoughts of teaching his son, though for the most laudable purposes, the early use of dice and gaming.

But how much I am charmed with a hint in Mr. Locke, which makes your Pamela hope, she may be of greater use to your children, even as they *grow up*, than she could ever have flattered herself to be. 'Tis a charming paragraph; I must not skip one word of it. Thus it begins, and I will observe upon it as I go along. § 177 : " But under whose care soever a child is put to be taught, during the tender and flexible years of his life, this is certain, it should be one who thinks Latin and language the least part of education."

How agreeable is this to my notions; which I durst not have avowed, but after so excellent a scholar ! For I have long had the thought, that much time is wasted to little purpose in the attaining of Latin. Mr. H., I think, says he was ten years in endeavouring to learn it, and, as far as I can find, knows nothing at all of the matter neither !—Indeed he lays that to the wicked picture in his grammar, which he took for granted (as he has often said, as well as once written) was put there to teach boys to rob orchards, instead of improving their minds in learning, or common honesty.

But (for this is too light an instance for the subject) Mr. Locke proceeds—" One who knowing how much virtue and a well-tempered soul is to be preferred to any sort of *learning* or *language*," [*What a noble writer is this !*] makes it his chief business to form the mind of his scholars, and give that a right disposition : " [*Ay, there, dear Sir, is the thing !*] " which, if once got, though all the rest should be neglected," [*charmingly observed !*] " would, in *due time,* [*without wicked dice, I hope !*] produce all the rest; and which, if it be not got and settled, so to keep out ill and vicious habits, *languages* and *sciences*, and all the other accomplishments of education, will be to no purpose, but to make the worse or more dangerous man." [*Now comes the place I am so much delighted with!* " And indeed, whatever stir there is made about getting of Latin, as the great and difficult business, his mother " [*thank you, dear Sir, for putting this excellent author into my hands!*] " may teach it him herself, if she will but spend two or three hours in a day with him," [*If she will! Never fear, but I will, with the highest pleasure in the world!*] " and make him read the Evangelists in Latin to her." [*How I long to be five or six years older, as well as my dearest babies, that I may enter upon this charming scheme!*] " For she need but buy a Latin Testament, and having got somebody to mark the last syllable but one, where it is long, in words above two syllables (which is enough to regulate her pronunciation and accenting the words), read daily in the Gospels, and then let her avoid understanding them in Latin, if she can."

Why, dear Sir, you have taught me almost all this already; and you, my beloved tutor, have told me often, I read and pronounce Latin more than tolerably, though I don't understand it : but this method will teach *me*, as well as your dear *children*— But thus the good gentleman proceeds—" And when she understands the Evangelists in Latin, let her in the same manner read Æsop's Fables, and so proceed on to Eutropius, Justin, and such other books. I do not mention this," adds Mr. Locke, " as an imagination of what I fancy *may* do, but as of a thing I have known done, and the Latin tongue got with ease this way."

He then mentions other advantages, which the child may receive from his mother's instruction, which I will try more and more to qualify myself for : particularly, after he has intimated, that " at the same time that the child is learning French and Latin, he may be entered also in arithmetic, geography, chronology, history, and geometry too; for if," says he, " these be taught him in French or Latin, when he begins once to understand either of these tongues, he will get a knowledge of these sciences, and the language to boot." He then proceeds: " Geography, I think, should be begun with : for the learning of the figure of the globe, the situation and boundaries of the four parts of the world, and that of particular kingdoms and countries, being only an exercise of the eyes and memory, a child with pleasure will learn and retain them. And this is so certain, that I now live in a house with a child, whom his MOTHER has so well instructed this way in geography," [*But had she not, do you think, dear Sir, some of this good gentleman's kind assistance?*] " that he knew the limits of the four parts of the world; would readily point, being asked, to any country upon the globe, or any county in the map of England; knew all the great rivers, promontories, streights, and bays in the world, and could find the longitude and latitude of any place, before he was six years old."

There's for you, dear Sir!—See what a mother can do if she pleases !

I remember, Sir, formerly, in that sweet chariot conference, at the dawning of my hopes, when all my dangers were happily over (a conference I shall always think of with pleasure), that you asked me, how I would bestow my time, supposing the neighbouring ladies would be above being seen in my company; when I should have no visits to receive or return; no parties of pleasure to join in; no card-tables to employ my winter evenings?

I then, Sir, transported with my opening prospects, prattled to you, how well I would try to pass my time, in the family management and accounts, in visits now and then to the indigent and worthy poor; in music sometimes; in reading, in writing, in my superior duties—And I hope I have not behaved quite unworthily of my promise.

But I also remember, what once you said on a certain occasion, which *now*, since the fair prospect is no longer distant, and that I have been so long your happy wife, I may repeat without those blushes which then covered my face; thus then, with a *modest* grace, and with that *virtuous* endearment that is so *beautiful* in *your* sex, as well as in *ours*, whether in the character of lover or husband, maiden or wife, you were pleased to say— " And I hope, my Pamela, to have superadded to all these, such an employment as—" in short, Sir, I am now blessed with, and writing of; no less than the useful part I may be able to take in the first education of your beloved babies !

And now I must add, that this pleasing hope sets me above all other diversions : I wish for no parties of pleasure but with you, my dearest Mr. B., and these are parties that will improve me, and make me more capable of the other, and more worthy of your conversation, and of the time you pass (beyond what I could ever have promised to my utmost wishes) in such poor company as mine, for no other reason but because I love to be instructed, and take my lessons well, as you are pleased to say; and indeed I must be a sad dunce, if I did not, from so skilful and so beloved a master. I want no card-table amusements :

for I hope, in a few years (and a proud hope it is), to be able to teach your dear little ones the first rudiments, as Mr. Locke points the way, of Latin, of French, and of geography, and arithmetic.

O, my dear Mr. B., by your help and countenance, what may I not be able to teach them, and how may I prepare the way for a tutor's instructions, and give him up minds half cultivated to his hands !—And all this time improve myself too, not only in science, but in nature, by tracing in the little babes what all mankind are, and have been, from infancy to riper years, and watching the sweet dawnings of reason, and delighting in every bright emanation of that ray of divinity, lent to the human mind, for great and happy purposes, when rightly pointed and directed.

There is no going farther after these charming recollections and hopes, for they bring me to that grateful remembrance, to whom, under God, I owe them all, and also what I have been for so happy a period, and what I am, which will ever be my pride and my glory; and well it may, when I look back to my beginning with humble acknowledgment, and can call myself, dearest Mr. B., *your honoured and honouring, and, I hope to say, in time, useful wife,*

P. B.

LETTER XCVII

My dearest Mr. B.,

Having in my former letters said as much as is necessary to let you into my notion of the excellent book you put into my hands, and having touched those points in which the children of both sexes may be concerned (with some *art* in my intention, I own), in hope that they would not be so much out of the way, as to make you repent of the honour you have done me, in committing the dear Miss Goodwin to my care; I shall now very quickly set myself about the proposed little book.

You have been so good as to tell me (at the same time that you disapprove not these my specimen letters as I may call them), that you will kindly accept of my intended present, and encourage me to proceed in it; and as I shall leave one side of the leaf blank for your corrections and alterations, those corrections will be a fine help and instruction to me in the pleasing task which I propose to myself, of assisting in the early education of your dear children. And as I may be years in writing it, as the dear babies improve, as I myself improve, by the opportunities which their advances in years will give me, and the experience I shall gain, I may then venture to give my notions on the more material and nobler parts of education, as well as the inferior : for (but that I think the subjects above my present abilities) Mr. Locke's book would lead me into several remarks, that might not be unuseful, and which appear to me entirely new; though that may be owing to my slender reading and opportunities, perhaps.

But what I would now touch upon, is a word or two still more particularly upon the education of my own sex; a topic which naturally arises to me from the subject of my last letter. For there, dear Sir, we saw, that the mothers might teach the child *this* part of science, and *that* part of instruction; and who, I pray, as our sex is generally educated, shall teach the *mothers ?* How, in a word, shall *they* come by their knowledge ?

I know you'll be apt to say, that Miss Goodwin gives all the promises of becoming a fine young lady, and takes her learning, loves reading, and makes very pretty reflections upon all she reads, and asks very pertinent questions, and is as knowing, at her years, as most young ladies. This is very true, Sir; but it is not every one that can boast of Miss Goodwin's capacity, and goodness of temper, which have enabled her to get up a good deal of *lost* time, as I must call it; for her first four years were a perfect blank, as far as I can find, just as if the pretty dear was born the day she was four years old; for what she had to *unlearn* as to temper, and will, and such things, set against what little improvements she had made, might very fairly be compounded for, as a blank.

I would indeed have a girl brought up to her needle, but I would not have *all* her time employed in samplers, and learning to mark, and do those unnecessary things, which she will never, probably, be called upon to practise.

And why, pray, are not girls entitled to the same *first* education, though not to the same plays and diversions, as boys; so far, at least, as is supposed by Mr. Locke a mother can instruct them ?

Would not this lay a foundation for their future improvement, and direct their inclinations to useful subjects, such as would make them above the imputations of some unkind gentlemen, who allot to their part common tea-table prattle, while they do all they can to make them fit for nothing else, and then upbraid them for it ? And would not the men find us better and more suitable companions and assistants to them in every useful purpose of life ?—O that your lordly sex were all like my dear

Mr. B.—I don't mean that they should all take raw, uncouth, unbred, lowly girls, as I was, from the cottage, and, destroying all distinction, make such their wives; for there is a far greater likelihood, that such a one, when she comes to be lifted up into so dazzling a sphere, would have her head made giddy with her exaltation, than that she would balance herself well in it: and to what a blot, over all the fair page of a long life, would this little drop of dirty ink spread itself! What a standing disreputation to the choice of a gentleman!

But *this* I mean, that after a gentleman had entered into the marriage state with a young creature (saying nothing at all of birth or descent) far inferior to him in learning, in parts, in knowledge of the world, and in all the graces which make conversation agreeable and improving, he would, as you do, endeavour to make her fit company for himself, as he shall find she is *willing* to improve, and *capable* of improvement: that he would direct her taste, point out to her proper subjects for her amusement and instruction; travel with her now and then, a month in a year perhaps; and shew her the world, after he has encouraged her to put herself forward at his own table, and at the houses of his friends, and has seen, that she will not do him great discredit any where. What obligations, and opportunities too, will this give her to love and honour such a husband, every hour, more and more! as she will see his wisdom in a thousand instances, and experience his indulgence to her in ten thousand, to the praise of his politeness, and the honour of them both!—And then, when select parties of pleasure or business engaged him not abroad, in his home conversation, to have him delight to instruct and open her views, and inspire her with an ambition to enlarge her mind, and more and more to excel! What an intellectual kind of married life would such persons find theirs! And how suitable to the rules of policy and self-love in the gentleman; for is not the wife, and are not her improvements, all *his own?—Absolutely*, as I may say, *his own?* And does not every excellence she can be adorned by, redound to her husband's honour because she is *his*, even more than to *her own?*—In like manner as no dishonour affects a man so much, as that which he receives from a bad wife.

But where is such a gentleman as Mr. B. to be met with? Look round and see where, with all the advantages of sex, of education, of travel, of conversation in the open world, a gentleman of his abilities to instruct and inform, is to be found? And there are others, who, perhaps, will question the capacities or inclinations of our sex in general, to improve in useful know-

414

ledge, were they to meet with such kind instructors, either in the characters of parents or husbands.

As to the first, I grant, that it is not easy to find such a gentleman: but for the second (if excusable in me, who am one of the sex, and so may be thought partial to it), I could by comparisons drawn from the gentlemen and ladies within the circle of my own acquaintance, produce instances, which are so flagrantly in their favour, as might make it suspected, that it is policy more than justice, in those who would keep our sex unacquainted with that more eligible turn of education, which gives the gentlemen so many advantages over us in *that;* and which will shew, they have none at all in *nature* or *genius.*

I know you will pardon me, dear Sir; for you are so exalted above your Pamela, by nature and education too, that you cannot apprehend any inconvenience from bold comparisons. I will beg, therefore, to mention a few instances among our friends, where the ladies, notwithstanding their more cramped and confined education, make *more* than an equal figure with the gentlemen in all the graceful parts of conversation, in spite of the contempts poured out upon our sex by some witty gentlemen, whose writings I have in my eye.

To begin then with Mr. Murray, and Miss Darnford that was; Mr. Murray has the reputation of scholarship, and has travelled too; but how infinitely is he surpassed in every noble and useful quality, and in greatness of mind, and judgment, as well as wit, by the young lady I have named! This we saw, when last at the Hall, in fifty instances, where the gentleman was, you know, Sir, on a visit to Sir Simon and his lady.

Next, dear Sir, permit me to observe, that my good Lord Davers, with all his advantages, born a counsellor of the realm, and educated accordingly, does not surpass his lady.

My countess, as I delight to call her, and Lady Betty, her eldest daughter, greatly surpassed the Earl and her eldest brother in every point of knowledge, and even learning, as I may say, although both ladies owe that advantage principally to their own cultivation and acquirement.

Let me presume, Sir, to name Mr. H.: and when I *have* named him, shall we not be puzzled to find any where in our sex, one remove from vulgar life, a woman that will not out-do Mr. H.?

Lady Darnford, upon all useful subjects, makes a much brighter figure than Sir Simon, whose knowledge of the world has not yet made him acquainted with himself.—Mr. Arthur excels not his lady.

415

Mrs. Towers, a maiden lady, is an over-match for half a dozen of the neighbouring gentlemen I could name, in what is called wit and politeness, and not inferior to any of them in judgment.

I could multiply such instances, were it needful, to the confutation of that low, and I had almost said, *unmanly* contempt, with which a certain celebrated genius treats our sex in general in most of his pieces, I have seen; particularly his *Letter of Advice to a new married Lady;* so written, as must disgust, instead of instruct; and looks more like the advice of an enemy to the *sex*, and a bitter one too, than a friend to the *particular Lady*. But I ought to beg pardon for this my presumption, for two reasons: first, because of the truly admirable talents of this writer; and next, because we know not what ladies the ingenious gentleman may have fallen among in his younger days.

Upon the whole, therefore, I conclude, that Mr. B. is almost the only gentleman, who excels *every* lady that I have seen; so *greatly* excels, that even the emanations of his excellence irradiate a low cottage-born girl, and make her pass among ladies of birth and education for somebody.

Forgive my pride, dear Sir; but it would be almost a crime in your Pamela not to exult in the mild benignity of those rays, by which her beloved Mr. B. endeavours to make her look up to his own sunny sphere: while she, by the advantage only of his reflected glory, in *his* absence, which makes a dark night to her, glides along with her paler and fainter beaminess, and makes a distinguishing figure among such lesser planets, as can only poorly twinkle and glimmer, for want of the aid she boasts of.

I dare not, Sir, conjecture whence arises this more than parity in the genius of the sexes, among the above persons, notwithstanding the disparity of education, and the difference in the opportunities of each. This might lead one into too proud a thought in favour of a sex too contemptuously treated by some *other* wits I could name, who, indeed, are the less to be regarded, as they love to jest upon all God Almighty's works: yet might I better do it, too, than anybody, since I am so infinitely transcended by my husband, that no competition, pride or vanity, could be apprehended from me.

But, however, I would only beg of those who are so free in their contempts of us, that they would, for *their own* sakes (and that, with such generally goes a great way), rather try to *improve* than *depreciate* us: we should then make better daughters, better wives, better mothers, and better mistresses: and who (permit me, Sir, to ask them) would be so much the better for these opportunities and amendments, as our upbraiders themselves!

On re-perusing this, I must repeatedly beg your excuse for these proud notions in behalf of my sex, which, I can truly say, are not owing to partiality because, I have the honour to be one of it; but to a far better motive; for what does this contemptuous treatment of one half, if not the better half, of the human species, naturally produce, but libertinism and abandoned wickedness? for does it not tend to make the daughters, the sisters, the wives of gentlemen, the subjects of profligate attempts?—Does it not render the sex vile in the eyes of the most vile? And when a lady is no longer beheld by such persons with that dignity and reverence, with which perhaps, the graces of her person, and the innocence of her mind, should sacredly, as it were, encompass her, do not her very excellencies become so many incentives for base wretches to attempt her virtue, and bring about her ruin?

What then may not wicked wit have to answer for, when its possessors prostitute it to such unmanly purposes! And as if they had never had a mother, a sister, a daughter of their own, throw down, as much as in them lies, those sacred fences which may lay the fair inclosure open to the invasions of every clumsier and viler beast of prey; who, though destitute of *their* wit, yet corrupted by it, shall fill their mouths, as well as their hearts, with the borrowed mischief, and propagate it from one to another to the end of time; and who, otherwise, would have passed by the uninvaded fence, and only shewed their teeth, and snarled at the well secured fold within it?

You cannot, my dearest Mr. B., I know be angry at this romantic painting: since you are not affected by it: for when at worst, you acted (more dangerously, 'tis true, for the poor innocents) a *principal* part, and were as a lion among beasts— Do, dear Sir, let me say *among*, this one time—You scorned to borrow any man's wit; and if nobody had followed your example, till they had had your qualities, the number of rakes would have been but small. Yet, don't mistake me, neither; I am not so mean as to bespeak your favour by extenuating your failings; if I *were*, you would deservedly despise me. For, undoubtedly (I *must* say it, Sir), your faults were the greater for your perfections: and such talents misapplied, as they made you more capable of mischief, so did they increase the evil of your practices. All then that I mean by saying you are not

417

affected by this painting, is, that you are not affected by my description of clumsy and sordid rakes, whose *wit* is *borrowed*, and their *wickedness* only what they may call *their own*.

Then, dear Sir, since that noble conversation you held with me at Tunbridge, in relation to the consequences that might, had it not been for God's grace intervening, have followed the masquerade affair, I have the inexpressible pleasure to find a thorough reformation, from the *best* motives, taking place; and your joining with me in my closet (as opportunity permits) in my evening duties, is the charming confirmation of your kind and voluntary, and I am proud to say, *pious* assurances; so that this makes me fearless of your displeasure, while I rather triumph in my joy for your precious soul's sake, than presume to think of recriminating; and when (only for this once) I take the liberty of looking back from the delightful *now*, to the painful *formerly* !

But, what a rambler am I again ! You command me to write to you all I think, without fear. I obey, and, as the phrase is, do it without either *fear* or *wit*.

If you are *not* displeased, it is a mark of the true nobleness of your nature, and the sincerity of your late pious declarations.

If you *are*, I shall be sure I have done wrong in having applied a corrosive to eat away the *proud flesh* of a *wound*, that is not yet so thoroughly *digested*, as to bear a painful application, and requires balsam and a gentler treatment. But when we were at Bath, I remember what you said once of the benefit of retrospection : and you charged me, whenever a *proper* opportunity offered, to remind you, by that one word, *retrospection*, of the charming conversation we had there, on our return from the rooms.

If this be not one of them, forgive, dearest Sir, the unreasonableness of your very impertinent, but, in intention and resolution, *ever dutiful*,

P. B.

LETTER XCVIII

From Mrs. B. to her Father and Mother

EVER DEAR, AND EVER HONOURED,

I must write this one letter, although I have had the happiness to see you so lately; because Mr. B. is now about to honour me with the tour he so kindly promised; and it may therefore be several months, perhaps, before I have again the pleasure of paying you the like dutiful respects.

You know his kind promise, that he would for every dear baby I present him with, take an excursion with me afterwards, in order to establish and confirm my health.

The task I have undertaken of dedicating all my writing amusements to the dearest of men; the full employment I have, when at home; the frequent rambles he has so often indulged me in, with my dear Miss Goodwin, to Kent, London, Bedfordshire, Lincolnshire, and to my lady Davers, take from me the necessity of writing to you, to my Miss Darnford that was, and to Lady Davers, so often as I formerly thought myself obliged to do, when I saw all my worthy friends so seldom; the same things, moreover, with little variation, occurring this year, as to our conversations, visits, friends, employments, and amusements, that fell out the last, as must be the case in a family so uniform and methodical as ours.

I have for these reasons, more leisure to pursue my domestic duties, which are increased upon me; and when I have said, that I am every day more and more happy in my beloved Mr. B., in Miss Goodwin, my Billy, my Davers, and now, newly, in my sweet little Pamela (for so, you know, Lady Davers would have her called, rather than by her own name), what can I say more?

As to the tour I spoke of, you know, the first part of Mr. B.'s obliging scheme is to carry me to France; for he has already travelled with me over the greatest part of England; and I am sure, by my passage last year, to the Isle of Wight, I shall not be afraid of crossing the water from Dover thither; and he will, when we are at Paris, he says, take *my* farther directions (that was his kind expression) whither to go next.

My Lord and Lady Davers are so good as to promise to accompany us to Paris, provided Mr. B. will give them our company to Aix-la-Chapelle, for a month or six weeks, whither my lord is advised to go. And Mr. H. if he can get over his fear of crossing the salt water, is to be of the party.

Lady G., Miss Darnford that was (who likewise has lately lain-in of a fine daughter), and I, are to correspond as opportunity offers; and she promises to send you what I write, as formerly: but I have refused to say one word in my letters of the manners, customs, curiosities, &c. of the places we see; because, first, I shall not have leisure; and, next, those things are so much better described in books written by persons who made stricter and better observations that I can pretend to make:

419

so that what I shall write will relate only to our private selves, and be as brief as possible.

If we are to do as Mr. B. has it in his thoughts, he intends to be out of England two years :—but how can I bear that, if for your sakes only, and for those of my dear babies !—But this must be my time, my *only* time, Mr. B. says, to ramble and see distant places and countries; for as soon as his little ones are capable of my instructions, and begin to understand my looks and signs, he will not spare me from them a week together; and he is so kind as to propose, that my dear bold boy (for every one sees how greatly he resembles his papa in his dear forward spirit) shall go with us; and this pleases Miss Goodwin highly, who is very fond of *him*, and my little Davers; but vows she will never love so well my pretty black-eyed Pamela.

You see what a sweet girl Miss is, and you admired her much : did I tell you, what she said to me, when first she saw you both, with your silver hairs, and reverend countenances?—" Madam, I dare say, your papa, and mamma, *honoured their father and mother :* "—" They did, my dear; but what is your reason for saying so? "—" Because *they have lived so long in the land which the LORD their GOD has given them.*" I took the charmer in my arms, and kissed her three or four times, as she deserved; for was not this very pretty in the child?

I must, with inexpressible pleasure, write you word how happily God's providence has now, at last, turned that affair, which once made me so uneasy, in relation to the fine Countess (who has been some time abroad), of whom you had heard, as you told me, some reports, which, had you known at the time, would have made you very apprehensive for Mr. B.'s morals, as well as for my repose.

I will now (because I can do it with the highest pleasure, by reason of the event it has produced), explain that dark affair so far as shall make you judges of my present joy : although I had hitherto avoided entering into that subject to you. For now I think myself, by God's grace, secure to the affection and fidelity of the best of husbands, and that from the worthiest motives; as you shall hear.

There was but one thing wanting to complete all the happiness I wished for in this life; which was, the remote hope I had entertained, that one day, my dear Mr. B. who from a licentious gentleman became a moralist, would be so touched by the divine grace, as to become in time, more than moral, a *religious* man, and, at last, join in the duties which he had the goodness to countenance.

For this reason I began with mere *indispensables*. I crowded not his gates with objects of charity: I visited them at their homes, and relieved them; distinguishing the worthy indigent (made so by unavoidable accidents and casualties) from the wilfully, or perversely, or sottishly such, by *greater* marks of my favour.

I confined my morning and evening devotions to my own private closet, lest I should give offence and discouragement to so gay a temper, so unaccustomed (poor gentleman!) to acts of devotion and piety; whilst I met his household together, only on mornings and evenings of the Sabbath-day, to prepare them for their public duties in the one, and in hopes to confirm them in what they had heard at church in the other; leaving them to their own reflections for the rest of the week; after I had suggested a method I wished them to follow, and in which they constantly obliged me.

This good order had its desired effect, and our Sabbath-day assemblies were held with so little parade, that we were hardly any of us missed. All, in short, was done with cheerful ease and composure: and every one of us was better disposed to our domestic duties: I, to attend the good pleasure of my best friend; and they, that of us both.

Thus we went on very happily, my neighbourly visits of charity, taking up no more time than common airings, and passing many of them for such: my *private duties* being only between my FIRST, my HEAVENLY BENEFACTOR, and myself, and my family ones personally confined to the day separated for these best of services, and Mr. B. pleased with my manner beheld the good effects, and countenanced me by his praises and his endearments, *as* acting discreetly, *as* not falling into enthusiasm, and (as he used to say) *as* not aiming at being *righteous overmuch*.

But still I wanted, and waited for, with humble patience, and made it part of my constant prayers, that the divine Grace would at last touch his heart, and make him *more* than a countenancer, *more* than an applauder of my duties; that he might for his own dear sake, become a partaker in them. "And then," thought I, "when we can, hand in hand, heart in heart, one spirit as well as one flesh, join in the same closet, in the same prayers and thanksgiving, what a happy creature shall I be."

I say, *closet*: for I durst not aspire so high, as to hope the favour of his company among his servants, in our Sunday devotions.—I knew it would be going too far, in *his* opinion, to expect it from him. In *me* their mistress, had I been ever so high-born, it was not amiss, because I, and they, *every one* of us, were *his*; I in one degree, Mr. Longman in another, Mrs. Jervis in another—But from a man of his high temper and manner of education, I knew I could never hope for it, so would not lose *every* thing, by grasping at *too much.*

But in the midst of all these comfortable proceedings, and my further charming hopes, a nasty masquerade threw into his way a temptation, which for a time blasted all my prospects, and indeed made me doubt my own head almost. For, judge my disappointment, when I found all my wishes frustrated, all my prayers rendered ineffectual; his very morality, which I had flattered myself, in time, I should be an humble instrument to exalt into religion, shocked, and in danger; and all the work to begin over again, if offended Grace should ever again offer itself to the dear wilful trespasser !

But who should pretend to scrutinize the councils of the Almighty?—for out of all this *evil appearance* was to proceed the *real good,* I had been so long, and so often, supplicating for !

The dear man *was* to be on the brink of relapsing : it was proper, that I should be so very uneasy, as to assume a conduct not natural to my temper, and to raise his generous concern for me : and, in the very crisis, divine Grace interposed, made him sensible of his danger, made him resolve against his error, before it was yet too late : and his sliding feet, quitting the slippery path he was in, collected new strength, and he stood the firmer and more secure for his peril.

For having happily put a stop to that affair, and by his uniform conduct, for a considerable time, shewed me that I had nothing to apprehend from it, he was pleased, when we were last at Tunbridge, and in very serious discourse upon divine subjects, to say to this effect : " Is there not, my Pamela, a text, *That the unbelieving husband shall be saved by the believing wife, whilst he beholds her chaste conversation coupled with fear ?* "

" I need not tell you, my dear Mr. B., that there is, nor where it is."

" Then, my dear, I begin to hope, *that* will be my case; for, from a former affair, of which this spot of ground puts me more in mind, I see so much reason to doubt my own strength, which I had built, and, as I thought securely, on *moral* foundations, that I must look out for a *better* guide to conduct me, than the proud word *honour* can be, in the general acceptance of it among us lively young gentlemen.

" How often have I promised (and I never promised but I

intended to perform) that I would be faithfully and only yours ! How often declared, that I did not think I could possibly deserve my Pamela, till I could shew her, in my own mind, a purity as nearly equal to hers, as my past conduct would admit of !

" But I depended too much upon my own strength : and I am now convinced, that nothing but RELIGIOUS CONSIDERATIONS, and a resolution to watch over the very *first* appearances of evil, and to check them as they arise, can be of sufficient weight to keep steady to his good purpose, a vain young man, too little accustomed to restraint, and too much used to play upon the brink of dangers, from a temerity, and love of intrigue, natural to enterprising minds.

" I would not make this declaration of my convictions to you, till I had thoroughly examined myself, and had reason to hope, that I should be enabled to make it good. And now, my Pamela, from this instant you shall be my guide ; and, only taking care, that you do not, all at once, by injunctions too rigorous, damp and discourage the rising flame, I will leave it to you to direct as you please, till, by degrees, it may be deemed worthy to mingle with your own."

Judge how rapturous my joy was upon this occasion, and how ready I was to bless God for a danger (so narrowly escaped) which was attended with the *very* consequences that I had so long prayed for ; and which I little thought the divine providence was bringing about by the very means, that, I apprehended, would put an end to all my pleasing hopes and prospects of that nature.

It is in vain for me to seek words to express what I felt, and how I acted, on this occasion. I heard him out with twenty different and impatient emotions ; and then threw myself at his feet, embracing his knees, with arms the most ardently clasped ! My face lifted up to Heaven, and to him, by turns ; my eyes overflowing with tears of joy, which half choked up the passage of my words.—At last, his kind arms clasping my neck, and kissing my tearful cheek, I could only say—" My ardent prayers, are at last—heard—May God Almighty confirm your pious purposes ! And, Oh ! what a happy Pamela have you at your feet ! "

I wept for joy till I sobbed again—and he raising me to his kind arms, I said—" To have this *heavenly* prospect, O best beloved of my heart ! added to all my *earthly* blessings !—How shall I contain my joy !—For, oh ! to think that he is, and will be mine, and I his, through the mercies of God, when this transitory life is past and gone, to all eternity ; what a rich thought is this !—Methinks I am already, dear Sir, ceasing to be mortal, and beginning to taste the perfections of those joys, which this thrice welcome declaration gives me hope of hereafter ! —But what shall I say, obliged as I was beyond expression before, and now doubly obliged in the rapturous view you have opened to me, into a happy futurity !"

He said, he was delighted with me beyond expression ; that I was his ecstatic charmer !—That the love I shewed for his future good was the moving proof of the purity of my heart, and my affection for him. And that very evening he joined with me in my retired duties ; and, at all proper opportunities, favours me with his company in the same manner ; listening attentively to all my lessons, as he calls my cheerful discourses on serious subjects.

And now, my dear parents, do you not rejoice with me in this charming, charming appearance ? For, *before* I had the most generous, the most beneficent, the most noble, the most affectionate, but *now* I am likely to have the most *pious*, of husbands ! What a happy wife, what a happy daughter, is *his* and *your* Pamela ! God of his infinite mercy, continue and improve the ravishing prospect !

I was forced to leave off here, to enjoy the charming reflections, which this lovely subject, and my blessed prospects, filled me with ; and now proceed to write a few lines more.

I am under some concern on account of our going to travel into some Roman Catholic countries, for fear we should want the public opportunities of divine service : for I presume, the ambassador's chapel will be the only Protestant place of worship allowed of, and Paris the only city in France where there is one. But we must endeavour to make it up in our private and domestic duties : for, as the phrase is—" When we are at Rome, we must do as they do at Rome ; " that is to say, so far as not to give offence, on the one hand, to the people we are among ; nor scandal, on the other, by compliances hurtful to one's conscience. But my protector knows all these things so well (no place in what is called the grand tour, being new to him), that I have no reason to be very uneasy.

And now let me, by letter, as I did on my knees at parting, beg the continuance of your prayers and blessings, and that God will preserve us to one another, and give us, and all our worthy friends, a happy meeting again.

Kent, you may be sure, will be our first visit, on our return, for your sakes, for my dear Davers's, and my little Pamela's sake, who will be both put into your protection ; while my

Billy, and Miss Goodwin (for, since I began this letter, it is so determined), are to be my delightful companions; for Mr. B. declared, his temper wants looking after, and his notices of every thing are strong and significant.

Poor little dear! he has indeed a little sort of perverseness and headstrongness, as one may say, in his will : yet he is but a baby, and I hope to manage him pretty well; for he notices all I say, and every look of mine already.—He is, besides, very good humoured, and willing to part with anything for a kind word : and this gives me hopes of a docile and benevolent disposition, as he grows up.

I thought, when I began the last paragraph but one, that I was within a line of concluding; but it is *to* you, and *of* my babies, I am writing; so shall go on to the bottom of this new sheet, if I do not directly finish : which I do, with assuring you both, that wherever I am, I shall always be thoughtful of you, and remember you in my prayers, as becomes *your ever dutiful daughter,*

P. B.

My respects to all your good neighbours in general. Mr. Longman will visit you now and then. Mrs. Jervis will take one journey into Kent, she says, and it shall be to accompany my babies, when carried down to you. Poor Jonathan, and she, good folks! seem declining in their health, which grieves me.—Once more, God send us all a happy meeting, if it be his blessed will! Adieu, adieu, my dear parents ! *your ever dutiful, &c.*

LETTER XCIX

My dear Lady G.,

I received your last letter at Paris, as we were disposing every thing for our return to England, after an absence of near two years; in which, as I have informed you, from time to time, I have been a great traveller, into Holland, the Netherlands, through the most considerable province of France, into Italy; and, in our return to Paris again (the principal place of our residence), through several parts of Germany.

I told you of the favours and civilities we received at Florence, from the then Countess Dowager of ——, who, with her humble servant Lord C—— (that had so assiduously attended her for so many months in Italy), accompanied us from Florence to Inspruck.

Her ladyship made that worthy lord happy in about a month

425

after she parted from us, and the noble pair gave us an opportunity at Paris, in their way to England, to return some of the civilities which we received from them in Italy; and they are now arrived at her ladyship's seat on the Forest.

Her lord is exceedingly fond of her, as he well may; for she is one of the most charming ladies in England; and behaves to him with so much prudence and respect, that they are as happy in each other as can be wished. And let me just add, that both in Italy and at Paris, Mr. B.'s demeanour and her ladyship's to one another, was so nobly open, and unaffectedly polite, as well as highly discreet, that neither Lord C. who had once been jealous of Mr. B. nor the *other party*, who had had a tincture of the same yellow evil, as you know, because of the Countess, had so much as a shadow of uneasiness remaining on the occasion.

Lord Davers has had his health (which had begun to decline in England) so well, that there was no persuading Lady Davers to return before now, although I begged and prayed I might not have another little Frenchman, for fear they should, as they grew up, forget, as I pleasantly used to say, the obligations which their parentage lays them under to dearer England.

And now, my dearest friend, I have shut up my rambles for my whole life; for three little English folks, and one little Frenchman (but a charming baby as well as the rest, Charley by name), and a near prospect of a further increase, you will say, are family enough to employ all my cares at home.

I have told you, from time to time, although I could not write to you so often as I would, because of our being constantly in motion, what was most worthy of your knowledge relating to every particular, and how happy we all have been in one another. And I have the pleasure to confirm to you what I have often written, that Mr. B. and my Lord and Lady Davers are all that I could wish and hope for, with regard to their first duties. We are indeed a happy family, united by the best and most solid ties !

Miss Goodwin is a charming young lady !—I cannot express how much I love her. She is a perfect mistress of the French language and speaks Italian very prettily ! And, as to myself, I have improved so well under my dear tutor's lessons, together with the opportunity of conversing with the politest and most learned gentry of different nations, that I will discourse with you in two or three languages, if you please, when I have the happiness to see you. There's a learned boaster for you, my dear friend ! (if the knowledge of different languages makes

426

one learned.)—But I shall bring you an heart as entirely English as ever, for all that !

We landed on Thursday last at Dover, and directed our course to the dear farm-house; and you can better imagine, than I express, our meeting with my dear father and mother, and my beloved Davers and Pamela, who are charming babies.—But is not this the language of every fond mamma?

Miss Goodwin is highly delighted now with my sweet little Pamela, and says, she shall be her sister indeed ! " For, Madam," said she, " Miss is a beauty !—And we see no French beauties like Master Davers and Miss."—" Beauty ! my dear," said I; " what is beauty, if she be not a good girl? Beauty is but a specious, and, as it may happen, a dangerous recommendation, a mere skin-deep perfection; and if, as she grows up, she is not as good as Miss Goodwin, she shall be none of my girl."

What adds to my pleasure, my dear friend, is to see them both so well got over the small-pox. It has been as happy for them, as it was for their mamma and her Billy, that they had it under so skilful and kind a manager in that distemper, as my dear mother. I wish if it please God, it was as happily over with my little pretty Frenchman.

Every body is surprised to see what the past two years have done for Miss Goodwin and my Billy.—O, my dear friend, they are both of them almost—nay, quite, I think, for their years, all that I wish them to be. In order to make them keep their French, which Miss so well speaks, and Billy so prettily prattles, I oblige them, when they are in the nursery, to speak nothing else : but at table, except on particular occasions, when French *may* be spoken, they are to speak in English; that is, when they *do* speak : for I tell them, that little masters must only ask questions for information, and say—" Yes," or—" No," till their papas or mammas permit them to speak; nor little ladies neither, till they are sixteen; for—" My dear loves," cry I, " you would not speak before you know *how;* and knowledge is obtained by *hearing,* and not by *speaking.*" And setting my Billy on my lap, in Miss's presence—" Here," said I, taking an ear in the fingers of each hand, " are two ears, my Billy; " and then, pointing to his mouth, " but one tongue, my love; so you must be sure to mind that you *hear* twice as much as you *speak,* even when you grow a bigger master than you are now."

" You have so many pretty ways to learn one, Madam," says Miss, now and then, " that it is impossible we should not regard what you say to us ! "

Several French tutors, when we were abroad, were recommended to Mr. B. But there is one English gentleman, now on his travels with young Mr. R. with whom Mr. B. has agreed; and in the mean time, my best friend is pleased to compliment me, that the children will not suffer for want of a tutor, while I can take the pains I do: which he will have to be too much for me: especially that now, on our return, my Davers and my Pamela are added to my cares. But what mother can take too much pains to cultivate the minds of her children?—If, my dear Lady G., it were not for these *frequent* lyings-in!—But this is the time of life.—Though little did I think, so early, I should have so many careful blessings!

I have as great credit as pleasure from my little family. All our neighbours here admire us more and more. You'll excuse my seeming (for it is but seeming) vanity: I hope I know better than to have it real—"Never," says Mrs. Towers, who is still a single lady, " did I see, before, a lady so much advantaged by her residence in that fantastic nation " (for she loves not the French) " who brought home with her nothing of their affectation!"—She says, that the French politeness, and the English frankness and plainness of heart, appear happily blended in all we say and do. And she makes me a thousand compliments upon Lord and Lady Davers's account, who, she would fain persuade me, owe a great deal of improvement (my lord in his conversation, and my lady in her temper) to living in the same house with us.

My Lady Davers is exceeding kind and good to me, is always magnifying me to every body, and says she knows not how to live from me: and that I have been a means of saving half a hundred souls, as well as her dear brother's. On an indisposition of my Lord's at Montpellier, which made her very apprehensive, she declared, that were she to be deprived of his lordship, she would not let us rest till we had consented to her living with us; saying that we had room enough in Lincolnshire, and she would enlarge the Bedfordshire seat at her own expense.

Mr. H. is Mr. H. still; and that's the best I can say of him; for I verily think, he is more of an ape than ever. His *whole* head is now French. 'Twas *half* so before. We had great difficulties with him abroad: his aunt and I endeavouring to give him a serious and religious turn, we had like to have turned him into a Roman Catholic. For he was much pleased with the shewy part of that religion, and the fine pictures, and decorations in the churches of Italy; and having got into company with a

428

Dominican at Padua, a Franciscan at Milan, and a Jesuit at Paris, they lay so hard at him, in their turns, that we had like to have lost him to each assailant: so were forced to let him take his own course; for, his aunt would have it, that he had no other defence from the attacks of persons to make him embrace a faulty religion, than to permit him to continue as he was; that is to say, to have none at all. So she suspended attempting to proselyte the thoughtless creature, till he came to England. I wish her success here: but, I doubt, he will not be a credit to any religion, for a great while. And as he is very desirous to go to London, it will be found, when there, that any fluttering coxcomb will do more to make him one of that class, in an hour, than his aunt's lessons, to make him a good man, in a twelvemonth. "*Where much is given, much is required.*" The contrary of this, I doubt, is all poor Mr. H. has to trust to.

We have just now heard that his father, who has been long ill, is dead. So now, he is a lord indeed! He flutters and starts about most strangely, I warrant, and is wholly employed in giving directions as to his mourning equipage.—And now there will be no holding him in, I doubt; except his new title has so much virtue in it, as to make him a wiser and better man.

He will now have a seat in the House of Peers of Great Britain; but I hope, for the nation's sake, he will not find many more like himself there!—For, to me, that is one of the most venerable assemblies in the world; and it appears the more so, since I have been abroad; for an English gentleman is respected, if he be any thing of a man, above a foreign nobleman; and an English nobleman above some petty sovereigns.

If our travelling gentry duly considered this distinction in their favour, they would, for the honour of their country, as well as for their own credit, behave in a better manner, in their foreign tours, than, I am sorry to say, some of them do. But what can one expect from the unlicked cubs (pardon the term) sent abroad with only stature, to make them look like men, and equipage to attract respect, without one other qualification to enforce it?

Here let me close this, with a few tears, to the memory of my dear Mrs. Jervis, my other mother, my friend, my adviser, my protectress, in my single state; and my faithful second and partaker in the comforts of my higher life, and better fortunes!

What would I have given to have been present, as it seems,

she so earnestly wished, to close her dying eyes! I should have done it with the piety and the concern of a truly affectionate daughter. But that melancholy happiness was denied to us both; for, as I told you in the letter on the occasion, the dear good woman (who is now in the possession of her blessed reward, and rejoicing in God's mercies) was no more, when the news reached me, so far off as Heidelburgh, of her last illness and wishes.

I cannot forbear, every time I enter her parlour (where I used to see, with so much delight, the good woman sitting, always employed in some useful or pious work), shedding a tear to her memory; and in my Sabbath duties, missing *her*, I miss half a dozen friends, methinks; and I sigh in remembrance of her; and can only recover that cheerful frame, which the performance of those duties always gave me, by reflecting, that she is now reaping the reward of that sincere piety, which used to edify and encourage us all.

The servants we brought home, and those we left behind, melt in tears at the name of Mrs. Jervis. Mr. Longman, too, lamented the loss of her, in the most moving strain. And all I can do now, in honour of her memory and her merit, is to be a friend to those she loved most, as I have already begun to be, and none of them shall suffer in those concerns that can be answered, now she is gone. For the loss of so excellent a friend and relation, is loss enough to all who knew her, and claimed kindred with her.

Poor worthy Jonathan, too, ('tis almost a misery to have so soft, so susceptible an heart as I have, or to have such good servants and friends as one cannot lose without such emotions as I feel for the loss of them!) his silver hairs, which I have beheld with so much delight, and thought I had a father in presence, when I saw them adorning so honest and comely a face, are now laid low!—Forgive me, he was not a common servant; neither are *any* of ours so: but Jonathan excelled all that excelled in his class!—I am told, that these two worthy folks died within two days of one another: on which occasion I could not help saying to myself, in the words of David over Saul and his son Jonathan, the name-sake of our worthy butler—
" *They were lovely and pleasant in their lives, and in their deaths they were not divided.*"

I might have continued on in the words of the royal lamenter; for, surely, never did one fellow-servant love another in my maiden state, nor servant love a mistress in my exalted condition, better than Jonathan loved me! I could see in his eyes a glisten-

430

ing pleasure, whenever I passed by him: if at such times I spoke to him, as I seldom failed to do, with a—"*God bless you too!*" in answer to his repeated blessings, he had a kind of rejuvenescence (may I say?) visibly running through his whole frame: and, now and then, if I laid my hands upon his folded ones, as I passed him on a Sunday morning or evening, praying for me, with a—"*How do you, my worthy old acquaintance?*" his heart would spring to his lips in a kind of rapture, and his eyes would run over.

O my beloved friend! how the loss of these two worthies of my family oppresses me at times!

Mr. B. likewise shewed a generous concern on the occasion: and when all the servants welcomed us in a body, on our return —"Methinks my dear," said he, "I miss your Mrs. Jervis, and honest Jonathan." A starting tear, and—"They are happy, dear honest souls!" and a sigh, were the tribute I paid to their memories, on their beloved master's so kindly repeating their names.

Who knows, had I been here—But away, too painful reflections—They lived to a good old age, and fell like fruit fully ripe: they *died the death of the righteous;* I must follow them in time, God knows how soon: and, *Oh! that my latter end may be like theirs!*

Once more, forgive me, my dear friend, this small tribute to their memories: and believe, that I am not so ungrateful for God's mercies, as to let the loss of these dear good folks lessen with me the joy and delight I have still left me, in the health and the love of the best of husbands, and good men; in the children, charming as ever mother could boast of—charming, I mean, principally, in the dawning beauties of their minds, and in the pleasure their towardliness of nature gives me; including, as I always do, my dear Miss Goodwin, and have reason to do, from her dutiful love of me, and observation of all I say to her; in the preservation to me of the best and worthiest of parents, hearty, though aged as they are; in the love and friendship of good Lord and Lady Davers, and my excellent friend Lady G.; not forgetting even worthy Mr. Longman. God preserve all these to me, as I am truly thankful for his mercies!—And then, notwithstanding my affecting losses, as above, who will be so happy as I? That you, my dear Lady G. may long continue so, likewise in the love of a worthy husband, and the delights of an increasing hopeful family, which will make you some amends for the heavy losses you also have sustained, in the two last years of an affectionate father, and a most worthy mother, and, in Mrs. Jones, of a good neighbour, prays *your ever affectionate friend and servant,*

P. B.

LETTER C

My beloved Lady G.,

You will excuse my long silence, when I shall tell you the occasions of it. In the first place, I was obliged to pay a dutiful visit to Kent, where my good father was taken ill of a fever, and my mother of an ague; and think, Madam, how this must affect me, at their time of life !

Mr. B. kindly accompanied me, apprehending that his presence would be necessary, if the recovery of them both, in which I thankfully rejoice, had not happened; especially as a circumstance I am, I think, *always* in, added more weight to his apprehensions.

I had hardly returned from Kent to Bedfordshire, and looked around, when I was obliged to set out to attend Lady Davers, who said she should *die*, if she saw me not, to comfort and recover, by my counsel and presence (so she was pleased to express herself) her sick lord who had just got out of an intermittent fever, which left him without any spirit, and was occasioned by fretting at the conduct of her *stupid nephew* (those also were her words).

For you must have heard (every body hears when a man of quality does a foolish thing !), and it has been in all the newspapers, that, " On Wednesday last the Right Honourable John " (Jackey they should have said), " Lord H., nephew to the Right Honourable William Lord Davers, was married to the Honourable Mrs. P., relict of J. P. of Twickenham, Esq., a lady of celebrated beauty and ample fortune."

Now, you must know, that this celebrated lady is, 'tis true, of the —— family, whence her title of *honourable ;* but is indeed so *celebrated*, that every fluttering coxcomb in town can give some account of her, even before she was in keeping of the Duke of —— who had cast her on the town he had robbed of her.

In short, she is quite a common woman; has no fortune at all, as one may say, only a small jointure incumbered; and is much in debt. She is a shrew into the bargain, and the poor wretch is a father already; for he has already had a girl of three years old (her husband has been dead seven) brought him home, which he knew nothing of, nor even inquired, whether his widow had a child !—And he is now paying the mother's debts, and trying to make the best of his bargain.

This is the fruit of a London journey, so long desired by him, and his fluttering about there with his new title.

He was drawn in by a brother of his lady, and a friend of that brother's, two town sharpers, gamesters, and bullies. Poor Sir Joseph Wittol ! This was his case, and his character, it seems, in London.

Shall I present you with a curiosity ? 'Tis a copy of his letter to his uncle, who had, as you may well think, lost all patience with him, on occasion of this abominable folly.

" MY LORD DAVERS,

"For iff you will not call me neffew, I have no reason to call you unkell; surely you forgett who it was you held up your kane to : I have as little reason to valew you displeassure, as you have me : for I am, God be thanked, a lord and a pere of the realme, as well as you; and as to youre nott owneing me, nor your brother B. not looking upon me, I care not a fardinge : and, bad as you think I have done, I have marry'd a woman of family. Take thatt among you !

" As to your personal abuses of her, take care whatt you say. You know the stattute will defend us as well as you.—And, besides, she has a brother that won't lett her good name be called in question.—Mind thatt !

" Some thinges I wish had been otherwise—perhapps I do.— What then ?—Must you, my lord, make more mischiefe, and adde to my plagues, iff I have any ?—Is this your unkelship ?

" Butt I shan't want youre advice. I have as good an estate as you have, and am as much a lord as yourselfe.—Why the devill then, am I to be treated as I am ?—Why the plague— But I won't sware neither. I desire not to see you, any more than you doe me, I can tell you thatt. And iff we ever meet under one roofe with my likeing, it must be at the House of Peeres where I shall be upon a parr with you in every thing, that's my cumfurte.

" As to Lady Davers, I desire not to see her ladyship; for she was always plaguy nimbel with her fingers; but, lett my false stepp be what itt will, I have in other respectes, marry'd a lady who is as well descended as herselfe, and no disparage-ment neither; so have nott thatt to answer for to her pride : and who has as good a spiritt too, if they were to come face to face, or I am mistaken : nor will shee take affruntes from any one. So my lord, leave mee to make the best of my

433

matters, as I will of youres. So no more, but that I am *youre servante*, H.

"P.S. I mean no affrunte to Mrs. B. She is the best of yee all—by G—."

I will not take up your time with further observations upon this poor creature's bad conduct: his reflection must proceed from *feeling;* and will, that's the worst of it, come too late, come *when* or *how* it will. I will only say, I am sorry for it on his own account, but more for that of Lord and Lady Davers, who take the matter very heavily, and wish he had married the lowest born creature in England (so she had been honest and virtuous), rather than done as he has done.

But, I suppose, the poor gentleman was resolved to shun, at all adventures, Mr. B.'s fault, and keep up to the pride of descent and family;—and so married the *only* creature, as I hope (since it cannot be helped), that is so great a disgrace to both: for I presume to flatter myself, for the sake of my sex, that, among the poor wretches who are sunk so low as the town-women are, there are very few of birth or education; but such, principally, as have had their necessities or their ignorance taken advantage of by base men; since birth and education must needs set the most unhappy of the sex above so sordid and so abandoned a guilt, as the hourly wickedness of such a course of life subjects them to.

But let me pursue my purpose of excusing my long silence. I had hardly returned from Lady Davers's, and recovered my family management, and resumed my nursery duties, when my fourth dear boy, my Jemmy (for, I think am I going on to make out the number Lady Davers allotted me), pressed so upon me, as not to be refused, for one month or six weeks close attention. And then a journey to Lord Davers's, and that noble pair accompanying us to Kent; and daily and hourly pleasures crowding upon us, narrow and confined as our room there was (though we went with as few attendants as possible), engrossed *more* of my time. Thus I hope you will forgive me, because, as soon as I returned, I set about writing this, as an excuse for myself, in the first place; to promise you the subject you insist upon, in the next; and to say, that I am incapable of forgetfulness or negligence to such a friend as Lady G. For I must always be *your faithful and affectionate humble servant,*

P. B.

My dear Lady G.,

The remarks, your cousin Fielding says, I have made on the subject of young gentlemen's travelling, and which you request me to communicate to you, are part of a little book upon education, which I wrote for Mr. B.'s correction and amendment, on his putting Mr. Locke's treatise on that subject into my hands, and requiring my observations upon it.

I cannot flatter myself they will answer your expectation; for I am sensible they must be unworthy even of the opportunities I have had in the excursions, in which I have been indulged by the best of men. But your requests are so many laws to me; and I will give you a short abstract of what I read Miss Fielding, who has so greatly overrated it to you.

The gentleman's book contains many excellent rules on education; but this of travel I will only refer you to at present. You will there see his objections against the age at which young gentlemen are sent abroad, from sixteen to twenty-one, the time in all their lives, he says, at which young gentlemen are the least suited to these improvements, and in which they have the least fence and guard against their passions.

The age he proposes is from seven to fourteen, because of the advantage they will then have to master foreign languages, and to form their tongue to the true pronunciation; as well as that they they will be more easily directed by their tutors or governors. Or else he proposes that more sedate time of life, when the gentleman is able to travel without a tutor, and to make his own observations; and when he is thoroughly acquainted with the laws and fashions, the natural and moral advantages and defects of his own country; by which means, as Mr. Locke wisely observes, the traveller will have something to exchange with those abroad, from whose conversation he hopes to reap any knowledge. And he supports his opinion by excellent reasons, to which I refer you.

What I have written in my little book, not yet quite finished on *this* head, relates principally to *Home Travelling*, which Mr. B. was always resolved his sons should undertake, before they entered upon a foreign tour. I have there observed, that England abounds with curiosities, both of art and nature, worth the notice of a diligent inquirer, and equal with some of those we admire in foreign parts; and that if the youth be not sent abroad at Mr. Locke's earliest time, from seven to fourteen (which I can hardly think will be worth while, merely for the sake of attaining a perfection in the languages), he may with good advantage begin, at fourteen or fifteen, the tour of Great Britain, now-and-then, by excursions, in the summer months, between his other studies, and as a diversion to him. This I should wish might be entered upon in his papa's company, as well as his tutor's, if it could conveniently be done; who thus initiating both the governed and governor in the methods he would have observed by both, will obtain no small satisfaction and amusement to himself.

For the father would by this means be an eye-witness of the behaviour of the one and the other, and have a specimen how fit the young man was to be trusted, or the tutor to be depended upon, when they went abroad, and were out of his sight: as *they* would of what was expected from them by the father. And hence a thousand benefits may arise to the young gentleman from the occasional observations and reflections of his father, with regard to expence, company, conversation, hours, and such like.

If the father could not himself accompany his son, he might appoint the stages the young gentleman should take, and enjoin both tutor and son to give, at every stage, an account of whatever they observed curious and remarkable, not omitting the minutest occurrences. By this means, and the probability that he might hear of them, and their proceedings, from his friends, acquaintance, and relations, who might fall in with them, they would have a greater regard to their conduct; and so much the more, if the young gentleman were to keep an account of his expences, which, upon his return, he might lay before his father.

By seeing thus the different customs, manners, and economy of different persons and families (for in so mixed a nation as ours is, there is as great a variety of that sort to be met with, as in most), and from their different treatment at their several stages, a great deal of the world may be learned by the young gentleman. He would be prepared to go abroad with more delight to himself, as well as more experience, and greater reputation to his family and country. In such excursions as these, the tutor would see his temper and inclination, and might notice to the father any thing amiss, that it might be set right, while the youth was yet in his reach, and more under his inspection, than he would be in a foreign country: and his observations, on his return, as well as in his letters, would shew how fit he was to be trusted; and how likely to improve, when at a greater distance.

After England and Wales, as well the inland parts as the

sea-coasts, let them if they behave according to expectation, take a journey into Scotland and Ireland, and visit the principal islands, as Guernsey, Jersey, &c. the youth continuing to write down his observations all the way, and keeping a journal of occurrences; and let him employ the little time he will be on board of ship, in these small trips from island to island, or coastwise, in observing upon the noble art of navigation; of the theory of which, it will not be amiss that he has some notion, as well as of the curious structure of a ship, its tackle, and furniture : a knowledge very far from being insignificant to a gentleman who is an islander, and has a stake in the greatest maritime kingdom in the world; and hence he will be taught to love and value that most useful and brave set of men, the British sailors, who are the natural defence and glory of the realm.

Hereby he will confirm his theory in the geography of the British dominions in Europe, he will be apprised of the situation, conveniences, interests, and constitution of his own country; and will be able to lay a ground-work for the future government of his thoughts and actions, if the interest he bears in his native country should call him to the public service in either house of parliament.

With this foundation, how excellently would he be qualified to go abroad ! and how properly then would he add to the knowledge he had attained of his own country, that of the different customs, manners, and forms of government of others ! How would he be able to form comparisons, and to make all his inquiries appear pertinent and manly. All the occasions of that ignorant wonder, which renders a novice the jest of all about him, would be taken away. He would be able to ask questions, and to judge without leading strings. Nor would he think he has seen a country, and answered the ends of his father's expence, and his own improvement, by running through a kingdom, and knowing nothing of it, but the inns and stages, at which he stopped to eat and drink. For, on the contrary, he would make the best acquaintance, and contract worthy friendships with such as would court and reverence him as one of the rising geniuses of his country.

Whereas most of the young gentlemen who are sent abroad raw and unprepared, as if to wonder at every thing they see, and to be laughed at by all that see them, do but expose themselves and their country. And if, at their return, by interest of friends, by alliances, or marriages, they should happen to be promoted to places of honour or profit, their unmerited preferment will only serve to make those foreigners, who were eye-witnesses of their weakness and follies, when among them, conclude greatly in disfavour of the whole nation, or, at least, of the prince, and his administration, who could find no fitter subjects to distinguish.

This, my dear friend, is a brief extract from my observations on the head of qualifying young gentlemen to travel with honour and improvement. I doubt you'll be apt to think me not a little out of my element; but since you *would* have it, I claim the allowances of a friend; to which my ready compliance with your commands the rather entitles me.

I am very sorry Mr. and Mrs. Murray are so unhappy in each other. Were he a generous man, the heavy loss the poor lady has sustained, as well as her sister, my beloved friend, in so excellent a mother, and so kind a father, would make him bear with her infirmities a little.

But, really, I have seen, on twenty occasions, that notwithstanding all the fine things gentlemen say to ladies before marriage, if the latter do not *improve* upon their husbands' hands, their imputed graces when single, will not protect them from indifference, and, probably, from worse; while the gentleman, perhaps, thinks *he* only, of the two, is entitled to go backward in acts of kindness and complaisance. A strange and shocking difference which too many ladies experience, who, from fond lovers, prostrate at their feet, find surly husbands, trampling upon their necks !

You, my dear friend, were happy in your days of courtship, and are no less so in your state of wedlock. And may you continue to be so to a good old age, *prays your affectionate and faithful friend,*   P. B.

LETTER CII

My dear Lady G.,

I will cheerfully cause to be transcribed for you the conversation you desire, between myself, Mrs. Towers, and Lady Arthur, and the three young ladies their relations, in presence of the dean and his daughter, and Mrs. Brooks; and glad I shall be, if it may be of use to the two thoughtless Misses your neighbours; who, you are pleased to tell me, are great admirers of my story and my example; and will therefore, as you say, pay greater attention to what I write, than to the more passionate and interested lessons of their mamma.

I am only sorry you should be concerned about the supposed

trouble you give me, by having mislaid my former relation of it. For, besides obliging my dear Lady G., the hope of doing service by it to a family so worthy, in a case so nearly affecting its honour, as to make two headstrong young ladies recollect what belongs to their sex and their characters, and what their filial duties require of them, affords me high pleasure; and if it shall be attended with the wished effects, it will add to my happiness.

I said, *cause* to be transcribed, because I hope to answer a double end by it; for, on reconsideration, I set Miss Goodwin to transcribe it, who writes a pretty hand, and is not a little fond of the task, nor, indeed, of any task I set her; and will be more affected as she performs it, than she could be by *reading* it only; although she is a very good girl at present, and gives me hopes that she will continue to be so.

I will inclose it when done, that it may be read to the parties without this introduction, if you think fit. And you will forgive me for having added a few observations, with a view to the cases of your inconsiderate young ladies, and for having corrected the former narrative in several places.

My dear Lady G.,

The papers you have mislaid, as to the conversation between me and the young ladies, relations of Mrs. Towers, and Lady Anne Arthur, in presence of these two last-named ladies, Mrs. Brooks, and the worthy dean, and Miss L. (of which, in order to perfect your kind collection of my communications you request another copy) contained as follows.

I first stated, that I had seen these three ladies twice or thrice before, as visitors, at their kinswomen's houses so that they and I were not altogether strangers to one another: and my two neighbours acquainted me with their respective tastes and dispositions, and their histories preparatory to this visit, to the following effects:

That Miss Stapylton is over-run with the love of poetry and romance, and delights in flowery language and metaphorical flourishes: is about eighteen, wants not either sense or politeness; and has read herself into a vein, more amorous (that was Mrs. Towers's word) than discreet. Has extraordinary notions of a *first sight* love; and gives herself greater liberties, with a pair of fine eyes (in hopes to make sudden conquests in pursuance of that notion), than is pretty in her sex and age; which makes those who know her not, conclude her bold and forward; and is more than suspected, with a mind thus prepared for instantaneous impressions, to have experienced the argument to her own disadvantage, and to be *struck* by (before she had *stricken*) a gentleman, whom her friends think not at all worthy of her, and to whom she was making some indiscreet advances, under the name of PHILOCLEA to PHILOXENUS, in a letter which she entrusted to a servant of the family, who, discovering her design, prevented her indiscretion for that time.

That, in other respects, she has no mean accomplishments, will have a fine fortune, is genteel in her person, though with some visible affectation, dances well, sings well, and plays prettily on several instruments; is fond of reading, but affects the action, and air, and attitude of a tragedian; and is too apt to give an emphasis in the wrong place, in order to make an author mean significantly, even where the occasion is common, and, in a mere historical fact, that requires as much simplicity in the reader's accent, as in the writer's style. No wonder then, that when she reads a play, she will put herself into a sweat, as Mrs. Towers says; distorting very agreeable features, and making a *multitude* of wry mouths with *one* very pretty one, in order to convince her hearers, what a near neighbour her heart is to her lips.

MISS COPE is a young lady of nineteen, lovely in her person, with a handsome fortune in possession, and great prospects. Has a soft and gentle turn of mind, which disposes her to be easily imposed upon. Is addressed by a libertine of quality, whose courtship, while permitted, was imperiousness; and whose tenderness, insult : having found the young lady too susceptible of impression, open and unreserved, and even valuing him the more, as it seemed, for treating her with ungenerous contempt; for that she was always making excuses for slights, ill manners, and even rudeness, which no other young lady would forgive.

That this docility on her side, and this insolence on his, and an over-free, and even indecent degree of romping, as it is called, with her, which once her mamma surprised them in, made her papa forbid *his* visits, and *her* receiving them.

That this however, was so much to Miss Cope's regret, that she was detected in a design to elope to him out of the private garden-door; which, had she effected, in all probability, the indelicate and dishonourable peer would have triumphed over her innocence; having given out since, that he intended to revenge himself on the daughter, for the disgrace he had received from the parents.

That though convinced of this, it was feared she still loved him, and would again throw herself in his way; urging, that his rash expressions were the effect only of his passion; for that she knows he loves her too well to be dishonourable to her; and by the same degree of favourable prepossession, she will have it, that his brutal roughness is the manliness of his nature; that his most shocking expressions are sincerity of heart; that his boasts of former lewdness are but instances that he knows the world; that his freedoms with her person are but excess of love and innocent gaiety of temper; that his resenting the prohibition he has met with, and his threats, are other instances of his love and his courage : and peers of the realm ought not to be bound down by little narrow rules like the vulgar; for, truly, their *honour* is in the greatest cases regarded as equal with the *oath* of a common gentleman, and is a security that a lady may trust to, if he is not a profligate indeed; and that Lord P. *cannot* be.

That excepting these weaknesses, Miss has many good qualities; is charitable, pious, humane, humble; sings sweetly, plays on the spinnet charmingly; is meek, fearful, and never was resolute or courageous enough to step out of the regular path, till her too flexible heart became touched with a passion, that is said to polish the most brutal temper, and therefore her rough peer has none of it; and to animate the dove, of which Miss Cope has too much.

That Miss Sutton, a young lady of the like age with the two former, has too lively and airy a turn of mind; affects to be thought well read in the histories of kingdoms, as well as in polite literature. Speaks French fluently, talks much upon all subjects; and has a great deal of flippant wit, which makes more enemies than friends. However, is innocent, and unsuspectedly virtuous hitherto; but makes herself cheap and accessible to fops and rakes, and has not the worse opinion of a man for being such. Listens eagerly to stories told to the disadvantage of some of her own sex; though affecting to be a great stickler for the honour of it in general : will unpityingly propagate them : thinks (without considering to what the imprudence of her own conduct may subject her) the woman that slips inexcusable; and the man who seduces her, much less faulty; and thus encourages the one sex in their vileness, and gives up the other for their weakness, in a kind of silly affectation, to shew her security in her own virtue; at the same time, that she is dancing upon the edge of a precipice, presumptuously inattentive to her own danger.

The worthy dean, knowing the ladies' intention in this visit to me, brought his daughter with him, as if by accident; for Miss L. with many good qualities, is of a remarkable soft temper, though not so inconsiderately soft as Miss Cope : but is too credulous; and, as her papa suspects, entertains more than a liking to a wild young gentleman, the heir to a noble fortune, who makes visits to her, full of tenderness and respect, but without declaring himself. This gives the dean much uneasiness; and he is very desirous that his daughter should be in my company on all occasions, as she is so kind to profess a great regard to my opinion and judgment.

'Tis easy to see the poor young lady is in love; and she makes no doubt that the young gentleman loves *her ;* but, alas ! why then (for he is not a bashful man, as you shall hear) does he not say so?—He has deceived already two young creatures. His father has cautioned the dean against his son. Has told him, that he is sly, subtle, full of stratagem, yet has so much command of himself (which makes him more dangerous), as not to precipitate his designs; but can wait with patience till he thinks himself secure of his prey, and then pulls off the mask at once; and, if he succeeds, glories in his villainy. Yet does his father beg of the dean to permit his visits, for he wishes him to marry Miss L. though greatly unequal in fortune to his son, wishing for nothing so much as that he *would* marry. And the dean, owing his principal preferment to the old gentleman, cares not to disoblige him, or affront his son, without some apparent reason for it, especially as the father is wrapt up in him, having no other child, and being himself half afraid of him, least, if too much thwarted, he should fly out entirely.

So here, Madam, are four young ladies of like years, and different inclinations and tempers, all of whom may be said to have dangers to encounter, resulting from their respective dispositions : and who, professing to admire my character and example, were brought to me, to be benefited, as Mrs. Towers was pleased to say, by my conversation : and all was to be as if accidental, none of them knowing how well I was acquainted with their several characters.

How proud would this compliment have made me from such a lady as Mrs. Towers, had I not been as proud as proud could be before, of the good opinion of four beloved persons, Mr. B., Lady Davers, the Countess of C. and your dear self.

We were attended only by Polly Barlow, who in some points was as much concerned as any body. And this being when Lord and Lady Davers, and the noble Countess, were with us, 'tis proper to say, they were abroad together upon a visit, from which, knowing how I was to be engaged, they excused me. The dean was well known to, and valued by, all the ladies;

and therefore was no manner of restraint upon the freedom of our conversation.

I was in my closet when they came; and Mrs. Towers, having presented each young lady to me when I came down, said, being all seated, "I can guess at your employment, Mrs. B. Writing, I dare say? I have often wished to have you for a correspondent; for every one who can boast of that favour, exalts you to the skies, and says, your letters exceed your conversation; but I always insisted upon it that *that* was impossible."

"Mrs. Towers," said I, "is always saying the most obliging things in the world of her neighbours: but may not one suffer, dear Madam, for these kind prepossessions, in the opinion of greater strangers, who will judge more impartially than your favour will permit you to do?"

"That," said Lady Arthur, "will be so soon put out of doubt, when Mrs. B. begins to speak, that we will refer to that, and to put an end to every thing that looks like compliment."

"But, Mrs. B.," says Mrs. Towers, "may one ask, what particular subject was at this time your employment?"

I had been writing (you must know, Lady G.) for the sake of suiting Miss Stapylton's flighty vein, a little sketch of the style she is so fond of; and hoped for some such opportunity as this question gave me, to bring it on the carpet; for my only fear, with her and, Miss Cope, and Miss Sutton, was, that they would deem me too grave; and so what should fall in the course of conversation, would make the least impression upon them. For the best instructions, you know, will be ineffectual, if the manner of conveying them is not adapted to the taste and temper of the person you would wish to influence. And moreover, I had a view in it, to make this little sketch the introduction to some future observations on the stiff and affected style of romances, which might put Miss Stapylton out of conceit with them, and make her turn the course of her studies another way, as I shall mention in its place.

I answered that I had been meditating upon the misfortunes of a fine young lady, who had been seduced and betrayed by a gentleman she loved, and who, notwithstanding, had the grace to stop short (indeed, later than were to be wished), and to abandon friends, country, lover, in order to avoid any further intercourse with him; and that God had blessed her penitence and resolution, and she was now very happy in a neighbouring dominion.

"A fine subject," said Miss Stapylton. "Was the gentleman a man of wit, Madam? Was the lady a woman of taste?"

443

"The gentleman, Madam, was all that was desirable in a man, had he been virtuous: the lady all that is excellent in woman, had she been more circumspect. But it was a first love on both sides; and little did she think he could have taken advantage of her innocence and her affection for him."

"A sad, sad story!" said Miss Cope: "but pray, Madam, did their friends approve of their visits? For danger, sometimes, as I have heard, arises from the cruelty of friends, who force lovers upon private and clandestine meetings, when perhaps there can be no material objection why the gentleman and lady may not come together."

"Well observed, Miss Cope," thought I. "How we are for making every case applicable to our own, when our hearts are fixed upon a point."

"It cannot be called *cruelty* in friends, Madam," said I, "when their cautions, or even *prohibitions*, are so well justified by the event, as in *this* case—and, *generally*, by the wicked arts and practices of seducers. And how happy it is for a lady, when she suffers herself to be convinced, that those who have lived *forty* years in the world, may know twice as much, at least, of that world, as she can possibly know at *twenty*, ten of which, moreover, are almost a blank! If they do *not*, the one must be supposed very ignorant; the other very knowing. But, Madam, the lady whose hard case I was considering *hoped* too much, and *feared* too little; that was her fault; which made her give opportunities to the gentleman, which neither *liberty* nor *restraint* could justify in her. She had not the discretion, poor lady! in this one great point of all, that the ladies I have in my eye, I dare say, would have had in her case."

"I beg pardon," said Miss Cope, and blushed. "I know not the case, and ought to have been silent."

"Aye," thought I, "so you would, had not you thought yourself more affected by it, than it were to be wished you were."

"I think," said Miss Sutton, "the lady was the less to be pitied, as she must know what her character required of her, and that men will generally deceive when they are trusted. There are very few of them who *pretend* to be virtuous, and it is allowed to be *their* privilege to ask, as it is the *lady's* to deny."

"So," replied I, "you are supposing a continual state of warfare between the two sexes; one offensive, the other defensive: and indeed I think the notion not altogether amiss; for

444

a lady will assuredly be less in danger, where she rather *fears* an *enemy* in the acquaintance she has of that sex, than *hopes* a *friend;* especially as so much depends upon the issue, either of her doubt, or of her confidence."

"I don't know *neither*, Madam," returned Miss Sutton, very briskly, "whether the men should be set out to us as such bugbears, as our mothers generally represent them. It is making them too considerable; and is a kind of reflection upon the discretion and virtue of our sex, and supposes us weak indeed. The late Czar, I have read," continued she, "took a better method with the Swedes, who had often beat him; when, after a great victory, he made his captives march in procession through the streets of his principal city, to familiarize them to the Russes, and shew them they were *but* men."

"Very well observed," replied I; "but then, did you not say that this was thought necessary to be done, because the Russes had been often *defeated* by the Swedes, and thought *too highly* of them: and when the Swedes, taking advantage of that prepossession, had the *greater contempt* of the Russes?"

She looked a little disconcerted; and being silent, I proceeded:—"I am very far, Madam, from thinking the generality of men very formidable, if our sex do justice to themselves, and to what their characters require of them. Yet, allow me to say, that the men I thought contemptible, I would not think worthy of my company, nor give it them, when I could avoid it. And as for those, who are more to be regarded, I fear, when they can be assured that a lady allows it to be their privilege to sue for favours, it will certainly embolden them to solicit, and to think themselves acting in character, when they put the lady upon hers, to refuse them. And yet I am humbly of opinion, with the poet:

"'He comes *too near*, who comes to be *deny'd*.'

"For these reasons, Madam, I was pleased with your notion, that it would be best to look upon that sex, especially if we allow them the privilege you speak of, in an *hostile* light.

"But permit me to observe, with regard to the most contemptible of the species, fops, coxcombs, and pretty fellows, that many a *good* general has been defeated, when, trusting to his great strength and skill, he has despised a *truly weak* enemy."

"I believe, Madam," returned she, "your observation is very just. I have read of such instances. But, dear Madam, permit me to ask, whether we speak not too generally, when

445

we condemn every man who dresses well, and is not a sloven, as a fop or a coxcomb?"

"No doubt, when this is the case. But you hardly ever saw a man *very* nice about his person and dress, that had any thing he thought of *greater* consequence to himself to regard. 'Tis natural it should be so; for should not the man of *body* take the greater care to set out and adorn the part for which he thinks himself most valuable? And will not the man of *mind* bestow his principal care in improving that mind? perhaps to the neglect of dress, and outward appearance, which is a fault. But surely, Madam, there is a middle way to be observed, in these, as in most other cases; for a man need not be a sloven, any more than a fop. He need not shew an utter disregard to dress, nor yet think it his first and chief concern; be ready to quarrel with the wind for discomposing his peruke, or fear to put on his hat, lest he should depress his foretop; more dislike a spot upon his clothes, than in his reputation; be a self-admirer, and always at the glass, which he would perhaps never look into, could it shew him the deformity of his mind, as well as the finery of his person; who has a taylor for his tutor, and a milliner for his school-mistress; who laughs at men of sense (excusably enough, perhaps in revenge because they laugh at him); who calls learning pedantry, and looks upon the knowledge of the fashions as the only useful science to a fine gentleman.

"Pardon me, ladies; I could proceed with the character of this species of men, but I need not; for every lady present would despise such an one, as much as I do, were he to fall in her way: or the rather, because he who admires himself, will never admire his lady as he ought; and if he maintains his niceness after marriage, it will be with a preference to his own person; if not, will sink, very probably, into the worst of slovens. For whoever is capable of one extreme (take almost the cases of human life through) when he recedes from that, if he be not a man of prudence, will go over into the other.

"But to return to the former subject" (for the general attention encouraged me to proceed), "permit me, Miss Sutton, to add, that a lady must run great risks to her reputation, if not to her virtue, who will admit into her company any gentleman who shall be of opinion, and know it to be *hers*, that it is *his* province to ask a favour, which it will be *her* duty to deny."

"I believe, Madam, I spoke these words a little too carelessly; but I meant *honourable* questions, to be sure."

"There can be but *one* honourable question," replied I;

" and that is seldom asked, but when the affair is brought near a conclusion, and there is a probability of its being granted; and which a single lady, while she has parents or guardians, should never think of permitting to be put to herself, much less of approving, nor, perhaps, as the case may be of denying. But I make no doubt that you meant honourable questions. A young lady of Miss Sutton's good sense, and worthy character, could not mean otherwise. And I have said, perhaps, more than I need upon the subject, because we all know how ready the presuming of the other sex are, right or wrong to construe the most innocent meetings in favour of their own views."

" Very true," said she; but appeared to be under an agreeable confusion, every lady, by her eye, seeming to think she had met with a deserved rebuke; and which not seeming to expect, it abated her liveliness all the time after.

Mrs. Towers seasonably relieved us both from a subject *too applicable*, if I may so express it, saying—" But, dear Mrs. B., will you favour us with the result of your meditation, if committed to writing, on the unhappy case you mentioned? "

" I was rather, Madam, exercising my fancy than my judgment, such as it is, upon the occasion. I was aiming at a kind of allegorical or metaphorical style, I know not which to call it; and it is not fit to be read before such judges, I doubt."

" O pray, dear Madam," said Miss Stapylton, " favour us with it *to choose ;* for I am a great admirer of that style."

" I have a great curiosity," said Lady Arthur, " both from the *subject* and the *style*, to hear what you have written : and I beg you will oblige us all."

" It is short and unfinished. It was written for the sake of a friend, who is fond of such a style; and what I shall add to it, will be principally some slight observations upon this way of writing. But, let it be ever so censurable, I should be *more* so, if I made any difficulties after such an unanimous request." So, taking it out of my letter-case, I read as follows :

" While the *banks* of *discretion* keep the *proud water* of *passion* within their natural channel, all calm and serene glides along the silver current, enlivening the adjacent meadows, as it passes, with a brighter and more flowery verdure. But if the *torrents* of *sensual love* are permitted to descend from the *hills* of *credulous hope*, they may so swell the gentle stream, as to make it difficult, if not impossible, to be retained betwixt its usual bounds. What then will be the consequence ?—Why, the *trees of resolution*, and the *shrubs of cautious fear*, which grew upon the frail mound, and whose intertwining roots had contributed to support it,

447

being loosened from their hold, *they*, and all that would swim of the *bank* itself, will be seen floating on the surface of the triumphant waters.

"But here, a dear lady, having unhappily failed, is enabled to set her *foot* in the *new-made* breach, while yet it is *possible* to stop it, and to say, with little variation in the language of that power, which only could enable *her* to say it, *Hither, ye proud waves of dissolute love, although you* HAVE *come, yet no farther* SHALL *ye come;* is such an instance of magnanimous resolution and self-conquest, as is very rarely to be met with."

Miss Stapylton seemed pleased (as I expected), and told me, that she should take it for a high favour, to be permitted, if not improper, to see the whole letter when finished.

I said, I would oblige her with all my heart.—"But you must not expect, Madam, that although I have written what I have read to you, I shall approve of it in my observations upon it; for I am convinced, that no style can be proper, which is not plain, simple, easy, natural and unaffected."

She was sure, she was pleased to say, that whatever my observations were, they would be equally just and instructive.

"I too," said the dean, "will answer for that; for I dare say, by what I have already heard, that Mrs. B. will distinguish properly between the style (and the matter too) which captivates the imagination, and that which informs the judgment."

Our conversation, after this, took a more general turn; which I thought right, lest the young ladies should imagine it was a designed thing against them: yet it was such, that every one of them found her character and taste, little or much, concerned in it; and all seemed, as Mrs. Towers afterwards observed to me, by their silence and attention, to be busied in private applications.

The dean began it with a high compliment to me; having a view, no doubt, by his kind praises, to make my observations have the greater weight upon the young ladies. He said, it was matter of great surprise to him, that, my tender years considered, I should be capable of making those reflections, by which persons of twice my age and experience might be instructed.—"You see, Madam," said he, "our attention, when your lips begin to open; and I beg we may have nothing to do, but to *be* attentive."

"I have had such advantages, Sir, from the observations and cautions of my late excellent lady, that did you but know half of them, you would rather wonder I had made *no greater* improvement, than that I have made *so much*. She used to think me pretty, and not ill-tempered, and, of *course* not incredulous, where I conceived a good opinion; and was always arming me on that side, as believing I might be the object of wicked attempts, and the rather, as my low fortune subjected me to danger. For, had I been born to rank and condition, as these young ladies here, I should have had reason to think of *myself*, as justly as, no doubt, *they* do, and, of consequence, beyond the reach of any vile intriguer; as I should have been above the greatest part of that species of mankind, who, for want of understanding or honour, or through pernicious habits, give themselves up to libertinism."

"These were great advantages," said Miss Sutton; "but in *you*, they met with a surprising genius, 'tis very plain, Madam; and there is not, in my opinion, a lady of England, of your years, who would have improved by them as you have done."

I answered, that I was much obliged by her good opinion: and that I had always observed, the person who admired any good qualities in another, gave a kind of *natural* demonstration, that she had the same in an eminent degree herself, although, perhaps, her modest diffidence would not permit her to trace the generous principle to its source.

The dean, to renew the subject of *credulity*, repeated my remark, that it was safer, in cases where so much depended upon the issue, as a lady's honour and reputation, to *fear* an *enemy*, than to *hope* a *friend;* and praised my observation, that even a *weak* enemy is not to be too much despised.

I said, I had very high notions of the honour and value of my own sex, and very mean ones of the gay and frothy part of the other; insomuch, that I thought they could have no strength, but what was founded in our weakness: that the difference of education must give men advantages, even where the genius is naturally equal; besides, they have generally more hardness of heart, which makes women, where they meet not with men of honour, engage with that sex upon very unequal terms; for that it is so customary with them to make vows and promises, and to set light by them, *when made*, that an innocent lady cannot guard too watchfully against them; and, in my opinion, should believe nothing they said, or even *vowed*, but what carried demonstration with it.

"I remember my lady used often to observe, there is a time of life in all young persons, which may properly be called *the romantic*, which is a very dangerous period, and requires therefore a great guard of prudence; that the risque is not a little augmented by reading novels and romances; and the poetical tribe have much to answer for, by reason of their heightened and inflaming descriptions, which do much hurt to thoughtless minds, and lively imaginations. For to those, she would have it, are principally owing, the rashness and indiscretion of *soft* and *tender* dispositions: which, in breach of their duty, and even to the disgrace of their sex, too frequently set them upon enterprises, like those they have read in those pernicious writings, which not seldom make them fall a sacrifice to the base designs of some wild intriguer; and even in cases where their precipitation ends the best, that is to say, in *marriage*, they too frequently (in direct opposition to the cautions and commands of their *tried*, their *experienced*, and *unquestionable* friends) throw themselves upon an *almost stranger*, who, had he been worthy of them, would not, nor *needed* to have taken indirect methods to obtain their favour.

" And the misfortune is, the most innocent are generally the most credulous. Such a lady would do no harm to others, and cannot think others would do her any. And as to the particular person who has obtained, perhaps, a share in her confidence, *he* cannot, she thinks, be so *ungrateful*, as to return irreparable mischief for her good-will to him. Were all the men in the world besides to prove false, the *beloved* person cannot. 'Twould be unjust to *her own merit*, as well as to *his views*, to suppose it: and so *design* on his side, and *credulity* and *self-opinion*, on the lady's, at last enrol the unhappy believer in the list of the too-late repenters."

" And what, Madam," said the dean, " has not that wretch to answer for, who makes sport of destroying a virtuous character, and in being the wicked means of throwing, perhaps, upon the town, and into the dregs of prostitution, a poor creature, whose love for him, and confidence in him, was all her crime? and who otherwise might have made a worthy figure at the head of a reputable family, and so have been an useful member of the commonwealth, propagating good examples, instead of ruin and infamy, to mankind? To say nothing of, what is still worse, the dreadful crime of occasioning the loss of a soul; since final impenitence too generally follows the first sacrifice which the poor wretch is seduced to make of her honour ! "

" There are several gentlemen in our neighbourhood," said Mrs. Brooks, " who might be benefited by this touching reflection, if represented in the same strong lights from the pulpit. And I think, Mr. Dean, you should give us a sermon upon this subject, for the sake of both sexes, one for caution, the other for conviction."

"I will think of it," replied he, "but I am sorry to say, that we have too many among our younger gentry who would think themselves pointed at were I to touch this subject ever so cautiously."

"I am sure," said Mrs. Towers, "there cannot well be a more useful one; and the very reason the dean gives, is a convincing proof of it to me."

"When I have had the pleasure of hearing the further sentiments of such an assembly as this, upon the delicate subject," replied this polite divine, "I shall be better enabled to treat it. And pray, ladies, proceed; for it is from your conversation that I must take my hints."

"You have only, then," said Mrs. Towers, "to engage Mrs. B. to speak, and you may be sure, we will all be as attentive to *her*, as we shall be to *you*, when we have the pleasure to hear so fine a genius improving upon her hints, from the pulpit."

I bowed to Mrs. Towers; and knowing she praised me, with the dean's view, in order to induce the young ladies to give the greater attention to what she wished me to speak, I said, it would be a great presumption in me, after so high a compliment, to open my lips: nevertheless, as I was sure, by speaking, I should have the benefit of instruction, whenever it made *them* speak, I would not be backward to enter upon any subject; for that I should consider myself as a young counsel, in some great cause, who served but to open it and prepare the way for those of greater skill and abilities.

"I beg, then, Madam," said Miss Stapylton, "you will *open the cause*, be the subject what it will. And I could almost wish, that we had as many gentlemen here as ladies, who would have reason to be ashamed of the liberties they take in censuring the conversations of the tea-table; since the pulpit, as the worthy dean gives us reason to hope, may be beholden to that of Mrs. B."

"Nor is it much wonder," replied I, "when the dean himself is with us, and it is graced by so distinguished a circle."

"If many of our young gentlemen, were here," said Mrs. Towers, "they might improve themselves in all the graces of polite and sincere complaisance. But, compared to this, I have generally heard such trite and coarse stuff from our race of would-be wits, that what they say may be compared to the fawnings and salutations of the ass in the fable, who, emulating the lap-dog, merited a cudgel rather than encouragement.

"But, Mrs. B.," continued she, "begin, I pray you, to *open* and *proceed* in the cause; for there will be no counsel employed but you, I can tell you."

"Then give me a subject that will suit me, ladies, and you shall see how my obedience to your commands will make me run on."

"Will you, Madam," said Miss Stapylton, "give us a few cautions and instructions on a theme of your own, that a young lady should rather *fear* too much than *hope* too much? A necessary doctrine, perhaps; but a difficult one to be practised by one who has begun to love, and who supposes all truth and honour in the object of her favour."

"*Hope*, Madam," said I, "in my opinion, should never be unaccompanied by *fear ;* and the more reason will a lady ever have to fear, and to suspect herself, and doubt her lover, when she once begins to find in her own breast an inclination to him. For then her danger is doubled, since she has *herself* (perhaps the more dangerous enemy of the two) to guard against, as well as *him*.

"She may secretly wish the best indeed : but what *has been* the fate of others *may be* her own; and though she thinks it not *probable*, from such a faithful protester, as he appears to her to be, yet, while it is *possible*, she should never be off her guard : nor will a prudent woman trust to his mercy or honour ; but to her own discretion : and the rather, because, if he mean well, he *himself* will value her the more for her caution, since every man desires to have a virtuous and prudent wife ; if not well, she will detect him the sooner, and so, by her prudence, frustrate all his base designs.

"But let me, my dear ladies, ask, what that passion is, which generally we dignify by the name of *love ;* and which, when *so* dignified, puts us upon a thousand extravagances? I believe, if examined into, it would be found too generally to owe its original to *ungoverned fancy ;* and were we to judge of it by the consequences that usually attend it, it ought rather to be called *rashness, inconsideration, weakness,* and thing but *love ;* for very seldom, I doubt, is the *solid judgment* so much concerned in it, as the *airy fancy*. But when once we dignify the wild mis-leader with the name of *love*, all the absurdities which we read in novels and romances take place, and we are induced to follow examples that seldom end happily but in *them*.

"But, permit me further to observe, that love, as we call it, operates differently in the two sexes, as to its effects. For in woman it is a *creeping* thing, in a man an *incroacher ;* and this ought, in my humble opinion, to be very seriously attended

452

to. Miss Sutton intimated thus much, when she observed that it was the man's province to ask, the lady's to deny :—excuse me, Madam, the observation was just, as to the men's notions; although, methinks, I would not have a lady allow of it, except in cases of caution to themselves.

"The doubt, therefore, which a lady has of her *lover's* honour, is needful to preserve *her own* and *his* too. And if she does him wrong, and he should be too just to deceive her, she can make him amends, by instances of greater confidence, when she pleases. But if she has been accustomed to grant him little favours, can she easily recal them? And will not the *incroacher* grow upon her indulgence, pleading for a favour to-day, which was not refused him yesterday, and reproaching her want of confidence, as a want of esteem; till the poor lady, who, perhaps, has given way to the *creeping, insinuating* passion, and has avowed her esteem for him, puts herself too much in his power, in order to manifest, as she thinks, the *generosity* of her affection; and so, by degrees, is carried farther than she intended, or nice honour ought to have permitted; and all, because, to keep up to my theme, she *hopes* too much, and *doubts* too little? And there have been cases, where a man himself, pursuing the dictates of his *incroaching* passion, and finding a lady *too conceding*, has taken advantages, of which, probably, at first he did not presume to think."

Miss Stapylton said, that *virtue* itself spoke when *I* spoke; and she was resolved to recollect as much of this conversation as she could, and write it down in her common-place book, where it would make a better figure than any thing she had there.

"I suppose, Miss," said Mrs. Towers, "your chief collections are flowers of rhetoric, picked up from the French and English poets, and novel-writers. I would give something for the pleasure of having it two hours in my possession."

"Fie, Madam," replied she, a little abashed, "how can you expose your kinswoman thus, before the dean and Mrs. B.?"

"Mrs. Towers," said I, "only says this to provoke you to shew your collections. I wish I had the pleasure of seeing them. I doubt not but your common-place book is a store-house of wisdom."

"There is nothing bad in it, I hope," replied she; "but I would not, that Mrs. B. should see it for the world. But, Madam" (to Mrs. Towers), "there are many beautiful things, and good instructions, to be collected from novels and plays, and romances; and from the poetical writers particularly,

453

light as you are pleased to make of them. Pray, Madam" (to me), "have you ever been at all conversant in such writers?"

"Not a great deal in the former: there were very few novels and romances that my lady would permit me to read; and those I did, gave me no great pleasure; for either they dealt so much in the *marvellous* and *improbable*, or were so unnaturally *inflaming* to the *passions*, and so full of *love* and *intrigue*, that most of them seemed calculated to *fire* the *imagination*, rather than to *inform* the *judgment*. Titles and tournaments, breaking of spears in honour of a mistress, engaging with monsters, rambling in search of adventures, making unnatural difficulties, in order to shew the knight-errant's prowess in overcoming them, is all that is required to constitute the *hero* in such pieces. And what principally distinguishes the character of the *heroine* is, when she is taught to consider her father's house as an enchanted castle, and her lover as the hero who is to dissolve the charm, and to set at liberty from one confinement, in order to put her into another, and, too probably, a worse: to instruct her how to climb walls, leap precipices, and do twenty other extravagant things, in order to shew the mad strength of a passion she ought to be ashamed of; to make parents and guardians pass for tyrants, the voice of reason to be drowned in that of indiscreet love, which exalts the other sex, and debases her own. And what is the instruction that can be gathered from such pieces, for the conduct of common life?

"Then have I been ready to quarrel with these writers for another reason; and that is, the dangerous notion which they hardly ever fail to propagate, of a *first-sight love*. For there is such a susceptibility supposed on both sides (which, however it may pass in a man, very little becomes the female delicacy) that they are smitten with a glance: the fictitious blind god is made a *real* divinity: and too often prudence and discretion are the first offerings at his shrine."

"I believe, Madam," said Miss Stapylton, blushing, and playing with her fan, "there have been many instances of people's loving at first sight, which have ended very happily."

"No doubt of it," replied I. "But there are three chances to one, that so precipitate a liking does not. For where can be the room for caution, enquiry, the display of merit and sincerity, and even the assurance of a *grateful return*, to a lady, who thus suffers herself to be prepossessed? Is it not a random shot? Is it not a proof of weakness? Is it not giving up the negative voice, which belongs to the sex, even while she is not sure of meeting with the affirmative one from him whose affection she wishes to engage?

"Indeed, ladies," continued I, "I cannot help concluding (and I am the less afraid of speaking my mind, because of the opinion I have of the prudence of every lady that hears me), that where this weakness is found, it is no way favourable to a lady's character, nor to that discretion which ought to distinguish it. It looks to me, as if a lady's *heart* were too much in the power of her *eye*, and that she had permitted her *fancy* to be much more busy than her *judgment*."

Miss Stapylton blushed, and looked around her.

"But I observe," said Mrs. Towers, "whenever you censure any indiscretion, you seldom fail to give cautions how to avoid it; and pray let us know what is to be done in this case? That is to say, how a young lady ought to guard against and overcome the first favourable impressions?"

"What I imagine," replied I, "a young lady ought to do, on any the *least* favourable impressions of the kind, is immediately to *withdraw into herself*, as one may say; to reflect upon what she owes to her parents, to her family, to her character, and to her sex; and to resolve to check such a random prepossession, which may much more probably, as I hinted, make her a prey to the undeserving than otherwise, as there are so many of that character to one man of real merit.

"The most that I apprehend a *first-sight* approbation can do, is to inspire a *liking;* and a liking is conquerable, if the person will not brood over it, till she hatches it into *love.* Then every man and woman has a black and a white side; and it is easy to set the imperfections of the person against the supposed perfections, while it is only a *liking.* But if the busy fancy be permitted to work as it pleases, uncontrolled, then 'tis very likely, were the lady but to keep herself in countenance for receiving first impressions, she will see perfections in the object, which no other living soul can. And it may be expected, that as a consequence of her first indiscretion, she will confirm, as an act of her judgment, what her wild and ungoverned fancy had misled her to think of with so much partial favour. And too late, as it probably may happen, she will see and lament her fatal, and, perhaps, undutiful error.

"We are talking of the ladies only," added I (for I saw Miss Stapylton was become very grave): "but I believe first-sight love often operates too powerfully in both sexes : and where it does so, it will be very lucky, if either gentleman or lady find reason, on cool reflection, to approve a choice which they were so ready to make without thought."

" 'Tis allowed," said Mrs. Towers, " that rash and precipitate love may operate pretty much alike in the rash and precipitate of both sexes : and which soever loves, generally exalts the person beloved above his or her merits : but I am desirous, for the sake of us maiden ladies, since it is a science in which you are so great an adept, to have your advice, how we should watch and guard its first incroachments and that you will tell us what you apprehend gives the men most advantage over us."

" Nay, now, Mrs. Towers, you rally my presumption, indeed ! "

" I admire you, Madam," replied she, " and every thing you say and do; and I won't forgive you to call what I so seriously *say* and *think*, raillery. For my own part," continued she, " I never was in love yet, nor, I believe, were any of these young ladies." (Miss Cope looked a little silly upon this.) " And who can better instruct us to guard *our hearts*, than a lady who has so well defended *her own* ? "

" Why then, Madam, if I must speak, I think, what gives the other sex the greatest advantage over even many of the most deserving ones, is that dangerous foible, the *love of praise*, and the desire to be *flattered* and *admired*, a passion I have observed to predominate, more or less, from sixteen to sixty, in most of our sex. We are too generally delighted with the company of those who extol our graces of person or mind : for, will not a *grateful* lady study hard to return a *few* compliments to a gentleman who makes her so *many* ? She is concerned to *prove* him a man of distinguished sense, or a polite man, at least, in regard to what she *thinks* of herself ; and so the flatterer shall be preferred to such of the sincere and worthy, as cannot say what they do not think. And by this means many an excellent lady has fallen a prey to some sordid designer.

" Then, I think, nothing can give gentlemen so much advantage over our sex, as to see how readily a virtuous lady can forgive the capital faults of the most abandoned of the other ; and that sad, sad notion, *that a reformed rake makes the best husband ;* a notion that has done more hurt, and discredit too, to our sex (as it has given more encouragement to the profligate, and more discouragement to the sober gentlemen), than can be easily imagined. A fine thing, indeed ! as if the wretch, who had run through a course of iniquity, to the endangering of soul and body, was to be deemed the best companion for life, to an innocent and virtuous young lady, who is to owe the kindness of his treatment to her, to his having never before accompanied with a modest woman; nor, till his interest on one hand (to which his extravag ance, perhaps, compels him to attend), and his impaired constitution on the other, oblige him to it, so much as *wished* to accompany with one; and who always made a jest of the marriage state, and perhaps, of every thing either serious or sacred!"

"You observe, very well," said Mrs. Towers: "but people will be apt to think, that you have less reason than any of our sex, to be severe against such a notion: for who was a greater rake than a certain gentleman, and who is a better husband?"

"Madam," replied I, "the gentleman you mean, never was a common town rake: he is a man of sense, and fine understanding: and his reformation, *secondarily*, as I may say, has been the natural effect of those extraordinary qualities. But also, I will presume to say, that that gentleman, as he has not many equals in the nobleness of his nature, so he is not likely, I doubt, to have many followers, in a reformation begun in the bloom of youth, upon *self-conviction*, and altogether, humanly speaking, *spontaneous*. Those ladies who would plead his example, in support of this pernicious notion, should find out the same generous qualities in the man, before they trust to it: and it will then do less harm; though even then, I could not wish it to be generally entertained."

"It is really unaccountable," said Mrs. Towers, "after all, as Mrs. B., I remember, said on another occasion, that our sex should not as much insist upon virtue and sobriety, in the character of a man, as a man, be he ever such a rake, does in that of a lady. And 'tis certainly a great encouragement to libertinism, that a worn-out debauchee should think himself at any time good enough for a husband, and have the confidence to imagine, that a modest woman will accept of his address, with a *preference* of him to any other."

"I can account for it but one way," said the dean: "and that is, that a modest woman is apt to be *diffident* of her own merit and understanding and she thinks this diffidence an imperfection. A rake *never* is troubled with it: so he has in perfection a quality she thinks she wants; and, knowing *too little* of the world, imagines she mends the matter by accepting of one who knows *too much*."

"That's well observed, Mr. Dean," said Mrs. Towers: "but there is another fault in our sex, which Mrs. B. has not touched upon; and that is, the foolish vanity some women have, in the hopes of reforming a wild fellow; and that they shall be able to do more than any of their sex before them could do: a vanity that often costs them dear, as I know in more than one instance."

457

"Another weakness," said I, "might be produced against some of our sex, who join too readily to droll upon, and sneer at, the misfortune of any poor young creature, who has shewn too little regard for her honour : and who (instead of speaking of it with concern, and inveighing against the seducer) too lightly sport with the unhappy person's fall; industriously spread the knowledge of it—" [I would not look upon Miss Sutton, while I spoke this], "and avoid her, as one infected; and yet scruple not to admit into their company the vile aggressor; and even to smile with him, at his barbarous jests, upon the poor sufferer of their own sex."

"I have known three or four instances of this in my time," said Mrs. Towers, that Miss Sutton might not take it to herself; for she looked down and was a little serious.

"This," replied I, "puts me in mind of a little humourous copy of verses, written, as I believe by Mr. B. And which, to the very purpose we are speaking of, he calls

> "'*Benefit of making others' misfortunes our own.*
>
> "'Thou'st heard it, or read it, a million of times,
> That men are made up of falsehood and crimes;
> Search all the old authors, and ransack the new,
> Thou'lt find in love stories, scarce one mortal true.
> Then why this complaining? And why this wry face?
> Is it 'cause thou'rt affected *most* with thy own case?
> Had'st thou sooner made *others'* misfortunes thy own,
> Thou never *thyself*, this disaster hadst known;
> Thy *compassionate caution* had kept thee from evil,
> And thou might'st have defy'd mankind and the devil.'"

The ladies were pleased with the lines; but Mrs. Towers wanted to know at what time of Mr. B.'s life they could be written. "Because," added she, "I never suspected, before, that the good gentleman ever took pains to write cautions or exhortations to our sex, to avoid the delusions of his own."

These verses, and these facetious, but severe, remarks of Mrs. Towers, made every young lady look up with a cheerful countenance; because it pushed the ball from *self* : and the dean said to his daughter, "So, my dear, you, that have been so attentive, must let us know what useful inferences you can draw from what Mrs. B. and the other ladies so excellently said."

"I observe, Sir, from the faults the ladies have so justly imputed to some of our sex, that the advantage the gentlemen *chiefly* have over us, is from our own weakness : and that it behoves a prudent woman to guard against *first impressions* of favour, since she will think herself obliged, in compliment to *her own* judgment, to find reasons, if possible, to confirm them.

"But I wish to know if there be any way that a woman can judge, whether a man means honourably or not, in his address to her!"

"Mrs. B. can best inform you of that, Miss L.," said Mrs. Towers: "what say you, Mrs. B.?"

"There are a few signs," answered I, "easy to be known, and, I think, almost infallible."

"Pray let's have them," said Lady Arthur; and they all were very attentive.

"I lay it down as an undoubted truth," said I, "that true love is one of the most *respectful* things in the world. It strikes with awe and reverence the mind of the man who boasts its impressions. It is chaste and pure in word and deed, and cannot bear to have the least indecency mingled with it.

"If, therefore, a man, be his birth or quality what it will, the higher the worse, presume to wound a lady's ears with indecent words: if he endeavour, in his expressions or sentiments, to convey gross or impure ideas to her mind: if he is continually pressing for *her confidence* in *his* honour: if he requests favours which a lady ought to refuse: if he can be regardless of his conduct or behaviour to her: if he can use *boisterous* or *rude* freedoms, either to her *person* or *dress*—" [Here poor Miss Cope, by her blushes, bore witness to her case.] "If he avoids *speaking* of *marriage*, when he has a *fair opportunity* of doing it—" [Here Miss L. looked down and blushed] —"or leaves it *once* to a lady to wonder that he does not:—

"In any, or in all these cases, he is to be suspected, and a lady can have little hope of such a person; nor, as I humbly apprehend, consistent with honour and discretion, encourage his address."

The ladies were so kind as to applaud all I said, and so did the dean. Miss Stapylton, Miss Cope, and Miss L. were to write down what they could remember of the conversation: and our noble guests coming in soon after, with Mr. B., the ladies would have departed; but he prevailed upon them to pass the evening; and Miss L., who had an admirable finger on the harpsichord, as I have before said, obliged us with two or three lessons. Each of the ladies did the like, and prevailed upon me to play a tune or two: but Miss Cope, as well as Miss L., surpassed me much. We all sung too in turns, and Mr. B. took the violin, in which he excels. Lord Davers obliged us on the violincello : Mr. H. played on the German flute, and sung us a fop's song, and performed it in character; so that we had an exceeding gay evening, and parted with great satisfaction on *all* sides, particularly on the young ladies; for this put them all in good humour, and good spirits, enlivening the former scene, which otherwise might have closed, perhaps more gravely than efficaciously.

The distance of time since this conversation passed, enables me to add what I could not do, when I wrote the account of it, which you have mislaid : and which take briefly, as follows :

Miss Stapylton was as good as her word, and wrote down all she could recollect of the conversation : and I having already sent her the letter she desired, containing my observations upon the flighty style she so much admired, it had such an effect upon her, as to turn the course of her reading and studies to weightier and more solid subjects; and avoiding the gentleman she had begun to favour, gave way to her parents' recommendations, and is happily married to Sir Jonathan Barnes.

Miss Cope came to me a week after, with the leave of both her parents, and tarried with me three days; in which time she opened all her heart to me, and returned in such a disposition, and with such resolutions, that she never would see her peer again; nor receive letters from him, which she owned to me she had done clandestinely before; and she is now the happy lady of Sir Michael Beaumont, who makes her the best of husbands, and permits her to follow her charitable inclinations according to a scheme which she consulted me upon.

Miss L., by the dean's indulgent prudence and discretion, has escaped her rake; and upon the discovery of an intrigue he was carrying on with another, conceived a just abhorrence of him; and is since married to Dr. Jenkins, as you know, with whom she lives very happily.

Miss Sutton is not quite so well off as the three former; though not altogether so unhappy neither, in her way. She could not indeed conquer her love of dress and tinsel; and so became the lady of Col. Wilson : and they are thus far easy in the marriage state, that, being seldom together, they have probably a multitude of misunderstandings; for the colonel loves gaming, in which he is generally a winner; and so passes his time mostly in town. His lady has her pleasures, neither laudable nor criminal ones, which she pursues in the country. And now and then a letter passes on both sides, by the inscription and subscription of which they remind one another that they have been *once* in their lives at *one* church together.

And what now, my dear Lady G., have I to add to this tedious account (for letter I can hardly call it) but that I am, with great affection, *your true friend and servant,*

P. B.

LETTER CIII

MY DEAR LADY G.,

You desire to have a little specimen of my *nursery tales* and *stories,* with which, as Miss Fenwick told you, on her return to Lincolnshire, I entertain my Miss Goodwin and my little boys. But you make me too high a compliment, when you tell me, it is for your *own* instruction and example. Yet you know, my dear Lady G., be your motives what they will, I must obey you, although, were others to see it, I might expose myself to the smiles and contempt of judges less prejudiced in my favour. So I will begin without any further apology; and, as near as I can, give you those very stories with which Miss Fenwick was so pleased, and of which she has made so favourable a report.

Let me acquaint you, then, that my method is to give characters of persons I have known in one part or other of my life, in feigned names, whose conduct may serve for imitation or warning to my dear attentive Miss; and sometimes I give instances of good boys and naughty boys, for the sake of my Billy and my Davers; and they are continually coming about me, "Dear Madam, a pretty story," now cries Miss : "and dear mamma, tell me of good boys, and of naughty boys," cries Billy.

Miss is a surprising child of her age, and is very familiar with many of the best characters in the Spectators; and having a smattering of Latin, and more than a smattering of Italian, and being a perfect mistress of French, is seldom at a loss for a derivation of such words as are not of English original. And so I shall give you a story in feigned names, with which she is so delighted, that she has written it down. But I will first trespass on your patience with one of my childish tales.

Every day, once or twice, I cause Miss Goodwin, who plays and sings very prettily, to give a tune or two to me, my Billy and my Davers, who, as well as my Pamela, love and learn to touch the keys, young as the latter is; and she will have a sweet finger; I can observe that; and a charming ear; and her voice is music itself !—"O the fond, fond mother !" I know you will say, on reading this.

Then, Madam, we all proceed, hand-in-hand, together to the

nursery, to my Charley and Jemmy: and in this happy retirement, so much my delight in the absence of my best beloved, imagine you see me seated, surrounded with the joy and the hope of my future prospects, as well as my present comforts.

Miss Goodwin, imagine you see, on my right hand, sitting on a velvet stool, because she is eldest, and a Miss; Billy on my left, in a little cane elbow-chair, because he is eldest, and a good boy; my Davers, and my sparkling-ey'd Pamela, with my Charley between them, on little silken cushions, at my feet, hand-in-hand, their pleased eyes looking up to my more delighted ones; and my sweet-natured promising Jemmy, in my lap; the nurses and the cradle just behind us, and the nursery maids delightedly pursuing some useful needle-work for the dear charmers of my heart—All as hush and as still as silence itself, as the pretty creatures generally are, when their little, watchful eyes see my lips beginning to open: for they take great notice already of my rule of two ears to one tongue, insomuch that if Billy or Davers are either of them for breaking the mum, as they call it, they are immediately hush, at any time, if I put my finger to my lip, or if Miss points hers to her ear, even to the breaking of a word in two, as it were: and yet all my boys are as lively as so many birds: while my Pamela is cheerful, easy, soft, gentle, always smiling, but modest and harmless as a dove.

I began with a story of two little boys, and two little girls, the children of a fine gentleman, and a fine lady, who loved them dearly; that they were all so good, and loved one another so well, that every body who saw them, admired them, and talked of them far and near; that they would part with any thing to one another; loved the poor; spoke kindly to the servants; did every thing they were bid to do; were not proud; knew no strife, but who should learn their books best, and be the prettiest scholar; that the servants loved them, and would do any thing they desired; that they were not proud of fine clothes; let not their heads run upon their playthings when they should mind their books; said grace before they eat, their prayers before they went to bed, and as soon as they rose; were always clean and neat; would not tell a fib for the world, and were above doing any thing that required one; that God blessed them more and more, and blessed their papa and mamma, and their uncles and aunts, and cousins, for their sakes. "And there was a happy family, my dear loves!—No one idle; all prettily employed; the Masters at their books; the Misses at their books too, or at their needles; except at their play-hours, when they were never rude, nor noisy, nor mischievous, nor quarrelsome : and no such word was ever heard from their mouths, as, ' Why mayn't I have this or that, as well as Billy or Bobby ? ' Or, ' Why should Sally have this or that, any more than I ? ' But it was, ' As my mamma pleases; my mamma knows best ;' and a bow and a smile, and no surliness, or scowling brow to be seen, if they were denied any thing; for well did they know that their papa and mamma loved them so dearly, that they would refuse them nothing that was for their good; and they were sure when they were refused, they asked for something that would have done them hurt, had it been granted. Never were such good boys and girls as these ! And they grew up; and the Masters became fine scholars, and fine gentlemen, and every body honoured them : and the Misses became fine ladies, and fine housewives; and this gentleman, when they grew to be women, sought to marry one of the Misses, and that gentleman the other; and happy was he that could be admitted into their companies ! so that they had nothing to do but to pick and choose out of the best gentlemen in the country : while the greatest ladies for birth and the most remarkable for virtue (which, my dears, is better than either birth or fortune), thought themselves honoured by the addresses of the two brothers. And they married, and made good papas and mammas, and were so many blessings to the age in which they lived. There, my dear loves, were happy sons and daughters; for good Masters seldom fail to make good gentle-men; and good Misses, good ladies; and God blesses them with as good children as they were to *their* parents; and so the blessing goes round !—Who would not but be good ? "

" Well, but, mamma, we will all be good :—Won't we, Master Davers ? " cries my Billy. " Yes, brother Billy. But what will become of the naughty boys ? Tell us, mamma, about the naughty boys ! "

" Why, there was a poor, poor widow woman, who had three naughty sons, and one naughty daughter; and they would do nothing that their mamma bid them do; were always quarrel-ling, scratching, and fighting; would not say their prayers; would not learn their books; so that the little boys used to laugh at them, and point at them, as they went along, for block-heads; and nobody loved them, or took notice of them, except to beat and thump them about, for their naughty ways, and their undutifulness to their poor mother, who worked hard to maintain them. As they grew up, they grew worse and worse, and more and more stupid and ignorant; so that they im-

463

poverished their poor mother, and at last broke her heart, poor poor widow woman !—And her neighbours joined together to bury the poor widow woman : for these sad ungracious children made away with what little she had left, while she was ill, before her heart was quite broken ; and this helped to break it the sooner : for had she lived, she saw she must have wanted bread, and had no comfort with such wicked children."

" Poor poor widow woman !" said my Billy, with tears ; and my little dove shed tears too, and Davers was moved, and Miss wiped her fine eyes.

" But what became of the naughty boys, and the naughty girl, mamma ? "

" Became of them ! Why one son was forced to go to sea, and there he was drowned : another turned thief (for he would not work), and he came to an untimely end : the third was idle and ignorant, and nobody, who knew how he used his poor mother, would employ him ; and so he was forced to go into a far country, and beg his bread. And the naughty girl, having never loved work, pined away in sloth and filthiness, and at last broke her arm, and died of a fever, lamenting, too late, that she had been so wicked a daughter to so good a mother !— And so there was a sad end to all the four ungracious children, who never would mind what their poor mother said to them ; and God punished their naughtiness as you see !—While the good children I mentioned before, were the glory of their family, and the delight of every body that knew them."

" Who would not be good ? " was the inference : and the repetition from Billy, with his hands clapt together, " Poor widow woman ! " gave me much pleasure.

So my childish story ended, with a kiss of each pretty dear, and their thanks for my story : and then came on Miss's request for a *woman's* story, as she called it. I dismissed my babies to their play ; and taking Miss's hand, she standing before me, all attention, began in a more womanly strain to *her ;* for she is very fond of being thought a woman ; and indeed is a prudent sensible dear, comprehends any thing instantly, and makes very pretty reflections upon what she hears or reads as you will observe in what follows :

" There is nothing, my dear Miss Goodwin, that young ladies should be so watchful over, as their reputation : 'tis a tender flower that the least frost will nip, the least cold wind will blast ; and when once blasted, it will never flourish again, but wither to the very root. But this I have told you so often, I need not repeat what I have said. So to my story.

464

"There were four pretty ladies lived in one genteel neighbourhood, daughters of four several families; but all companions and visitors; and yet all of very different inclinations. Coquetilla we will call one, Prudiana another, Profusiana the third, and Prudentia the fourth; their several names denoting their respective qualities.

"Coquetilla was the only daughter of a worthy baronet, by a lady very gay, but rather indiscreet than unvirtuous, who took not the requisite care of her daughter's education, but let her be over-run with the love of fashion, dress, and equipage; and when in London, balls, operas, plays, the Park, the Ring, the withdrawing-room, took up her whole attention. She admired nobody but herself, fluttered about, laughing at, and despising a crowd of men-followers, whom she attracted by gay, thoughtless freedoms of behaviour, too nearly treading on the skirts of immodesty: yet made she not one worthy conquest, exciting, on the contrary, in all sober minds, that contempt of herself, which she so profusely would be thought to pour down upon the rest of the world. After she had several years fluttered about the dangerous light, like some silly fly, she at last singed the wings of her reputation; for, being despised by every worthy heart, she became too easy and cheap a prey to a man the most unworthy of all her followers, who had resolution and confidence enough to break through those few cobweb reserves, in which she had encircled her precarious virtue; and which were no longer of force to preserve her honour, when she met with a man more bold and more enterprising than herself, and who was as designing as she was thoughtless. And what then became of Coquetilla?—Why, she was forced to pass over sea to Ireland, where nobody knew her, and to bury herself in a dull obscurity; to go by another name, and at last, unable to support a life so unsuitable to the natural gaiety of her temper, she pined herself into a consumption, and died, unpitied and unlamented, among strangers, having not one friend but whom she bought with her money."

"Poor Lady Coquetilla!" said Miss Goodwin; "what a sad thing it is to have a wrong education; and how happy am I, who have so good a lady to supply the place of a dear distant mamma!—But be pleased, Madam, to proceed to the next."

"Prudiana, my dear, was the daughter of a gentleman who was a widower, and had, while the young lady was an infant, buried her mamma. He was a good sort of man; but had but one lesson to teach to Prudiana, and that was to avoid all sort of conversation with the men; but never gave her the right turn

465

of mind, nor instilled into it that sense of her religious duties, which would have been her best guard in all temptations. For, provided she kept out of the sight and conversation of the gentlemen, and avoided the company of those ladies who more freely conversed with the other sex, it was all her papa desired of her. This gave her a haughty, sullen, and reserved turn; made her stiff, formal, and affected. She had sense enough to discover early the faults of Coquetilla, and, in dislike to them, fell the more easily into that contrary extreme, which a recluse education, and her papa's cautions, naturally led her. So that pride, reserve, affectation, and censoriousness, made up the essentials of her character, and she became more unamiable even than Coquetilla; and as the other was too accessible, Prudiana was quite unapproachable by gentlemen, and unfit for any conversation, but that of her servants, being also deserted by those of her own sex, by whom she might have improved, on account of her censorious disposition. And what was the consequence? Why this: every worthy person of both sexes despising her, and she being used to see nobody but servants, at last throws herself upon one of that class: in an evil hour, she finds something that is taking to her low taste in the person of her papa's valet, a wretch so infinitely beneath her (but a gay coxcomb of a servant), that every body attributed to her the scandal of making the first advances; for, otherwise, it was presumed, he durst not have looked up to his master's daughter. So here ended all her pride. All her reserves came to this! Her censoriousness of others redoubled people's contempt upon herself, and made nobody pity her. She was finally turned out of doors, without a penny of fortune: the fellow was forced to set up a barber's shop in a country town; for all he knew was to shave and dress a peruke: and her papa would never look upon her more: so that Prudiana became the outcast of her family, and the scorn of all that knew her; and was forced to mingle in conversation and company with the wretches of her husband's degree!"

"Poor, miserable Prudiana!" said Miss—"What a sad, sad fall was hers. And all owing to the want of a proper education too!—And to the loss of such a mamma, as I have an aunt; and so wise a papa as I have an uncle!—How could her papa, I wonder, restrain her person as he did, like a poor nun, and make her unacquainted with the generous restraints of the mind?

"I am sure, my dear good aunt, it will be owing to you, that I shall never be a Coquetilla, nor a Prudiana neither. Your

466

table is always surrounded with the best of company, with worthy gentlemen as well as ladies : and you instruct me to judge of both, and of every new guest, in such a manner, as makes me esteem them all, and censure nobody; but yet to see faults in some to avoid, and graces in others to imitate; but in nobody but yourself and my uncle, any thing so like perfection, as shall attract one's admiration to one's own ruin."

" You are young, yet, my love, and must always doubt your own strength; and pray to God, more and more, as your years advance, to give you more and more prudence, and watchfulness over your conduct.

" But yet, my dear, you must think justly of yourself too; for let the young gentlemen be ever so learned and discreet, your education entitles you to think as well of yourself as of them : for, don't you see, the ladies who are so kind as to visit us, that have not been abroad, as you have been, when they were young, yet make as good figures in conversation, say as good things as any of the gentlemen ? For, my dear, all that the gentlemen know more than the ladies, except here and there such a one as your dear uncle, with all their learned education, is only, that they have been *disciplined*, perhaps, into an observation of a few accuracies in speech, which, if they know no more, rather distinguish the *pedant* than the *gentleman :* such as the avoiding of a false concord, as they call it, and which you know how to do, as well as the best; not to put a *was* for a *were*, an *are* for an *is*, and to be able to speak in mood and tense, and such like valuable parts of education : so that, my dear, you can have no reason to look upon that sex in so high a light, as to depreciate your own : and yet you must not be proud nor conceited neither; but make this one rule your guide :

" In your *maiden state*, think yourself *above* the gentlemen, and they'll think you so too, and address you with reverence and respect, if they see there be neither pride nor arrogance in your behaviour, but a consciousness of merit, a true dignity, such as becomes virgin modesty, and untainted purity of mind and manners, like that of an angel among men; for so young ladies should look upon themselves to be, and will then be treated as such by the other sex.

" In your *married state*, which is a kind of state of humiliation for a lady, you must think yourself subordinate to your husband; for so it has pleased God to make the wife. You must have no will of your own, in *petty* things; and if you marry a gentleman of sense and honour, such a one as your uncle, he will look upon you as his equal; and will exalt you the more for your abasing

467

yourself. In short, my dear, he will act by you, just as your dear uncle does by me : and then, what a happy creature will you be ! "

" So I shall, Madam ! To be sure I shall !—But I know I shall be happy whenever I marry, because I have such wise directors, and such an example, before me : and, if it please God, I will never think of any man (in pursuance of your constant advice to young ladies at the tea-table), who is not a man of sense, and a virtuous gentleman. But now, dear Madam, for your next character. There are two more yet to come, that's my pleasure ! I wish there were ten ! "

" Why the next was PROFUSIANA, you may remember, my love. Profusiana took another course to *her* ruin. She fell into some of Coquetilla's foibles, but pursued them for another end, and in another manner. Struck with the grandeur and magnificence of what weak people call the *upper life*, she gives herself up to the circus, to balls, to operas, to masquerades, and assemblies; affects to shine at the head of all companies, at Tunbridge, at Bath, and every place of public resort; plays high, is always receiving and paying visits, giving balls, and making treats and entertainments; and is so much *above* the conduct which mostly recommends a young lady to the esteem of the deserving of the other sex, that no gentleman, who prefers solid happiness, can think of addressing her, though she is a fine person, and has many outward graces of behaviour. She becomes the favourite toast of the place she frequents, is proud of that distinction; gives the fashion, and delights in the pride, that she can make apes in imitation, whenever she pleases. But yet endeavouring to avoid being thought proud, makes herself cheap, and is the subject of the attempts of every coxcomb of eminence; and with much ado, preserves her virtue, though not her character.

" What, all this while, is poor Profusiana doing? She would be glad, perhaps, of a suitable proposal, and would, it may be, give up some of her gaieties and extravagances : for Profusiana has wit, and is not totally destitute of reason, when she suffers herself to think. But her conduct procures her not one solid friendship, and she has not in a twelvemonth, among a thousand professions of service, one devoir that she can attend to, or a friend that she can depend upon. All the women she sees, if she excels them, hate her : the gay part of the men, with whom she accompanies most, are all in a plot against her honour. Even the gentlemen, whose conduct in the general is governed by principles of virtue, come down to these public places to partake of the innocent freedoms allowed there, and oftentimes give themselves airs of gallantry, and never have it in their thoughts to commence a treaty of marriage with an acquaintance begun upon that gay spot. What solid friendships and satisfactions then is Profusiana excluded from !

" Her name indeed is written in every public window, and prostituted, as I may call it, at the pleasure of every profligate or sot, who wears a diamond to engrave it : and that it may be, with most vile and barbarous imputations and freedoms of words, added by rakes, who very probably never exchanged a syllable with her. The wounded trees are perhaps also taught to wear the initials of her name, linked, not unlikely, and widening as they grow, with those of a scoundrel. But all this while she makes not the least impression upon one noble heart : and at last, perhaps, having run on to the end of an uninterrupted race of follies, she is cheated into the arms of some vile fortune-hunter; who quickly lavishes away the remains of that fortune which her extravagance had left; and then, after the worst usage, abandoning her with contempt, she sinks into an obscurity that cuts short the thread of her life, and leaves no remembrance, but on the brittle glass, and still more faithless bark, that ever she had a being."

" Alas, alas ! what a butterfly of a day," said Miss (an expression she remembered of Lady Towers), " was poor Profusiana !—What a sad thing to be so dazzled by worldly grandeur, and to have so many admirers, and not one real friend ! "

" Very true, my dear; and how carefully ought a person of a gay and lively temper to watch over it ! And what a rock may public places be to a lady's reputation, if she be not doubly vigilant in her conduct, when she is exposed to the censures and observations of malignant crowds of people; many of the worst of whom spare the least those who are most unlike themselves."

" But then, Madam," said Miss, " would Profusiana venture to play at public places ? Will ladies game, Madam ? I have heard you say, that lords, and sharpers but just out of liveries, in gaming, are upon a foot in every thing, save that one has nothing to lose, and the other much, besides his reputation ! And will ladies so disgrace their characters, and their sex, as to pursue this pernicious diversion in public ? "

" Yes, my dear, they will too often, the more's the pity ! And don't you remember, when we were at Bath, in what a hurry I once passed by some knots of genteel people, and you asked what those were doing ? I told you, whisperingly, they were gaming; and loath I was, that my Miss Goodwin should stop to see some sights, to which, till she arrived at the years of discretion, it was not proper to familiarize her eye; in some sort acting like the ancient Romans, who would not assign punishments to certain atrocious crimes, because they had such an high idea of human nature, as to suppose it incapable of committing them : so I was not for having you, while a little girl, see those things, which I knew would give no credit to our sex, and which I thought, when you grew older, should be new and shocking to you : but now you are so much a woman in discretion, I may tell you any thing."

She kissed my hand, and made me a fine curtsey—and told me, that now she longed to hear of Prudentia's conduct. " *Her* name, Madam," said she, " promises better things than those of her three companions; and so it had need : for how sad is it to think, that out of four ladies of distinction, three of them should be naughty, and, *of course*, unhappy."—" These two words, *of course*, my dear," said I, " were very prettily put in : let me kiss you for it : since every one that is naughty, first or last, must be *certainly* unhappy.

" Far otherwise than what I have related, was it with the amiable PRUDENTIA. Like the industrious bee, she makes up her honey-hoard from every flower, bitter as well as sweet; for every character is of use to her, by which she can improve her own. She had the happiness of an aunt, who loved her, as I do you; and of an uncle who doated on her, as yours does : for, alas ! poor Prudentia lost her papa and mamma almost in her infancy, in one week : but was so happy in her uncle and aunt's care, as not to miss them in her education, and but just to remember their persons. By reading, by observation, and by attention, she daily added new advantages to those which her education gave her. She saw, and pitied, the fluttering freedoms and dangerous flights of Coquetilla. The sullen pride, the affectation, and stiff reserves, which Prudiana assumed, she penetrated, and made it her study to avoid. And the gay, hazardous conduct, extravagant temper, and love of tinselled grandeur, which were the blemishes of Profusiana's character, she dreaded and shunned. She fortifies herself with the excellent examples of the past and present ages, and knows how to avoid the faults of the faulty, and to imitate the graces of the most perfect. She takes into her scheme of that future happiness, which she hopes to make her own, what are the *true* excellencies of her sex, and endeavours to appropriate to herself the domestic virtues, which shall one day make her the crown of some worthy gentleman's earthly happiness : and which, *of course,* as you prettily said, my dear, will secure and heighten her own.

"That noble frankness of disposition, that sweet and unaffected openness and simplicity, which shines in all her actions and behaviour, commend her to the esteem and reverence of all mankind; as her humility and affability, and a temper uncensorious, and ever making the best of what she said of the absent person, of either sex, do to the love of every lady. Her name, indeed, is not prostituted on windows, nor carved on the barks of trees in public places: but it smells sweet to every nostril, dwells on every tongue, and is engraven on every heart. She meets with no address but from men of honour and probity: the fluttering coxcomb, the inveigling parasite, the insidious deceiver, the mercenary fortune-hunter, spread no snares for a heart guarded by discretion and prudence, as hers is. They see, that all her amiable virtues are the happy result of an uniform judgment, and the effects of her own wisdom, founded in an education to which she does the highest credit. And at last, after several worthy offers, enough to perplex a lady's choice, she blesses some one happy gentleman, more distinguished than the rest, for learning, good sense, and *true politeness,* which is but another word for *virtue* and *honour;* and shines, to her last hour, in all the duties of domestic life, as an excellent wife, mother, mistress, friend, and Christian; and so confirms all the expectations of which her maiden life had given such strong and such edifying presages."

Then folding my dear Miss in my arms, and kissing her, tears of pleasure standing in her pretty eyes, "Who would not," said I, "shun the examples of the Coquetilla's, the Prudiana's, and the Profusiana's of this world, and choose to imitate the character of PRUDENTIA !—the happy, and the happy-making PRUDENTIA."

"O Madam ! Madam !" said the dear creature, smothering me with her rapturous kisses, "PRUDENTIA is YOU !—Is YOU indeed !—It *can* be nobody else !—O teach me, good God ! to follow *your* example, and I shall be a SECOND PRUDENTIA— Indeed I shall !"

"God send you may, my beloved Miss ! And may he bless you more, if possible, than Prudentia was blessed !"

And so, my dear Lady G., you have some of my nursery tales; with which, relying on your kind allowances and friendship, I conclude myself *your affectionate and faithful*

P. B.

CONCLUSION

The Editor thinks proper to conclude in this place, that he may not be thought to deserve a suspicion, that the extent of the work was to be measured by the patience of its readers. But he thinks it necessary, in order to elucidate the whole, to subjoin a note of the following facts.

Mr. B. (after the affair which took date at the masquerade, and concluded so happily) continued to be one of the best and most exemplary of men, an honour to his country, both in his public and private capacity; having, at the instances of some of his friends in very elevated stations, accepted of an honourable employment abroad in the service of the state; which he discharged in such a manner, as might be expected from his qualifications and knowledge of the world : and on his return, after an absence of three years, resisting all the temptations of ambition, devoted himself to private duties, and joined with his excellent lady in every pious wish of her heart; adorning the married life with all the warmth of an elegant tenderness; beloved by his tenants, respected by his neighbours, revered by his children, and almost adored by the poor, in every county where his estates gave him interest, as well for his own bountiful temper, as for the charities he permitted to be dispensed, with so liberal a hand, by his lady.

She made him the father of seven fine children, five sons, and two daughters, all adorned and accomplished by nature, to be the joy and delight of such parents; being educated, in every respect, by the rules of their inimitable mother, laid down in that book which she mentions to have been written by her for the revisal and correction of her consort; the contents of which may be gathered from her remarks upon Mr. Locke's Treatise on Education, in her letters to Mr. B., and in those to Lady G.

Miss Goodwin, at the age of eighteen, was married to a young gentleman of fine parts, and great sobriety and virtue : and both she and he, in every material part of their conduct, and in their behaviour to one another, emulate the good example set them by Mr. and Mrs. B.

Lord Davers dying two years before this marriage, his lady went to reside at the Hall in Lincolnshire, the place of her birth, that she might enjoy the company and conversation of her excellent sister; who, for conveniency of the chapel, and advantage of room and situation, had prevailed upon Mr. B. to make it the chief place of his residence; and there the noble lady lived long (in the strictest friendship with the happy pair) an honourable relict of her affectionate lord.

The worthy Mr. ANDREWS, and his wife, lived together in the sweet tranquillity set forth in their letters, for the space of twelve years, at the Kentish farm : the good old gentlewoman died first, full of years and comfort, her dutiful daughter performing the last pious offices to so beloved and so loving a parent : her husband survived her about a year only.

Lady G., Miss DARNFORD that was, after a happy marriage of several years, died in child-bed of her fourth child, to the inexpressible concern of her affectionate consort, and of her dear friend Mrs. B.

Lord H., after having suffered great dishonour by the ill courses of his wife, and great devastations in his estate, through her former debts, and continued extravagance (intimidated and dispirited by her perpetual insults, and those of her gaming brother, who with his bullying friends, terrified him into their measures), threw himself upon the protection of Mr. B. who, by his spirit and prudence, saved him from utter ruin, punished his wife's accomplices, and obliged her to accept a separate maintenance; and then taking his affairs into his own management, in due course of time, entirely re-established them : and after some years his wife dying, he became wiser by his past sufferings, and married a second, of Lady Davers's recommendation, who, by her prudence and virtue, made him happy for the remainder of his days.

Mr. LONGMAN lived to a great age in the worthy family, much esteemed by every one, having trained up a diligent youth, whom he had recommended, to ease him in his business, and who, answering expectation, succeeded him in it after his death.

He dying rich, out of his great love and gratitude to the family, in whose service he had acquired most of his fortune, and in disgust to his nearest relations, who had perversely disobliged him; he bequeathed to three of them one hundred pounds a-piece, and left all the rest to his honoured principal, Mr. B.; who, as soon as he came to know it, being at that time abroad, directed his lady to call together the relations of the old gentleman, and, after touching them to the heart with a just and effectual reproof, and finding them filled with due sense of their demerit, which had been the cause of their suffering, then to divide the whole, which had been left him, among them, in greater proportions as they were more nearly related : an action worthy of so generous and ennobled a spirit; and which procured him the prayers and blessings, not only of the benefited, but all who heard of it. For it is easy to imagine, how cheerfully, and how gracefully, his benevolent lady discharged a command so well suited to her natural generosity.